The Great Ideas

Man

Mathematics

Matter

Mechanics

Medicine

Memory and Imagination

Metaphysics

Mind

Monarchy

Nature

Necessity and Contingency

Oligarchy

One and Many

Opinion

Opposition

Philosophy

Physics

Pleasure and Pain

Poetry

Principle

Progress

Prophecy

Prudence

Punishment

Quality

Quantity

Reasoning

Relation

Religion

Revolution

Rhetoric

Same and Other

Science

Sense

Sign and Symbol

Sin

Slavery

Soul

Space

State

Temperance

Theology

Time

Truth

Tyranny

Universal and Particular

Virtue and Vice

War and Peace

Wealth

Will

Wisdom

World

Rear view of the Centre National d'Art et de Culture Georges Pompidou, Paris, showing exposed elevators, power ducts, gantries, air shafts, and other service elements.

The
Great Ideas
Today

1977

Encyclopædia Britannica, Inc.

Chicago • London • Toronto • Geneva • Sydney • Tokyo • Manila • Seoul

The Great Ideas Today 1977

"On the Theory of Transformations, or the Comparison of Related Forms," is reprinted from *On Growth and Form*, volume two, by D'Arcy Wentworth Thompson, second edition, 1952, by permission of the publisher, The Cambridge University Press.

"The Victory of the Good over the Evil Principle and the Founding of God on Earth," translated with an introduction and notes by Theodore M. Greene, and Hoyt H. Hudson, is reprinted from *Religion within the Limits of Reason Alone* by Immanuel Kant, by permission of The Open Court Publishing Company, La Salle, Illinois, copyright 1934 by The Open Court Publishing Company, Chicago.

Printed in the U.S.A. Library of Congress Catalog Number: 61-65561
International Standard Book Number: 0-85229-335-6
International Standard Serial Number: 0072-7288

Contents

Preface   1

PART ONE   **A Symposium on Culture and Society**

Introduction   4

The Growth of Public Patronage
  Waldemar A. Nielsen   7

The Need for a Comprehensive Cultural Policy
  Jacques Rigaud   28

State Subsidy and Artistic Freedom
  Arnold Goodman   41

Public Funding of the Arts in America
  Michael Straight   53

Patronage through the Ages
  Philipp Fehl   74

PART TWO   **Current Developments in the Arts and Sciences**

Human Fossils: The New Revolution
  Charles E. Oxnard   92

The Idea of a Modern Museum
  Roy McMullen   154

PART THREE   **The Contemporary Status of a Great Idea**

The Idea of Religion—Part One
  John Edward Sullivan, O.P.   204

PART FOUR   **Reflections on a Great Books Author**

The Philosophy of Kant
  Anthony Quinton   278

PART FIVE   **Additions to the Great Books Library**

The Comparison of Related Forms
  D'Arcy Wentworth Thompson   320

Religion within the Limits of Reason Alone
  Immanuel Kant   368

The Utility of Religion
  John Stuart Mill   404

The Golden Flower Pot
  E. T. A. Hoffmann   426

A NOTE ON REFERENCE STYLE

In the following pages, passages in *Great Books of the Western World* are referred to by the initials *'GBWW,'* followed by volume, page number, and page section. Thus, *'GBWW*, Vol. 39, p. 210b' refers to page 210 in Adam Smith's *The Wealth of Nations*, which is Volume 39 in *Great Books of the Western World*. The small letter 'b' indicates the page section. In books printed in single column, 'a' and 'b' refer to the upper and lower halves of the page. In books printed in double column, 'a' and 'b' refer to the upper and lower halves of the left column, 'c' and 'd' to the upper and lower halves of the right column. For example, 'Vol. 53, p. 210b' refers to the lower half of page 210, since Volume 53, James's *Principles of Psychology*, is printed in single column. On the other hand, 'Vol. 7, p. 210b' refers to the lower left quarter of the page, since Volume 7, Plato's *Dialogues*, is printed in double column.

Gateway to the Great Books is referred to by the initials *'GGB,'* followed by volume and page number. Thus, *'GGB*, Vol. 10, pp. 39-57' refers to pages 39 through 57 of Volume 10 of *Gateway to the Great Books*, which is James's essay, "The Will to Believe."

The Great Ideas Today is referred to by the initials *'GIT,'* followed by the year and page number. Thus *'GIT* 1968, p. 210' refers to page 210 of the 1968 edition of *The Great Ideas Today*.

Preface

This year's issue of *The Great Ideas Today* is arranged in the usual manner. The volume begins with a symposium in which a number of well-informed persons express themselves on a topic of current interest, in this case the question of government support for the arts. Their discussion is followed by two articles that review, respectively, a science—physical anthropology—which we have not heretofore considered, and the visual arts, or more exactly the setting in which most people confront the visual arts, that is, the museum. Then comes the first part of a long essay on one of the great ideas, the idea of religion (the second part will appear next year); this is followed by an explication of one of the authors in *Great Books of the Western World*, Immanuel Kant, the importance of whose writings in the development of Western thought is as great as the difficulty they present to the reader of them; and at the end of the volume will be found four brief works by various authors which may be regarded as worthwhile additions to the Great Books library.

It will be observed that several of these writings are related in their subject matter, and in fact that the contents of the volume as a whole arrange themselves under as few as four headings. One of these, *art*, is the concern not only of the symposium, and of the article by Roy McMullen on the Georges Pompidou National Center of Art and Culture, which has recently been constructed in Paris; it is also the subject of "The Golden Flower Pot," one of the tales of Hoffmann, with which the book ends. Under the heading of *science* may be placed both Professor Oxnard's article on physical anthropology and the selection from D'Arcy Thompson's earlier work in the same field. *Philosophy*, of course, is Professor Quinton's preoccupation in his essay on Kant, and *religion* is the concern of Father Sullivan, J. S. Mill, and Kant himself, in the writings that appear beside their names.

Readers interested in the subject of religion may wish to compare discussions that have appeared in earlier issues of *The Great Ideas Today*. Among them are the symposium entitled "Should Christianity Be Secularized?" which appeared in 1967, and which included an account of the idea of religion in *GBWW*, and an essay by Etienne Gilson, "The Idea of God and the Difficulties of Atheism," which appeared in 1969.

On the influence of Kant, see W. T. Jones, "The Widening Gyre: Philosophy in the Twentieth Century," in the volume for 1973; for an earlier piece by Roy McMullen that deals with contemporary music, painting, and sculpture, see the volume for 1967; for other works by J. S. Mill, see the volumes for 1964 ("A Review of Toqueville"), 1966 ("The Subjection of Women"), and 1969 ("Inaugural Address at St. Andrews").

Recent subscribers, who will not have these earlier and now out-of-print issues of *The Great Ideas Today* at hand, may wish to know that a selection of what seemed the best original articles from them has recently been published by the Arno Press in four volumes. The volumes are entitled, respectively, *The Humanities Today, The Social Sciences Today, The Sciences Today,* and *Contemporary Ideas in Historical Perspective,* and any one of these or the four of them as a set may be ordered from Arno Press, Inc., Three Park Avenue, New York, N.Y. 10016.

A Symposium on Culture and Society

Introduction

Our symposium this year deals with the subject of arts patronage and how it is evolving these days—how in most countries it has already evolved—into the subject of arts subsidy. The evolution is, in essence, from something that if not always private was usually personal and for the most part upper-class into what increasingly is public and therefore, in the typical modern situation, both institutional and democratic. It thus raises questions about the role of government as a sponsor of cultural enterprises, and forces us to think in general terms about the relation between culture and society.

The contributors to the symposium accept this evolution as inevitable, given the social and economic trend of our times. They would like as much private patronage retained as possible, but they do not think there can be enough of it henceforth to sustain cultural life. What concerns them is the kind of public support that is being made available to the arts, the degree of control over cultural activity that it entails, and the effect it is likely to have on future cultural development. These are questions raised by the various cultural policies that have been established in one country or another since the Second World War, when the responsibility of the public sector in this area began to be generally recognized. While some of these policies have been in effect for two decades or more, and while in most cases they reflect settled principles of social practice in the countries where they exist, they are as yet too new, particularly where they have had to be altered in the face of changing circumstances, for their value to be entirely established. They are therefore open to discussion of the sort the symposium provides, which reflects the much more extensive consideration of the subject that is going on elsewhere.

An introductory essay by Waldemar A. Nielsen, director of the Aspen Institute Program for the Study of Pluralism and the Commonweal, sets the stage by examining the different cultural programs that have been adopted by France, Britain, Sweden, and the United States. Although Mr. Nielsen has views of his own as to the merits of these programs, he is admirably balanced in the account he gives of them, indicating both the strengths and weaknesses, as well as the particular history and the probable prospects, of each one. He thus provides a useful survey of what in their various ways are really model undertakings in the field, though perhaps none of them, owing to their peculiar national characteristics, is altogether imitable.

The three essays that follow explain in more detail the French, British, and American programs and defend the policies that underlie them. In each case the argument is made by a person of wide experience and exceptional qualifications. Thus, the cultural policy of the French government is set forth by Jacques Rigaud, who has served as bureau chief of the French Ministry of Cultural Affairs; British policy is described by Arnold Goodman, who has been chairman of the British Arts Council as well as a member of numerous other arts organizations; and American policy at the federal level is expounded by Michael Straight, deputy chairman of the National Endowment for the Arts in Washington, D.C. These statements should not be taken as in any sense official, but short of that it is clear they are as informed and authoritative as it is possible to have.

A fifth essay, by Philipp Fehl, professor of the history of art at the University of Illinois, takes a somewhat longer look at the subject of patronage, considering how it has developed, particularly since the Renaissance, into a tradition the influence of which may be clearly seen in the cultural programs of modern states. Such a prospect raises interesting and somewhat disturbing questions about the historicism, the lack of critical judgment, and the generally academic character of much arts scholarship nowadays, as it does also about the showmanship of those theater and museum directors who in their efforts to make art popular sometimes misrepresent or otherwise distort it.

Of the contributors who defend specific policies — Jacques Rigaud, Arnold Goodman, and Michael Straight — it will be noted that, as they all accept the idea that the arts should to some extent be publicly supported, so they all agree that this support will, or should, leave cultural life with the freedom they believe it requires to function. They agree, further, that if this is done the effect on cultural development of public support will be beneficial. Where they do not agree is over the kind of support that government ought to provide. Jacques Rigaud, reflecting French tradition, maintains that such support should be the instrument of a comprehensive cultural policy whereby the government would, as in France, take general responsibility for cultural life. Opposed to this idea is Arnold Goodman, equally reflective of British tradition, who maintains that government assistance should go only to cultural endeavors that have got started on their own, without presuming to say where and what they ought to be, and then should be forthcoming only to the extent that such endeavors cannot overcome the deficits they are likely to run up if left to themselves. The difference between these two conceptions, it seems fair to say, is the difference between the French Ministry of Cultural Affairs and the British Arts Council. And the difference between both of those institutions and the National Endowment for the Arts in Washington may be taken as the difference between

European thinking in this field and that of America. For this last seems, by Michael Straight's account, to reflect an attempt to find a middle way— difficult, perhaps, to maintain—between the all-embracing, respectful, and enlightened control over cultural activity that is assumed in France and the disinterested, even detached—if also concerned and thoughtful—approach of the British.

Whether *any* of these policies (and we should include among them the Swedish plan described by Mr. Nielsen) will be adequate to sustain the cultural life of the countries that have conceived them is not more certain, of course, than whether, ideally speaking, one of them is preferable to the others. The fact is that, because of rapidly increasing costs and limited financial resources in many parts of the world, it may not be possible to sustain indefinitely certain of the arts and arts institutions—opera, theater, museums, and so forth—that are highly valued, at least on the scale to which we have been accustomed, no matter what scheme for doing so is devised. This is the context within which the symposium must be understood, and which indeed it endeavors to explain.

Moreover, even if sufficient funds can be found, it may not seem as clear as once it would have how they should be used. The time when sums could be allocated to cultural affairs on the decision of public officials remote from—and, in their taste, incomprehensible to—the population at large is drawing to an end. This is so in part because the sums required are now so great that the public at large cannot fail to notice them. It must seem interesting to the ordinary Frenchman that the largest single item in the government's budget for cultural activities is the subsidy for the Paris Opera, which in a given year only one Frenchman in forty ever gets to hear. Apparently it was more than interesting, it was repugnant to a mob that raged through Milan recently during a performance at La Scala, which is heavily subsidized by the hard-pressed Italian government, in protest that so much was being spent for the entertainment of so few. If a visible part of the national budget is henceforth to be devoted to culture, there is going to be public demand for a much wider distribution of the money than was formerly thought necessary and a much greater say in the sort of cultural life that society, through its institutions, should undertake to foster. It is this prospect to which the contributors to the symposium ultimately feel obliged to address themselves, although they can do little more than suggest the possibilities of a public attitude that is not yet fully formed. It is at this point that the question of public subsidy turns into the much more serious question of social desires and the common good.

The Growth of Public Patronage

Waldemar A. Nielsen

Trained as an economist and political scientist, Waldemar A. Nielsen has been a university teacher, government official, diplomat, consultant, and foundation director. He has served as special assistant to the secretary of commerce (1947–48) and has been deputy director for the behavioral sciences division and assistant to the president of the Ford Foundation (1952–55); deputy director of that foundation's international affairs program (1956–61); head of a White House study of U.S. cultural and informational programs overseas (1960); president of the African-American Institute (1961–70), during which period he wrote three books on Africa; consultant to the State Department on international youth activities, to the Department of Housing and Urban Development, and to government and philanthropic organizations (1966–68); board member of such organizations as UNESCO and International Planned Parenthood Association; and philanthropic consultant to the Empress of Iran (1970). He is author of the widely discussed study *The Big Foundations* (1972), written for the Twentieth Century Fund.

Mr. Nielsen is currently director of the Aspen Institute's new program on the problems of American pluralism. As a natural outcome of his involvement with cultural programs in Europe, Asia, and Africa, he has become interested in similar undertakings in America. Especially in New York, where he lives, he is known for his devotion to the arts and his many contributions to cultural affairs.

Patronage of the arts has a long, checkered, and confusing history. The Chinese and Egyptian courts thousands of years ago practiced it, as did the Athenians. Both private and official patronage was so developed among the Romans that Seneca, the philosopher and statesman, wrote a book on how to be a generous but not oppressive benefactor. The Catholic popes, the medieval Italian and German princes, the doges of Venice, and great bankers like the Fuggers of Augsburg were devoted, and sometimes highly competitive, patrons.[1] In the period since the Industrial Revolution, the Rothschilds, Mellons, and Rockefellers have prominently continued the tradition.

Much of the art produced over the centuries, whatever the system of patronage, has been mediocre or worse. But periodically in most cultures there have occurred bursts of outstanding creative activity, usually in several art forms simultaneously and often in parallel with great advances in science and technology. We do not know why this is so. The output of great art seems to have some relationship to the wealth of a society, but the triumphs, century after century, of Chinese culture emerged out of an eternal ocean of general poverty. Great art seems to have something to do with the enlightenment and cultivation of leadership, but it has flourished under the hand of ruthless Italian princes and barbarous Sassanian nomads, not to speak of Papuan and Congolese tribal chiefs. We may suppose art to have something to do with human freedom, but it has thrived amid the slavery of Athens and the repressiveness of the inquisitorial Spanish Court. About all that can be said for sure is that the thrust of artistic creativity has somehow persisted through every obstacle and outrage inflicted upon it. One might even be tempted to conclude that misery, oppression, and great art go together, since nearly all of it has been produced under those circumstances.

In recent decades, and especially in the period since the end of the Second World War, most advanced democratic societies have felt impelled to try to provide encouragement and support to the arts and to cultural activities. Their efforts are as varied as their national traditions. A comparison of these undertakings in four countries—France, Great Britain, Sweden, and the United States—as to the problems of cultural policy and its prospects is instructive.

France: prestige and patrimony

France is a country with a rich cultural tradition, of which it is keenly conscious and very proud. It is also a country in which the State has long taken a strong interest in culture as a national responsibility and as an instrument for radiating French prestige and influence abroad.

Many of the great cultural institutions of contemporary France were created by the State long before the twentieth century, some—the Louvre museum, the Paris Opéra, the various Académies—even before the Revolution. Napoleon I signed the decree regulating operation of the Comédie-Française during the winter he occupied Moscow.

This long and active involvement of the State has not resulted in the establishment of a totalitarian culture; that is, it has not meant the manipulation of creative artists in the service of an ideology or to further the immediate political purposes of government. The deeply ingrained respect for the autonomy of the artist in France has taught politicians and the bureaucracy the unacceptability of any such effort. What they have also learned, however, is that they can shape French culture by selectively rewarding achievements in accordance with their tastes and interests, so long as the initiative and privileged moral status of the artist is not violated. The result has been the imposition of an "official culture"—a monolithic, aristocratic, and scholastic culture nurtured and protected by government distribution of preferences, status, and subsidies.

Enforcement of official norms was until recently both sustained and severe. As one French social critic has said, "It banished the giants of Impressionism and left them to eat out of garbage cans in Montmartre while subsidized academic nonentities were banqueting at the Beaux-Arts."[2] Yet, for a long time this did not stifle artistic creativity. On the contrary, it was paradoxically invigorating. In the nineteenth and early twentieth centuries, for example, the rigidity of official artistic standards excluded the most creative spirits and at the same time provoked them to destroy the prototypes venerated by the Establishment. A state of permanent warfare between official culture and the artist was born, along with the concept of the avant-garde. The effect was to stimulate, almost to necessitate, radical artistic innovation.

By the Second World War, however, the bloodless norms of official culture had been so discredited that they were no longer even a source of provocation. The consequence was a notorious decline in the brilliance of French culture. Theater, opera, ballet, music, literature, sculpture, and even painting passed under a cloud of mediocrity. This development was of concern to a succession of French governments, which tried to counteract it. The Fifth Republic, under President Charles de Gaulle, had among its aims the restoration of the "grandeur" of France. In 1958 it created the first Ministry of Culture and named the late André Malraux to head it. According to the decree defining its tasks, the ministry was "to insure a vast audience for our cultural inheritance" and to "encourage the creation of works of art . . . which enrich this culture." Its ideal was thus the historic one, "one culture for one nation," and the goals were preservation of the heritage, its dissemination, and the reenforcement of it by the "guidance" of new creativity.

It has become apparent that these objectives are unattainable. Their premise, which was that the only barriers to mass participation in traditional culture were financial or educational, has been challenged by new and undeniable evidence of French behavior and preferences. Surveys show, for example, that most of the French people, like the citizens of many other industrialized countries, never read books, seldom go to a museum, rarely attend the theater, almost never appear at a concert or the opera. On the other hand, their outlays have tripled in recent years for sports and camping equipment, holiday trips, tobacco, gambling, and radio and television sets. Despite all official efforts to "ensure a vast audience" for it, the French have little appetite for classical culture.[3]

Likewise, attempts to guide new creativity toward the reenforcement of the traditional culture have run aground on the rapidly expanding reefs of popular culture. Among the young, especially, a general indifference to the classics is combined with a voracious appetite for comic books, western movies, and pop music. In addition, diverse expressions of underground and counterculture have vigorously emerged. These, however chaotic, have confirmed the impossibility of administering a universal culture by official action and design.

Recognition of this has been painful for a country with the history of France, but the fact has now been grasped and acted upon. In 1969 the Sixth Plan Commission laid down a new policy which represented a major break with the past. The old premises were dropped and, as a principle, the State henceforth is to promote the unrestricted expansion of diverse expressions of creativity, to bring about conditions most propitious for such activity, and to promote public awareness through appropriate means of dissemination. To this end, and notwithstanding the disappointments of the past, the State has over the last fifteen years tripled the level in real value of its direct subsidies, which now total about 1 percent of its budget. A series of special national taxes and indirect subsidies has been adopted: a tax on publishing and printing houses for the benefit of writers; a tax on profitable private theaters to subsidize those in deficit; a tax on art dealers for the benefit of artists; special credits available to film producers; special tax exemption for "art and experimental" cinema houses. Significantly, some diversification of support has been encouraged, by the *départements* and the municipalities, and even by private patrons. Limited tax incentives have been provided for the establishment of foundations and for the purchase of works and art which are to be donated by the buyer to the State.

The results to date have been beneficial. The old nationalism has been replaced by a new cosmopolitanism. Exiled artists such as Pierre Boulez are being called back; a German, Rolf Lieberman, has been hired to revive the decayed Paris Opéra; a vast new international center for the arts, the Centre National d'Art et de Culture Georges Pompidou, familiarly known as the Beaubourg, has been built in Paris. At least a limited artistic revival seems to have begun.

The avowed intention of current policy is to create a more open, flexible, diverse environment for cultural development. But in the allocation and administration of the increased resources being provided, the weight of old habits is apparent. The "prestige" centers of the traditional culture in Paris receive the lion's share. (The government provides a $40 subsidy to every seat for every performance of the Paris Opéra.) Likewise, the assistance given to regional theaters is administered by a centralized bureaucracy in Paris, which is more inclined to promote presentations of the classics than to respond to local tastes and initiatives.

In this difficult period of transition, France has responded to new forces, but with compromise and contradictions. It has opted for evolution, but under strong State tutelage. There are those, particularly in academic circles, who hope that the invention of some new pedagogy will make it possible to restore the sovereignty of the classical heritage and close the gulf between it and the general population. There are those of the counterculture who fervently believe that the old tradition is dead and will be succeeded by a radically new culture of participation, free self-expression, spontaneity, and what they see as "relevance."

What is indisputable is that, in France, culture remains of great importance in public policy, and that a break with the past has been achieved. Whether the new official eclecticism will prove fruitful in creative terms remains to be seen.

Great Britain: patronage and passivity

The contrasts between Britain and France, which are striking, have their origins in the distant reaches of history. In France, the medieval pattern of royal and Church patronage was ruptured by the Revolution and, beginning in the late eighteenth century, was formally replaced by installation of the secular state as the provider of the arts. But in Britain that abrupt displacement was averted, and until recently patronage of the arts remained primarily in private hands.

Among its other consequences for Britain, the Second World War destroyed much of the basis of wealth and privilege on which the tradition of private patronage had rested. This breakdown, and the necessity of shifting to some new kind of public support, reached crisis proportions in the postwar period.

Immediately after the cessation of hostilities, a new Arts Council was created by royal charter. It was to be a permanent government agency, but in a peculiarly British sense. The new agency was to be the principal vehicle for distribution of official support for the arts; at the same time, elaborate measures were taken to ensure its formal independence. The council is composed of private citizens who are appointed by the government but who have complete authority for setting policy and for distributing the funds it receives. The politicians leave the council free to spend as it thinks fit. Parliament provides the funds but does not lay down purposes or priorities for which they must be spent. This arm's length, indirect method to "decontaminate" government money passing into sensitive fields such as education, science, and the arts is a special British invention.

Several other features of the British approach designed to buffer the arts from official influence are also noteworthy: the volume of central government assistance has been intended to draw forth other and greater resources from local governments and from private patrons, which it has successfully done. This has been partly by necessity, for the council's resources, by comparison with those of its counterparts on the Continent, have been rather small. But it has also been by design, in the belief that the independence of recipient institutions and the ability of each "to stand on its own bottom" are essential to the balance of the entire subsidy system. Such diversification and decentralization of support is considered to be not only a political protection but also a guarantee of broad public involvement.

The council itself, in its operations, has emphasized the democratization of procedures. It relies heavily upon the participation of artists and other private citizens in its advisory committees and specialized panels, and no grant is made without their recommendation. These panels are carefully composed of persons differing in age, artistic outlook, and experience; they are chosen from different parts of the country; membership on the panels rotates rather rapidly. The council is also in the process of devolving responsibility for decision making to regional arts associations and to the Scottish and Welsh arts councils.[4] Finally, the council insists that its role is to be a service agency, not a promoter or organizer of the arts. It prides itself on its planlessness, its policy of responding to the initiatives of artists and cultural institutions rather than advancing initiatives of its own.

British opinion is not inclined to spare the country's institutions from criticism, and in the arts this is at least as true as in other fields. The Arts Council has been attacked repeatedly on grounds of untidiness, passivity, and capriciousness. It has been accused both of excessive dispersion and excessive concentration of grants. It has been denounced as excessively establishmentarian and also as excessively responsive to provincial, amateurish, and counterculture elements. Such complaints are difficult to sort out. What seems clear is that, on the whole, the council has been neither as planless, decentralized, or purely reactive as its public posture sometimes suggests. There has been, for example, consistently heavy stress on institutional support rather than direct assistance to the individual artist; heavy emphasis on the performing arts rather than the creative arts; heavy concentration of financial support on a handful of great prestige organizations and the "high culture" tradition they embody. And while all these patterns of priority are now being diluted or even reversed, they have been until recently the rule, suggesting that the council, for all its formal independence, has operated in coordination, if not with British government, then at least with the preoccupations and preferences of that upper class of individuals whose influence has long been decisive both in official life and in many areas of private life.

Whatever the particular contours of Arts Council policy, British cultural life in many fields has flourished during the period of its existence. London has regained its position as a world center of drama, music, opera, and dance. Its actors, actresses, and directors have given it a leading position on the international stage. The country has made a remarkable record in finding new playwrights and choreographers. For the first time since Purcell, Britain has produced composers who have attracted international admiration. The least that can be said for the government's aid to the arts, therefore, is that it has avoided the danger of official stultification.

Looking to the future, however, it seems likely that the problems of maintaining the delicate balance between centralization and decentralization, between older and newer institutional claimants, between the various forms of artistic expression, and between various class and regional interests will become rapidly more difficult. Most disturbing to the workability of the system is the fact that the unusual degree of national consensus on which the British constitutional system has depended in the past seems to be breaking up on the rocks of class bitterness, economic decline, and profound changes in social values. If this should continue, no aspect of national life will be more powerfully affected than its cultural institutions and cultural life.

Sweden: the sociological way

If France and Britain are countries with a long and rich tradition of cultural achievement, which are now being drawn somewhat reluctantly toward decentralization and "democratization" of culture, Sweden is one with a rather modest cultural heritage, which is now leading the charge in those new directions.

Official Swedish interest in cultural matters is very recent, the first comprehensive program in the field having been enacted only in 1961. That program resulted in increased state assistance to arts education in the schools and increased support for artists and arts institutions. It also resulted in a decade of intensifying debate about cultural policy. That debate involved not only questions of levels of financial support but fundamental differences about values and objectives. Some argued that the aim of cultural policy should be to guarantee "every citizen's right to free communication with others"; others held that cultural activity should be supported as a means of presenting a social or political message, not merely to produce artifacts or facilitate social interaction.

The question of "cultural equality" has also been much discussed. The view has become more and more common that traditional art forms are an embodiment of aristocratic or bourgeois values. Many therefore feel that cultural institutions have to be reorganized on the basis of a new concept of culture "without the curtailing effect of traditional concepts based on esthetics."

During the 1960s, while these arguments were going on, political developments relating to more practical issues were also occurring. Unions of "cultural workers" were able to win large pay increases for their members and also to increase greatly their influence over the form and distribution of state grants. By the end of the decade they had won the right to control the distribution of the funds appropriated by the parliament for the benefit of artists, writers, and performers. In this process the unions and professional associations have carefully avoided making qualitative assessment of individual applicants and have insisted upon nondiscriminatory formulas for making their allocations.

In 1969 a National Council for Cultural Affairs was appointed to develop a new cultural policy. The report of this citizens' group was presented to the public and to the parliament in 1974. In 1975, after a further year of consultations, its proposals became law.

The thorough and systematic way in which the new cultural policy was developed is suggested by the fact that the council worked for nearly five years on proposals that involved more than 200,000 individuals participating in committees and groups at every level and reflecting every significant viewpoint. After the report was drafted, it was sent to some 400 authorities, institutions, and organizations for their reactions; these in many cases distributed it to their subsidiary bodies. Their voluminous response was then considered by the parliament, along with the council's recommendations, before action was taken, some six years after the start of the enterprise.

Because of the process by which it was developed, and because it was subsequently enacted by the Swedish parliament almost without a scratch, the council's report is probably the most representative statement of the viewpoint of a modern society on cultural issues in existence. It is appropriate, therefore, to give the ideas in it special attention.

In the Swedish fashion, it speaks in the vocabulary not of aesthetics but of management, ideology, and sociology. As regards the question of the relationship between government and private activity, the report proceeds on the unchallenged assumption that the welfare state should be an enlightened, benevolently paternalistic, but nonetheless comprehensive provider of society's needs. It offers a blend of democratic theory with a large dose of centralized practice.

"By cultural policy, the National Council for Cultural Affairs means a concentrated structure for societal measures in the cultural field," the report begins. "The Council proposes that the GENERAL GOAL of cultural policy be to contribute towards creating a better social environment and promoting increased equality. . . ." This undertaking is justified on the ground that

> cultural activity aims mainly at satisfying the needs of human beings for experiences, expression, and contact and at being the tool for the investigation of reality and the critical examination of society. . . . Cultural policy should be seen as part of society's engagement in environment policy as a whole. . . . Society can never count on the free market to create diversified cultural production and cultural activity evenly distributed all over the country or a reasonable living for cultural workers. . . . If the demands for equality and justice are to be met, society's work in cultural policy cannot be limited to the task, great as it may be, of making resources available for those who, because of their training or other circumstances, want such activity. Special drives must be made in culturally backward environments and with underprivileged groups.[5]

If the "GENERAL GOAL" is to be achieved, seven subgoals, according to the council, have also to be met. These are:

1. *Decentralization:* "State support of cultural activity has long been concentrated on institutions in larger cities. . . . It is an economically just demand that the state support the building up of independent regional cultural activity."
2. *Coordination and differentiation:* "This may involve coordination with physical planning and the planning of social services and with educational or social policy. . . . The goal of differentiating measures is . . . to break through . . . isolation and debarment and to create the prerequisites for a broader sense of community."
3. *Community and activity:* "From a practical point of view and from the point of view of organizations, it is natural to give priority to forms of collective activity."
4. *Freedom of expression:* "Measures of cultural policy . . . shall create the prerequisites for a cultural life marked by manifoldness, both in content and in forms of expression."
5. *Artistic renewal:* "Radio and television have created new forms of art and new forms of information and entertainment. . . . It is important that various groups of people working artistically be offered the possibilities of working within these media and, in their own fields, contributing to their development."
6. *Preservation of older culture:* "Technological advances have had the result that our possibilities of preserving the culture of older areas have im-

proved considerably. . . . This technical progress, however, . . . may . . . be used in ways involving risks for cultural life. The commercial exploitation of television satellites, tapes, and television cassettes and the increased dependence upon the international book market are examples of such tendencies."

7. *Society's responsibility*: "Most of the production and distribution of culture today is in private hands. . . . The state's activities in the future should be aimed to a greater extent at offering alternatives to the private cultural activity in various sectors."

The entire statement of policy is presented with logic, vision, and generosity of spirit. It desanctifies culture by considering it as a concern of state policy coordinate with housing, education, the improvement of working conditions, and the relocation of industry. The values which underlie it are not aesthetic but functional and social—justice, equality, communication, community building, and individual development. It sees culture as a proper object of comprehensive state responsibility, and it is equally concerned with freedom on the one hand and with the employment of culture as a political instrument on the other. The decentralization it stresses is a decentralization in which the chosen vehicles are county and municipal authorities—that is, other elements of government.

Yet, the report is silent about artistic excellence. The hope seems to be that a multiplicity of interests and support sources—municipal, county, and state authorities, popular education and trade union movements, the press, and an increasingly educated consumer public—will provide self-regulating safeguards against both political interference and poor standards.

The NCCA, by act of parliament in adopting the new policy, has now been transformed into the central agency for carrying it out. Though independent, it is still an arm of government and is therefore required to execute government policies mandated to it. A good deal of the funds it receives are earmarked, and decisions made by the parliament during the financial year may specifically direct certain allocations. The government thus spends its money via the council to carry out government objectives. It is not, as in Britain, a matter of the council's seeking government money to carry out its own policies.

The new policy has improved the incomes of journeymen artists and performers; it has increased the level of government support for culture; it has quantitatively increased cultural activity throughout the country. But the standard of artistic production in Sweden remains generally disappointing, and the most notable single cultural event since the adoption of the new policy has been the self-exile and departure of the country's best known artistic figure, the filmmaker Ingmar Bergman. At this point, one can be pessimistic and say that the apparent lack of real imagination and excellence in Swedish artistic manifestations is the result of too much abstract theorizing and bureaucratic planning; or one can be optimistic and say that the combination of a carefully thought out policy from the center, allowing plenty of freedom for maneuver by the local and independent partners, will in time have a broadly beneficial effect both on the art and on the quality of Swedish life. Convincing evidence to support either view is yet to come in.

The United States: the mixed economy of culture

American policy in support of the arts has developed against this swirling background of tendencies in Europe—contradictory tendencies as regards the role of the State and the emphasis to be given social or aesthetic aims, but common tendencies toward greater government support for the arts and wider opportunities for popular participation in them.

American culture and ideas about culture, like American religious, political, and economic ideas, were initially imported from Europe. To think about art was to borrow the seventeenth-century European distinction between the "fine" and the "decorative," or "minor" and "practical," arts. The legacy of the great European royal academies and conservatories and of the patronage traditions of the titled and the wealthy firmly linked

"The road to governmental involvement was little by little opened. . . . [In 1964] Congress authorized a $15.6 million grant for construction of a national cultural center as a memorial to the late President Kennedy."

art in the United States with ideas of high culture, educated taste, and elite society.

In the nineteenth century the nation's preoccupations gradually shifted from political development to economic development, and the personal fortunes acquired in the process paved the way for the cultural development that followed. The wealthy have been the leaders, the patrons, and the tastemakers of American high culture from then down to the present. They have provided the funds and the prestige on which the nation's symphony orchestras, opera companies, and ballet companies have been built.[6] Their art collections have formed the core around which the major museums have been developed. (The principal exception is the theater, which until recent decades was commercially profitable and self-supporting.) These patrons financed activities which appealed to their taste, and what is now accepted as "culture" and "excellence" has been defined by their standards.

In the first half of the twentieth century the pattern of the previous century was modified, first, by the inclusion in 1917 of tax incentives for charitable giving in the recently enacted income tax law, and second, by the expenditures of the Works Progress Administration in 1935 to alleviate unemployment among musicians, artists, actors, and writers. By the former, the support of the wealthy for the arts was subsidized and institutionalized; by the latter, the wall against federal funding of the arts was massively, although fortuitously and only temporarily, breached. Thus, $45 million was spent in the years 1935–39 by the Federal Theatre Project for theatrical performances throughout the country, but then the Congress, for political reasons, abruptly cut off the funds.

Curiously enough, and despite the interest and generosity of many wealthy individuals in giving to the arts, the major philanthropic foundations and business corporations which were controlled by the same social class gave little to them until rather recent years.

The period following the Second World War was a time of general prosperity, increasing leisure, rising levels of education, and rapidly increasing expenditures for recreational cultural activities. Americans took more piano lessons, joined more art classes, bought more records and hi-fi equipment, bought more books, saw more plays, and went more often to museums than ever before. They multiplied the number of symphony orchestras, opera companies, theater groups, and dance companies in the United States at the same time that they were going more often to the movies, watching more TV, taking more vacations, and buying more fishing tackle and photographic equipment. Some kind of major shift in tastes and habits was quite dramatically under way, but commentators were in sharp disagreement as to just what it was.

Some applauded it as a "culture boom." Others were less sanguine, pointing to the fact that most of the expansion in the arts was amateur and that professional companies and organizations were in unending financial dif-

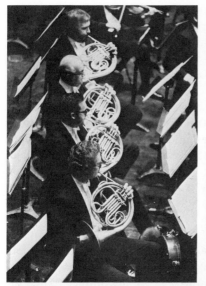

"The wealthy have been the . . . tastemakers of American high culture . . . and what is now accepted as 'culture' and 'excellence' has been defined by their standards." Above, performances of the Chicago Symphony Orchestra (top, left), the Metropolitan Opera (top, right), and the Guthrie Theater (bottom).

ficulty. Harold Schonberg, the respected music critic of the *New York Times*, seeing many young talented American musicians and singers forced to go abroad to find employment because of the lack of opportunities at home, called the reported cultural prosperity "phony."[7]

As time was to reveal, the issue was falsely drawn, for not one but two contradictory trends were intertwined. There was indeed a vast surge under way in recreational activity, entertainment, and amateur arts. At the same time, although there was a modest increase in public attendance and support, nothing that could be called a boom in the traditional forms of art had occurred. Despite the construction of new cultural centers in many cities and notwithstanding an increase in personal incomes, interest in opera, classical music, ballet, and the theater remained specialized minority tastes; their audiences were predominately upper-income, better educated individuals, living largely in and around New York and largely of German, Jewish, or Italian background. The great mass of the population preferred popular culture and participatory culture. The evidence of the bottom line was incontrovertible: the temples of high culture were impoverished, while the purveyors of recreation and entertainment were rolling in profits.

To some, the conclusion to be drawn was that the old rituals of culture were dying, that the authority of the old elite in matters of taste had been broken, and that new forms of artistic expression were about to take over. But to many distinguished leaders of society and professionals in the arts, the lesson was quite the opposite, namely that there was an urgent need to come to the rescue of the established arts organizations and to take advantage of the new interest in amateur arts so that great new audiences for high culture by education and encouragement might be built. The situation was seen as a call to action to avert a danger and to seize an opportunity.

The first significant new response came from the Ford Foundation. Beginning in 1957, largely as a result of the initiative of W. McNeill Lowry of the staff, the foundation launched what became the first national effort by philanthropy to strengthen arts organizations. Over the next twenty years the foundation poured some $300 million into its program, a private effort of unprecedented scale. It was focused primarily on the performing arts— theater, music, and dance—rather than the visual arts; on professional artists and arts organizations, not avocational artists or educational institutions; and it was intended to develop their long-term capacity to sustain themselves on an independent, private basis. No definitive history or assessment of the program has yet been done, but without question it has profoundly changed the artistic landscape of the country. Dozens of national and regional theaters, ballet companies, and symphony orchestras are now far stronger and more fully developed than they would have been without Ford assistance.

While many might disagree with the foundation's choice of priorities, none could disagree with its consistency and courage in attempting to do what a private institution uniquely has the freedom and capacity to do—to set independent goals and to make discriminating choices, thereby contributing a distinctive quality and coloration to the tapestry of national activity in any major field.

While Ford was launching its program, however, a number of forces, both cultural and political, were converging to demand that the arts be given status as a responsibility of government, especially the federal government. The time was the crest of the cold war, and many of the supportive arguments were consequently geopolitical and nationalistic. It was said to be backward of the United States not to subsidize culture as generously as did West Germany and France, for example; we could not compete in the global "battle for men's minds" without a stronger show of governmental interest in the arts; for the government to recognize the arts officially would give them dignity and "prove to the world" that Americans are culturally serious; and so on. In parallel, the bread-and-butter case was insistently put forth: without more government subsidy, culture simply could not survive.

A few voices were raised against the whole idea. Russell Lynes of *Harper's Magazine* argued that the less the arts have to do with politics, "the healthier they will be, the more respected, the more important to Americans, and the more productive." John Sloan, the painter, wrote: "Sure it would be good to have a Ministry of Fine Arts. Then we'd know where the enemy is."[8] But the road to governmental involvement was little by little opened. The milestones along that road were the following:

1958: Nelson Rockefeller, who had long been interested in the arts, and who as coordinator of Inter-American Affairs during World War II had directed extensive official cultural programs with Latin America, became governor of New York. He successfully pushed for legislation in his first year to create a state Arts Council and to provide substantial funding for it.

1962: Pres. John F. Kennedy named August Heckscher to the newly created post of special consultant on the arts to prepare a report on the role of government in the arts, a document which helped lay the basis for subsequent legislative action.

1964: Under Pres. Lyndon Johnson, Congress authorized a $15.6 million grant for construction of a national cultural center as a memorial to the late President Kennedy. It also voted to establish the National Council on the Arts, created by executive order by President Kennedy shortly before his assassination, on a more permanent basis.

1965: A panel of prominent leaders in the arts assembled by a private foundation, the Rockefeller Brothers Fund, at the instigation of John D. Rockefeller III, issued an important report on the problems and prospects of the performing arts in the United States. It had a powerful effect in that for the first time it gave blue-ribbon respectability to the idea of government funding. Later that same year the Congress approved a three-year program providing for the first time for direct federal support of the arts through the creation of a National Endowment for the Arts.

These developments were the result of a change in attitude and policy which had come about in a peculiarly American way. Belated as compared with Europe, it was largely the result of initiatives from the private sector, and from the economic and philanthropic potentates of that sector. The resulting bias can be clearly seen if we compare the approach of the Rockefeller panel, for example, with that of the subsequent legislation creating the endowment.

The privately composed panel included wealthy connoisseurs and arts professionals of great prestige. They confined their attention essentially to theater, dance, and classical music. They were confident to the point of righteousness in their taste, and evangelical in their zeal to convert the multitudes to high culture. Their aim was to improve the financing of professional arts organizations from both private and—especially—government sources. But their horror was that this additional financial support and these vast new audiences might expose the arts to vulgarization. "We must never allow the central focus on quality to weaken or shift," the panel said. "Popularization in any realm often leads to a reduction of standards. ... Democratization carries with it a peril for the arts, even as it does for education."[9] Nevertheless, the panel was careful to avoid castigation of commercialization as a factor tending in this same direction. It was tolerant toward amateurism, but only if it contributed to the audience for and appreciation of the professional arts.

In contrast, the legislation creating the National Endowment and the programs which it has subsequently developed reflect a far broader range of objectives and the accommodation of a wider range of influences and values than the Rockefeller panel. The endowment is in fact a fascinating assemblage of conceptual and political compromises reflective of the actual complexities of contemporary American thinking.

It is, for example, an "independent" agency of government, but not too independent. Its policies and programs are formulated with the advice of a National Council on the Arts made up of twenty-six private citizens appointed by the president. But it is also subject to specific directives from the president and to designated appropriations from the Congress.

Its programs and policies are capacious enough to include the old elite and the new populists, the professionals and the amateurs, and both high and popular culture. The National Advisory Council is composed principally but not quite exclusively of the high culture Establishment, and in many of the endowment's statements the theme of "excellence"—artists "of the highest talent," organizations "representing the highest quality"—is repeated, perhaps not with the obsessiveness of the Rockefeller panel but still insistently.

On the other hand, the "arts" as defined by the endowment include not only the classical forms but also folk art, photography, industrial design, costume design, television, and radio. In addition to "arts exposure" programs to build audiences for high culture, there are crafts programs for prison inmates, the handicapped, and the elderly. Indeed, there are offerings which permit almost everyone to witness or to join in cultural activity of some kind, from urban ethnics and ghetto dwellers to those in the smallest rural communities and the backwoods of Appalachia.[10]

By the diversity of its programs, the endowment has greatly broadened its constituency throughout the country. It has sagaciously headed off fears of domination from Washington by distributing block grants to the arts councils in every state, and it has placed heavy stress on matching grants to induce expanded private, state, and municipal contributions, thereby keeping the federal share of funding in a minority position.

The overall result is a program that is pragmatic, diverse, and responsive, and one for which almost everyone has some enthusiasm and some criticism. The elitists are pleased that it has made a brave effort to hold to standards of quality in its grant making, but they fear the growing attention given the amateurs and the "artsy-craftsy" advocates. The offbeat and avant-garde elements of the cultural community suspect the endowment's heart is still with the old Establishment, but they are satisfied that they have been able to win at least a piece of the action. In private philanthropy, there are those who deplore what they regard as too much scatteration in the endowment's grant making, charging that it does little more than sprinkle dew on every leaf without watering or deepening any roots. But even they are impressed by the fact that the endowment, under the leadership of Nancy Hanks, has been able in a particularly delicate political environment to persuade the Congress and three successive presidents to increase its annual budget from $10 million to more than $70 million in the span of a decade.

The evolution of American support for the arts has been essentially ad hoc. It is now a patchwork program of private and public elements which operates without a philosophy, without even a philosophy that it should have no philosophy. But so far, at least, it works.

The need for pluralism

Between now and the approaching end of the century, the problems confronting the United States in the field of cultural policy are likely to become much more difficult and dangerous.

The first of these is financial. Clearly, the old basis of financing the arts by earned income and private gifts has become inadequate and in the future will become even more so. Some possibilities, probably limited, exist for stimulating further private support. There are also possibilities of easing budgetary strains by better, more efficient institutional management. But the likelihood is that costs will increasingly outstrip earnings and gifts, and the widening deficit can be filled only by greater and greater government subsidy.

Whether or not this will be adequately forthcoming is uncertain. The fact that the National Endowment has managed to persuade the Congress to increase its annual budget eightfold in the span of a decade is no guarantee that such a rate of increase can be sustained. The easy, euphoric spending mood of Washington in the 1960s has ended. Concern about government deficits has now intensified. The competition for government resources is increasing as the number of claimants multiplies. There are serious reasons to believe that the American economy, because of rising energy costs and a growing capital shortage, may be entering a period of sustained slow growth. The advocates for the arts will have to make their case, therefore, in an increasingly crowded and clamorous political arena, and in an atmosphere of increasing budgetary stringency at all levels of government.

On balance, the prospect is that government subsidy will not increase as fast as the deficits of arts organizations but that the volume will become greater, causing the government portion of funding for the arts to become increasingly preponderant in relation to private support. That leads directly to the second problem, which is the danger of bureaucratization and politicization.

Although the National Endowment for the Arts has in its first years been a well-run agency with élan and even flair, this happy situation must inevitably erode. Programs in the arts confront any bureaucracy with a maximum of the kinds of decision for which it has the maximum distaste, namely those which require discriminating choices to be made on the basis of nonobjective, nonquantifiable criteria. The logic of modern management will tend to drive the endowment, and state arts councils as well, in the direction of fixed formulas in the allocation of funds—formulas relating to geography, population, audience size, and ratios of subsidy to institutional earnings.[11] Likewise, the tendency will be to retreat from funding the arts and artists as such, because of their controversiality and unquantifiability, and toward the more comfortable areas of research in the arts and of arts education. This trend will be powerfully encouraged by the great organized power of the educationists, who at present are acutely hungry for more jobs, grants, and contracts.

The prospects for politicization are not less worrisome than those for bureaucratization. At the high ideological level there is little possibility, whatever degree of financial dependence on government funding may develop, that any single political viewpoint can be enforced upon the arts. The tradition of assertive diversity in the American body politic provides strong bulwarks against that danger.

But there are more primitive forms of political intrusion which could well be troublesome. In New York, to take a concrete instance, the legislature has now required the Arts Council to distribute "arts services" on a basis of seventy-five cents per capita per county. Also, hundreds of thousands of dollars are now channeled by the legislature directly to certain projects— in one case for a Bicentennial barge that plied the waterways of the state during 1976. It is not difficult to foresee the possibility, indeed the likelihood, of pressure groups of all kinds—ethnic, religious, trade union, and other—persuading Congress and state legislatures in the future to require similar allocations to their special clienteles.

Other forms of possible intrusion arise from what might be called Archie Bunker and superpatriotic politics. These have been rather frequent in the past. The Federal Theatre Project in New Deal days was prevented by the government from raising the curtain on one of its shows because it criticized Mussolini's Italy. Later, the entire project was summarily demolished by a House committee on grounds that it was un-American. In 1946 the State Department organized an exhibition of modern paintings to be circulated in Europe. When a member of the House Appropriations Committee criticized some of the pictures as "weird" and "unnatural," the department promptly ordered the exhibition shipped home. Later it sold the paintings as "war surplus." In the McCarthy era, the infamous investigatory team of Cohn and Shine compiled a list of "subversive" volumes on the shelves of United States Information Service libraries overseas and successfully demanded that they be withdrawn. More recently, the Nixon administration sought to establish partisan control over the programming of the Corporation for Public Broadcasting, an effort which was beaten back only with great difficulty.

Thus far the Endowment for the Arts has been spared such trials, but judging from the record, its day in the dock or on the rack will come. It will come, that is, unless the danger is squarely faced, which has not been done in recent years, when the drive for government funding was gathering momentum. There is no alternative to seeking such money. Government dollars may be hazardous to the health of the arts, but so is starvation. The question is how to obtain them without paying an unacceptable price.

If there is any way to do this, it must be a pluralistic one. Financially, that means reliance upon all available sources—earnings, private gifts, corporate and philanthropic contributions, grants from government at all levels —to the greatest possible extent. Such a mix provides some protection against sharp fluctuations in the level of government support. More important, it enables arts organizations to talk back to their government donors, in some degree at least, and thereby to impose some restraint on any official tendencies to become oppressively bureaucratic or aggressively programmatic.

If the first requirement of a prudent course is a multiplicity of funding sources, the second is deliberate governmental passivity on the British model, in the distribution of its subsidies. As an explicit commitment, official policy should be loose and responsive, leaving initiative and innovativeness to the living forces of art and the artist. Such a policy would do more than provide protection against official intrusion. There are important collateral advantages which a system open to the interplay of all ideas and tendencies provides at this point in cultural history.

This is a time when the boundaries between art, recreation, and social therapy are blurring. It is a time when the standards of judgment appropriate to art are in violent dispute. "High and low are really separate cultures," writes sociologist Herbert Gans. "Each has its own artistic standards, its own concept of good taste, its preferred arts and artists. Which culture people prefer depends on their income, occupation, and cultural education at home and at school."[12]

However radical such a view may seem to traditionalists, it is a mild reflection of the spreading revolt against what is seen as the "colonial approach," by which is meant the endeavor to transmit cultural values downward from a cultivated elite to the masses. There is a rapidly growing public, involved in everything from square dancing to wood carving, which is unwilling to allow its activities to be characterized as mere expressions of uneducated taste. It is insistent that the primary aim of cultural policy should be to encourage active participation in the arts, not passive exposure to the art object or performance. At the outer fringe there is a militant minority, small but influential, which rejects all traditional culture in favor of discordant, politically motivated art forms.

In the context of such dispute about definition, standards, and role of art, it is hardly surprising that a flood of new modes and forms of artistic expression has appeared—electronic music, computerized light shows, multimedia performances, self-destructive art, temporary art, mega-art, micro-art, and anti-art. Professor Steven Marcus has suggested that the present chaotic period signals the interruption of an aesthetic stream which has lasted from the Middle Ages until now. "When a phase of culture comes to an end or to a kind of end, it does not simply vanish and leave not a wrack behind," he writes. Instead, "what it usually does is to go into a state of decomposition. It is that state that we are passing through now."[13] Yet he believes that the existing disarray contains within itself the seeds of fundamentally new developments which at some point will begin to make themselves decisively felt. However this may be, evolutionary changes as profound as those now under way cannot be foreseen or guided. The clash of views cannot be resolved by any court or critic. There is no final theoretical answer to the competing concepts. They can only be left to work themselves out.

Thus the positive reasons for a pluralistic approach to cultural policy in the United States are both prudent and practical: to sustain the arts in a period of difficult changeover from primary reliance on private support to growing reliance on government, and at the same time to protect them from official manipulation in their new dependency. But the negative virtues of such an approach are equally important. In a time of cultural transition and of the possible advent of some new epoch, it is the one least likely to abort or deform the deep, mysterious processes of artistic gestation and rebirth.

---

[1] For a detailed view of the tough and demanding terms of the Church, the guilds, the Medicis, the doges, and the other principal patrons of the period, and of their contentious relationships with the great artists of the time, *see* David S. Chambers, *Patrons and Artists in the Italian Renaissance* (London: MacMillan, 1970).

[2] Gérard Bonnot, in conversation with the author, 1975.

[3] For a stimulating and opinionated discussion of the problems of French cultural policy, *see* the article by Gérard Bonnot on this subject in *The Arts, Economics, and Politics: Four National Perspectives* (New York: Aspen Institute for Humanistic Studies, 1975). Full statistical data on the French subsidy system can be found in the article by Claude G. Menard in the same document.

[4] See *The Twenty-Ninth Annual Report and Accounts, 1973–74*, of the British Arts Council, especially the Secretary General's Report, for a more complete discussion of its policies and procedures. A report by Lord Redcliffe-Maud published by the Gulbenkian Foundation in 1976 in London, *Support for the Arts in England and Wales*, presents an excellent analysis and recommendations regarding the role of local authorities and regional associations and councils in the execution of British arts policy.

[5] The full text of the report, *New Cultural Policy in Sweden*, has been published in English by the National Council for Cultural Affairs and the Swedish Institute, Stockholm (1973).

[6] A more precise picture of the successive stages of wealthy support is given by William Wright in his lively piece, "The Sound of Money: The Plight of Our Symphony Orchestras," in *Town and Country* (October 1976), p. 146: "The solitary backer gave way to a group of wealthy backers, usually rich blue bloods who regarded the orchestra as a cultural *cosa nostra*; as the old guard got tired of giving or ran out of money to give, it gave way to new money that in turn gave way to large corporations that were as eager to show off their civic responsibility as the parvenus were to parade their bank accounts."

[7] This is quoted in the first-rate study by William J. Baumol and William G. Bowen, *Performing Arts—The Economic Dilemma* (Cambridge, Mass.: MIT Press, 1968), p. 38. It was this study which argued with impressive documentation and analysis that arts organizations are doomed to operate at a progressively greater financial disadvantage because they are labor intensive units unable to increase their productivity by mechanization in an increasingly productive and technological society.

[8] See Russell Lynes, *Confessions of a Dilettante* (New York: Harper & Row, 1948).

[9] From *The Performing Arts: Problems and Prospects*, Rockefeller Panel report on the future of theater, dance, music in America (New York: McGraw-Hill, 1965), p. 207.

[10] See, for example, *National Endowment for the Arts—Guide to Programs, 1975–76*.

[11] For a knowledgeable discussion of some of these problems, *see* the paper prepared for the Aspen Institute by Eric Larrabee, former head of the New York State Arts Council, "The Public Funding Agency" (8 October 1975).

[12] See the *New York Times*, 9 February 1975, sec. 2, p. 1.

[13] Steven Marcus, "Notes on Some Problems in the Humanities Today," *Partisan Review* 41, no. 4 (1974): 506–20.

The Need for a Comprehensive Cultural Policy

Jacques Rigaud

Jacques Rigaud is assistant director-general of UNESCO in Paris. A native Parisian, he holds a degree in law and is a graduate of the Institute of Political Studies in Paris. He also studied at the French National College of Administration, from which he graduated in 1954. M. Rigaud served as a government commissioner to the French Council of State from 1964 to 1969 and, from 1965 to 1969, as a deputy advocate for the Constitutional Council. He has been a master of requests for the Council of State since 1960 and a judicial adviser to the French minister of public works since 1961. His professorship at the Institute of Political Studies at the University of Paris began in 1958.

Following his service as bureau chief for Jacques Duhamel, the French minister of agriculture, M. Rigaud continued in this role when Duhamel became minister of cultural affairs in 1971. He was also briefly bureau chief for Duhamel's successor, Maurice Druon, in the spring of 1973. Since then he has maintained an active interest in the problems of cultural development and the administration of cultural affairs. His book, *La Culture pour vivre* (1975), explored this subject. He has also written *Débat sur la France de demain,* published in 1961.

Can culture and the arts flourish in our day without government or public support? This question troubles those who think that state aid and cultural freedom are incompatible because government intervention necessarily entails government control.

The object of this study is to define and illustrate a public cultural policy which guarantees freedom of creative expression and initiative.

Our age is witnessing a growing awareness of the responsibility of government for culture. Since 1970, when the world conference on cultural policies organized by UNESCO was held in Venice, more than forty governments have created some form of department or ministry of culture.

These governments have approached the problem of culture in roughly three different ways. The socialist countries were the first to concern themselves in a systematic manner with the role of the state in cultural matters. From the perspective of socialist ideology and the kind of state it fosters, culture is a basic element of social cohesion. Cultural activity must be organized and directed like any other activity, perhaps more so, in that uncontrolled it can foster turmoil and subversion. The artistic professions, therefore, must be organized and supervised by the government. Furthermore, socialist egalitarianism fosters easy access to the benefits of cultural experience for the masses and equal opportunity for all those who have artistic gifts. Socialist countries are typified by a tight network of state-directed cultural institutions competent in sponsoring, inspiring, diffusing, and preserving the arts. These cultural institutions eliminate the role of private enterprise and the influence of the marketplace.

A second approach is that of liberal countries which have developed a tradition of intervention in cultural affairs. The activities of these states have certain common characteristics. Intervention is partial. The government does not deem itself totally competent in cultural matters and admits that certain areas, particularly creativity, escape its control. Intervention is generally directed toward the national heritage—monuments, museums, archaeological excavations, and such traditional institutions as the theater and the opera. Furthermore, the state is not the exclusive agent of intervention but yields responsibility to cities, provinces, or foundations. Last, intervention is discreet and respectful of traditional cultural freedom. Such is the classic pattern in this type of society. It is a pattern based not on the conception of culture as an aspect of a political program but on a recognition of the traditional role of the state in the fine arts. As we shall see, this traditional role eventually leads to an even deeper and more extensive intervention on the part of the state. As yet, however, the actions of most liberal governments conform merely to the pattern we have described.

The developing nations take a third approach. One could argue that these countries do not constitute a separate category. In regard to political and social structure they draw their inspiration from either the socialist or the liberal model. Cuban cultural policy, for example, is closer to East European policy in many respects than to the cultural policy of Tunisia or Kenya. Nevertheless, most developing countries share certain convictions that culture is not a luxury for the elite but "the very axis of development," as the African ministers of culture assembled in Accra, Ghana, in October 1975 phrased it.

Many of the developing countries have a cultural heritage that is frequently rich but generally unrecognized and threatened by an overhasty or badly assimilated course of modernization. The growing demand for "cultural identity" indicates the desire of these countries to modernize without losing their unique character. That desire coexists with the wish to utilize everything in their past, in their traditions, in their unique character, which permits them to affirm their personality and enables them to participate more fully in the growth of international culture. Developing nations usually have rather imaginative cultural policies, at least in those cases where the policymakers are not tempted by limited resources and easy profits to vulgarize their cultural heritage for the sake of the tourist trade.

Such is the context of the growing international awareness of cultural problems. In both the socialist and developing nations the intent is essentially political, since the object is either to ensure social cohesion or to shape development. This approach is more or less constraining according to what methods are employed, but it is always a component of a broad political program.

The situation is much less clear in the liberal countries, which are, in fact, the concern of this study. In these countries, social cohesion is either a historical development or something formally consented to by the citizenry. The government does not consider itself authorized to impose cohesion by force. In such societies pluralism is esteemed as a value, not merely regarded as a fact. Social and economic development results from the relatively free interplay of economic forces and the competition of social equals. Even when it aspires to direct this development, the state does not regard itself as competent to establish unilaterally the ways and means of that development.

It follows that intervention by the state in cultural affairs appears to be less necessary in liberal societies than in socialist or developing societies. As mentioned earlier, the mission of government in liberal countries has been most often limited to preserving the national heritage. The rich cultural history of these countries shows quite clearly that the arts have not required government action to bring them to fruition. Even if kings and churches have patronized the arts in the past, for at least three centuries the aristocracy, followed by the bourgeoisie, have constituted a sufficient audience of amateurs, readers, spectators, and collectors to offer all the arts adequate support.

Today, such class support of the arts seems to belong to an age gone by. For one thing, in spite of very considerable economic progress, the shifting distribution of wealth and increasing organization of the economy have disrupted the traditional forms of patronage. Art patrons have become less common. Intense economic competition has curtailed disinterested actions. The spirit of consumer society tends to impede personal artistic expression. The artist finds his place uneasily in a world that is increasingly complex and cynical. Those cultural enterprises which used to seek funds from business and the public now turn to the state and ask for financial cooperation.

On top of this, the progress of democracy entails reexamination of the very foundation of middle-class culture. In former times the masses were excluded de facto if not de jure from the culture of the elite, in which they could participate only after social advancement. Today universal education, the demand for equality, and the growth of mass media oblige us to recognize the right to culture of the vast majority of people, even if the people do not place this right at the top of their list of priorities.

Faced with these conditions, the state can respond in one of two ways. It can act in a limited, sporadic, and incidental fashion, or else systematically. In the first case it will grant temporary or permanent support to cultural institutions undergoing crisis or will agree to assume responsibility for those activities no longer sustained by private enterprise. Nevertheless, the state will stop short of defining an overall cultural policy. Cultural activity, whether on the part of the artist, the public, or the promoters, will remain the prerogative of the individual.

In the second case the state will overcome its scruples and try to synthesize a methodical approach to cultural problems. It will define a cultural policy and create or encourage institutions and proceedings which will bring culture to the vast majority of people.

We can find one or the other of these formulas in much of the Western world. Statistically, the first and more pragmatic method still prevails over the second and more systematic one. In the ensuing pages, I would like to demonstrate why the second, more systematic method is preferable and suggest in my conclusion how a national cultural policy can be reconciled with artistic freedom.

Justification of a comprehensive policy

There are several reasons why a comprehensive cultural policy is preferable to any number of sporadic and incidental responses to the needs of culture and the fine arts.

Even a modern democracy, which is anxious to safeguard private initiative, is led increasingly to intervene in the affairs of its citizens. When such a government corrects or softens the effects of economic advantage and social status, usually it does so to enhance the quality of life. Clearly, culture is or should be an essential component of the quality of life. Thus inevitably we confront the question whether government action should extend to cultural concerns. As a practical matter, the question may be posed in these terms: Should urban policy, whether it involves building cities and new neighborhoods or renovating the historical centers of towns, take into account the cultural aspects of city life? Should it take into account the preservation of traditional architectural harmony, the creation and maintenance of cultural facilities, the fostering of new architectural design, the procurement of modern works of art to adorn a city?

The examples of Scandinavian urban development and the new towns built around Paris demonstrate that city planning cannot ignore cultural questions. Even if the government does not directly oversee planning, organization, and construction, it does assume legal, financial, and social responsibility as part of its urban policy, and assists local groups and all kinds of local promoters. These activities are necessarily influenced by the emphasis or lack of emphasis placed on their qualitative aspects, which in the largest sense are cultural. One might draw a parallel to the policy of regional development, where the intention is to correct the effect of economic forces by a redistribution of economic activity. Whether it is involved in rejuvenating depressed areas or accelerating the growth of developing areas, the government must consider the cultural situation, if only to ensure efficient implementation of its program. Economic stimulation must be balanced by enhancement of the cultural heritage of regions which have one; the government must encourage the growth of spiritual and aesthetic values in regions where such a heritage is deficient.

The French policy of regional development seeks to achieve a balance within the country. Specifically, it endeavors to counteract the excessive concentration of business in Paris by creating other centers of equal economic attraction. This policy had little impact until it began to take cultural considerations into account. Similarly, an educational policy cannot be established without providing for the awakening of aesthetic sensitivity and artistic creativity in children. It is no longer a question, as it was in the past, of simply appending drawing, singing, and needlepoint—what are called "accomplishments"—to the traditional curriculum but rather one of infusing a scientific and utilitarian education with humane values. Nor can the diplomatic policy of a country ignore culture. The ascendancy of a nation depends on its culture as much as on its economic and tactical strength. Without becoming propagandistic, cultural activity is at least the complement of all those activities which promote the greatness of a nation. In the past, international cultural exchange was spontaneous, the work of individuals, social groups, or institutions that were naturally inclined to be cosmopolitan. Today the division of the world, the complex nature of international dealings, and the general politicization of international relationships make cultural exchange more difficult and costly. As a result, cultural considerations have become an aspect of international politics, whether we wish it or not.

Culture then is not merely a separate consideration in formulating public policy. If it were only that, it could be easily dismissed by government. Culture is actually a new dimension of public life, a tonality, an accent, which must influence all political intervention. It must be ever present in the minds of those who are responsible for planning and implementing an integrated vision of national development. The great Western democracies more and more frequently seek out new areas of endeavor, as if the growing complexity of public affairs and the fragmented nature of government actions have created a sense of frustration among politicians and the public. The desire for new frontiers and new challenges, which springs from both fear and hope, helps to explain the interest in such topics as ecology and the quality of life. But this interest might be confined to purely materialistic concerns if it were not enhanced by cultural implications which are infinitely richer and more humane. Indeed, it can fairly be said that culture transforms the quality of life into the dignity of life.

There is another reason to concern ourselves with a cultural policy. Modern society is constantly confronted by problematic choices and decisions. In our age choices are governed by the natural fluctuations of the market, by the increasingly sophisticated manipulations of businessmen, or by a subtle mixture of both. By their very nature, cultural affairs are particularly vulnerable and may easily become the victim of these two forces. The preoccupation with the market and profit, as it exists in our society, leads either to the neglect of cultural endeavors, which are by nature costly, risky, and unmarketable, or to their exploitation to meet the immediate needs of the public or the artist. The mediocrity of television in most countries, the difficulties of innovative cinema, theater, and writing, and the domination of architecture by real-estate speculation are cases in point.

But if fluctuations of the market fail by their nature to promote the arts, the actions of political leaders do little to remedy the situation. In democratic societies leaders tend to satisfy the needs which the public regards as most pressing, and the public is much more inclined to demand hospitals, schools, athletic facilities, and transportation from the state than theaters, museums, concert halls, and libraries. Needs such as these are not regarded as having priority. If the state attempts to redirect the demands of the public in the general interest, it will spend money on national defense, external action, or justice more readily than it will on culture. In contemporary democratic societies normal economic and political forces do not guarantee optimal satisfaction of the seemingly peripheral but real needs of the culture. To guarantee that culture is taken into account as societies make decisions, it must figure as an integral part of any social plan, one not imposed on, but rather proposed to, the public. In the past, popular culture as well as high culture was sustained either by consensus—the single spiritual and moral breath of an entire community—or by the choices and caprices of princes, kings, churches, or patrons among the aristocracy or business community. Today we can no longer depend upon these traditional sources, which have disappeared or are impoverished. Culture must have a place in the debate and policymaking by which a democratic society defines its future. If it does not, the natural tendencies of cultural life will be to widen the gap between the elaborate, sophisticated culture of the elite and the increasingly limited culture of the masses.

The third and final reason to support a coherent cultural policy is less easily formulated. When a government limits itself to more or less sporadic support of needy artists or institutions, it risks errors which could have strong cumulative effect. This kind of ad hoc patronage may benefit only those petitioners who are the best connected, the shrewdest, or the most reassuring. Thus it may encourage academic and cultural conservatism. Or, conversely, intellectual snobbery or political calculation may lead the government to favor those artists and promoters who make the most noise and are best publicized. In neither case is aid necessarily granted to those who most merit it. Furthermore, the government may be tempted to establish permanent criteria for intervention which result in rigidity. Or it may refuse to establish permanent criteria and allow administrative councils, experts, or financiers to make decisions case by case. Either method of proceeding may result in arbitrary decisions and humiliation for artists, who in modern society object as much to being regarded as pensioners as they do to the notion that they are "misunderstood." There will always be some on the fringe of society who challenge our norms on principle and for the sake of art, but it is a mistake to suppose that all artists are in revolt against a society from which they feel excluded. Dickens and Balzac, Van Gogh and Pollock, Chaplin and Béjart were certainly not docile, contented citizens, but it would be difficult to demonstrate that their art was inspired by whatever persecution or rejection they may have suffered. It is even less demonstrable that society had a duty to mistreat or neglect them in order to encourage their creativity. Sufficient is it for the artist to struggle with himself. A liberal society should not be interested in turning artists into civil servants or salaried employees of show business and commercial arts; nei-

"Today universal education, the demand for equality, and the growth of mass media oblige us to recognize the right to culture of the vast majority of people, even if the people do not place this right at the top of their list of priorities." Above, the Louvre, Paris.

ther should it make outcasts of them. In formulating the operations of a cultural policy which is to go beyond the framework of sporadic aid to the arts, the government, controlled by public opinion, can set terms which, without dictating regulations to the artist, will permit him to define his place and purpose in a society that continues to need him.

Is a comprehensive policy compatible with freedom?

Such an appeal for a cultural policy in liberal societies may not convince those who sincerely believe that artistic freedom is and always will be irreconcilable with any kind of state intervention. I would like in the following portion of this paper to suggest that these two principles are indeed compatible and that a cultural policy may be conceived and implemented to serve and protect cultural freedom.

What should be the objective of such a policy? Under no circumstances should it assume the directing or molding of the cultural life of a country. It should have only two specific goals: First, it should foster conditions conducive to free development in all areas of cultural endeavor. Second, it should guarantee to all people free and equal access to cultural activity. Freedom as an established fact and equal opportunity as a definite goal are the imperatives of a democratic cultural policy. It is true that spontaneous cultural activity in Western society usually preserves this freedom and opportunity, but it can work in the opposite direction. When that happens, government must correct and compensate. In this sense the role of the state is both fundamental and subsidiary to cultural affairs. It is fundamental in that, if it does not intervene, cultural freedom may be twisted to benefit only a few, and equal opportunity may never be realized. It is subsidiary in that government ought to intervene only when no other individual or group is capable of assuming responsibility. Limited to a specific goal, intervention should cease when citizens, communities, or associations are ready to assume responsibility. Culture is not, properly speaking, a public service. Government should intervene only to ensure its autonomous growth.

The paradoxical nature of such a cultural policy—at once fundamental in principle and subsidiary in procedure—requires personalities and methods that are sensitive to subtle and opposing imperatives. One does not administer culture as one would the postal service or the customs office. Cultural administration should be marked by discretion, modesty, and delicacy. Its function is not to direct culture or those who create it but to elicit, encourage, and coordinate private initiative. The strength of this administration derives not from coercion but from benevolent influence. It should act as though it were dealing not with subordinates but with equals.

Such a cultural policy should normally encompass four functions, each corresponding to one of the four major aspects of culture. The importance of each of these functions will, of course, vary from country to country and from epoch to epoch.

1. *Preservation:* This is the least disputed responsibility of the state with respect to cultural affairs. The cultural heritage is a national treasure, whether owned by state, city, or private citizens. Through appropriate legislation the state must protect this heritage, avoid its destruction or disintegration, define and promote its role in modern society. This heritage consists of more than just monuments or widely known works of art, although these things may come to mind first. There is also a heritage of art and of popular traditions—an invisible heritage, of which language (or several national languages) is the most precious element—which deserves equal recognition and protection. Whether this protection is legislative, financial, technical, intellectual, or administrative, whether it consists of assuming direct control of the national heritage or of delegating that responsibility, the state cannot shirk its role as protector. This is particularly true in our age of rapid change, when traditional safeguards of the spiritual and physical heritage have lost their efficacy.

2. *Training:* Society recognizes government's general responsibility in matters of education. On the same principle the state must assure professional instruction for those involved in cultural vocations, from architects to musicians, from painters to filmmakers. While the government may not provide this training directly, it must make sure that schools or universities offer programs conducive to the future development of national culture. It must do more. Education cannot be limited, particularly in our age, to the intellectual development or vocational training of young people. Regardless of other pragmatic concerns, artistic sensitivity, innate in all of us, must be stimulated and developed in a child when he or she is still very young. Equal cultural opportunity requires that every child be offered the chance to discover the scope of his interest, taste, and capacity in artistic matters. Here again it is possible that the existing school system assumes this responsibility of its own accord. But if it does not, the government must step in.

3. *Stimulation of creativity:* This is more controversial. Creation is by definition a free activity that does not lend itself to public intervention. Although the government may intend to act discreetly, its actions may prove untimely or arbitrary, or at least may be thought so. But whenever the free enterprise system fails to sustain creative activities, the state cannot evade the responsibility to act. It must establish a network of programs which offers those artists who want it recourse to the kind of assistance that is compatible with their own creative freedom. By establishing programs which mediate between itself and the artist, the state can guard against inadvertent abuses. These programs will offer counsel and distribute public funds fairly, provided of course that they do not grow too large or too conservative.

4. *Promotion:* Here we have the most diffuse, the most recent, and surely the most difficult function to define. It is a modern manifestation of the need for mediation between art and the public, the need to awaken artistic

sensitivity in the public, the need for the identification of cultural activity with community effort. Promotion may take the form of a doctrine, a technique, or an attitude. Its goal may be to define a priori what the cultural life of a new city ought to be or to elicit a more active public interest in theaters, museums, or public sites. Cultural promotion is in our day a rich and often uncertain area of experimentation. The government should not conduct or even sponsor these experiments itself. Instead it should make them possible, then study and publicize the results in order to ensure further work along the most promising lines.

The state must first determine the nature and degree of its responsibility with respect to these four cultural functions. Having accomplished that task, it must then decide what methods it will employ to discharge them. The choice of methods is a sensitive matter, for cultural freedom will be directly affected by the selection.

The state must take precautions to avoid abuses and to guarantee and develop pluralism, which is the very foundation of a free and vibrant culture. These precautions are in a sense the principles of a good, working cultural policy.

The definition of this policy must be neither unilateral, clandestine, nor inflexible. Culture is a living activity, constantly renewing and reshaping itself. In a liberal society cultural policy should be formulated in the open, not behind closed doors. It should involve full public debate among all concerned parties—the public, the consumer, and the artist. To the greatest possible degree the policy should be developed by consensus, not by unilateral decision of the government. Furthermore, it should be revised periodically to keep pace with the evolution of needs, tastes, and opportunities and to profit from the lessons of experience.

Cultural policy is not the business of the state alone, nor is direct collaboration between state and artists a valid means of implementing it. For then the artist risks becoming a civil servant and losing not only his freedom but also his creativity. The state must deal with actual partners who will be its interlocutors, its link to artists and professionals, indeed, its challengers. These partners may well be local groups, regions, provinces, counties, or towns who may be the state's associates and may also create autonomous centers of cultural development. There is a network of institutions such as churches, universities, businesses, or trade associations which may play a role in cultural matters. This list demonstrates that a cultural policy cannot be dictated by the state and implemented by docile executors. On the contrary, it will require the united efforts of independent groups, efforts in which the state may play only a conciliatory, promotional, or complementary role, if it is to be carried out. And the list of possible partners does not stop here. If a society is truly alive, it creates communities: citizens interested in protecting a significant site or organizing a celebration, the public interested in using a library or a museum, an audience devoted to radio or television stations. Such groups are all potential partners or inter-

*"The government does not deem itself totally competent in cultural matters. . . .
Intervention is generally directed toward the national heritage—monuments, museums . . .
and such traditional institutions as the . . . opera."* Above, the Paris Opera House.

locutors of the state. The state may even find it useful, as did Great Britain, to set up organizations of independent people whose job is to define and implement the cultural policy in a given area. However, the state must provide for a continual restaffing of these groups in order to avoid the dangers of both a technological bureaucracy and an inflexible elite.

A cultural policy must be innovative, because contemporary cultural life is characterized by continual change. An avant-garde trend in film, dance, or music quickly becomes accepted and is confronted by a new trend. When an avant-garde movement becomes established, it will attempt to hold its hard-won ground against new trends and styles. The state is always in danger of being restricted by the progress it has fostered and losing contact with newer artistic trends. Once established, an artistic movement may inhibit the state's sensitivity to new departures. Cultural policy must always remain open to innovation, must provide opportunities to artistic endeavors which do not fit preexisting categories. This neglected aspect of the matter cannot be too much emphasized.

As often as possible, cultural support should be rendered on a contract basis. Artists can and must make commitments in return for public support, though only after full discussion and with a prospect of sufficient duration. In France the experiment with three-year contracts has taught us a great deal.

Conclusion

The principles which I have been formulating are not the product of theoretical reflections. They are conclusions drawn from actual observation of cultural policies developed by such countries as Sweden, Great Britain, France, Canada, and West Germany. The policies of these countries differ greatly in spirit. They differ particularly in regard to the degree of dominance exerted by state, regional governments, cities, or private institutions. All these countries are experimenting; none claims to have found definitive solutions. But they would all profit from a mutual exchange of information and experience inasmuch as they are all confronted by the same challenge, that of shaping cultural development to benefit the greatest number of people without violating artistic freedom. More than a challenge, they are confronting a veritable paradox, for culture is both the expression of collective certainties and the denial of these certainties. Culture is a continual revolt against an established order, a sovereign need for emancipation. The state is naturally distrustful of so subversive a force. But if it truly subscribes to the democratic ideal, it must risk disturbing the status quo in order to promote social progress.

The experience I have had with French cultural policy, during a period when the government was conscious of the importance of such a program, has convinced me that it can be compatible with liberty. Certainly cultural intervention requires patience, generosity, and constant vigilance. The risk is great that intervention will become partisan or bureaucratic. But, in this regard, liberalism must not become an element of political strategy or a simple administrative technique. It ought to be above all an ethic. Those responsible for cultural policy must not attempt to impose their taste or base their decisions on voter appeal. They must put themselves at the disposal of those who create culture and those who have need of it. Should they be tempted to believe in their own power, they have only to remember that there are more things in culture than can be contained in any policy.

State Subsidy and Artistic Freedom

Arnold Goodman

Born in 1913, Arnold Goodman has for many years played an important advisory role in British public life. A solicitor by profession, with an exceptional legal mind (he took a double first in law at Downing College, Cambridge, of which he is an honorary fellow), he is a senior partner of the London firm of Goodman, Derrick and Company. He has been a consultant to many public figures, among them the late Richard Crossman, minister of housing, during the Labour government of 1964–70, to whom he gave advice on rental policy. He has also been a mediator in difficult negotiations, among them the efforts made by the Conservative administration of 1970–74 to bring about a Rhodesian settlement.

Created a life peer in 1965, Lord Goodman was chairman of the Arts Council of Great Britain from then until 1972. He has also been chairman of the Newspaper Publishers Association (1970–76); chairman of the Observer Trust; a member of the South Bank Theatre Board, under whose auspices a National Theatre building was recently constructed in London; chairman of British Lion Films Ltd.; a director of the Royal Opera House, Covent Garden, and of the English National Opera Ltd.; a governor of the Royal Shakespeare Company; and president of the National Book League.

Lord Goodman is the holder of several honorary doctorates, among them an LL.D. from the University of London. In August 1976 he was appointed master of University College, Oxford. He is unmarried. In private life he is a collector of pictures. His recreations are music and the theater.

It is a current belief that in a free society without state intervention man is free. This extends to a further belief that in such a society the artist is freer than he would be where he has to rely on state support.

In fact, the artist is no more free in a capitalist society or a democratic society than he is under a system of state subsidy. I do not deny that there are certain political organizations, such as a Communist or a syndicalist society, where the concept of artistic freedom has quite a different quality and character than it does with us, and where different considerations are weighed when it comes to granting financial support. In these societies, for good or ill, artistic freedom is rated below industrial or political organization. There is a deliberate and calculated policy to ensure that the artist does not utter a syllable that is at variance with current opinion and thought. Whether the benefits that derive from a society so organized can compensate for the loss of intellectual freedom is a question on which men may disagree. To me and to those who think like me the ultimate denial of human right is a refusal to allow man to express or publish his thoughts.

But what we are discussing here is something very different. It is whether in a society which on the whole is devoid of malign intentions or of a calculated plan to suppress nonconformist utterances it is nevertheless better to leave the support and sustenance of the artist to the accident of public favor, or to private patronage, or to the myriad of other methods which exist to assist him in self-support, rather than to have direct subsidy from the public purse seeking to attain the same purpose.

This is a very interesting speculation. There is no easy answer and no clear-cut answer. It must depend on the individual circumstances. No man is totally untrammeled. A man marooned on a desert island is probably subject to more restraints and inhibitions than a man who lives in a London suburb or a New York apartment house. He can walk no farther than the width or length of the island. He will not wander into the wood because of his apprehension that a wild bear may be prowling there, even if the nearest wild bear is to be found in Sydney Zoo. The freedom that has value and requires support is the freedom of the mind. If a man thinks he is free, he is free. This is a crucial proposition when considering state subsidy of the arts. If a man believes that the receipt of a state subvention places him under an obligation or leaves him less able to say what he wants to say, or paint what he wants to paint, or sing what he wants to sing, then, however fanciful this belief, it is nevertheless a clog on his freedom.

Personal patronage by way of payments or personal services may be totally innocuous or highly vicious. I do not know anything about the old Margate landlady who looked after Turner so assiduously, but I would rate this as the very best form of patronage. He may have been terrified of her, afraid to stay late in bed on her account, but in no circumstances is she likely to have exercised an intellectual or artistic influence or, even worse, an intellectual or artistic coercion. She would not have threatened to forfeit his breakfast unless he painted a sea scene in a particular color. She is unlikely to have refused to light the fire until he expressed willingness to paint a portrait rather than a seascape. In short, whatever influence she brought to bear was totally innocent in creative terms. Subsidy that produces this result is good subsidy. Subsidy that produces any other result is bad and can be wicked subsidy. I have chosen in Turner's landlady—to whom I offer the most profuse apologies for hypothesizing her on a basis of total igno-rance—one extreme of the subsidy polarization. Good, virtuous, innocent, free from pressure, her warming pans and hot-water bottles, her stews and her joints, her hot mulled drinks and all the other figments of my imagina-tion in relation to her could do no evil to Turner's work, except possibly to overfeed him.

One moves along the spectrum in directions where a litmus paper test is no longer a possibility. A rich patron who has to be satisfied, mollified, propitiated—can one always say that he exercised no influence at variance with the full and free operation of a natural talent? There may be clear-cut cases. The proprietor of a newspaper who directs his contributors to write contrary to their beliefs is plainly doing something wrong. Whether he is doing something inartistic cannot be readily determined. The pressures of financial exigency do not necessarily impair artistic quality. Oliver Gold-smith and Samuel Johnson were always writing at the point of a publisher's pistol, but only the Almighty can determine whether that writing was better or worse because of the constraint.

Moreover, is it financial exigency alone that provides a corrupting or disturbing influence? May not the reverse be the case? There is a disagreea-ble, sentimental notion that the artist works best under the prick of poverty. There is certainly evidence to show that artists do not necessarily write badly under the benign influence of opulence. Charles Dickens lost neither genius nor diligence when he was emancipated from the blacking factory. Marcel Proust was a rich man, but the money was an irrelevancy; it came into the picture only for the negative reason that it was about the only thing he did not need to worry about. Tolstoy frittered away a great fortune and never knew poverty, although he drove his family to distraction by extrava-gance and want of concern.

Almost without exception the high geniuses of Russian czarist life in the nineteenth and twentieth centuries were bothered by improvidence, but rarely by poverty. Chekhov was an exception in that as the grandson of a serf he had no inherited wealth; nevertheless, he earned enough from medicine and writing for his needs. Tchaikovsky, like Turner, would appear to have found an absolutely ideal patron. Nadezhda von Meck was a wealthy widow who provided him with a generous annuity on the ideal basis that, although they corresponded copiously, they never met. Such patronage I recommend to everyone, but, alas, the likelihood of encountering it is slender.

A history of private patronage often discloses generosity, breadth of mind, a willingness to indulge the whims and caprices of the artist, and a discriminating perception of genius long before its general recognition. But it often also discloses meanness, pettiness, an overproprietary disposition, and a willingness to jettison the artist at some crucial moment. These instances of bad qualities are inclined to make the artist rightly suspicious of private patronage. A history of patronage would also demonstrate variations and permutations to an infinite degree. There is the good patronage of personal friendship. When Theodore Watts-Dunton rescued Swinburne, he provided him with a home and support and security and, so far as I know, no serious interference with his work methods and a respectable urging to output.

On the other hand, if we contrast the great patronage of the princes of Italy, different questions arise. The discipline of being required to be suspended upside down for years to paint the Sistine Chapel produced a great masterpiece. I do not know whether Michelangelo wanted to paint the ceiling of the Sistine Chapel or instead would have preferred to paint portraits of some lovely lady. The world has benefited by the imposition of the discipline. Michelangelo can be said to have benefited. But whether artistic freedom was, in fact, deferred to is a matter of consideration for those concerned with the philosophy of aesthetics.

Almost all the great old masters conformed to a discipline of one kind or another, imposed by their patronage. The Church was the great patron of most old masters, and the Church imposed a rigid discipline, although probably not a limitation on freedom. Freedom is the ability to roam in the areas where you want to roam. The fact that the great artists of the Venetian Republic and of Florence and of the other city-states were satisfied to paint religious works and to work for the Church did not erode their freedom in the slightest. It was only if they were dissatisfied, hated religious conceptions, and wanted to embark on other areas that freedom was involved. Again, this is an important consideration where subsidy is concerned.

We have today arrived at a position where all civilized countries accept that the maintenance of their artists and their artistic institutions is possible only with collateral support from somewhere. Private as opposed to state subsidy is, of course, one route which is not, in my view, a wholly satisfactory route. A rich man or a rich company will provide a production at an opera house or present an old master or an impressionist to an art gallery or museum. But what you cannot do with a rich man is to organize a scientific and systematic support of the arts across the board. In the result, the metropolitan museums in the great conurbations will find themselves loaded with impressionists, but some small town in a remote county or state will lack a repertory theater or an art gallery or an orchestra or even a music group. This is not to disparage the value of personal subsidy or the quality of impressionist paintings or the value of benefactions from private sources—these are indeed a very useful supplement.

Moreover, subsidy, according to our notions, should not be the principal source for artistic support. The principal source should always be the customer. Books, especially, about which I say a word below, should be largely self-supporting from the purchases made by readers. The theater, too, should be largely self-supporting from the purchases of seats, and concerts likewise. It is true, at the end of the day there is a need for support that is not fully provided from commercial sources. In some cases this is because the audience is at best a limited one. You can probably fill a concert hall if you have a great soloist and a popular program. You cannot fill a concert hall, however distinguished the orchestra and even, alas, however distinguished the conductor, if you play modern or little-known music. Subsidies for such programs can be justified on the ground that it would be a crime against musical culture if modern and little-known music were never played. It would be a crime against the visual arts if modern and contemporary artists, the so-called avant-garde, could not procure an exhibition and even purchase. So too with the serious theater, which can barely survive on the basis of being self-supporting from the customers. We subsidize such undertakings in the belief that a full exposure of artistic activity, representing all facets and satisfying all reasonable tastes, is a crucial need in societies where materialist conceptions need desperately to be corrected. But we must never lose sight of the fact that the major provider for the arts is that element of the population at large capable of understanding them, appreciating them, and supporting them.

It is easy to confuse two quite different considerations because they are so interlinked and often inextricably linked. The first consideration, which is the subject of our theoretical discussion, is the source of subsidy—private or public, eleemosynary or statutory. The second consideration is one that might conceivably arise quite independent of subsidy but in fact never does —the nature of the organization required to distribute support for the arts and to encourage the arts to burgeon under the best conditions. The state may provide one in the form of state subsidy or both in the form of state encouragement, but it is rare for the state to provide the encouragement without some form of financial support. Having had a good many years' involvement in the support of the arts, it is my considered belief that a state system of subsidy, coupled with a state-promoted—but not operated— administrative system to organize and support the arts in the areas where the "customer" element is inadequate, is the best that can be contrived, notwithstanding the imperfections which exist, as they must in all human institutions.

The ideal is to seek a means whereby the "customer" element can be self-sufficient. In the worlds of painting, drama, and music this would not seem to be, with society as now organized, a possibility. In the world of literature it is not a total possibility but nearer a possibility than in the other arts. There are a great number of explanations for this, of which the principal and simplest one is the relative cost. It is possible to publish a book at an expense which bears no relationship to the expense of producing a play, promoting a concert, or especially promoting some operatic production. And the size of the reading public is such that most authors entertain the hope—frequently forlorn—that enough of their books will be bought to keep them alive. In fact, artists at large are seldom successful even to this extent. Still, the author just manages to keep alive at bare subsistence level, so that, on the whole, organized state subsidy for authors is not a high priority in artistic programs. Moreover, in England at least, and I believe to an appreciable extent in the United States, the publishing ranks have contained cultivated men conscious of their responsibilities to literature, who have given continuing support to promising talents until they have nurtured them into bloom. But, where the other artistic activities are concerned, an organized system of administrative help sustained by state subsidy is probably the best system that can be devised, so long—as I have said —as it is an auxiliary to customer support.

In the United Kingdom the major system of state support for the arts, both as a route for subsidy and as an administrative organization, is the Arts Council of Great Britain. This is at present a nonelected body, although there are people who mistakenly believe election to be a possibility in these areas of high specialization. The council consists of some twenty members and a vast number of panels and committees to advise them. It has no responsibility for permanent galleries and museums, nor for the quasi arts —I use the phrase in no derogatory sense—such as architecture, the crafts, and cognate activities, although it has recently ventured gently into the world of photography. The cinema is represented by a different organization, which maintains both a film school and a number of quality cinemas.

The Arts Council is almost entirely manned by volunteers, with a small but highly expert professional staff. It is impossible to assess the influence of the permanent staff as against the chairman and the council except day by day. Inevitably, a permanent staff, if able and dedicated and concerned, must exercise a very great influence, and it is hypocritical to suggest that any detrimental effects of such influence will be wholly corrected by the council. On the other hand, the chairmanship of the council changes at relatively brief intervals—five to seven years—and the membership of the council every three years. As a result the council has been a potent body in determining the distribution of subsidy. It has happily not been—and in a democratic country never should be—a potent influence on the shape of

"The serious theater . . . can barely survive on the basis of being self-supporting from the customers. We subsidize such undertakings in the belief that a full exposure of artistic activity . . . is a crucial need in societies where materialist conceptions need desperately to be corrected." Above, the National Theatre, London.

the arts. The artist will, of course, be influenced by the society he lives in, but he will not be influenced by a small body of distinguished dilettantes, clucking impeccable sentiments in relation to what an artist should or should not do. It is because this proposition has been widely recognized by the Arts Council and its membership that the council enjoys a good reputation and has done good work. It has been—although often under challenge —a liberally minded body in the sense of recognizing that the most discerning of eyes have failed to identify all or even most of the real talent of their own generation.

The acceptance of this truism poses two very different risks. The first and the most condign is to refuse to provide for any talent that is not immediately identifiable in contemporary terms. This is safe, but it is pusillanimous and immensely damaging. The second is to accept the most lunatic of all propositions—that if you cannot identify all talent during its day, you must subsidize all claimants, however seemingly bogus and preposterous they may be.

There are, of course, no rules, no artistic standards that will provide a course of prophetic accuracy between these two dangers. One has only to remember the artists who died unrecognized and in privation—the Mozarts and the Chattertons of their day—to realize how splendid it might be if such possibilities could be obviated for the future. They cannot be obviated, but they do enjoin a policy in relation to subsidy of some daring. If you do not go over the edge, the risk will always be that you will remain too far from the edge. And to the subsidizing body, I would urge an assessment of the relative triviality of the risk they are taking. In England there is a well-trained chorus of strident disapproval of any artistic expenditure that can be designated ridiculous or socially damaging. But Socrates, Galileo, Copernicus, Ibsen, Shaw, the impressionists, the surrealists, and the cubists were all so designated. The more difficult question is how to identify them from the imposters. There is no rule. We must rely on the gut reaction of wise and educated men, and we must give weight not to a single opinion but to a great number of opinions, so that if twenty wise men condemn an essay in artistic novelty and one wise man approbates it, some support should be forthcoming. The corollary is that the voices of 200 influential cretins should go unheeded. But all this is the counsel of perfection and demonstrates something that is not the topic of this article—how to assess artistic quality which has not yet captured popular taste. This is one of the most difficult questions that a society concerned for its artists has to face.

There are two basic criteria to which an organization concerned to promote the arts should conform. They are complementary. The first is that although the money must necessarily, or at least in large part, come from the government purse, the organization itself should not be answerable to the government except in terms of accounting and probity. It should be answerable to its own conscience, and the test is whether, despite the inevitable grousing and grumbling of the artistic world—containing some of the most experienced grumblers in any community—there is nevertheless a general sense of approval that the artist is being honorably done by. Thus, an arts council or any similar body should not merely refuse to conform to any government direction in relation to how or where to give its grants but should leap at the throat of any government which presumes to give any such direction. Subsidy free from such direction is of social benefit. Subsidy accompanied by any such direction is worse than no subsidy. It is not easy to find governments or purse bearers who recognize that high virtue reposes in leaving the subsidized body alone to determine its own policy.

On the whole, governments in the United Kingdom have an honorable record of noninterference in relation to the Arts Council. Every so often some member of the public stirs the government into an apprehension that subsidized performances are politically or socially undesirable and that government intervention is called for. The Arts Council has over the years possessed sufficient muscle to protect itself against such interventions, largely because successive governments have recognized the impropriety of intervention. But it is a matter for constant vigilance. There will always be the well-intentioned busybody who believes that his or her views on a particular book or production should be imposed on the rest of mankind. This is a matter for quite different discussion. Whatever other public forces exist to invigilate authors or production, they should not be contained within the machinery of an arts council.

Separate argument will go on forever about how far public prosecutors and the police should exert themselves over books and plays and pictures. There can be little doubt that far into eternity some prosecuting donkey will continue to prosecute D. H. Lawrence or Thomas Hardy—who, in fact, only just escaped prosecution for what they called "Jude the Obscene." Even in England in the present decade prosecution was threatened (or may even have been launched) over the works of Aubrey Beardsley.

It is not easy for public bodies who have public responsibilities to resist such pressures, but resisted they must be. The test for a grant is an artistic claim, and that is not vitiated by anyone's sense of moral outrage, although it may well be the case that crudity, vulgarity, and obscenity are factors which nullify the artistic claims. Some while ago the Arts Council was asked to issue a directive urging its customers to exercise greater control in sexual terms over the productions for which it was responsible. I am happy to say that beyond a mild injunction to ensure that productions unsuitable for children exercised proper precautions to exclude them, it declined to indulge in any moral exhortations. There are, happily or unhappily, quite enough other people only too anxious to perform such functions.

The second criterion for an Arts Council—for state subsidy—is that when the administrative machine has reached its decision upon whom to shower its bounty, the beneficiary should then be left in peace, subject to probity and accounting, to use the money as it pleases. The time for decision making is before the check is sent off. The eligibility of the recipient should be tested and carefully, but once the grant has been made, the expenditure of the money and the choice of works, of actors, and of scenes is a matter for those who run each organization. These policies are often condemned as timid, as showing a willingness to delegate without responsibility. Properly carried out, the reverse is true. They show a courage to accept the responsibility for decisions, to have confidence in the persons selected, and to leave them in peace.

To attain the working of a system operating on these two principles is a matter of high sophistication. Some years ago one of the Arts Council advisers came to me in some gratitude to say she had recently been advising a local authority of a virtuous but uninformed nature on the purchase of a picture and had sought to persuade them to buy one of the works of a now established modern master, which they had viewed askance. To her delight they sent for her after she had withdrawn to say they had decided to make the purchase on her advice and on the basis of an observation they had heard me address to some conference of local authorities, when I had urged them in artistic matters "not to be afraid of their own opinions — but to be terrified of them." The temptation to intervene by a body which is holding the purse strings is often irresistible. This article will have done a lot of good if it sounds in the minds of persons involved in such bodies even a scintilla of doubt about the justification of such interventions.

In short, if I may enunciate Goodman's Rules for artistic subsidy, they are:

1. It should be a supplement to the resources available from the customer.
2. It should never be used so as to seek to influence public taste in any particular direction, except for the general advancement of all knowledge. (Artistic subsidy will theoretically and in a perfect world cease to be necessary when we have an adequate system of education. Since we will never have an adequate system of education, we will always need some artistic subsidy.)
3. The attaining of the subsidy should be a matter of right and not of grace. No applicant should feel beholden to the organization concerned either because of an application or because of its success. No artist should feel in the least degree diminished because he has applied for what should be his inalienable right under whatever the rules may be, if he can satisfy the artistic claim. No subsidizing body should be subject to any political or artistic control in general or in total from government or treasury or from any private contributor. The latter is probably the greater risk. Occasionally one encounters the amiable tycoon, anxious to promote his girl friend (or his boy friend) in a play or ballet or opera. Such a one, when he approaches any state-subsidized organization, or for that matter, any self-respecting organization, should be flung from the gallery into the pit and left for observation by succeeding audiences.

4. Finally, no artistic organization, no theater or gallery, no opera house or concert hall should be subject to any coercion or pressure accompanying the grant or any part of it. The beneficiary should be as free as the air provided he comes up with the results, and the results should be tested by reasonable expectation. Here again there is no meter for measuring whether a grant has successfully justified its award. It is right to say that the size of the audience should not be a determining factor, but it is idiotic to say it should not be a factor at all. The total absence of a popular response is an indication that the work does not justify a claim, but that that response may be small can argue quality, and here again informed and knowledgeable opinion and experience must be the only guides. It is perhaps surprising that no fuller work devoted entirely to the criteria for subsidy for the arts exists.

An almost unavoidable situation, but one that every effort should be made to avoid, is the conflict between the promotion of the arts and those, totally indifferent to the arts, who resent any expenditure on them. The motivation of these people is mixed. Some genuinely believe that anything provided to satisfy the taste of one segment of the public should be paid for entirely by that segment. The absurdity of this proposition really needs no refuting. It would, in fact, wholly exclude expenditure on higher education unless it were totally vocational and harnessed to state need. The motivation of others is even less creditable. It is a sense of bitter resentment that something should be provided on advantageous terms that cannot be enjoyed by the objectors. The facility with which this argument is deployed is unfortunately supported by the general belief that an assessment of artistic value can be made from a position of total ignorance. A man who would hesitate to express any view on an engineering or mechanical or scientific topic will spout imbecilities on literature, painting, and music without the slightest compunction or any sense of the absurdity of such a performance. That you cannot understand pictures without having looked at a great many pictures, that you cannot appreciate music without having heard a lot of music, and that you cannot assess a book without having read many books is difficult to maintain to those who have never looked at pictures, listened to music, or read books. Of course, it is not, unfortunately, always the case that the uninformed criticism comes from the illiterate and the analphabetics. It often comes from those educated in depth but on too narrow a front—blinkered intellectuals who have a knowledge of the classical past and declare that no one has written a novel since Jane Austen. These in many ways are the more potent enemies of support for the arts. They can enunciate with fervor and persuasion the virtues of a particular school, nearly always of decades if not centuries back. By so doing they lend a plausible denigration to anything of modernity.

The artistic subsidy is there principally to help to produce art from present practitioners, for now and for the future. If all artistic performance is restricted to what was created long ago, art will soon stagnate and possibly even die. For that reason the views of the ignorant and the views of the archaists must be rejected with firmness. But, in so doing, high discretion is needed. You cannot thrust art or culture down the throats of free people. If the mass of the population leaves culture alone, culture should leave them alone, except to the extent of dangling at a safe distance the allure to which their children will succumb. If they do not succumb, a civilized nation does not press-gang its people into concerts, theaters, or art galleries; it simply makes such works available. Hence, there must be unrequited expenditure; there must be empty seats, unsold books, galleries to the exhibitions of which only a few people are drawn. All this is needed for a rounded supply. All this calls for subsidy—intelligent and discriminating subsidy.

I am gratified that the publishers of this book have asked for a contribution on this topic—however ill-advised their choice of a contributor. More people should think about it. More people should recognize both the importance and the difficulty of the subject, and that it is solved only by courage and determination and a refusal to succumb to the clamant voices of ignorance. A community which gives sensibly and freely to support the arts is a community of which its population can be proud. It is a pleasant reflection that although the might and glory of the British Empire in military terms and in terms of power have diminished and in some respects even vanished, its intellectual virility has been maintained, and that there is better music and better theater and many other better manifestations of the mind in London and other parts of the country than there has been at any time in the past. This is largely due to the intelligent use of subsidy. Of course, there is much to be done and many improvements called for.

However inadequate, and indeed they are inadequate, may be these few comments, they derive from many years of experience and many hours of thought. I believe that state subsidy in my own country has not been badly conducted. Its conduct depends not on vast committees, hotly contested elections, and the other nonsense that has nothing to do with the arts but upon the availability of knowledge, judgment, fair-mindedness and above all the inculcation of the belief that the artist's contribution to society exceeds in its purpose and value that of any other.

Public Funding of the Arts in America

Michael Straight

Michael Straight, who has served since 1969 as deputy chairman of the National Endowment for the Arts, is also a patron of the arts—as well as a painter, a musician, and even a former dancer with the Martha Graham company—in his own right.

Born in 1916 into a prominent New York family, he attended the London School of Economics and Cambridge University, from which he received an M.A. From 1937 to 1940 he was a writer-researcher for President Franklin D. Roosevelt and an economist with the Department of State. In the latter year he became contributing editor from Washington to *The New Republic,* a magazine of which he was subsequently editor and publisher.

During the Second World War, in which he was a bomber pilot for the Air Force, he wrote a book, *Make This the Last War* (1943), a study of U.S. war aims and the emerging United Nations. In 1954 he published *Trial by Television,* an account of the Army-McCarthy hearings in Congress. A former board member of the Washington Theater Club, and vice-chairman of the National Repertory Theatre, he is the author of a play about the seventeenth-century Italian painter Caravaggio. He has also written two novels.

Mr. Straight is head of the William C. Whitney Foundation, which makes grants to the performing arts. In addition, he collects paintings and has contributed works to the White House, the Corcoran Gallery, the National Collection of Fine Arts, the Cleveland Museum of Art, and Cornell University.

For the past ten years, Congress and the state legislatures have provided direct funding in support of the arts in America. This funding has grown rapidly in a decade marked by resistance to the further encroachment of government in our lives. During that interval, arts institutions have flourished, audiences have multiplied, contributions to the arts from private sources have sharply increased, artists themselves have set out to regain the role they once held at the center of our society. Public funding is not the root cause of these advances, but it has been an essential ingredient. The federal government and the state governments have provided the working capital needed for expansion, and they have provided it without seeking domination or control.

The legislative framework

The framework for this rapid growth in public funding has been provided by the governing statute of the National Endowment for the Arts: the National Foundation on the Arts and the Humanities Act of 1965, which also established a National Endowment for the Humanities. Its provisions, like those which govern the state arts agencies, are based upon six underlying concepts.

1. Excellence

Throughout the act, emphasis is placed upon excellence as the criterion by which all arts activities must be judged. The arts endowment is directed to support "productions which have substantial artistic and cultural significance, giving emphasis to . . . the maintenance and encouragement of professional excellence." It is further directed to support "projects that will encourage and assist artists . . . to achieve standards of professional excellence." And, in directing the endowment to transfer a portion of its funds to state arts agencies, the Congress adds that the state projects and productions must also meet the standards of excellence set forth in the act.

The impact of this principle can be felt day by day in the operations of the endowment. At the time of its creation it was widely believed that government funding of the arts would lead to the support of mediocrity. Instead, the endowment, armed with this guiding principle, has been able to resist whatever pressures have been brought to bear upon it to support activities which are entertaining rather than enlightening, or, in terms of performance, second-rate.

2. *Independence*

The act, in its Declaration of Purpose, holds that "it is necessary and appropriate for the Federal Government to help create and sustain . . . a climate encouraging freedom of thought, imagination, and inquiry." It goes on to state that "the Endowment shall be headed by a Chairman . . . appointed by the President, by and with the advice and consent of the Senate." The chairman serves, not "at the pleasure of the President," but for a term of four years. And while the endowment's budget is set, first by the president's executive arm, the Office of Management and Budget, and then by the Congress, neither the OMB nor the oversight committees of the Congress interfere with the prerogatives of the chairman in determining how and where the funds appropriated to the endowment are to be spent.

The chairman is advised by the National Council on the Arts and, once again, the act, in creating the council, ensures that it will not be a means of injecting political considerations into the endowment's decisions. The council is purely advisory to the chairman. Qualifications for membership are stern and require that appointees must be either "practicing artists, civic cultural leaders, members of the museum profession" or other art-related professions; they may also be "citizens . . . who are widely recognized for their broad knowledge of, or expertise in, or their profound interest in, the arts."

By these means the independence of the endowment is effectively safe-guarded. Safeguards have been given added force over the past decade because the Democratic and Republican parties and the press have understood that the nonpolitical, nonpartisan nature of the endowment must be respected if it is to carry out its assigned role of supporting excellence in the arts. The two individuals who have been selected thus far to be chairman have been outstanding professionals in arts-related fields. They have submitted their recommendations on appointments to the council to the White House, and while their recommendations have not been taken on all occasions, successive presidents have respected the standards for council membership set forth in the act. It is of course true that the sums appropriated for the endowment have been small in comparison with those administered by other federal agencies. It is also true that as appropriations increase, patronage, rather than artistic purpose, may become the cement which holds the endowment in place. The Congress, in reauthorizing the endowment in 1976, amended the act to provide that, henceforth, appointments to the council will be subject to the advice and consent of the Senate. While this adds stature to the council, it could in time lead to the kind of political intrusion which has weakened other independent agencies of government.

3. Nonintervention

The third principle embodied in the act, of great importance, is nonintervention by the government in the operations of organizations and institutions to which public funds are given.

The fear that government patronage would lead to government censorship and control was widely held at the time of the endowment's creation. In recognition of that concern, section 4(c) was written into the act. It provides that:

> In the administration of this Act, no department, agency, officer, or employee of the United States shall exercise any direction, supervision, or control over the policy determination, personnel, or curriculum, or the administration or operation of any school or other non-Federal agency, institution, organization, or association.

This provision is as vital to the integrity of the Congress and of the endowment as it is to the freedom and independence of the grantees. The past decade has been a turbulent one, marked by women's liberation, the black revolution, and opposition to the war in Vietnam. Each of these upheavals has found expression in the arts. The expression has been characterized by frankness, bitterness, anger, and militancy. It has extended the vocabulary of literature, of film, and of the theater to words and phrases which in past years have been widely held to be offensive. The endowment, in its commitment to seriousness of intent and excellence in execution, has funded many of these activities. And, understandably, taxpayers and their elected representatives have been upset. The endowment on occasion has been called upon to bring its grantees into line with prevailing values, or else to cut off their funds. In each instance, it has cited section 4(c) of the act. Congressmen, in turn, have acknowledged the force and wisdom of the section and have allowed common sense to prevail.

4. Nondomination

More insidious than outright censorship, because it is less visible, is the threat that government may come to dominate the artistic life of the nation through its predominance in funding arts institutions and organizations. This threat, foreseen by the Congress, was countered by the provisions of the act which limit the proportion of arts budgets which may be funded by the endowment. Save for contracts, which it may enter into for its own purposes, and for a small portion of grants, given in exceptional circumstances, the act provides that the endowment shall not fund more than 50 percent of the cost of the projects and productions which it supports.

The wisdom of this provision is demonstrated day by day in administrative as well as artistic terms. At the level of 5 to 15 percent funding, which prevails for most performing arts institutions, the endowment with its small staff (220 in all) exercises a minimum degree of oversight. The survival of each institution turns on its own inner vitality and on the response of the constituency which it serves. In contrast, at 50 percent funding, the endowment would, sooner or later, be drawn into questions of management: unions, contracts, salary scales, the competence of key personnel, the nature and composition of boards of directors. Its support, or lack of support, could become a matter of life or death—a nightmare which the endowment has been spared thus far.

The endowment, guided by the National Council on the Arts, has clung tenaciously to the 50 percent rule. In developing its own guidelines, it has absolved itself of the psychological pressures that flow from a parental relationship by specifying that it will not fund a theater company, for example, until it has been in existence for two years. In positive terms, the endowment has supported arts organizations and institutions in ways that encourage them to obtain increased funds from private sources. An oversight committee of the Congress, reviewing the record of the endowment in 1970, concluded:

> The fear that Federal support would mean that the traditional private sources of funds for the arts would withdraw proved unfounded. On the contrary, it has proved a stimulus to private funds from sources never before involved with the arts.

5. Decentralization

Section 5(g) of the National Foundation on the Arts and the Humanities Act authorizes the chairman of the endowment to carry out a program of grants-in-aid to the several states in support of the arts.

This provision, added almost as an afterthought to the legislation, has been a key element in the success of public funding over the past ten years.

Only five states had functioning arts agencies when the act was passed in 1965. It was accompanied by an appropriation of $25,000 to each state to assist in the creation of a state arts agency. The response was immediate: within a year, state agencies were operating with appropriated funds in twenty-two states and in Puerto Rico; by 1974, agencies were functioning in every state and special jurisdiction.

In addition to the basic state agency grant, the endowment provides matching funds to the state agencies. It gives them administrative responsibility for a number of programs, including the Dance Touring Program and the Artists-in-Schools Program.

By these means, public support for the arts has been decentralized.

Given the rapid growth in public funding, the alternatives to decentralization would have been either formula funding, with a consequent loss of oversight of artistic standards, or else the emergence of a massive federal bureaucracy in the endowment. In contrast, the federal-state partnership has enabled the endowment to safeguard its standards during a decade of growth, and yet to remain small.

6. Professionalism

Public patronage of the arts, like private patronage, is ultimately measured by the taste and perception of those who make the artistic judgments on which funding is based.

Section 10(a)(4) of the act authorizes the chairman of the endowment to "utilize from time to time, as appropriate, experts and consultants, including panels of experts." The first chairman, Roger Stevens, moved promptly to carry out this provision and appointed panels of professional advisers in most program areas. When Nancy Hanks became chairman in 1969, added emphasis was given to the panel structure. A congressional oversight committee, reporting in 1973, noted that:

> Professional advisory panels now play a major role in Endowment
> programming with 185 individuals residing in 68 communities in 31
> states, assisting ten different Endowment program areas.

Panelists are appointed by the chairman of the endowment; they may serve up to four years. They are selected primarily for their professional competence but also with the need for maintaining a balance within each panel of background, residence, and artistic viewpoint. The panels review the 20,000 applications that are now received each year. They also review the categories within which the applications are submitted. The National Council on the Arts advises the chairman on the allocation of funds between art forms, but the chairmen of the standing panels attend council meetings and speak out on the art forms which they represent.

The panels make the basic recommendations on which grants are given. While these recommendations are only advisory, the council and the chairman rarely overturn them, and almost never for artistic reasons. The panels are protected by confidentiality and by the assurance that artistic merit must always be their primary consideration. Thus they are insulated against external pressures. Nonetheless, as the endowment's appropriations mount and its grants grow in size, it would be naive to suppose that these pressures will not increase.

It is of critical importance that until now neither the White House nor the oversight committees of the Congress have encroached upon the chairman's authority to select individual panelists. However, the committees have instructed the chairman on how they are to be selected. Thus, in hearings held in 1973, members of the Congress decided that too large a proportion of the endowment's funds was being allocated to urban centers in New York and California. They came, in turn, to the belief that a disproportionate number of panelists had been drawn from these centers. In consequence, section 10(a)(4) of the act, which gives the chairman the power to appoint the panels, was amended to read:

Provided, however, That any advisory panel appointed to review or make recommendations with respect to . . . funding shall have broad geographic representation.

Again, in 1976, the two authorizing committees dealt with the panel structure in a general way, the House committee calling for "frequent rotation of the panel members in order to foster a greater involvement of the public in the decision-making process" and the Senate committee urging "the broadest possible representation of viewpoint on each panel so that all styles and forms of expression which involve quality in the arts . . . may be equitably treated."

These generalized comments are sound enough, given the commitment of our nation to democracy and to cultural pluralism. They do not damage the endowment. In contrast, were the Congress to undertake to control the selection of panelists, it would undermine the endowment's ability to recruit the nation's leading artists and critics as its professional advisers and to give free rein to their insights and skills.

The current programs of the endowment

The endowment's current programs can be summarized in a table, showing estimates by program area for 1977.

Architecture + Environmental Arts	$ 3,470,000
Dance	5,622,077
Education	4,488,000
Expansion Arts	5,591,000
Federal-State Partnership	15,764,960
Literature	2,150,000
Media Arts	7,102,040
Museums	9,550,563
Music	12,880,655
Special Projects	4,819,705
Theater	5,921,000
Visual Arts	3,650,000

These programs have developed in their own ways, and they vary substantially in their impact upon the constituencies they serve.

"Grants were made to assist new works and, more importantly, to encourage touring, an activity . . . which furthered the endowment's purpose of making the arts available to all Americans." Above, a performance of *The River* by the American Ballet Theatre.

"Public funding of the arts has worked well for a decade. Its success was heightened because so much else that government did . . . seemed misguided or wrong." Top, Gary Chryst in the Joffrey Ballet production *Trinity,* and Patricia McBride and Jean-Pierre Bonnefous of the New York City Ballet in *The Nutcracker* (bottom).

Architecture ✛ *Environmental Arts*

The program began in 1967 with eleven small grants, mostly in support of environmental design projects. Ten years later, in addition to awarding grants, the architecture office has undertaken to raise standards of design, of architecture, and of graphic work throughout the federal government. It has organized national and regional design assemblies to increase design awareness among federal officials. It has recruited teams of nationally known designers to improve the graphic materials of forty-six federal agencies. It has published task force reports on the opportunities and the constraints which determine the quality of federal architecture.

Dance

The program, established in 1966, soon moved into massive support for large companies whose audiences were multiplying and whose financial problems were acute. Grants were made to assist new works and, more importantly, to encourage touring, an activity which for the first time provided continuous employment for dancers and which furthered the endowment's purpose of making the arts available to all Americans.

In 1977 the touring program has allocated $1,180,000 in grants which provide 30 percent of the company's minimum weekly fee to sponsors of the American Ballet Theatre, the Joffrey Ballet, and the New York City Ballet. It also has provided $2.1 million in support of touring by smaller companies, a program administered through regional agencies and through the state arts councils.

The program, as the Senate Committee on Labor and Public Welfare noted in its 1976 report, has been instrumental in raising the number of resident professional dance companies in America from ten to sixty in a single decade.

Education

In its second meeting in June 1965, the National Council on the Arts called for an expanded role for the arts in education, one that would advance professional training as well as awareness and appreciation of the arts.

The council went on to set in motion two collaborative efforts with the Office of Education. The first, the Laboratory Theater Project, was innovative, daring, expensive, and short-lived. The second, which the Office of Education helped to fund for only two years, became the federal government's most notable art-in-education program. The program, to which $3,392,000 was allocated in 1977, is directed by the endowment but administered by the state arts agencies. Matching funds are offered to the states in recommended categories for the employment of actors, architects, craftsmen, dancers, filmmakers, poets, painters, sculptors, photographers, printmakers, jazz, folk, and classical musicians, and other artists. The selection of the artists is made by the state agency and the participating schools. The program, which began with six schools in 1969, is operating in 7,500 schools in all the states and the special jurisdictions.

Expansion Arts

In the first four years of its existence, the endowment gave a few grants within its program areas to projects involving ethnic minorities or the residents of inner cities. These grants were plainly inadequate, and in 1971 a new program office, Expansion Arts, was created to support arts activities among groups whose cultures had been historically undervalued or ignored. The program, building on the prior efforts of the Ford Foundation and the Rockefeller Brothers Fund, quickly identified a large number of professionally led, community-based enterprises. Its support of these enterprises was then extended to professional artists at work in social contexts, most notably in prisons and hospitals.

The money allocated to the program in 1977 is being spent for workshops and performances in a wide variety of art forms. Grants are almost entirely in the $5,000–$30,000 range, but, since the scale of operations is small, the endowment's contribution may be 20 to 30 percent of the budget of an expansion arts grantee as against the 3 to 5 percent contribution which the endowment makes to the nation's leading symphony orchestras and opera companies.

Federal-State Partnership

The largest component of this program is the basic state agency grant allocation, which this year is $11,935,000. This allocation is given in equal amounts to the arts agencies of the states and the special jurisdictions.

The sums set aside for the state agencies were once determined by the chairman of the endowment. Since 1973 they have been set by the Congress, under an amendment to the act which provides that the state agencies and regional associations shall receive no less than 20 percent of the endowment's program funds.

The act requires that the basic grant be matched within the states. The additional funds advanced to the state agencies, for regional associations, for community councils, and for specific projects are given on a matching basis on the recommendations of the federal-state panel.

In principle, in order to be eligible for the basic grant, the state agencies must meet the qualitative standards set forth in section 5 of the act. In practice, review of the state programs has, so far, been minimal. In contrast, applications by the state agencies for project assistance have been subjected to qualitative review.

Literature

This program has been allotted a small share of the endowment's funds, although fine writing is basic not only to literature but to theater, to film, and to other art forms. The reason is two-fold: government finds it difficult to gear itself down to the individual writer, and writers in turn are loners, neither trained nor organized to deal with government in meeting their needs.

The Writers-in-the-Schools program has, in fact, made it possible for poets to earn their living as poets in America. In addition, the Literature Program, in alternate years, provides fellowship awards of $7,500 to writers to advance work-in-progress. Applications from 2,500 published writers were reviewed in 1976 by the program's professional advisers, and 165 awards were given.

The program has not provided general support for creative writing courses or for workshops for teachers of English. It has given direct support to small presses which publish contemporary work. It has provided indirect support to over 200 literary magazines through the Coordinating Council of Literary Magazines. It has funded innovative efforts to bring contemporary poetry and fiction to wider audiences and it has supported service organizations such as PEN.

Media Arts

One-third of the Media Arts budget is allocated to the American Film Institute. A grant of $1.1 million supports the institute's Center for Advanced Film Studies in Los Angeles and other activities; contracts, awarded to the institute, are for filmmaker fellowships and for film preservation.

In addition to these sums, the Media Arts Program awards direct grants in support of film, radio, and television. Programs in film include grants to forty-six regional film centers, grants for workshops, study courses, and festivals, and awards to individuals engaged primarily in making documentary and experimental films. Programs in radio include grants to Minnesota Public Radio for live presentations of poetry and folk music and for "Earplay," a series of plays produced for public radio by the University of Wisconsin. Programs for television include fellowships for young filmmakers in residence at cable television stations and for projects funded jointly with private corporations and foundations and the Corporation for Public Broadcasting and carried over the public television network.

Museums

The act creating the endowment listed museums as one of its legitimate concerns. A report prepared in 1968 for the Federal Council on the Arts and the Humanities found that "a pervasive and insistent financial crisis" confronted the nation's museums and added: "A strong case can be made for Federal support."

The small size of the endowment's budget made a program in support of museums impracticable in its early years. Pilot grants were made to three art museums in 1967 to help them "stimulate awareness of the visual arts and to make their collections more readily available to a wider public."

A second category of support, begun in 1968, provided matching funds to museums for the purchase of works by living American artists. Then, in November 1970, the council approved a report calling for the creation of a new program of project support for all types of museums.

The program now provides a wide range of assistance to museums in mounting and touring exhibitions, in training professional staff members, and in conserving collections through restoration of works of art and renovation of the buildings in which they are housed. General support is not provided, and endowment grants to museums amount to less than 2 percent of their operating costs each year. Congress in 1976 added a new title to the act of 1965 entitled the Museum Services Act. The title established within the Department of Health, Education, and Welfare an Institute of Museum Services. It authorized appropriations of $15 million for the institute in 1977 and $25 million in 1978. If funds are in fact appropriated for the institute, it will be enabled to provide general operating support for museums of all kinds. It is understood that the arts endowment and the humanities endowment will continue to provide project support to museums.

Music

Projects in support of music were undertaken at the inception of the endowment in a wide-ranging, somewhat arbitrary way. The small size of the endowment's budget made categorical support impracticable; in fact, the minutes of an early council meeting record an occasion on which the trustees of the Ford Foundation, prior to approving their own $80-million allocation to the nation's symphony orchestra associations, asked for and were given an assurance that the endowment was not about to fund the orchestras.

The symphony orchestra associations, as late as 1968, held that they did not want or need federal funds. Then, in October 1969, they reversed their stand and held that endowment support was essential to their survival. In turn, they were instrumental in mobilizing sentiment behind President Nixon's request that the Congress double the appropriations of the two endowments in 1970.

For seven years the orchestras have been assured of limited but continuing support from the endowment. Thirty major orchestras, with annual budgets of over $1,500,000, received $4,710,000 in 1977; that is, about 4 percent of their gross receipts. Sixty-five regional and metropolitan orchestras, with annual budgets between $100,000 and $1,500,000, received $1,700,000, a sum less than 4 percent of their gross receipts.

In principle, the grants are given in support of projects such as touring, youth concerts, and summer concerts in parks. In practice, at a time when orchestras are committed to year-round employment of musicians, the endowment funds have amounted to general support.

In support of opera, forty-six professional companies were granted $3,201,000 for the 1976–77 season. The grants range from $7,500 to the Nevada Opera Guild to $600,000 to the Metropolitan Opera Association.

In other categories, $850,000 is allocated to support of jazz, ethnic, and folk music in 1977; $1,058,280 to training and career development; $172,995 to contemporary music performance; and $400,000 to composers and librettists to advance work-in-progress. A small sum, $70,000, is allocated to support of choral music and none to chamber music as such.

Special Projects

The Office of Special Projects has funded programs which do not fall into categories set by art forms. Currently it encompasses folk arts, service organizations, art centers and festivals, fellowship exchanges with Great Britain, and "City Spirit," a program to assist communities which seek to employ the arts as a catalytic force.

Theater

In signing the act of 1965, President Johnson stated: "We will create a national theater." This concept of one predominant and heavily subsidized institution on the European model proved to be ephemeral and inappropriate. Instead, the endowment undertook to encourage the decentralization of professional theater in America by providing continuing support to a growing number of resident professional theater companies. Its grants, given as general support rather than for projects, coincided with and reinforced the rapid expansion of these companies across the nation. Fifty-six companies in forty-one cities, all operating with Equity contracts, were given grants for the 1976–77 season. The total allocation of $3,780,000 is about 7 percent of their gross receipts for the year.

In other categories, the Theater Program supports experimental companies of national or regional standing; companies performing for short seasons, and for children; service organizations; and some training institutions. A new category of support provides funds for state arts agencies to encourage touring by professional companies within their areas.

Visual Arts

The program, operating without a standing panel, has developed a wide range of categories of support. The largest, with a total allocation of $1,350,000 for 1977, provides fellowships for visual artists, printmakers, photographers, craftsmen, and art critics. A second category provides $600,000 in matching funds to communities for the commissioning of works of art in public places. In a comparable program, the visual arts office has assisted the General Services Administration in carrying out a program under which 0.5 percent of the cost of new federal buildings has been set aside for works of art.

Challenge Grants

A supplemental appropriation provided the endowment with $9 million for challenge grants in 1977. The grants, given for one-time projects, are intended to encourage forward planning by cultural institutions. They thrust the endowment itself in a new direction by imposing criteria such as financial reliability, managerial competence, and community responsiveness onto the panels and the council whose judgments up to now have been based solely upon artistic merit.

Issues in search of a concept

Public funding of the arts has worked well for a decade. Its success was heightened because so much else that government did during the decade seemed misguided or wrong. Yet innovative ideas often harden into restrictive categories, and the programs that generated growth in one decade may inhibit it in the next. Continuity is essential. But a new chairman, working with a new administration, will need to consider certain underlying issues which up to now have not been confronted, let alone resolved.

Institutions of national standing

One of the purposes for which endowment grants are given is preservation of our cultural heritage. At the center of this heritage are certain key institutions of national and international standing. The following table lists the total expenditures of a group of these institutions in 1976, along with the endowment's grants to these institutions and the grants as percentages of the total expenditures of each institution.

(1) Institution	(2) Total expenditures	(3) Arts endowment grants	(4) Percentage (3) of (2)
American Ballet Theatre	$6,619,200	$627,790	7.8
New York City Ballet	6,334,000	267,330	4.2
Guthrie Theatre	2,443,825	150,000	6.1
American Conservatory Theatre	3,006,000	150,000	4.9
Chicago Symphony	6,420,456	150,000	2.3
Los Angeles Symphony	5,975,000	150,000	2.5
Metropolitan Opera	27,833,000	600,000	1.1
San Francisco Opera	5,189,522	150,000	2.9
Metropolitan Museum	27,733,000	308,480	1.1
Cleveland Museum	4,005,000	84,750	2.1
Museum of Modern Art	8,700,000	290,644	3.3

Many of the institutions listed here are in serious financial difficulties. In some instances dissolution may be inevitable; in others, greatly increased public funding may be the price of survival. What will the response of government be?

In Europe the response presumably would be massive support for the preeminent institutions. A comparable response in America is more problematical. We are committed to the view that government should not be a predominant patron. Moreover, the concept of preeminence is abhorrent to us. Therefore, funding that is provided to one institution must be offered to many others.

Leading advocates for the arts have argued that the federal government should shift from project support to general support and from varying levels of support to a minimum level of 10 percent funding of arts institutions.

While projections are uncertain, 10 percent funding of arts institutions of regional or national standing would point to expenditures of this magnitude in 1980:

	Total expenditures	Arts endowment grants
106 symphony orchestras	$204,000,000	$20,000,000
46 opera companies	114,000,000	11,400,000
55 theater companies	77,000,000	7,700,000
79 dance companies	68,000,000	6,800,000

In addition, if the operating costs of the nation's museums are estimated at $800 million in 1980, then the combined funding provided by the two endowments and the new Institute of Museum Services would amount to $80 million.

Expenditures of this magnitude would suggest an annual budget for the arts endowment in 1980 of $160 million. It could operate effectively at this level within the principles set forth in the act. But even at 10 percent funding, the future of the key institutions would by no means be assured.

The training of professional artists

If the federal government is to provide $100 million and more each year in support of arts organizations, it must be concerned with the institutions in which professional artists are trained.

The National Science Foundation has made $900 million available in support of the training of scientists. In contrast, no funds have been granted for the training of artists by the Office of Education or any major federal department. The endowment's record by art form has been:

> Literature, visual arts, dance: no support.
> Architecture, museums: fragmentary project support.
> Films, music, theater: limited institutional support.

In films, support has been given to only one institution, the American Film Institute. In theater, pilot funding of some professional training institutions was judged unsuccessful, and funds are given to only nine university departments affiliated with professional theater companies. In music, support has so far been limited to small grants given to nine conservatories. To take three examples in 1976:

(1) Institution	(2) Annual expenditures	(3) Arts endowment grants	(4) Percentage (3) of (2)
Juilliard School	$6,872,000	$55,000	0.8
Cleveland Institute	2,090,225	40,000	2.0
Peabody Institute	2,763,497	40,000	1.4

Speaking on behalf of five private universities and colleges, Grant Beglarian, a dean of the University of Southern California, told the National Council on the Arts in September 1976 that the costs of professional training were mounting beyond the capacity of students and private institutions to bear. He proposed that:

It shall be a prime objective of the National Endowment for the Arts
to help the education of future professionals in the arts through
programs designed to share a part of the heavy financial burden
carried by qualified students and the institutions they attend.

The statement was not adopted by the council. But the problem remains and demands serious consideration, and a committee of the council has been established to address this concern.

Beyond the professional core

Beyond the boundaries of the professional core for which the endowment has accepted limited responsibility lies the much larger constituency of nonprofessional artists and arts institutions.

In Alabama there are no professional resident theater companies, but there are eighteen community theaters. If the live experience of the arts is important for the participant and for the audience, then community theaters deserve attention. If the endowment will not directly assist them, does it follow that the state agencies will accept this responsibility? The Alabama State Council on the Arts and Humanities does in fact make grants to community theaters. Many state councils do not. No state agency program is worked out in collaboration with the endowment; no federal program is prepared in conjunction with the states; no division of roles has ever been defined between the endowment and the states.

In principle, it might seem logical that the endowment should accept primary responsibility for funding institutions of national and regional standing and that the state agencies should accept responsibility for all others. In fact, this division of roles has been unacceptable to the state agencies. Many of them feel that they must fund the major institutions in order to obtain their backing in the state legislatures. In addition, many state agencies sense that for the endowment to take the best and to leave them the good is to relegate them to second-class status.

It may well be that the state legislatures should accept some funding responsibilities for their major institutions, just as New York State does today. It may be that no uniform division of roles can be agreed on by the arts agencies of the nation. Nonetheless, if a community orchestra or theater company or dance troupe is advised by the endowment to seek funds from its state agency, only to be told in turn that the state agency has allotted its funds to the endowment's grantees, the result is exasperation.

A new factor in this situation is the community arts council. Ten years ago there were 125 community councils; today there are 1,000. Their combined budgets are over $50 million a year. In the past, these councils have had to seek federal funds through the state agencies. As they grow, they may well insist upon direct and substantial support. In the process of becoming a partnership, the federal-state relationship may be enlarged to include community councils, above all, in the big cities.

Support or employment

In his statement on the arts of October 21, 1976, Jimmy Carter declared:

> The greatness of the Roosevelt years as compared to the past eight
> years was that Roosevelt did not view the arts merely as something to
> be supported. Roosevelt treated artists as an integral part of society—
> workers who had an important job to do in rebuilding our nation.

He added:

> We must again have a government that is prepared to make active use
> of the arts.

The president's view, in my opinion, is sound. To hold that society must *support* its artists is to separate the artists from society. It is demeaning, because it implies that artists are unable to support themselves. It is self-defeating, because it incites resentment and scorn in those who provide support for those who seek it. The old French fable about the cricket and the ant is a variation on this theme. It ends badly for the cricket when winter comes.

In the long run, whatever its initial success may be, a public agency dedicated to supporting one class of citizens at the taxpayer's expense is likely to find that it has enclosed itself within invisible boundaries, for the basic ethic on which it operates is against the American grain.

But if support for artists is ultimately a self-defeating concept, what about support for arts organizations and institutions? Museums plainly are educational institutions, entitled to public support. Performing arts centers may be included in the category of physical facilities which each municipality must maintain. However, no such historical sanction exists in this nation for symphony orchestras, opera companies, and theater and dance groups.

In requiring its grantees to conform to the guidelines it prepares, the endowment is providing more than *support* but far less than *employment*. It is a public foundation, operating within the framework that has legitimized all foundations over the past fifty years. The growth of foundations during this period is impressive, but it should not blind us to recent trends. There is ample evidence in congressional actions and in studies, such as the Report of the Filer Commission, that the foundation, like the spirit of philanthropy which gave birth to it, has seen its best days. As a democratic people gain in self-esteem, they are increasingly intolerant of the notion that the privileged are entitled to the nation's gratitude if they bestow a part of their bounty upon the less privileged.

In contrast to the narrowing horizons of *support, employment* of artists offers immense opportunities of expansion at a time when more and more citizens find their lives frustrating and seek enrichment through the arts. The Artists-in-Schools program of the endowment is one pilot program of proven worth. Prisons, hospitals, community centers, and centers for the aging are among the social contexts in which artists are now at work. The actors who work for the Cell Block Theater or the poets, painters, potters, and weavers who work as a team for COMPAS in St. Paul may not stand at the peak of their professions. But they are committed professionals, and by their own testimony their perceptions have been deepened and their skills strengthened by the work they do.

If President Carter carries out his commitment, we can expect a shift in emphasis toward employment of artists and of organizations such as symphony orchestras and dance companies which today receive grants from the endowment for services they perform in parks and in schools.

Awards to individuals

The first grants announced by the National Council on the Arts included awards to individuals (an action questioned by the writer at that time). Awards were given to painters and sculptors, undergraduate students of architecture, and elderly poets.

The Congress objected. In reauthorizing the two endowments in 1968, it struck the term *individuals* from the relevant sections of the act. Notwithstanding, the council and the chairman insisted on continuing awards to individual artists. The Congress relented and permitted awards to be made to "individuals of exceptional talent."

The endowment has continued and expanded its programs in support of individual artists.* In 1976 it provided the following fellowships:

---

* Save for apprentice jazz musicians, performing artists are not directly assisted in advancing their careers.

Program	Number	Amount
Architecture	50	$428,935
Dance	95	532,964
Literature	245	1,230,580
Media arts	34	286,965
Museums	29	137,741
Music	328	847,070
Visual arts	326	1,399,000
Total	1,107	$4,863,255

These awards are unanimously supported by the council, the chairman, and the program directors of the endowment. In my opinion they are misguided, for these reasons:

First, the competitive nature of all awards sets artists against each other and is contrary to what Robert Henri called "the art spirit." The lasting benefit gained by the hundreds of artists who are given grants is problematical. The damage done to the thousands who apply and are rejected is indisputable. Belief in self is essential to the artist's creativity. Rejection can only undermine it. Rejection by a private jury may be discounted by the artist. Rejection in the name of the United States may do great harm.

Second, individual awards are a misuse of the resources of government. The proper role of government is to raise the general level of aesthetic awareness in the nation, not to pick and choose among the end products of the arts. The proper role of a small agency such as the endowment is to provide vision, to apply leverage, to employ its pennies in order to activate the dollars of others in employment in the arts. This role cannot be assumed by program offices overburdened with the peripheral tasks of handing out $5 million a year to one in one thousand of our professional artists. To say "overburdened" may seem an exaggeration, but no one who has watched panelists and staff members poring for hours over manuscripts, transparencies, and tapes, and who has seen the corridors of the endowment barricaded by piles of unopened packages from individual applicants, can doubt that the term is fair.

Third, in a democratic culture aesthetic judgments should, as far as possible, be dispersed.

The endowment can and must assess the relative merits of symphony orchestras and theater companies. But no such rating system can be applied to individuals. In literature a panel of acknowledged authorities may reach a consensus on the relative talents of applicants. A second and a third gathering of experts may confirm the conclusions of the first. In contrast, in the visual arts the formlessness of the "form" makes any such consensus illusory. In its determination to keep abreast of every passing fad, the endowment has, through its awards, funded activities which I can only characterize as frivolous.

All this is not to say that public funds cannot be effectively channeled to individuals. A current program provides matching funds to museums for the purchase of works by contemporary Americans. The program in my opinion is effective, first, because it disperses among many authorities the aesthetic judgments which must be made, and second, because it ends in a transaction, not a handout. The program, I believe, can and should be greatly expanded.

The endowment in its first decade has operated in contrasting ways. Its flexibility has been its strength, but the pressures upon it are mounting. Substantial institutions are clamoring for substantial assistance. Neglected areas as large as the Western Reserve are crying out for settlement. Pilot programs endure, but like the unborn they have a period of gestation that cannot be extended for long.

Is the endowment, in its primary emphasis, to become a leadership agency or an operating agency? Will it be a catalytic force or an integral part of a large department of the federal government?

In itself, the endowment is unimportant, but from now on the federal government is bound to have a substantial impact upon the development of our culture. It may act consciously and purposefully; it may act in a fragmented manner, without comprehension of or concern for the aesthetic impact of its actions.

If President Carter and his advisers sense that aesthetic values are important, the coming decade may see the emergence of a policy which relates the two endowments, the Office of Education, the Corporation for Public Broadcasting, the State Department, and the social agencies in a series of collaborative efforts, all in the service of an overarching design. If, on the contrary, aesthetic values and the arts are thought not greatly to matter, the endowments may go their separate ways, gaining just enough in appropriations to keep up with inflation, letting the human environment be shaped only by the blind, contending forces of the marketplace. Other questions may seem more pressing, and perhaps they are. But there is wisdom in the poet's insight: *Life is short, art is long; the song outlives the singer; the coin, Tiberius.*

Patronage through the Ages

Philipp Fehl

Philipp Fehl was born in Vienna, Austria, in 1920. Obliged to flee Nazi persecution in 1938, he immigrated to the United States in 1940, studied painting for two years at the Art Institute of Chicago, and then joined the Army to fight in World War II. The end of this found him serving as an interrogator with American forces at the Nuremberg trials. In 1943 he became an American citizen. He holds a bachelor's degree in romance languages and a master's degree in the history of art from Stanford University. His doctorate is from the University of Chicago.

Mr. Fehl taught widely in the United States before coming to the University of Illinois at Urbana-Champaign as professor of the history of art in 1969. Recognition of his scholarship has come from both this country and abroad. As art historian, he has been associated with the Brussels Art Seminar, Belgium; the American Council of Learned Societies; the Warburg Institute of the University of London; the American Academy in Rome; and the College Art Association of America. He is at present on the councils of the Gazette des Beaux Arts, the Institute of International Education, and the Midwest Art History Society.

His views on the aims of art are to be found in *The Classical Monument* (1972). He is editor and translator of *A Course in Drawing* by Nicolas Cochin and Denis Diderot (1954) and the author of many articles. An admirer of the picture stories—the capricci—of Tiepolo and Rodolphe Toepffer, Mr. Fehl has himself published two books of drawings, *The Bird* (1970) and *Capricci* (1971). Some of these have also been exhibited internationally and reproduced in literary magazines.

The establishing of the tradition

Vanity and luxury are great promoting powers of private patronage. Ignorance or prostitution of the good, for the sake of success and vainglory, motivate the artist in catering to corrupt demands. If the lawgiver be not wise, state patronage will but contribute to making private ills public and, worse, by a skillful appeal to the emotions and by deception (to which the arts that present illusions are ever prone), will contribute to the endurance of an unjust state. Because it evokes convincing likenesses and moves the passions, art can be a constant source of error, can subvert our minds, and can even corrupt our desire to arrive at just judgments; to be gripped in emotion will be all. At its worst, art, by the very exercise of the best efforts of its skills, through images that pretend to be true representations and through tales attractively told, will give us false notions of the gods.

Thus speaks the voice of accusing philosophy, in the formidable arguments of Plato. It is seconded, furthermore, by the awesome authority of the Bible. The second commandment expressly forbids the making of images of any kind, and the Psalms are full of verses mocking the pagans who put their trust in statues.

> They have mouths, but they speak not: eyes have they, but they see not. . . . They that make them are like unto them; so is every one that trusteth in them [Psalm 115].

Modern lovers of art tend to make short shrift of the biblical injunction; it may have suited, one likes to say, the days and the circumstances for which it was written, but it was not meant to apply to contemporary conditions, either of art or of life. Plato often fares no better. His argument is so at odds with the rewards we receive from looking at works of art that we are tempted not to take it seriously. The modern response to Plato's challenge rather tends to take it for granted that he did not know anything about art, certainly not about the art of his time, which marked so obviously a turning point in the history of art. There is a theory, however, that Plato was a reactionary, and if this was the case it may be supposed that he rejected Greek classical art because it was modern in his time and stood for progress. On the same assumption one may argue, of course, that he was well aware of the newly gained skill and power of art at his time and for that very reason feared it the more. Artists, who had become capable of producing with ease compelling and, by their very beauty, seductive likenesses of figures and actions, were now as dangerous in their power to confuse and obscure truth and the search for truth as poets and rhetoricians had been all along. Since seeing and *believing* are so very closely allied, the visual arts could even be deemed potentially more dangerous (and more ridiculous) than the art of Homer, the source, as it were, and procreator of all man-made poetic arts.

Plato's successors, concerned as they were with reintroducing the arts to the republic for the good that was obviously in them, took his criticism seriously. They made distinctions between what was true in the arts and what fiction, and what in the framework of fiction itself was a likeness of truth and what a falsehood, what could be believed and endorsed, what respected, what merely tolerated ("here Homer nodded"), and what should be expunged.

The Church, even though it passed through a number of iconoclastic crises, did likewise. It very earnestly sponsored the visual arts on a variety of levels, from use in the simple instruction of those who could not read to celebrations of divine virtue and compassion in representations which equaled in their refinement (if they did not transcend) the power of words.

The reasoning behind what at first glance (and to the iconoclasts always) appears to be a circumvention of the second commandment is actually an interpretation of its sense on premises ultimately derived, intriguingly enough, from Plato's philosophy. The gist of the argument was, in fact, taken over from the pagan defense of the use of statuary in divine and imperial rites against Judaeo-Christian allegations of idol worship, at a time in Rome when the commission of cult statues represented the highest form of state patronage. I give the argument in the words of the last pagan emperor, Julian the Apostate:

> Therefore, when we look at the images of the gods, let us not indeed
> think they are stones or wood, but neither let us think they are the
> gods themselves; and indeed we do not say that the statues of the
> emperors are mere wood and stone and bronze, but still less do we say
> they are the emperors themselves. He therefore who loves the
> emperor delights to see the emperor's statue, and he who loves his son
> delights to see his son's statue, and he who loves his father delights to
> see his father's statue. It follows that he who loves the gods delights to
> gaze on the images of the gods, and their likenesses, and he feels
> reverence and shudders with awe of the gods who look at him from
> the unseen world.[1]

We know perfectly well that we do not gaze upon the gods themselves when we contemplate the images of the gods, this clearly says (*pace* the second commandment), but we are pleased by the images, nevertheless, because we take pleasure in what they stand for, and are made the more reverent thereby (*pace* Plato).

The defense of art in the renaissance follows the theory of poetry (such

"We do not gaze upon the gods themselves when we contemplate the images of the gods." Above, "The Creation of Adam," detail of the ceiling fresco in the Sistine Chapel, 1508–12 by Michelangelo.

as we find it exemplified in Sir Philip Sidney's *Defence of Poesie*) that accepts and happily builds on those premises of philosophy and religion that restrict art. In other words, it defends a reformed art, one that is above reproach and will serve the will of God as well as the republic of men under God. The writers as a rule are themselves artists or, like Leon Battista Alberti (1404–72), at least experienced in the arts. What they wish to do is rediscover, from the study of the surviving works of art and the literary remains, the lost theory of classical art (which they deemed to be a perfect system and in keeping with the cautions of the philosophers) and apply it to the even more obligating demands of a world that has received the true knowledge of divine revelation.

The chief impact on society, and on the rank and file of artists, was not made, of course, by the writings of the theoreticians but by the demonstrations provided by the most thoughtful works of great artists. These stand out as landmarks of humanistic accomplishment, and even today the dignity, grandeur, and ultimate serenity which are alive in them make them places of pilgrimages and continue to protect, without the need for argument, the good name of the practice of art. Such works are not just "art." They represent the quintessence of reflection on the nature of art and its highest purposes. The great minds presiding over this new republic of the visual arts are Michelangelo and Raphael. They are at the heart of the first great history of art, Vasari's *Lives of the Most Eminent Italian Architects, Painters and Sculptors* (1550, enlarged ed. 1568), which was written primarily to benefit the education of young artists and advance the enlightenment of patrons; the same two figures dominate another great instrument dedicated to the same purposes over two hundred years later, Sir Joshua Reynolds's *Discourses* on art.

The highest recommendation of the works treated in these writings is in moral terms; it is the good and noble we perceive that gives pleasure, or the beauty of the work that attunes us to the finest desires of the good. Small wonder that other books, on manners and on the education of the gentleman, included injunctions on the usefulness of the visual arts in that process. They help in the acquisition of the spiritual refinement which makes the gentleman worthy of his station and fit to exercise the power he holds by virtue of his title. Not that it was ever put to a nobleman that he should himself strive to be an artist. This would lead to a neglect of the duties to which he was born and would demean him. His glory was in military and political action. The nobleman was, however, encouraged to practice his hand at art and to acquire enough knowledge of it to sponsor artists with just discrimination. It is from this realm of sensible advice that we have received the now so unhappily discredited terms *amateur*, a lover of art, and *dilettante*, one who delights in it.

All this striving for virtue and refinement in the arts of the Renaissance does not mean that vice and error and vanity and sin were eradicated from the practice and the sponsorship of art. On the contrary, they flourished, and the arts continued in need of defense. Artists and their works, styles, and beauty were debated, sometimes perversely, sometimes dearly, in the language of virtue, and critics could and did justify, derogate, or extol the value of works of art according to their views of artistic license and the working of the laws of decorum in given circumstances. The battles of the styles we call Renaissance, *maniera*, baroque, rococo, and even neoclassicism are, in their original constellations, essentially debates about propriety, a family quarrel in the house of the Greater Renaissance.

What about patrons who cared chiefly to procure themselves vulgar pleasure in their commissions? There certainly was no lack of artists to supply the need, but the owners could be proud of their cherished acquisitions only in a qualified way. Such works of art were kept under lock and key or behind curtains and displayed to like-minded friends as delights of pornography, perhaps, rather than as triumphs of art. Artists in turn put the mantle of mythology over the exquisite nudes (for which there was ever a ready market) and thus practiced and catered to hypocrisy, save where an artist of genius (as did Titian in the *Rape of Europa*) would elevate a lewd topic to a most affecting—and yet appropriately cheerful—representation of the drama of love.

The framework for the discussion of what was proper was the hierarchy of genres. Works of art were considered more or less worthy depending on the nobility or worthiness of their subject matter, provided they could live up to the particular requirements that a given subject posited. The higher a subject was on the scale of artistic values, the more rewarding in turn were the benefits the accomplished work would bestow upon its audience. In painting, the largest variety of representation was permitted by history painting, the just representation of affecting or inspiring deeds; art of this kind was regarded as an entrance gate to the understanding of acts of greatness and piety. Christian history, with representations which at once were also evocations of the Passion as the greatest story, led the field; then came mythological history and history proper, in which were esteemed first the heroes of classical antiquity who figured in the life of Christ—that is, the Passion—then the events of biblical history, mythological history, and secular history, ancient and modern, in that order. All these stories, on different levels, dealt with the sublime and were considered to be capable of moving the mind of the viewer to great and sublime ideas.

Next in the hierarchy came genre painting proper. In this, peasants, artisans, shepherdesses, shepherds were the rule. The subject matter was humble; it might be touching or visible, and it even might instruct or point a lesson, but it was not meant to inspire awe. Its chief function was to entertain, to help us pass the time. Accordingly, as we look at it now, we see that a different atmosphere prevails. Different keys of expectation are struck, and our pleasure in the passing scenes before us is correspondingly different—simpler, undemanding, but, for these reasons, not necessarily less precious to us than the great organ tones of accomplished history painting.

Still further down in the hierarchy was portrait painting, an art always needed and usually the bread and butter of artists waiting for commissions in which their imaginations could flourish more grandly; yet it was still a noble art, and a great wonder, making the absent near, the dead come to life, and the living immortal. Then came landscape (heroic and plain), animal painting, and finally still life—the painting which had the least story to tell and yet in the hands of a master could show us a world. Not allowed was rhyparography, the representation of sordid or pornographic subjects: which does not mean (as we have said before) that it did not prosper.

No element of the academic tradition is more despised today than the system of genres. Perhaps we can arrive at a better understanding of this hierarchy if we see in its ordering of the value of pictures by the stories they tell a concern for the expectations which are elicited in us when a given subject or story puts forth its claim to our attention or, better, invites our interest and love. It is only when these expectations have been raised that we can hope to see fully what in fact is before us in all the complexity of a particular encounter with a work of art.

The genres are but one of a number of essential links between the world of art and moral significance. Additional connections become best apparent through the abstract, or seemingly abstract, art of architecture. There is left to us but one of the classical treatises on the art of architecture, the work of Vitruvius, which is dedicated to the emperor Augustus in the hope of securing his patronage:

> But I observed that you cared not only about the common life of all men, and the constitution of the state, but also about the provision of suitable public buildings; so that the state was not only made greater through you by its new provinces, but the majesty of the empire also was expressed through the eminent dignity of its public buildings. Hence I conceived that the opportunity should be taken at once of bringing before you my proposals about these things. . . . For I perceived that you have built, and are now building, on a large scale. Furthermore, with respect to the future, you have such regard to public and private buildings, that they will correspond to the grandeur of our history, and will be a memorial to future ages. I have furnished a detailed treatise so that, by reference to it, you might inform yourself about the works already complete or about to be entered upon. In the following books I have expounded a complete system of architecture.[2]

Vitruvius's complete system of architecture in fact is chiefly a practical handbook for building—full of useful advice, from the mixing of lime to the laying out of a city or, for that matter, its destruction with the help of war machines. In the eighteenth century it was still an eminently practical acquisition for a gentleman's library. But it was also more—a guide to giving beauty and dignity to building. Architecture, said Sir Joshua Reynolds, is called a polite or liberal art not for its practical function but because it is "capable of inspiring sentiment, and of filling the mind with great and sublime ideas.[3]

Vitruvius himself is not by any means a great writer. What he has to say on the beauty and majesty of buildings is culled from earlier writers greater than he and is poorly put together by him, but nonetheless he makes us comprehend that architecture at its finest touches the moral sense. The architect (who is to be well educated in the liberal arts) comprehends that the success of his work depends on a regard for the correspondence of parts, which will differ with the different tasks he undertakes. This concern for what is appropriate in given circumstances is what really underlay the hierarchy of genres, too, of course, in the same period.

Vitruvius distinguishes six elements of what one might call the proper care of the architect in the planning of his building. They are order (*ordinatio*), arrangement (*dispositio*: "the fit assemblage of details, and, arising from this assemblage, the elegant effect of the work and its dimensions, along with a certain quality or character"), proportion (*eurythmia*), symmetry (*symmetria*: "the appropriate harmony arising out of the details of the work itself; the correspondence of each given detail among the separate details to the form of the design as a whole"), decorum (*decor*), and distribution (*distributio*, or economy).[4]

All of these basically point out the same concern, but from different vantage points at different stages of planning. The last one is of the greatest importance to patrons. *Distributio*, says Vitruvius, "is the suitable disposal of supplies and the site, and the thrifty and wise control of expense in the works." But it also obtains, he goes on to say,

> when buildings are variously disposed for the use of owners or with a view to the display of wealth or lofty enough to suit the most dignified eloquence. For manifestly houses should be arranged in one way in towns; in another way for persons whose income arises from country estates; not the same for financiers; in another way for the wealthy men of taste; for the powerful, however, by whose ideas the state is governed, there must be special adjustment to their habits. And generally the distribution of buildings is to be adapted to the vocations of their owners.[5]

True, Vitruvius repeats himself, and at times it is difficult if not impossible to understand what he means exactly by his terms. It was left to the theoreticians of the Renaissance to study the ruins of Roman buildings in the light of his text, and to examine the text in the light of the buildings. Then, in effect, his teachings were returned in clarified form for the use of the modern age. The pioneering work in which this was done, which also remains the broad and massive basis on which later efforts rest, is Leone Battista Alberti's *Ten Books on Architecture* (1452; first printed 1485). It is an all-embracing work, at once eminently practical and high-minded. Alberti, humanist that he is, is earnestly concerned about the public responsibility of the architect and the patron. In a chapter titled "Of Monuments raised for preserving the Memory of publick Actions and Events" (bk. 7, chap. 16), he offers us a history of monumental art in antiquity that indicates the range of his researches:

> *Alexander*, not to mention many others, besides those cities which he built in Honour of his own Name, went so far as to build one after the Name of his Horse *Bucephalus.* But in my Opinion, what *Pompey* did was much more decent; when having defeated *Mithridates* in the lower *Armenia*, he built the City *Nicopolis* (or of Victory) in the very place where he had been Conqueror.[6]

And we may read in other chapters, "Whether Statues ought to be placed in Temples, and what Materials are the most proper for making them" (bk. 7, chap. 17) or "Of little Chapels, by way of Sepulchres, Pyramids, Columns, Altars and Moles" (bk. 8, chap. 3):

> I cannot be pleased with these enormous Structures [the pyramids] serving to no good Purpose whatsoever. There is something much more commendable in the Tomb of *Cyrus*, King of the *Persians*, and there is more true Greatness in his Modesty, than in the vain Glory of all those haughtier Piles. . . . in a little vaulted Temple built of square

Stone, with a Door scarce two Foot high, lay the Body of *Cyrus*, inclosed in a golden Urn, as the Royal Dignity required; round this little Chapel was a grove of all Sorts of Fruit-trees, and a large green Meadow, full of Roses and other Flowers and Herbs of grateful Scent, and of every Thing that could make the Place delightful and agreeable. The Epitaph was adapted to the Structure:

> Cyrus *am I that founded* Persia's *State,*
> *Then envy not this little Place of Rest.*[7]

Stories of art and patronage

The stories that follow are not necessarily true stories; they speak of a truth and illustrate it, often in a homely fashion, like adages. They are told again and again, without a diminution of the pleasure they give; they are assertions of truths we hold dear, not discoveries — ornate platitudes, we may call them, that invite life-enhancing echoes. The majority of my tales are from classical antiquity. All were retold with delight in the Renaissance, when they caught on and gave occasion for the rise of new tales involving Renaissance artists; these then seemed to have joined the ancients or, conversely, the ancients seemed to have moved on to the modern world, until the stories became "contemporary" or timeless in the lesson they point.

Vitruvius (preface, bk. 2) tells us the tale of Dinocrates, a Macedonian architect who had a scheme for what he deemed to be the most glorious monument to Alexander the Great. Dinocrates could never gain access to Alexander to present him with his project. As, however, he was "of ample stature, pleasing countenance, and the highest grace and dignity," he finally dressed himself in spectacular nudity, garbed only with a lion's skin and carrying a club as if he were Hercules himself, and marched to a public place where Alexander was giving judgment. This naturally caused a sensation, and Dinocrates was led before the king. He told Alexander that he had a plan to transform Mount Athos into a statue of him — a statue that in its left hand would hold "the ramparts of a very extensive city" and in its right "a bowl to receive the water of all the rivers which are in that mountain."

Alexander appeared to like the plan. He never doubted that it could be executed but with true royal concern asked if there were fields about which would supply the people in that monumental city with corn. Dinocrates suggested import by sea freight, and Alexander promptly proceeded to give Dinocrates a lesson in the higher duties of architecture and true patronage:

> I note, Dinocrates, the unusual formation of your plan, and am
> pleased with it, but perceive that if anyone leads a colony to that place,
> his judgment will be blamed. For just as a child when born, if it lacks
> the nurse's milk cannot be fed, nor led up the staircase of growing life,
> so a city without cornfields and their produce abounding within its

ramparts, cannot grow, nor become populous without abundance of food, nor maintain its people without a supply. Therefore, just as I think your *planning* worthy of approval, so, in my judgment, the *site* is worthy of dispproval; yet I want you to be with me, because I intend to make use of your services.

And so, when the time was ripe, and Alexander came upon a suitable site in Egypt, "a port naturally protected, an excellent market, cornfields all over Egypt, the great advantages of the huge Nile river, he ordered Dinocrates to lay out a city in his name, Alexandria."[8]

So much for a triumph over vanity that redounds to glory. Needless to say, there were a number of Renaissance artists who came forward with projects of their own to turn mountains into colossal statuary. None was realized, the prospective patrons perhaps having been better readers of Vitruvius than the artists. But we also owe the creation of St. Petersburg and Washington, D.C., to the account of Alexander's greathearted founding of the city of Alexandria. Alexander was buried, according to his will, in the Library of Alexandria at the very heart of the city. Similarly, there is a provision for the tomb of George Washington in a crypt in the Capitol building in Washington.

Another story about the magnanimity of Alexander the Great: Alexander had a favorite mistress, Campaspe, whose beauty he admired so much that he commissioned Apelles, the artist who excelled all others by "a certain grace," to paint her in the nude; "but perceiving that Apelles had fallen in love with her, with great magnanimity and still greater self-control he gave her to him as a present, winning by the action as great a glory as by any of his victories. He conquered himself and sacrificed . . . not only his mistress but his love, and was not even restrained by consideration for the woman he loved, who, once a king's mistress, was now a painter's!"[9]

Now that is patronage! Renaissance artists on occasion represented the high point of the story: Apelles staring at the maiden, his brush on the painting, unable for emotion to go on with his work. And Alexander comprehends as, differently moved, does his mistress. Needless to say, there is no record of an act of comparable magnanimity in the annals of modern patronage. The closest we come is a story about Titian (a new Apelles), who while painting the portrait of Charles V dropped one of his brushes. The emperor himself bent down to pick it up and, observing the amazement of the courtiers, said that he could always create another count of the realm but he could not make another Titian.

But now to a once-famous poetical account of the moral significance of history painting: In the first book of Virgil's *Aeneid* we meet Aeneas and Achates, enveloped by the grace of Venus in clouds so that they become invisible, wandering through the newly founded city of Carthage and wondering apprehensively what kind of reception the refugees from Troy might be accorded in this unknown land. In the center of the city they come upon the temple of Juno:

On brazen steps the marble threshold rose,
And brazen plates the cedar beams inclose:
The rafters are with brazen cov'rings crown'd;
The lofty doors on brazen hinges sound.
What first Aeneas in this place beheld,
Reviv'd his courage, and his fear expell'd.
For while, expecting there the queen, he rais'd
His wond'ring eyes, and round the temple gaz'd,
Admir'd the fortune of the rising town,
The striving artists, and their arts' renown;
He saw, in order painted on the wall,
Whatever did unhappy Troy befall:
The wars that fame around the world had blown,
All to the life, and ev'ry leader known.
There Agamemnon, Priam here, he spies,
And fierce Achilles, who both kings defies.
He stopp'd, and weeping said: "O friend! ev'n here
The monuments of Trojan woes appear!
Our known disasters fill ev'n foreign lands:
See there, where old unhappy Priam stands!
Ev'n the mute walls relate the warrior's fame,
And Trojan griefs the Tyrians' pity claim."
He said (his tears a ready passage find),
Devouring what he saw so well design'd,
And with an empty picture fed his mind.[10]

The reliefs on the door (which Virgil goes on describing, in words that make us see, no longer the pictures, but the war itself in some of its most piteous moments) are the result of two combining forces: a magnanimous commission and its execution by an artist capable of representing nature convincingly, so that his figures seem to live. The artist himself must have been moved by the suffering he represented so truthfully. Where such compassion with alien grief is alive and cultivated, there, Aeneas concluded, he might find a nation that would be gracious to the Trojan refugees.

This account of the power of art for the good inspired Dante—ever guided by Virgil—to describe a number of reliefs which he finds on his journey through purgatory. They are placed there by the will of God (who is now patron and artist in one) to assist the sinners in the work of their repentance. First, Dante encounters three reliefs which share the beauty of humility. They are upright on the wall of the circle he and Virgil ascend and are so beautiful "that not only Polycletus, but Nature there would be put to shame." The subjects are "The Annunciation," "David Dancing before the Ark" and "The Justice of the Emperor Trajan." Each of the scenes is represented so vividly that the figures seem to move and speak or sing, and they are described by the poet in such a way that we not only hear what they are saying but also are touched by the beauty of their souls.

The second sequence of reliefs is carved on the pavement of the circle of the proud, with representations of the proud brought low from the fall of Lucifer to the destruction of Troy. In contemplating that scene of sorrow, Dante is moved by art and, humbled in his pride, exclaims:

Dead seemed the dead, and the living, living.
He saw not better than I who saw the reality of all that
I trod upon while I was going bent down.[11]

"Dead seemed the dead, and the living, living." Vasari thus begins his description of Michelangelo's *Last Judgment*. In the picture, he says, "we are shown the misery of the damned and the joy of the blessed." The painting speaks to the heart, he implies, as do Dante's reliefs, but Michelangelo makes it possible for all of us to see what Dante could only have seen for himself. Michelangelo, in the representation of his awesome topic, assists us with a gift in the renewal of our souls even more vivid in its reality than Dante's. There can be no higher praise for a work of art. Vasari makes it the high point of his *Life* of Michelangelo and thus also the keystone which holds together the edifice of his history of art.

But to return once more to Virgil's doors in the *Aeneid*. Surely their affecting splendor and, as it were, their civic use were a source of inspiration for the commission of the three great doors of the Baptistry of Florence, of which the finest were done by Lorenzo Ghiberti. They must have affected Ghiberti's own definition of his artistic purpose in fashioning the work which took up the better part of his life. These doors show the history of the world from the Creation to the meeting of Solomon and the queen of Sheba in scenes allusive to the redemption of man through Christ. In these reliefs the beauties of visual splendor and moral dignity and grace are so inextricably joined that they inspired Michelangelo (and here legend and truth probably coincide) to call them the Gates of Paradise.

National sponsorship, museums, and the history of art

In the eighteenth century one could look back four hundred years and more on the visual arts that both tradition and Vasari himself asserted had commenced with Giotto, "who, by God's favour, rescued and restored the art [of painting], even though he was born among incompetent artists." It took two hundred years before artists, in a sequence of discoveries building one upon the other, altogether succeeded in rendering the likeness of nature with such a sublime freedom that looking at works of art was like looking at nature herself, a nature purged of the dross of accident and lovely as it can be only in the life of poetry. These two hundred years in Vasari's account are two hundred years of progress until we reach the great figures of Leonardo, Michelangelo, and Raphael, whose works are said to shine with such truth to nature, joined to the truth or virtue of poetry guided by reason, that they can be compared favorably even to the art of classical antiquity.

At the end of his description of Michelangelo's *Last Judgment*, Vasari exclaims:

> This great painting is sent by God to men as an example to show what can be done when supreme intellects descend upon the earth, infused with grace and divine knowledge. It takes captive those who think they know art, who tremble at the genius of the master in seeing his handiwork, while in regarding his labours their senses are overcome by thinking how other pictures can possibly bear comparison with them. Happy indeed is he who has seen this stupendous marvel of our century. . . . Artists born in this century owe Michelangelo a great debt, for he has removed the veil from all imaginable difficulties in his painting, sculpture and architecture.[12]

Vasari considers himself and his contemporaries blessed that they can be followers of the great. Only in the light of such an example does one fully know what art is about, he indicates. There is no point in aiming at progress beyond perfection, but wonders can still be performed, not by striving to outdo the masters, but rather by working under the protection of their accomplishments. The ideals of art and the technical means of realizing them were in the keeping of a new generation. Being so well instructed, they could enrich the world with art, if only they were properly supported! Vasari's preface to the third and last part of the *Lives* ends on a plea:

> It is undeniably true that if the artists of our own time were justly rewarded they would produce even greater works of art [than they are already producing, without encouragement], far superior to those of the ancient world. Instead, the artist struggles to ward off famine rather than to win fame, and this crushes and buries his talent and obscures his name. This is a shame and disgrace to those who could come to his help but refuse to do so.[13]

This cry of the artist dedicated to aims higher than readily suits his patrons' needs and interests would be heard again and again in succeeding generations.

Vasari was, however, successful in founding an Academy in Florence under the protection of the grand duke, Cosimo I—the Accademia del Disegno, the first of its kind (1562). The Accademia di San Luca of Rome followed (founded 1577 but not opened until 1593). Neither, however, was very effectively supported by the state; it was more a matter of artists helping themselves, their activities being endorsed and protected by the authorities, than of patronage. Artists and students would meet in regular sessions for instruction and practice, especially in drawing from the nude and copying the classics. At more or less regular intervals there would also be lectures on the theory and the history of art, and on anatomy. Another function of the academies, and a very important one, was to arrange regular exhibitions of the work of members and selections from that of students.

The academies also functioned as confraternities. Members jointly attended religious and civic functions and had the privilege of burial in a chapel set aside for the use of the academy.

It was not until the foundation of the Académie Royale de Peinture et de Sculpture in Paris (1648), and most signally with its reorganization under Louis XIV's powerful minister Colbert (completed 1664), that a government solemnly made the regulation and protection of the arts its own proper business. The Académie was at once an organization of carefully selected artists and a school of art. It had about two hundred members, among them twelve professors and eight associate professors. Its president was also "premier peintre du roi." The Académie virtually became the authorized arbiter of taste of the land, with everything done to give students the opportunity to develop their genius. Above all the best of them were sent to Rome, to the Académie's school there, where those who did well naturally looked forward to a future rich in opportunity and fame. Very important in the life of the Académie, and events in polite society, were the exhibitions of the members. There the artists proved their worth; there gossip flourished, criticism was tested, taste was made, and reputations rose and fell.

The French Academy was the envy of the artists of all of Europe. Owing chiefly to their pressure—and to the desire of monarchs to conform to French precedent—a number of academies were founded in the course of the eighteenth century on the pattern of the Académie Royale. Most noteworthy among them were those of Madrid, Vienna, Dresden, Berlin, but above all the Royal Academy of the Arts in London, under the presidency of Sir Joshua Reynolds. Reynolds's *Discourses*, which were delivered at special academic occasions and are principally addressed to the students, remain to this day the best introduction to the meaning and challenge of the Renaissance tradition in art.*

The flourishing of the academies and the regular exhibition of the work of the academicians was accompanied by the rise of the museum, the natural ally of academic instruction in art. The museum is to the artist and the lover of art what the library is to the writer and the lover of literature. And as the library is administered and its holdings perused and the meaning of text ever clarified (or obscured, as the case may be) by scholars, so the rise of the museum also brings into existence the professional historian of art.

In the eighteenth century a number of princely collections were reorganized and turned into art galleries. From the sixteenth century, gentlemen travelers and artists as a rule could count on being admitted to collections as a favor readily granted, but now projects were being devised to turn the galleries into museums open (at proper occasion and with due restrictions) to the educated public. In Rome the art-loving Pope Clement XI Albani

---

* See *The Great Ideas Today*, 1976, pp. 336–427.

(ruled 1700–21) initiated a program for a museum of Christian antiquities that was realized by Clement XII in 1734 when he opened the Capitoline Museum to the public. It contained a large collection of classical sculpture donated by the Albanis and later enlarged by Benedict XIV with the addition of the famous Capitoline Venus, among other works. The statues, in keeping with plans for the restoration of the Capitol going back as far as the fifteenth century, are exhibited as much as witnesses of the greatness of ancient Rome as for their value as works of art. In 1775 Pope Clement XIV established another great museum of classical sculpture, the Museo Pio-Clementino, in the Vatican.

The Louvre contained a great royal picture gallery installed by Louis XIV in connection with the establishment of the French Academy (1681). In the course of the eighteenth century several attempts were made to create a museum for the public exhibition of treasures from the royal collection, but it was not until the French Revolution that the plans were seriously taken up; then they were realized with a force and enthusiasm that altogether transformed the idea of a public museum. The Louvre was turned into a collection point and national museum for works of art dispossessed from the royal collections, convents, and monasteries, as well as from the emigrés who had fled the country, until it became a monument of overwhelming splendor to the power of the Revolution and its intransigent public-spiritedness. Thus the glory of art and of France were joined into one. The director of the committee in charge of the affairs of the institution was the painter Jacques-Louis David. Soon works of art requisitioned from the conquered or "liberated" nations of Europe also began pouring in.

The Revolution, and later on Napoleon, looked upon Paris as another Rome, a new capital of the empire of liberty, brotherhood, equality, justice, and progress which was to be adorned with all the trimmings of glory and the wherewithal of the instruments of civilization. The yearning for art, which is in itself a product of the academic enterprise, and the systematic confiscation of works of art, which is characteristic of the revolutionary, combined eventually with the Napoleonic wars to advance these acquisitions. The French academicians and critics—with the one marvelous exception of Quatremère de Quincy, who published a pamphlet protesting the transfer of the Italian patrimony of art to Paris—in their published statements and, presumably, in their hearts, all thought it a great triumph of civilization that the Louvre now offered a virtually complete survey of the history of art in the form of masterpieces there collected in the original. After Napoleon's ascent to power the museum was called the Musée Napoleon. The emperor elected to marry Marie-Louise of Austria in the Grande Galerie of the Louvre, the richest promenade the world had ever seen, for what was meant to be the most auspicious wedding of all time. The very choice of such a show contradicted the poetical dignity and taste which had given the works of art Napoleon used there to celebrate his triumph the reputation that had made them the valuable possessions he craved to be adorned with. The service of art had turned upon itself and become the abuse of art, and not for the last time in history.

After the fall of Napoleon the works of art robbed from abroad were, by and large, returned to the countries to which they belonged. The Louvre, however, still remained a marvel, and the memory of the Musée Napoleon impressed itself upon the age. New museums were created all over Europe, as instruments of a national purpose. Purged (one hoped) from the excesses of Napoleon's acquisitiveness and, certainly, not having available his opportunities, the museums continued to serve the academic ideals of the cultivation of art, but with a signal difference. What in the eighteenth century had been available only to the happy few was now offered to the many, in the ever so high-minded hope of improving and delighting their understanding of the values of truth and beauty by the gift of art. The art-loving citizen was also to be a good citizen, provided that he was animated by a just love of art. The museums, in purpose as well as appearance, become veritable temples of art and national shrines. As the nineteenth century advanced, these ideals, ludicrous as perhaps they were in the exclusiveness of their focus and sense of mission (and, in extreme cases, their fear of laughter), came to be challenged by a number of forces transforming social life which we cannot discuss here, but most directly and cogently the challenge came from within the walls of the museum itself, in the name of historical accuracy. The history of art, a child of the Renaissance understanding of the exemplary character of classical art, came of age in the vastness of the offerings which were collected in the new museums. It became irresistibly clear that beauty does not speak in one tongue only, and that one cannot judge the perfection or the moral significance of works of art from an inflexible position.

A healthy pluralism led to the introduction of the art of extra-European cultures into the world of the museums, and works on once-despised styles, European as well as others, came to be studied and presented to the public in the terms of a new discovery of their values. But the more the museums were enlarged and the art historians' telescopic view expanded with them, the more, by the desire to be "objective," did the profession slip into cultural relativism. The historian of art now finds his escape in "pure" scholarship, divorced from the language of criticism and the praise of beauty (one prefers instead to speak of "quality" which is believed to be a materially verifiable "fact" of a work of art), and the museum director, equally a professional, is concerned with attendance records and the engaging display of works of art in habitat situations that will satisfy our curiosity about the ever changing progress of autonomous styles across the stage of history. Let the public be its own judge of value, according to individual pleasure. Hindsight, one trusts, eventually will let us see this as but the historically conditioned taste of the age. Needless to say, museums built in keeping with such persuasions no longer look like temples but rather like drive-in exhibition halls, accentuating in their structure not the timelessness of beauty but rather the fact that they are of our time, the museum itself being the ultimate museum object.

A dream

We have come full circle. It will not do, in a time of plenty as far as sponsorship is concerned (no matter how hungry the artists who have become redundant in society), to end on a note of unqualified pessimism. How can one reunite the purposes of patronage with morally and socially defensible standards for the love of art?

A dream took me by the hand and showed me an art school. It was a modern academy. The students were ten to thirteen years old, modern teenagers dressed in blue jeans. Some were drawing from life, attentively measuring, reflecting. It was a long pose, and drawing was an act of responsibility. Others were copying drawings by Rubens, Raphael, Michelangelo. "Who are your teachers?" I asked a young boy who was seated in front of the Apollo Belvedere, sketching it in charcoal. "The old masters themselves," said the boy, "but you can't see them today." "Do you have any art history?" "Yes." "And who are your teachers?" "The same old masters," said the boy, "and Michelangelo is my favorite." "What does he talk about?" "Very little, but yesterday he took me to Florence and showed me the Gates of Paradise. 'There', he said to me, 'you can see the grace and dignity of our art. Draw the panel of the Creation'." "What will you be when you grow up?" "A modern sculptor," said the boy; "I want to make gates for airports and space stations." "Who endows your school?" "I do," said the dream, and I awoke.

---

[1] Trans. Wilmer C. Wright, *The Works of the Emperor Julian*, Loeb Classical Library (London, 1913), 2 : 311.

[2] Vitruvius, *On Architecture*, trans. Frank Granger, Loeb Classical Library (London, 1931), 1 : 3–5.

[3] *Discourses on Art*, ed. Robert Wark (San Marino, Calif.: 1959), p. 241.

[4] Vitruvius, *On Architecture*, 1 : 25–31.

[5] Ibid., pp. 31–33.

[6] Leon Battista Alberti, *Ten Books on Architecture*, trans. James Leoni (London: Alec Tiranti, 1955), p. 158.

[7] Ibid., pp. 166–67.

[8] Vitruvius, *On Architecture*, 1 : 73–75.

[9] K. Jex-Blake and Eugenie Sellers, *The Elder Pliny's Chapters on the History of Art* (London, 1896), p. 125.

[10] *Virgil's Aeneid*, trans. John Dryden, Harvard Classics (New York: P. F. Collier & Son, 1909), 13 : 91; cf. *GBWW*, Vol. 13, p. 115.

[11] Dante Alighieri, *The Divine Comedy* (Purgatorio, Canto 12), trans. Carlyle-Wicksteed, (New York: Modern Library, 1932), p. 260; cf. *GBWW*, Vol. 21, p. 71.

[12] Giorgio Vasari, *The Lives of the Painters, Sculptors and Architects* (London: J. M. Dent & Sons, 1927), 4 : 143–44.

[13] Ibid., 2 : 155.

PART TWO

Current Developments in the Arts and Sciences

Human Fossils: The New Revolution

Charles E. Oxnard

Charles E. Oxnard is professor of anatomy, anthropology, and evolutionary biology at the University of Chicago, where he is a popular and highly respected teacher. He holds honorary appointments at the Field Museum, Chicago; the University of Birmingham, England; and the University of Hong Kong. A native of England, he received his medical qualifications at the University of Birmingham in 1958, and his scientific doctorate in 1962 under the training of Sir Solly (now Lord) Zuckerman. He became a senior lecturer at Birmingham prior to his departure for the University of Chicago in 1966.

His work commenced in 1954 with traditional functional anatomical studies of primates involving dissection and osteometry; it progressed to more complex methods of functional anatomy using the techniques of experimental stress analysis, and to more complicated osteological investigations using the approaches of multivariate statistics. In recent years his interests in the analysis of form and pattern have taken him into such areas as image analysis and cluster finding procedures. He is author of more than one hundred papers and has contributed chapters to several recent volumes on primate evolutionary morphology. Among his books are *Primate Locomotion* (with Jack T. Stern, Jr.; 1973), *Form and Pattern in Human Evolution* (1973), and *Uniqueness and Diversity in Human Evolution* (1975).

The times in which we live are exciting for everyone who cares about the evolution of man and his nearest living relatives, the apes and monkeys. They are so because of the well-publicized fossil finds that have been made in Africa in the last few years. After many decades during which all that was available was a tooth here, a fragment of cranium there, often scarcely datable with any degree of accuracy, we are now suddenly confronted almost day by day with discoveries of extensive fossil conglomerations. These often include remnants of several parts of the same individual, even fragments of more than a single individual, and they often come from a variety of fossiliferous sites allowing a wide range of determinable dates. Such discoveries have not been accidental or unaided. Those at East Turkana, for instance, as in the Omo, at Laetolil, and in the Afar Valley, have rather come about by the assiduous work of teams of investigators led by Richard Leakey, Clark Howell, Mary Leakey, Donald Johanson, and Maurice Taieb. The finds increase, by orders of magnitude and through many millions of extra years, our knowledge of creatures presumably related to man.

Although most of these fossil fragments have not been fully studied as yet, their mere existence, together with some early tentative estimates as to their dates, suggests that the conventional notion of human evolution must now be rejected and new concepts explored. No longer can the idea be held that there exists a single lineage from *Homo sapiens* back through *Homo erectus* to *Australopithecus africanus* (including "*Homo habilis*," from which *A. africanus* has not been clearly differentiated, and *Homo africanus*, which is a recently invented synonym), with *Australopithecus robustus* being a closely related but probably parallel line to *A. africanus* (fig. 1).

Now, whatever the details may turn out to be, we must be willing to envisage a number of different lines, undoubtedly of different degrees of relatedness, with the genus *Homo* itself going back perhaps five million years and even longer. This contrasts with the half million years previously guessed for *Homo* upon the basis of earlier finds of *Homo erectus*. We must even be prepared to see a link with early African apes that at its most recent is ten million years old and perhaps very much more; this, too, contrasts with the three million- and five million-year guesses that were made not long ago. We must be prepared to remove both australopithecine species to positions in which they lie on lineages at best only parallel to that of man,

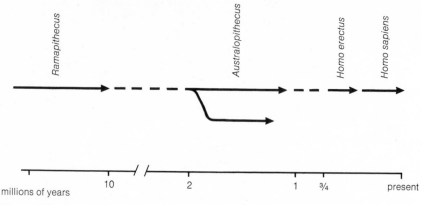

Figure 1. The conventional notion, somewhat simplified, of the human lineage.

and perhaps for rather long periods of geological time. We must even be prepared to see yet other lineages as possibilities, for some of the new finds do not seem to fit even within this much more complicated scheme (fig. 2).

The task has thus changed from one in which it seemed necessary to fit each succeeding fossil into a single lineage to one in which a radiation of many forms must be assumed, and of these presumably only one, *Homo sapiens*, is still extant. This concept of a radiation fits far better with biological ideas about evolution and is thereby the more acceptable to biological anthropologists.

The picture is also, therefore, turning from one in which certain attributes were thought to be basically human, and were believed to have evolved only once (for example, bipedalism, toolmaking and tool using, high intelligence, perhaps even some social and cultural developments), to one in which it is conceivable that some of these features have evolved more than once, albeit presumably in related lineages. Fossil evidence of such possibilities has now to be sought; they must be strongly denied before we can ever return to the old view. Certainly, new studies of different capabilities of the living great apes (toolmaking, tool usage, communication, even perhaps a limited degree of conceptual thought) suggest the likelihood of repeated and overlapping evolutionary trends.

This new picture also means that we have to return to a state of ignorance about the site of origin of the genus *Homo*. Now that *Homo* is at least contemporaneous with, and indeed very probably predates, the various australopithecine fossils, we have no non-*Homo* progenitor from Africa. And though remains of *Homo* of this degree of antiquity are still known only from Africa (some alleged finds from China have yet to be studied), it must be acknowledged that Africa is virtually the only region that has been searched with any degree of intensity. The possibility must be opened up again that man may as likely have originated in Asia as in Africa. Only further discoveries will provide evidence on these matters.

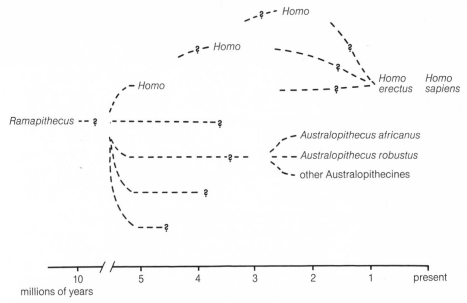

Figure 2. Human ancestry viewed as a radiation. Many of the connections implied by this diagram must remain in considerable doubt at this time. Ancestral connections not labeled imply fossil finds not yet placeable.

Finally, the new picture forces us to look again at the nature of our relationships with the African great apes, those creatures to which, among living forms, man is most closely related. The nature of that relationship must be far more complex than previously thought, and in all likelihood must have been far more ancient than has been supposed in recent years. This inevitably follows if we have to push *Homo* almost ten times farther back in time. It must especially follow if there is any truth in the idea that there has been a radiation of near-human forms in the course of evolution rather than a single human lineage. One wonders whether this radiation must not have involved the African great apes, or if it was subsequent to their connections with prehuman ancestors. One even wonders, too, whether there might not be evidence that the African apes themselves underwent a radiation of sorts, of which the chimpanzee and gorilla are the only surviving remnants. Perhaps some of the fossil remnants that pose problems for human evolution actually belong to ape evolution.

There is thus much reason for excitement in the world of human evolution, and much reason to anticipate the next few years with very open minds.

However, it is necessary to understand that the discovery of new fossils is not the only source of the new visions that are opening up. Every bit as important, but less well known to the wider public, because of their more esoteric and difficult nature, are developments in the many disciplines that act as handmaidens in all evolutionary investigations.

The first of these relates to our ability to make better assessments of dates. Without a series of new tools for the study of absolute and relative time, much of the story would yet remain hidden. There have been for some years now two basic approaches in the dating of primate fossils. One depends upon relative time scales in which sequences from successive geological layers are determined; the other is absolute and derives from certain physical parameters (such as degree of radioactivity of rocks) that change with time. As a result of advances in both of these general areas, much more precise dates can be arrived at now than formerly. Many dates long accepted in the literature of human evolution are now known to be incorrect; at the same time, these new methods impress upon us sources of error inherent in the different dating methods. The effect of these new methods has thus been not only to change actual dates but also to make us aware of the need for increased rigor in all studies of human evolution.

A second set of tools enhances our ability to assess the fossil environment. New investigations pertinent to assessing the biotic and physical environment of these fossil creatures are freeing our ideas from conventional constraints. Earlier concepts led us to envision a relatively arid, certainly treeless (or almost so), savannalike environment for almost all of the primate fossils of that time. Such conceptions compelled us to look only for savannalike niches and behaviors in the fossils; analogous behaviors today, for example, include the quadrupedalism of baboons, together with the kind of society that goes with it. As a result, studies of baboon behavior have been much utilized in order to make assessments of behaviors of prehuman ancestors. These traditional ideas prevent us from seeing, for instance, the possibilities that might exist within a heavily wooded or forested environment: hiding, climbing, leaping, and acrobatic activities among the branches, and the different social and feeding milieus that go with such environments. Recent advances in the rigor and clarity of paleoecological investigations now mean that we have to change our idea rather completely from the conventional picture, and in particular, they suggest behavioral possibilities for those fossils that could stem from perhaps as wide a range of environments as exists anywhere in Africa today.

Yet further methods have become important in the studies of human evolution. Although information about changes over time of the various molecular and biochemical materials that are the very stuff of evolution cannot be obtained (except in those rare cases where residues of actual materials are entrapped within the fossils), knowledge of molecular and biochemical elements—for instance, protein structure and immunological relationships in living species—tells us a considerable amount about what the changes may have been. Such studies are really quite old (for instance, the first were carried out at the end of the last century, and an early summary by Zuckerman in 1933 looked toward a time when we would have such information in abundance). Yet it has required the molecular revolution in biology since 1950, together with the extensive comparative work of very recent years, to provide a sufficiently large data bank for these methods to contribute to the solution of such evolutionary problems.

Even as we come to look at the evolution of behavior, there are now major new data to examine. Some of these stem from studies of morphology and relate to the very simple, perhaps we could call them primary, kinds of behaviors which have their effect upon morphology, mainly through their biomechanical effects upon the bones, muscles, and joints of the animals. Others result from investigations of many secondary and yet more complex aspects of behavior (social, sexual, communicative, etc.,) now being studied in ways that were not well recognized years ago; in their turn, although they have not yet yielded the very large body of information that will be necessary in order to understand better the evolution of behavior in man and primates, a time is coming when they will indeed do so. This too was foreseen by Zuckerman in 1932. Knowledge of these new studies is thus also important new information, and contributes much—will certainly in the future contribute more—to the new picture of human evolution.

Finally, without new methods and ideas which have been developed for the study of the fossil specimens themselves, we would still remain fixed at the level of scientific deduction that is imposed by the conventional or classical ways of looking at fossils. On the one hand, the new methods free us so that we can "see" information in the fossil forms that is not available to visual observation. On the other hand, modes of interpretation are such that we no longer look immediately to genetic relationship as the primary explanation of morphological similarity in fossils; rather, we now look toward similarities of function within overall behavior. This also allows the possibility of information from the fossils themselves melding with molecular, ecological, behavioral, and environmental data obtained from some of the other modes of study. One clear evidence of this change relates to our way of viewing the structural relationships of the australopithecine fossils with men and with the living great apes. The older view has been interpreted to mean that the fossils are humanlike rather than apelike. And humanlike morphologies have been interpreted to mean humanlike functions (bipedalism, toolmaking) for the fossils. New views of some of these morphologies may mean that we now have to envisage a range of functions for the fossils quite different from those seen in any present-day form, either human, ape, or even monkey. This also then allows us to include in our investigations all those pieces of information which were ignored in prior attempts to make these fossils fit the conventional picture (or if they were not ignored, they were provided with curious ad hoc arguments to suggest why they existed).

It is fascinating that in each of these different areas: dating, environment, molecules, behavior, and study of the fossil fragments themselves, the new investigative methods are becoming developed to the extent that each can be used as a genuine tool in its own right and need not be merely presented as an example of what the future will bring. However, the future does shine with the hope of what will be discovered as these investigational batteries are brought to bear upon more and more materials, upon wider and wider questions, and with greater and greater abilities for extending our inferences about the evolution of man.

It is also of great interest to realize that developments within each of the different academic areas that are capable of contributing to our understanding of human evolution have already provided information predating the discoveries of the new fossils. Although it has taken the excitement of the new fossil finds of the last three years to bring to most minds a realization that human evolution must be far more complicated and the human lineage of far greater ancestry than previously thought, in fact the germs of these ideas could already be detected in prior studies. Thus, quantitative investigations of the fragments of fossils that have been available for many years have continually suggested to some investigators the likelihood that the australopithecines were not as closely related to man as implied by the conventional wisdom. The doubts thus raised have, within the last ten years, been transformed by further quantitative studies into positive suggestions as to what, indeed, the australopithecines might have been, given that they were not direct human ancestors. But such investigations do not have the excitement and publicity of new fossil finds, and thus we have had to await the new fossils to confirm suggestions. Now, however, that such confirmation is available, it is worthwhile looking more closely at some of these new quantitative studies in order to understand what they are capable of revealing and how they have supplied additional information about the problems of human evolution. And the actual bulk of the new fossils is so great that the application of the quantitative methods to them, as they become available to scientists, suggests that yet more will follow in our understanding of human evolution. It is to the methods and results now available for studying fossil structure that the remainder of this article is directed.

Assessment of fossil fragments: the observational technique

The traditional method of assessing fossils has been through visual observation, sometimes aided by measurement for estimating the overall sizes of specimens. This method has enormous strengths stemming from the fine powers of recognition and discrimination that are shown by the human eye and mind. But it has many weaknesses. The human eye is not very good at assessing variation among specimens within a group and among different groups. Moreover, visual observation has great difficulty when faced with large data sets. It is especially poor in arriving at assessments of the more complicated interrelationships of structures such as association and regres-

Some Difficulties in Cluster Analysis

bridges between clusters

nonspherical
clusters

linearly
nonseparable
clusters

unequal
cluster
populations

Figure 3. Problems of finding groups in data. Examples showing data in two dimensions
with some possible group configurations. These groups are easy to see by eye in two
dimensions as displayed here. They are difficult to recognize in many dimensions even
with computational help because they present irregular arrangements.

sion between features, or autocorrelation and cross-correlation among
characters, and so on. And although visual assessment is often fairly good
at recognizing groupings in data, it is much less able to recognize situations
where data are arranged in more or less continuous fashion, or where there
are overlaps between groups or even other more complicated data interrelationships. Examples of some of these difficulties are provided in figure 3.

In addition, however, the visual approach may suffer because of difficulties in interpretation; that is, from the problem of making assessments of
the biological meaning of the observed morphologies. Biological assessments may relate to such matters as the extent to which the perceived shape
differences among living and fossil forms provide information about differences among individual specimens of the same species, between the sexes,
among differently aged specimens, between geographic, racial, or sub-
specific groups, and resulting from pathology. All of these may, in turn, be
intermixed with more important differences (more important in an evolutionary context) that may relate to biological function, hereditary relationship, biotic and physical environment, and systematic classification. All of
these biological inferences are entwined in the problem of deciding what
species of creature we are dealing with and where it fits into the evolutionary picture.

Not only may it be difficult, using the eye, to distinguish these biological
assessments; it may not even be possible. Indeed, many workers do not
attempt to separate the comparison of structure from its biological evalua-

tion; the whole thing is often done at one step in an intuitive manner. And while the human mind is certainly capable of such a complex task, it is also capable of making major mistakes—of falling into hidden traps— with such a methodology. The method of visual inspection and mental estimation easily leads into unsuspected circularities between the two steps mentioned above. It also suffers more than most techniques from the unconscious defect of subjectivity because we, ourselves, are the object of study.

Morphological investigations of extant primates and of fossils already well known have, in general, been limited to the techniques of dissection of soft tissues, when available, and observation of hard structures. Such findings as have been made thereby have certainly succeeded in providing new information, but this has usually resulted in the closure of relatively minor gaps in an already fairly well-known pattern rather than in the creation of new vistas.

There is no doubt that the self-sufficiency of the techniques of *dissection* and *observation* has prevented researchers from utilizing new methods. Both of these older techniques are time-consuming and laborious, yet neither can be relegated to technical help; both require the complete attention, the experience, and the expertise of the researcher himself and leave little room for other technical experimentation.

It is also true that the early use of newer, quantitative methods (involving, for example, measurement and statistical analysis) was laborious. Much of this work was rejected by some investigators as mere number grinding; some anatomists and anthropologists still look upon quantitative morpho- logical studies as extravagant expenditures of time and man power, often for results that seem to add little to our knowledge. There can be no doubt that criticism of this type is superficial. Without the laborious but pioneer- ing studies of early biometrics, often rendered more difficult by the lack of techniques and equipment nowadays regarded as indispensable (such as computers and computer programs), it would not now be possible to go beyond the confines provided by interpretation based upon personal ob- servation and dissection. For it has been only the use of the older formulae to the extreme of their capabilities that has conferred upon modern inves- tigators the competence to help propose yet better approaches.

But one of the chief stumbling blocks in the adoption of newer techniques lies in what has been thought to be the "difficult" nature of the methods, and in a lack of understanding of the extent to which they may be valuable. Thus it is that, having myself attempted to apply a number of these ways of looking at evolutionary differences in the shape of primates, I have been led to some understanding of how they work and of what new insights they are capable of providing. A sufficient number of studies have now been carried out so that some of the research strategies and tactics involved can be evaluated.

Newer investigative methods for morphological assessment

These various criticisms of the observational method have in fact been apparent for many years. And a few really great minds have been brought to bear upon the problems. D'Arcy Thompson's theory of transformations for revealing how one creature may be described by a simple distortion of another, Fisher's discriminant functions for distinguishing between closely related plants and animals, Huxley's allometric studies of growth as an exponential phenomenon akin to the "growth" of a bank account, Woodger's ideas of comparing animals by "mapping," mathematically, from one to another—all readily spring to mind. But in the interval since those studies, the manner of investigating evolutionary change in shape has scarcely improved, though we recognize the fascinating but difficult theoretical work of Thom using "catastrophe theory" to model discontinuities in animal development, and the creative use of trend-surface analysis borrowed from geology by Sneath for comparing adult forms one with another.

In some ways it is easy to see the reason for lack of improvement over so many years. The earlier masters (Huxley, D'Arcy Thompson, etc.) include within their writings clear indication of the difficulty—lack of an ability to make large numbers of algebraic calculations with, therefore, excessive reliance on the geometric approach. They had gone as far as was possible with the tools available to them. Just as microscopists awaited the electron microscope before being able to venture from the microscopic to the ultrastructural level, so morphologists needed new tools before venturing far from assessment of gross shape by observation (occasionally backed by measurements and simple analysis) toward more complex evaluation of underlying factors of shape. However, the evolution of a number of modern tools (especially the electronic computer and computer software) provides mechanisms for new orders of investigation. With the development and use of these tools have also arisen a more overt recognition of the nature of the different logical steps used in the investigations, a rationale for avoiding circularity of argument, and certainly an overt attempt at increasing objectivity.

The new approach comprises, first, the application of new methods for characterizing and comparing complex morphologies and, second, advances in our understanding of biological causation that allow better assessments of the meaning of the morphological comparisons.

The methods of characterizing and comparing complex morphologies stem from developments in many different scientific areas. It is possible, however, to think of them in two broad groups: those that utilize characterizations of structures based upon measurements of individual parts of the structure, and those that involve manipulation of the structure as a whole.

101

The metrical approach

The first of these can involve rather simple metrical descriptions of the bones of the living and fossil species followed by the use of computational techniques that allow sensitive comparisons of such descriptions. They are capable of tracing subtle variations of bone shape and fossil form; they do not depend upon prior conjecture as to the origin or function of the specimens; they make it possible to compare differences between several groups of animals while yet allowing for the variations within each group; they improve understanding of the difference between size and shape; and they often reveal complex gradations of form with which we have to deal. They can be used in different situations either as hypothesis-testing devices or as hypothesis-free descriptive tools. Such techniques have already been used fairly extensively and have been among the major factors in the development of the new views of human evolution that we began by noting.

The core of one of these techniques, the multivariate statistical approach, is the following. If we suppose that a single object can be defined by two measurements, then that object can be represented as a point on a two-dimensional plot or graph. A group of similar objects will then appear as a cloud of points lying relatively close together on the graph. Other different groups of objects will appear as other clouds in other positions on the graph. If the original measurements defining the objects are uncorrelated with one another, then the original system of axes on the graph may well best describe the arrangement of clouds. If, however, the original measurements defining the objects are correlated with one another to some or other degree, then the true relations among the clouds may be best seen from the vantage point of some other oblique axis obtained by rotating the graph under the original coordinate system. In this way the separation may be reduced from two axes to one—a situation easier to understand (fig. 4).

Figure 4. A diagram of two-dimensional data (left frame) showing three clouds (circles) plotted within the framework of two dimensions—X and Y. Rotation of the three clouds into a new position (right frame), as indicated by the arrows, allows their representation by means of only one new axis—λ. This is a geometric description of the algebraic process of multivariate statistics.

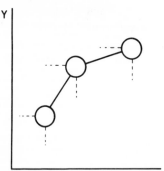
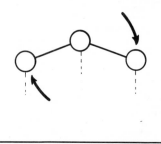

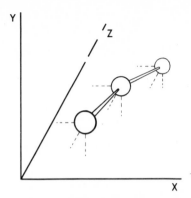
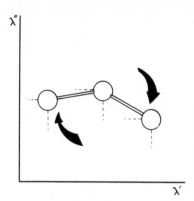

Figure 5. A diagram of three-dimensional data (left frame) showing three clouds (circles) plotted within the framework of three dimensions—X, Y, and Z. Rotation of the three clouds into a new position (right frame), as indicated by the arrows, allows their representation by means of two new axes—λ' and λ". This is a second geometric description of the algebraic process of multivariate statistics.

In terms of three measurements taken on each object, this procedure is the equivalent of constructing and viewing from one position the three-dimensional model of the clouds and then rotating and viewing the model from a new position that best separates the clouds. Again, the new view may reduce from three to two or even one the number of new axes necessary to describe the positions of the clouds (fig. 5).

If we can extrapolate such two- and three-dimensional descriptions to an example where we have taken many measurements on each object, then the problem is many-dimensional. We cannot draw or construct a many-dimen-

Figure 6. An explanation of the minimum spanning tree. Two-dimensional data as represented by the positions of the dots in the left frame can be grouped according to the set of minimum connections shown in the right frame. This process is, of course, usually carried out with multidimensional data where we do not have the visual representation to guide us.

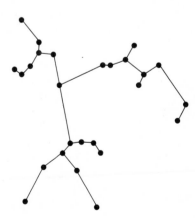

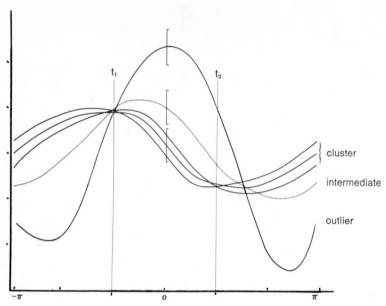

Figure 7. An explanation of the representation of many-dimensional data by embedding them within a sine-cosine function. The position of a cloud of points in, say, a ten-dimensional space can be represented by a single wavy line in the plot. Three groups which are close to one another in the ten-dimensional space are represented, as shown, by three very similar wavy lines. A fourth group that is very far distant from the first three is represented by a fourth wavy line that is markedly different in shape from the others; we are thus able to distinguish an outlier even though we cannot "see" the ten-dimensional data. A fifth group that is intermediate between the group of three and the outlier is represented by a wavy line that is also intermediate. This mode of display was invented by Professor D. F. Andrews, now of the University of Toronto, Ontario.

sional model for ourselves, but we can represent such a model in the computer. The computer can then "rotate" this model to look for the new view that best separates the multidimensional clouds; in so doing it may discover that the many dimensions can be reduced to a number small enough to understand.

Once such analyses have been performed, however, these techniques may still produce information that is truly of dimensionality higher than three and that, accordingly, is rather difficult to display. One way of demonstrating the results inherent in these more complicated situations is to use any one of a variety of group-finding procedures. The simplest of these is a technique that examines the shortest distances between the various groups. This is known as the "minimum spanning tree" and was evolved in part from the very practical problem of discovering the minimum length of wire required to link a group of towns into a telephone grid. In exactly the same way, the minimum spanning tree can provide a picture of the links

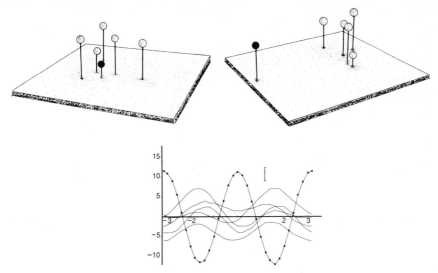

Figure 8. The interpolation of an unknown specimen among a set of known extant groups. The upper left frame shows that interpolation can provide a spurious answer suggesting that the unknown, the dark ball, actually "belongs" with the set of known groups when in fact we may know that it does not. Reanalysis with this point in mind can provide a picture (upper right frame) in which we are left in no doubt that the unknown does not "belong" with the known groups. Andrews's high-dimensional display (as explained in figure 7) also makes clear (bottom) that the unknown specimen (the dotted wavy line) does not "belong" with the known groups represented by the solid wavy lines.

between data representing groups of animals even when those data are high-dimensional (fig. 6).

Yet other methods of display may be required. One of these is to embed multidimensional information from a multivariate statistical analysis within the infinite-dimensional space of some well-known mathematical function. This can be readily achieved using sine-cosine functions, but others are also appropriate. Thus, if we suppose that it takes, say, ten anatomical dimensions to represent the evolutionary position of a group of animals, we can represent that group as a single wavy line by using those ten dimensions as ten coefficients in a sine-cosine plot. Three similar groups, even though existing within ten dimensions, will show as three similar wavy lines on such a plot. Groups that are quite different and that are intermediate can also be visualized, and we have avoided the impossible task of constructing a ten-dimensional model (fig. 7).

These methods are of value not only for the examination of a series of known groups, i.e., data from living animals, but also for investigating the position, relative to known groups, of unknown specimens, i.e., fossils. Clearly, a fossil specimen can be interpolated so that relationships pertinent to biological investigations are preserved and can be examined. Of course, biological speculations about unknown groups are more easily

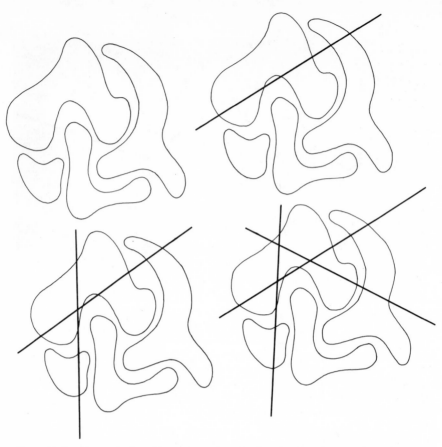

Figure 9. The shapes and positions of a series of curiously shaped groups in a picture (top left frame) may be defined by throwing a series of random lines across the picture. The top right frame shows "recognition" of part of one of the shapes by a first random line. The bottom left frame shows additional information through the laying down of a second random line. The bottom right frame shows the next steps in the process. Eventually most of the information the picture contains can be seen in terms of such random lines. They may be more readily treated for analysis than the original picture itself (after Professor Jack D. Cowan).

made from these analyses when the unknown groups are reasonably close to other groups that are known. If the fossils are far distant, we can say little about them biologically except that they are unique. But the related problem, of knowing when a fossil group is really out of place among a series of extant forms, is easily solvable with these analyses and displays (fig. 8).

Even with such methods, it is still not easy to view a small number of groups at one time unless the data are fairly strongly clustered. Again, we recognize a limitation in our abilities to visualize data in many dimensions. However, the entire battery of methods taken together may be able to supply information additional to that required in understanding these more complicated situations.

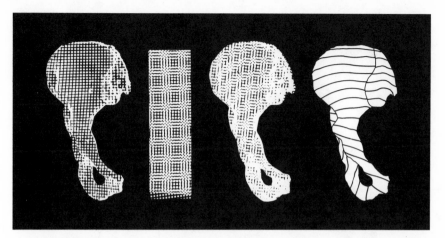

Figure 10. The representation of a complex surface (the pelvic bone) through the use of moiré fringes. The first frame shows a grid shadowed upon the bone. The second frame shows a calibration specimen where two plane grids superimposed at an angle to one another provide a set of moiré fringes. The third frame shows the moiré fringe pattern produced when the grid, distorted because it is shadowed upon the bone, is superimposed upon a grid shadowed upon a plane. For clarity, the fourth frame shows the fringes diagrammatically.

The pictorial approach

A second group of tools is also being developed to help reveal the information hidden within the complex shapes and structures of bones. These tools include some of the techniques of image analysis. Here the rationale is to attempt to avoid the problems inherent in measurements of structures and to include the information held in the pictorial, holistic view that is lost in the use of measurement but that is too complex to be taken in by observation alone. This may be done by a series of ad hoc digital methods using the information in the picture as obtained from laying down nonbiological patterns upon the picture: for example, a grid, or scanning lines (as in a television image) or random points, lines or planes, or by a number of other mechanisms (fig. 9).

But it may also be done by transforming the entire information presented in a picture into some other more easily understood diagram or plot. Such transformations may be done computationally with computers. Fortunately, however, many of them may be made more simply using optical techniques with the laser.

One preliminary attempt that is currently being investigated is the use of moiré fringe analysis (stemming from discoveries in optics over many years now) for contouring and comparing complex shapes. In theory, at any rate, a complicated form such as the pelvic girdle, or a complex curvature of the surface of a joint cavity, may be characterized by this method (fig. 10). Another approach that is being used is that of medial axis transformation

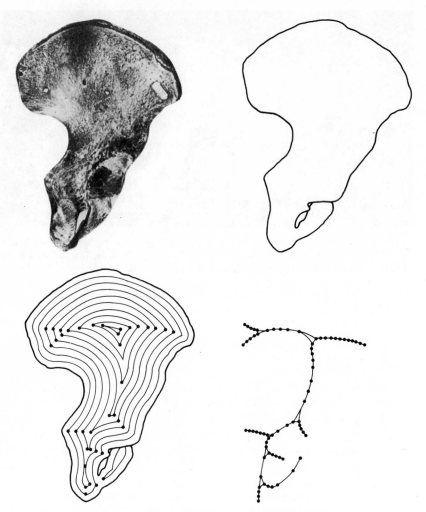

Figure 11. The representation of a complex shape (the pelvic bone) through the use of the medial axis transformation. The bone itself (top left frame) has the outline shown in the top right frame. Collapse of this boundary into itself in regular steps produces the figure in the bottom left frame. The process can be thought of as analogous to the burning of a bone-shaped field of dry grass, lighted simultaneously all around its perimeter, on a day when there is no wind. The field will burn inward, and when the burning process meets itself coming from the other side, the flames will travel along the pathway defined by the central dots. These form the medial axis shown in the bottom right frame.

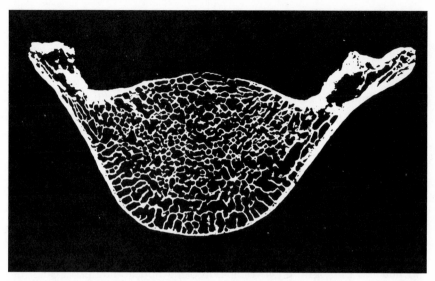

Figure 12. The more complex structure evident within a bone. A photograph of a section of a vertebra displaying not only the thin rim of compact bone that forms its surface but also the many small plates (trabeculae) of bone lying internally.

stemming from pattern recognition studies. This is achieved by allowing the outline of the shape of a bone to collapse into itself in a direction normal to its boundary and at a constant rate. Such a procedure defines a "medial axis" where the opposite collapsing boundaries meet one another. The mathematical function of this medial axis, together with the order and speed of propagation of the collapse along it, completely define the shape (fig. 11). Reductions such as these are achieved without defining any special points along the perimeter of the bone, although if it be necessary to incorporate information about such points—for example, points of possible biological import such as the edge of a joint, articular surface, or the margin of a muscular attachment—this could be done.

When, however, interest in defining form and pattern reaches into such complex forms as these, it perhaps ought to include the totality of information presented by a bone. For a bone consists of very much more than the three-dimensional envelope of its outer surface. One of the persistent problems that has vexed those interested in the functional significance of bone form over many years has been the description of the architecture *within* a bone. This architecture, often observable in fossils, is the network of trabecular plates that can be seen with the eye or, at most, a hand lens or low-power dissecting microscope, and which is evident in normal radiographs of bones and some fossils (fig. 12). How can these more complex patterns be characterized?

Usually the delineation of such patterns depends upon defining major bundles of trabeculae and the most prominent parts of the compact shell

109

of the bone. The primary problem, a more complete characterization of the trabecular network, has scarcely been tackled. It is clear why this is so. For instance, one way to characterize such patterns is to measure the length, width, and orientation of each trabecula in a given section of bone. But it is most time-consuming to measure hundreds of trabeculae for even one section of bone; the comparison of many such sections within even a single bone would be a proportionately greater task; the final comparison of many single bones of one group of animals with many single bones of each of several other groups of animals becomes virtually impossible.

However, it happens that other scientists are also interested in avoiding all of this work. Computational and optical methods for studying images have evolved as fallout from modern technological advances related to the exploration of space and the development of instruments such as lasers and computers. The best known examples are found in the transmission and improvement of pictures taken by artificial satellites in space probes, in pattern recognition studies utilizing powerful computers, and in holographic and photographic investigation using optical data processing (fig. 13). A by-product of many of these methods is the realization that in the procedure of reconstruction of an improved picture an intermediate stage exists in which the pictorial data are transformed into a nonpictorial form. Both computational and optical processing, for instance, transform the original picture in some quantitative manner. It is this intermediate transformation that may provide an analysis of the picture. In the case of pictures or X rays of bones, the intermediate transformation may supply succinct yet comprehensive information about the details contained within complex trabecular lattices, and although this can be done using mathematical manipulations with a computer to create Fourier transforms of a picture, it can also be done optically. That is because one property of a lens system forming a real image is that it performs an optical Fourier transform on the input signal. Using such optical equipment, specified visual items in the original picture that are defined by size and orientation can also be identified in the transform. Moreover, this identification can be easily quantified so that the contributions of the specified items relative to the whole picture may be obtained (fig. 14).

Such procedures can be used in an exploratory manner; that is, the technique may be employed in an empirical way as a searching tool. The Fourier analysis may be used as a "fingerprint" of the bony patterns for the purposes of recognizing individual patterns and of comparing one bony pattern with another. The technique may also be used explicitly as a hypothesis-testing device; for instance, in the studies of bones one guiding theory might be that the trabecular network is the realization of a random process. From the Fourier analysis, unique and sufficient parameters may be obtained that characterize the network and afford a test of the actuality of the random nature of the bone fabric. An alternative model that may be more useful to test is one relating the idea that the bony trabecular plates

Figure 13. A regular pattern is obvious in the picture shown upper left. The picture on the lower left does not show any readily evident pattern. Optical data processing of each picture (right respective frames) shows that, in fact, the pattern of the upper figure is contained within the lower figure—the same pattern of dots exists within the optical transform of each. This revelation may be perceived far more easily through optical data processing than by eye, although, with hindsight, the eye can detect those elements in the lower picture that replicate the upper one.

lie at right angles to one another, for it is believed by some investigators that this relates to stress bearing in bone during function. Such a model may be more realistic than the idea that bone is the realization of random processes.

It is possible to utilize filters to screen out some of the data, thereby allowing other information in the picture to present itself more readily. For instance, if it is obvious that a certain number of the shadows in a radiograph are clearly oriented in a particular direction, a filter can be inserted which will screen out all items oriented in that way. The resulting reconstruction may allow one to see more clearly what remains (fig. 15). Again, it may be that the pattern of a certain size of radiographic shadow is very

111

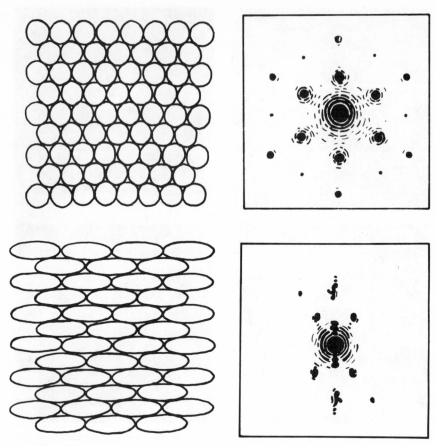

Figure 14. Optical data analysis of a pattern of touching circles (top) and of a uniformly squashed pattern (bottom). The orientational change evident in the second picture is also evident in the second optical transform (after Professor H. J. Pincus).

obvious; if so, appropriate filters can be used once more to screen out items of that size, permitting inspection of the pattern of other less obvious shadows (fig. 16).

Filtering techniques may be taken yet further. The Fourier analysis of one specimen can itself be used as a filter for the examination of a second specimen. This process then results in, first, a reconstruction of the image of the actual differences between the specimens and, second, the production of the Fourier transform of some of the differences between the specimens. From these may be calculated the parameters of the differences, and such comparisons consist of the true differences of the many elements in the picture, not just those of the major trends that are evident to the naked eye (fig. 17).

Finally, there is the very special application of filtering methods for the

112

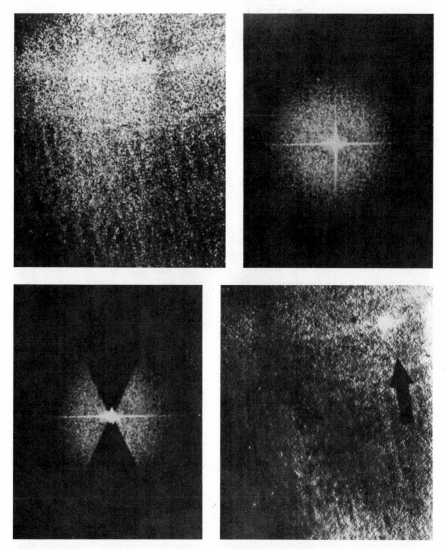

Figure 15. Optical filtering of a radiograph of part of the head of a tibia (much enlarged). The top left frame reproduces the trabecular pattern within the bone; its main directions are vertical. The second frame (top right) shows the optical transform of the radiograph. The bottom left frame shows the optical transform with a horizontal sector-shaped filter in place to screen out all items oriented vertically in the original (there is a ninety-degree shift between orientational information in an original and in a transform). The final frame shows the reconstruction from the filtered transform. The major bulk of vertical trabecular shadows are now removed, and there is revealed a small shadow shown by subsequent histology to be a small (approximately one millimeter sized) ivory osteoma.

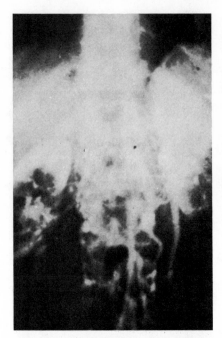

Figure 16. Optical filtering of a radiograph of the abdomen in which one ureter is filled with a radio-opaque medium thus outlining what is ordinarily a soft tissue structure not visible on X ray. The left frame is the usual view: much of the information is hidden by many other shadows due to other tissues. The right frame shows the resulting reconstructed radiograph after a filter has been used that removes many of those shadows. It emphasizes the edges of objects, and in addition to revealing the edges of the vertebral column, it much more clearly reveals the ureter (which is abnormally coiled).

reconstruction of the patterns in fossils. Radiographs of fossils often delineate quite clearly trabecular and other architectural patterns. But in addition the picture of internal structure relating to the original bone of the fossil is often obscured by crystalline and other patterns associated with geological processes of fossilization. With the technique of optical filtering described above, it is possible to subtract the unwanted (for biological purposes) pattern from that of the entire fossil. What is left then relates to those elements of the fossil that are associated with the original architecture of the bones (fig. 18).

These general methods are very widely applicable throughout science. They are already well established in a variety of nonbiological studies. These include automatic processing of aerial photographs, distinction between ground and cloud patterns in meteorological studies, automatic tracking of particles in spark, bubble, and cloud chambers, and automatic signal analysis for monitoring explosions. They now are starting to become powerful weapons for the morphologist interested in the identification, characterization, and comparison of complex biological patterns present in

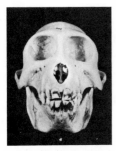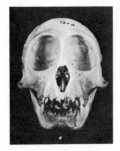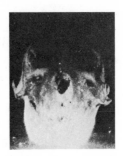

Figure 17. (Left and center) Photographs of skulls of a mangabey (*Cercocebus*) and a green monkey (*Cercopithecus*). (Right) The reconstruction that can be made when the reverse transform of *Cercopithecus* is used as a filter in the examination of *Cercocebus*. In this third picture the information that is of interest is not contained within the shape; it is demonstrated by the flux or intensity of light within the picture. Thus, the fact that very little light passes in the region of the forehead shows that, in this region, the information in the two pictures is similar. The fact that the brightest part of the reconstruction is in the area of the jaws and teeth indicates that it is this anatomical region in which the two pictures most differ. This is truly comparative anatomy of the most complete kind.

bones and fossils. But they do not supersede the other methods we have described: visual observation, and measurement together with analysis. Rather they add to our armamentarium for studying shape and pattern. They are able to demonstrate that there is a good deal of information within bone form and pattern that cannot be obtained by simple observation and measurement; they allow us to test out faults in assessments inher-

Figure 18. The same principle is evident in this series. An original pattern (left frame) was sprinkled with rug fibers (center frame). A filtering procedure (right) shows how well the original picture can be reconstructed. In a similar manner, nonbiological patterns in an X ray of a fossil might be removed to better reveal the original structure of the fossil. Again the appropriate further studies are under way.

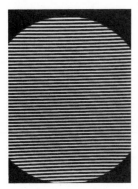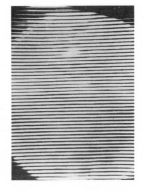

ent in the axioms of the other techniques; they allow us to confirm inferences because similar results may be obtained through the use of independent methods; and they allow us more easily to reject assessments because they cannot be confirmed with the new tools.

Newer biological interpretations of morphological differences

A major problem in understanding animal morphology is one inherent in the association between the structures that animals possess and the functions they display. This interface has loomed ever larger as our abilities to understand the complexities of both structure and behavior have increased. Although at one time structure itself could be described rather simply by its appearance to the naked eye, both directly and through dissection procedures, the application of the techniques just described shows that animal structure is more complicated.

It is also now becoming clear that the functions organisms display cannot be observed in all their complexities through anecdotal descriptions of behavior (the functional analogue of visual observation in morphology). Although, in general, organismal function has not been investigated as fully as organismal structure, evidence abounds that its complexity is no less; in fact, it may be much greater.

When we come to define the nature of the association between function and structure, we run into further problems, for the association may be studied at a number of different levels. *One* is the understanding of the mechanisms that lead, from the genetic materials, through the developmental process within an individual, to a particular functional-structural association in that individual. Thus, a simple embryonic limb bud may become, through such mechanisms, a prehensile, five-digit hand. A *second* is the study of how the functional-structural bond changes over geological time in evolving organisms. A prehensile five-digit extremity, for instance, may become reduced to a single digit associated with the evolution of galloping. A *third* attempts to understand the direct impact upon structure of function through biomechanics. For example, mechanical interference in an organism produces marked structural changes such as the formation of a new joint or changed bony pattern. Our understanding of this has recently received an impetus from the discovery of various mechanoelectrical phenomena within biological materials whereby impressed mechanical forces can be shown to have direct effects upon the form of bone and other tissues.

None of the above attacks on the problems of evolutionary biology is isolated; each depends upon the other for full understanding. Yet disentangling the functional-structural interrelationship often starts with the understanding of biomechanics as supplying one set of constraints within which heredity and evolution must operate.

Biomechanics can be studied at a relatively simple level: it is easy to see, for instance, that the physical principles embodied in the hip joint determine some of its limits as a biological form, and that as a result land animals equipped with such a bone cannot exist above a certain size. But biomechanical studies have become complex as a result of many modern developments such as equipment miniaturization and computer simulation. Moreover, experimental methods such as cineradiography and force-plate studies are providing information about biomechanisms that hone our understanding and in many cases provide entirely new views of traditional subjects. It has been shown by cineradiography, for instance, that when chimpanzees walk upright, they do it using their regular quadrupedal locomotion within a new upright position; they do not adopt bipedalism after the fashion of man. Such a finding may help us to define in detail how both human and ape hips differ from those of some fossils. It has been demonstrated by experimental stress analysis utilizing strain gauges in vivo not only that the vertebral column helps to bear obvious loads associated with posture and locomotion but that each individual vertebra expands and contracts like a concertina as a result of hitherto generally neglected and apparently small cyclical forces such as those of the heartbeat and respiratory rhythm. This may have applications to the understanding of fossil vertebrae. Other studies can be cited that today are providing new information about functional-structural relationships in living species and that by analogy may provide estimations about fossil forms. Although we have no immediate extant biological equivalents in living species to the "sails" of pelycosaurs or the "crests" of hadrosaurs with which to study their possible functions experimentally, in the case of many of the problems relating to human evolution reasonable inferences may be made about fossil structures from models provided by study of closely related living species.

The model may be entirely theoretical. For example, utilizing theoretical stress analyses it has been suggested that the form of the metacarpals in some fossil apes is well adapted to use in palmigrade postures and gaits. The adoption of digitigrade modes of locomotion, as in some terrestrial monkeys today, or of knuckle-walking, as in the terrestrial living African apes, would appear to lead to greater stresses than are efficient in restricted parts of the fossil metacarpals. This indicates the unlikelihood of digitigrade or knuckle-walking locomotor patterns in dryopithecine apes; it may indicate that these fossil apes were arboreal rather than terrestrial. Major differences from modern African ground-dwelling monkeys and apes are thus suggested.

In a similar way, experimental stress modeling has been applied to fossil shapes in comparisons with the structures of extant species the functions of which are known. It has been shown that the complicated architectures of the finger bones in the living apes relate fairly well to primary functions during locomotion and foraging, whether of the terrestrial, knuckle-walking African apes, the gorilla and chimpanzee, or of the arboreal, hanging-climbing Asian great ape, the orangutan. A fossil finger bone from Olduvai has been shown, in related comparisons, to be mechanically more efficient in the arboreal mode and to be nothing like that of man; these bones have, accordingly, been removed from consideration as possibly of human ancestry.

Both these studies suffer from a major deficiency in that the bone areas modeled, whether theoretically or experimentally, are treated as though they were uniform elastic bones. Bone is not, of course, a "homogeneous, isotropic material" operating as a "uniform elastic body" under "infinite beam theory." There is now every reason for believing that bone may be better considered as an anisotropic, poroelastic material and that finite element elastic theory may be more appropriate to the study of it, especially for complexly shaped anatomical regions. It is to be hoped, however, that the inferences derived from models, whether theoretical or experimental, are reasonably accurate despite the simplifications adopted.

Another, indirect, method is also available for the study of animal form. This consists of allowing the structures to speak, as it were, for themselves. The approach is a good deal less directly aimed at biomechanics than the experimental methods discussed above. And because the structures do not always speak very clearly when they tell us about themselves, we may run into different sets of problems. Nevertheless, while the results must be inferred from complex comparisons rather than neatly displayed by experiment, the inductive approach is, in some important aspects, decidedly superior to the experimental. It is better able to deal with populations than individuals, something that is usually prohibitive in experimental work. It can cope with different anatomical regions and a diversity of taxonomic groups of animals (including many rare species) such as can scarcely be involved in carefully planned experimental studies with adequate controls. It is capable of dealing with fragmentary and incomplete specimens in a manner difficult to arrange in experimental studies and can therefore be used with fossils. And it may require only examination of museum materials already collected, without the need to interfere with living animals, many of which are undergoing severe population reductions at the present time.

Nevertheless, the inductive method is not at variance with the direct techniques. In fact, the converse is true. The various approaches are complementary rather than competitive; concordance among them is an important strength in evaluating results; disagreement should make each investigator look to the problems in his own approach.

The inductive approach may involve a methodology as simple as associating, visually, functional observations with morphological information. Of course, one must proceed with care. A rough association between function and morphology readily springs to mind, whatever the function and whatever the morphology happen to be. Once we become interested in shades of difference, however, the complex nature of bone form and pattern and the complicated series of developmental, evolutionary, and biomechanical processes that are responsible for its precise expression defy facile explanation. Thus, the causal relationship between structure and function seems not usually to be between primary elements of function and primary elements of structure. Each particular function as observed must be associated causally with several structures; each structure must have impinging upon itself the effect of several functions; the association between function and structure must be more complicated than any simple one-to-one relationship.

That this is likely to be so has always seemed intuitively obvious to those who have a "gestalt" whole-organism view. It has recently become more obvious as a deeper understanding of biological correlation reveals that any given primary functional feature must be partially correlated with each of several different pieces of structure. Likewise, the idea can be read in reverse: particular morphological structures can rarely be aligned totally with particular functions; structure has to be partitioned out, through correlation, with several, perhaps many, elements of function. This seems to suggest that the morphological-behavioral interface is unbelievably complicated. Fortunately, the development of ideas like correlation, and the analytical methods that go with it, provides us with tools for investigating the situation.

The biomechanical approach suggests that we can hope to make real inroads into studying the morphological-behavioral interface. This is evident from a very large bulk of experimental work carried out over the last two centuries and culminating, during the last two decades, in a new burst of activity into the nature of the adaptation of biological materials to impressed mechanical forces. It has never been doubted that hereditary mechanisms play their part in the origin of mammalian structures, especially of the structure of the bone-joint-muscle unit, and particularly, therefore, of bone (the only material whose direct study allows us insight into fossils). But the new studies indicate that hereditary mechanisms are not implicated in a direct way in the development of the detailed form of those structures involved in biomechanisms. Genetic and epigenetic mechanisms are clearly involved in the laying down of *a* bone, *a* joint, or *a* muscle, in the production of *an* epiphyseal plate, or *a* sesamoid bone at a particular locality, in the formation of *the* basic shape of the femur or pelvis; but it now seems clear that the part these hereditary mechanisms play in the emergence of ultimate detailed external shape and internal structure is at the level of inheritance of adaptability toward mechanical stimuli during ontogeny (both intrauterine development and postnatal growth). Even though it is not clearly understood how the hereditary mechanisms are able, through evolution, to anticipate approximate final adult shape, the plasticity of the entire mammalian organism is such that that anticipation is fully realized only when external functions no different from those of ancestors are placed upon the structures. Much experimental evidence suggests that should something occur which alters function (for instance, prevention of movement in utero, or production of new forms of movement through experimental interference postpartum) in a particular organism, that organism's structure has no difficulty in changing to a new form or pattern in relation to the changed mechanical demand.

There are two questions here. One, to which we will not address ourselves, is how such adaptations (which appear superficially Lamarckian) become subsequently included within the hereditary mechanisms in an evolutionary time scale, given that the changes might be those occurring naturally. The other is how such changes in function actually affect the changes in structure during ontogeny. This is no less important if we are to understand the adaptation of bone form to function, and a partial answer is available. Much work suggests that the mechanism of the adaptation is through the "resultant or average biomechanical situation."

What that means is rather complicated, because the idea of the term "resultant or average biomechanical situation" must be defined. It does not mean the "resultant force" as customarily defined in mechanics: an average of a number of vector quantities. Rather must it mean some much more complicated average that has to take into account at least some of the following factors. *First,* this average must presumably reach a certain critical value before it starts to have any effect at all in causing adaptational changes in structure; this is the idea of a scalar threshold. *Second,* it is likely that the situation must exist for some minimum length of time before it has effects: the notion of a temporal threshold. A *third* idea affecting the "resultant or average biomechanical situation" may relate to the existence and effect of cyclically changing forces such as those due to the heartbeat and respiration, perhaps those of repetitive reflex movement in utero and locomotor cycles postpartum. A *fourth* is the effect of the spatial arrangement of the forces: the vectorial element in computing "averages" in all of the above matters. A *fifth* is the likelihood that the adaptation of bone form in relation to average biomechanical situations is unlikely to be linear. And, *finally,* these elements of the "average" of any single identifiable functional element must be averaged against all those other features also acting during the period of time in which the morphology is being influenced. It all adds up to the final influencing factor being not any particular force and certainly not any particular function but a curious "resultant or average biomechanical situation" that can take appropriate account of each of these different forms of individual force.

Obviously we can never understand the precise *real* value of this "resultant or average biomechanical situation"; but do we have to? It is almost like asking for average pressures based upon determinations of the actual position of each atom in a gas. Quantum mechanics has shown that we do not need that detailed information about each atom in order to be able to understand the gas pressure laws. And in an analogous way some simpler estimate of the biomechanical situation may be all that is necessary in order to understand functional-structural arrangements in particular biological systems.

In an example where many of the forces contributing to the resultant biomechanical situation are small, and a rather small number of the forces are overwhelmingly large, some estimate of the "resultant" can be made from the latter alone. For the "resultant" will be largely affected by the small number of large forces, and affected scarcely at all, in comparison, by all the many small ones. That is because, unless the small forces are similar in all of their parameters, including direction, they do not sum in the formation of the average. Although, for example, the gorilla and chimpanzee can both use the fingers for a fairly wide variety of manipulative activities that cause many small forces to act upon the fingers, the functions which exert by far the biggest forces upon the finger bones are those that occur when the hand is used in heavy compression during knuckle-walking and in high tension during climbing. Examination, then, of these major forces alone provides us with a reasonable estimate of the "resultant biomechanical situation," and it will be to this resultant that the form and architecture of the finger bones will be most clearly related.

Usually, therefore, in the study of man and the primates, except for special regions—for instance, the skull—most of the major features of bones will be most clearly associated with a "resultant biomechanical situation" that is influenced to the greatest extent by a relatively small number of locomotor activities involving the large forces generated in behaviors such as traveling, foraging, and escaping; postures and other movements involving small forces, however frequent or prolonged they may be, relatively speaking, are unlikely to have much effect on major aspects of morphology. On that basis, study of fossil specimens may utilize information about living forms to provide assessments of the "resultant biomechanical situation" that may have acted upon the specimens during life. It is this part of the information contained within fossils that has become so much more clearly understood at the present day.

However, realization of these arguments severely limits what we can learn from fossils. In the examination of individual anatomical parts of living creatures, logical argument may progress from all of the detailed behaviors of living forms, through some resultant biomechanical situation, to the detailed structures of bones, muscles, and joints. But in making the opposite assessment about the equivalent anatomical regions of the fossils, we can legitimately progress only from the detailed structures of fossil bones to "resultant biomechanical situations." We cannot then pass to an estimate of the detailed behaviors of the fossil forms, because many different sets of behaviors may be associated with the rather simpler "resultant biomechanical situations" in a given anatomical region. Assessments of possible fossil ecologies and behaviors, when based upon examinations of individual fossil bones, should thus be understood to be exactly what they are: guesses, which cannot be tested without further independent information. But estimations that confine themselves to descriptions of "resultant biomechanical situations" are far more than guesses and can indeed be tested through examination of forms and functions of other, parallel, living species. On the other hand, evaluations of fossil skeletal remnants (of the postcranium at any rate) that attempt to pass directly to the genetic relationship or taxonomic position without passing through stages relating to assessments of biomechanical situations have little validity. The all-pervasive effect of function and structure—especially, at any rate, within the postcranial skeleton—is such that it is highly unlikely that any major quantitative features will be identifiable that are entirely hereditary in the primary sense.

Applications to man, ape, and monkey

We can apply any of these advances in understanding (*a*) structure or (*b*) the structural-functional interface to the study of fossils. Their novelty demands that we apply them first, however, to extant animals so that we can clearly understand their implications. This applies as much to the various techniques for defining form and pattern as it does to the arguments about the functional meaning of the forms and patterns themselves.

The primates are inevitably, and in some ways unfortunately, the most interesting of animals to us—ourselves a species that belongs to the same order. No other group of mammals has been so well studied, just as no other species is so well known as man. Indeed, more is known about the systematics of man and other primates, and of man's place among the living primates, than about any other group. On top of that, the evidence upon which primate systematics is grounded is itself very widely based.

Nevertheless, there is no totally agreed classification for the primate group, although many would say that the amount of agreement there is is perhaps surprisingly high. There is only a small measure of agreement in the consideration of *fossil* primates, which is not surprising at all. That is because, for the great majority of fossil representatives of this group, there is a relative paucity of information as compared with vast bodies of data that exist for many other fossil organisms.

If the overall classification of the primates has been fairly well settled for quite a long period, individual points are still challenged from time to time. Most work attempts nowadays to produce a marginally better picture; and though in some minds marginal changes in nomenclature are deemed valid, other workers agree that to make such changes sometimes produces more confusion than help in our present state of knowledge. Such a disagreement has occurred, for example, over the basic division of the primates into the two groups: Prosimii and Anthropoidea. Although, at this level, there would seem to be some reality in the suborder Anthropoidea, most workers nowadays agree that there is little reality to the term Prosimii. Yet for most investigators, to do away with that term appears less than useful,

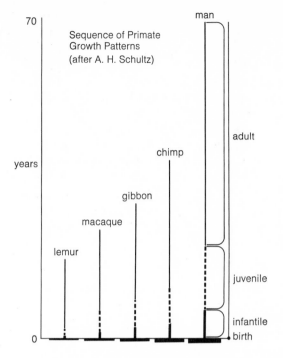

70

Sequence of Primate
Growth Patterns
(after A. H. Schultz)

man

adult

chimp

years

gibbon

macaque

lemur

juvenile

infantile
birth

0

Figure 19. Studies by the late Professor A. H. Schultz on growth patterns in primates show an arrangement of some primates that entirely accords with views about the classification of the order. The forms are arranged with prosimians at one extreme, monkeys intermediate, then apes and man at the other extreme.

and so it is retained. Another example of controversy in primate systematics is at the opposite end of the order with respect to the generic names *Gorilla* and *Pan*. Here also there is probably no doubt in the minds of most workers that the gorilla and chimpanzee are genetically far closer to each other than is represented by the use of separate generic designations, and a number of workers have, on reasonable evidence, suggested that they be grouped as a single genus *Pan*. The usage is starting to catch on. But the consensus about the basic information is probably good enough so that many believe there is no real need to make the nomenclatorial change; most workers will undoubtedly try to reduce confusion in the literature by retaining the older terms while yet accepting the newer relationship.

When, therefore, we view the systematics of the primates, we are looking at a series of pragmatic compromises as well as at attempts to carry systematic studies as far as possible. Much of the data base upon which primate classification and systematics is grounded is rather classical in nature; it depends upon a series of morphological features at the organ and organismic level such as external appearances of the face, cheiridia and genitalia, structures of the skull and teeth, and superficial features such as coat color and other pelage characteristics.

Similar evidence is contained in the overall proportions of the bodies of these creatures, especially as revealed in the extensive lifetime studies of the late Professor A. H. Schultz of Zurich (although data of this type were not initially used in primate systematics). But it is certainly to Professor Schultz

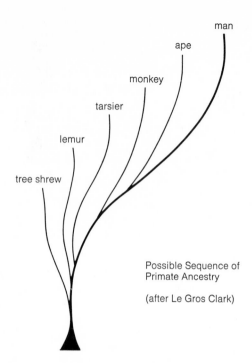

Figure 20. An arrangement of the primates, somewhat simplified after W. E. Le Gros Clark, and based upon studies of cranial and dental features together with superficial facial, genital, and pelage characteristics, shows a linear arrangement of the primates similar to figure 19.

Possible Sequence of Primate Ancestry

(after Le Gros Clark)

that we may turn for a picture (fig. 19) that can summarize the essential relationships these various creatures seem to present. This is a pattern of relationship that, with appropriate gaps and groupings, sees the living primates very much as a linear series with many prosimian forms being most like presumed "stem" mammals and least like man; monkeys lie intermediately and, of course, the apes are most like man. In such studies it is always rather clearly presented that man is indeed, structurally, a member situated at one extreme of the group (but not a "terminal" member in any evolutionary manner, for, of course, all these species are "terminal" in the sense that they are all alive today).

The relatively linear sequence (fig. 20) has also been summarized in many classical studies, of which those by Professor Sir Wilfred Le Gros Clark are most well known. They are based upon assessments about phylogeny resting essentially upon organismic information primarily from teeth, jaws, crania, and external features.

However, our knowledge of the relationships of primates does not rest upon organismic data alone. Whereas some at least of the organismic information has been known for centuries, data of a different form, relating to biomolecular entities, have been available for many decades, although only in the last two has the bulk of the data loomed large enough to be used in a practical manner in primate systematics. There is little doubt that this information, in general, supports the classical picture to a quite remarkable degree. The evidence consists of a rather wide range of types of infor-

124

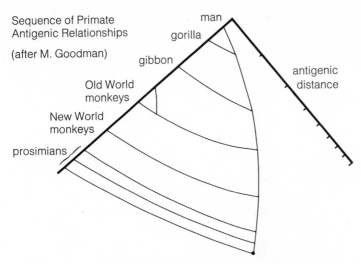

Sequence of Primate
Antigenic Relationships

(after M. Goodman)

man

gorilla

gibbon

Old World
monkeys

New World
monkeys

prosimians

antigenic
distance

Figure 21. Study of some antigenic distances by Professor Morris
Goodman (reoriented for comparison with organismic results of figures
19 and 20) demonstrates a basically similar linear arrangement of the
primates by biomolecular data.

mation: blood group distributions, chromosome analyses, protein sequencing, immunological tolerances, antigenic distances, and so on. It is really remarkable how closely this set of relationships parallels those obtained from the organismic data. Again, species can be arranged in a linear sequence (fig. 21), with the prosimians at one end as before, and man can again be viewed as a species at the other end of this sequence—an end that he shares, as before, with the apes. There are some gaps, to be sure, but many examples of investigations of such biomolecular data provide a generally similar scheme.

Of course, these two taxonomic pictures, the organismic and the biomolecular, are not identical. What are the points of difference? There are indeed some, and they are concentrated in particular places. For instance, the biomolecular techniques are more likely to place man in close relationship with the chimpanzee and gorilla as compared with the Asiatic apes. This contrasts with most organismic methods, which place the African great apes with the Asiatic great apes in the Ponginae, and with man rather separate at one side and the gibbons rather separate at the other. Similarly, the biomolecular techniques usually produce somewhat different groupings of New World monkeys, as compared with those traditionally arrived at from the standpoint of most organismic studies that recognize the families and subfamilies of New World monkeys of the present day. Other differences are apparent between the two systems. But we must, in the main, be pleased at the general degree of conformity which the two groups of studies produce.

When it comes to judging fossil data, it is not possible to include fossils in either of the above ways of classifying the primates. Of the various informational items useful in making judgments on the basis of organismic methods, really only one, comparison of teeth, jaws, and crania, is available for fossils, although, to a somewhat greater degree nowadays, information is starting to come from the postcranial skeleton. From the viewpoint of biomolecular investigations, no information whatsoever is known or can be known for most fossil materials. On the other hand, fossil materials do sometimes provide some data about time, and to this extent new information is available which is of value in discussing primate relationships.

For fossils, therefore, the data must, in the first instance, be judged piecemeal. Comparisons must be drawn among fragments that represent the same anatomical region in different species. Once this has been done, it is possible to add the data from different anatomical regions for a given species, but, of course, this must be done in such a way that information from one worker about one region is not used to help to make judgments about a second region; data from some other worker about the second region may already have been used to help to make judgments about the first, resulting in a circularity of reasoning. Moreover, when we add together osteological data from many different anatomical regions in order to make judgments about fossils, it is important that we be aware of the consequences. A test can be made by adding osteological data from different anatomical regions for extant species, where the results can be compared with the vast body of other data available.

Forelimbs

Let us look at the consequences of examining parts of organisms, rather than whole organisms. Let it be done using the new biometrical tools so that we can gain some idea of quantitative relationships. A number of such studies have been carried out in recent years. First, a series of studies on shoulder, arm, forearm, and forelimb as a whole has been carried out in which the rationale of examination is to choose a series of definable and repeatable measurements on the various anatomical regions and then to compound them in a manner allowing for the correlations among them, using a multivariate statistical treatment.

The result of carrying out these procedures is primarily that the various primates are strung out in a relatively linear sequence. This resembles the studies already described. But once we examine the sequence of genera within this linear sequence, it is readily apparent that there is little true relationship with the systematic classification. Thus, while apes are indeed at one end of the sequence as before, the various prosimians are not all grouped near the other end. In fact, Anthropoidea and Prosimii are, with the exception of the apes, strung out along the sequence in approximately parallel series. Tarsiers and bush babies (prosimians) lie near one extreme with baboons and patas monkeys (Old World monkeys); squirrel and saki

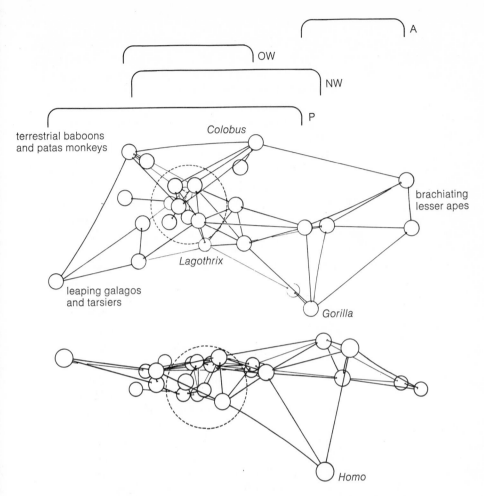

Figure 22. Study, using multivariate statistical methods, of various dimensions of the forelimb in the primates provides an arrangement of the nonhuman genera that is essentially linear within a broad band. But the disposition of the various groups of primates within that linear array is not similar to that shown in figures 19, 20, and 21. In fact, almost all groups of the primates overlap with one another—P=prosimians, N=New World monkeys, O=Old World monkeys, and A=apes. Turning the model through ninety degrees (lower frame) demonstrates that man is unique. The arrangement is best associated with the function of the forelimb as explained in the text.

monkeys (New World monkeys), macaques and mangabeys (Old World monkeys), and lemurs and tree shrews (prosimians) lie not too distantly from one another along the sequence; while colobus, woolly monkeys, pottos, and sifakas (yet another mixture of Old and New World monkeys and prosimians) share, to a degree, loci even further along a spectrum that terminates with the apes and the spider and woolly-spider monkeys of the New World. This arrangement (fig. 22) is quite different from the systematic one posited earlier.

127

An obvious feature concerns the position of man. His place is not within the linear sequence at all but is uniquely defined. He is so far distant from the sequence of nonhuman forms that his closest relationships are equivocal, being with several quite different species—some apes, some Old World monkeys, some New World monkeys, and even some prosimians.

An initial reaction to these results might be to question them because they are so different from the overall picture presented by primate taxonomy. However, numbers of workers have either replicated the investigations or carried out studies that are essentially parallel, and it can be easily shown that their results are basically similar.

If, then, these results are valid, what can be the explanation for them? The explanation seems to reside in the idea that when one characterizes the form of a localized anatomical region, one is presumably characterizing a morphology which is associated with the "resultant or average biomechanical situation" within which that anatomical region performs. Viewing the skull in this way does not easily give a coherent functional picture, because the skull itself is not a single functional region but a compound of several, some of which are among the most complicated to be found in the body. But visualizing the primate forelimb in this way probably does provide some kind of overall average view of the functional-structural relationships within that anatomical member.

It is thus not unexpected that gibbons, siamangs (lesser apes), orangutans (great apes), and spider and woolly-spider monkeys (New World monkeys) should fall near one another: these are all animals in which (irrespective of the details of actual behavior) the limb operates more frequently than in most primates in raised positions, in which limb mobility is high in all planes in space, and in which the limb as a whole frequently bears tensile forces. It is not unexpected that a large number of regular four-footed running and climbing animals are near the other end of the spectrum (e.g., baboons, patas monkeys [Old World monkeys], squirrel monkeys [New World monkeys], lemurs [prosimians]): these are creatures in which, however wide the range of activities that may on occasion be carried out, forelimbs are mostly used in a lowered position as compared with the previous species, in which mobility in the forelimb is somewhat more confined to a two-dimensional craniocaudal plane rather than the three-dimensional picture in the previous forms, and in which, as a consequence of all the many locomotor, foraging, feeding, and other activities in which they engage, the forelimb bears less general tensile force and more compressive force than in the prior animals. Predictably, too, we find, along the spectrum between the extremes, species that fit in a general way with these concepts.

It is not surprising either that the position of man is outside this morphological spectrum. That man lies uniquely apart presumably relates to the unique functions of the human forelimb, which is employed for a rather wider range of smaller force-bearing activities than is the case in most other primates, and perhaps more particularly to the fact that, of course, man is the only primate that does not use the forelimb for locomotor purposes at all.

The above links between morphological information and such biomechanical resultants of behavior as can be visualized in our present state of information are evident mainly from examination of those genera (e.g., terrestrial baboons, brachiating lesser apes) that are rather extreme in their behaviors.

It turns out that similar patterns can be observed if we confine our attention to animals that are generally recognized as being less extreme, whose locomotor behavior at any rate is often characterized as regular quadrupedalism. These latter genera are rather similar, yet even within species usually lumped as quadrupeds, anatomical separations exist that seem to relate to lesser differences in the use of the forelimb but in terms of somewhat similar positions of action, overall mobility, and degrees of tension-bearing, as above. Thus, among many different lesser groupings of primates, the separations of the genera are from those which are most quadrupedal, through those which are intermediate, to those that are most highly acrobatic (fig. 23). Even studies that have been undertaken at the species or species group level, for groups such as the langurs, mangabeys, vervets, or the different species of bush baby, show such functional relationships. One already suspects that groups of howler monkeys, or saki monkeys, or macaques, or lemurs move in different ways and have equivalent differences in structure. Comparative, functional, and structural examinations, carried out more widely throughout the primates, are therefore required.

Pending such studies, there is considerable information here suggesting that, even among relatively regular quadrupedal animals, variations in forelimb morphology can be observed that seem to be associated with variations in biomechanical evaluations derived from behavioral and ecological observations.

Bearing all these data and interpretations in mind, we might suppose that we had an excellent tool for making speculations about the behavior of a particular fossil, given that we had for it roughly comparable morphological information. In fact, of course, we cannot suppose that to be the case. Although an association between some behaviors and some morphologies can be readily seen, it must be recognized that this association acts through the interface of the smaller set of factors: those situations that result from the behaviors and that by their actions (through both ontogenetic and evolutionary mechanisms) impinge upon and "shape" the anatomical structures concerned.

It is not at all unreasonable to expect that different behaviors might produce a rather similar resultant situation in a particular anatomical region. This is presumably the case for the fairly close associations in terms of certain aspects of forelimb structures that can be seen, for instance, between sifakas and proboscis monkeys, between pottos and woolly mon-

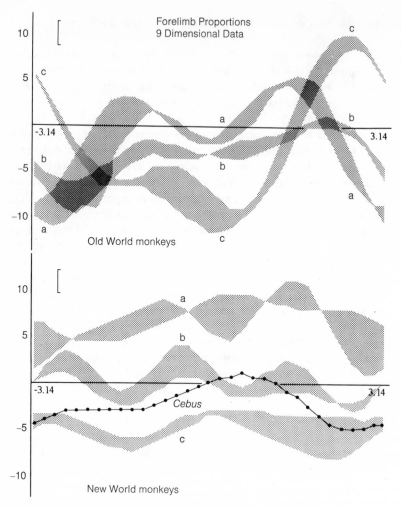

Figure 23. Those species that are generally characterized as regular quadrupeds (and enclosed within the dotted circle in figure 22) are here displayed using Andrews's high-dimensional method. The species are separated into groups a, b, and c as indicated. These groups are not especially closely related in an evolutionary sense but are clearly related functionally. Group a includes those species that are least acrobatic in the trees, group c those that are most highly acrobatic, and group b those that are generally intermediate. The same picture holds for both Old and New World monkeys as indicated, although, of course, the precise functional (locomotor) descriptions vary for the two groups. Among the New World monkeys, the capuchin (*Cebus*) falls in an equivocal position, and even this has functional sense in terms of what is known about its methods of movement.

keys, or among squirrel monkeys, macaques, and lemurs. None of the members of these sets of genera moves in similar ways. Yet there are certain morphological similarities. Knowing what we do of the ways in which their forelimbs function, we can only surmise that, different as the overall behavior is, the resultant situations are similar enough to produce (through development and evolution) somewhat similar morphologies. Thus, sifakas and proboscis monkeys, although progressing in different ways, both employ their forelimbs in a relatively three-dimensional manner as compared with such closer taxonomic relatives as lemurs and macaques. Pottos and woolly monkeys move quite differently, yet both employ their forelimbs in such a way that they may be under resultant forces of tension to a somewhat greater degree than, respectively, in many other prosimians and New World monkeys. Squirrel monkeys, macaques, and lemurs all move in different manners and could not be mistaken for one another when compared through locomotor profiles; yet the functions of their forelimbs are such that, compared with some of the other primate species described here, they presumably function with overall smaller resultant ranges of movement, an overall lower resultant position of action, and an overall resultant compressive force to extents greater than most other genera.

It is thus clear that using comparable data from the forelimb in a fossil does not allow, of itself, any strong evidence for reaching specific conclusions as to the behavior of the fossil animal. It merely allows us to make some deduction about the resultant mechanics that may have obtained in the forelimb during function in that fossil. Nothing further is possible without additional study of some sort.

Hindlimbs

The arguments advanced above are sound only if they can be confirmed through examination of other anatomical areas. Let us therefore look toward the hindlimb. Here a lesser range of investigations is available, studies of the pelvis, the talus, and the overall proportions of the hindlimb being the main evidence. Research is in progress to test these ideas in other anatomical elements of the hindlimb. In the case of the above anatomical areas, the result parallels that seen in the forelimb: there is no resemblance to the general systematics of primates. Not only are the relationships of individual genera not at all similar to their overall systematic relationships; the general form of the arrangement differs even from that for the forelimb in that it is not a linear spectrum. The picture (fig. 24) is more a star-shaped, or multipolar, spectrum than anything else. As with the studies on the various forelimb regions, man himself does not fall at any particular locus within the star-shaped spectrum; rather is he uniquely separate from all other species.

Again, the initial reaction to these results might be to question them because they are so different from those pertaining to the general systematic picture. But, again, replicate studies have confirmed the general

131

result for this anatomical region. If the results are real, what can be the explanation for them? A glance at the arrangement produced by the structural analysis suggests it is related not to the systematics or evolution of the animals but to aspects of hindlimb function within their behaviors.

Here, even more clearly than in the forelimb, there are juxtapositions of genera that presumably relate to biomechanical realities. Why otherwise would tarsiers and bush babies share affinities with mouse lemurs? These are animals from three different taxonomic groups. They presumably share these anatomical features because all are animals capable of leaping in a particular way, although to different degrees. Similarly, baboons and patas monkeys presumably share a locus together because, although their nearest taxonomic relatives are other genera and not each other, they, and they alone among Old World monkeys, are most heavily terrestrial in the functions of their hindlimbs as compared with other closer but more arboreal relatives of each. The functional analogies of some groups are a little less obvious because the taxonomy happens to coincide with functional patterns (e.g., the unique locomotor *and* taxonomic positions of the lorisines among the Lorisiformes, of the indriids among the lemurs, and of the pitheciines among the New World monkeys). Again, there may be some discrepancies in the positions of particular genera, although it would appear that these, if they exist, are rather less easily recognized than is the case in the forelimb studies.

It is also not surprising that man does not lie somewhere within the star-shaped spectrum of living nonhuman primates. He is uniquely separate from all genera, although he is, of course, nearer to some than to others. Those with which he has closest connections, although still very far distant, are the great apes and certain prehensile-tailed New World genera, together with the uakaris and saki monkeys of the New World. Presumably such distant relationships mean little. That man lies uniquely apart, however, means a great deal. The fact that he is bipedal may not be the only reason for this. It is true that man is habitually bipedal and that most other primates, although capable of bipedality to far greater degrees than most mammals, are nevertheless not adapted for bipedality in the same way that man is; but, in addition, a large part of man's unique structure may devolve not only upon his *acquisition* of habitual bipedality but also, and perhaps mainly, upon his *loss* of quadrupedal and climbing abilities in the hindlimb. Man is totally unable to move quadrupedally, notwithstanding the fact that a poor type of quadrupedality may form part of his ontogenetic pattern at an early age. Moreover, man is not by any means an accomplished climber. It is true that, through training, he can become an acrobat, but he is able, however skilled he may be, to carry out such activities for only a very short period of time. It is a fact that natural man may also be capable of a fair degree of arboreal activity in a field situation (witness the climbing abilities of the Tasaday), but this still falls far short of the arboreal abilities of all nonhuman primates.

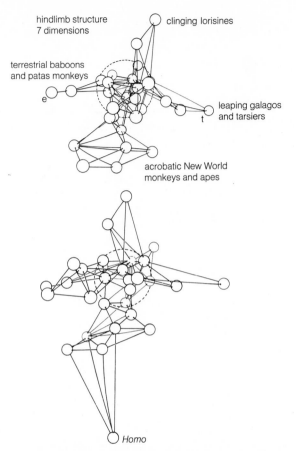

hindlimb structure
7 dimensions

clinging lorisines

terrestrial baboons
and patas monkeys

e

leaping galagos
and tarsiers

t

acrobatic New World
monkeys and apes

Homo

Figure 24. Study, using multivariate statistical methods, of various dimensions of the hindlimb in primates provides an arrangement of the species that does not resemble at all the linear arrangements of figures 19, 20, and 21. In this case the arrangement is generally star-shaped (although this model is locally correct only in three dimensions—the real model is actually of dimensionality higher than three and cannot be fully represented by this mode of display). The star-shaped arrangement is best associated with the function of the hindlimb as explained in the text. All those species in the center of the star (enclosed within the dotted circle, top) are those generally regarded as ordinary quadrupedal animals. Many of those species out in the arms of the star seem to be those that are united (in each separate arm respectively) because their hindlimbs participate in similar extreme modes of movement. Thus, the ray labeled ''t'' contains the most extreme prosimian leapers, the spectral tarsier, the less extreme bushbaby, and the least extreme mouse lemur—each from a different taxonomic subgroup of the prosimians. The ray labeled ''e'' contains patas monkeys and baboons, both highly terrestrial monkeys but each more closely related to other Old World monkeys than to each other.

The bottom frame demonstrates a rotated position of the model in which the unique position of man is shown.

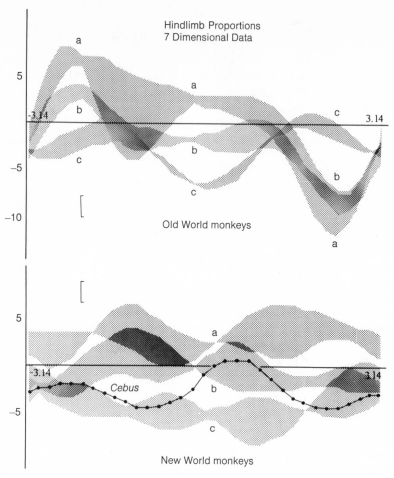

Figure 25. This figure represents the arrangement of the generally quadrupedal species of figure 24 as shown through the medium of Andrews's high-dimensional display. The arrangement does not resemble taxonomy; as for figure 23, the closest association of the various species seems to be in terms of degree of acrobatic activity in the trees. Thus, group a includes the least acrobatic forms, group c the most acrobatic, and group b, which always lies in an intermediate position in terms of the morphology, includes those that possess intermediate locomotor abilities. Again, among the New World monkeys the functionally equivocal species *Cebus* (the capuchin) is also morphologically equivocal.

As with the forelimb information, so with the hindlimb analyses. Differences can be observed among those many genera that are not extreme, that are crowded together, and that share biomechanical resultants dependent upon the fact of hindlimb function within locomotor modes that can be characterized as regular quadrupedalism. These genera are far from identical, however, and again, looking more closely into the morphological variation within them reveals separations that make sense in terms of differences in locomotion of smaller grade (fig. 25). In each case the nature of the relationship is such that it is most easily interpretable as being associated with locomotor and ecological features. The separations of the different animals are associated with degrees of arboreal activities in the hindlimb within what are usually regarded as rather regular quadrupedal modes. Similar findings are evident at the species-group and species levels, and again, further studies at these very low taxonomic levels are clearly required to discover just how widespread such finely tuned adaptation is among primates.

There is thus here very considerable support for the idea that major aspects of hindlimb structure, as visualized in these investigations, are associated through biomechanical adaptations of structure with major elements of behavior. As with the forelimb, overall information about the hindlimb or some of its parts, if known for some fossil, might provide for us evidence that would relate to the "resultant or average biomechanical situation" for that fossil. As with the forelimb, however, the same caveat must be extended. That is, although associations can be rather readily seen for extant forms for which we have a great deal of information, for fossil forms for which we may have only fragments of the lower limb, deductions are less easily made about overall behavior; sometimes all that can be said with confidence is about resultant mechanics of that behavior in the particular anatomical region. And because more than one behavior may have given rise to similar resultant mechanics, we have to be most careful.

However, in the case of the hindlimb, the caveat actually seems to work in the opposite direction. Here we are able to discern differences in morphology presumably related to differences in resultant mechanics when, to the casual view, the behavior seems remarkably similar. An obvious example is the major force-producing aspect of locomotion in many prosimians that are capable of great leaping. Although the indriids on the one hand and tarsiers and bush babies on the other are capable of big leaps and have enormously lengthened lower limbs, comparative morphology suggests that these behaviors are achieved in ways that are very different and associated presumably with very different resultant mechanics. This insight has allowed revisualization of how these two groups of animals actually leap, so that one can recognize a leaping pattern of tarsiers and bush babies often involving passage of the body through the air curled up—a leaping golf ball (fig. 26). This may be compared with leaping in the various indriids, where, at least in large leaps, there is considerable evidence of a stretched out

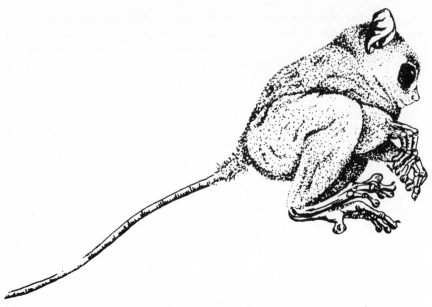

Figure 26. The spectral tarsier in mid-leap (after Walker, 1948).

midair posture that presumably utilizes aerodynamic factors in a totally different way (fig. 27). Many other primates also leap, e.g., macaques, spider monkeys, and gibbons, but when carried out by most of these forms, the midair posture is much less specialized and consists of neither opened out nor closed up postures but merely positions in which the limbs hang down and sometimes also cycle, in efforts to maintain midair positions preparatory to landing (fig. 28).

To summarize: examination of the hindlimb as well as the forelimb does not speak specifically to direct behavior of a fossil, though it may well allow interpretation about the resultant mechanics that lie at the interface between the morphology and the function of that anatomical part. As with the forelimb, the information that apparently is projected here is at variance with that contained in those overall systems which appear to be associated with the systematic arrangement of the primates (reviewed in the introduction to this article).

Other anatomical regions

It is, of course, possible to look at multivariate statistical agglomerations of data taken from other anatomical regions of the body such as the trunk and the head. It is also possible to view data sets chosen, not as representing particular anatomical regions, but as characterizing other types of anatomical phenomena, such as overall widths or overall lengths, as separate entities.

Studies of the head and trunk, either separately or taken in combination,

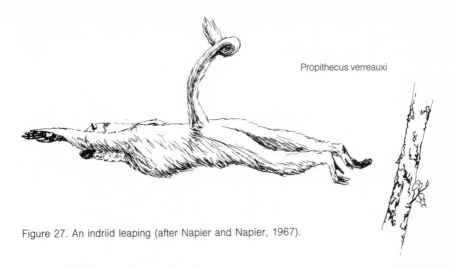

Propithecus verreauxi

Figure 27. An indriid leaping (after Napier and Napier, 1967).

provide information that is complex, separating out many individual species of the primates. It is of interest that the particular species so separated are those that are usually regarded as being somewhat more different from their fellows than most other species. Among the Prosimii, such analyses tend to isolate, in different ways, genera such as aye-ayes, tree shrews, and pottos. Among the Anthropoidea, genera such as patas monkeys from among the cercopithecines, proboscis monkeys from among the colobines, uakaris and howler monkeys (separately) among the New World monkeys, and, of course, man among the hominoids tend to be most separated.

In general, it is rather difficult to place any detailed biomechanical interpretation upon such results other than that these genera tend to be extreme in various ways, but the lack of such biomechanical interpretation does not mean that the separations are not real nor of very distinct biological (perhaps systematic) importance; certainly the scale of these separations

Figure 28. Leaping postures in (left) a macaque (after Pilbeam, 1970), a spider monkey (center, after Mittermeier and Fleagle, 1976), and a gibbon (right, after Baldwin and Teleki, 1976). Awkward positions with the limbs hanging down and cycling movements are evident.

is such that they not only are statistically significant but also must be taken into account in any assessment even if, at this time, we do not know what they signify.

Studies of dimensions arranged such that all transverse dimensions are taken together, or all longitudinal measures are compounded, are somewhat easier to interpret biologically. Analysis of transverse dimensions does not provide any very meaningful arrangement of primate genera; it does separate in a fairly uniform manner the sexes of individual primate genera where these are known. Given the nature of transverse measures, it is rather likely that what is being reflected here is degree of robusticity. Robusticity is frequently easily seen in univariate examinations of transverse measures, and differences between sexes appear to depend to at least a considerable degree upon differences in robusticity. Examination of a series of longitudinal measures provides information that is fairly closely linked with those of the limbs that we have already examined. This is perfectly reasonable because, of course, the majority of the measurements of the proportions of the limbs already discussed are in themselves measures of longitudinal elements of the body.

Overall body structure

Does this mean that from fossil fragments we can never obtain more complete information (*a*) about behavior or (*b*) about systematics? It does not. But in order to be able to make more complete assessments for any given fossil, we must have information from at least several different anatomical regions. A fragment of clavicle alone, the lower end of the radius alone, a toe bone alone can tell us only something about the resultant mechanics in shoulders, wrists, and toes, respectively, in the given fossil. We must be able to add together, independently, information from several areas if we are to evaluate the creatures more fully.

This is an impossible request for some fossil species at the present time. We have only a few jaws and teeth of *Ramapithecus*; we have even less of other creatures. But the finds of paleontologists in the field are progressing so well that soon we can truly hope to add together information from a number of different fossils. Though it will be rather rare that the information will be about a single specimen, exceptions do occur—e.g., Johanson and Taieb's find in the Afar Valley (fig. 29). Information will more usually be about a single species—*Australopithecus africanus* as a single species is now known in many different anatomical regions (fig. 30). Most commonly, however, information will be available at the species-group or generic levels; e.g., for australopithecines as a subfamily. Even here difficulties exist in being certain that associations among fragments are being drawn correctly. Yet we can look to the day when such additions are possible; indeed this has already been attempted for the australopithecines as a subfamily or genus.

The result of performing on living species such a total multivariate statis-

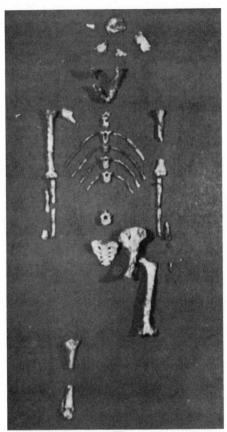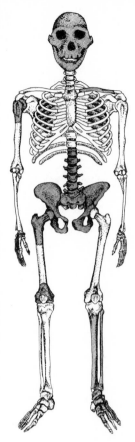

Figure 29 (left). A photograph of the remains of a single individual found by Don Johanson and Maurice Taieb in the Afar Valley. Figure 30 (right). Some of the fragments available for *Australopithecus* from Sterkfontein.

tical study of all regions of the body combined is most surprising. Notwithstanding the functional result that obtains from examination of individual body segments, the overall result provides no recognizable functional answer, but it does resemble most closely the generally accepted taxonomic subdivisions of the primates (fig. 31). Not only are the various major groups of the Prosimii clearly evident (e.g., indriids, galagines, lorisines) but so also many of the subgroups of the Anthropoidea are obvious (Old World monkeys, and within them cercopithecines and colobines; New World monkeys; Hominoidea).

Closer scrutiny reveals, however, that in the details of this picture there are a number of departures from systematics as currently recognized using the organismic methods. One example is the Hominoidea, where in these new studies the orangutan is associated with the lesser apes rather than with the African great apes. However, although this result is contrary to the

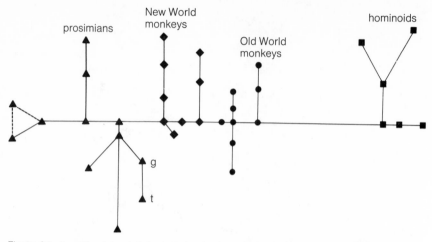

Figure 31. A multivariate statistical study of many dimensions of the entire carcass of primates displayed using the minimum spanning tree. In contrast to the functional arrangements of figures 22 and 24 for similar analyses of data from the fore- and hindlimbs alone, but markedly similar to the taxonomic arrangements of figures 19, 20, and 21, the primates form a linear array from prosimians at the left through the various monkeys to the apes and man at the right.

assignment of the orangutan to the pongids as by classical organismic taxonomy, it is entirely concordant with the evaluation provided by both biomolecular studies and by the fossil records that place the African apes closer to man and the orangutan closer to the gibbon and siamang. Other, similar detailed departures are evident within each of the various subdivisions of the primates, and in most of these examples the results recorded in this study are similar to those obtained from classifications based upon biomolecular studies, not organismic ones.

The position of *Tarsius* is of special interest for a different reason. The close linkage between the bush babies and the tarsiers may be almost entirely due to the fact of the locomotor specializations of these two species (at the same time the most extreme of all primates, and also heavily convergent). It is possible that in this case the locomotor information overshadows the taxonomic content. Such an explanation would account for the only major taxonomic discrepancy in these results (the tarsier and the bush baby actually being in separate infraorders). However, if we ignore the bush baby–tarsier link (i.e., ignore the functional convergence between them) and study the remainder of the results, we find that while the next nearest links of the bush baby remain with other prosimians, the next nearest links of the tarsier are with a variety of monkeys. Such a finding is of considerable interest in the light of (*a*) many older suggestions based on organismic methods, and (*b*) many new biomolecular data, that the affinities of *Tarsius* are with the Anthropoidea (fig. 32).

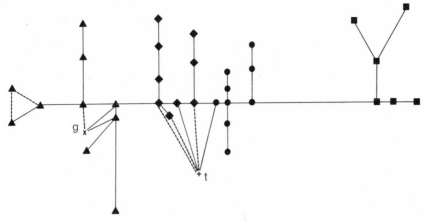

Figure 32. In figure 31 the spectral tarsier (t) and the bushbaby (g) lie close to one another, a propinquity which does not accord with their markedly different taxonomic positions, but which is concordant with the extreme functional convergence of these two leaping primates. In this figure the link between the two is disconnected; the next nearest neighbors of the bushbaby are a number of other prosimians, but the tarsier is found to be closest to many monkeys. This agrees with many new views of the taxonomic relationships of these two species.

Irrespective, however, of these lesser differences in detail, over which systematists may wish to argue, a most interesting aspect of these multivariate studies of proportions taken from many anatomical regions is the degree to which they mirror the general results of primate systematics, whether obtained from organismic or biomolecular data. The general correspondence between biomolecular data and primate systematics seems fairly obvious; after all, the molecules are the very stuff of evolutionary change. But what, we may ask, in the case of the multivariate study of overall bodily proportions may be the reason for its close correspondence with classical primate systematics? This question is especially important when we remember that equivalent study of individual regions gives the opposite, functional result (*see* sections summarizing forelimb and hindlimb).

One answer is the circular possibility: that in some nonquantitative, perhaps intuitive way, systematists have already included information about overall proportions of animals within their systematic assessments. But study of the systematic literature reveals the opposite; these judgments have not been made upon the basis of overall dimensions of animals, whether assessed by the eye or by ruler. Rather, the morphologies that have been employed in such studies have truly been those features enumerated earlier, to wit, features of the skull (teeth, jaws, orbits, middle ear, cranial base, etc.), of the external form of the face, cheiridia, genitalia, and pelage, and sometimes a few measurements especially of the skull and teeth. Information about overall bodily form has not been entered, either overtly or covertly, into primate systematic assessments. In fact there is considerable evidence that, being readily recognized as of functional (locomotor) significance, these features have actually been avoided by primate systematists.

In any case, when the individual proportions of the body are examined one by one (all that has been possible until now), they provide the functional, not the systematic, result; it is only the multivariate comparison, which includes the new information about patterns of variances and covariances among the bodily proportions, that gives the new, taxonomic picture.

Presumably, therefore, the correspondences obtaining between these multivariate studies of overall bodily proportions and those stemming from general primate systematics must result from the fact that, whether or not dimensions of individual anatomical parts reflect the functions of those parts, the addition of many such different parts provides the information that results in the systematic association. In reflecting a totality of different functions (for the limb girdles, the limbs themselves, the trunk, the head, the neck, and so on), the multivariate statistical approach (while allowing for correlation and avoiding, therefore, duplication) provides as good an estimate as that obtained from the intuitive addition of separate bits of information in the assessments normally arrived at by primate systematists. In fact, this methodology actually provides a far better estimate than that arrived at by classical primate systematics, given that when the latter differs from the biomolecular results, it is the biomolecular result that is confirmed.

Whatever the ultimate rationale for these results, the findings are most encouraging for the analysis of fossils because they suggest that whenever it is possible to add together, by the multivariate statistical approach or its equivalent, many items of information from many restricted anatomical regions of fossils, and even if only skeletal tissue is represented, there is real hope for a good estimate of systematic position.

But it is also clear that overall assessments of either systematic position or behavioral pattern for fossils are problematical if they are based on studies of single individual postcranial bones, joints, or single functional complexes alone. In our present state of knowledge, investigations of such anatomically localized postcranial fragments seem generally to result in some sketchy first approximation to "resultant or average biomechanical situation in the given anatomical region."

Applications to fossils

Conventional studies of australopithecines

For some time after their first discovery there was a great deal of controversy about those fossils from Africa ultimately designated australopithecines; some workers assessed them as more related to the living apes, others as more closely linked with man. For many years now, however, the general consensus has been that these fossils are very close to the human lineage and that particular subgroups (variously known as *Australopithecus africanus*,

Homo africanus, H. habilis) are direct human ancestors. Others (the robust australopithecines) are generally thought to be sidelines that are a little way from a direct line to man. Most of the primary evidence stems from studies of crania, jaws, and teeth and depends upon the notion that these particular anatomical areas provide information relating fairly directly to the phylogenetic relationships of primates.

Somewhat more recently, information has started to flow from a series of studies of postcranial fragments of australopithecines. The previous section has indicated that in studies of such fragments it is becoming more generally recognized that they speak less directly to phylogenetics, although sometimes the studies have been interpreted in that way. Most workers believe now that study of such fragments tells more about aspects of the behaviors that "shaped" (in both evolutionary and developmental senses, of course) these particular anatomical parts. Assessments of the possible behaviors of the australopithecines have therefore been attempted, but in the main the results of these studies have been read as confirming the phylogenetic speculations advanced on the basis of the cranial and dental evidence. For example, earlier studies of the australopithecine pelvis seem to suggest that this is a pelvis involved in bipedal locomotion. And although there is some slight disagreement as to how similar to man's locomotion that may have been, there is general agreement that what we are assessing here is indeed a line leading to the evolution of human bipedality. Similarly, initial study of a series of hand bones seems to suggest rather clearly that the hands of at least some of the australopithecines are essentially similar to the hands of man, and that in viewing these fragments we are assessing information that speaks directly to the evolution of the free forelimb of man. A third series of studies of the evolution of postcranial functions in the australopithecines that seems to have generally stamped these creatures as similar to man is on the foot. A major part of the foot of *Homo habilis* discovered at Olduvai has been examined, articulated, reconstructed, and pronounced to be the foot of a creature that is clearly bipedal; for this reason it is said to be a human ancestor. Thus we can see that although the method of study of the postcranial fragments has sometimes been slightly different from that of the crania and jaws (although not entirely so, as some of the cranial features have also been used to support behavioral arguments, for instance about bipedality), the overall opinion remains the same: that these creatures are closely involved in human ancestry and that some of them, the gracile australopithecines, are directly ancestral to man.

On the other hand, most of these studies have been carried out using man as the model for comparison; the idea that the relationship was indeed to man was the underlying notion that the studies purport to support. But the fossil fragments should also be viewed against the background of the diversity of locomotor patterns that are known among extant nonhuman primates. Possibly at almost all times during the evolution of the primates there have been species variously adapted for quadrupedal running, leap-

143

ing, and climbing in the trees, and in many of these it is likely that specializations with emphases on the hindlimb (e.g., such as is involved in extensive leaping: bush babies, colobus monkeys) and on the forelimb (e.g., in acrobatic climbing activities: woolly monkeys, orangutans) have broadened the diversity of quadrupedal forms into the complex arrangements described in the previous section. For it must be from one or another part of this diverse quadrupedal mosaic that human bipedalism has been derived.

Such a series of comparisons is rarely attempted, it being commonplace for investigators to compare the australopithecines only with living man and African apes. Even the inclusion of pongids in the comparisons is usually either to confirm resemblances to man or to deny similarities to nonhuman species. It is somewhat less often that investigators make comparisons with a wide spectrum of primate species in order to determine relative degrees of convergence, parallelism, and divergence.

The questions we are interested in asking here about any postcranial fragment of the australopithecines stem from the discussion of the previous sections and are the following: to what extent does the morphology of the australopithecine fragments indicate (*a*) close *functional* similarity with extant man (i.e., similarly bipedal), or (*b*) some functional similarities with any of a wide diversity of essentially quadrupedal forms as represented today by the living nonhuman primates, or (*c*) a pattern of functional associations that point to intermediacy between man and one or another part of the nonhuman matrix, or even (a question rather less frequently asked) (*d*) a pattern of functional associations that may be unique to themselves. Answers to any of these questions would provide useful and interesting data for primate evolution, although we must bear in mind that, for australopithecines, the first possibility is generally believed to be the case.

New studies of australopithecines

The application of new methods to this particular taxonomic group is now suggesting a picture that is rather different from the conventional one. New studies do not deny that the australopithecines bear many resemblances to man that may betoken functional features in the australopithecines—some forms of bipedality, for instance, and some abilities with a free forelimb— but these studies are also suggesting additional ideas. Thus, other similarities of the australopithecines include features somewhat reminiscent of those of arboreal apes and monkeys and may reflect quadrupedal and arboreal abilities such as are not possessed by man today. Most important of all, information about architectural features or combinations of features actually renders the australopithecines uniquely different from all of the living hominoids, and these differences are every bit as great as those already separating man from the African apes.

It is possible that such findings may be referring to some mode of behavior of australopithecines that is totally different from anything that we see today or, indeed, have so far guessed at. It is more likely, however, that the morphological uniqueness of the australopithecines actually rests, not in a totally unique behavior, but rather in a combination of activities, no one of which is special by itself but of which the combination in a single animal is truly unique. Thus, these creatures may have been capable of a form of bipedality far more efficient and habitual than that of any ape at the present day, combined with a form of quadrupedalism, perhaps including abilities in a climbing environment, far more sophisticated than that of which man is capable at the present time.

The various studies that have been performed allow us to go into these matters in considerable detail. Some of the Olduvai hand bones, for instance, seem to relate to abilities for grasping with power somewhat reminiscent of the orangutan (though care is required here, as it is entirely possible that these hand bones do not form a single assemblage). One Olduvai ankle bone is undoubtedly quite unlike those of the present African apes and man and finds its closest morphological model with other fossil ankle bones from Africa that probably belong to other nonhuman primates of those eras. This fragment also finds some resemblance with an ankle bone of a living form that is principally arboreal: the orangutan. Even the remaining bones of the Olduvai foot may resemble man less than once was thought, because the foot bones of several of the apes can be rearticulated with arches, and when this is done they display the same curious features as are found in the rearticulated Olduvai foot. Studies of the pelvis show some features representing adaptation to upright posture and movement, but other features are clearly reminiscent of those of different ape pelves that may betoken their various quadrupedal and acrobatic activities. Taken as a whole, however, these postcranial studies seem to indicate a unique arrangement of australopithecine anatomy that denies the conventional assessments noted earlier.

Similarities of the fossils with extant primates are either in characteristics so basic that they can merely be said to be hominoid (i.e., similar to all apes and men), or in special characteristics that are mirrored in both bipedal and arboreal creatures. Presumably these indicate tentative functional similarities such as might be possessed by some intermediately sized hominoid form. These fossils may have done some of the things that arboreal animals do (for instance, acrobatic climbing and arboreal quadrupedality) but also enough other things (probably bipedality) whereby they are rendered unique in the frame of reference of present-day forms. There is certainly no evidence of functional similarity with the African apes, and no evidence of the kind of bipedality that is characteristic of modern man. Such a conclusion is rather speculative, although it is now based upon studies of a number of the anatomical regions.

Is there any other way to study these fossils? Is there any other information that we can bring to bear upon this matter of uniqueness and diversity?

It would seem that one of the best ways to do this would be through multivariate statistical analysis of all the data combined, as described in the previous section. Sets of perhaps twenty measurements each could be taken of each of twenty anatomical regions located upon available specimens of, say, forty genera of extant primates. This would certainly be a major study, and for all except the larger computers it might well occur that the number of measurements taken upon each complete skeleton could be so great as to exceed the capacity of the computer for some of the matrix manipulations that would be required. Another practical reason why we are a long way from such a study, however, is the coordination that would be required to obtain such an extensive data set from so many anatomical regions of the same specimens of so many genera of extant primates.

When it comes to the matter of trying to interpolate the various fossil fragments, they would have to be combined as though they presented information about the approximate mean values that might be obtained for the fossil genera. Inevitably, one would have to pool data from fossil remnants that might well, in truth, belong to separate species, or perhaps even separate genera. However, this last limitation is not new and is with us all the time. The real problem is the immensity of the study that would be required to tackle all anatomical regions in an equivalent way.

Thus it is that we must look for other ways of investigating the problem. Many of the new ideas carry less weight because they are expressed through a relatively new technology that is not easily understood and not readily accessible to those who do not themselves utilize it. Attempts have been made to provide appropriate visual comparisons of some of the individual bones of the australopithecines, and these seem to confirm that there are aspects of bony structure that have not generally been taken into account in their assessment. Classical study of, for instance, the scapula, the upper and lower ends of the humerus, and the upper ends of the radius and ulna has suggested to some workers that these fragments are more like those of man than any ape; other studies of the pelvis, upper end of femur, upper end of tibia, lower end of tibia, talus, and some foot bones have been similarly assessed. Yet a simple visual comparison of differences in proportion between upper and lower limb articular surfaces in the apes, man, and the fossils shows most convincingly that human lower limb articular surfaces are large in comparison with upper limb articular surfaces; this presumably befits their bipedal status whereby the lower limb takes most of the weight. This same visual comparison reveals that ape upper and lower limb articular surfaces have a more nearly equal relationship than is the case in man, and this presumably relates to the more frequent quadrupedal habitus of these creatures. It is of extreme interest that in such a set of comparisons the information that is available for the australopithecine fossils shows that they resemble the apes (and among the apes, the orangutan) more closely than they do man (fig. 33). This fact should be set alongside the comment of Richard Leakey, who reports that "preliminary indications point to a relatively short lower limb and a longer forelimb" for *Australopithecus* and suggests that this raises the doubt as to

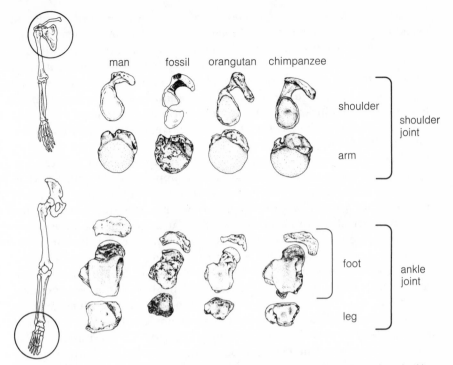

Figure 33. A visual comparison of the shoulder (scapular and humeral joint surfaces) with the ankle (lower end of tibia, ankle bone [talus] and foot bone [navicular]) for man, *Australopithecus*, orangutan, and chimpanzee. The diagrams are scaled so that the shoulder fragments are the same size. As a result, the lower limb fragments for man are much larger (lower limbs bear all the weight in man). Lower limb fragments for the two apes are smaller (both upper and lower limbs in the apes bear the weight of the body). The relative proportions for the fossil accord more closely with the apes, and especially the arboreal orangutan, than they do with man. Of course, while the specimens for the living forms are from single individuals, those for the fossils are not; such a finding could be due to the accident of having shoulder fragments from large fossil specimens and ankle fragments from small ones. However, comparison of the relative proportions of many different fragments for the fossils throughout the upper and lower limbs confirms this general picture.

"whether the australopithecine pattern of bipedal adaptation really reflects a transitional phase" with man. One can only come to the conclusion that, however able these animals were at bipedality, they were also convincing quadrupeds, and this is a feat denied to man today (his ontogenetic quadrupedal stage is inefficient in the extreme).

The meld, or otherwise, with earlier investigations

A major criticism that can be made about these ideas relates to the fact that the number of anatomical regions and the number of fossils actually examined with these new techniques is too limited to convert most paleoanthropologists. Most workers would say that the fossil record of human evolution is now too complete and too well studied for multivariate analyses of less than a dozen isolated fossil bones and a few additional studies to change many minds. Yet although there have indeed been a great many papers published about the australopithecines in the years since their first discoveries, even the entire output of the twentieth-century fossil hunters has not provided an overly large number of useful fragments for study.

It has been only in the last two or three years that really large and numerous finds have been made (e.g., Richard Leakey at East Turkana, Clark Howell in the Omo, Mary Leakey at Laetolil, Johanson and Taieb in Ethiopia), and these new discoveries do not support the conventional view. In fact, so far as they suggest that man must be far older than previously realized, they actually support the new views that have stemmed from the small number of multivariate studies of the australopithecine finds previously available for study. Thus, just as a different form of behavior postulated for australopithecines denies them a close link with the human lineage so do (1) the finding, at East Turkana, of an old skull at approximately two million years that is not necessarily *Homo* but that has a much bigger cranial capacity at 800 cc than is usual for one-million-year australopithecine skulls at 400–500 cc, (2) the recovery of a talus also from East Turkana that is both much older than the australopithecine talus from Olduvai and also far more like man than the Olduvai specimen, (3) the discovery of a very old skull, about 3.8 million years, that seems to be *Homo* from Laetolil, and (4) the existence of a humeral fragment from Kanapoi that is almost five million years old yet is indistinguishable in shape from many modern human humeri (younger australopithecine humeri are vastly different from modern man's). At the same time, however, we hear every day of new fossil specimens, some of which are much more like man than previously known australopithecine specimens, yet some of which, at the same time, are as old as or even far older than many australopithecine specimens. The original australopithecines had to have been a long way from the lineage leading to man, and the human lineage itself must be much older than generally recognized. Conventional wisdom would have the genus *Homo* less than a million years old and a link with some ape ancestor at three million, five million, or perhaps eight million years (all guesses put forward in the last decade).

However, although, prior to the present spurt of fossil finding, the actual number of fossils known was rather small, the total number of investigations performed upon those fossils and reported is voluminous. It includes many older studies of jaws, teeth, and crania, and in the main it is upon these that the conventional picture of the australopithecines is based. To what degree do the results of these studies actually meld with, or oppose, the new views? Do they, in truth, negate the new ideas?

There are good reasons to reexamine them. It is quite possible that the earlier controversies drove the earlier participants into extreme, perhaps untenable, positions. In the uproar, at that time, as to whether or not these creatures were truly men or apes, the *opinion* that they were men won the day. This may well have resulted not only in the defeat of the contrary *opinion* but also in the burying of that part of the *data* upon which the contrary opinion was based. If so, it should be possible to unearth this other part of the evidence. A reassessment could then be made with the possibility in mind that the australopithecines might be, not like either African ape or man, and certainly not intermediate, but something uniquely different from both. Let me present a few examples.

The various controversies over the shapes and sizes of the different australopithecine teeth are a case in point. Although many studies have been carried out, the general consensus is that the evidence from these teeth clearly supports their manlike status.

What, however, are the facts? Certain studies show that in some features (incisors, canines, and lower first premolars) the australopithecines are manlike, and these have been emphasized. But in other features (remaining premolars and molars), studies show that they are apelike. Assessment, with hindsight, of some of the results (e.g., for the milk canine) shows that some features are neither manlike nor apelike, but different from each. In the light of the foregoing discussion of the postcranial fragments, the totality of these older results is not incompatible with the idea that these creatures possessed a combination of dental features rendering them unique.

Another controversy results from the various studies of the basicranial axis, a feature of the base of the skull. The fact that the angle of the forepart of this axis in the australopithecines is markedly similar to that in man has been seized upon in many prior arguments. The fact that the angle of the latter part of the basicranial axis in the fossils is markedly similar to those of apes has been neglected. Recent restudy of this area shows that in combination these characters render the fossils unique.

Yet another example includes the facial area and its contained infraorbital foramina. The fact that there is only a single infraorbital foramen in both man and the fossils is well publicized. The other part of the evidence is that in the position of the foramina on the face the fossils are much more like the apes. Taking these two facts together and with others which they mirror, the fossils thus exhibit still further anatomical arrangements that render them unique.

One final example that may be cited includes a recent new study of the back region of the skull. This shows that the position of the occipital condyles, the joint surface that allows movement of the head upon the neck, is, in the fossils, convincingly apelike (*pace* descriptions worded in such a way as to suggest the possibility that the opposite is true), but this feature is combined with an angulation of the condyles upon the skull base that is markedly human. These facts may possibly relate to upright posture in a creature with an apelike skull. Once again, therefore, the new theory is supported.

Australopithecines, man, and the evolution of locomotor function

The foregoing are the end products of a fairly large number of studies involving many different anatomical regions spread over the whole of the skeleton (skull, shoulder, elbow, hand, pelvis, hip, knee, ankle, and foot). They are provided mostly by a series of multivariate statistical procedures that are capable of revealing facets of information that are hidden from more usual visual inspection. At the same time they are consonant with a series of studies that utilize visual inspection as the primary method but that view the fragments in a manner not usually attempted. The results are generally corroborative of one another when seen separately and independently. They continue to provide the same story when attempts are made to "add" them together (albeit, by techniques that can, at this stage, only be somewhat speculative) in order to try to obtain an overall view. They are even consistent with older studies where these are reevaluated to include all aspects of the data.

The result is the following: in terms of morphology, the various australopithecines, viewed as a single group at the higher taxonomic level, are generally more similar to one another than any individual specimen is to any living primate. They are uniquely different from any living form to a degree comparable at least to the differences among living genera. The manner in which they are similar to living hominoids is such that it either is applicable to all living hominoids or displays special morphological resemblances to arboreal species. In few ways are they more similar to either man or the terrestrial African apes than these latter are to each other.

The meaning of this result is difficult to disentangle. It does not rest upon genetic propinquity, as it is surely clear that genetically, man, the African apes, and presumably the australopithecines are all far closer to one another than are any of them to living arboreal hominoids. Because of the interpretations that can be made from functional anatomy, it is far more likely that the patterns of uniqueness and diversity that have been uncovered relate to the biomechanical resultant of locomotion and related behaviors.

Accordingly, the more speculative deductions these results speak to are the following. The australopithecines, in displaying uniqueness in morphology, may likewise have been functionally unique from all living hominoids. This surely means that they were not arboreal in the different manners of the Asiatic apes; they were not terrestrial in the knuckle-walking mode of the African apes; they were not solely bipedal like man. They therefore displayed either a totally new and unknown manner of locomotion, which would be totally unique and which we will judge rather unlikely, or they display such a mixture of locomotor abilities, therefore anatomical adaptations, and therefore bony morphologies, as to be rendered unique through being a mixture of different intermediates.

The modes in which they are similar to man indicate propensities for a type of bipedality. But the ways in which they are similar to arboreal apes may well also indicate abilities for quadrupedal movement, presumably in an arboreal environment and with acrobatic climbing abilities such as are reminiscent of all apes when they are in an arboreal milieu or, just possibly, a clifflike terrain.

Let us be clear that the nature of these suggestions is not merely an extension of human capabilities. Man can climb using methods like those of apes, not like those of monkeys. But his abilities to live in a climbing setting are almost nonexistent. Likewise man can, and does when an infant, move on all four limbs, but in fact his quadrupedal facility is zero. Man's true abilities in both these directions cannot be said by anyone to be other than a total liability in any conceivable life framework where they might be required. Such was presumably not the case with *Australopithecus,* although we are not able to disentangle the time relationships of these abilities. *Australopithecus* may display these morphologies because it had both sets of abilities or because, while performing the one as a new acquisition, it had not yet lost the hallmarks of the other, older, mode.

Finally, we may make the further speculation as to what all this means for human evolution and the position of the australopithecines within it. It is still possible that these results are consonant with australopithecines as close to the pathway of the evolution of bipedality as expressed in the evolution of man. This is the standard view. If true, however, it suggests that bipedality arose by some markedly complicated process involving genetic intermediates that are very much unlike man and that this all occurred in an extremely short period of time. The results are actually far more consonant with the simpler idea that *human* bipedality was not the only experiment in this direction. The australopithecines may well be displaying for us another experiment, and one that failed. The reasons why this may have happened are speculative in the extreme and unnecessary to consider here.

One may expect that Leakey and others will find more evidence of earlier forms that are considerably more human in all respects. On present evidence, these forms would be more like man than are the australopithecines, even though the latter must also have existed at earlier periods of time. Certainly, the numbers of fossil remnants that are now appearing through the work of many investigators in Africa would yield a great deal of information if compared with living species by the methods used in this essay. We may well have to accept that human bipedality is far older than previously guessed, and that australopithecine locomotion included one or more unsuccessful parallel experiments. We may well have to accept that it is rather unlikely that any of the australopithecines, including "*Homo habilis,*" can have had any direct phylogenetic link with the genus *Homo.*

Broader implications for human evolution

All of this makes us wonder about the usual presentation of human evolution in encyclopedias and popular publications, where not only are the australopithecines described as being of known bodily size and shape but, in addition, such characteristics as bipedality, tool using, and even facial features are confidently (and nonscientifically) reconstructed.

There is now a rather strong body of information relegating the conventional australopithecines to a side role in human evolution. This raises a series of further fascinating possibilities. *First,* it is rather likely that *Homo* as a genus has existed an order of magnitude longer than previously guessed (five million years rather than half a million). He must surely have been contemporaneous with the australopithecines as we now know them, and he may have extended back considerably farther. Such a time span is so much greater than that currently believed to be the case that it allows a very much longer period for the psychosocial evolution of the genus. It is possible, therefore, that those features of man in which he differs most markedly from animals—behavioral, cultural, intellectual, and creative— may depend rather less upon prior social behavior in his animal forebears and much more upon this extra amount of evolutionary time.

Second, the simple abilities of man that relate to bipedality and a free forelimb may also have existed for longer than we had previously thought. This in turn almost certainly means that these simple biological features may have evolved not once, not even twice, but perhaps several times. Such a radiation would closely resemble what zoologists generally recognize in evolution as spread into a new adaptive zone or a new niche. It would also inevitably mean, however, that in this new adaptive zone, *Homo* as we know him at the present time may have been the only *successful* evolutionary experiment along these lines.

Finally, these ideas also mean that the evolution of the various australopithecines may be a most interesting separate set of problems in their own right. What were the actual behaviors of the various creatures that made up this particular genus? What were their relationships with the human genus? They presumably represent some of the experiments that failed. We may be able to see more clearly the flowering (and withering) of this entire group of creatures once we are able to remove from our minds the idea of the australopithecines as direct human ancestors.

It is especially fascinating that the new investigative methods described here have proved capable of forecasting the situation as confirmed by the new fossil finds. They are thus to be reckoned as a set of very powerful tools that have been added to the armamentarium of the evolutionary morphologist. Findings resulting from the application of such methods, once they have been thoroughly checked, should not lightly be discarded even if they are at some variance with the conventional wisdom. Indeed, such controversial results may well be the source of more thoughtful assessments of human evolution and may help us to escape from the bonds that traditional thinking sometimes lays upon us.

* * *

The best single account of the traditional story of human evolution is still Sir Wilfred Le Gros Clark's *The Antecedents of Man* (Edinburgh: Edinburgh University Press, 1959). However, descriptions including conventional studies of some of the newer fossil materials may be obtained from three recent books: *Primate Evolution: An Introduction to Man's Place in Nature* by Elwyn Simons, *The Ascent of Man: An Introduction to Human Evolution* by David Pilbeam, and *The Evolution of Primate Behavior* by Alison Jolly (all New York: Macmillan Publishing Company, 1972).

Some of the earliest recognition that there might be new methods and new insights to be obtained in primate evolution may be obtained from *The Social Life of Monkeys and Apes* (1932) and *Functional Affinities of Man, Monkeys, and Apes* (1933), both by Solly Zuckerman (London: Kegan Paul, Trench, Trubner & Co.). More recent doubts about the conventional story of human evolution are expressed in *Form and Pattern in Human Evolution: Some Mathematical, Physical, and Engineering Approaches* (1973) and *Uniqueness and Diversity in Human Evolution: Morphometric Studies of Australopithecines* (1975), both by Charles Oxnard (Chicago: University of Chicago Press).

The most recent fossil discoveries from Africa that support the new ideas about human evolution have not yet appeared in book form but may be read in the original in recent numbers of *Nature* (London) and in popular form in recent numbers of the *National Geographic* magazine.

NOTE TO THE READER

The science discussed here by Professor Oxnard is based upon techniques of measurement never dreamed of by the authors of *GBWW*. Measurement itself is discussed, however, in references listed under Chapter 52 of the *Syntopicon*, MATHEMATICS, Topic 5a, and under Chapter 76, QUANTITY, Topic 6b. It would be instructive also to look at the references in Chapter 10, CHANGE, especially Topic 8, which deals with changes of size, and Topic 9b, where changes of quality that come about with the vital alterations familiar in biology are discussed.

In addition, see Chapter 24, EVOLUTION, Topic 1, where references will be found to passages in the Great Books that discuss the classification of animals; see also, in the same chapter, Topic 3a, which considers heredity, the inheritance of acquired characteristics, and the use and disuse of parts; Topic 6a, which talks about the significance of fossil remains; and Topic 6c, which says something about comparative anatomy.

Professor Oxnard's article deals at length with the difficulties of arriving at hypotheses adequate to explain the data his measurements provide. In this connection the passages indicated in Chapter 36, HYPOTHESIS, under Topic 4, would be interesting to look up. So would those in Chapter 51, MAN, under Topic 8c, where man is discussed as a natural variation from other forms of animal life.

The Idea of a Modern Museum

Roy McMullen

American-born, Roy McMullen has lived in Paris since the end of World War II and has acquired an extensive knowledge of contemporary European culture. A journalist of distinction, he has written widely on music, the visual arts, and literature for such publications as the Paris *International Herald Tribune, Saturday Review, Horizon, Time, Art News, High Fidelity, The American Scholar, Connaissance des Arts,* and *Réalités.* He has also done two documentary films on twentieth-century painting and a television show, "Art for Tomorrow," dealing with modern art, science, and technology, with Walter Cronkite (CBS, 1969).

Since 1963 Mr. McMullen has been a consultant on the fine arts for the *Encyclopaedia Britannica* and served on the planning board for the new 15th edition of that work. To this he also contributed feature articles on Braque; Chagall; Style in the Arts; J.-L. David; Léger; Kandinsky; Primitive, Folk, and Popular Arts; Matisse; and Rouault. He is the author of *Art, Affluence, and Alienation* (1968) and of separate volumes on the Mona Lisa, on Chagall, and on Whistler. In preparation is *Degas: A Biography.* A previous article on "Music, Painting, and Sculpture" by Mr. McMullen appeared in *The Great Ideas Today, 1967.* He is married to the French abstract painter Simone Bellet.

M uch of our terminology for discussions of culture is old, unspecific, and notoriously liable, like Polonius, to produce what information theorists call noise. We need a filter to get useful signals out of the semantic buzz emitted by the word *art,* for instance, or by *culture* itself. There are some words, however, which have lost their meaning through shrinkage rather than from any expansion of this kind. *Museum* is a case in point. Although old, it can almost be said to have reversed the normal lexical aging process and hence to be suffering today from an excess of exactitude, a senile dearth of overtones.

In classical Greece a museum, or *mouseion,* was at first simply a seat, or haunt, of the Muses, which were not yet sharply differentiated deities assigned to particular arts and sciences. The best known of such dedicated places was the one on Mount Helicon that was marked by a temple and a grove, where a theater existed and numerous statues were set about. During the Hellenistic era such installations were secularized without losing their comprehensiveness. Accounts of the celebrated Mouseion of Alexandria, created around 300 B.C. by the Ptolemies, suggest a cross between an English university and an American think tank; it included faculties of literature, mathematics, astronomy, and medicine, plus a library, a botanical garden, a lecture hall, colonnaded walks for peripatetics, a combined restaurant and commons room, and even a menagerie. The large connotations of the term survived into the Renaissance; as late as 1554 the *Lexicon-Graeco-Latinum* of French scholar Guillaume Budé could still define a museum, with magnificent imprecision, as a place "where one engages oneself in noble disciplines." By that date, however, the word, or one of its vernacular derivatives, was already being used to mean a collection of aesthetic, scientific, historical, or freakish objects installed in a special room or building, and soon this new, narrow sense was dominant. The broad Greek connotations were largely forgotten.

This loss of meaning is regrettable. On the one hand, it tends to limit both lay and professional notions of the possible activities of whatever happens to call itself a museum. (For example, Gertrude Stein once grumbled that the New York Museum of Modern Art was a contradiction; it could be a museum or be modern, she felt, but not both. And Henry James, in 1907, rightly observed that the New York Metropolitan Museum of Art had money "for *all* the most exquisite things except creation.")[1] On the other hand, we are left with no convenient word, nothing with the right historical resonance, for an enterprise which, although it may call itself an institute or, more fashionably, a center, is actually an approximation of the Greek place dedicated to the Muses in general.

A number of relatively new institutions of this latter sort are now functioning in Europe and the United States. Some are devoted to the performing arts; others are the results of an expansion of the traditional aims of public galleries of painting and sculpture. The most recent, however, and for many people easily the most spectacular and controversial, is the Centre National d'Art et de Culture Georges Pompidou, which opened officially in Paris on January 31, 1977, and which Parisians usually refer to as the Centre Beaubourg, or simply Beaubourg, because of the name of the Right Bank square on which it stands.

Although it is thoroughly up-to-date and is not dedicated to all the Muses that were favored by its remote ancestors, the Centre Beaubourg can be called Greek—generously inclusive, that is—in its conception and organization. Its steel, glass, and concrete building, a sizable part of which is below ground, shelters four major components, or subinstitutions: (1) the Musée National d'Art Moderne, which stages temporary shows of painting, sculpture, and allied arts in addition to presenting a permanent collection; (2) the Bibliothèque Publique d'Information, which provides Paris with a needed large library open, unlike the Bibliothèque Nationale, to everybody; (3) the Institut de Recherche et Coordination Acoustique/Musique, which groups composers, performers, scientists, and technologists under one roof for an analysis of new musical possibilities; and (4) the Centre de Création Industrielle, which studies and invents new approaches to industrial design, visual communication, dress, architecture, town planning, and transportation. Helping to make the whole complex work as intended are meeting halls, reading rooms, a film library, a theater, a restaurant, computers, and a staff recruited from many countries besides France.

In short, a remarkable cultural undertaking. The Beaubourg is not, of course, functioning in a climate of academic detachment. It is a long way from being ripe for the judgment of history, and it is definitely not to everyone's taste today. Although it has been praised extravagantly as a "factory for dreams" and a "cathedral of modern art," it has been derided, even more extravagantly, as "the Beaubourg folly," a cultural "supermarket," and "the Pompidoleum." Both the architecture and the program strike many sensitive people, who are not necessarily artistic reactionaries, as being deliberately provocative—a revival of the tiresome old modernist campaign to shock the bourgeoisie. But one can argue that the violent reactions, whatever the supposedly judicious future may decide about them, are at least evidence of an innovation in museology that is touching the quick of our culture and that is consequently worth examining with as much historical perspective and as much serenity as can be mustered.

The rest of this article will attempt such an examination. It will also use the Centre Beaubourg, occasionally along with somewhat analogous institutions in the United States and Europe, to focus a look at a few of the problems implicit in the whole idea of a modern museum — or *mouseion*, for here the word *museum*, given the nature of Beaubourg, will have to carry both its usual and its ancient senses.

An act of the sovereign

Who, or what, should create museums? Oversimplifying only slightly, one can say that the average American is likely to give an Adam Smith sort of answer, whereas the average Frenchman is likely to give a Louis XIV sort.

Granted, in the United States today there appears to be a growing inclination to leave museum-making to universities, municipalities, federal agencies, and other public bodies. But a reliance on private initiative and philanthropy, coupled perhaps with an appeal for local or national government help after a project is launched, can still be called the traditional American approach, and it can be credited with an impressive list of achievements. The Smithsonian Institution, for example, which since its foundation in 1846 has grown into a vast, many-faceted descendant of the Mouseion of Alexandria, owes its existence to an unexpected bequest from a pro-American English scientist, James Smithson. The Metropolitan, now the greatest museum, in the art-gallery sense, in the hemisphere, was created in 1870 by a group of New York businessmen motivated by civic pride, social ambition, and elitist tastes — with perhaps a hope for remission, through art, of their sins. An extraordinary gift from Andrew W. Mellon, who combined a passion for paintings with his talent for banking and industry, made possible the National Gallery of Art in Washington, D.C., which opened in 1941 and rapidly expanded into a rival of the Metropolitan.

Moving closer to the subject of Beaubourg, one can cite the success of the American donor system in the field of galleries devoted primarily to contemporary painting and sculpture. The pioneer and now almost venerable Museum of Modern Art, which dates back to 1929, owes enough to the vision and money of Mrs. John D. Rockefeller, Jr., to have been referred to, not inappropriately, by Nelson A. Rockefeller as "Mother's museum." Other New York avant-garde institutions with a strongly personal history are the Whitney Museum of American Art, which was created in 1931 by the heiress Gertrude Vanderbilt Whitney, and the Guggenheim museum, which opened in 1939 with the Solomon R. Guggenheim private collection of abstract paintings as a nucleus. The Hirshhorn Museum and Sculpture Garden in Washington, D.C., which was opened in 1974 (and which, like the National Gallery, is officially a part of the Smithsonian Institution), offers monumental proof of the continuing vitality of the tradition. Here the government provided the housing, but a single private citizen, uranium millionaire Joseph H. Hirshhorn, provided the some four thousand paintings and two thousand pieces of sculpture.

In France, too, there are museums founded by private initiative. Some, like their American counterparts, are the results of the generosity, or the status-seeking, of wealthy collectors; others are the creations of associations interested in a particular art, craft, or science; and some are shrines donated by artists or their heirs. None, however, is anywhere near the size of the Metropolitan, the Washington National Gallery, or the New York MOMA; and nearly all, along with most of the French municipal and provincial galleries, are part of the network of roughly nine hundred *musées nationaux, musées classés,* and *musées contrôlés* administered by a central state authority, the *Direction des Musées de France,* which is itself controlled by the minister, or the secretary of state, for cultural affairs. In sum, private initiative is merely incidental in the system, which assumes that museums are the business of the national government, in general, and more specifically that the creation of a really important museum is an act of the sovereign (or an appropriation of the outcome of such an act, which comes to the same thing). The system has obvious political and emotional roots in a long history of authoritarianism, from monarchism through Bonapartism to Gaullism. It reflects the same habit of mind that has made court styles dominant in French furniture production. And it has been strengthened by a functionarism that has engendered, particularly since the French Revolution and the First Empire, an almost unbelievable centralization. France, although composed of culturally distinct, naturally centrifugal regions (and partly for that very reason), is the exact opposite of a federal state.

In our context the Louvre, of course, comes first to mind. Although opened by the National Convention in 1793, in the midst of the Revolution, it qualifies easily as an act of the sovereign: it was conceived under Louis XVI, its building is an old royal palace, and the core of its contents is the old royal collection. But the Louvre is not alone in its odor of monarchism. The palaces of Versailles, Fontainebleau, and Compiègne are now museums. The zoo, botanical garden, and scientific collections of the former Jardin du Roi, in Paris, now constitute the Muséum National d'Histoire Naturelle. The recently renovated Musée des Antiquités Nationales, which occupies the chateau of Saint-Germain-en-Laye and offers one of the finest collections of prehistoric art and artifacts to be seen anywhere, was one of Napoleon III's happier inspirations. Even the Musée National d'Art Moderne that is now in the Centre Beaubourg is a continuation of the defunct Musée du Luxembourg, which was opened on the Paris Left Bank by Louis

XVIII as a sort of testing place for the admission of works to the Louvre
—and became the world's first museum devoted exclusively to contemporary art.

To be appreciated fully for what it is, the Centre Beaubourg as a whole
has to be seen in this peculiarly French perspective. It, too, in ways difficult
to imagine for an American accustomed to private-initiative museums, is a
product of the massive intervention of a centralized government in cultural
affairs. It, too, with proper allowances for the difference (which is not
immense) between French monarchism and French republicanism, can be
described as an act of the sovereign, and as a quite arbitrary act. In brief,
it is a monument, as its official name indicates, to the rule of Georges
Pompidou, president of the republic from June 1969 until his death in
April 1974. Beaubourg without Pompidou is as inconceivable as Versailles
without Louis XIV.

Pompidou was an unusual politician; in fact, for much of his adult life he
was not a career politician at all. Like Jean-Paul Sartre and many other
eminent Frenchmen, he was a graduate of the École Normale Supérieure,
the most prestigious of the French colleges that concentrate on the humanities; and he was always—paradoxically, in view of the rest of his personality
—something of a literary intellectual, fond especially of poetry. After a
period as a teacher, he joined Charles de Gaulle's personal staff and rapidly
became one of the general's principal advisers. He continued his rise by
entering the Rothschild Bank in Paris and becoming one of its directors.
When he was appointed premier in 1962, he had never run for office, and
although later elected to the National Assembly and finally to the presidency, he never developed an excessive concern for majority opinions. He
liked automobiles, airplanes, expressways, computers, trade centers, big
cities, big business—the second half of the twentieth century in general.
Helped by an unprecedented French growth rate, he gave the Gaullist
politique de grandeur a strongly economic orientation and encouraged the
first important urban renewal Paris had undergone since the reign of
Napoleon III. Aided by his wife, Claude, he collected modern art with
discernment and boldly used it to alter the neoclassical atmosphere of the
presidential apartment in the Elysée Palace. Given his tastes, his ambitions
for France, and the fact that he had a mostly docile parliament, a project
like the Centre Beaubourg was almost inevitable.

The idea emerged in private conversations immediately after the presidential elections of 1969. By December of that year it was firm enough for
Pompidou to inform the Ministry for Cultural Affairs that the new institutions should include "not only a vast museum for painting and sculpture"
but also some "special installations" for music, films, books, and the theater.
Soon he was stressing the need to involve living artists. "My ardent wish,"
he announced, "is that Paris should possess a cultural center that is at once
a museum and a center of creation." To make certain that the project would
not be hampered by considerations of economy he specified that construc-

tion costs must be, in finance ministry language, *hors enveloppe*—outside the regular state budget for culture.

A planning group was formed under the chairmanship of Sébastien Loste, a brilliant young technocrat in the Ministry for Cultural Affairs. Robert Bordaz, an able administrator who had been the director of the state-owned radio and television network and more recently the government commissioner for the French section of the Montreal world's fair, was named president of the center for the period of its realization. Under the supervision of these two men and of Pompidou himself, the "ardent wish" began to take shape with little of the delay and fumbling common to big cultural enterprises. The state purchased, for 99 million francs (about $20 million), the Beaubourg site from the city of Paris. By the spring of 1972 the bulldozers were at work. Soon the four main departments were being organized and were being authorized to function in a dispersed fashion, without waiting for the completion of the building. (The art museum and the industrial-design department had only to modify already existing structures.) Supporters of the project had reasons for alarm in the summer of 1974, after the death of Pompidou, for the new president of the republic, Valéry Giscard d'Estaing, had a reputation for being unenthusiastic about modern architecture and about modern art in general. But by that time things were too far advanced for any serious thought of stopping them. And so, in the winter of 1974–75, a largely "Pompidolien" measure giving the undertaking its final legal form was voted by the National Assembly and the Senate and signed by Giscard d'Estaing.

This law, as elaborated by a decree of application in 1976, gives Beaubourg the status of a government-subsidized "public establishment" endowed with a "legal standing and financial automomy" and organized ostensibly as a reduced replica of the Fifth French Republic—a cultural state within the Gaullist state. A president, named for a renewable term of three years and invested with a good deal of both policymaking and executive power, runs the establishment. He is assisted by a Conseil de Direction, a sort of cabinet or council of ministers, whose members include notably the heads of the art museum, the library, the musical-research institute, and the industrial-design department. A twenty-seven-man Conseil d'Orientation plays the part of a parliament—without legislative power, however. Five of the members represent the minister for cultural affairs, three the National Assembly, three the Senate, two the city of Paris and its suburbs, and three the minister of education, the state secretary for universities, and the minister for industry and research. Eight are representatives-at-large, not necessarily French, who are chosen by the minister for cultural affairs because of their special competences in fields related to Beaubourg, and the remaining three are elected by the Beaubourg personnel.

Legally, the center has much of the independence of a private business firm, or of an American private-initiative museum like the New York Metropolitan. It can invest in other enterprises, accept contributions of capital from nongovernmental sources, acquire and exploit literary and artistic properties, patent an invention (a new industrial design, for instance), and in general engage in whatever commercial transactions are necessary for the accomplishment of its cultural mission. Its annual budget is prepared by the president, discussed by the Conseil d'Orientation, and finally approved by a vote of the Conseil de Direction. (The Bibliothèque Publique d'Information and the Institut de Recherche et Coordination Acoustique/Musique are given an extra measure of managerial and financial freedom by being defined as "associated," rather than fully integrated, parts of the complex.) Exhibitions, concerts, and other activities are decided on, according to scope, by the four departments separately or by the president and the Conseil de Direction. Broad policy decisions are made by the same executives with the help of advice from the Conseil d'Orientation.

A model arrangement, one might say at first glance. It combines many of the advantages of capitalism with those of socialism; it offers, in the Conseil de Direction and the Conseil d'Orientation, opportunities for the expression of a wide variety of cultural opinions. It bears, however, the marks of its origins as an act of the sovereign. The Conseil d'Orientation is after all merely a consultative assembly, and sixteen of its twenty-seven members are appointed by ministers, who are themselves appointed by the president of the republic. The four department heads are named by the minister for cultural affairs, and when they sit as the Conseil de Direction their decisions are subject to the approval of a government commissioner who attends all their sessions. The president of the center is named by a decree of the national Council of Ministers, and his budget, which of course involves a large state subsidy, is subject to acceptance by the minister for cultural affairs, the finance minister, and to a lesser degree the rest of the government. Thus the entire institution, although nominally independent, is in fact under the fairly immediate tutelage of ministers and ultimately under the control of the president of the republic. Every morning of his seven-year term of office the latter has the power, if he chooses to exercise it, to make the sun shine or the rain fall on Beaubourg.

The dangers in such a concentration of cultural control are quite evident, and they are not, as will be pointed out farther on in this article, all being avoided by the present French government. But they should not be exaggerated, for they are constantly being countered by at least three checks — three antidotes that are influencing the development of modern museums not only in France but also in many other Western democracies.

The most subtle, although by no means the least effective, of these checks is the accelerating decline in the direct influence of art patrons and the concomitant growth of the idea of the autonomy of the world of culture in general and of art in particular. In terms of anecdotal history this decline may be said to have begun during the Italian Renaissance, when Leonardo da Vinci announced that painters were gentlemen, not just manual workers, and when Michelangelo decided to ignore the tantrums of Pope Julius

II. By the second half of the seventeenth century, the sculptor Gian Lorenzo Bernini could defy the wishes of Louis XIV, and by the second half of the eighteenth Dr. Johnson could proudly and publicly reject a patronage proposal from Lord Chesterfield. Soon the Romantic notion of the artist as a lonely, godlike genius, or as a Bohemian eccentric, was by implication reducing the formerly authoritative connoisseur-purchaser of painting and sculpture to the status of an inferior outsider—a humble admirer, a suspected philistine. Soon, too, the growth of the art market was wrecking the old system of personal commissioning, with the important result that the patron found himself at the severe disadvantage of negotiating with the artist, if he did so at all, only *after* a work had been executed. In music the proliferation of public concerts had a comparable result: whereas Haydn and Mozart had been servants, Berlioz and Liszt were marketers. (The change brought new kinds of servitude, of course, but that's another story.) The modern movement in all the arts further reduced the leverage of the consumer, at first by depriving him of his traditional criteria and eventually by suggesting that, since he had been demonstrably, absurdly wrong about several innovations, he had better be wary about rejecting anything at all.

The upshot of all this is an American and Western European situation that is without precedent in cultural history. Artists of every sort are increasingly regarded as constituting, rather like scientists and clergymen, a corporation that must be allowed to pursue its own ends, regardless of the desires of the people who put up the money. Works and performances can be criticized but not controlled in advance—not without violating our code of seemliness. Even in architecture, where the ancient practice of direct commissioning has continued to a degree, clients have become remarkably submissive when confronted by designers who have strongly personal manners. And, increasingly since the advent of specialized art history and stylistic analysis at the end of the nineteenth century, the independence conceded to creators has been extended to museum directors and curators. Hence the president of the French republic has to be cautious, and above all quiet, in exercising his power, real as it is, to control Beaubourg; he has to resort to the manipulation of funds and appointments, and avoid, whatever his personal tastes may be, any overt meddling in artistic matters, any appearance of censorship, any discernible attempt to impose an official style. He has to remember that, given the code that has emerged from the decline of the patron, a state-owned museum cannot decently be an organ of government policy, a sort of Quai d'Orsay for the arts. Indeed, even the Ministry for Cultural Affairs cannot be such an organ, for in theory, if not quite always in fact, a modern, secular, nontotalitarian state can no more have an aesthetic than it can have a chemistry, a biology, or a religion. Like a twentieth-century private patron, it is supposed to pay the cultural piper without pretending to call the tune.

The other two checks on any inclination to play the museological tyrant are more obvious. They are that, in Western Europe as in the United States, cultural policy issues have been highly and sometimes inflammably politicized during the last fifteen years or so, and that during the same period the volume of printed, broadcast, and otherwise diffused cultural criticism has increased to an extraordinary extent. All the major French political parties now have their cultural specialists, their cultural departments, and their programs for bringing art to the people, encouraging creators, and preserving the nation's cultural patrimony; and almost any item of cultural news—a minor financial crisis at the Paris Opéra, for example, or a decision to demolish an eighteenth-century town house—is apt to make the front pages of the daily papers and to inspire comment in the intellectual weeklies. Some of the public debate, like some of the argument over pollution, growth rates, the liberation of women, and similarly popular subjects, is perhaps just a political and a journalistic exploitation of a fashion. But much of it is undoubtedly based on a realization that art is not a frill and that culture, however difficult it may be to define, is everybody's business in an ostensibly egalitarian society.

Many of the above remarks apply to private-initiative museums. The decline in the influence of art patrons, for instance, can be seen in the fact that the New York Metropolitan is today run largely by its professional staff, not by its trustees, and is quite open about preferring donors who contribute cash instead of works that restrict the freedom of curators. Few private institutions, however, can illustrate the complexity of the idea of a modern museum as well as Beaubourg does. Created by an act of the sovereign, the Center is supposed to become an instrument of cultural democracy. Independent on paper, it is actually under the control of a centralized government. Yet the latter is restrained by cultural history, by political expediency, and by an alert corps of critics. (To be fair, one should add that the present French government is also restrained by its own belief in democracy and cultural freedom. But here we are talking about the abuses that the system permits.) Thus the pendulum swings, and it does so not only at the level of rather abstract entities but also at that of concrete things—the Beaubourg building, for example.

A changing participatory space

What sort of architecture is proper for a museum? A complete answer is difficult even under the most simple conditions, since it involves, for a conscientious designer, finding adequate solutions for a formidable series of conflicts, all overlapping, between contents and container, function and symbol, interior and exterior, utility and beauty, openness and security, conservation and presentation, didacticism and aestheticism, contemporaneousness and historicism, neutrality and expressiveness, democracy and elitism, friendliness and dignity, variety and unity, uniqueness and legibility, economy and monumentality, accessibility and urbanism—and so on and on. When the conditions are not simple, when the museum in question is a complex, a *mouseion*, like Beaubourg and not just a painting and sculpture gallery, the conflicts are of course multiplied, and they are multiplied again when the art to be exhibited, performed, studied, preserved, or perhaps created is supposed to be avant-garde.

During the period of intense museological activity that began in the latter part of the eighteenth century and that today shows no sign of ending, two sorts of museum buildings, the palace and the temple, have been especially favored. Many of the palace-museums are former royal or aristocratic residences whose stately halls and chambers have been transformed, sometimes chopped up, into exhibition spaces; familiar examples in this category are the Louvre in Paris and the Uffizi in Florence. Temple-museums, however, are designed as such; they are exhibition spaces masquerading, often with the help of just a Romantic Classical facade, as Greek or Roman sanctuaries. Well-known examples are the London National Gallery, erected between 1834 and 1838 by the architect William Wilkins, and the Washington National Gallery of Art, designed by the academic, eclectic, but immensely competent John Russell Pope shortly before his death in 1937.

These period-style edifices, with their monumental colonnades, high ceilings, grand staircases, and rich decoration, can create, for a tuned sensibility, the sort of atmosphere that is sometimes thought suitable for aesthetic contemplation. They are containers that ennoble and sanctify their contents. They also have the advantage, for a thoughtful traditionalist, of being rich in historical associations — of providing oil for what Ruskin called the Lamp of Memory in architectural appreciation. After all, palaces were for many centuries, long before ministers of culture took them over, something like museums: at one point there were more than two thousand pictures at Versailles. And, although only the more scholarly of Romantic Classical architects may have been aware of such a justification for their stylistic revivals, in classical antiquity collections of art were in fact often housed in important temples, miscellaneous sanctuaries, and such adjoining structures as porticoes and storehouses. By the fourth century B.C. the temple of Hera at Olympia contained among other things an already ancient cedar chest carved with mythological scenes, a score of statues in the Archaic Greek style, some bronze, gold, and ivory figures by the fourth-century sculptors Cleon and Leochares, and — the masterpiece of the collection — Praxiteles' lazily sensuous marble statue of Hermes with the child Dionysus (which still exists, if one accepts the verdict of a number of specialists). At the temple of Asclepius on the island of Cos a visitor could see paintings by the celebrated Apelles, and in the treasuries at Delphi a fantastic accumulation of sculptures, pictures, vases, and metalwork that included the poet Pindar's iron chair and a golden throne allegedly donated by King Midas. A section of the Propylaea, the monumental entrance to the Acropolis of Athens, was transformed into a *pinakotheke*, a picture gallery, in which works by Polygnotus, the earliest of the great Greek painters, were displayed. Since a museum is partly in the eye of the beholder, all that such art-laden sanctuaries needed to become museums was for the gods to die —and by the Hellenistic period they were sinking rapidly in the mind of a sophisticated Greek tourist.

The Lamp of Memory and an ambience of royal pomp or old heathen religiosity are not, however, very suitable for an exhibition of modern art. What is worse, converted palaces and imitation temples are often cursed with bad lighting, illogical circuits for viewers, and a lack of space for reserves, offices, documentation, laboratories, postcard stands, bookstores, toilets, and restaurants. Hence the twentieth century has seen a long list of attempts to replace the palace-museum and the temple-museum with something more specifically functional—with what might be called the museum-museum. Among the interesting results are Louis I. Kahn's Yale University Art Gallery at New Haven (1953), Philip Johnson's garden court for the Museum of Modern Art (1953) and his Sheldon Memorial Art Gallery for the University of Nebraska in Lincoln (1963), Frank Lloyd Wright's Guggenheim (completed in 1959 but designed some fifteen years earlier), Jørgen Bo and Vilhelm Wohlert's Louisiana Museum at Humlebæk, Denmark (1958), Marcel Breuer's Whitney (1966), Ludwig Mies van der Rohe's Nationalgalerie in Berlin (1968), Gordon Bunshaft's Hirshhorn (1974)— the enumeration could easily be continued. Many of these museum-museums have in common a neutral, clinical interior that, unlike the heavily decorated halls of the converted palaces and the imitation temples, does not clash with the works on display. Several, however, exhibit in their shapes, spaces, and patterns a stylistic willfulness that can be almost as awkward for a curator as colonnades and red plush, and that can be a strong deterrent to any inclination toward flexibility and expansion. Mies's industrial classicism, although beautifully austere and consistent, is more rigid than Romantic Classicism; and Wright's Guggenheim snail, although fascinating as a piece of hollow sculpture, is notoriously a museological absurdity, imposed on a client who took the decline in the power of the patron rather too seriously.

Thus Pompidou did not lack possible models, both good and bad, to consider when he turned to the problem of giving his "ardent wish" its architectural form. But he, too, had accepted the code of seemliness that had emerged from the decline of the power of the art patron, and so he announced that the choice of a building was to be made through a competition open to every architect in the world, "even if he is young and without financial resources."[2] Projects were to be submitted anonymously to an international jury of nine "wise men" with experience in both modern architecture and the planned activities of the Centre Beaubourg, and no member of the French government was to intervene, however unhappy he might be about what was being decided. Surprisingly, in view of the authoritarian habits of Paris ministers and functionaries, these instructions were carried out, and the jury that was selected by Pompidou and his advisers was as competent and fair as anyone could have imagined. Its members were Philip Johnson, who qualified both as a practicing architect and as a critic and historian who had been the first director of the architectural department of the Museum of Modern Art in New York; Jean Prouvé, the French architectural engineer who had been one of the pioneers of curtain walling and of prefabricated construction; Oscar Niemeyer, best known as the brilliant designer of the main public buildings (including a museum) in Brasilia; Emile Aillaud, one of the most imaginative (even fantastic) and socially conscious of the older generation of French architects; Sir Frank Francis, former director of the British Museum; Willem Sandberg, former director of the municipal museums of Amsterdam; Michel Laclotte, curator in chief of the paintings department at the Louvre; Gaëtan Picon, a French writer on art and literature noted for his philosophical and psychological analyses; Herman Liebaers, director of the Bibliothèque Royale in Brussels. Pompidou invited them all to the Élysée Palace but carefully abstained from giving them any hint of what he might like in the way of a Beaubourg building. He promised his full support for their choice and added: "As a Frenchman I would prefer that the winner [of the competition] be a Frenchman. If, however, he is a foreigner, he will be a foreigner."[3]

To help the competing architects in their planning, the group of technocrats headed by Sébastien Loste prepared a book that explained in detail the objectives, organization, and possible activities of the future center. Seventeen hundred architects eventually requested it, after a publicity campaign that mobilized French ambassadors, consuls, and cultural attachés and bombarded professional publications with announcements. Meanwhile, the jury prepared for its own guidance a set of criteria that emphasized the need for an aesthetic and functional integration of the center in the Beaubourg section of Paris, for a close agreement between architectural thinking and the Beaubourg program, for carefully articulated volumes and surfaces, for links between different categories of activities, for clear, inviting, and logical entrances and visiting circuits, for simple structural members that might be produced industrially, and for a flexible, expandable space that could be easily adapted to changing or growing requirements. Nothing was said about the Lamp of Memory.

A majority of the architects who had requested the official book of specifications backed away when they saw the complexity of the program. Six hundred and eighty-one projects, however, were on hand in Paris by the beginning of July 1971, when the competition closed, and an astonishing 491 were from outside France. One could not have asked for a more complete panorama of architectural trends in the last third of the twentieth century. There were palace-museums, temple-museums, museum-museums, and some manifestations of the gray regionalism and eclectic anti-Miesian historicism current in the United States. There were a few countercultural propositions that questioned the whole idea of Beaubourg.

A particularly ardent modernist and symbolist suggested a building in the form of a giant hand of Le Corbusier. The jury rapidly eliminated some five hundred of the projects on the grounds that they were merely what one member called "grand architectural gestures," and then a commission of technical experts joined the "wise men" for the final stages of sifting. On July 15, by a vote of eight to one, the contract was awarded to a thirty-four-year-old Italian, Renzo Piano, and his thirty-eight-year-old English partner, Richard Rogers. They had been helped in their planning notably by another Italian, Gianfranco Franchini, and by a British engineering firm, Ove Arup & Partners.

Although both of the winning architects had already distinguished themselves in several international competitions, neither was very well known outside professional circles. Both had done a good deal of intermittent teaching, Piano notably at the Politecnico of Milan, Columbia University, and the School of Architecture at the University of Pennsylvania, and Rogers notably at Cornell, the Massachusetts Institute of Technology, Princeton, and Yale (where he had done graduate work). In their teaching and in their practice as a team based in London, Genoa, and Paris, they had developed a strong interest in the possibility of a rational use of modern technology to solve not only construction problems but also social and ecological ones. They had designed, mostly for Italian and British clients, a wide variety of factories, laboratories, pavilions, and office buildings and had experimented extensively in mass-production prototypes, structural shell systems, elastic and inflatable roofs, space frames, and general-purpose sheds. Neither had ever built a museum, although Piano had worked for a time with the Italian architect Franco Albini, whose Museo di Palazzo Bianco (1951) and Museo del Tesoro di San Lorenzo (1956), both in Genoa, are among the few generally acknowledged masterpieces of postwar museum design.

The Beaubourg building as finally erected is essentially what Piano and Rogers had imagined for the competition, although some modifications proved advisable in the course of construction. It is a rectangular, largely transparent, steel-and-glass box that rises to a height of six stories in its main section and covers an area that is almost exactly that of two football fields. The word *box*, however, is scarcely appropriate, for there are no closed facades of the traditional sort, and no smooth curtain walls of the modern sort. Instead there is an exposed metal structural grille whose lattice beams, crisscrossing struts, and nodal points can remind a viewer variously of ordinary wooden or pipe scaffolding, of tent stakes and ropes, of Meccano and Erector assemblages, of the Eiffel Tower, and of American carpentered balloon frames—although none of these analogies is adequate in engineering terms. This frank externalization of what is usually an internal skeleton is accompanied by an equally striking externalization of what are usually internal organs. Snaking up across one of the long sides of the building, like an immense alimentary canal, is a tubular, glass-enclosed escalator that affords direct access to the center's upper-floor components and finally to a restaurant at the top. (As the visitor goes up, a splendid view of Paris unfolds: first the nearby church of Saint-Merri and the Tour Saint-Jacques and most of the historic center, and finally the whole city, with Montmartre and its white Basilica of Sacré-Coeur on the horizon.) On the other long side, also attached to the structural grille, are elevators, power ducts, gantries, air shafts, and other service elements. All of these clipped-on funnels, flues, cubes, and tubes are painted in vivid blues, greens, reds, and yellows that stand out dramatically against the dominant glitter of steel and glass.

The floors are supported by a series of steel beams, each 158 feet long, that link the two main sides of the building and rest on special sections of the structural grille designed to maintain the proper tension and take up all movement due to imposed loading and changes in the temperature. (Incidentally, these giant beams, which were made as single pieces in a steel plant outside Paris, posed a formidable delivery problem when they reached the city. They were finally mounted on massive wheels and hauled to the construction site in the traffic-light hours of the night, through streets that had to be carefully selected to make it possible to turn corners.) The combination of this system with the externalized skeleton and service elements makes the interior a collection of vast loft spaces completely free of columns, pillars, and weight-bearing walls. Zones are assigned to particular Beaubourg activities, but the assigning is largely arbitrary, or at least not predetermined by the architecture, for there is nothing to prevent almost any imaginable utilization of such a fluid, flexible area of roofed-over emptiness.

All in all, the building is remarkably resistant to the usual sort of critical categorizing and labeling. It is certainly, for anyone who is not systematically antimodern, a stimulating pattern of shapes and colors, but it is not beautiful or monumental in any conventional way. It is *functionalist,* if one wants to employ that confusing adjective to point out merely that there are no ornaments and that the exposed structures and equipment express their practical purposes; but it is not functionalist in the sense of having been obviously designed for a specific use, as banks may be designed for banking, or railroad stations for railroading. Nor, by the same token, is it symbolic of a particular cultural function, as a church may be. It offers points of comparison with twentieth-century sculpture and painting: the structural grille with Constructivism, for instance, the transparent, spidery, inside-outside space with certain phases of Cubism, the escalator with Expressionism, and the brightly painted pipes and other equipment with Pop art and the work of Fernand Léger. But such comparisons do not take us very far. Nor do those that might be made with some of the dominant currents in twentieth-century architecture; indeed, Beaubourg breaks with the commercial steel-and-glass slab, with what used to be called the International Style, almost as radically as it does with the palace-museum and the temple-museum. It is closer in many ways to Joseph Paxton's great glass-and-iron Crystal Palace, erected in London in 1851, than it is to strongly stylized museum-museums like Breuer's rather monastic Whitney and Bunshaft's decidedly military (on the outside) Hirshhorn. After noticing what the edifice is not, we are left with what can be described as an open museum, or an exploded museum, or even an antimuseum, and also with an important batch of politico-cultural considerations. Piano and Rogers have in fact consistently avoided the word *museum* in talking about their creation.[4] Instead they have referred to it as "an urban machine," a simple "shed," and "a participatory space." They have insisted that Beaubourg must be "not just an elitist cultural monument made up of a number of watertight departments, but a people's center, a university of the street," and that "the people of both today and tomorrow, the curators, the specialists and the amateurs, must have the possibility of designing their own changing needs into the building, as far as possible freed from the limitations of the architectural form." Returning with enthusiasm to the idealism and hopefulness that marked the early years of the Soviet Union, they have adopted as a sort of slogan a quotation from the Russian poet and Futurist Vladimir Mayakovsky: "We do not need a dead mausoleum of art where dead works are worshipped, but a living factory of the human spirit." One can wonder a bit about their awareness of complexity. But there is no reason to doubt the sincerity and generosity of their intentions, nor the deliberateness of the attempt to convert those intentions into steel and glass. If the Beaubourg building is difficult to "read" as an art gallery, or even as a conventional cultural institution of any kind, the explanation is partly that it is not supposed to be read as such.

The design, the reader will have noticed, follows fairly closely many of the criteria set up by the jury, in particular those concerning flexibility, simplicity, and clarity. It also takes into account, to a degree that is apt to surprise a visitor accustomed to the sharply delimited area, the elitist isolation, of the average museum, the jury's demand for an integration of the center in the Beaubourg section of Paris. The "participatory space" extends out from the building into a plaza, about two and a half acres in its total extent, that slopes gently, invitingly, amphitheatrically toward the main entrance and the external escalator. The slope and the flagstone paving testify to the architects' admiration for the great medieval and Renaissance squares in Italian towns—and especially, it would seem, for the scallop-shaped Piazza del Campo in Siena. Automobiles are of course banned, and the entire plaza is serviced with a grid of outlets for electricity, sound, and water, intended to make possible what Piano and Rogers list as "a flower market, chess tables, a magic circus, poetry reading, participatory activities, art exhibitions, blood donations, cinemas, zoos, meetings, audio-visual presentations, happenings, laser shows, mimes, picnic spaces, dancing, etc." Present or scheduled early in 1977 (when this article was being written) were only a few hints of such animation. But there was no reason to doubt

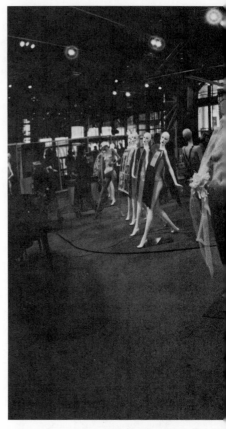

"Although it is thoroughly up-to-date and is not dedicated to all the Muses that were favored by its remote ancestors, the Centre Beaubourg can be called Greek—generously inclusive, that is—in its conception and organization."

that it would develop eventually. Several Paris experiments with automobile-free zones have demonstrated that the Beaubourg architects are quite right in their belief that, as they put it, "exciting things happen when a variety of overlapping activities meet in a flexible environment opening up the possibility of interaction outside the normal confines of institutional limits." In any event, on a suitably mild evening (the center stays open till ten o'clock for the benefit of working people) the plaza is a fine place from which to watch the spectacle of Beaubourg itself—the mass of steel glittering coldly in the darkness, the light and color emerging warmly through the tracery of the structural grille, and the silhouettes gliding up through the glass tube of the escalator and dispersing themselves in the lofts of the interior. You need not be a fanatical believer in progress to feel that the twentieth is not such a bad century after all, and you can be tempted to walk in, leaf through a book, take a ride in the escalator, look at a couple of Georges Braque's robust still lifes, and have a cup of coffee. Which of course is exactly what Piano and Rogers hoped you would do.

Beyond the plaza, on the western and southern sides, two smaller squares and a tangle of a dozen narrow streets, most of them only a block long, are also reserved for pedestrians. Beaubourg planners dream of extending this stroller's paradise in one direction toward the historic town houses of the Marais quarter and in the other direction perhaps as far as the Avenue de l'Opéra. So far, however, the project has been blocked by politicians who continue to regard the automobile as a sacred object.

Cultural politics and cultural economics

Many of the problems raised by the Centre Beaubourg concern primarily, although not exclusively, the components of the institution. Before moving on into these specific contexts, however, we can conveniently pause for a moment longer in the general context and look at some of the broad objections the creation of the whole complex has provoked. Several of these objections may seem very French at first. But in slightly different forms they are likely to occur in any country, including the United States, where important museums increasingly are being founded with state aid—where, in other words, art is being socialized and ostensibly democratized.

Even in bare outline the story of the beginnings of Beaubourg leads a cultural historian or critic deep into a maze of paradoxes and ambiguities. The sovereign act by which Pompidou decreed the birth of the center was beyond question a manifestation of nationalism, elitism, and authoritarianism, and at the time it was vigorously denounced as such by many French artists, intellectuals, and Socialist or Communist politicians. Yet, largely because Pompidou was an intelligent, sophisticated man, anxious to observe the noninterventionist code of the modern patron, the originally arbitrary decision led to a jury of impeccably independent experts, to an open ar-

chitectural competition involving the safeguard of anonymity, to an interna-
tionalism without precedent in such matters, and finally to a building that,
at least in the minds of its two designers, is intended to shelter the exact
opposite of the elitist cultural institution. Could such an outcome have been
produced by private initiative? Possibly, but not very probably, if one thinks
of the architecture of American private-initiative museums. Could it have
been produced by an initiative from the French National Assembly or by
a direct consultation of French voters? Almost certainly not: French depu-
ties accepted Beaubourg only after it had become an irreversible enterprise, and a poll taken in the spring of 1976, less than a year before the
opening of the center, revealed that 70 percent of French adults disliked
modern architecture.

The moral of the story might thus be that cultural democracy is best
achieved by cultural dictatorship. But there is no need to push things that
far. What is required of an honest observer is merely an admission that
there is indeed a fundamental contradiction between cultural democracy
and the democratic process as it is usually conceived and that therefore a
bit of enlightened despotism, surrounded by some effective checks, can be
a good thing in the business of making a modern museum. Cultural democracy, while we are waiting for the millennium of a classless society of equally
endowed, equally educated art appreciators, cannot be reconciled with
majority opinions; it can in practice be only an attempt to provide a minority
with enlarged opportunities, with protection against philistine dema-
goguery, and, above all, with a chance to remain open to new members.
Such an attempt often calls for a Pompidou at the head of a government.
(These remarks suppose, of course, a rather restricted definition of *culture;*
they do not apply if the word is taken to mean almost any sort of behavior
from whittling to watching football on television.)

The art-loving minority that is being encouraged, protected, and perhaps opened up does not, however, exist in isolation, and it may find itself
in conflict with other minorities, or with the majority, not just at the level
of opinions but at that of actions. The difficulties that may then arise can
be sampled by glancing again at the integration of the Centre Beaubourg
in its section of the centuries-old Parisian urban fabric. We have seen that
this integration is on the whole very successful when considered from the
viewpoint of Piano and Rogers: it is an extension of the center. But how does
it look from the viewpoint of the inhabitants of the quarter and from that
of the average antimodern Frenchman?

The Beaubourg neighborhood is a small, rather amorphous zone across
the Seine from the Latin Quarter, two blocks north of the Hôtel de Ville,
and three blocks east of Les Halles, the former food-market "belly" of Paris
that is now being transformed, amid much controversy, into an underground facility and a surface park. The zone does not have a very distinguished history: it grew out of the medieval village of Beau-Bourg, so
named by derision because of the unsavory reputation of its population of

173

thieves and prostitutes, and in 1834 it witnessed a massacre of rioting workers that inspired one of Honoré Daumier's most powerful lithographs, the *Rue Transnonain.* Nor, aside from the Gothic church of Saint-Merri and some picturesque facades of the seventeenth and eighteenth centuries, does it have much in the way of architectural distinction; in fact, the Plateau Beaubourg, on which the center now stands, became available as a site because of the demolition, begun in the 1930s, of deteriorated, unsanitary structures. The remaining buildings, however, which are mostly in the academic styles that became popular during the Second Empire, do have a sort of pleasant, washed-out, old-fashioned unity; and one cannot deny that the steel-and-glass "urban machine" erected by Piano and Rogers is a noticeable break in that unity. The local population refers to the building as "the oil refinery" or simply "the monster" and feels strongly that it should have been put somewhere else—perhaps out at La Défense, the new sky-scraper development in the western suburbs of Paris.

The aesthetic objections are accompanied by economic and social ones. The inhabitants of the quarter are mostly factory workers, artisans, and small merchants. Many are poor, and many of their apartments are sadly dilapidated and unequipped. It takes, however, a great deal of living to make a slum, and now that kind of living has been brutally disrupted by the Centre Beaubourg. It has become almost as chic, in the minds of many Parisians, to have an address near the new institution as to have one across the river near the ministries in the Seventh Arrondissement, long considered the most socially desirable section of the city. Rents and land values have been soaring, and expulsions of tenants have been multiplying. In their corner cafés, over their espressos and shots of calvados, old residents complain that the neighborhood has been invaded by arrivistes, junior executives, art dealers, Left Bank types, tourists, and homosexuals. Until recently one of the ancient, crumbling walls near the center bore the eloquent graffito *"Et le bonheur?"* ("And happiness?") Again a frequent argument is that "the monster" should have been exiled to La Défense.

There are good answers to that argument. In the long run, to reject modern architecture in the older parts of the city is to turn them into burrows for the underprivileged, or collections of stylistic fakes (which does not mean, of course, that truly historic quarters should be violated). To have isolated the "participatory space" of the Centre Beaubourg out among the commercial skyscrapers at bourgeois La Défense, where what community life there is tends to flicker out when the offices close and the secretaries take the metro home, would have been an evident absurdity; and it would have been bad town planning at the same time, for the eastern part of Paris (like the eastern parts of many big cities, for sometimes mysterious reasons) has long been in need of renovation, stimulation, and more variety in its class structure. Also, the center is expected to attract some ten thousand visitors a day when everything is in full operation, and one need not be a disciple of Jeremy Bentham to feel that the sum of their pleasure will eventually compensate for the present unhappiness of the old residents. Also, fresh money will be flowing into the quarter, which has long been a business backwater. Understandably, however, none of these answers is apt to impress a lover of Second Empire architecture or a worker who has just lost his apartment to an art dealer, and finally a cultural critic is obliged to grant that cultural democracy of the Beaubourg sort has its price in human disarrangement.

It also has its price in public appropriations, and hence in loud protests from politicians, taxpayers, and the supporters of cultural institutions and activities that are competing for state funds. The protests began as soon as Pompidou announced his "ardent wish"; they subsided a little while the building was going up; they swelled to an angry chorus when the bills began to come in. Shortly before the opening day even Mme Françoise Giroud, the state secretary for cultural affairs, seemed about to join the complainers. The center, she remarked during a television interview, "is an ambitious enterprise conceived during a period of financial euphoria, and it poses a financial problem that must be solved." (Incidentally, it is perhaps indicative of a change in the French politico-cultural climate that since the death of Pompidou the cabinet member for culture has been demoted from the rank of minister to that of a mere state secretary.) A week later, in another interview, she made a valiant effort to present the other side of the question. "France," she said, "exists because of her culture. It is not because of her military power, or her diplomacy, or her economic development, that she has been exceptional in the world. . . . When people say to me that we are spending too much on the Opéra, too much on Beaubourg, I feel like replying that in certain cases one must be ready to spend too much."[5] The impression remained, however, that the government was not very friendly toward the new "oil refinery."

The coolness was not without cause. The cost of building the center was nearly a billion francs (about $200 million at the exchange rate of early 1977), and the cost of operating it during its first year of existence was an estimated 130 million francs ($26 million). Although such sums were arguably quite small in the context of modern state spending for things like highways and weapons, they seemed very large, as Mme Giroud realized, to the average Frenchman, who was being reminded every day of how much the economic situation of his country had changed for the worse since Pompidou's sovereign act of 1969, and who was not enthusiastic about seeing his tax money go to the minority that liked modern art. Moreover, the amounts involved raised some serious questions about cultural priorities. Germain Bazin, art historian, former curator in chief for paintings at the Louvre, and a member of the Institut de France, angrily evoked the situation in a newspaper article that appeared while the building was getting its final touches. "Sound the trumpets," he wrote; "beat the drums that announce the new spectacle. Sound them loudly, so that we may cease to perceive the lugubrious squeaking of the doors of the Louvre as they are being closed."[6] He was exaggerating, of course. But it was true that the Louvre and some other French public art galleries were being forced to close certain departments two or three days a week because of a shortage of guards. (The situation had not changed when this article was being written. So don't try to see a van Eyck at the Louvre without first making inquiries.) It was also true that all over France there were monuments, musicians, dancers, actors, writers, libraries, and film directors imploring the government for subsidies. And it was true that what Bazin called "this museological Concorde," with nearly a thousand relatively well-paid employees and modern equipment that included an impressive number of computers, was getting more public money than thirty national museums put together. In fact, according to one estimate that apparently lumped some lingering construction credits in with operating costs, it was getting an astonishing 14 percent of the total annual state budget for culture.

The complaint that Beaubourg was getting more than its fair share of the cultural budget was sometimes accompanied by the complaint that it was an example of the government's tendency to favor Paris and neglect the cultural needs of the rest of the country. Here the issue was what Americans are familiar with as that of the big cities versus the cultural hinterland. In France the issue has always had a special capacity for provoking bitterness, partly because Paris is the only really big city in the country and partly because of a long history of centralization and a disposition among residents of the capital to regard people in the provinces as hopeless if rather amusing yokels—equivalents of what the proverbially ignorant and slow-witted peasants of ancient Boeotia were in the eyes of sophisticated Athenians. And it was difficult to deny that the new center increased the evidence of cultural concentration. It meant, when added to the other large state-owned Paris institutions (including notably the Opéra, whose budget for 1977 was a whopping 142 million francs), that henceforth the city would be receiving nearly half of the funds voted by the National Assembly for the arts.

Pro-Beaubourg people had some replies to the budget-based criticism. They argued that a sprinkling of subsidies all over the map, although favored by politicians eager to please all the voters, was less apt to yield cultural results than a concentration of the available means in a few large institutions. They pointed out that Paris and its surrounding territory contained, after all, about a quarter of the population of France. Moreover, they said, the Centre Beaubourg was going to function as a national cultural distributor, a centralizer for decentralization and a catalyst for regionalism, by welcoming talent and initiatives from outside Paris and by sending art shows, traveling libraries, performing musicians, industrial designs, and cultural experts out into the provinces—with the intention, not of imposing a Parisian uniformity, but of cooperating with local institutions. All this in addition to encouraging French painters and sculptors everywhere by bolstering the waning prestige of Paris as a world art capital.

Gradually it became apparent to nearly everybody except diehard enemies of modernism that the whole subsidy controversy was being badly focused. The real trouble was not that Beaubourg and Paris were getting too big a slice of the pie but that the pie was too small. France, like most Western democracies, had had a rapid increase in cultural activity: in fifteen years the number of museum visitors, for instance, had tripled; the production of books had doubled; the production of phonograph records had quintupled. The French government had responded to the growing demand by agreeing on help, to an extent that varied from very little to total support, for just about everything, whether state-owned or not, and it had thus set in motion wave after wave of rising expectations. By 1977 it was faced with outstretched hands not only from such major undertakings as the Louvre, the Paris Opéra, the Comédie Française, the Orchestre de Paris, and Beaubourg but also from such smaller ones as 938 museums, 840 artistic associations, 800 schools of music, 200 theaters, 153 theatrical troupes, and 48 Établissements d'Action Culturelle (very roughly describable as little, provincial Beaubourgs). It was subsidizing opera houses at an annual rate of 280 francs ($56) per seat and concerts at 30 francs per seat. It was advancing sums to film producers and art galleries (if they were staging first one-man shows), helping to maintain some thirty thousand historic monuments ranging from cathedrals and chateaus to Art Nouveau doorways, and trying to save some fifty-five square kilometers of medieval stained glass menaced by atmospheric pollution. To pay for all this and many other commitments, Mme Giroud had a 1977 cultural-affairs budget that came to 1,958,000,000 francs ($391 million). This was about a fortieth of the defense budget and a microscopic 0.55 percent of the total national budget.

Obviously, the government had to make up its mind. Either it was going to abandon its aid-for-all cultural policy for a more selective one, or it was going to spend more money. Early in 1977 it chose the second alternative and announced that the 1978 budget for cultural affairs would be considerably larger. The moral of this part of the story would seem to be that if you want to further cultural justice and cultural democracy you should not be afraid to start by being apparently unjust and provocatively undemocratic, for a boldly expensive new institution aimed at a minority can easily become a locomotive for a general advance. Because of Beaubourg, the Louvre and other French museums will probably have more, not fewer, guards and curators, and the French provinces will have more Mozart, Molière, and modernism.

With that reminder of the possible ramifications of our subject, and of its possible ambiguities and ironies, serving as a transition, we can now move on to the components of the center, beginning with the gallery of modern painting, sculpture, and allied arts.

From Fauvism to tomorrow

The Musée National d'Art Moderne, MNAM to its habitués, was created officially in 1937 as a replacement for the nineteenth-century Paris gallery of contemporary art, the Musée du Luxembourg, but because of World War II it was not ready for visitors until 1947. Until its transfer at the end of 1976 it was lodged in a rambling monument, sometimes called the Palais de Tokyo, that had been erected on the Right Bank opposite the Eiffel Tower as part of the world's fair of 1937. It now occupies the entire fifth level of the Beaubourg building and sections of three other levels, and its 16,550 square meters make it, in terms of floor space, the largest institution of its kind in the world. Its permanent collection, however, is only moderately large—some eight thousand paintings, sculptures, drawings, prints, photographs, and films. The director is a Swede, K. G. Pontus Hulten, who attracted a good deal of attention in the early 1960s as the innovating chief curator of the Moderna Museet in Stockholm.

These facts may not suggest anything extraordinary, and indeed MNAM is in many respects quite similar, architecture aside, to Washington's Hirshhorn, New York's Whitney, Guggenheim, and MOMA, and even London's Tate Gallery. But partly because of those similarities, and also because it is new, big, and ambitious, it offers a good occasion for meditating on the difficulty of transposing the great ideas of traditional museology—history, knowledge, art, memory, quality, beauty, education, and democracy—into the cultural context of the last quarter of the twentieth century.

First, some perspective. Gertrude Stein's feeling that there was something contradictory in the notion of a museum of modern art had, of course, a fairly solid justification in the realities of human psychology and practical curatorship. Apparently people have always had a peculiarly fervent admiration for the art of the past, and museums, or their ancient prototypes, have always catered to that admiration. Excavations have revealed, for example, that a Mesopotamian temple of the second millennium B.C. was apt to exhibit treasures dating back to the third millennium. The palace collection of Nebuchadrezzar II of Babylon, in the first half of the sixth century B.C., contained statues, reliefs, stelae, and clay cylinders to which specialists have assigned dates running from about 700 B.C. back to 2400 B.C. The painter Polygnotus, who flourished in the middle of the fifth century B.C., was already an old master when his works were exhibited in the entrance to the Acropolis of Athens, and around A.D. 160 he was still being venerated as such by connoisseurs like the guidebook-writer Pausanias. This sort of veneration reached a new pitch of intensity when the Renaissance set out to imitate Graeco-Roman antiquity (and at the same time created a boom in art collecting), and it reached another pitch when the Romantic movement brought into play a rich compound of stylistic revivalism, popular archaeology, sentimental historicism, hagiographic biography, and masterpiece worship. The industrial revolution contributed to the trend by making the present seem ugly in comparison with an idealized, aestheticized bygone era, and also by generating a class of newly rich, often untutored entrepreneurs eager to legitimate themselves and their wealth by displaying the tastes of the old landed aristocracy. The institutionalized results were the great museums of the nineteenth century, which took it for granted that their mission was primarily the conservation of the art of the past. Sometimes the mission was made surprisingly specific: at the Louvre the rule was that only the works of artists who had been dead for at least ten years could be considered for admission.

To be sure, there were occasional breaks in this rather cemeterial sort of museology; as early as 1889 the New York Metropolitan was persuaded to accept two Manets. And in fairness one should not forget that the nineteenth century saw the emergence of a series of museums devoted entirely or mostly to contemporary art: the Paris Musée du Luxembourg, for instance, in 1818, the Munich Neue Pinakothek in 1853, the Berlin Deutsches Museum in 1875, and the London Tate Gallery in 1897. But the breaks occurred very occasionally indeed, and in thinking about the contemporary-art institutions one should be careful not to project onto them an image derived from our own era. They were largely a response to a patriotic demand for more recognition for native artists; they were at first respectively French, German, or English in outlook, and only somewhat accidentally contemporary. (Oddly, in view of the amount of Yankee nationalism in other domains, this trend toward galleries that reached the contemporary through the indigenous did not manifest itself effectively in the United States until well after World War I, when it finally led to the creation of the Whitney Museum of American Art.) Moreover, for a long while the contemporaneousness of such institutions was merely temporal; in terms of style they were almost as conservative as their past-conserving counterparts. In the 1890s the Musée du Luxembourg and the Deutsches Museum could still make a fuss about admitting Impressionist works, and until the early 1920s the Tate Gallery strongly reflected the taste of reactionary members of the Royal Academy.

Two points are evident even from a survey as brief as the above: (1) A museum of modern art, although not a contradiction in the Gertrude Stein sense, is certainly an anomaly, a product of a rupture, in the history of aesthetic appreciation, and it is therefore bound to be a rather unstable thing. (2) Such a museum, if it is to have any important cultural significance, must not be simply an exhibition hall for a miscellany of artists who have little in common aside from being alive or only recently dead; on the contrary, it must be a place that rules out academicism and traditionalism, rejects the common confusion of the modern with the merely modish or merely contemporary, and opts clearly for the modern as a period style — in the sense in which the Baroque, for example, can be called a period style. That definition may seem too militant, but in fact it fits fairly well such institutions as the New York MOMA, the Hirshhorn, the Guggenheim, and

Beaubourg's MNAM. All these places have a firm, exclusive stylistic commitment that makes them radically different from the old Luxembourg or even the Tate, which continues to mix international modernism with British nationalism. Their common ancestor is not to be found in the nineteenth century but rather in the first American modern-art museum, an unconventional enterprise that called itself the Société Anonyme and owed its birth, in 1920, to the private initiative of the wealthy bluestocking Katherine Dreier. The Société had advice from Marcel Duchamp and Man Ray, and a fine motto: "Traditions are beautiful—but to create them, not to follow."[7]

A commitment to modernism as a period style raises the question of when the period can be supposed to have begun, and hence of how far back in time the museum's permanent collection should extend. The question is not, of course, precisely answerable; it is like asking at what point the water in an estuary becomes salty. But if we assume, as most people do, that the chief stylistic constant of modern art is a refusal of strict representationalism, of the illusionism invented by the Renaissance, we find ourselves with a limited number of reasonable answers. A case can be made for going back to the almost abstract patterns of color and luminosity painted by J. M. W. Turner in the 1840s, or to the flickering sketches produced in the 1860s and 1870s by the Impressionists and their fellow revolutionaries. (André Malraux, who liked to dramatize art history, was of the opinion that the whole modern movement began at the precise moment when Édouard Manet decided to add an apparently gratuitous blob of paint to one of his otherwise quite realistic compositions.) Cases can also be made for taking as the point of rupture Fauvism, Cubism, Futurism, or another of the manifestations of antitraditionalism that appeared in the early 1900s. Believers in a heroic theory of history can choose an individual act of defiance: something as rich in consequences as Pablo Picasso's decision, in 1906, to paint the proto-Cubist *Demoiselles d'Avignon*, or Wassily Kandinsky's decision, around 1910 or perhaps a little later, to paint what has been called the first purely abstract work in history.

At Beaubourg, Pontus Hulten has chosen to start—after a small sampling of late-nineteenth-century trends—with the Fauves. The choice was dictated partly by practical considerations: the museum was already rich in the work of such onetime Fauves as Henri Matisse, Maurice de Vlaminck, and André Derain, and the French Impressionists were already installed in their own Paris gallery, the Musée du Jeu de Paume (which is officially a part of the Louvre). It is easily defended, however, on other grounds. Fauvism, which created a resounding scandal at the Paris Salon d'Automne of 1905 (where its practitioners were dubbed *les fauves*, "the wild beasts"), was the first of the important pictorial isms of the twentieth century. In its flat distortions and its violently unrealistic colors it anticipated by several years the antirepresentationalism of Cubism. It made Turner look like a

Romantic visionary, and even Impressionism seemed by comparison only the last phase of Realism, or at most a transition toward modernism.

Having decided where, historically speaking, to start the collection, Hulten and his assistants were faced with the problem of how to control its inevitable growth. This sort of problem confronts all museums, of course; the curators of the Louvre and the New York Metropolitan spend a lot of their time pleading for display space for recent acquisitions. But a curator who is committed only to past periods can slow down, or even halt, his acquiring without suffering any consequences more serious than regret over not having this or that masterpiece, whereas a modern-art curator, committed as he is to the present period, must in theory go on acquiring year after year in an effort to keep up to date. He is condemned, it would seem, to eventually stuffing his gallery to death. Moreover, whereas a Louvre curator, given the automatic admiration aroused by sheer pastness in art, can feel happy about the fact that his collection is receding deeper into the past year by year, a modern-art curator cannot contemplate the aging process without misgivings. At the New York MOMA, which will soon be half a century old and which is entangled in a definition of the modern period that extends the collection back into Postimpressionism and even a bit beyond, such misgivings have long been acute. At the Beaubourg MNAM they are bound to become so, for 1905 and Fauvism are already a good while ago and will soon seem strangely far back to museum visitors who assume mistakenly, under the influence of the semantic buzz in our cultural terminology, that "modern" in the sense of a label for a historical style is somehow always equivalent to "modern" in the widespread sense of "contemporary" or "recent."

The situation is complicated for Hulten by the fact that MNAM, although authorized under certain conditions to buy paintings and sculptures, or to acquire them as gifts, is not authorized—as American private museums commonly are—to sell any apparently surplus or inferior pieces. Everything, including future acquisitions, is supposed to remain the inalienable property of the state. French authorities have tried to ward off the danger of a collection plagued by excessive growth and old age. A paragraph in the law of 1976 stipulates that the works of artists born before 1870 cannot be admitted to Beaubourg without special authorization, and an administrative ruling says that "in order to preserve the contemporary character of the collection" the center should "periodically transfer" to other French museums its older works, in general a hundred and twenty years after the births of the artists concerned. But will these measures have much effect? One can doubt that they will and feel that they should not. It is hard to believe that Hulten will ever refuse a masterpiece by Matisse, for example, who was born in 1869. It is almost impossible to imagine that future Beaubourg curators will really get rid of their Kandinskys in 1986, their Matisses in 1989, their Vlamincks in 1996, their Picassos in 2001, their Braques in

2002, and so on. And if such amputations were to occur, the result would be a sadly, senselessly mutilated collection, a museological monster neither modern fish nor contemporary fowl.

Is there no good solution, then, to the growth-and age problem? There is, of course, although it may not be one that the directors of the new Paris center—and the heads of similar institutions in the United States—like to contemplate. It is simply to grant that a museum of modern art, if consistent with its own nature, must eventually commit suicide. If what we call "modern" is in fact a period style with a discernible beginning in time, say around 1905, it will necessarily, like all historical phenomena, come to an end one day. When that day arrives the semantic buzz of "modern" and "contemporary" will be filtered out, for "modern," presumably under a different label, will be completely a style of the past. And when that day arrives the Beaubourg MNAM, along with its sister galleries elsewhere, will have to accept the logical consequences—or founder in eclecticism and incoherence. If it wants to keep its accumulated paintings and sculptures it will have to choose a cutoff date, change its name (perhaps to something like the Musée National du Vingtième Siècle), and resign itself to being a past-period museum in about the same category as the Impressionist Jeu de Paume. If it wants to continue calling itself a modern-art gallery, it will have to relinquish most of its present permanent collection, choose a new point of rupture in stylistic history, suffer anew the popular confusion surrounding "modern" and "contemporary," and start all over again the hazardous business of trying to conserve and present the art of a historical period that is not yet completely historical, that is still a fluid mixture of being, becoming, and beginning.

Such speculation cannot be dismissed as a mere fantasy of the remote future, as an art historian's version of science fiction, for there is a sober (and to many people dismaying) possibility that we have already entered, if not exactly a new period, at least a transitional phase that can be described as post-modern. One cannot stroll through the Beaubourg gallery without noticing a striking change that sets in roughly in the rooms devoted to the 1960s and continues in later sections. Such movements as Fauvism, Cubism, Futurism, Surrealism, and the various kinds of abstractionism, Action Painting included, do not prepare a period-conscious viewer for developments like Pop Art, Op Art, Minimal Art, Kinetic Art, Process Art, Conceptual Art, Earth Art, Body Art, Photo-Realism, Hyper-Realism, and the several sorts of meta-art, of art about art. Links, of course, can be found, if a special effort is made, for everything is connected with something. But even when there are links between earlier and later work, the later is apt to have a quite different emphasis. On the whole, and in spite of some obvious exceptions, art since about 1960 has become less visual, less aesthetic, less decorative, less dignified, and more intellectual, more rude, more derisive, more questioning. The locus of appreciation has shifted from the retina into the cerebrum. Whereas the Fauves and Cubists looked back to Paul Cézanne, today a large number of painters, sculptors, and miscellaneous conceptualists and gagsters regard Marcel Duchamp as the great father figure—a fact recognized by Hulten, whose first temporary exhibition at the new Paris center was an overpoweringly complete Duchamp retrospective, accompanied by a four-volume catalog.

A Beaubourg stroll can also bring to mind a number of standard museological questions which, while perhaps less exciting than those concerning the sweep of art history, have nevertheless their share of cultural significance. How, for instance, should additions to a museum's permanent collection be made? Like similar institutions elsewhere, MNAM has had to depend heavily on gifts and loans, and it has had to endure the usual disadvantages of such dependence—the donor who wants his stylistically disparate collection kept together in one room, the loyal widow anxious to preserve and enhance the reputation of her artist husband, the wealthy eccentric who has to be cultivated socially by busy curators, the meddler who feels that the gift of a single picture means he can determine museum policy. In 1976 a group of French donors balked strenuously at having their treasures transferred from the Palais de Tokyo to Beaubourg; they feared that their gifts would not be properly exhibited, or perhaps not exhibited at all, in the new building, and they felt that Hulten was not making a proper distinction between the work of established twentieth-century masters and the work of younger artists. In January 1977 a group of American artists and art dealers, partly under pressure from the New York Jewish community, threatened to withdraw their promised gifts and loans to the Paris center because of anger at the French government's release of a suspected Palestinian terrorist. Both the French and the American groups eventually showed signs of behaving more rationally, and Beaubourg did not collapse under the huffing and puffing. Memories of the pressure will remain, however, as reminders of how vulnerable a museum dependent on donations can become.

The answer, of course, is to be rich enough to buy what is wanted. And Beaubourg, although not exactly rich, does have an annual budget for acquisitions, which was 7.5 million francs ($1.5 million) for 1977 and will be adjusted upward in coming years to keep pace with the market. The museum also hopes to receive cash donations from private citizens and corporations. Normally, works of art will be purchased by the state secretary for cultural affairs on the advice of a special Commission d'Acquisition composed of curators, critics, and historians. Up to 10 percent of the purchasing budget, however, can be spent by Hulten about as he pleases, the only requirement being that he explain to the commission what he is doing. The system is intended to provide a certain guarantee of quality—a guarantee that inevitably becomes less and less certain as the works become more recent—and at the same time allow for the experimental buying that is one of the functions of a modern-art curator.

Although it is too early to be definite, one can form a notion of how

183

experimental Hulten will be by glancing at his career and at some of his expressed opinions. He began his serious concern with art by making avant-garde films that were a bit too avant-garde to earn money and then wrote a doctoral thesis on the relationship of the philosophy of Benedict Spinoza to the paintings of Jan Vermeer. In 1958, when he was thirty-four, he helped to open the Moderna Museet in his native Stockholm, and in 1961 he attracted European attention by staging, first in Amsterdam and then in Stockholm, a large exhibition of kinetic art. During the next few years he brought to Sweden the work of such American Pop or semi-Pop artists as Jim Dine, George Segal, Robert Rauschenberg, and Roy Lichtenstein and organized in New York a show called "The Machine at the End of the Mechanical Age." He has written a book on the Swiss kinetic and junk sculptor Jean Tinguely. On the existence of countercultural art in a capitalist context he has said:

> There is a race of birds that lay their eggs in the nests of other birds. The artist belongs to such a race. I believe that in our so-called liberal societies the state must accept, and even pay for, criticism of itself.[8]

On the future of painting and sculpture:

> The avant-garde is always somewhere else than where you expect it. In twenty years our opinion of the present time will be very different from what it is today, and we'll be very surprised.[9]

He has declared that he is in general "not convinced that one should not be a utopian."[10]

Once a permanent collection is formed, how should it be presented to the public? At Beaubourg the gray, beige, and sometimes pink panorama of the city of Paris, visible from three sides of the art gallery, is very much a part of the show. So is the building itself, with its massive exposed steel beams, its great loft space, and its occasional terraces extending out toward the external structural grille. In the daytime the light from the sky merges with the unobtrusive artificial light so as to produce a diffused, uniform glow, uninterrupted by spots of dramatization. The container and its environment merely condition, however, the presentation of the contents; they do not, as in many museums, control it. Low, easily movable partitions and panels, painted an off-white, form a neutral, clinical background against which the sculptures and paintings, the latter without heavy frames, seem to float, each in its own little isolated universe. But the isolation is only relative, for the partitions are arranged so as to create rooms, alcoves, and corridors that are devoted, whenever possible, to particular styles or modern movements, and these compartments are arranged in a roughly chronological order. Thus the place is both an art museum and a history museum, both an enclosure for concentrated aesthetic contemplation and an information center—even something of a teaching machine.

The combination is not at all original. Indeed, it has become so standard in Europe and America that we are apt to forget that it has not always existed, that it is the product of a cultural evolution, and that, although mostly satisfactory, it does have its inconvenient aspects. As recently as the end of the nineteenth century a museum visitor, accustomed to seeing pictures jamming the walls from floor to ceiling, would have felt cheated by an institution like MNAM, which manages to exhibit at one time only a meager twelve hundred of the eight thousand items in its collection. (The situation is somewhat alleviated by the fact that six hundred of the paintings in the reserves are attached to panels that slide down from overhead coffers at the touch of a button.) He would have regarded, not without some justification, the practice of keeping pictures widely separated as a lingering consequence of aestheticism, art for art's sake, the Japanese fad, Walter Pater's "gemlike flame," and all that. As for the chronological visiting circuit, he would probably have accepted it, being a nineteenth-century man brought up on historicism, evolutionism, and biological metaphors. But his grandfather, having been brought up perhaps on the old Baroque notion of an art collection as a splendid miscellany, might have been horrified by such a rational presentation. He might have protested that a historical arrangement encouraged viewers to see works of art as mere documents, that the purpose of a museum was not to instruct but to delight, and that anyway if you really wanted to teach appreciation the best method was to force people to look at paintings and sculptures as such, without an apparatus of dates, names, and stylistic labels. And he might have added that it was a nuisance to have Matisses, for instance, scattered all over the place simply because they were not all painted in the same year.

Probably the best answer to such objections is that a mixture of aestheticism and history was inevitable, given the present state of museological thinking and the disadvantages in other kinds of presentation. But one can hope that Hulten and his assistants will find ways to vary their formula in the future. One such way might be to introduce a little more in the way of value judgments: the viewer's journey through the twentieth century might be interrupted now and then by strong points that ignored chronology. Or perhaps the curators, reviving an idea that was a success at the Louvre and the Uffizi in the nineteenth century, might try crowding a choice of acknowledged, stylistically contrasting masterpieces into a single, central, well-publicized room. The experiment might demonstrate that people today are not as allergic to juxtaposed pictures as they are supposed to be, and in any event it might help to correct one of the almost unavoidable defects of a historical presentation (and of art history in general)—the tendency to upgrade second-rate works because they illustrate a stylistic change, and to neglect some first-rate works because they do not.

Would the experiment create a bit of old-fashioned temple-museum atmosphere? Admittedly it might, and it would then certainly run into opposition from Hulten. On this subject he has written:

> Since the war the typical museum has evolved in its structure and its function. It was at first what it had been in the nineteenth century—a place for conservation, a place for contemplation where one could see and admire the works of the past, objects that had lost their original social, sacred, or other functions, beautiful fossils from a bygone period or civilization. The museum was a catalyst for a collective memory. It prolonged a cult for works that had been sanctified. But such notions, once taken for granted, are now out of date. Since the 1960's new forms of communication have led to new relationships between art and life, between creation and diffusion. Information and criticism have situated and prolonged the work of art in new perspectives. . . . We are headed toward a society in which art will play a very great role. Dialogues, information, and debates should elucidate a work in a living perspective, instead of maintaining it as the object of a passive cult.[11]

He is counting on the "participatory space" designed by Piano and Rogers for help in the process of desanctification and demythologization, and also on the museum's exceptionally large documentation service. In the meantime, as a first step toward making visitors feel at ease, he has substituted informally dressed hostesses and concealed television cameras for the usual uniformed guards, and roaming impromptu commentators for the usual guides and lecturers.

To talk of "information" and "new perspectives" is to raise the problem of special exhibitions. These have become an increasingly important museum activity since World War II, and also an increasingly severe headache. They call for long preparation, expensive yet merely temporary facilities, and costly insurance against damage and the constantly growing danger of theft. They often mean transporting a precious, fragile painting or sculpture over immense distances and exposing it during a few weeks to more shocks and changes in temperature and humidity than it would have endured during years of tranquil existence in its home gallery. Often, too, the home gallery is deprived of one of its chief attractions for several weeks or even months, and expectant, serious tourists are left to discover, too late, that they have come to the wrong place. Perhaps worst of all, a temporary exhibition, especially if it is of the common kind with a theme, can tempt the organizing curator into trying to impose, without adequate reason, a new order and hence a new significance on familiar works. He may thus cease being a properly humble scholar and become instead a sort of theatrical or operatic producer, an artist whose material is other men's art, and the result may be a show that should have been, if anything, a mere suggestion in a learned journal. But none of these disadvantages seems likely to prevail against such facts as that special exhibitions, if carefully organized, can illustrate important aspects of art history, reveal new trends and new artists, and considerably enlarge a museum's public.

And so the Beaubourg MNAM is committed, even addicted, to them. On its schedule for the first part of 1977, in addition to the Duchamp retrospective, were four one-man shows for contemporary artists, three group shows, also contemporary, and a large historical affair, entitled "Paris–New York–Paris," documenting the give-and-take between France and the United States which since 1905 has contributed to the development of modern art.

In spite of all this, French painters and sculptors have not been by any means unanimously favorable toward Beaubourg. Many feel that Pompidou's desire for an institution that would be "at once a museum and a center of creation" has not been respected. Others fear that MNAM's international outlook will in the long run simply mean a surrender to American influence. Still others object to a museum of any sort, on the grounds that it provides an unfair consecration for certain works and certain artists, encourages the development of academic or official styles, and creates for art an entirely artificial setting, cut off from economic, social, and psychological realities. There is some justification, of course, for each of these reactions. But defenders of Beaubourg can reply that MNAM could not have been transformed into a collection of studios, that a museum can help to bring about the conditions for a local renaissance (as the New York MOMA unquestionably did after World War II), that the inventiveness of American painters and sculptors during the last thirty years is as much an inescapable fact of modernism as the inventiveness of the School of Paris during the first part of the twentieth century, and that the opposition of artists to museums is one of the stock, constantly recurring ironies of art history. In 1822 John Constable, several of whose landscapes are now among the glories of the London National Gallery, wrote to a friend:

> Should there be a National Gallery (which is talked of), there will be
> an end of the art in poor old England, and she will become, in all that
> relates to painting, as much a nonentity as every other country that has
> one. The reason is plain; the manufacturers of pictures are then made
> the criterion of perfection, instead of nature.[12]

Camille Pissarro, whose landscapes are now among the glories of the Jeu de Paume, once remarked that in the interest of artistic sincerity it might be a good idea to burn down the Louvre—and he was neither the first nor the last painter to make such an anarchistic suggestion. Victor Vasarely, whose checkerboard abstractions grace the MNAM permanent collection and whose monumental Op portrait of Pompidou greets visitors in the Beaubourg entrance hall, was in principle a member of the opposition as recently as 1970:

> I want to finish once for all with everything that is precisely what
> makes a museum a museum—the unique and irreplaceable work of
> art, the pilgrimage, the contemplation by a passive public.[13]

187

Perhaps the moral here is that the big museums of the nineteenth and twentieth centuries, being largely bourgeois institutions, possess the bourgeoisie's notorious ability to co-opt everybody eventually. Or perhaps, somewhat on the contrary, it is that Hulten is right in thinking that artists are birds that lay their eggs in other birds' nests.

Information without intimidation

Many of the problems that confront the curators of the Beaubourg art gallery have their parallels in those that confront Jean-Pierre Seguin, the director of the Beaubourg Bibliothèque Publique d'Information (the BPI). He too must worry about such matters as space, presentation, cutoff dates, acquisitions, growth, age, and the complaints of creators and consumers (although admittedly writers and readers tend to be more quiet than painters and viewers, and to refrain from suggesting arson at the Bibliothèque Nationale). He too feels the pressure of the past, for the history of libraries and librarianship closely resembles the history of museums and museology. The sanctuaries of classical Greece often had their collections of books along with their collections of paintings and statues, and Imperial Rome saw the creation of a number of fairly large public libraries. After being nursed through the Middle Ages mostly in monasteries, the idea flowered again in the great national libraries of the European seventeenth and eighteenth centuries, and by the middle of the nineteenth, notably in England, it was yielding the free, local, bourgeois-democratic institutions that became the direct ancestors of the BPI—although usually housed, of course, in the library equivalents of palace-museums and temple-museums.

In fact, the BPI is itself, on paper at least, one of these nineteenth-century institutions, for it was conceived during the reign of Napoleon III, who during his years of exile in Great Britain had developed a profound admiration for the English approach to cultural problems. The project remained a project, however, until 1967, when it was actively revived by General de Gaulle, destined for the vacant Plateau Beaubourg, and entrusted to Seguin, a former member of the staff of the Bibliothèque Nationale who had made a reputation as an administrator in the Ministry of Education. In 1969 it was incorporated into Pompidou's plan for the new cultural center.

By that date the need for such a library in Paris, and for literally thousands of smaller versions out in the provinces, had long been evident, and Seguin made an extended tour of foreign libraries and came home convinced that France was about a hundred years behind the United States and Great Britain in terms of public reading facilities. In 1975 François-Régis Bastide, well known as a writer, broadcaster, and publisher, came to a similarly embarrassing conclusion:

It is frightening to notice the backwardness of France [in this respect], not only by comparison with our own estimates of minimal needs but also by comparison with what other European nations are doing. Statistics show that England is beating us by about nine to one—and it is best not to think about any comparisons with the Scandinavian countries. We have less than a thousand municipal libraries, and we need at least five thousand. And let's not talk about our university libraries. Nor, above all, about our general lack of funds for library personnel, acquisitions, and upkeep.[14]

How had the country of Denis Diderot and the Enlightenment got itself into such a scandalous situation? Several explanations have been offered. It has been said that Frenchmen do not much like reading in public places, which can scarcely be demonstrated in the present state of affairs, and that profit-minded French writers and publishers dislike free libraries, which although probably true is also probably true of British writers and publishers. (In fact, a number of the latter have been quite vocal on the subject in recent years.) Perhaps the best explanation is that in a country like France, which has a weak tradition of private cultural philanthropy and a strong tradition of centralized governmental responsibility for cultural activity, there is an inevitable tendency to spend the available money on things that are more visible and audible—more immediately impressive—than bookstacks and reading rooms. One can wonder what would have become of the BPI project if it had not been hitched to a prestige operation involving painting, sculpture, architecture, and music.

The new library, however, cannot in fairness be said to show any signs of having been stinted. It occupies 15,445 square meters of floor space on the second, third, and fourth levels of the Beaubourg building and thus comes close to the size of the art gallery. When operating at full capacity it will have about 1,000,000 books, 4,000 subscriptions to newspapers, magazines, and learned journals, 300,000 slides devoted to art and science, 45,000 microfiche, 30,000 microfilms, 10,000 phonograph records or tapes, and 1,500 documentary films. There are 1,300 places for readers at small, widely spaced desks and tables; this is more than three times the number of places in the main reading room of the Bibliothèque Nationale and is supposed, with allowance for departures, to assure rapidly available seats for about four thousand readers a day. Two hundred and fifty of the places are variously equipped for looking at slides, reading microfiche or microfilms, listening to records or tapes, or learning a language with audiovisual aids. Outside the library proper there are rooms reserved for exhibitions, lectures, films, and children's activities.

Seguin's policy is to provide information for "people from all walks of life without distinction,"[15] and with a minimum of the formalities and restraints that might intimidate a potential but inexperienced user of the establishment. There are no fees, no cards, and no request slips at the BPI, and no surveillants enthroned behind a pulpitlike desk. The arriving reader is merely asked to leave his briefcase or the equivalent with the cloakroom attendants (who are not allowed to accept tips). After that he has free access to everything in the stacks except microfiche, tapes, and phonograph records. If he wants to use some of the viewing or audio equipment, he reads the instructions and goes ahead. Members of the staff leave him strictly alone unless he asks for help in finding something or in operating a machine. Since the BPI is not a lending library, he leaves his book or other document on a table when he decides to go home. (If he tries to smuggle anything out, a little metal plate inside it will set off an alarm as he goes through the door.)

Trying to be useful for "people from all walks" has raised a difficult question. What should be on the shelves? Seguin has been attempting to decide this with an acquisitions policy that is a mixture of refusals, hypotheses, and experimentation. He has rejected the possibility of becoming a legal-deposit institution like the Bibliothèque Nationale and of thus receiving free copies of every French publication, for that would mean a flood of mostly unwanted material. (France is now publishing roughly 24,000 book titles a year.) Archives, primary sources, rare works, and other things of interest primarily to scholars have been ruled out on the grounds that the BPI, while often presenting the results of specialized research, should not attempt to furnish the means for such research. Nor, its director feels, should it attempt to play the role of a university or lycée library, for this would mean shelves controlled by professors' outside-reading lists, and seats and equipment monopolized by students. What these refusals have led to is a collection that plays down literature and emphasizes general information in the fields of science, art, and history. Usually only the most recent works on a given subject—preferably those published during the preceding five years—are offered, although a classic in the field may be included. The idea, Seguin has explained, is "to satisfy contemporary needs for permanent education." But all this is being kept extremely tentative and flexible: there were only 300,000 books on the shelves for the opening day, and the buildup toward 1,000,000 is being accomplished slowly on the basis of studies of demand. If the readers want more on space travel and less on anthropology, that is what they will get.

The interior designed by Piano and Rogers lends itself admirably to such a flexible acquisitions policy. Since there are no weight-bearing walls, expanding or reducing a section of the library is largely just a matter of moving some of the low, light, freestanding bookstacks to another place on the floor of the loft. There is always, of course, the task of making the required changes in the catalog, the classification system, and the prepared bibliographies that are available for readers, but here too everything has been simplified. The catalog is edited by a computer. The use of the Universal Decimal Classification (which is somewhat similar to the Dewey system favored by most American libraries) permits a rapid regrouping, under the same number, of all the documents treating a given subject. The computer also takes care of bibliographies—which in any event are not much of a problem for the average reader at the BPI, since free access to the stacks means that bibliographies of a sort are before his eyes in the form of the books themselves.

Is the final effect rather disconcertingly new-fashioned and cold? Admittedly, the little metal reading tables and the freestanding bookstacks, painted in an aggressively cheerful combination of creamy white and bright green, are a long way from the warm wood and the high, multitiered, wall-covering stacks of many nineteenth-century libraries, and there is nothing very cozily romantic about the great hall with its strong light and exposed steel beams. Certain aspects of Seguin's flexible acquisitions policy can suggest cultural market research, and the batteries of visual and audio equipment can remind one unpleasantly of some of Marshall McLuhan's notions about the future of print. There is something vaguely troubling, too, about the constant use of the word *information* in the institution's handouts, to the point of implying that stimulating the imagination and transmitting values are not part of the proper business of a library. But one shouldn't carp, for the BPI is young, optimistic, and obviously determined to promote knowledge and democracy, and its many gadgets are, after all, the servants, not the masters, of the book.

In favor of amnesia

Pompidou may have been thinking of the future Institut de Recherche et Coordination Acoustique/Musique (IRCAM) when he said that he wanted a center of creation. In any event, this component of the Beaubourg complex does indeed attempt to foster artistic creation—although it does so by methods that are not, at first glance, particularly artistic.

The principal idea behind IRCAM is simple. It is to act as a marriage broker for modern music and modern science, to get the two disciplines under one roof, and to trust that the offspring—with some help from modern technology—will turn out to be new and excellent kinds of musical composition. Composer and conductor Pierre Boulez, who founded and now directs the institute, has explained his objectives in the following terms:

> The creator working with only his intuition is powerless to provide a complete translation of musical invention. He must collaborate with the scientific research worker in order to envisage the distant future, to imagine less personal, broader solutions. . . . As for the scientist, we are of course not asking him to compose, but to conceive with precision what the composer, or instrumentalist, expects of him, to understand the direction contemporary music has taken, and to orient his imagination along these lines. . . . In this way we hope to forge a kind of common language that scarcely exists at present, while training a staff that will be basically oriented towards musical creation.[16]

Why cannot composers just go on working as they have for the past few centuries? Because, Boulez says, electronic and computer technology has put us on the threshold of vast developments in sound, and because a composer can neither ignore this new technology nor master its complexities all by himself. To work toward the desired mastery of these techniques, IRCAM has assembled an international team of fifty-four composers, performers, researchers, technicians, thinkers, managers, and plain secretaries. Although many of these people, like Boulez himself, have other commitments to worry about, they have all been devoting a lot of their time to the job in Paris. Among the composers, in addition to the director, are the Yugoslav (although French-born) Vinko Globokar, professor at the Staatliche Musik Hochschule in Cologne and best known as an astonishing virtuoso on the trombone; the Italian Luciano Berio, who brings to IRCAM the experience he gained as a founder of the Studio di Fonologia Musicale in Milan; the Frenchman Jean-Claude Risset, whose career has included five years of research at the Bell Telephone Laboratories in New York; the American Gerald Bennett, recently the director of the conservatory of Basel; and the Frenchman Michel Decoust, formerly the director of a conservatory at Pantin, on the outskirts of Paris. Among the men who have been making important contributions on the scientific and technical side are Max Mathews, research director in acoustics and psychology at the Bell Telephone Laboratories, and acoustics expert Manfred Schroeder, director of the Physikalische Institut of Göttingen (and also a Bell Laboratories veteran).

Globokar heads the important Instruments and Voice Department, whose multiple assignment is to discover, invent, and disseminate innovations in traditional Western instrumental and vocal techniques; study Asian and other non-Western techniques without condescension and without "colonizing" them; develop new instruments, or devices that radically transform old instruments; and investigate the psychology, the physiology, and the contemporary social role of the performing musician. Berio heads the Electro-Acoustics Department, which is officially charged by IRCAM with "studying the means of processing electronic sound production in real time and introducing digital techniques for generating and processing signals (particularly intermodulation and voltage-control techniques)."[17] Risset, who runs the Computer Department, is required to do research on sound and the synthesis of sonic material with computers. He must also study the man–machine relationship in the field of music, improve present methods of computer-assisted composition, probe the many psychoacoustic phenomena that affect our enjoyment of music, and take care of IRCAM's general need for scientific calculations, data processing, circuit simulations, trial runs, and automatic controls. Bennett heads the Diagonal Department, which—as its name is intended to imply—slants across the organization chart, coordinates the various branches of research, instigates the transplanting of techniques from one department to another, and looks into the links between music theory and other areas of inquiry. Decoust is in charge of the Pedagogic Department, which is scheduled to start functioning sometime late in 1978, when the results of IRCAM research will presumably begin to pile up in usable amounts. The department will study ways to train people for a new music and will provide advanced conservatory students with the technical facilities they need for becoming familiar with new instrumental techniques and new ways to compose. Boulez hopes that the pedagogy that emerges will have an effect outside the avant-garde and will eventually help to make all sorts of music, including the non-Western, more accessible to the average listener.

Something of the spirit in which these men are approaching their assignments can be gathered from a sampling of their remarks during IRCAM press conferences. "In my opinion," Globokar has said, "the sonic material that is available to us today, at a time when everything is permitted, has become grayer and grayer, and it is precisely because of this grayness that musical sounds are no longer capable of communicating a message."[18] Berio, taking a more optimistic line, has promised that "the Electro-Acoustics Department, and IRCAM as a whole, will not be a hospital for sick music, first of all because I believe that music itself is never sick—it is what society and the composer make of it."[19] Risset has been cautious but hopeful: "Direct synthesis makes the computer the most general of sound sources, potentially capable of producing any sound, but one must learn how to use these new possibilities."[20] Bennett has been antiromantic: "Contemporary music has at the moment less need of individual souls and their vagaries than of common effort to explore its own innermost nature, to explore sound itself."[21] Decoust has emphasized a methodical approach: "We must clarify things from the inside. . . . It is only by developing a feeling for fundamental research that we can have an evolving society, a society that does not, for example, raise idiotic questions like whether or not electronic music has a heart."[22]

Finding the right spot in the loft spaces of the Beaubourg building for such a specialized enterprise proved difficult, and so Piano and Rogers finally decided to put it all underground. The result, which has been referred to as Boulez's Nibelheim (an allusion to his conducting of Wagner's *Ring* at Bayreuth), is a warren of studios, laboratories, halls, offices, and study rooms beneath a pedestrian square that lies between the main Beaubourg plaza and the church of Saint-Merri. The whole structure, which has a total floor area of about 4,800 square meters and a maximal depth of 16 meters, is encased in thick insulating materials that increase the sonic isolation provided by the surrounding earth. A glassed-over zone helps to prevent claustrophobia and gives curious Parisians a chance to peer in and see what some of the modern-music Nibelungs are doing. The most spectacular part is an auditorium, called the Espace de Projection, that accommodates about four hundred people and functions as a combination of concert hall, experimental theater, recording studio, and scientific laboratory. There are mobile ladders and bridges for performers, bouquets of colored lights, and a large collection of loudspeakers and tape machines. The ceiling goes up or down in three separate sections, flexible metal partitions divide the room as desired, and 172 pivoting, prismatic wall elements reflect or absorb sound waves to the exact degree that is wanted. These devices are controlled by an electronic console that can be coupled to a computer, so that the resulting spatial and acoustical configurations can be programmed, or memorized for future experiments. To counteract the possible impression that what he has created is a closed, mysterious domain, an underground ivory tower for a few far-out musicians and wizards, Boulez has been carefully cultivating his relations with the public. A special mobile unit, carrying experimental equipment, has been created and given the mission of diffusing the results of avant-garde research. Programs of concerts, lectures, and debates have been organized for French provincial cities and have been animated by Globokar, Berio, Risset, Bennett, Decoust, and Boulez in person. An "exhibition" of sound, with works performed by various combinations of electronic equipment and modified traditional instruments, has been staged at Beaubourg. A documentation service has been set up to supply interested persons with publications, tapes, and audiovisual material (in certain cases, of course, for a fee). The most ambitious manifestation so far, however, has been a gigantic, yearlong modern music festival, entitled "Passage of the Twentieth Century" and intended as a salute to the opening of the new Paris cultural center. Concerts have been given (or were scheduled when this article was being written) in the main Beaubourg building, at the Opéra, and in seven other Paris halls or theaters, by eighteen French and foreign symphony orchestras or smaller ensembles and by a procession of sixty soloists—including such international stars as Cathy Berberian, Yvonne Minton, Aurèle Nicolet, Heinz Holliger, Daniel Barenboïm, Maurizio Pollini, Itzhak Perlman, Pinchas Zuckerman, and Mstislav Rostropovitch. In a preface written before the first concert, Boulez explained his intentions and those of his institute:

> Before devoting itself completely and exclusively to research, IRCAM
> wants to focus, in public, on what exists as an immediate or distant
> reality and also on what ought to exist in the perspective of the future.
> . . . What we have as our constant aim is the transition from works that
> have become models to experiments that are courageous and
> adventurous.[23]

Actually, as a look through the full festival program revealed, what was being offered to listeners was a musical equivalent for the Beaubourg museum of modern painting and sculpture. Compositions by 116 composers, from Gustav Mahler to youngsters born since the end of World War II, were listed. Nearly everything from Impressionism to Computerism was sampled. But not quite everything, for a second look made it clear that to Boulez "twentieth century," like "modern" to Hulten, means a period style, not just a stretch of time. Claude Debussy was represented, but not Maurice

Ravel; Arnold Schoenberg, but not Richard Strauss; Charles Ives, but not Percy Grainger.

Members of the IRCAM staff are aware that what they are attempting is not very new. After all, ingenious minds have been dreaming of electromechanical or electronic musical instruments since at least the closing years of the nineteenth century, when an American scientist, Thaddeus Cahill, developed his Dynamophone, or telharmonium. (Like many of its successors, it was fascinating in theory and rather depressing to listen to.) During the 1920s and 1930s there were extraordinary, although usually short, bursts of enthusiasm for a long list of such devices—the spherophone, the partiturophon, the etherophone or theremin, the Trautonium, the *Ondes Martenot*, the mellertion, the dynaphone, the emicon, and the hellertion, to name only some. Tape music has been familiar since the 1940s, the synthesizer since the mid-1950s, and computer composition since the late 1950s. Operations similar to IRCAM's have long been sponsored by many American universities, beginning with the establishment of the Experimental Music Studio at the University of Illinois in 1958 and the creation of the Columbia-Princeton Electronic Music Center in 1959. European radio networks, beginning with the formation of a studio at Cologne in 1951, have been working in the same direction.

Moreover, in this context Paris was far from being a laggard when Boulez launched his new institute. Here, in the late 1940s, Pierre Schaeffer and Pierre Henry developed the type of musical collage called *musique concrète* and pioneered, for all practical purposes, the whole concept of tape music. Schaeffer's Groupe de Recherches Musicales, financed by Radio France and directed by the talented François Bayle, has continued as a very active organization. The French composer Pierre Barbaud has been working with computers for nearly twenty years. So, with more fanfare, has the Paris-based Greek composer Yannis Xenakis, who has also, since the early 1960s, been doing a good deal of fundamental musical research with a team of mathematicians and physical scientists.

In the light of such facts, was IRCAM really needed? Wouldn't Pompidou have been more effective, and more just, if he had simply distributed his subsidy among already existing musical activities? These questions are variations on those that have often been asked about Beaubourg as a whole, and general answers are not hard to come by. Boulez, however, has some specific ones of his own. Other musical research centers, he argues, are on the whole too small and too dependent on larger undertakings with different aims. The electronic studios attached to radio networks, for example, are often subject, so far as diffusion is concerned, to program policies that mostly ignore electronic—and in fact all modern—music; and the studios sponsored by American universities are often subject to standard music departments that are inclined, quite naturally and almost inevitably, to emphasize the works of the great composers of the past. Also, these smaller centers tend to be staffed mostly by musicians and thus tend to isolate music

195

from science and technology. By contrast with all this, IRCAM is large enough to have its own priorities and to get composers, scientists, and technicians together in one place. Will the new institute annex or destroy the enterprises of people like Bayle, Barbaud, and Xenakis? Here Boulez has been a bit vague, remarking simply that he has no Napoleonic ambitions and that he is ready to cooperate with everybody. Understandably, he has been inclined to talk more about IRCAM's large purposes than about its connection with French musical politics.

He has insisted repeatedly on the importance of technology—of new instruments and new sonic material—in the stylistic history of music. "It's like architecture," he has argued. "A new style followed the invention of glass and steel. You can't build a Greek temple with glass and steel. The material itself is central."[24] He has a point, of course, for it is easy to see links between technical factors and stylistic change in all the arts. Pottery changed with the invention of the wheel; Renaissance painting emerged with the use of the oil technique. The links are particularly evident in musical history. Without the new sonic material—the more powerful, more brilliant, more expressive effects which the violin produced—European music would not have evolved as it did from the middle of the sixteenth century to the middle of the eighteenth, and the classical symphony would not have appeared. The new sonic material generated by the piano can be cited as another of the many possible examples, for without it the accentuations, crescendos, diminuendos, strong rhythms, and singing passages characteristic of Romantic keyboard music can scarcely be imagined. Neither the force of a Beethoven sonata nor the poetry of a Chopin nocturne can be obtained from a harpsichord.

To maintain, however, that in the stylistic evolution of Western music technical innovations and new sonic material have always been "central" would be, as Boulez himself would undoubtedly admit, to exaggerate for the sake of the IRCAM argument. Obviously, a lot of social, psychological, philosophical, politico-economic, aesthetic, and general cultural factors have also been at work and have often been determinant. During the series of important changes, from roughly the eleventh century through the fifteenth, that gave rise to fully elaborated polyphony, European composers concentrated largely on choral writing, and thus their sonic material remained practically unaltered. The revolutionary notions of key and tonality arose gradually in the sixteenth century from an internal process of erosion and consolidation of the medieval modal system, not from the introduction of a new technology. Schoenberg dropped them and eventually developed his dodecaphonic system by a somewhat similar process of erosion and consolidation, without help from Cahill's telharmonium or any other new instrument. Such evidence, which could be added to without much trouble, does not, to be sure, prove that technology has been important only on rare occasions. But even that admission could do with some qualification, for there are good reasons for thinking that new instruments with a real stylistic impact are always, like other inventions that count, responses to felt needs. In other words, they are preceded by perceptible changes in musical sensibility. The fact that the violin rapidly replaced the medieval rebec and the Renaissance fiddle strongly suggests that it was wanted before it existed, and we know from the testimony of eighteenth-century musicians that the piano was born out of their dissatisfaction with the harpsichord.

Is there a felt need for new instruments today? More specifically, has there been a change in musical sensibility that calls for the new sonic material produced by electronic equipment? That there are some signs of such a felt need and such a change cannot be denied. One can cite, for example, the success of electronic popular music in recent years, the growing number of musical-research centers, the growing number of musicians who know something about such formerly esoteric things as sine and saw-tooth waves, and Globokar's already quoted opinions that conventional musical sound has become grayer and grayer and incapable of communicating a message. But all this evidence looks very slight when placed in the full context of contemporary musical activity. Performers are continuing with their old instruments, much as they have since the beginning of the nineteenth century. The electronic-music public is a small minority inside the modern-music minority. Most significantly, the immense majority of modern composers, including Boulez himself, have continued—a generation after the introduction of tape, synthesizers, and computers—to favor the old instruments, the old sonic material. It is as if Claudio Monteverdi had composed for the rebec, and Felix Mendelssohn for the harpsichord.

Given the situation, IRCAM cannot be regarded as simply a response to a demand, a product of normal stylistic evolution. In fact, it reverses the usual process in which a change in sensibility leads to technical innovation; it attempts, through technical innovation, to persuade composers to change their sensibilities. Even more radically, it tries to persuade them to abandon the last traces of historicism in their art, to get rid of the residual pastness that is always present in a traditional instrument, and to take a fresh, scientific, and hence ahistorical look at fundamentals. For, of course, electronic equipment does not just produce new sounds; it also renders obsolete nearly all the musical structures that have been devised, in both East and West, during the past several thousands of years. You can play a Haydn harpsichord piece on a piano, but you cannot play a Debussy piano piece on a synthesizer, not without indulging in a tour de force as absurd as reproducing a Greek temple in steel and glass. And that this sort of forced, total break with the past is what Boulez has in mind has been made abundantly clear. As long ago as 1971, in an essay entitled "Style or Idea?" and subtitled "In Praise of Amnesia," he was already denouncing historicism:

> Ah, how good it would be to wake up and find that one had forgotten everything, absolutely everything! Each of us, at each instant, has at his disposition a cultural encyclopaedia, all the memory in the world. It

has become almost impossible to ignore history, not only the history of our own culture, but also that of other civilizations, the most distant, the most recent.[25]

In 1976, shortly before the opening of the Centre Beaubourg, he added:

I have always thought that the strong civilizations are those that laugh at preceding civilizations and know how to forget them, or destroy them.[26]

Conservative composers cannot say that they have not been warned.

Beyond museology

Although the French critics who have scoffed at Beaubourg as merely a cultural supermarket have been grossly, deliberately unfair, they have at least had the merit of calling attention to the fact that the new center is something more than an innocent haunt of the Muses, and something more than an example of socialized art patronage. For it does exist, after all, in a capitalist society, and it cannot help having a sometimes ambiguous relationship with that society. Nothing, one may feel, could be more remote from the marketplace than the disinterested musical research that is the principal concern of IRCAM. Yet that kind of research today means, inevitably, that you are improving the public image of a computer corporation, for example, and helping to sell its products. Nothing, one may feel, could be more innocent than a painting that has been admitted to the sacred, clinical corridors of the Musée National d'Art Moderne. It ceases, once inside those purifying precincts, to be a piece of merchandise; it becomes Art with a capital *A,* and an inalienable part of the French national patrimony, forever unsalable. Yet it immediately increases the market value of other works by the same artist, and of works in the same stylistic category. Indeed, the mere existence of a place like Beaubourg increases the market value of all modern art, upgrades the importance of Paris in the international art business, and stimulates in general the turnover in paintings and sculptures. It is not by accident that in the streets around the museum there are now some eighty private galleries, whereas five years ago there were only three or four.

IRCAM in its underground quarters and the BPI and MNAM on their upper levels usually give the impression of ignoring, with the dignity proper in cultural agencies, these crude economic realities. The Centre de Création Industrielle (the CCI) does not. Situated as it is at the plaza level of the main building, and thus at one of the main nexuses of the "participatory space," it suggests rather a cheerful, informal readiness to enter the melee of modern daily life. Although with its 3,730 square meters of floor space it is the smallest of the four main Beaubourg components, it is easily, according to attendance records so far, the most popular. Also—a fact that does not make for much popularity with French industrialists and certain ministries—its staff is easily the youngest, the most unionized, and politically the furthest to the left.

The CCI began in 1969 as a branch of the Union Centrale des Arts Décoratifs, and until its transfer to the Beaubourg building it staged most of its exhibitions at the Musée des Arts Décoratifs, which occupies a wing of the nineteenth-century part of the Louvre. Its mixed ancestry includes the English arts and crafts movement led by William Morris, the somewhat similar but less medievalist movement in nineteenth-century Scandinavia, the Bauhaus of the 1920s and its later offshoots, the various organizations that have been created, particularly since World War II, to defend American consumers, and the countercultural movement that got under way in the United States and Western Europe in the 1960s and eventually came to include a good deal of environmentalism. This mixture of romanticism and rationalism has not always made for a unified outlook among the eighty-five members of the staff, but in general one can say that the CCI regards itself as a diffuser of information on the relations between the modern individual and spaces, objects, and signs—which comes down in practice to a concern with urbanism and architecture, industrial design, and publicity, the graphic arts, and visual communication as a whole. To make the diffusion as efficient as possible, the organization is divided into five more or less distinct "services": Specialized Documentation, Product Information, Exhibitions, Publications and Productions, and Studies and Projects. (So far these services have been changing their names every few months, and they may continue to do so after this article is in print. But the five sorts of activity are not apt to change.)

The Specialized Documentation Service includes a library of 220 magazines, both French and foreign, and 3,000 exhibition catalogs, professional directories, lengthy technical reports, and other books; extensive files on industrial designers, graphic artists, illustrators, architects, and town planners, with a computerized index; files and card indexes on such subjects as color, signs, playgrounds, transportation, and city street equipment; a collection of slides on urbanism, architecture, building materials, color theory, and such more specific subjects as exhibitions and trademarks; and a collection of films on such people as Breuer, Charles Eames, Alvar Aalto, and Charles Rennie Mackintosh. The service publishes catalogs of fundamental works on design, a yearly directory of designers, a monthly bibliographical bulletin, and a quarterly one, in English, for the International Council of Societies of Industrial Design. It does special studies on request, a recent one being a survey of signal systems in subways, done for the planning group of the Paris Metro. It will even answer questions on the telephone, if they are not too complicated.

The Product Information Service feeds, manages, and offers to the public a computerized accumulation of facts pertaining to the *valeur d'usage*, the "use value," of more than 30,000 French brands of durable manufactured objects—razors, vacuum cleaners, and so on. With the help of an operator (although the CCI hopes that people will eventually learn to handle the computer console themselves) a consumer tells this data bank roughly what he wants to buy and how much he would like to pay. He gets back the sort of information that never appears in advertisements; he discovers, for example, that a dozen French dishwashing machines are absolutely identical on the inside, and that he may pay as much as 40 percent more for a stylish shape and some fancy control buttons. What if he simply wants to buy some good-looking chairs? The computer will then remain silent, for it knows nothing about anything as subjective as what the CCI cautiously refers to as *valeur d'estime*, "esteem value." The inquiring consumer will, however, be given a list of chairs selected by a committee of human judges whose tastes are presumably good because formed by experience.

The other three services are perhaps adequately described by their names. So far the more important "studies and projects" have been undertaken at the request of ministries and municipal councils and have been concerned with public buildings and *micro-urbanism*—a term that refers to planning, not for an entire town, but for a new complex in an existing town layout. The more important "publications and productions" have been manuals and films for teachers, monographs on categories of objects in daily life, and a slick quarterly magazine, called *Traverses*, each issue of which has been devoted to a theoretical discussion of a single theme: functionalism, for example, and, less expectedly, "places and objects of death." Among the 1977 "exhibitions," by which the CCI means not only shows of objects and images but all sorts of staged events that give rise to encounters between the public and designers, were "Archaeology of a City," "Anatomy of a Building," "Furniture for Learning," "A Day of Women," "Who Decides for the City?," "Fifteen Posters for Amnesty International," and "Pinned-on Clothes."

Each of these activities has revealed the ambiguity in the cultural mission of the CCI and has raised hard questions for conscientious staff members. Should the agency be a show window for the products of French industry? Or should it be a constant, although constructive, critic of those products? Should it be, as the Bauhaus was, optimistic about the possibilities in modern technology or, as a lot of serious people are today, mostly pessimistic? Should it place industrial design, architecture, town planning, visual communication, and related matters in their full ideological and social contexts? If so, how can this be done without getting into politics?

During the months immediately preceding the inauguration of the Centre Beaubourg, the French government, along with many of the French businessmen who supported the government, became increasingly vexed by the answers that were being given to such questions. A CCI show called "Factory, Work, Architecture" had taken what a conservative politician called a negative approach to the issues involved. Another exhibition, "Alternative Architecture in the United States," had included panels with texts by such iconoclastic types as Herbert Marcuse and Allan Ginsberg. An event entitled "What Is a Publicity Campaign?" had been rather ironic about the posters of an important Paris bank. A film about recent Paris architecture had not taken exactly a positive approach. Finally François Mathey, the founder and director of the CCI, was persuaded by the state secretary for cultural affairs to withdraw and become simply the chief curator of the Musée des Arts Décoratifs, and his principal CCI assistant, François Barré, was dismissed for what was officially termed "a lack of maturity." Staff members staged a twenty-four-hour strike and denounced what they called "a takeover by a centralized and hierarchical administration."[27] But the government held firmly to its decisions and eventually named as the new director Jacques Mullender, a respected civil servant who had spent much of his career in the Ministry of Equipment and the Société Nationale Indus-rielle Aérospatiale, which had helped to build the supersonic Concorde. He immediately took the positive approach that had allegedly been lacking:

> The CCI ought not to forget that the second "C" in its initials stands for creation. All calling into question should be accompanied by concrete proposals. We must foster a hope that everyone can do something. Our final objective is to transform fifty million consumers into fifty million creators.[28]

Since then the crisis appears to have subsided. The presence, however, of a state official at the helm of the CCI, whereas the BPI, MNAM, and IRCAM are run respectively by a librarian, a curator, and a composer, can be taken to indicate that down there among the electric razors and dish-washing machines the Centre Beaubourg begins to move beyond the functions of even a *mouseion*—and beyond the scope of the present article.

[1] Calvin Tomkins, *Merchants and Masterpieces: The Story of the Metropolitan Museum of Art* (New York: E. P. Dutton & Co., 1970; paperback ed., 1973), p. 100.

[2] *Lettre d'Information No. 1* (Paris: Centre National d'Art et de Culture Georges Pompidou, 1975), p. 2.

[3] Ibid., p. 3.

[4] For all the quotations from Piano and Rogers see *Architectural Design*, May 1975, pp. 307–8.

[5] *Le Monde*, 4 November 1976, p. 17.

[6] *Le Monde*, 1 July 1976, p. 13.

[7] Barbara Rose, *American Art since 1900: A Critical History* (New York: Frederick A. Praeger, 1967), p. 113.

[8] *Art Press*, July–August 1975, p. 12.

[9] Ibid., p. 12.

[10] Ibid., p. 12.

[11] Centre Beaubourg press release, 1976 (otherwise undated), p. 5.

[12] Philip Hendy, *The National Gallery, London*, rev. paperback ed. (London: Thames and Hudson, 1968), p. 16.

[13] *Encyclopaedia Universalis* (Paris, 1974), vol. 2, p. 449.
[14] *Le Monde*, 21 February 1975, p. 22.
[15] Centre Beaubourg press release, 1976 (otherwise undated), p. 22.
[16] *IRCAM* (Paris: Centre National d'Art et de Culture Georges Pompidou, 1976), p. 6.
[17] Ibid., p. 15.
[18] Ibid., p. 14.
[19] Ibid., p. 15.
[20] Ibid., p. 16.
[21] Ibid., p. 17.
[22] *Le Monde*, 2 October 1975, p. 19.
[23] *Passage du XXe siècle (Festival program, 1977), p. 1.*
[24] *Newsweek*, 7 February 1977, p. 68.
[25] *Musique en Jeu*, no. 4 (1971), p. 13.
[26] *Le Monde*, 23 December 1976, p. 11.
[27] Press release by the CCI staff, 21 May 1976.
[28] *Le Nouvel Observateur*, 24 January 1977, p. 82.

BIBLIOGRAPHY

In addition to the books and articles cited in the notes, the following may be consulted:
AFFEULPIN, GUSTAVE. *La Soi-disant Utopie du Centre Beaubourg.* Paris: Éditions Entente, 1976.
L'Arc, no. 63 (1975; special issue on Beaubourg).
Créé, 25 January 1977 (special issue).
DAVIS, DOUGLAS. "The Idea of a 21st Century Museum." *Art Journal*, Spring 1976, pp. 253–58.
MOLLARD, CLAUDE. *L'enjeu du Centre Georges-Pompidou.* Paris: Éditions 10/18, 1977.
Les Nouvelles Litteraires, 27 January 1977 (special issue).

NOTE TO THE READER

Save as they are mentioned in Homer, there is no discussion of the Muses in *GBWW*. References to inspiration as the source of art may be found, however, under Topic 5 of Chapter 4, ART, in the *Syntopicon*. In the same chapter the references listed under Topic 7a dealing with art as a source of pleasure, and those under Topic 10b, where the political regulation of the arts for the common good and the problem of censorship are considered, all bear on the subject of public concern with, and support for, the arts.

See also Chapter 20, EDUCATION, the references under Topic 8b dealing with the economic support of educational institutions; Chapter 56, MEMORY AND IMAGINATION, the references under Topics 4a and 4b, which are relevant insofar as the museum is the embodiment of cultural memory; and Chapter 90, STATE, where references to the importance of the arts in political life will be found under Topic 7b.

PART THREE

The Contemporary Status of a Great Idea

The Idea of Religion—Part One

John Edward Sullivan, O.P.

In 1973 John Edward Sullivan became associated with the Institute for Philosophical Research in Chicago and undertook a lengthy study of the idea of religion. A shortened version of this was subsequently prepared in the form of the following essay. It is in two parts, of which the second part will appear in *The Great Ideas Today* next year.

A Roman Catholic priest and scholar, Father Sullivan entered the Dominican Order in 1952 and was ordained in 1959. Educated at the University of Michigan, and at the Dominican houses of study in River Forest, Ill.; Dubuque, Iowa; Washington, D.C.; and Rome, he holds degrees in Thomistic philosophy and in systematic Catholic theology.

Two years after his ordination he accepted the post of professor of historical theology at the Aquinas Institute in Dubuque. He remained at the institute until 1968, serving as associate dean from 1964 to 1966. In 1969 he became professor of philosophy at St. Albert's College in Oakland, Calif., and professor of the philosophy of religion at the Graduate Theological Union in Berkeley. For the past two years he has been visiting professor of philosophy and religion at St. John's College in Camarillo, Calif.

The Image of God, a study of Saint Augustine, was published by Father Sullivan in 1963, and *Prophets of the West* in 1970. He is the author of articles on religious freedom, man in history, the spirituality of Teilhard de Chardin, and other subjects.

I.   Need for a prolegomenon 206
     A. The method to be used.. 210
         1. Agreement and disagreement 211
         2. Issues and controversies 212
         3. Hypothesis and evidence.. 214
     B. The hypothesis in outline 216
II. The kinds of religion 218
     A. Basic agreement and disagreement.. 219
         1. Basic conceptual agreement about religion................ 219
         2. Basic conceptual disagreement about religion 222
     B. The basic kinds of religion.. 224
         1. Ceremonial religion.. 224
         2. Moral religion.. 226
         3. Mystical religion 229
         4. Revealed religion.. 234
         5. Secular religion 241
     C. Atypical kinds of religion.. 244
III. Conceptual controversy among the kinds of religion 247
     A. Existential and conceptual issues.. 247
     B. Issues on which four kinds side together against one.......... 249
         1. Issues concerning the religious object........................ 249
         2. Issues about the concept of religious activity............ 251
     C. Issues on which the five kinds are more or less evenly
         divided 253
         1. Issues concerning the religious object........................ 253
         2. Issues concerning the religious activity...................... 255
     D. The secular repudiation: a conceptual counterattack 256
IV. A dialectical understanding of religion in general 258
     A. The problem of religion in general 258
     B. Religion in general.. 260
         1. Transcendent goodness 261
         2. Reverence.. 264
         3. Reverence for transcendent goodness 267

I. NEED FOR A PROLEGOMENON

Philosophical thought is not itself a collaborative undertaking. Nevertheless, headway is gained in the pursuit of truth through the combined efforts of many men. Such was the claim of Aristotle, the intellectual heir of Plato and Socrates, at the very beginning of the philosophical thought of the West. "We contribute little individually," Aristotle writes in the *Metaphysics*, Book II, chapter 1, but, he adds, "by the united effort of all a considerable amount is amassed."* It does not detract from the contributions of the great philosophers to say that their creative thought must be supplemented by collective endeavor.

For philosophy to live up to the demands of its collective dimension, certain conditions have to be met.[1] In the first place, philosophers must somehow confront one another in the light of their differences or conduct their own inquiries against the background of the total philosophical diversity to which they are themselves contributing. To the extent that philosophical diversity involves genuine disagreements, rational debate becomes an essential part of the philosophical enterprise as a whole. The existential conditions of the philosophical pursuit of truth are such that disagreement, rather than agreement, is generally regarded as the mark of its health and competence. Yet disagreement is profitable only when it is capable of resolution through the rational debate of fundamental issues.

Another condition to be met before philosophy can become a collective endeavor is that there be an impartial clarification of the whole relevant tradition of thought about the controverted subjects. Rational debate cannot be jointly carried on and enriched by the latest generation of philosophers except as it has before it the main outlines of the controversies which so far have developed. Nor can the individual philosopher relate his own theories to the thoughts of others without some knowledge of the agreements and disagreements that already exist on the subjects with which he is concerned. Before any striking progress toward the collective acquisition of truth in controversial matters can be reasonably hoped for in philosophy, it is necessary that such controversy and debate that already exist on the subject be made explicitly available for study. What is needed is a map of the controverted philosophical terrain, a map which is impartial, like the ordinary road map, in that it leaves all the critical decisions to the one who wishes to undertake the journey.

Among all philosophical subjects, religion is surely the most controversial. It occupies an extraordinarily ambiguous position in the minds of both reflective thinkers and ordinary human beings, as H. J. Paton has pointed out.[2] Serious thinkers may differ in their theories about art or science, for instance, but they are broadly agreed about the kind of activity that characterizes the artist or scientist. More than that, few philosophers would deny

---

* Cf. *GBWW*, Vol. 8, p. 511c.

all value to art and to science. This is not the case with religion. What some thinkers regard as religion is regarded by others as not religious at all. Others hold that religion is superstition and say that it should be abolished. If it be true that philosophy in general needs impartial maps of its controverted terrain, how acute must the need be in the philosophy of religion, where there appears to be no universally acceptable answer even to the basic question of what religion is. In such a case, where no conceptual agreement exists as to the nature of the subject under debate, the territory to be charted and clarified is the controversy about the very concept of religion itself.[3]

Any detailed illustration of the conceptual variations that are to be found on the theme of religion would be out of place here, but one or two instances may be noted. A famous formulation is offered by Fielding's Mr. Thwackum, in *Tom Jones*, who has no doubt at all what entity the term *religion* must refer to. "When I mention religion," he states, "I mean the Christian religion; and not only the Christian religion, but the Protestant religion; and not only the Protestant religion, but the Church of England."[4] Such an identification of a species of religion with its genus is not peculiar to eighteenth-century English divines. It is a standing temptation for the Western world to assume that *religion* means divinely revealed religion or religions. The attitude thus expressed may not be as narrow as that of Thwackum, but there can be little doubt that the implication of this identification of revealed religion with the whole of religion is that if one is not a Christian, or a Jew, or a Muslim, one is not really *religious* at all.[5]

Nor should it be thought that the identification of the whole range of religion with one kind is a conceptual temptation reserved for proponents of religion. The great foes of traditional Western religion in the nineteenth and early twentieth centuries, Karl Marx and Sigmund Freud, have much the same concept of religion as their opponents. "One would like to mix among the ranks of the believers in order to meet those philosophers who think they can rescue the God of religion by replacing him with an impersonal, shadowy and abstract principle, and to address them with the warning words: 'Thou shalt not take the name of the Lord thy God in vain!' " Freud writes. "Let us return to the common man and to his religion . . . the only religion which ought to bear that name."[6]

At the opposite extreme is the equally arbitrary expansion of the range of *religion* to cover things not formerly comprehended by the word. John Stuart Mill, for example, does this in *Three Essays on Religion*, where he claims that "the essence of religion is the strong and earnest direction of the emotions and desires towards an ideal object, recognized as of the highest excellence, and as rightfully paramount over all selfish objects of desire." Such a definition allows Mill to argue that "the Religion of Humanity" is "justly entitled to the name" of religion, for it fulfills all the essential conditions implied in the usage of the term. More than that, the Religion of Humanity is "not only entitled to be called a religion: it is a better

207

religion than any of those which are ordinarily called by that title."[7] A similar determination to redefine *religion* is to be found in the pioneering work of Auguste Comte. More recently has come a holding of the United States Supreme Court, which in the 1960s felt compelled to admit an expanded area of applicability for the term. Stating that its new interpretation of religion embraced "the ever broadening understanding of the modern religious community," the Court did not hesitate to recognize Secular Humanism and Ethical Culture as religions.[8]

Another source of confusion about the very concept of religion is the usage of some major contemporary Christian theologians. This usage is so distinctive that it merits special mention. We are referring to those theologians, such as Dietrich Bonhoeffer and Karl Barth, who speak of "religionless" Christianity. What has been and still is usually taken to be the paradigm case of religion in the West, the Christian faith, is now to be excluded from the genus of religion, or so it seems. Barth, for instance, devotes a lengthy section of one volume of his *Church Dogmatics* to "The Abolition of Religion," in which he makes very pointed remarks about Christian faith and religion. "The genuine believer," he writes, "will not say that he came to faith from faith, but—from unbelief, even though the attitude and activity with which he met revelation, and still meets it, is religion." Hence, Barth claims that "religion is the contradiction of revelation . . . [and] directly opposed to faith."[9] For Barth, apparently, Christian faith is something that falls outside the range of the concept of religion, for it is truly something *sui generis*.

In the face of such a variety of conflicting views about what is or what is not to be considered religion, some thinkers have had recourse to desperate strategies. In *The Meaning and End of Religion*, a noted Islamic scholar, W. C. Smith, asserts that "the concepts of religion and the religions . . . in practice [are] being dropped in part," and states his belief that such concepts "in principle ought to be dropped altogether."[10] The advantage of such a proposal is not at all clear, inasmuch as Smith has to use two terms, *cumulative tradition* and *personal faith*, to do the duty of the banished *religion*. Less extreme, yet equally ineffectual, is the solution of D. A. Wells in *God, Man, and the Thinker*. The thing to do in the face of the welter of definitions of religion, according to Wells, is to consider one and all as no more than "stipulative," by which he means that the values of truth and falsity do not apply to them, and that they do not refer to any existential state of affairs other than the definitions themselves."[11] Wells seems to be unaware that at the end of the road of stipulation one comes face to face with Lewis Carroll's Humpty Dumpty. "When *I* use a word," Humpty Dumpty said, "it means just what I choose it to mean—neither more nor less. . . . The question is . . . which is to be master—that's all."[12] Presumably, Wells means to stop short of such complete arbitrariness, but no limit appears in his statement of principle: "Let us decide to allow each person and group to define religion."[13] If opponents need have no more in common than the mere word *religion*, then rational debate and argumentation about the subject are impossible. Individual mastery of meaning has its consequences, just as public mastery does.

This is not to say that there cannot be a stipulative definition of religion in philosophy. It is to make a distinction between the formulations of philosophers who have tried to understand the real nature of religion and expressions that serve only to indicate the meanings men wish to assign to words. The former, "real," definitions, not the latter, merely verbal ones, are the main sources of conceptual confusion about religion. Most authors as a matter of course take the serious statements of philosophers about religion to be at least approximations to real definitions, or to what are also called "theoretical" definitions.[14] These are regarded as inherently assertive. As Irving Copi puts it: "To give a theoretical definition amounts to affirming the correctness of the theory in whose terminology the definition is formulated."[15] Copi also observes that it is in connection with such real or theoretical definitions that most disputes over definitions occur. To propose a theoretical definition of religion is in effect to propose the acceptance of a theory of religion, and theories are notoriously debatable.

The trouble is that they cannot be debated, with respect to this subject, until they are clarified. This requires an impartial sorting out and locating of these competing definitions and theories of religions in a neutral conceptual context. Or so we maintain. We are happy to note that some philosophers of religion themselves recognize as much. W. A. Christian, for example, speaks plainly about the problem. "We need," he says,

> a set of concepts about religion within which popular preachers,
> Jehovah's Witnesses, Karl Barth, contemporary religious humanists,
> and so on, can clearly say what they want to say, and within which
> their opponents can say what *they* want to say also, without entangling
> themselves or each other in verbal contradictions. Only so can the real
> contradictions and disagreements be discerned.[16]

Without such a conceptual framework, proposals and counterproposals about religion pass each other like ships in the night, and no one knows what the questions are to which the different proposals are responding. Without an objective context, we cannot be sure of the degree or the depth of the dissension in the controversy about religion, or even whether any real dissension exists.

The need for neutral concepts entails a need for neutral terms as well. What we must ultimately have is a linguistic medium in which all the problems that each of the contending parties to the dispute about religion finds challenging can be stated, and in which all promising solutions can be expressed, without the sacrifice of particular perspective or presupposition. E. A. Burtt points to the route that must be taken if such a linguistic medium is to be constructed.

> When conflicts come to light between two or more philosophic
> positions, with respect to their implicit or explicit definitions of this or
> that key term, the appropriate thing to do is to form a neutral
> definition of that term about which the contending parties are
> concerned. . . . This neutral formulation thus set up will constitute the
> "generic" definition of the term involved, and the partisan ideas . . .
> will become species under this genus, now capable of being
> differentiated from each other by impartial adjectives or descriptive
> phrases.[17]

A linguistic medium through which competing views about religion can
be expressed, and a conceptual framework within which partisan views of
religion can be located, so as to reveal the real issues of debate among them
without prejudice to one view or another, is equivalent to an impartial
mapping of the controversy about religion. Such a map, we maintain, is an
essential condition of rational debate and collective progress in the philosophy of religion. It is what the following essay undertakes to present. In so
doing, it sets forth as well what may be understood as the *prolegomenon* to
the study of religion.[18]

A. The method to be used

Religion itself, or the religious phenomenon, does not constitute the object
of our analysis, but theories about religion or the religious phenomenon.
The literature about religion provides the materials for our investigation,
but only that portion of the literature which is expository and analytical in
character concerns us. Much if not most of the literature about religion is
thereby excluded from consideration. Theories (or definitions) of religion
that are intended to delineate and to account for the religious fact constitute the object of our analysis. Theories of this kind are to be found most
often in the philosophical literature about religion, it is true, but we have
not considered ourselves obliged to observe what are often no more than
artificial divisions of labor in the study of religion. Any theory of religion,
whether it comes from philosophy, theology, sociology, psychology, anthropology, history, or general literature, in principle should find a place
on our map and in our analysis, if it lays claim to specify and explain the
religious fact.

As we have already noted, if that map is to be similar to ordinary maps,
it will do no more than coordinate different concepts and theories of
religion in an objective framework that makes no critical decisions about
the choice of destination for its users. Our map of the conceptual controversy about religion must be nonpartisan, or neutral, if it is to be the
prolegomenon to the philosophy of religion that is needed. Neutrality,
however, cannot and does not mean a mind empty of every theoretical
commitment or presupposition. Some presuppositions or theoretical commitments are present, at least by implication, in the very project that we
have set for ourselves. Among them is the belief that objective truth in

religious matters is both possible and good, though we are not concerned with that truth here. Without this basic assumption there would be no point at all to our prolegomenon. Another belief or presupposition is that the extreme contextualist or historicist approach to the history of thought can be successfully challenged and should be. If radical historicism were true, every theory of religion would be so permeated with the total historical context of its author's thought that none would have a common point of reference with any other; all appearance of real agreement and disagreement about religion would be illusory.[19] Our assumption is to the contrary, that there are real disagreements and agreements, though we do not debate the matter. Without this assumption there would be no possibility of such a prolegomenon to the philosophy of religion as we propose to construct. Neutrality, as we see it, cannot mean the abdication of the very conditions of our analysis of theories of religion. What it does mean is the exercise of all reasonable impartiality in treating the conflicting theories, even though some views of religion may be preferred over others.[20]

Even this is not enough. However necessary neutrality or impartiality may be for an objective charting of religious controversy, a logically disciplined approach to the theories of religion is also required. The method we use to arrive at this is the dialectical method of the Institute for Philosophical Research.[21] A brief outline of the Institute's central concepts and procedures is in order here.

1. Agreement and disagreement. In general, men are said to *agree* when they affirm the same proposition about a particular subject. They are said to *disagree* when they make conflicting or incompatible statements about the same subject. One should distinguish between *topical* agreement or disagreement and *categorical* agreement or disagreement. Agreement and disagreement are to be called topical if they concern the subject of the discussion and categorical if they concern statements about the subject under discussion. Topical agreement may be *minimal*, that is, an agreement about the subject under discussion only, or *complete*, that is, including a further agreement about the question to be answered about the common subject.

Categorical agreement and disagreement about religion presuppose, as a necessary condition, a complete topical agreement with respect to it— which is to say, an agreement as to the subject under discussion and a common understanding of the question to be answered about that religious subject. If there is no topical agreement whatsoever among the discussants, their statements about religion are completely *irrelevant* to one another, for they are in fact discussing two quite different subjects, though they use the same word (*religion*) to designate those subjects. If, on the other hand, there is only minimal topical agreement among the parties to the discussion—a common religious subject in view, but not the same question about that common subject—the parties are said to *differ* from one another concerning religion but not to disagree (or agree) categorically about it. Only if there is complete topical agreement by the different parties about religion can verbally differing statements about religion be said to *disagree* categorically, or verbally identical (or equivalent) statements about religion be said to *agree* categorically. Categorical agreement about religion requires identical propositions about what is or is not true with regard to the same question about the same religious subject. Categorical disagreement about religion requires incompatible or contradictory propositions about what is or is not true with regard to the same question about a common religious subject.*

These distinctions indicate why the interpretation of an author's position about religion is seldom an easy matter. One cannot take the use of the same word, especially a word as ambiguous as *religion*, as an infallible sign of *minimal topical agreement*—that is, as an indication that an author is referring to precisely the same subject as others who use the same word. Nor, on the contrary, is the use of a word other than *religion* an absolutely certain sign of the absence of a minimal topical agreement about a religious subject. The same caution must be observed with regard to the second essential ingredient of *complete topical agreement*, that is, with respect to the question raised about the common religious subject. One author, for instance, may claim that the "essence of religion" is such and such, while another claims that the "essence of religion" is so and so. These statements do not constitute infallible evidence that their authors are in complete topical agreement, and thus in the condition of categorical disagreement as well. Each could, and indeed may, have a different question in mind when he speaks of the "essence" of religion.[22] If so, they differ about religion but do not necessarily disagree. Even if they should have the same question in mind when they speak of the "essence" of religion, the two apparently contrary statements about the essence of religion may never meet in debate, if by "religion" they understand two different religious subjects—that is, two distinct facets of the religious phenomenon. In the case of the use of a word as ambiguous as *religion*, it is almost always necessary to go behind the language of the author to the thought he intends to express. It is imperative to discover whether his statements about religion are relevant to those of others who seem to be discussing the same religious subject, and whether they could possibly disagree or agree categorically with those of others who seem to be answering the same question about the common religious subject.

2. Issues and controversies. An *issue* about a certain subject can arise only when the conditions for categorical disagreement are satisfied. Unless there is complete topical agreement among the discussants, there cannot be an issue at stake. One and the same religious subject must be in mind, and one

---

* Rational argumentation is impossible when debating opponents share no ground at all. Between the man who holds to the rule not to contradict himself and the man who finds nothing repugnant in answering "yes" and "no" to the same question, there can be only shouts, or silence.

and the same question raised about that common religious subject if an issue is to arise about religion at all. In addition, the parties to the discussion must put in a claim to truth for their answers to the question, or at least claim superiority for their answer over the answers given by others. If no such transsubjective claim to truth is made for the statement about religion, at least implicitly, the statement is completely irrelevant to the discussion, constituting no more than a report about a subjective condition of its author. Purely stipulative definitions of religion, it should be observed, find their proper place here.

Three factors enter into the composition of an issue: the subject in question, the question raised about that subject, and the opposed answers given to, or the positions taken on, the question. Of these three factors, it is the second that determines the type of issue. At least three types of issues can be distinguished in dealing with the subject of religion, and these can be quickly exemplified by three types of questions which have been raised about religion: (1) What is religion, or what does religion or religious activity consist in? (2) Can or does religion as identified or conceptualized really exist? (3) Should religion as identified exist? These questions do not exhaust the variety of questions that belong to each type of issue, but they give some indication of three types: (1) *conceptual* issues, (2) *existential* issues, (3) *normative* issues.

Conceptual issues about religion are issues raised by questions about the nature of religion, or by questions about its qualities, kinds, or number. Conceptual issues have a decided priority over the other types of issues, and among conceptual issues, disagreements about real definitions of religion have an obvious primacy. Minimal topical agreement is required for the formation of every genuine religious issue; that is, the participants in a debate about a religious issue must have the same religious subject in mind. Conceptual issues as a group, and definitional issues among them, are concerned precisely with an adequate delineation of the religious subject —that is, with basic topical agreement. Issues about the reality or factual existence of religion, or existential issues, and issues about the value or worth of religion, or normative issues, of necessity presuppose some topical agreement about the conception of religion. Existential issues about religion call for judgments of fact about religion, while normative issues about religion call for judgments of value about religion. Neither kind of judgment about religion, whether factual or evaluative, can be made logically until what is being judged is conceptualized or defined in some way, and for either kind of judgment about religion to become an issue in a controversy, prior agreement about that concept of religion (a minimal topical agreement) is demanded.

An issue derives its unity from the topical agreement that underlies its formation. The parties to an issue must be considering a common subject and must share a common understanding of the question raised about it. They must be in complete topical agreement. Parties to a controversy, on the other hand, need only be in minimal topical agreement—that is, in agreement about the subject only. A *controversy*, as it is to be understood here, consists in a single set of issues which derives its unity from minimal topical agreement alone. The unity of a controversy, like that of an issue, depends on a topical unity or agreement, but that topical agreement need only be *minimal* (the same subject) in the case of a controversy, whereas it must be *complete* (the same subject and the same question about that subject) in the case of an issue.

A controversy is more complex than an issue. Not only does it involve a number of issues which are related by having a common subject; it also takes a certain form or structure from the other ways in which these issues may be related. One of the component issues of a controversy may be logically *dependent* on another in the sense that the position that an author takes on one issue is in some manner determined by the position he takes on another issue. Or two issues in a controversy may be logically *interdependent* in the sense that the position an author takes on either one is in some manner affected by the position he takes on the other issue. But even if two issues are logically *independent* of one another, they still belong to the same controversy if they have a common subject.

3. Hypothesis and evidence. We have applied our dialectical method to the confusing diversity of opinion that exists on the subject of religion without partiality. Selective one must be with regard to these opinions, but our selectivity has been consciously controlled by our purpose. That purpose is neither a pure history of ideas of religion nor a critique of theories of religion. From our reading and interpretation of writings about religion we have sought to lay out a map of the issues and controversies the subject has created. Eventually, we found it possible to arrive at a comprehensive hypothesis about these issues and controversies, the most tenable that could be developed on the basis of the evidence known to us. The hypothesis is on the whole a construction created out of materials given in the literature, from the views it provides of religion; it is not a historical reconstruction of the past.

By *construction* we mean two things: first, a painstaking effort to construe what the authors mean from what they say; second, an attempt to formulate in neutral language and without prejudice to any point of view the understanding of religion and the positions about it that we were able to discern as common to a number of authors. Such constructions have enabled us to compare and relate what diverse authors say in diverse ways about religion. Only by such constructions can we identify the various concepts of religion about which different groups of authors are in topical agreement. Only thus can we identify the underlying topical agreement that is the general understanding of religion which is commonly, if only implicitly, shared by all. Only thus, finally, can we formulate from the literature the controversies that are either actually or only potentially present in it. To formulate the controversies about religion we must state, in our own neutral language, the commonly understood questions, which create the issues in each controversy, the positions shared by a number of authors, which represent the sides taken on each issue, and finally the opposed arguments that constitute the debate of the issues.*

The identification we give of the subjects of religious controversy, and the formulations we present of the religious issues, are meant to be as neutral as possible. Hence they are not to be found in the literature, at least in those precise terms. Nor are the statements we make in the course of expounding our hypothesis mere repetitions of the statements made by the authors. The authors are writing about religion, and their statements express their conceptions of it or their opinions about it, while we write about controversies that are often present only potentially in their discussion, and our statements express a construction of these controversies that we regard as most tenable in the light of the data. This difference is often reflected in the difference between the language of the authors and our language, but even where verbal difference is slim or absent, conceptual difference can be presumed to be present.

At the same time, it should not be thought that the issues and controversies set forth about religion are purely fictitious. Undoubtedly, at many points we make statements different from any explicitly expressed in the works of the authors. Reading all their works would not by itself provide a comprehensive statement of the larger controversy in which we consider their remarks to have a logical place. Nevertheless, a firm and irreplaceable foundation in given data—that is to say, in other men's words and thoughts—is claimed for our hypothesis. Refinement, indeed, these data have required, in order to serve our purpose, but the refined data always retain some character of the given about them. Like any other hypothesis that is based on observed data, it is to be judged in the light of the evidence that can be offered in its support, and must submit to the test of whatever additional evidence can be offered to challenge it. And as with any other hypothesis, what can be said for our dialectical map of the religious terrain as it has appeared to thinkers is that it is the one most tenable in the light of the data.

The documentary materials we have examined require more or less extensive interpretation on our part. Three degrees of interpretation can be involved in the construction of the questions which create the issues in each controversy: (1) The language of some authors is such that the question formulated does no more than put in interrogative form the very words used declaratively by the writers themselves. (2) The language of other authors is such that it is necessary to interpret the intent of their

---

* This method of "construction" is not novel. It is employed by historians of ideas and philosophy who adopt neutral formulations to express what a number of thinkers have in common. Our use of this method, however, is more sustained and systematic, and is used for the clarification of the discussion about religion rather than for a historical study of ideas.

declarations, so that, on the basis of their direct intent rather than their actual words, we can construe them as facing and answering the questions. (3) The language of still other authors is such that it is necessary to discern implications of the intent of what they actually say, though this involves making certain assumptions about what they say. In the light of these assumptions, we can draw from actual statements their implied views on the point in question. Here the question we construe them as facing and answering is farthest from the actual words they use, yet no violence is done to their thought, if views are attributed to them on the basis of what the intent of their remarks necessarily implies.

B. The hypothesis in outline

The comprehensive hypothesis we have formed with respect to the discussion of religion is shaped in its main outlines by the complexity of that discussion as given in the literature. It is not religion itself but theories about religion that constitute the object of our investigation. Nor are the theories with which we deal fully explored. A theory of religion may cover much territory and include many topics and subtopics. This is so because religion is often taken as a kind of umbrella topic covering a wide variety of problems and considerations. For our purpose, however, much of this diversity can be ignored. The sole object of concern in this essay is the concept or idea of religion that a given author has—what he says religion is, or consists in, explicitly or implicitly. There exist many such concepts or ideas of religion, in fact as many as there are writers on the subject, since any one author departs in some respect from what others have said about it. Yet all the concepts are not equally close or remote from one another. They tend to fall into more or less definitely marked groups, or families of concepts, as follows:

1. Two different discussions about the nature of religion should be kept distinct. One focuses its attention on what can be called the *kinds* of religion; the other concentrates on what can be called the essential characteristics or fundamental *qualities* of religion.

2. Five distinct subjects of discussion can be clearly identified within the general discussion about kinds of religion. We have designated these distinct subjects as *Ceremonial* religion, *Moral* religion, *Mystical* religion, *Revealed* religion, and *Secular* religion. Each of these identifications expresses a topical agreement that we have found among a particular group of authors. Of these, Revealed religion is the principal subject of discussion within the Western tradition. It is also the most complex of the five kinds, encompassing, within its theocentric perspective, ceremonial, moral, and mystical features. In fact, revealed religion even includes some secular features.

3. Three main subjects of discussion can be clearly identified within the general discussion about the basic qualities of religion. We have designated these subjects as *ultimacy,* or the quality of holding the highest place in the hierarchy of values of the human; *integrativity,* or the capacity for combining

the disparate aspects of the human in a harmonious whole or unity; and *voluntarism,* or the characteristic of being grounded ultimately in the willing side of the human. Each of these designations expresses a topical agreement to be found among a particular group of authors.

4. A common understanding of what religion is in general is present implicitly in the discussion. We have formulated that general understanding of religion as *reverence for transcendent goodness.* This formulation expresses the minimal topical agreement we have found among all the authors who engage in the discussion of religion. It is the underlying thread that ties together the special understandings of religion referred to in (2) and (3) as parts of a single whole. If no meaning for *religion* were common to the authors who use that word, they would have nothing in common except the word itself. What must be understood to unify the discussion of religion as a whole, and what prevents the participants in this discussion from being in a state of complete irrelevance to one another, is this minimal topical agreement on the subject of religion in general. It is, therefore, a fundamental point in our hypothesis about the discussion of religion that its various aspects and phases can be related as parts of an intelligible whole, which is unified by a general understanding of religion that is shared implicitly by the writers concerned.

5. There is a *general controversy* about religion, and religion in general is its unifying subject. Part of the general controversy involves all five kinds of religion referred to in (2). In this part of the general controversy, each of the five kinds of religion which has been identified is subject to dispute. On the one side of the issue about each of the kinds of religion are authors who conceive that kind of religion to be the true religion. On the other side are authors who reject that kind of religion as either a false religion or no religion at all. Another part of the general controversy concerns the three subjects referred to in (3), a controversy about the fundamental characteristics of religion. On the one side of the issue about each of these qualities are writers who conceive the quality in question to be a characteristic or even *the* characteristic of religion, while on the other side are those who reject the quality in question as in any way characteristic of religion.

A final, distinct part of the general controversy about religion is concerned with the existential plurality of religions, On the one side of the issue are authors who reject the plurality of religions and maintain that true religion is one, while on the other side are those who accept the plurality of religions, maintaining that true religion is many, or more than one.

6. In addition to the general controversy about religion, there are *special controversies* about religion. Each of the identifiable subjects that have been discussed in the name of religion is a possible subject of special controversy. The authors who could be parties to the special controversies are those who agree sufficiently about this or that kind or quality of religion to be represented as having a common understanding of its broad features, while at the same time differing about it in detail. In the literature, however, the

217

special subjects of actual religious controversy are principally Revealed religion, among the five kinds, and integrativity and voluntarism, among the three fundamental qualities.

The foregoing statements outline the main points of the comprehensive hypothesis we have developed for the purpose of clarifying the discussion of religion that is present in the analytical literature. Our hypothesis enables one to see the relation of the major concepts of religion without methodological commitment to the truth of any one of them, and without the complications arising from their historical connections.[23] Abundant evidence in the form of detailed documentation could be presented in support of the hypothesis. However, given the confines of this essay, we shall have room only for references to authors chosen as representatives of a point of view on religion that is common to many. In so doing, we think we shall have indicated everything that is most important in the literature. Of all that has been written on a particular subject, only part, usually a relatively small number of books, or other documents, sets forth the original contributions men have been able to make on that topic. The rest consists of unwitting repetitions or intentional restatements by disciples or followers. In our effort to envisage the controversy about religion, we pay special attention only to those authors whose views enlarge or change its scope.

II. THE KINDS OF RELIGION

The very first problem to be faced in dealing with the discussion of religion is to determine what controversies it might contain—whether there is one controversy that comprises all the major issues with all the principal authors party to it, or several distinct but related controversies, each comprising a set of issues about a distinguishable subject, with some of the authors involved in each case, and some not. To put it differently, the problem is to decide how many distinct subjects of discussion can be identified. Do all the authors agree or disagree about a single common subject to which they give the name "religion," or are they talking about different subjects, and in the latter case, do the different subjects have something in common that enables them to be denominated as "religion," without stretching the term beyond all reasonable limits?

In our judgment, the literature provides evidence for a number of controversies about the concept of religion: special controversies that include controversies about particular kinds of religion, especially the Revealed, and controversies about particular qualities of religion, notably integrativity and voluntarism; also, a general controversy that involves not only the question of whether religion must be conceived to be of this or that kind but whether it must be conceived to have this or that quality or characteristic. In the remaining sections of this essay we intend to develop our hypothesis in some detail. This section sets out that portion of the hypothesis which

maps the conceptual controversy about the question whether religion consists in a certain distinctive kind of activity. However, this question presupposes a common subject called "religion." Is there any concept of religion
that is universally implied in all the discussion about religion?

A. Basic agreement and disagreement

1. Basic conceptual agreement about religion. One must begin the mapping of
the discussion of religion by taking into account two conceptual presuppositions about the general nature of the subject that are present in the literature. Often taken for granted, and without explicit recognition, these two
conceptual perspectives on religion are universally presupposed in the
accounts of religion. They are not a matter of debate or controversy among
the authors.

The first presupposition is the universal implication with regard to the
most basic kind of being that religion is. Before religion is conceived to be
anything else, it is commonly implied and sometimes asserted that religion
must be viewed as a *relation,* or relationship—that is, as having a relational
kind of existence. In other words, whatever else religion may turn out to
be in the varied specific conceptions of the authors, it has the most general
nature of a relational being. We find this stated by Augustine, among
others, who, in the very midst of lamenting that there was no completely
adequate term in Latin for the worship of God alone, points to the basic
relational character of the word *religio,* which eventually came to stand
exclusively for that worship in the West. "The word 'religion'," he writes,
"might seem to express . . . the worship due to God alone, . . . " "Yet," he
continues, "as not only the uneducated, but also the best instructed, use the
word religion to express human ties, and relationships, and affinities, it
would inevitably introduce ambiguity to use this word in discussing the
worship of God."[24]

Well before Augustine, among both Latin and Greek writers, it is clear
that religion, whatever else it might be conceived to be, was regarded as a
relational entity. Cicero, for instance, implies this when he speaks of religion
(*religio*) as "justice towards the gods."[25] Much the same implication is to be
found in the first analytic work on the idea of religion in the West, Plato's
dialogue *Euthyphro.* There, Plato, through the character Euthyphro, speaks
of religion, or piety (ευσεβες τε και οσιων), as that part of the right, or
just, attitude that "attends to the gods," and constitutes "a kind of service
to the gods."[26]

By the time of Aquinas, the sense of the term as indicating a relationship
with the divine is well established. Aquinas himself says, "Whether religion
takes its name from frequent reading [Cicero's interpretation], or from a
repeated choice of what has been lost through negligence [one of Augustine's interpretations], or from a bond [another interpretation of Augustine, and that of Lactantius], it denotes properly a relation to God."[27] The
relational character of the term is likewise asserted by more recent authors.

John Baillie, for instance, says that "religion is essentially a relation between two terms, or more exactly, a communion between two personal existences, the human soul and God."[28] Erich Przywara states that "religion is the relation between absolute God and relative man."[29]

Even among recent authors who exhibit a growing reluctance to identify the object of the religious relationship as "divine" in any straightforward sense of that term, one still easily finds express statements about the relational character of religion. "Religion ... shall mean for us," writes William James, "the feelings, acts, and experiences of individual men in their solitude, so far as they apprehend themselves to stand in relation to whatever they may consider the divine."[30] We find the same conception in the celebrated definition of religion (or piety) of Friedrich Schleiermacher. "The self-identical essence of piety," Schleiermacher writes, "is ... the consciousness of being absolutely dependent, or, which is the same thing, of being in relation with God."[31] Whether this is so—that is, whether being conscious of being absolutely dependent is the same thing as being related to God, or not— religion is plainly relational for Schleiermacher, as for others. Even Auguste Comte, the founder of a new religion in the nineteenth century, refers to his religion as "the new Man in his relation to the new God."[32] Though Comte's "new God" is no more than Humanity, or Man writ large, his new religion preserves the old, or perennial, relational status of all religion.

Other modern authors, while disagreeing as to the nature of the religious object, are perfectly clear about the relational character of religion itself. Hegel calls religion "a relation of the spirit to absolute Spirit."[33] Josiah Royce asserts that "religion, in its higher sense always involves a practical relation to a spiritual world."[34] For Tolstoy, "true religion is a relation, accordant with reason and knowledge, which man establishes with the Infinite Life surrounding him, and it is such as binds his life to that Infinity, and guides his conduct."[35] Auguste Sabatier writes: "[Religion] is a commerce, a conscious and willed relation into which the soul in distress enters with the mysterious power on which it feels that it and its destiny depend."[36] And even Paul Tillich, who does not accept any of these replacements for the traditional divine object of religion, agrees that "religion is directedness toward the Unconditional."[37]

Precisely because it leaves out every specification or determination save one, the common presupposition of the literature that religion must be conceived as relational constitutes, in effect, the most general conception of what religion is.[38]

The relational character of religion, however, is only the first presupposition about the concept that is universal in the literature, at least by implication. It is also invariably presupposed that religion is a *human* relationship, i.e., a relation in which man constitutes one of the terms. The frequent proposition of man as the religious animal reflects this assumption. It is what Hegel had in mind when he rejected the definition of religion proposed by Schleiermacher. For, Hegel said, if it were true that the "essence" of piety, or religion, consists in the *feeling* of absolute dependence, as Schleiermacher could be understood to assert, then Hegel's dog, rather than any human, would be the most religious animal.[39]

That religion is a human relationship is no more a matter of debate in the literature than that it is relational, though the proposition is seldom expressly affirmed. When it is, the affirmation as to the "humanness" of the religious relationship is apt to be put in very strong terms. Lactantius claims that "religion ... alone distinguishes us from animals."[40] Moses Maimonides considers "people who have no religion ... as irrational beings, and not as human beings."[41] Calvin maintains that "the worship of God . . . is the only thing which renders men superior to beasts."[42] Lord Herbert of Cherbury asserts that "religion is the ultimate difference of man . . . [not] rationality."[43]

Other authors, while not as extreme, agree that religion must be conceived of as an exclusively human phenomenon. Across the centuries, Marsilio Ficino answers Xenophon's rhetorical question "What race of living things other than man worships gods?"[44] with the response that "the worship of God is as natural to men as neighing is to horses, or barking to dogs."[45] Even writers as suspect to traditional religionists as Thomas Hobbes and Ludwig Feuerbach agree that religion must be conceived as a human phenomenon exclusively. Hobbes confidently claims that "there are no signs nor fruit of religion but in man only."[46] Feuerbach, less confident of such fruit, says only that "religion has its basis in the essential difference between man and the brute—the brutes have no religion."[47]

What is meant by "human" in our identification of the basic conceptual agreement about religion must be qualified, however. In the first place, we intend no more than a vague, generic sense of *human*. Without prejudice, the term is intended to cover the human individual and the human community, human attitudes and human activities, both inner and outer, and furthermore the stable products or objectifications of human activities and attitudes, that is, human institutions. The word *human* must be understood in as broad a sense as is necessary to cover concepts or definitions of religion which are poles apart, if it is not to beg a disputed question.

Second, when we assert that there is basic conceptual agreement about religion to the effect that it must be conceived of as a human relationship, this must not be taken to mean that religion is a relationship that is wholly and exclusively human, one that is humanly initiated, humanly sustained, and humanly consummated. Any number of Western religious thinkers dispute that view of religion, holding to the view that religion (at least the "true religion") must be conceived to be divinely initiated and even divinely sustained. Abraham Heschel, for example, writes: "The way to God is a way of God. Israel's religion originated in the initiative of God, rather than in the efforts of man. It was not an invention of man, but a creation of God . . . God's relation to man precedes man's relation to Him."[48]

221

Hence, however true it is that religion is universally conceived by the authors to be a human relationship, it is not at all universally conceived to be only a human product. If one is not to beg still another disputed question at this point, one must leave open the question whether resources other than the human may be involved in the admittedly human phenomenon of religion.[49]

2. Basic conceptual disagreement about religion. Religion as a human relationship, the universally implied basic conceptual agreement about the subject, is the point of departure for our identification of the basic conceptual *disagreement* about it. From an abstract point of view, a relational entity such as religion is invariably taken to be can subsist only between a subject (or referend) and object (or referent). Not only that, but relations have a way of reacting to any variation that occurs in the conception of the object, or of the subject. For example, the way in which the religious object is conceived must affect the way in which the relationship *to* that object, which is *religion*, is conceived; otherwise the whole conception is incoherent and without rationale. Granted that the term *human* in the basic conceptual agreement about religion already specifies in some vague way the religious subject, or the subject of the religious relationship, it would seem that the primary conceptual disagreement about religion should derive from varying conceptions of the religious object. And so it does. There is a great divide in the literature over the way in which the religious object must be conceived, and, in consequence, just as great a divide among the authors over what the religious relationship to the religious object is—which is to say, over what religion itself is. Basic conceptual disagreement about religion is most often the by-product of basic conceptual disagreement about the religious object.

Five major distinct kinds of religious object are variously proposed in the literature, as follows:

1. The object of the religious relationship is a number of suprahuman, personal beings who are freely active in human affairs in a beneficial way.
2. The object of the religious relationship is an entity of the highest moral character that is not active in any way in human affairs.
3. The object of the religious relationship is the one and only really real, which is not finally distinct from the best in human beings.
4. The religious object is the revealing God, the one and only supreme creator, a personal being of moral excellence, who is freely active in human affairs in a beneficial way, and who has intervened definitively in human history to reveal himself and to establish a visible community as the bearer of the true religion.
5. The religious object is an intrahistorical idealized humanity which lies within the active powers and capacities of mankind.

Corresponding to these five distinctive kinds of religious object are five distinctive kinds of human activity that are proposed by the authors in the literature as characterizing the religious relationship, or religion:

1. Religious activity consists of actions and words that express a real and continuing dependence on the beneficent activity of suprahuman personal beings.
2. Religious activity consists of the exercise of the sociomoral virtues in imitation of, or in conformation with, the ultimate moral being.
3. Religious activity consists of an inner quest for realization of unification with the one really real that entails a process of disengagement from otherness and individuality.
4. Religious activity consists of a complex, divinely aided human response to a unique divine initiative: the elements of this response are faith in the revealing God and obedience to divine commands that require distinctive ceremonial activities, sociomoral living, and the love of God and man.
5. Religious activity consists of all human activity that effectively and consciously cooperates in the realization of idealized humanity in history.

It will be seen from these two sets of propositions, one dealing with the objective side, the other with the subjective side of the human relationship called religion, that to specify the religious object in a given way is in effect also to specify the kind of human activity involved in the religious relationship, and vice versa. Our identification of the five basic kinds of religion in the literature is the result of the conjunction between the one set of specifications and the other, where the correspondences of religious objects with religious activities are easily recognized.

Thus, the kind of religion we call Ceremonial in the outline of our hypothesis is a compound of the first pair of specifications, one from the side of the religious object, the other from the side of human activity. In the same manner, Moral religion is a compound of the second pair of specifications; Mystical religion is a compound of the third pair; Revealed religion is a compound of the fourth; and Secular religion is a compound of the fifth and final pair of specifications.

In the end, however, it seems that the conceptual disagreements about the kinds of religion stem from a conceptual disagreement about the entitative status of the religious object. The different options exercised with regard to the conception of the religious object have immediate and decisive impact on options exercised in the conception of the activity that is taken to characterize the religion—or religious relationship—in question. Without any doubt, *that* objective conceptual disagreement is ordinarily due, in its turn, to conflicting judgments of fact about the existence of the proposed religious object. The proponents of any and all of the five kinds of religions always assume the existence, actual or possible as the case may be, of their favored religious object.

B. The basic kinds of religion

Our hypothesis about the basic concepts of religion maintains that there is one set of such conceptions to which the designation of "kind" of religion can be justly applied. Kinds of religion, to be sure, can be and often are identified from different points of view. As we have said, the kinds of religion that constitute our basic kinds are distinguished by the application of what we consider a fundamental criterion of distinction. This is the conception of the religious object, which in turn calls for a specific conception of religious activity. Our basic kinds of religion, consequently, are constructed out of compound affirmations, one about the nature of the religious object, the other about the nature of the human activity characteristically involved in a religious relationship to that object.

In addition, our hypothesis maintains that within this basic conception of religion there are five families of conceptions that are irreducibly distinct from one another: Ceremonial religion, Moral religion, Mystical religion, Revealed religion, and Secular religion. So far, we have given no more than a sketch of these five basic kinds. To complete their identification and to provide some documentary evidence that such kinds of religion actually occur in the literature are the tasks of this section of our essay. The references to be given here are to the writings of authors that we call "paradigmatic authors." Not only do these authors represent points of view that are common to many others; they also assert, or come very close to asserting, the constitutive propositions of each basic kind of religion as we have formulated it.

1. Ceremonial religion. We designate our first basic conception or kind of religion Ceremonial because of a singular emphasis of its proponents. Religion for these authors is ceremony or ritual, though ceremony of a distinctive kind. The single-minded accent placed on the outer, social expressions of religion, that is, on actions and words that symbolize inner religious attitudes, is unmatched in any other concept of religion. If by *ceremony* is meant an outward, symbolic expression or form, then the advocates of this first kind of religion merit the title of "ceremonialists," for that is the point of stress in their religious theory.

By Ceremonial religion we mean the conception of religion which gives an affirmative response to this set of questions: (1) Is the religious object a number of suprahuman, personal beings who are freely or spontaneously active in a beneficial way in human affairs? (2) Does religious activity consist primarily in symbolic activities that acknowledge a continuing, real dependence on that activity? The Ceremonialist alone responds in the affirmative to these questions. Every other major family of religious theoreticians responds in the negative to these questions. The non-Ceremonialists deny both assertions of the Ceremonialist, repudiating at once "the gods" as the authentic religious object, and, consequently, ceremonial activity directed to them as a kind of authentic religious activity.

On the whole, this concept of religion is an ancient view and does not appear to represent a contemporary living option—not, at least, so far as the analytical literature indicates. The authors we have chosen as representative of the Ceremonial theory come from the ranks of the ancient Greek and Roman thinkers. Plato and Cicero are its paradigmatic representatives.

The first proposition of the Ceremonialists is that the authentic religious object is a number of suprahuman, immaterial beings whose personal agency is beneficial to humans. From this it follows, for Plato, that religion is some sort of "service of the gods." It may be true, if we look at Plato's works as a whole, that the meaning of the word *god* (and *gods*) develops from one period of his life to another. Yet from first to last, from the *Euthyphro* to the *Laws*, it is Plato's belief that there are some kinds of higher, spiritual, personal beings who worked for good among humans. In the *Laws*, Plato's last word on the subject of the gods and religion, the theology prescribed by the Lawgiver in the ideal State is set forth through the Athenian. Among the opinions about the gods to be forbidden by law is one which would regard the gods as indifferent to human affairs, concerned only with their own. Because this opinion appears to militate directly against the perfection and goodness of the divine, it is to be proscribed in the ideal State. Indeed, Plato claims, the gods are providentially concerned with all human affairs, large and small.[50] It is impious to hold that the gods are either indolent or lazy and impotent, for they are powerful agents who actively help humans in a cosmic struggle between good and evil.[51]

Cicero's conception of the gods as a religious object does not differ significantly from Plato's. Not only are the gods the authentic referent of religious activity; they must be conceived after the Platonic model if traditional religion is to survive at all.[52] The principal matter for debate about the gods, according to Cicero, is not the issue of their existence, nor that of their moral probity—both of which he considers true enough—but the question of their beneficial activity among humans.[53] Epicurean theology viewed the eternal happiness of the gods as precluding any divine concern for, or any divine intervention in, human affairs. If this were true, Cicero thought, the death of traditional, ceremonial religion could not be forestalled. In his view, as in Plato's, religion or piety consisted in rendering "justice towards the gods," and how could it survive if humans neither have received nor can hope to receive any benefits from such beings? "Epicurus, in abolishing divine beneficence and divine benevolence, has uprooted and exterminated all religion from the human heart," Cicero charges.[54] In his view, religion cannot or at least should not exist if the gods have no care for human affairs.[55] For if that is so, there is no point at all to worship and prayer, to sacrifices, petitions, and vows—no point, that is, to Ceremonial religion.

The second proposition of the Ceremonialists asserts that religious activity is a special sort of activity consisting of distinctive words and actions that express a real, continuing dependence on the beneficial activity of the gods. This dependence is here called "real" in order to distinguish it sharply from a dependence which is "ideal" only. In the case of the Epicurean gods, for instance, it could be claimed that there is a sort of human dependence on the internal activity of these gods, the sort of dependence there is on a model or exemplar. Religion, in this hypothesis, could be conceived as an imitation of the gods.[56] There is no need to deny that the gods of Plato and Cicero can and do function in this way. Imitation of the gods is by no means alien to the moral views of these ancient thinkers, but it is not religion. Their conceptions of religion focus, not on the gods as exemplars of the good or happy life, but on the beneficent interventions of the gods in human affairs —that is, on the external, efficacious activity of the gods. For both Plato and Cicero, religion consists of words and actions that express a real and continuing dependence on this activity. It consists, in short, of prayer and sacrifice.

From the *Euthyphro*, Plato's first work on religion, to the *Laws*, his last dialogue, this view of religion is persistently maintained. In the *Euthyphro*, reverential service to the gods consists in prayer—that is, in "making requests" of them—and in sacrifice—that is, in honoring them with symbolic "tributes" which are express acknowledgments of gratitude and praise for their benefactions.[57] In the *Laws*, the Athenian claims that the noblest and truest of all the regulations in the ideal State is "to engage in sacrifice and communication with the gods continually by prayer and offerings, and by devotions of every kind."[58]

For Cicero, too, religion is a form of ceremonial activity that is an expression of justice toward the gods. Among his listing of moral virtues the youthful Cicero included religion, which "consists in offering service and ceremonial rites to a superior nature that men call divine."[59] If one were to sum up in a word or two the ceremonial activities that seemed acceptable to Cicero, the expression "prayer and sacrifice" pretty well hits the mark. Cicero goes on to insist, however, that prayer (of petition) and sacrifices (of praise and thanksgiving) are fittingly directed to the gods only if the gods are true benefactors of mankind. "Piety," he asserts, "like the rest of the virtues, cannot exist in mere outward show and pretence."[60]

2. Moral religion. In calling the second basic conception of religion *Moral*, we mean to indicate an almost exclusive emphasis on moral qualities by the proponents of this theory. The emphasis is plain in the two basic areas of specification of the human relationship called religion, in the specification of the religious object, and in the specification of the corresponding religious activity. Not only does the religious object proposed by the advocates of the Moral theory have moral characteristics, as do the objects of both the Ceremonial and Revealed theories; moral goodness is its basic characteris-

tic, if not necessarily its only quality. Similarly, the religious activity advocated in the Moral theory is predominantly, if not always exclusively, moral in character.

By Moral religion we refer to that conception of religion which gives an affirmative response to this set of specific questions: (1) Is the religious object a moral entity of the highest character that is inactive in human affairs? (2) Does religious activity consist predominantly in the practice of the sociomoral virtues as an imitation of or conformation with that moral being? To both of these questions the Moral religionist alone responds in the affirmative. To these same questions, proponents of every other basic kind of religious conception give negative replies. The non-Moralist denies that the authentic religious object is an inactive moral entity, even of the highest sort, and he then denies that religious activity consists predominantly in conforming to that moral being.

Two authors have been chosen as the leading representatives of the Moral theory, Jean Jacques Rousseau and Immanuel Kant. They have been chosen not just because of their philosophical prominence but because they represent two extremes among the Moral theorists themselves. If Rousseau tends strongly in the direction of a sentimental moral theism, Kant tends no less strongly toward a purely rational moral idealism.[61]

The first proposition of the Moralists states that the authentic religious object is a moral ultimate that is inactive in human affairs. Unlike the Ceremonialist, the Moralist believes that religion must be directed toward an ultimate entity. However far the religious objects of Rousseau and Kant may be from the traditional God of the West, they remain supreme entities, the one and only ultimates to which religion should be referred. Yet neither Rousseau nor Kant views ultimacy alone, even were it divine, as a sufficient condition for the authentic religious object. Above all else moral goodness must characterize the religious object, for without this quality no object, however ultimate or divine it may be, deserves the religious response of the human.

Rousseau, in *Émile*, is clear about the moral goodness of his God. So prominent are moral qualities in Rousseau's concept of divinity that they constitute the unique standard by which religion and religious education are to be judged. The religious education of children, for example, should be confined to the "little circle of dogmas which are related to morality."[62] Indeed, the Savoyard Vicar ignores "those dogmas which have no effect upon action or morality."[63] Not satisfied with setting aside as irrelevant doctrines about the religious object which have no bearing on moral living, Rousseau is even more concerned to eliminate any doctrines from religion that conflict with his concept of the moral God. Teachings about God that lay claim to some divine revelation or origin must meet his moral standard, Rousseau believes, for an immoral God is no God at all.[64] Intelligence and omnipotence do not of themselves qualify a divine ultimate to be an authentic religious object. Only a thoroughly moral God fits the specifications laid down by Rousseau for the religious object. To qualify as the object of Rousseau's religion, divine omnipotence and intelligence must be exercised with a morally good will, and with evenhanded justice.

Kant is even more demanding. To begin with, he claims that the very idea of God is generated by practical, moral considerations, not by some theoretical considerations of nature and its order.[65] Born of the highest moral expectations, the Kantian concept of the moral God meshes perfectly with the demands of Kantian moral religion. "A God who desires merely obedience to commands for which absolutely no improved moral disposition is requisite," Kant writes, "is ... not really the moral Being the concept of whom we need for a religion."[66] Kant spells out the moral attributes required of God by practical, moral reason. In authentic moral religion God is served "under three specifically different moral aspects," that is, under the three moral aspects of "holiness, mercy, and justice."[67] Beyond the concept of a "moral Governor" of the world it is neither possible nor necessary to go, Kant believes, if it is a question of a rational religion—that is, a question of Kantian moral reason and moral religion.[68]

To any description of the moral ultimates of Rousseau and Kant must be added a negative quality that concerns the activity of their moral Gods. Spontaneous intervention in human affairs by the divine, which is presumed in the Ceremonialist and Revealed theories of religion, finds no place at all in the Moralist version. By comparison, the moral ultimates of both Rousseau and Kant must be viewed as inactive Gods. This is not to say that they are without any causal influence and effective agency, as in the case of the Epicurean gods. Omnipotence, or an unlimited effective agency, is a prime feature of the Moralist God. Above all, divine omnipotence is required for the "exact coincidence" between human happiness in the afterlife and human moral goodness in this life assumed by Kant and Rousseau.[69] What is effectively ruled out by both Rousseau and Kant is any spontaneous exercise of divine power between the initial formation (or creation?) of the universe and its moral consummation in the afterlife. While Rousseau and Kant do not consider divine interventions in human affairs to be absolutely inconceivable or impossible, neither do they appear to admit any factual instance of divine miracle or divine revelation.[70] Such admissions in their view would compromise the rational basis of religion and the moral goodness of God. The God of the Moralist is inactive in human history.

There is one important difference between Kant and Rousseau, however. That the authentic religious object is an ultimate entity, that it is moral, that it is inactive in human affairs are points on which they are agreed. Where they disagree is with regard to the ontological status of the moral ultimate. Is the moral ultimate a real being, or is it an idea only? Such a question would scarcely occur to Rousseau, convinced as he is of the real existence of that personal, moral ultimate which he calls God.[71] The question does occur to Kant, however, and it seems that for him the pure idea of a moral

God suffices for the authentic religious object and authentic religion. Religion, Kant claims, "needs merely *the idea of God*," and "it need not presume that it can certify the objective reality of this idea."[72]

From the Kantian religious object it is not much of a step for the frank religious agnostic to another kind of moral ultimate, a moral ideal, as the authentic religious object. Thomas Huxley, for instance, claims to be both an agnostic and a religious person. "No two people agree as to what is meant by the term 'religion'," he writes, "but ... I think it ought to mean, simply the reverence and love for the ethical ideal, and the desire to realize that ideal in life, which every man ought to feel."[73] From an inactive moral God, the religious object of Rousseau, to a moral ideal, the religious object of Huxley, may seem too long a step for the Moralist to take, and perhaps it would be such if in between there did not stand the religious object of Kant, for whom God is a moral *idea*. Our purposely vague description of the religious object of Moral religion is meant to span that wide range of moral religious objects.

The second proposition of the Moralist deals with religious activity and asserts that this consists chiefly of practicing sociomoral virtues in conformity with the moral ultimate. The citation from Huxley is a case in point. Similar statements are to be found in Rousseau and Kant. The Savoyard Vicar of *Émile* does not engage in sacrifice, needless to say, but, and this is more surprising, neither does he pray to the moral God, at least not in the sense of making requests of him. Prayer of that kind is rash and impious because it presumes that the divinely planned order of things is so poorly planned that it needs adjustments from time to time in response to human petitions.[74] The "real duties" of religion are independent of such purely human institutions as sacrifice and prayer, Rousseau claims; the "true temple" of god is the "righteous heart." In short, "there is no religion that absolves us from our moral duties," for "these alone are really essential."[75]

Kant is even more emphatic. "Religion is (subjectively regarded)," he writes, "the recognition of all duties as divine commands." This definition of religion, Kant continues, rejects "the erroneous representation of religion as an aggregate of *special* duties having reference directly to God." Ceremonial religion, or that which Kant calls "courtly obligations," has no place at all in Moral religion. Over and above "the ethico-civil duties of humanity (of man to man)," there are no practices that should characterize religion and religious activity.[76]

3. Mystical religion. We call the third basic conception of religion Mystical because both the ultimate reality of which its proponents conceive and the religious activity to which they subscribe have this character. The term itself can be used in either sense. Thus, mystical can refer to an ultimate reality which is mysterious and not apparent to the ordinary ways of human cognition. On the other hand, mystical can also refer to the human concern for direct communion with ultimate reality. Both meanings come together

in the theory. It combines a stress on the cognitional transcendence of the religious object with a stress on concern for the realization of unity with that object.

By Mystical religion we refer to that conception of religion which gives an affirmative reply to this set of specific questions: (1) Is the religious object the one and only ultimate reality, not finally distinct from what is truly real in humans? (2) Does religious activity consist in an inner quest for realization of unification with the ultimately real, a quest that entails a process of disengagement from otherness? Only the Mystical religionist responds in the affirmative to both of these questions. For him, religious activity consists of whatever is necessary to realize his true unity of being with what can be called the One, which is both the only fully authentic reality and the only authentic religious object. To these same two questions the proponents of other religious theories respond in the negative. The non-Mystical religionist denies that the religious object is finally one with the genuine human self, as he denies that religious activity is or ought to be a quest for the realization of that mysterious unity.

The proponents of Mystical religion are much more interested in suggesting ways of realizing unification than in detailing a general religious theory. Hence in stating their position we have to rely more on the implications and general drift of their statements than we do in other cases. In addition, the highly individualistic, not to say idiosyncratic, character of Mystical religion makes it especially difficult to single out paradigmatic authors. We have selected two—Plotinus, the third-century neoplatonist, and Sankara, founder of the Hindu school of Advaita Vedanta in the ninth century—as representative. At one in their affirmation of the two basic propositions of the Mystical concept of religion, these writers are nevertheless at polar extremes within the Mystical family. Distinction from the One, or individuality and otherness, has a foundation in reality for Plotinus, whereas ignorance is the sole basis of all distinction of the self from *Brahman* for Sankara.

The first proposition of Mystical religion states that the authentic religious object is the one and ultimate reality. On this concern with the ultimate, the Mystical religionist agrees with the Moralist and not with the Ceremonialist. But, whereas the ultimate of the Moralist is a moral entity or being of some kind, that of the Mystic is simply the real—indeed, what is regarded as the only true and fully real.

Plotinus's One is an example. "Think of The One as Mind or as God, you think too meanly," Plotinus claims. "Use all the resources of understanding to conceive this Unity and, again, it is more authentically one than God, even though you reach for God's unity beyond the unity the most perfect you can conceive. For This is utterly a self-existent, with no concomitant whatever."[77] The One or self-existent conceived by Plotinus eludes our terms or names and is best described by means of negative assertions. However, positive things can be said about it. Thus "the First is no being," yet it is "precedent to all Being," and thus the First "has no origin" itself, yet it is "generative of all" beings.[78] But there is only one unqualified positive assertion that can be made of the One. "One seeing That [i.e., the One] as it really is will lay aside all reasoning upon it and simply state it as the self-existent."[79]

In all of this, Plotinus is expressly "seeking the statement of an experience" of his own,[80] an experience that "baffles telling," as he puts it. Within that experience of the One, it is impossible to isolate the object (the One) from the subject (the self) and describe accurately the object by itself. "If we have seen something thus detached we have failed of the Supreme which is to be known only as *one with ourselves*."[81]

Here, we believe, Plotinus is approaching an affirmation of the second part of the first proposition of the Mystical theory of religion: the claim that the authentic religious object is not finally distinct from the truly real or best in human beings. The One and the self are one in the peak experience of the religious quest, Plotinus writes:

> In our self-seeing There, the self is seen as belonging to that order, or rather we are merged into that self in us which has the quality of that order. It is a knowing of the self restored to its purity. No doubt we should not speak of seeing; but we cannot help talking in dualities, seen and seer, instead of, boldly, the achievement of unity. ... *There is no two.* The man is changed, no longer himself nor self-belonging; he is merged with the Supreme, sunken into it, *one with it*; centre coincides with centre, for on this higher plane things that touch at all are one.[82]

Plotinus repeatedly asserts that in the state of "absorbed contemplation" there is no longer any duality, but rather a "two in one."[83] In this state or experience, man has "become the Unity," for nothing within him, nor outside him, is able to introduce any diversity or distinction from the One.[84] This is not to say that the Plotinian identity with the One is a permanent state of affairs. If not precisely a momentary thing, the unitive experience is a transitory condition, at least in this life. Throughout the duration of the experience "all distinction fades," it is true, but inevitably, so long as the self is in the body, a moment of descent from identity with the Supreme takes place.[85] Why this should be so remains something of an enigma for Plotinus.

At the foundation of Sankara's interpretation of Hindu thought lies the conviction that *Brahman* alone exists and is truly real. "*Brahman* is real, the universe is unreal."[86] Such a conviction, the result of "right discrimination," according to Sankara, runs directly counter to the ordinary person's view of the character of the religious object, and of the world. However, the ordinary religious person, immersed as he is in day-by-day existence, is "buried under *Maya* and the effects of *Maya*," in the view of Sankara.[87] In that condition, the ordinary religious practitioner views the ultimate reality as a personal Lord and God who is responsible for the production of a real world teeming with multiplicity and change. Apprehended as having attributes and personal characteristics, *Brahman* may well be the "object of devotion," that is, the object of the common religious relationship. But, apprehended in that way, *Brahman* is also an "object of ignorance."[88] Bemused by *maya*, or cosmic illusion, the ordinary religious devotee is in the grip of the deepest ignorance of the true nature of *Brahman* and of the Self (*atman*). *Brahman* is without any quality or form, personal or otherwise, and is identical with *atman* (the eternal Self).

"*Atman* and *Brahman* are one."[89] As fundamental to Sankara's thought as the conviction that only *Brahman* exists is the companion conviction that there is one *atman* in all (if that expression can be permitted), and that it is identical with *Brahman*. The empirical phenomena that appear to surround human selves (the world of bodies) are, like the very multiplicity of selves (empirical egos), completely unreal, the product of illusion and ignorance.

> The highest *Brahman* [the object of knowledge] constitutes ... the real
> nature of the Self, while its second nature, i.e., that aspect of it which
> depends on the fictitious limiting conditions, is not its real nature. For
> as long as the individual self does not free itself from ignorance in the
> form of duality ... and does not rise to the knowledge of the Self,
> whose nature is unchangeable, eternal cognition—which expresses itself
> in the form 'I am *Brahman'*—so long it remains the individual self.[90]

Sankara's basic conviction about the radical identity of *atman* and *Brahman* is summed up in his flat assertion that "the difference between the individual Self and the highest Lord is owing to wrong knowledge only, not to any reality."[91]

Both Sankara and Plotinus can be interpreted as agreeing with the first proposition of Mystical religion, which is that the authentic religious object is not finally distinct from the truly real in humans. But that agreement is accompanied by decidedly different views about the character of the initial distinction of humans from the ultimate. For Plotinus, it appears that real distinction and individuality are present at the outset, and that a real change, or becoming, is involved in achieving unity with the One. For Sankara, all distinction and individuality is the result of illusion and ignorance, and no more than a change in one's knowledge is required for the goal of unity with *Brahman*.

The second proposition of Mystical religion asserts that authentic religious activity consists in the quest for realization of unification with the ultimate, and that this quest requires a process of disengagement from otherness or individuality. There is no question that unification with the ultimate is the supreme goal of both Plotinus and Sankara, nor is there any doubt that otherness or individuality, real or illusory, is viewed by both to be the main obstacle to the realization of that unification. Hence, necessarily implied in the pursuit of unification for both is the overcoming of otherness, a process which both conceive as pertaining to the inner man, or self.

Neither of these Mystics finds any room in this process for the characteristic activity of Ceremonial religion. Plotinus aligns religious ritual with the magical arts, explaining both in the same terms.[92] It is known that he shocked some of his disciples with his casualness toward the gods and the religious rites of his time. Sankara is perhaps more tolerant in this matter, but even he writes: "Men may recite the scriptures and sacrifice to the holy spirits, they may perform rituals, and worship deities — but, until a man wakes to knowledge of his identity with the *atman*, liberation can never be obtained."[93]

Toward the activities characteristic of Moral religion — that is, the practice of the sociomoral virtues — Plotinus and Sankara are perhaps less negative, though it is clear that their religious ultimates, the One and Brahman, do not have any noticeable moral features about them. Virtues may play some part in the purification stage of the ascent of the Plotinian man to unification, but they are principally individualistic or introspective virtues. The social virtues receive little attention from Plotinus.[94] For Sankara, "liberation" is attained in one way only, and "right actions" or "good works" do not appear to be essential to that way. "Neither by the practice of yoga . . . nor by good works, nor by learning, does liberation come," writes Sankara, "but only through realization that *atman* and *Brahman* are one — in no other way."[95]

In effect, both Plotinus and Sankara propose new religions for their times. Plotinus explicitly intends his teachings and his spiritual practices to replace the religious beliefs and observances of his contemporaries. If one wishes to live "the life of gods and of the godlike and blessed among men,"[96] Plotinus claims, he "must withdraw from all the extern" and be "pointed wholly inwards."[97] If we are in search of unity, "from many, we must become one,"[98] that is, self-collected and centered. In pursuit of identity with the One, one must "put otherness away,"[99] thereby enabling the self to merge with the Supreme in whom there is no otherness. Calling this spiritual journey "the passing of solitary to solitary,"[100] Plotinus sees it as no more than the return of the soul or the self to its origins. "This state is its first and its final," he writes, "because from God it comes, its good lies there, and, once turned to God again, it is what it was."[101]

If Sankara did not want to repudiate all ordinary religious beliefs and practices, because of their pedagogical value, he certainly presents his view of religion as the final truth. "The complete comprehension of *Brahman*," he claims, "is the highest end of man, since it destroys the root of all evil such as ignorance, the seed of the entire *samsara*."[102] Right discrimination, a discrimination that begins with the knowledge of one's identity with *atman* and accepts that only *Brahman* is real, is the path along which one must climb "to the height of union with *Brahman*."[103] "The spiritual seeker who is possessed of tranquillity, self-control, mental poise and forbearance,

233

devotes himself to the practice of contemplation, and meditates upon the *atman* within himself as the *atman* within all beings. Thus he completely destroys the sense of separateness . . . and dwells in joy, identifying himself with *Brahman*."[104] Here, according to Sankara, lies ultimate bliss and peace: the realization that one is *Brahman*, "one without a second."[105]

4. Revealed religion. If it were not prejudicial and misleading, the fourth basic conception of religion would be called "divine" because of the unique emphasis placed upon the divine by its proponents. Not only is the proposed religious object looked upon as divine in the strong sense of the term—that is, as the one and only God—but it is thought of as a God who is divinely revealed, God as known to himself alone and manifested through divine initiative. Moreover, the authentic religious activity appropriate to this "doubly-divine" religious object is held to bear the mark of the divine in every respect, for it is conceived of as both initiated and even specified by direct divine intervention, and as dependent upon continuing divine support. With all this in mind, the kind of religion that results might even be called, in strictest accuracy, "Divinely Revealed and Aided Religion." But as that is unwieldy, and as "Divine" alone is misleading, we have settled on "Revealed religion" as the name for it.

By Revealed religion we mean to refer to a conception of religion that gives an affirmative answer to this set of questions: (1) Is the religious object the revealing God, the one and only supreme Creator, who is freely active in human affairs in a beneficial way, and who has intervened definitively in human history to reveal himself, and to establish a visible community as the bearer of true religion? (2) Does authentic religious activity consist in a complex, divinely aided human response to the definitive divine initiative, a response that involves both the response of faith in the revealing God and the response of obedience to divine commands that require distinctive ceremonial activities, sociomoral living, and the love of God and man? Only the proponents of Revealed religion answer in the affirmative to these questions. Every other major family of religious thinkers gives a negative response to them. The upholders of non-Revealed religion reject divine revelation and, consequently, the religious activities that are demanded by and directed to the revealing God.

Three theologians, who speak out of different traditions, have been chosen as representatives of Revealed religion: Philo of Alexandria (fl. 20 B.C.–A.D. 40), a Jewish religious philosopher; Saint Augustine (A.D. 354–430), an early Christian thinker; and al-Ghazali (A.D. 1058–1111), an Islamic theologian. In agreement with one another when it is a question of the two propositions that form the Revealed theory of religion, they part company and disagree when it comes to its concrete identification. Their disagreement is rooted in a fundamental difference of opinion about the identification of the definitive divine spokesman, or prophet. Moses is the prophet of prophets for Philo the Jew, whereas Jesus is the greatest of prophets, indeed, more than a prophet, for Augustine the Christian, and Muhammed is *the* prophet for Ghazali.

The first proposition of Revealed religion contains several distinct claims about the character of the authentic religious object. First among these claims is that the genuine object of true religious activity is the one and only God, the supreme, spiritual, personal being who has freely created all other than himself. Philo, in his commentary on the Mosaic account of the creation of the world, sums up what he takes to be the Mosaic teaching: Moses teaches "that God is, and is from eternity, and that He that really Is, is One, and that He has made the world, and made it one world."[106] Despite the Platonic flavor of his thought, Philo also appears to view the God of Mosaic revelation as a Creator in the full sense of that term, that is, as a personal being who has freely created the world out of nothing.[107] To him alone "who really Is," Philo believes, belongs a truly creative power of bringing "into being what was not."[108]

Free creation, in time and out of nothing, of all that is other than himself, is so much a feature of the God worshiped by Augustine that he returns time and again to the exposition of the theme in his writings.[109] It is also a leading feature of the God worshiped by Ghazali, who writes: "Everything besides Him [Allah] is an originated thing which He created by his power from nothing, and made from nought, since He existed in eternity by Himself, and there was not along with Him any other."[110] Ghazali goes on to insist that divine creation is not in any way a matter of necessity, as if God were somehow moved by something other than his own will to create, but rather it is an act of absolute divine freedom.

Creation is also an act of divine generosity and pure magnanimity, according to these authors. "To those who ask what the origin of creation is," Philo writes, "the right answer would be, that it is the goodness and grace of God. . . . For all things in the world, and the world itself, are a free gift and act of kindness and grace on God's part."[111] To those who might ask the very same question about the origin of man, Ghazali responds that "man's very existence and man's attributes are nothing else but the gift of God, but for whose grace and kindness man would never have emerged from behind the curtain of non-existence into the visible world."[112] Augustine would agree with Philo and Ghazali that divine goodness is the only motive for creation, and adds: "All men engage in contest over the excellence of God, and no one can be found to believe a being is God if there is any being more excellent. Hence, all men agree that He is God whom they esteem above all things."[113]

Closely associated with this is the claim that God continues to be freely active in human affairs in a beneficial way. Belief in a providential God who is not indifferent to his creation or to human affairs is common to these authors, as it is to the Ceremonialists. "It stands to reason," Philo observes, "that what has been brought into existence, should be cared for by its Father and Maker."[114] Providential care for man especially, for groups as well as individuals, is viewed by all three writers as an indispensable attribute of the good God worshiped in genuine religion. "I cannot believe that there is anyone who considers himself religious," asserts Augustine, "who does not hold at least that divine providence looks after our souls."[115]

However differently these authors might explain the workings of divine providence or, as it is sometimes called, divine governance, they all agree that divine responses to petitionary prayers are part of that process.[116] Philo sums it up when he speaks of "the gracious Being Who assents to prayers." "Surely," he continues, "that Being will grant fulfillment to prayers, seeing that He is kindly by nature, and deems worthy of His special favour those who give Him genuine service."[117] Acknowledgment in petitionary prayer of a real, continuing dependence of man on God for benefits, both temporal and eternal, is no less evident in the writings of Augustine and Ghazali. Ghazali, once again, insists that the beneficence manifested in the divine response to prayer is not to be thought of as a matter of obligation on the part of God, as if some claim in justice could be made on God by man. Though God must be reckoned as incomparably more just than man, according to Ghazali, divine responses to petitionary prayers are not a matter of justice at all, but of divine mercy.[118] Augustine is concerned to point out that neither petitionary prayer nor the free divine response to it falls outside the plan or order of divine providence. "Prayers are of avail," he says, "to procure those things which He foreknew that He would grant to those who offered them."[119]

Not only is God conceived to be freely active in human affairs through his response to prayer, according to this group of theologians; he is also conceived as intervening from time to time in a much more dramatic way through the working of miracles. At the very peak of such interventions in human history is a definitive intervention that consists of a special revelation of God's will to mankind through humans divinely chosen to be divine spokesmen, or prophets. "The prophets are interpreters of God," says Philo, "Who makes full use of their organs of speech to set forth what He wills."[120] Prophetic mediation of the divine will is not confined to the spoken word of the prophets, according to Philo, but must also be attributed to the "sacred books" of the Hebrews.[121] Philo also insists that the prophetic knowledge of God, and of the divine will, is not attained through any reasoning process but only through "divine instruction."[122]

Augustine and Ghazali, along with Philo, are firm believers in a revelation of God that comes from God himself, not from human insight or reasoning of any kind.[123] They are also convinced that divine revelation has been transmitted by prophets and divine spokesmen, among whom they number Jewish prophets and especially Moses, and has been written down with divine help in sacred books or scriptures, among which they number the Hebrew scriptures. Where Augustine and Ghazali begin to disagree most sharply with Philo, and with one another, is on the identity of the divine spokesmen and the sacred books, and, above all, on the identity of the definitive spokesman. For Augustine, the definitive divine revelation is not mediated by Moses, nor is it to be found in the Hebrew scriptures, but is mediated through Jesus and his apostles and is found in the Christian scriptures.[124] For Ghazali, the definitive revelation is mediated neither by Moses nor by Jesus, but by Muhammad, and is found neither in the Hebrew nor in the Christian scriptures, but in the Quran.[125]

One final point remains regarding the first proposition of Revealed religion. It is the claim that the revealing God, through his chosen spokesmen, has established a visible community as the bearer of divine revelation and of true religion. This claim would be no more a matter for debate among Philo, Augustine, and Ghazali than the other items from the first proposition. No doubt, there are differences of note regarding the structure and role of authority in that community—differences, too, regarding the distinction of that community from ordinary civil societies, and differences as well regarding membership in that community in relation to final salvation. Yet all three writers agree that genuine divine revelation and true religion have been committed to a community which exists in time and in history, and which is perceptible by ordinary means.

Philo is of the opinion that "the highest and greatest source of the unanimity [of the Hebrews] is their creed of a single God."[126] He is also convinced that if the Hebrew community excels its neighbors, that excellence is due solely to its worship of the one God, and the practice of "true religion,"[127] and not to any other source. For Augustine, the visible community that is the bearer of final divine revelation, and of final true religion, is the Christian church, the "new people of God" or the "spiritual Israel," which by divine intervention has replaced the Hebrew community in the history of religion and salvation.[128] Ghazali thinks the Islamic community, "the people of the truth," is the bearer of final revelation and authentic religion, for by divine intervention it has replaced the Christian community.[129]

The second proposition of Revealed religion makes a number of claims about the character of authentic religious activity. It begins with the general statement that religious activity in Revealed religion is a human response to a divine initiative or intervention in human history, thereby ruling out purely human initiative as its source. This is actually a restatement, from the side of the religious subject, of what is asserted in the first proposition from the side of the religious object. The same general statement asserts that the authentic religious response to the divine initiative is at once divinely aided, and complex. Also included within the second proposition are attempts to isolate and identify in generic terms the essential elements of this response. Beginning with the assertion that faith in the revealing God is fundamental, the proposition passes on to claim that ceremonial activities, the practice of the sociomoral virtues, and the love of God and man combine to form an integral religious response of obedience to divine commands. We shall rapidly review the evidence of these concerns in the works of our three theological writers.

By *faith,* the fundamental religious response in Revealed religion, we refer to a religious activity that must be understood to encompass two rather different attitudes: (1) An inner acceptance of divinely revealed truth, of which the principal tenet is that there is one supreme providential God who has intervened in history to manifest his will to men; (2) A confident trust in the God of revelation, in his promises and his providence. When Philo, for instance, speaks of "faith," or "faith in God," as the "one sure and infallible good," or again as "the most sure and certain of virtues," or finally as "the queen of the virtues," he has both this acceptance and this trust in mind.[130] There can be little question that Philo considers "faith" (*pistis*) in these two senses to be the fundamental element in the religious response called for by Revealed religion. He constantly associates "faith" with "piety" and puts the former on a par with the latter.[131]

Much the same conception of the fundamental religious response appears in the writings of Augustine and Ghazali, though their emphasis and their terms may differ. When Augustine speaks of the fundamental relationship of the Christian to God, he refers to "faith" (*fides*) as constituting that relationship, and when Ghazali speaks of the fundamental relationship of the Muslim to Allah, he too refers to "faith," or "belief" (*iman*), as that element.[132] It may be true, as compared with the Philonic concept of faith, that both Augustine and Ghazali stress more the first attitude of mind, the inner assent to divinely revealed truth.[133] Yet the second attitude, of trust, characteristic of Philonic faith, is likewise present in the concepts of faith of Augustine and Ghazali. In addition, both speak of a trust in God called "hope," which appears to be distinguishable if not separable from "faith," according to their points of view.[134] Neither Augustine nor Ghazali would any more divorce trust *in* the revealing God from beliefs *about* the God of revelation than would Philo.

There is little need to delay over that part of the second proposition of Revealed religion which claims that ceremonial activities constitute an essential element of religious response. No doubt, authors differ as to the specific forms that ceremonial activity should take. What is common to all, however, is both an affirmation of ceremonial activity as authentically religious and an insistence on the presence of what is taken to be the heart of the matter, which is the inner attitude symbolized by the outer form. "That which in common speech is called sacrifice," Augustine claims, "is only the symbol of the true sacrifice." To this Philo adds that "the true oblation" in sacrifice is nothing other than "the devotion of a soul which is dear to God."[135] For, if ritual observances, including both prayers and sacrifices, are admitted to be essential elements of the integral religious response in Revealed religion—though sacrifice (external) is increasingly deemphasized, as we pass from Philo to Augustine to Ghazali—yet the external rite is not the most important factor. As the visible embodiment of an inner religious attitude, ceremonial activity is a proper response of an embodied human to the revealing God. Without the inner attitude, however, it is like the body without the soul.[136]

Public worship of God through ritual forms that are thought to derive ultimately from the divine will is not the whole of the authentic religious response in Revealed religion, of course. "Where honor is rendered to the God Who Is," writes Philo, "the whole company of the other virtues must follow in its train as surely as in the sunshine the shadow follows the body."[137] The practice of the moral virtues, especially the social virtue of justice, is essential to being religious, at least for Philo. "The nature which is pious is also kindly," he says, "and the same person will exhibit both qualities, holiness to God and justice to men."[138] Piety in the narrow sense of a special virtue is for Philo inextricably connected with the practice of all the moral virtues, especially the sociomoral virtues, because of divine command. Observance of the Ten Commandments includes not only duties that refer directly to the service of God but duties that refer directly to human relationships as well.

Yet Philo does not consider the response of Revealed religion to be complete even when one has included the practice of the sociomoral virtues commanded by the decalogue. Not only the honoring of God but the love of God and not only social justice but the love of man are also divinely commanded. Without the love of God and man, the response of Revealed religion is incomplete. Perhaps this is why Philo felt obliged to add a new social virtue called "humanity" (*philanthropia*) to the traditional Greek list of moral virtues.[139] In any event, when Philo speaks of those who are "especially devout in the service of God," he asserts that they take for their "defining standards" three loves: "the love of God, the love of virtue, and the love of men."[140]

The practice of the moral and social virtues is likewise viewed by Augustine as essential to the response of Revealed religion. Christianity, for Augustine, connotes actions which include the works of the traditional moral virtues; he complains of those who would wish to bear the name of Christian and do not practice such virtues.[141] However, Augustine is much more concerned that charity (*caritas*) be present in the religious response. "All the divine commandments are directed toward charity," Augustine claims. "This charity embraces both love of God and neighbor," he continues, "and on these two commandments depend the whole Law and the Prophets, and . . . the Gospel and the Apostles."[142] The practice of the twofold divine precept of love of God and love of neighbor is the crowning element in the religious response and contains "the perfection of the moral life."[143] Indeed, Augustine suggests that one could redefine virtue as "the perfect love of God." In that perspective he speaks of the fourfold virtue of the ancients (temperance, fortitude, justice, and prudence) as "various dispositions of love."[144]

A life of virtue is just as essential to the religious response demanded by Ghazali as it is to that of Philo and Augustine, though his listing of moral virtues may not coincide exactly with theirs. "Belief is perfected," Ghazali says, "through the fulfillment of good works."[145] Along with Philo and Augustine, he gives pride of place among good works to those qualities that relate to fellow humans, that is, to virtues such as "beneficence, sympathy, and mercy,"[146] which are undoubtedly the sources of the distinctive Islamic practice of almsgiving (*zakat* or *sadaqa*). The love of God as an essential part of the religious response is not slighted by Ghazali, for it is a matter of divine command for him, as it is for Philo and Augustine.[147] In fact, Ghazali goes so far as to say that "the essence of religion is love [of God]." But there are degrees in the love of God, in Ghazali's view, and as that love grows in strength, so too does the love of man and of creation. "If one's love [of God] is strong," he asserts, "he will love all men, for all are God's servants; nay, his love will embrace the whole creation, for he who loves anyone, loves the works he composes and his handwriting."[148]

In addition to claiming that authentic religious activity includes the fundamental response of faith in the revealing God and a further complex response consisting of ceremonial activity, the practice of sociomoral virtue, and the love of God and man, the second proposition of Revealed religion asserts that the religious response is divinely aided. By "divine aid" is meant something more than a divine revelation or a divine command that specifies the content of the religious response. For Philo, Augustine, and Ghazali, it appears to mean something like a true causal influence that is somehow efficacious with respect to genuine religious activity. "It becomes God to plant, and to build virtues in the soul," Philo writes, and "when God sows and plants noble qualities in the soul, the mind that says 'I plant' is guilty of impiety."[149] Augustine, treating the question of gratuitous divine aid for human activity, or "grace," makes clear that faith and good works (including the love of God), and perseverance in faith and good works to the end, are gifts of God and the work of divine grace, though not to the exclusion of human freedom and action.[150] Faith and good works, of course, are Augustinian terms for what Revealed religion as a whole requires. Along with the others, Ghazali considers special divine aids, or graces, to be necessary for genuine religious activity. However, if his general view that all causation is divine be taken into account, one may wonder how he can regard religious activity as a truly human response.[151]

Before leaving Revealed religion, one final point should be raised. Setting aside the different concepts of the religious object which are involved, it is not unreasonable to claim that the believer in Revelation is in partial agreement with the Ceremonialist and the Moralist on the character of authentic religious activity. With the Ceremonialist, the believer in Revelation asserts that ceremonial activity *can* be genuinely religious, and with the Moralist, he asserts that sociomoral activity *can* also be genuinely religious. The question remains whether the same judgment can be made about the activity postulated by Mystical religion.* Could the believer in Revealed religion agree partly with the Mystic that an inner quest for realization of unification with the religious object can be an authentically religious quest? The answer would appear to be No. The absolute and eternal transcendence of the God of Revelation from every single creature, and from the whole of creation, rules out even this limited partial agreement with the Mystic for Philo, Augustine, and Ghazali.[152]

However, if Mystical religion's key term of *unification*, which implies the final identity of the religious subject with the religious object, were changed to *union* or *communion*, either of which implies an enduring distinction of the religious subject from the religious object, then Ghazali, Augustine, and Philo could say Yes. For each of these theologians of Revealed religion it is possible to experience some sort of immediate contact with the God of Revelation in this life, whether it is called a "God-possessed ecstasy" (Philo), an "experience of the Absolute" (Augustine), or a "direct communion with the most Holy" (Ghazali).[153] Undoubtedly, this is a rare experience, reserved for those who love God for himself, not for his benefits, and attained only with divine aid.[154] Yet for all of that it is not wholly dissimilar to the terminus of the quest of the Mystic.

5. Secular religion. To designate the fifth and final distinctive conception or kind of religion we use the term *Secular religion*. Our choice of the term *secular* calls for some explanation. We consider it appropriate for two reasons especially. One is the character of the religious object proposed by adherents of this theory. Unlike the religious objects of any other religious theory that we have seen, the object of this theory is a secular object in the basic sense of that term; it is part and parcel of "this world" and of "this world-age." The other reason for calling this concept of religion Secular religion is the character of the religious activity called for by it. Insistent upon the denial of any distinction between the *sacred* and the *secular*, Secular authors are hard pressed to isolate and identify any human activity as distinctively religious.[155] Authentic religious activity, for them, is every sort of human activity that can be construed as cooperating in the realization of the secular religious object. Thus, religious activity appears to be no less secular than is its object.

By Secular religion we refer to that conception of religion which gives an affirmative reply to this set of specific questions: (1) Is the religious object an intrahistorical idealized humanity which lies within the active powers and capacities of mankind? (2) Does religious activity consist in all human activity that consciously and effectively cooperates in the realization or actualization of idealized humanity in history? Only the Secularist responds

---

* The same question should also be asked about the activity postulated by Secular religion, that is, activity which cooperates in the actualization of idealized humanity in history. Certainly, some believers in Revealed religion would assert that such activity *can* be genuinely religious activity.

in the affirmative to both of these questions. To these same questions every other major family of religious authors responds in the negative. For the non-Secularists the religious object is not an idealized humanity in the process of realization in time, nor, consequently, is authentic religious activity to be conceived as human activity that is productive of such an idealized humanity.

From among a number of authors, two have been chosen to be representatives of this position: Auguste Comte and Ludwig Feuerbach. Pioneers among the Secular religionists in the early nineteenth century, they were also independent thinkers whose views of religion blend at certain key points only. Feuerbach was content with the role of secular prophet, unmasking what he took to be theological idols and predicting the advance of a humanistic religion in the future. Comte, on the other hand, was a secular religious founder who established a highly organized secular religion, the religion of Humanity, complete with creed, code, cult, and community.

The first proposition in the composite statement of Secular religion claims that the religious object is an idealized humanity that is in the process of conscious actualization in the new and final religion. Properly understood, according to Comte, the word *religion* expresses a state of "perfect unity," both social and psychological, which obtains "when all the constituent parts of man's nature ... are made habitually to converge towards one common purpose." To Comte, the pioneer historical sociologist, a major gap was developing in the social structures of his time as a result of the inability of traditional religion to perform its perennial role, that of unifying human affairs. "At bottom, there is but one religion at once universal and final," Comte claims, and "to it all the partial and provisional religions more and more pointed, so far as the whole state of things at the time allowed."[156] What is allowed and even demanded by the times, in Comte's view, is the emergence of final, universal religion. Such a religion must abandon the "primitive" theological conception of its object and be directed wholly and plainly toward its unifying role in society and in the individual. What is needed is a replacement for the discredited traditional divine religious objects, a new religious object to go along with the newly discovered truth of religion and its role.

Not any object will do, however. The need is for some attractive, coherent object upon which all human faculties and institutions can converge, and by means of which all things human can be brought together in harmony and unity. Comte's choice for the new and final religious object is the "Great Being" of Humanity, an intrahistorical idealized humanity which has been in the process of being formed unconsciously by human activities for centuries. The times are ripe, Comte says, for conscious orientation of human activity and religious commitment toward the focal point of the Great Being of Humanity, "a composite and progressive existence, the only limits to which, in time and space, are the limits fixed by the constitution of the planet it occupies."[157]

Writing at almost the same time as Comte, Feuerbach comes to a conclusion about the religious object which is similar to Comte's. What has passed for the object of traditional Western religion, God, is really no more than the idea of the human raised to the power of the species, Feuerbach maintains. "There is no other essence which man can think, dream of, imagine, feel, believe in, wish for, love and adore as the *absolute*," he writes, "than the essence of human nature itself."[158] Anthropology is the "secret" of theology, and atheistic humanism is the "secret" of religion. "Man in religion — in his relation to God — is in relation to his own nature."[159] However the religious object may be conceived in different religions, and in different phases of the evolution of religion, what is ever worshiped in truth is human nature, that is, humanity as it is present ideally in the potentialities of human species. There is no need to think that the discovery of this truth entails the death of religion, though it certainly entails the death of an illusion (the death of the God-concept, among others). "What yesterday was still religion," Feuerbach claims, "is no longer such today, and what today is atheism, tomorrow will be religion."[160] Conscious of the "secret" of religion, that is, conscious that Man is "the beginning, middle and end of religion," the religion of the future will expressly acknowledge that Man is God, that "*Homo homini Deus est.*"[161]

Before passing to the second proposition of Secular religion, it should be observed that the religious object of this theory is *not* conceived to be the ultimate reality, or absolute, whatever that might be. This is clearly the case for Comte, whose whole philosophy is agnostic with respect to any trans-phenomenal absolute or ultimate, and who maintains the same attitude in his version of Secular religion.[162] "The object of Positivist worship is not like that of theological believers an absolute, isolated incomprehensible Being," he says; "the Great Being whom we worship . . . is relative . . . and as such is eminently capable of growth."[163]

Feuerbach is not agnostic to the same degree, if he is at all, in his philosophy of the future, or in his version of Secular religion. He is at once convinced that "the *absolute* to man is his own nature," and that "Nature is the ground of man." These ideas can come together in an evolutionary perspective that sees man as the culmination of the process of nature. In such a perspective, where humanity is seen not as something apart from nature but as situated within and at the apex of its development, there would seem to be an ultimacy of some kind.[164] Feuerbach does not appear to regard it as such, however. For him, as for other secularists, the religious object is not an ultimate entity. He thus stands, as they do, against the Moralists, Mystics, and believers in Revealed religion, and with the Ceremonialists, at this point.

The second proposition of Secular religion claims that authentic religious activity consists in whatever consciously and effectively cooperates in the actualization of idealized humanity in time. This means, as Comte makes clear, that idealized humanity, religious object though it may be, must rely on the activities of its devotees, if it is to survive and develop in history. It requires the support of their thoughts and affections as well. Indeed, for Comte, religious service, in the religion of Humanity, encompasses all deliberate human activity, the whole of conscious human life.[165] "Towards Humanity . . . we, the conscious elements of whom she is composed, shall henceforth direct every aspect of our life, individual or collective." Human life and living itself, Comte concludes, can be viewed "as a continuous and earnest act of worship," if it is ordered to the development of Humanity.[166]

Feuerbach agrees. "The relations of child and parent, of husband and wife, of brother and friend—in general, of man to man," he says, ". . . are *per se* religious."[167] What is common to all these human relationships, at least in their ideal states, is the bond of love. In the end, for Feuerbach, it is human love that is at once divine and religious. The Christian claim that "God is love" should be reversed, to "Love is God, love is the absolute being."[168] Where one loves individual humans for their sake, not for God's sake, one's love has risen to the love of the human species as a whole, and is truly universal. "Love is the subjective reality of the species."[169] Genuine humanity and authentic divinity meet and are to be identified at the intersection of ideal human loves. There, too, for Feuerbach is true religious activity, and religion.

A final point should be made before we leave the subject of secular religion. The reader may have noticed that no reference has been made to what a number of thinkers view as *the* signal instance of it, Marxist Communism. We have omitted any such reference because Communism does not view itself in that way. The only religion acknowledged by the classical Communist is the traditional one that includes a divine object, which he rejects, and that assumes the existence of a "world" other than this secular world, in which he does not believe.[170] Hence, for the classical Communist, neither Communism nor any secular humanism should be called a "religion." This term is reserved for a human concern to which he is in all essential respects opposed. There is thus no reason to discuss such a concern with reference to him.

C. Atypical kinds of religion

The positions of the five basic concepts of religion have now been presented in their main outlines. These concepts or kinds of religion are basic in that they establish one of the two fundamental perspectives from which the entire controversy about religion may be viewed. That is because they provide types or paradigms according to which other concepts of religion can be compared and identified; or, in other words, they provide a set of basic coordinates for our map of religious controversy. We have found no conception of religion, that is, no notion of religious activity relative to its congruent religious object, that cannot be classified by reference to one of the five basic conceptions we have identified.

This does not mean that every such theory of religion fits easily and comfortably into one of the basic types or kinds. Some authors develop theories of religion that are "atypical" in that they fall outside the strict parameters of the five basic types. Nevertheless, atypical as these views of religion are, they can be referred to one or other of the five basic kinds, either as some *combination* of them in the case of all except Revealed religion, or, in that case, as a *variant* that singles out one or more of its aspects for special emphasis. In the following brief section, we shall make some suggestions as to how our map of the controversy about religion can accommodate atypical conceptions of religion, as well as the five basic types.*

Of all the combinations of the four conceptions of religion other than the Revealed, perhaps the most familiar is that which unites the *Ceremonial and Moral* (the latter in a modified sense). All that is required for this union of basic religious conceptions is for a Ceremonialist to attach a distinct religious significance to the moral goodness of his divine religious object, and to view imitation of the divine moral goodness as an essential element in authentic religious activity. Such a synthesis is characteristic of the religious theory of the Roman Stoics, especially that of Epictetus.[171]

Another combination joins the Ceremonial conception with the Mystical one. What is required for this version of religion and religious activity is for a Ceremonialist to view union or communion with the divine religious object, rather than mere communication, as an essential aim and possibility of religious activity. If the Ceremonialist goes on to conceive communion with the divine to be achieved through an appropriate ceremonial form, perhaps a sacred meal, then a synthesis, which we may call *Ceremonial and Mystical*, has been effected. Of course, the elements of the combination are both somewhat modified. Such a concept of religion is present among ancient authors, especially among those who refer to or promote the ancient oriental mystery religions.[172]

Still another combination of the basic concepts of religion appears to be present in the religious theory of Henri Bergson. "Dynamic" religion, the form that Bergson strongly commends in comparison to the form he calls "static," gives the appearance of consisting in a combination we may call *Mystical and Moral*, of which the elements, again, are modified. In Bergson's view, only if religious activity somehow aims and indeed arrives at an immediate contact with, or direct experience of, the divine creative energy and love is it on the path to religious authenticity. Religious activity becomes fully "dynamic," and thus authentic, when the divine contact generates an

---

* A fuller presentation would allow for *variants* of religions other than the Revealed. In some forms of Mystical religion, for example, Nature is taken to be the religious object. This appears to be the case in the religious theories of Giordano Bruno and Benedict Spinoza.

extraordinarily active love for mankind, and for life itself. Without this energetic imitation of the divine creative love, Bergson says, religion is essentially incomplete, no matter how moving the mystical experience may be.[173]

A final and rather unexpected combination of basic conceptions of religion seems to be present in the religious theory of Alfred North Whitehead. Here we find an unlikely combination that we may call *Moral and Secular*, assuming we have understood rightly the unusual concept of a God-in-process. This religious object of Whitehead's is divine, but it is a limited (or finite), immanent (and secular) divinity whose agency in the world is not one of effective power but one of persuasion and attraction. In other words, the divinity that Whitehead proposes as a religious object is a real being that functions in the world as an ideal or locus of values only. This divinity is not a finished thing for Whitehead, since he views it as attaining in time a fuller reality and being that is at least partly the effect of human activity. The religious activity called for by such a religious object appears to be an active conformity with divine aims and values that not only must be moral but must also be conceived as co-creative of the richer, consequent being of the divinity wherein the victory of good over evil finds an everlasting home.[174]

When we come to Revealed religion, we find that because of the complexity of the religious response for which it calls, some of its proponents confine their attention to one or more but not all of the elements considered essential to it by the paradigmatic authors. In this way, another class of atypical concepts of religion emerges, the class we have called the *variants* of Revealed religion.

Though they have their Jewish and Islamic counterparts, the plainest of these variants are to be found among the Christian forms of Revealed religion as propounded, for example, by Martin Luther, John Locke, and Friedrich Schleiermacher. Thus Luther, the great Reformer of Christianity, so stresses the element of faith in religious activity that his concept may fairly be called a *Fideistic* variant of Revealed religion.[175] On the other hand, Locke, who tends toward a Deistic variety of Christianity, gives such great prominence to the sociomoral side of the religious response that his variant should rather be termed a *Moralistic* one.[176] As for Schleiermacher, at least his early speeches strongly suggest that the experience or consciousness of union with the Infinite is the very heart of Christianity—an emphasis that can be taken as a *Mystical* variant of Revealed religion.[177]

Instances of pronounced emphasis on two rather than one of the elements that are considered essential to Revealed religion may be found among other Christian authors. A *Ceremonialist-Mystical* variant seems to be recommended by some Eastern Orthodox Christian writers who stress the ceremonial (or liturgical) dimension of Revealed religion, together with a loving union or communion with God that is often liturgically mediated.[178] Also, certain Quaker authors accentuate a nonceremonial communion with the divine along with a special stress on the sociomoral side of Revealed religion. Their concept would seem to merit being described as a *Mystico-Moralist* variant of that religion.[179]

Before leaving the question of atypical concepts of religion, a unique form of religion in the United States called *civil religion* should be taken into account. Robert N. Bellah, the major proponent, admits that most of the symbolic content of American civil religion is "selectively derived" from the Judaeo-Christian tradition as that has been believed to be embodied in the American experience. Yet, Bellah insists that this is a new form of religion, one that is concerned only with those events that are public in nature and national in scope.[180] No single classification of *civil religion* would seem to be accurate. For some Americans it could be a *nationalistic variant* of either Secular or Moral religion that makes free use of biblical symbols. For others, perhaps most, civil religion could be a *secularistic,* or political, *variant* of Revealed religion.

III. CONCEPTUAL CONTROVERSY AMONG THE KINDS OF RELIGION

A major part of what needed to be done in order to construct a map of the controversies about religion has now been completed. With the identification and formulation of the five kinds of religion we have obtained a set of basic concepts that allow disagreements to occur and give rise to controversy. These disagreements concern not only the individual kinds themselves but the very concept of religion in general. The section that follows will be devoted to this general controversy about religion, particularly as it concerns the basic kinds.

With respect to each of the kinds, issues arise from questions which have been formulated in the literature, and which elicit answers so different as to distinguish one kind of religion from another. One could proceed to fill in this part of the map of the controversy with the arguments that have been advanced on these issues, of which some are existential in character, while others are purely conceptual. To attempt this, however, would be a very lengthy process, and also a confusing one. For simplicity's sake, we will concentrate on the conceptual issues. As a still further simplification, we will attempt only to identify those conceptual issues from which controversy can arise, without documenting any actual controversy that has occurred. We intend to construct an outline of these as they derive from the different concepts of religion implicit in the five kinds.

A. Existential and conceptual issues

To avoid misunderstanding, it is important to be clear about the distinction between "existential" and "conceptual" issues. In existential issues the concept is also involved, but only to the extent that one or more of its elements must have some sort of existence (real or ideal) if the religion as so conceived is to have real existence. To deny the existence of a particular kind of religion, one must deny the existence of one or more of its elements as asserted by those who uphold it. For example, one denies existence to the Revealed kind of religion by denying the reality (or possibility) of divine revelation or the revealing God. In general terms, an issue is existential when the ground for rejecting a particular kind of religion is the denial of existence to the elements stipulated or presupposed by that concept.

In conceptual issues, on the other hand, it is the concept of religion itself that is directly attacked. The existence of the elements it asserts may be conceded, but it is denied that what is so conceived conforms to the general idea of religion: what is called "religion" is said to be not religion at all, but a counterfeit of it. Secular religion is often subjected to such a conceptual rejection. Proponents of the Secular theory maintain that theirs is a genuine religion, properly conceived according to the general understanding of religion. Their opponents deny that it is. In general terms, an issue is conceptual when the ground for rejecting a particular kind of religion is that it does not satisfy the common meaning of the concept of religion.

Each of the five basic kinds of religion constitutes an answer to the question "What is (true) religion?" Given the distinction between existential and conceptual issues, there are two markedly different senses to the question whether this or that proposed phenomenon constitutes "true religion." Understood existentially, it is a question about the existence or nonexistence of the elements stipulated or presupposed by that concept. Accordingly, to claim that it is "true religion" is to assert the existence of its elements, while to claim that it is "false religion" is to deny existence to those elements. Understood conceptually, however, the question whether suchand-such is "true" or "false" religion is whether or not it meets the criteria of the common meaning of *religion*. Accordingly, to claim that it is "true religion" is to assert no more than that it does fall within the common meaning of the concept of religion, whereas to claim that it is "false religion" is to deny that it falls under that common meaning.

In this section we shall be solely and exclusively concerned with the conceptual issues among the five basic kinds of religion, i.e., with the conceptual controversy among the five kinds.

The conceptual controversy can be divided into three parts according to the way in which the five kinds align themselves on a given conceptual issue:

1. On certain issues, four of the kinds side together in charging that the fifth on a given issue fails to meet the common understanding of *religion*.* There is thus a *many-one relation* in the controversy in that four share a common understanding that is denied in some respect by the fifth.

---

* The "common understanding" used as the standard is a common understanding of religion internal to a hypothetical controversy involving the five kinds. As common, it must be a matter of agreement by at least two kinds; as giving rise to controversy or disagreement, it must be disputed by at least one kind.

2. On other issues, several of the kinds side together in charging that several of the others deviate from the common meaning of *religion*. Here there is a *many-many relation* in which on one side there is a group sharing a common understanding of *religion*. In this case, of course, the shared understanding is not as wide as in the first case, where four of the kinds share a common understanding on a given issue.

3. Finally, there is the case in which one of the kinds repudiates the criteria used as a norm for the common concept and claims that they are prejudicial and misleading. Proponents of the Secular theory could take this position, since their own view of religion would be dismissed by the other four kinds as not being religion at all. This is a *one-many* relation.

Among the conceptual issues, still another distinction can be drawn according as the focus of concern is upon the religious object or upon the religious activity. Though these are inseparable in fact, they are conceptually distinct and thus provide ground for distinct conceptual issues.

B. Issues on which four kinds side together against one

1. Issues concerning the religious object

   a) Objections to Ceremonial religion: Although Ceremonial religion is the oldest claimant to the title of religion, it is not immune to conceptual criticism because of its historical priority. Proponents of the other kinds of religion would agree in making the Ceremonial concept of the religious object the focus of their criticism. They would do so on the ground that beyond the gods, who are the religious object of Plato's version of Ceremonial religion, there is another sphere of absolute, unchangeable reality that is independent of the gods and superior to them. This sphere, the realm of the Ideas, constitutes what is really real, the supreme or ultimate reality, superior to all else, including the gods. The inferiority of these beings as religious objects at once opens Ceremonial religion to criticism from all the other kinds except the Secular, since for all of them save that one the religious object must be conceived of as supreme and *ultimate*. There can be little doubt that the One of Mystical religion, the moral ultimate of Moral religion, and the Creator God of Revealed religion are ultimate entities in at least one, if not in every, order of things. And it is even arguable that the proponents of Secular religion would join in this conceptual objection to Ceremonial religion. For these proponents—in particular, for Comte—the religious object is an idealized humanity to be realized only in history and is thus not an ultimate, yet it *is* an ultimate as the supreme value in the universe of possible human knowledge. To that extent, therefore, all four kinds would agree, in common opposition to Ceremonial religion, that some sort of ultimacy or supremacy is essential to the concept of the religious object.

   At still another point the Ceremonial theory is subject to attack from the other four. Not only are the gods of the Ceremonialist not ultimate; they also are many and not one. The gods of both Plato and Cicero may comprise one class of beings, but they are many in number, many individual beings. Ceremonial religion is directed toward the gods, not as a class of superior beings, but as many different individuals who confer different benefits on the worshiping community. Because of the plurality of gods, Cicero, and Plato as well, could easily conceive of many religions (*religiones*), one for this god or family of gods and its favored community, another for that god or family of gods and *its* favored community. But, for all the other four kinds of religion the authentic religious object must be conceived as one in being. This one being may be conceived of as a real or an ideal being. It is a real being in the case of the One of Mystical religion, in the case of the Creator and Revealer of Revealed religion, and in the case of the moral God of theistic Moral religion. It is an ideal being in the case of the moral ideal of Moral religion and in the case of the idealized humanity of Secular religion. But in each such case the religious object is conceived of as one. Hence, the religious object of the Ceremonialist would be rejected by proponents of all the other four kinds because it denies an essential conceptual element of the religious object, namely its oneness.

b) Objections to Secular religion: Of all the five kinds, the one that is most subject to conceptual criticism is Secular religion. All except the upholders of Mystical religion would concede the high value of the human ideal of the Secularist and might not even question the possibility of its eventual realization in time and history. Yet all would reject such an ideal as the authentic religious object because of its "secularity." None would accept, as the Secularist does, that an authentically religious object can be conceived of as a possible part or element of this spatiotemporal world or age. However else they may differ about the distinctiveness of the religious object, all four kinds agree that it must be transsecular, i.e., that it must transcend in one way or another the spatiotemporal limits of this world and age. The gods of the Ceremonialist, the moral God of the Moralist, the revealing God of the believer in Revealed religion, and the One of the Mystic are all conceived of as belonging to a realm that is radically different from that of ordinary human activity (though it must be admitted that the ontological status of the moral ideal of some upholders of Moral religion is far from clear). Yet for the Secularist, the religious object *must* be conceived as belonging in all ways to this same secular world of ours, for it is here, as idealized humanity, that it is to be realized.

This conceptual criticism of the Secularist's religious object is advanced even by writers who are themselves strongly opposed to religion. The founders of Communism harshly criticized Feuerbach's brand of Secular religion. Their opposition was based on conceptual, not existential, grounds. Marx and Engels rejected the idea that any secular humanism, even a Communist version of it, could constitute a "religion," since they maintained that such a concept is inextricably bound up with the notion of a divine religious object and a world other than this one. Even the atheist Bertrand Russell held that the concept of religion demands something more than a secular humanistic ideal. "Those who attempt to make a religion of humanism, which recognizes nothing greater than man," he wrote, "do not satisfy my emotions."[181] Although he called himself a humanist, Russell felt that religion requires a transhuman kind of object.

On still another count the object proposed by the Secularist is subject to conceptual criticism; this criticism applies also to one version of Moral religion. The idealized humanity that is the religious object for the Secularist is an ideal existent, i.e., an entity whose existence is dependent upon human thought, even though in its realization there is ultimately a reference to the real order, i.e., to an order of entities independent of human thought. But for the opponents of Secular religion, the religious object must be conceived of as real, not as an ideal entity dependent upon human thought. The gods of the Ceremonialist, the One of the Mystic, the Creator-God of the believer in Revealed religion, and the moral God of one version of Moral religion are all beings whose existence is in no way dependent upon human conception or thought. Real existence is essential to the concept of the religious object for all the basic theories except the Secular and one version of the Moral.

c) Objections to Mystical religion: The religious object of Mystical religion, especially in Sankara's version of it, is also subject to conceptual criticism. According to Sankara, only *Brahman* is truly real—the many are no more than illusion, or *maya*—but the genuine or transcendental self, the *atman*, is identified in fact with *Brahman*. The religious object is thus identified with the self. But for the other four kinds of religion this identification would betray a false conception of the authentic religious object, since for all four the religious object must be conceived as other than the self. Distinction from the self is clearly a feature common to the gods of the Ceremonialist, the moral God or ultimate of the Moralist, and the Creator-God of the believer in Revealed religion. The distinction between self and object is found in Secular religion as well, though in some versions of this the ideal self seems to merge with the ideal humanity in the future. Thus, all four kinds join in common opposition to Mystical religion on the ground that some sort of otherness, some degree of distinction from the self, is essential to the concept of the religious object.

2. Issues about the concept of religious activity

a) Objections to Secular religion: Again, it is this kind of religion that offers the easiest target to conceptual criticism. For the Secularists, religious activity is conceived of as at least partly constitutive of the religious object itself, since the concrete realization of an idealized humanity is the result at which it aims. But for the other four kinds of religion this feature would betray a misconception of religious activity, which they all agree must be conceived of as passive with respect to the being or constitution of the religious object. The gods of the Ceremonialist, the moral God of some versions of Moral religion, the One of the Mystic, and the Creator-God of Revealed religion are all conceived of as independent of human activity. All four theories would agree that the mark of passivity with respect to the inner being of the religious object is essential to an authentic concept of religious activity.

On still another count, Secular theory is open to conceptual criticism. It conceives of religious activity as any and all human activity that consciously cooperates toward the eventual realization of an ideal humanity on earth. But if this is accepted, it becomes difficult if not impossible to identify any feature that would serve to distinguish religious activity from other human activity. It is certainly impossible to distinguish religious activity from the activity expected of an ideal citizen of the community, whether national or international. For the other four kinds of religion, authentic religious activity must be conceived of as different and distinct from the activity of a good citizen. There must be something, some feature either external or internal, to make religious activity distinguishable from the activity of the ideal citizen or the ideal humanist.

b) Objections to Moral religion: The Moralist theory of religion, in some versions, is open to the same criticism. If religious activity is identified as activity that conforms to the moral ideal, it becomes impossible to distinguish religious activity from the activity of the morally good person. Religion then is no different from morality. For the other theories, there must be some feature that makes religious activity distinguishable from the activity of the morally good person, however closely the two may be associated. Once again, this need not be a feature that is externally perceptible, since moral activity is also a requirement, either in part or as a whole, of religious activity in some theories. But that religious activity is distinct from moral activity as such is asserted by all the basic theories of religion except the idealist version of Moral religion.

c) Objections to Mystical religion: Religious activity for Sankara, as we have seen, consists in a quest for unification with a religious object that is not really distinct from the true or transcendental self. Such a quest, to be successful, requires that the human subject meet quite unusual conditions, and it may well terminate in quite an extraordinary experience. Nevertheless, it can still be asked how this quest is to be distinguished from any other energetic pursuit of self-knowledge and self-experience. However much the Ceremonial, Moral, Secular, and Revealed theories may disagree about religious activity, all agree that it is not identical with the quest for self-knowledge and self-experience. This is not to deny that an extraordinary perception or knowledge of the self may be claimed to accompany the high practice of religious activity—a feature that is especially true of Revealed religion—but to insist that such a result is an accompaniment or side effect of activity that has another aim.

Another criticism, similar to this one, is directed against the disembodied character of religious activity according to Mystical religion. This seems to demand or require no external activity at all, for the quest for unification appears to be exclusively internal or interior, and external activity is regarded as a distraction if not an obstacle. In the view of the other four kinds of religion, religious activity cannot be purely internal but must be embodied in external activity. Secular religion is inconceivable apart from the external activity that is needed for the historical realization of its ideal humanity. The same can be said of the Ceremonial and Moral religions, as well as of Revealed religion insofar as it includes activities similar to those two. This is not to say that external activity is all that is required, or is even the heart of the matter, for any of the four—especially not for Revealed religion. They would agree, however, that it is a misconception of religious activity not to include within it some form of external activity.

With this we complete our survey of the conceptual issues on which four of the theories side in common opposition to the fifth. It should be noted that on the different issues it is not the same four in agreement, nor the same one that is criticized. In fact, the only theory so far exempt from conceptual attack has been Revealed religion (about which we will have more to say later). It may also be noted that since the issues considered have been those which have received the largest measure of agreement among the five (i.e., of four against one), these issues can be considered the primary or fundamental conceptual issues in the general controversy about religion. Briefly, they are the issues raised when opposite answers are given to the following questions:

1. Does the concept of religion require that its *object* be:
    a) an ultimate that is one in being?
    b) a transsecular entity that is a real existent?
    c) an entity other than the self?
2. Does the concept of religion require an *activity* that is:
    a) passive with respect to the constitution of its object?
    b) distinguishable from the activity of:
        (1) the ideal citizen?
        (2) the morally good person?
        (3) one seeking self-knowledge or self-experience?
    c) external and not purely internal?

C. Issues on which the five kinds are more or less evenly divided

1. Issues concerning the religious object. Among the five basic kinds of religion a clear line can be drawn separating a theistic from a nontheistic group, i.e., between those who conceive the religious object in a traditional theistic way and those who do not. Their concept of the divine is by no means the same,

but for the Ceremonial theory, for the theistic version of Moral religion, and for Revealed religion the religious object must be conceived of as divine in some way. Not only do the proponents of these theories agree with one another that the object must be real in being and distinct from the self and any secular entity; they also commonly conceive the divine religious object to be *personal in being*, i.e., a self-conscious, intelligent subject or subjects. However much the gods of the Ceremonialist, the moral God of the Moralist, and the creating God of Revealed religion may differ, all are conceived of as beings to whom the concept of person can be legitimately applied. On the other hand, it is clear that the ideals that constitute the religious object for both the Secularist and the nontheistic Moralistic religions are *not* personal beings in any way. It is also very doubtful whether the One of Mystical religion is a personal being; the descriptions of it given by both Plotinus and Sankara seem to place it outside that category.

Another issue, similar to this one, concerning the personal status of the religious object, is that which has to do with its activity or agency. For the theistic group, the religious object is clearly a personal being or beings capable of freely initiated, effective agency in the world. More than that, all agree that the exercise of divine power or agency is indispensable to the successful outcome of mankind's major concerns. For the Ceremonialist, such divine activity seems to be restricted to this life only; for the theistic Moralist, it is reserved exclusively for the afterlife; for Revealed religion it is operative in both; but for all, divine agency is considered essential to man's success and happiness. Needless to say, the nontheistic group hold no such view. The ideals of both Secular and nontheistic Moral religion are radically incapable of any real or effective agency of their own. So, too, despite the rich reality attributed to it, the One of Mystical religion appears to be wholly "self"-contained and "self"-concerned.

Still another issue regarding the concept of the religious object concerns its knowability. For both Mystical religion and Revealed religion the religious object is veiled in mystery and has a dimension that is absolutely incomprehensible. Although not unknowable completely and in every respect, the object is mysterious and hidden in a way that differs not only in degree but also in kind from every other mystery in the universe. Augustine expressed this view for all when he wrote: "If you have comprehended it, it is not God."[182] But if incomprehensibility is essential to the concept, then the ideal objects of both Secular and the nontheistic Moral theories of religion would be rejected as inadequate, for they can function as ideals only to the extent that they *are* comprehensible. It would appear, too, that the gods of Ceremonial religion are open to the same criticism; if there is any mystery about their being and activity, it does not seem to differ in kind from any other mystery in the universe. Whether the same judgment should be made about the moral God of the theistic version of Moral religion is not clear. What evidence there is would seem to indicate that the moral God is only relatively incomprehensible.

2. Issues concerning the religious activity. These are closely connected with issues that concern the religious object. For example, if the religious object is conceived of as a personal being, the kind of religious activity directed to it should reflect its personal character as well as the personal character of the religious subject. In other words, authentic religious activity should be conceived of as interpersonal or intersubjective in order to measure up to the personal status of both the object and the subject in the religious relationship.

The same argument would hold with regard to personal agency. If the religious object should be conceived of as a personal agent whose activity is indispensable in one way or another to mankind, the religious activity directed to such an object should reflect that sort of dependence. Religious activity then would have to be conceived of as an activity that expresses real dependence on the religious object.

Of the basic theories, only the theistic group would maintain the affirmative position on these two issues. For the Ceremonialist and the theistic Moralist, as well as for the believer in Revealed religion, any view of religious activity as impersonal (or apersonal), or as an activity incapable of expressing real dependence on the religious object, would be a misconception of religious activity.

There is one issue concerning religious activity that seems to arise independent of the concept of the religious object. This is the issue concerning its social or communitarian dimension. For both Ceremonial and Revealed religion, religious activity must be conceived of as something more than a purely private and individual activity. Indeed, for the Ceremonialist it is much more an activity of the community than it is of the private individual. While the Revealed theory would not go as far as that, it would still insist that religion is as much an activity of the community as it is of the individual, as much public as private. So, too, the Comtean version of Secular religion seems to go as far as the Ceremonial in stressing the communal character of religion. These three theories would reject the view of religious activity propounded in Mystical religion, Moral religion, and the Feuerbachian version of Secular religion, each of which makes it an individual or purely private affair.

This completes our survey of the conceptual issues on which the basic theories are more or less evenly divided. They might be described as secondary in comparison with the primary and fundamental issues on which four side against one. And here again, as with the primary issues, the proponents are not the same on each issue, although on the first two the theistic group join in opposing the nontheistic group.

These secondary issues, in brief, are the ones raised when opposite answers are given to the following questions:

1. Does the concept of religion require that its *object* be:
   a) personal in being?

b) a personal agent whose power is indispensable to human affairs?

c) a mysterious and incomprehensible being?

2. Does the concept of religion require an *activity* that is:

   a) interpersonal in character?

   b) an expression of dependence on the personal activity of the religious object?

   c) communal and not purely private, or individual?

D. The secular repudiation: a conceptual counterattack

It should be noted, indeed emphasized, that among the five basic theories only one has been exempt from conceptual criticism, i.e., from the charge of having misconstrued or betrayed the very concept of religion. If our analysis of the understanding of the concept found in the five theories is sound, only Revealed religion is fully faithful to the concept.

This result should not be seen as surprising. Scholars of religion assure us that both the concept and term are the products of Western civilization and do not have any exact counterparts in other cultures or civilizations. If it is a fact that the very concept of religion derives from and expresses a massive traditional Western phenomenon, its range of meaning could scarcely lie beyond the Revealed theory of religion, for the two possess the same existential referent. The concept of religion, what we mean by it today, is the result of the teaching and practice of Judaism, Christianity, and Islam, these three being the main proponents of the kind or theory of religion that we have called Revealed religion. Of course, this in no way implies that Revealed religion is immune from other kinds of attack and criticism. All that its exemption from conceptual criticism implies is that it can claim to be fully included within the common meaning of the term *religion*. In other words, Revealed religion is truly a religious proposal. On the existential plane, Revealed religion is as open as are all the others to criticism, attack, and repudiation. Conceptually sound it may be, but it can be and in fact frequently has been repudiated as existentially false religion or superstition.

As we have seen, the claims to the title of religion made for the other four kinds are more or less subject to criticism on purely conceptual grounds. This means that even if one were to concede their existential claims—i.e., the real existence of the gods of the Ceremonialist, the ideal existence of the objects of the Moralist or the Secularist, and the One of Mystical religion —it could still be maintained, on one count or another, that such objects fail to meet the standard of an authentic religious object. Only an object that is fully divine—either the creator God of Revealed religion or the moral God of the theistic version of Moralist religion—seems to escape the possibility of denial as an authentic religious object; accordingly, only the human activity that is commensurate with such an object seems to be regarded as undeniably authentic religious activity.

What response can the opponents of Revealed or theistic moral religion make to this claim of authenticity? Is the concept of religion indissolubly wedded to the concept of one God and to the activity that befits such an object? If it is, must the concept of religion be regarded as dependent upon the concept of God? Or is there something about religion that can and should survive the death, verified or presumed, of the God-concept? There are a number of thinkers who would reply with a resounding Yes to this last question. In so responding, they would be charging, in effect, that the common understanding we have been claiming for and using to analyze the five basic kinds of religion is prejudicial and misleading.

Among the five kinds, it is the Secular theory, as we have seen, that is most open to conceptual criticism. Perhaps for this reason, its proponents mount the strongest and most articulate conceptual counterattack. Comte, for example, is convinced that the nature of religion has been almost universally misunderstood. Its central feature, he maintains, has always been a striving for the goal of human integration, social as well as individual; in his view this feature can be seen to underlie all historical forms of religion once the traditional divine religious objects are no longer believed in. Religion ever aims at "perfect unity, the distinctive mark of man's existence, both as an individual and in society," he writes. Such a unity is achieved only "when all the constituent parts of man's nature, moral as well as physical, are made habitually to converge toward one common purpose."[183] Hence, as long as there is some object or conception upon which all human faculties and institutions can converge, religion still survives, even though God—or the gods, or the One—is no longer believed in. So too, according to Comte, man will always stand in need of religion, because he will always need a principle of unification and integration.

Comte's position amounts to a direct attack upon the concept of religion we have used in constructing the conceptual controversy about the kinds of religion. It holds, in effect, that religion ought not to be approached from the viewpoint of its objects and the activity they elicit, that it is just this approach which is responsible for the conceptual rejection of the Secular theory. A concept of religion derived from this objective side of religion may be accurate within its limits, but it is limited by its perspective. Important questions about religion, including the most important one of all, are largely lost sight of, according to Comte. The most important question to be asked concerning religion is not what it is or what it consists in but why there is such a thing. A concept of religion that takes this as the central question may well maintain that authentic religion is relatively indifferent to conceptions of the religious object and activity. Hence, given his understanding of that purpose, Comte can claim that his concept of an idealized humanity, together with the activity capable of realizing that ideal, meets the specifications of authentic religion.

There is no need to accept Comte's claim in its entirety in order to acknowledge that exclusive reliance upon the objective approach does miss important questions and fails to do justice to some theories of religion. Such are the theories which focus on qualities claimed to be characteristic of religion as a whole, or as a unitary phenomenon, and which tend to refer more immediately to man, the religious subject, than to the religious object. From that perspective, the religious object—although still necessary, of course—tends to become merely functional and secondary in importance.

This being the case, the map we have so far sketched of the general controversy about religion remains incomplete. It needs to provide a better account of those concepts of religion that are missed or inadequately treated from the objective approach we have taken so far. This will be accomplished in Part Two of this essay by a consideration of those qualities of religion which the controversy about it have taken to be fundamental.

IV. A DIALECTICAL UNDERSTANDING OF RELIGION IN GENERAL

In the outline of our hypothesis it was maintained that the various aspects and phases of the discussion of religion in the literature can be related as parts of an intelligible whole. What is required for this, however, is a minimal topical agreement on the subject of religion in general that is shared in some way by all the authors. According to our hypothesis, the underlying thread that ties together the special understandings of religion of the various authors—the different basic conceptions called "kinds"—is a general understanding of religion which we have formulated as *reverence for transcendent goodness*. In this section we intend to show how this formulation of religion in general adequately represents what is common to the specific concepts of religion of the paradigmatic authors, that is, represents what is common to the five kinds.

A. The problem of religion in general

Our problem is to establish and identify the subject of general controversy about religion, or religion in general.* The diverse concepts or kinds of religion cannot be regarded as offering conflicting views about religion unless the five subjects, each of which may be defended or challenged as a kind of religion, have something more in common than the name "religion." Without a common subject, no categorical disagreement about religion is possible, because the participants are in that case talking about different things. Is there a subject that unifies the discussion of religion in an intelligible whole and thereby prevents participants in this discussion from being in a state of complete irrelevance to one another? What we are seeking is a minimal topical agreement on the subject of religion that is

---

* The general controversy about religion is distinguished from the other or special controversies by the fact that religion in general is its unifying subject. The special controversies have other subjects—namely, the individual kinds and qualities of religion. It is through the general controversy about religion that the special controversies can be seen as related to one another.

shared, if only implicitly, by the authors who propose the typical concepts of religion called "kinds."

The problem, or question, should not be misunderstood. Our interest here is not in asking the various groups of authors, each representative of a typical theory of religion, to say severally what each group thinks religion is. What we are seeking is a collective answer to the question, or at least to find out if one is possible. It is clear that few if any of the authors have asked or tried to answer the question in these forms.[184] The authors who affirm one or another of the five kinds of religion do not ordinarily even concern themselves with what they have in common with fellow proponents of their favored kind of religion. They have been content to state and defend their particular conceptions. But the dialectical task begins at this point. It consists, as preceding sections have shown, in discerning among these diverse conceptions what it is they have in common, and what, therefore, identifies the kind of religion to which they belong. So, here, after the identification of the five kinds, the dialectical task is to discover and formulate that which is common to all of them, by which we can identify religion in general.

In one respect the problem of identifying religion in general is like the problem of identifying the basic kinds. That is, formulations have to be constructed about religion which are not to be found explicitly in the literature, and neutral terms are required to formulate the identifications constructed. What is more, the test of a satisfactory solution is the same for both problems. The constructions must fit the evidence. Or, in other words, the common points which those constructions make explicit must be seen to exist implicitly in the conceptual diversities that constitute the actual literature about religion.

However, there are two important respects in which the problems of identifying religion in general and one of the basic kinds of religion are not alike. One derives from the fact that religion in general does not represent a genus of which Ceremonial, Moral, Mystical, Revealed, and Secular religions are species. It stands for what is *analogously*—not generically or univocally—*common* to the meanings of Ceremonial and the other basic kinds of religion. In contrast, the identification of Revealed religion, for instance, expresses elements which are generically common to a whole family of conceptions (Philonic, Augustinian, Ghazalian), and which are univocally present, under further specifications, in each of the specific conceptions that is a member of this family.

A second respect in which the problem of identification differs is that the identification of any particular kind of religion is the identification of a subject actually discussed in the literature. It is a generalization or abstraction drawn from the actual conceptions of Philo, Augustine, and al-Ghazali and is only one step removed from the concrete materials or literature. In contrast, the identification of religion in general will involve a generalization or abstraction that is two steps removed. It will not be drawn directly from the literature but instead from the identifications that have already been constructed on the basis of that literature, namely the identifications of Ceremonial, Moral, Mystical, Revealed, and Secular religions. This amounts to saying that the identification of religion in general is the identification of a subject which is not actually discussed in the literature. It is *not* proposed as a definition of religion but as a dialectical understanding constructed for the purposes of enabling proponents of the five typical kinds of religion to be participants in one and the same general controversy about religion.

Though some authors contribute insights which can be used in solving our problem, the materials principally used as the basis for constructing the identification of religion in general are the five identifications already constructed. Since the identification of Revealed religion, for instance, states what is common in a basic way to a whole family of conceptions (Philonic, Augustinian, Ghazalian), and similarly in the case of the other four identifications, it follows that if the identification of religion in general succeeds in stating what is common to the five kinds of religion, it will also state what is common to all the members of the five kinds.

B. Religion in general

Before attempting to justify our identification of religion in general, it will be helpful to give brief summary statements of the common understanding of each of the five typical kinds of religion. They are as follows:

1. To be religious is to offer prayer and sacrifice to the gods. (Ceremonial)
2. To be religious is to do good to one's fellow humans in conformity with the moral ultimate. (Moral)
3. To be religious is to seek unification with the one true reality. (Mystical)
4. To be religious is to respond with faith in and obedience to the God of revelation with divine help. (Revealed)
5. To be religious is to cooperate in the realization of ideal humanity. (Secular)

Now, let X stand for a summary statement of the general understanding of religion that is analogously common to such diverse understandings of religion as are expressed in these statements. Statement X must be determinate enough to be meaningful in itself, yet indeterminate enough, relative to those statements, so as not to exclude the positive content which each of them adds; that is, X must be a determinable of which 1, 2, 3, 4, and 5 are determinations. In effect this means that the dialectical statement of religion in general (Statement X) must be indefinite or vague about the points in question among the five kinds. That is because on each of these points the five typical theories of religion are precise and definite, insisting that the point in question be specified in one way rather than another. It is only by remaining indefinite on these same points that the dialectical statement can be general enough to state what is common to the whole range of specific theories.

As will be recalled, the points in question among the five kinds are two: (1) the character of the religious object; (2) the character of the activity that is proposed as genuinely religious. That these are the focal points of diverse specification is also reflected in the summary statements of the five kinds just given. Thus, the dialectical problem of religion in general contains two questions: (1) What is common to the variety of religious objects proposed in the five kinds? (2) What is common to the variety of activities proposed as religious in the same five kinds?

1. Transcendent goodness. What we are seeking is a dialectical concept of the religious object that expresses no more than the feature (or features) common to the religious objects proposed in the five kinds. What is common to (1) the gods; (2) the moral ultimate; (3) the One true reality; (4) the Creator-God of revelation; and (5) ideal humanity?

As we have already seen in the conceptual controversy, a number of features have been ruled out as *not* common to the variety of the proposed religious objects. Ultimacy in any order of things, unity of being, transsecularity, reality of being, and absolute otherness, on the one hand, and, on the other, personality, personal agency, and incomprehensibility are all matters of conceptual debate among the five kinds. Whatever the religious object is commonly conceived to be, it is *not* commonly conceived to be one, transsecular,* real, ultimate that is wholly other than the self, and who is a personal being and powerful agent beyond human comprehension. What does appear to be a characteristic common to all the concepts of the religious object is its *goodness*.

a) The meaning of goodness: By using the term *goodness* for the initial common character of the religious object, we mean that it is always conceived to be in the order of the desirable, the worthwhile, and valuable. That there is something desirable or worthwhile in one way or another about the religious objects of the broadly named theistic group (the gods, the moral God, and the Creator-God of revelation) and in other ways about the religious objects of the nontheistic group (the moral ideal, the One reality, and the ideal humanity) is easily confirmed by brief reflection on their individual qualities. Indeed, it does not seem to be an overstatement to claim that it is precisely their goodness which constitutes them as religious objects and which in each case calls forth the religious responses to them.

To claim that the religious object is conceived to be good and desirable is not to claim that it is always conceived to be morally good or morally

---

* To be transsecular and to be transcendent are not coextensive, at least in our usage. Hence, to deny that the common religious object is transsecular is not thereby to deny every form of transcendence to it.

desirable. The goodness of one of the proposed religious objects seems to be nonmoral, and the categories of moral good and moral evil appear to be irrelevant to it. This is the One of Plotinus and the Brahman of Sankara, which appear to be outside or beyond the moral categories. Their goodness is conceived as pertaining exclusively to the ontological order and consists in the fullness or perfection of reality or being. Hence, the term *goodness* in our dialectical formulation must not be understood solely in the ordinary sense of moral good, else it will rule out one specific conception of the religious object, the One true reality of Mystical religion.

If the understanding of *goodness* must be broadened to include a kind of goodness other than moral, this does not mean that a religious object could be conceived as evil in the moral sense. No author we have read suggests that the religious object as such—that is, as the referent of the religious relationship—could be morally evil. Traditional Western theologians would view such a thought as blasphemous, while untraditional philosophers of religion would consider it absurd.

One of the issues about the concept of God among modern Western philosophers concerns this very question. These philosophers assume that in any irreconcilable clash between the infinite power of the traditional God and his moral goodness, believers to a man would abandon any claim to infinite power and would cling to the moral goodness of God as the indispensable attribute. In other words, these thinkers assume that the concept of an infinite God will always be reduced to the concept of a finite God by traditional believers, if thereby the moral goodness of God is preserved unblemished.

John Stuart Mill is an early exponent of this view. He insists that "there is no subject on which man's practical belief is more incorrectly indicated by the words they use to express it, than religion." However much the traditional Western believer may talk about divine omnipotence, Mill claims, he is always willing to sacrifice the ontological perfection of infinite divine power to the needs of divine moral goodness. "Those who have strengthened in goodness by the sympathizing support of a powerful and good God," Mill writes, "have . . . never really believed that Governor to be, in the strict sense of the term, omnipotent. They have always saved his goodness at the expense of his power."[185]

Bernard Bosanquet goes farther. It is not merely the God of traditional Western religion or such gods as may be worshiped elsewhere that are good in his view. No religious object whatsoever can be morally evil, he asserts, for "there cannot be a religious attitude towards an object recognized as bad."[186]

What must be understood by the term *goodness* in our dialectical concept of the religious object, in summary, is a broad sense of goodness. It is intended to signify no more than a desirable perfection which may be moral or nonmoral (or both) but is never immoral.

b) Transcendence and its meaning: While it is true that each of the religious objects proposed in the five kinds belongs to the order of the desirable or worthwhile, the term *goodness* does not by itself suffice to identify their common feature. If no further specification or qualification were added to goodness, the field of religious objects would be open to any object whatsoever so long as some degree of goodness could be presumed to belong to it. This is not the collective view of the proponents of the five kinds. Though they specify the goodness of their religious objects in different and conflicting ways, there is something common to their specifications that limits the field of possible religious objects. For the religious object is conceived collectively not only as belonging to the order of goodness but as belonging to the order of *transcendent*, or transcending, goodness.

Our addition of the term *transcendence* to the goodness of the religious object is meant to point to a certain eminence in the ranking of its goodness.[187] Not any degree at all of goodness suffices for the religious object. It must be within the expanse of what we understand by transcendent goodness, which ranges between the boundaries of *relative transcendence* and *absolute transcendence*. At one extreme, the minimal boundary of relative transcendence, is found a goodness that goes beyond and surpasses any and every goodness actualized in the ordinary world of everyday experience. At the other extreme of the range of transcendent goodness, the maximal boundary of absolute transcendence, is found goodness that goes beyond and not only surpasses the everyday empirical world with its goods, actual and possible, but also transcends the whole universe of beings and goods, actual or merely possible.

If it is to encompass in its meaning such a range of goodness, *transcendence* can mean no more than a going beyond or surpassing that which is given in the world of ordinary human experience. The goodness to which the religious relationship is collectively conceived to refer by the proponents of the typical kinds of religion must be a goodness without a superior in rank, and even without a peer in status, among the actual goods of the world of expectable human experience.

Absolute transcendent goodness, or maximal transcendent goodness, is exemplified most plainly in the God of revelation, the object of Revealed religion. He is conceived as surpassing or transcending in both moral and nonmoral goodness not only the actual universe but all possible universes of beings and goods. Relative transcendent goodness, or minimal transcendent goodness, on the other hand, is exemplified most clearly in ideal humanity, the object of Secular religion. This is conceived as surpassing or transcending only the actual goods of human achievement in the world, individual and collective, as a high ideal ever outstrips actual performance, but not as something which goes beyond, or transcends, the collective capacities of mankind. Somewhere in between the absolute transcendent goodness of the God of revelation and the relative (or temporal) transcendent goodness of ideal humanity stand the other proposed religious objects.[188] The God of Moral religion and the One of Mystical religion approach the extreme of absolute transcendent goodness, though in different ways. The gods of Ceremonial religion and the ideal of Moral religion are closer to the extreme of relative transcendence.

What is common to the variety of religious objects proposed in the five kinds can be summed up in the following manner. The common religious object is dialectically conceived as *transcendent goodness*, that is, as a goodness, moral or nonmoral (or both), which permanently* transcends the perfection or goodness of the objects (persons or things) given in the ordinary world of human experience.

2. Reverence. The second and final question to be resolved in the dialectical problem of religion in general concerns the variety of activities proposed as religious by the five kinds. What is being sought is the dialectical concept of religious activity that best expresses the feature (or features) common to the five proposals. Though it should not be overlooked, there is no need to delay over the fact that each is a form of *human* activity. The question is what, other than humanness, is common to (1) offering prayer and sacrifice, (2) doing good to one's fellow humans, (3) seeking unification, (4) divine faith and obedience, and (5) constructing ideal humanity?

Some likely possibilities have already been ruled out in the conceptual controversy. Religious activity is *not* collectively viewed by the proponents of the five kinds as a kind of interpersonal activity, nor as a form of group or communal activity. The activities of Mystical, Secular, and Moral (in part) religions are not interpersonal in character, nor are those of Mystical, Moral, and Secular (in part) religions forms of group activity. Furthermore, religious activity is *not* collectively viewed as a matter of external action or embodied activity, because the religious activity of Mystical religion pertains exclusively to the inner dimension of the human. Finally, religious activity is *not* collectively conceived as either an expression of real dependence on the object, as in Revealed religion, Ceremonial religion, and Moral religion (in part), or as purely passive with respect to the constitution of the object, as in Revealed, Mystical, Ceremonial, and Moral religions.

Taking into account these negative boundaries on the collective concept of religious activity, it appears that the feature common to all five proposals must first of all be something that is inward or *internal*, that is, an inner or interior activity, or attitude, or disposition that may or may not be given expression in external actions and behavior. Second, the proposed religious activities, whether inner only (as in Mystical religion) or also outer (as in the other kinds), must be presumed to be intimately related to the common internal element, that is, related to it as apt expressions of its character. If this be so, then the common interior activity or attitude or disposition is

---

* The transcendence of the goodness of the religious object must also be conceived to be permanent, or, at the very least enduring throughout the temporal span of the religious relationship.

more crucial to the common religious relationship than the various activities proposed, for it seems to stand behind them as their proximate principle and cause. In any event, the common internal principle will have to be open to the varied specifications of religious activity that are proposed in the five kinds as its fitting expressions.

What must also be taken into account in our attempt to identify the feature common to the religious activities proposed is the character of the common religious object. If it be true that religious activity answers to the quality of the religious object, then the feature common to the variety of religious activities should be commensurate with the quality common to the variety of religious objects, that is, commensurate with transcendent goodness. It may very well also have to be an internal principle that generates this or that kind of expression, but above all else the feature common to the proposed activities must be a matter of a fitting relation to transcendent goodness, for it is precisely this sort of relation to the religious object that makes these activities to be religious activities.

Reverence is the term we use to name and to identify that which is common, in the end, to the variety of activities proposed as religious in the five kinds. Each of these activities, we maintain, must be understood as a form of "reverential" activity, and as an expression of "reverence" for the specific transcendent goodness involved. Hence, by the term *reverence* we wish to designate not only the feature common to the activities proposed as religious but also, and more important, the sort of relationship which must exist between the human and a religious object for that relationship to be called religious at all.

a) The meaning of reverence: Religion, at bottom, is collectively understood by the authors to be a matter of a fitting or congruent relationship between that which is in some pronounced and highly significant sense inferior (the human) and that which is superior in the same sense, a transcendent superior (transcendent goodness). As a consequence, religion involves a subordination of the human to a transcendent superior of goodness. More, it involves deep respect for, and the high honoring of, transcendent goodness. This attitude is what we mean by *reverence*, which, as we intend it, stands for the internal subordination, respect, and honor that is fittingly given to transcendent goodness.

To avoid misunderstanding the meaning we give to *reverence*, it is well to recall that there are two remarkably different kinds of transcendent goodness. What is fitting reverence for an absolutely transcendent goodness does not appear to be properly given to what is only a relatively transcendent goodness, and vice versa. Augustine, for instance, in *The City of God*, makes a sharp and deep distinction between reverence given to "the gods" (the good angels), or to relatively transcendent goodness, and the properly religious reverence given to the Creator-God of revelation.[189] Plato, on the other hand, does not refer religious reverence to the Idea of the Good, his absolute transcendent good, but to the gods, or relative transcendent goodness.[190] In the face of diversity of this sort, *reverence*, as we use the term, cannot be understood in either the specific Augustinian or the specific Platonic sense. As the common religious object ranges between relative and absolute transcendent goodness, so must the reverence common to the five kinds be understood to range between a reverence befitting a relative transcendent goodness and one befitting an absolute transcendent goodness.

Another possible misunderstanding of the meaning we give to *reverence* should be avoided. The word *reverence* comes from an ancient Latin word for *fear* (*vereor*). Because of this derivation, the word *reverence* very often bears a note of fear. However, to understand our dialectical concept of reverence as one in which fear is necessarily present is to misunderstand it. *Reverence*, as we use the term, is meant to be a concept that is empty of specific emotional content, though not of specific meaning. Indifferent in itself to any emotional specification, the dialectical notion of reverence is open to a further determination by proponents of this or that kind of religion which may or may not include fear among its components.

Traditional theistic religious objects can be objects of a religious reverence that includes fear as one of its components. The reason is plain. In one way or another, human affairs are conceived as really dependent on the autonomous exercise of divine power in Ceremonial, Revealed, and Moral (in part) religions. Rudolph Otto's *The Idea of the Holy* is a classic exposition of a kind of religious reverence that includes fear as one of its essential components. Otto uses the word *numen* for the religious object, but there is little doubt that he has a traditional theistic object in mind. Among other things Otto views the numinous as that on which the human is totally dependent, and, consequently, he gives fear a prominent place in the constellation of emotions which he views as proper to religious reverence.[191]

Reverence for the nontheistic religious objects proposed, on the other hand, does not include fear as one of its emotional components. For fear to be a reasonable response on the part of the human, a real threat of avoidable evil must be at stake. If evil can exist in the monistic systems of Plotinus and Sankara, it cannot be attributed to their self-contained religious objects, the One or Brahman. Fear has no place in reverence for the One or Brahman.[192] Much the same must be said of idealistic religious objects — the moral ideal of some of the Moralists and the ideal humanity of the Secularists. In and of itself, an ideal is incapable of being the effective source of anything real. However, to exclude fear from reverence is not thereby to eliminate reverence. Comte is clear about that. "Our love for her [Humanity] is tainted by no degrading fears," he writes, "yet it is always coupled with the most sincere reverence."[193]

Our response to the question about what is common to the variety of activities proposed as religious in the five kinds can be summed up in the following statements. First, religious activity must be dialectically conceived as reverential activity, that is, as an expression of an internal, habitual* reverence that constitutes the religious relationship.[194] Second, reverence itself must be dialectically conceived as no more than an internal subordination to, respect for, and honoring of the superiority or goodness of the religious object. Third, and finally, religious reverence must be dialectically conceived as transcending any reverence to be given to any object in the everyday world of ordinary experience, for it must be conceived as commensurate with the transcendence (common) of the dialectical religious object.

3. Reverence for transcendent goodness. Putting together the dialectical concept of the religious object with the dialectical concept of religious activity (and the religious relationship) in one brief statement, we claim that *reverence for transcendent goodness* is an adequate formulation of religion in general. Each of the terms in this statement carries a carefully stipulated neutral meaning that does not prejudice the statement in the direction of any one of the five specific conceptions of religion. It represents the collective response of the authors we have considered to the question "What is religion?" in that it identifies what is common to their five religious proposals. Such, at any rate, is the hypothesis we propose as the solution of the dialectical problem of religion in general.

Religion in general, it will be recalled, is the subject of the general controversy about religion. A successful identification of the subject of the general religious controversy is extremely important for our map of the religious terrain; it identifies what might be called the country of religion. If it be accurate that religion in general is reverence for transcendent goodness, then that which meets this specification has a place on the map of religion, and that which does not meet this specification is not comprehended by the religious terrain. A correct formulation of the general understanding of religion demarcates a distinct area of conceptual discourse and controversy and sets it off from any other such area. In so doing, it sets conceptual boundaries within which controversy and discourse must fall, if it would lay claim to being discourse and controversy about religion as it is commonly conceived.

The dialectical concept of religion in general not only takes in, as belonging to the general controversy about religion, such concepts as the five kinds (and the atypical kinds); it also rules out some other concepts as not genuinely religious. A few samples of the latter, which may be called *false concepts of religion*, can be given. First of all, where the reverential note is not present

---

* No author we have considered conceives religion to be constituted by a single, isolated act. Furthermore, only a habitual, or quasi-permanent, reverence is commensurate with the permanent superiority of the religious object.

at all in a relational concept, it has no claim to being a concept of religion. Among conceptions ruled out by this criterion is the concept of *magic*. If magic is "an attitude of command, of assertion, of the exercise of powers to deal with practical problems," as Ducasse conceives it, along with a number of authors, then magic is wholly outside the conceptual terrain of religion.[195] In this common view, magic is conceived as a relationship of authority, of a superior to an inferior, whereas religion is the exact reverse. Religion is commonly conceived to be the relation of an inferior to a superior, indeed to a transcendent superior, or what we have identified as reverence.

Second, even where the reverential note is present in a relational concept, this does not by itself guarantee that the concept is a religious one. Religion, dialectically conceived, is not reverence for any object at all, but reverence for transcendent goodness. Where a transcendentally good object is absent from a relational concept, the note of reverence, even if present, cannot claim to be nor should it be confused with a concept of religion. Among conceptions ruled out by this criterion are the concepts of *filial piety* and of *patriotism*. Reverence for parents and for country may be proper responses on the part of children and citizens, to be sure, but neither parents nor country are ordinarily conceived as transcendent superiors, that is, as possessing a goodness that goes beyond every perfection actualized in the everyday world, singly and collectively. Hence, a transcending reverence is not called for either in filial piety or in patriotism, while it *is* called for in the concept of religion.

In addition to ruling out some concepts apt to be mistaken for concepts of religion, which as such are false, the dialectical concept of religion can give definite content to certain *concepts of false religion*,* concepts such as idolatry, superstition, and hypocrisy. In terms of the dialectical concept of religion, *idolatry* can be identified as giving a transcending reverence to that which is not truly transcendent goodness, e.g., to one's country. *Superstition*, on the other hand, is to be identified as a reverence given to transcendent goodness that is grossly unfitting or unbecoming. Consisting mainly in practices, e.g., the mere repetition of acts, and in the associated beliefs, e.g., usually the belief implied in the practice, superstition is a highly improper expression of religious reverence.[196] Finally, *hypocrisy* (religious) can be identified as a reverence given to transcendent goodness that is wholly external, that is, as an action that is not an expression of internal reverence, this being entirely lacking.

---

* False concepts of religion are concepts that are *conceptually* false, that is, category mistakes. Concepts of false religion, on the other hand, are concepts dealing with *existentially* false religious phenomena.

¹ The position defended here about philosophy as a collective endeavor, and the need for rational debate and an impartial mapping of controversial subjects, is indebted to the lengthy treatment of the same points to be found in Mortimer J. Adler, *The Idea of Freedom*, 2 vols. (Garden City, N.Y.: Doubleday & Co., 1958), vol. 1, chaps. 8 and 9.

² H. J. Paton, *The Modern Predicament: A Study in the Philosophy of Religion* (London: Allen & Unwin, 1955), chap. 4, pp. 59–60. *See also* "Religion," chap. 79 of the *Syntopicon* (*GBWW*, Vol. 3), and "The Idea of Religion in *Great Books of the Western World*," in *GIT* 1967, pp. 70–80.

³ *See*, for example, A. N. Prior, "Can Religion Be Discussed?" in Antony Flew and Alasdair MacIntyre, *New Essays in Philosophical Theology* (New York: Macmillan, 1955), pp. 1–11.

⁴ Henry Fielding, *Tom Jones*, bk. 3, chap. 3; see *GBWW*, Vol. 37, p. 39b.

⁵ *See* William A. Christian, "Some Varieties of Religious Belief," *The Review of Metaphysics* 4, no. 4 (June 1951): 597–98.

⁶ Sigmund Freud, *Civilization and Its Discontents* (New York: Norton, 1962), p. 21; cf. *GBWW*, Vol. 54, p. 771b.

⁷ J. S. Mill, "The Utility of Religion," in *Three Essays on Religion*, 2d ed. (London: Longmans, 1874), p. 109; see *GIT* 1977, pp. 420–21.

⁸ *See* United States v. Seeger, 380 U.S. 163 (1965), and Torcaso v. Watkins, 367 U.S. 488 (1961).

⁹ Karl Barth, *Church Dogmatics*, Eng. trans. (Edinburgh: T. & T. Clark, 1956), vol. 1, pt. 2, pp. 302–3.

¹⁰ W. C. Smith, *The Meaning and End of Religion* (New York: Mentor, 1964), chap. 5, p. 138; cf. chap. 2, pp. 47–49.

¹¹ Donald A. Wells, *God, Man, and the Thinker* (New York: Dell, 1967), chap. 2, pp. 24–26.

¹² Lewis Carroll, *Through the Looking Glass*, chap. 6. The exchange between Viola and the Clown in Shakespeare's *Twelfth Night*, act 3, scene 1, is also relevant; see *GBWW*, Vol. 27, p. 14.

¹³ Wells, *God, Man, and the Thinker*, chap. 2, p. 40.

¹⁴ The more or less classic critical studies of the definitions of religion, James H. Leuba, *A Psychological Study of Religion* (New York: Macmillan, 1912), chap. 2 and the Appendix, and Vergilius Ferm, *First Chapters in Religious Philosophy* (New York: Round Table Press, 1937), chap. 2, may consider previous attempts at defining religion more or less wrongheaded, but they do not take them as exercises in private meanings.

¹⁵ Irving Copi, *Introduction to Logic* (New York: Macmillan, 1961), 2d ed., chap. 4, pp. 96–103. "A theoretical definition serves the purpose of explaining theoretically, that is, of formulating a theoretically adequate or scientifically useful characterization of whatever it is to which the definiendum is applied" (p. 102). Copi also observes that a theoretical definition can be phrased in emotive language, thus intended to influence attitudes as well as instruct. In this case, the definition is at once persuasive and theoretical.

¹⁶ Christian, "Some Varieties of Religious Belief," p. 599. C. J. Ducasse, in *A Philosophical Scrutiny of Religion* (New York: The Ronald Press, 1953), pp. 20–21, writes: "In the theory of religion ... questions of fact are inseparably bound up with questions of terminology; so that as soon as inquiry attempts to penetrate below the surface of a topic, and to establish anything not already familiar, the need becomes imperative to be clear as to which things exactly one means to indicate by the name one employs, and what character exactly one means to predicate by one's key adjectives. Without this, neither the reader nor one's self really knows what one is speaking about or what one is asserting about it. The steps taken to avoid this predicament may be somewhat tedious, but without their benefits, disquisitions on technical problems are at best literary essays, and establish nothing."

¹⁷ E. A. Burtt, "The Generic Definition of Philosophic Terms," *The Philosophical Review* 62, no. 1 (January 1953): 52–53. Burtt is no stranger to the problems of an impartial analysis of issues in the philosophy of religion: *see* his *Types of Religious Philosophy* (New York: Harper & Row, 1939).

¹⁸ William P. Alston suggests another approach to the problem of defining religion, making use of the Wittgensteinian conception of family resemblances to clarify the broad applications of the term *religion*. *See* his article "Religion" in the *The Encyclopedia of Philosophy* (New York: Macmillan, 1967), vol. 7, esp. pp. 142–43. Rem B. Edwards takes the same approach in his *Reason and Religion* (New York: Harcourt Brace Jovanovich, 1972), pp. 14–38, but does not appear to be convinced that the Wittgensteinian approach is fully adequate, since several family traits of religion seem to be almost universal. In any event, both Alston and Edwards

note that it is not the presence of a number of "religion-making" characteristics that is decisive in the debate over the application of the term *religion* but the relative *importance* assigned to this or that characteristic. How, in the end, a decisively important characteristic of religion differs from a more traditional essential property is not at all clear.

[19] *See* the author's *Prophets of the West* (New York: Holt, Rinehart & Winston, 1970), pp. 141 ff. for R. Collingwood's version of historicist-contextualism. For a contextualism that comes close to the extreme form, *see* Anders Nygren, *Meaning and Method: Prolegomena to a Scientific Philosophy of Religion and a Scientific Theology*, trans. Philip S. Watson (Philadelphia: Fortress Press, 1972), pp. 351–71.

[20] "A purely formal logic or semantic analysis entirely indifferent to the nature of reality [or the object-term of investigation] is not possible. Every system of categories exercises a legislative function to what counts as real in the world of existent reality described by means of these categories, and every such system establishes an order of priority as to which elements of the scheme will be regarded as 'primitive' in relation to the others." John E. Smith, "The Encounter between Philosophy and Religion," *Thought* 39, no. 152 (Spring 1964): 27. But *see also* Joseph M. Bochenski, *The Logic of Religion* (New York: N.Y.U. Press, 1965), pp. 14–17, 23–26.

[21] For an extensive treatment of the dialectical method of the Institute for Philosophical Research, *see* Mortimer J. Adler, *The Idea of Freedom*, 1: 3–105. An initial formulation is to be found in Adler's *Dialectic* (New York: Harcourt, Brace & Co., 1927).

[22] As C. I. Lewis notes, "It is desirable or even necessary to have some manner of marking this distinction between characters or properties of a thing which are essential to its being named by the term in question and other characters which are not thus essential. . . ." Yet the classification of things is often determined pragmatically, and even when not, there is "nothing which is not classifiable in more than one way. Also what is, for one such classification, essential, may be non-essential for another." *An Analysis of Knowledge and Valuation* (LaSalle, Ill.: The Open Court Publishing Co., 1946), pp. 41, 105.

[23] "In philosophy . . . the temporal sequence of thinkers cannot be identified with an inherent movement of doctrinal improvement. Philosophers do not replace each other in a linear series of ever more adequate minds, but rather take their own place at the open conference table. The dialogue grows more complex and the later thinkers have the advantage of a leisurely acquaintance with previously presented arguments, but there is a remarkable staying power exhibited by every participant, regardless of his time of entry into the discussion," James Collins, *The Emergence of Philosophy of Religion* (New Haven: Yale University Press, 1967), p. 419. *See also* John H. Randall, Jr., *How Philosophy Uses Its Past* (New York: Columbia University Press, 1963), pp. 20 and 30.

[24] Augustine *The City of God* 10. 1; *GBWW*, Vol. 18, p. 299b.

[25] Cicero *On the Nature of the Gods* 1. 41; cf. 1. 2.

[26] Plato *Euthyphro* 14 and 15; cf. *GBWW*, Vol. 7, p. 198a–c.

[27] Thomas Aquinas *Summa Theologica* 2. 2. 81.1, *corp.*

[28] John Baillie, *The Interpretation of Religion* (Edinburgh: T. & T. Clark, 1929), p. 448.

[29] P. Erich Przywara, *Polarity,* trans. A. C. Bouquet (London: Oxford University Press, 1935), p. 22.

[30] William James, *The Varieties of Religious Experience* (New York: Longmans Green, 1902), p. 30.

[31] Friedrich Schleiermacher, *The Christian Faith,* Eng. trans. (Edinburgh: T. & T. Clark, 1928), p. 12. At this point in his career, Schleiermacher prefers the term *piety* to that of *religion.*

[32] Auguste Comte, *A General View of Positivism,* trans. J. H. Bridges (New York: R. Speller, 1957), p. 378.

[33] Georg Hegel, *Lectures on the Philosophy of Religion,* trans. E. B. Speirs and J. B. Sanderson (London: Kegan Paul, 1895), 1: 205. Hegel also speaks of a special "relation of spirit with Spirit that lies at the foundation of religion." Ibid., p. 101.

[34] Josiah Royce, *William James and Other Essays on the Philosophy of Life* (New York: Macmillan, 1911), p. 89.

[35] Leo Tolstoy, "What Is Religion and Wherein Lies Its Essence?," in *On Life and Essays on Religion,* trans. Aylmer Maude (London: Oxford University Press, 1934), p. 233.

[36] Auguste Sabatier, *Outlines of a Philosophy of Religion,* trans. T. A. Seed (London: Hodder & Stoughton, 1902), p. 27.

[37] Paul Tillich, *What Is Religion?,* trans. James L. Adams (New York: Harper & Row, 1969), pp. 35, 59, and 162. Tillich's later, and more famous, definition of religion as "ultimate concern" will be considered later.

[38] Gerardus van der Leeuw, *Religion in Essence and Manifestation*, trans. J. E. Turner (London: G. Allen & Unwin, 1938), bases his influential analysis of the religious phenomenon on the relational character of religion.

[39] Hegel, *Lectures*, 1: 132: "Man alone has religion, not the beasts."

[40] Lactantius *Epitome Institutionum Divinarum* 37.

[41] Moses Maimonides *The Guide of the Perplexed* 3. 51.

[42] J. Calvin, *Institutes of the Christian Religion*, bk. 1, chap. 3.

[43] Herbert of Cherbury, *De Veritate*, trans. M. H. Carré (Bristol: J. W. Arrowsmith, 1937), p. 295.

[44] Xenophon *Memorabilia* 1. 4. 13.

[45] Marsilio Ficino *Theologica Platonica* 14. 9.

[46] T. Hobbes, *Leviathan*, pt. 1, chap. 12; *GBWW*, Vol. 23, p. 79b.

[47] Ludwig Feuerbach, *The Essence of Christianity*, trans. George Eliot, 2d ed. (New York: Harper & Row, 1957), p. 1.

[48] A. J. Heschel, *Between God and Man* (New York: Free Press, 1965), p. 78.

[49] Augustine has no doubt that the angels are at least as religious as humans; cf. *On True Religion*, trans. John H. S. Burleigh (Chicago: Regnery, 1959), p. 103. Another author seems to wish to extend religion in the direction of animals, rather than of angels. "The reverential and worshipful emotion spent is the essence of religion, and wherever this is found among the lowest animals or the highest specimens of mankind, there is religion." H. M. Stanley, "On the Psychology of Religion," *Psychological Review* 5 (May 1898): 258.

[50] Plato *Laws* 10. 902; *GBWW*, Vol. 7, p. 767a–b.

[51] Ibid., 906; p. 769a–b.

[52] Cicero *Laws* 2. 9. 22 and 2. 16. 41.

[53] Cicero *On the Nature of the Gods* 1. 1–2.

[54] Ibid., 1. 40–42; cf. 1. 43–44.

[55] Cf. ibid., 2. 28.

[56] Neither Epicurus nor his Roman follower Lucretius (*On the Nature of Things*; *GBWW*, Vol. 12, pp. 1–97) was of the opinion that the abolition of the activity of the gods entailed the abolition of all piety or religion, though they were very well aware that it meant the end of traditional, ceremonial religion.

[57] Plato *Euthyphro* 14; *GBWW*, Vol. 7, p. 198.

[58] Plato *Laws* 4. 716; cf. *GBWW*, Vol. 7, p. 683a.

[59] Cicero *De inventione* 2. 53.

[60] Cicero *On the Nature of the Gods* 1. 2; see also *On Divination* 2. 72.

[61] We use Rousseau's *Émile* (1762) and Kant's *Religion within the Limits of Reason Alone* (1793) [*GIT* 1977, pp. 371–402] as primary sources for their respective concepts of religion. Other works of Rousseau and Kant are referred to only when some additional light is needed to remove obscurities found in their principal works on religion.

[62] Rousseau, *Émile*, trans. Barbara Foxley (London: J. M. Dent & Sons, 1911), bk. 5, p. 344.

[63] Ibid., bk. 4, p. 272.

[64] Ibid., p. 263.

[65] Kant, *The Critique of Practical Reason*, pt. 1, bk. 2, chap. 2, in *Immanuel Kant: Critique of Practical Reason and Other Writings in Moral Philosophy*, ed. and trans. Lewis Beck (Chicago: University of Chicago Press, 1949), p. 242; cf. *GBWW*, Vol. 42, p. 345.

[66] Immanuel Kant, *Religion within the Limits of Reason Alone*. trans. Theodore M. Greene and Hoyt H. Hudson (New York: Harper & Row, 1960), bk. 3, pp. 117–18; see *GIT* 1977, p. 390.

[67] Ibid., pp. 131–32; pp. 397–98.

[68] Ibid., pp. 130–31, "This idea of a moral Governor of the world is a task presented to our practical reason. It concerns us not so much to know what God is in Himself (His nature) as what He is for us as moral beings; although in order to know the latter we must conceive . . . attributes of the divine nature . . . which, in their totality, are requisite to the carrying out of the divine will in this regard. Apart from this context we can know nothing about Him." See *GIT* 1977, p. 397.

[69] Rousseau's Savoyard Vicar admits, "I know not whether he has created matter, body, soul, the world itself. The idea of creation confounds me . . . so far as I can conceive it, I believe it. But I know that he has formed the universe and all that is, that he has made and ordered all things." *Émile*, bk. 4, p. 248.

[70] Cf. Rousseau, *Émile*, bk. 4, pp. 262 and 271. For Kant *see*, e.g., *Religion within the Limits*, bk. 2, pp. 80–84, and bk. 3, pp. 131–36. *GIT* 1977, pp. 397–400.

[71] Cf. *Émile*, bk. 4, p. 245.

[72] Kant, *Religion within the Limits*, bk. 4, p. 142, footnote.

[73] T. Huxley, "Agnosticism," *Science and Christian Tradition: Essays* (New York: D. Appleton & Co., 1898), pp. 249–50.

[74] Rousseau, *Émile*, bk. 4, p. 257.

[75] Ibid., p. 276. In *The Social Contract*, Rousseau writes, "The religion of man . . . has neither temples, nor altars, nor rites, and is confined to the purely internal cult of the supreme God and the eternal obligations of morality . . . [it] is the religion of the Gospel, pure and simple, the true theism . . . [the] holy, sublime, and real religion." See *GBWW*, Vol. 38, p. 437a–c.

[76] Kant, *Religion within the Limits*, bk. 4, p. 142, and footnote. "Whatever, over and above good life-conduct, man fancies that he can do to become well-pleasing to God is mere religious illusion and pseudo-service of God." Ibid., bk. 4, p. 158. "The illusion of being able to accomplish anything in the way of justifying ourselves before God through religious acts of worship is religious *superstition*, just as the illusion of wishing to accomplish this by striving for what is supposed to be communion with God is religious *fanaticism*." Ibid., p. 162.

[77] Plotinus, *The Six Enneads*, trans. Stephen MacKenna and B. S. Page, 6. 9. 6; *GBWW*, Vol. 17, p. 357b.

[78] Ibid., 6. 9. 3 and 6. 8. 10; pp. 355c and 347d. Cf. 6. 8. 5–6; 6. 8. 8; 6. 8. 11; 6. 7. 38; 5. 5. 13.

[79] Ibid., 6. 8. 19; p. 352c.

[80] Ibid., 6. 9. 3; p. 355d.

[81] Ibid., 6. 9. 10 (emphasis added); p. 360a.

[82] Ibid. (emphasis added); pp. 359d–60a.

[83] Cf. ibid., 6. 7. 34–35; pp. 338b–39c.

[84] Cf. ibid., 6. 9. 11; p. 360a.

[85] Cf. ibid., 4. 8. 1; p. 200d.

[86] Sankara, "Crest-Jewel of Discrimination," v. 20, in *Vedanta: An Anthology of Hindu Scripture, Commentary, and Poetry*, ed. Clive Johnson (New York: Harper & Row, Bantam Books, 1971), p. 131.

[87] Ibid., v. 67, p. 135.

[88] "The Vedanta Sutras with the Commentary by Sankarakarya," in *A Source Book of Indian Philosophy*, ed. Sarvepalli Radhakrishnan and Charles A. Moore (Princeton: Princeton University Press, 1957), p. 517.

[89] Sankara, "Crest-Jewel," v. 58, in *Vedanta: An Anthology*, p. 134.

[90] Sankara, "The Vedanta Sutras," in *A Source Book of Indian Philosophy*, pp. 514–15.

[91] Ibid., p. 515.

[92] Cf. Plotinus, e.g., *The Six Enneads* 4. 4. 26 and 4. 4. 40–43; *GBWW*, Vol. 17, pp. 171b–c and 180b–81c.

[93] Sankara, "Crest-Jewel," v. 6, in *Vedanta: An Anthology*, p. 130.

[94] Cf. Plotinus, e.g., *The Six Enneads* 1. 2. 1–7; *GBWW*, Vol. 17, pp. 6b–10a.

[95] Sankara, "Crest-Jewel," v. 55, in *Vedanta: An Anthology*, p. 134; *see also* v. 11, p. 130.

[96] Cf. Plotinus, *The Six Enneads* 6. 9. 11; *GBWW*, Vol. 17, p. 360d.

[97] Cf. ibid., 6. 9. 7; p. 358a.

[98] Cf. ibid., 6. 9. 3; p. 355b.

[99] Cf. ibid., 6. 9. 8; p. 358d.

[100] Cf. ibid., 6. 9. 11; p. 360d.

[101] Cf. ibid., 6. 9. 9; p. 359b.

[102] Sankara, "The Vedanta Sutras," in *A Source Book of Indian Philosophy*, pp. 510–11.

[103] Sankara, "Crest-Jewel," vv. 6–11 and v. 20, in *Vedanta: An Anthology*, pp. 130 and 131.

[104] Ibid., v. 356, p. 135.

[105] Cf. ibid., vv. 525–26, p. 136.

[106] Philo *On the Creation* 61. 172.

[107] *See* Harry A. Wolfson, *Philo*, 2 vols. (Cambridge, Mass.: Harvard University Press, 1947), 1: 180.

[108] *See* Philo *Moses* 2. 100 and 267.

[109] *See* in Augustine *On True Religion* 17. 35; *The City of God* 10. 31, 11. 4–6, 12. 15–20 [*GBWW*, Vol. 18, pp. 319, 324–25, and 351–57]; *Confessions* 12. 8 [*GBWW*, Vol. 18, p. 101]; and his three exegetical works on the book of Genesis.

[110] Al-Ghazali, *The Foundations of the Articles of Faith*, trans. N. A. Faris (Lahore, Pakistan: Sh.

Muhammad Ashraf, 1963), sec. 1, p. 7. This work is a translation of the second book of the first quarter of Ghazali's *Ihya ulum al-din.*

111 Philo *Allegorical Interpretation of Genesis.* 3. 22. 78.

112 Ghazali, *The Alchemy of Happiness,* trans. Claud Field (Lahore, Pakistan: Sh. Muhammad Ashraf, 1964), chap. 8, p. 120.

113 Augustine *On Christian Doctrine* 1. 7; cf. *GBWW,* Vol. 18, p. 626c. Cf. *The Enchiridion* 9.

114 Philo *On the Creation* 2. 10.

115 Augustine *The Catholic and Manichaean Ways of Life* 1. 6. "What could be called more kind and generous than divine providence which, although man had fallen away from its law . . . did not abandon him? For that most just Power, in marvelous and incomprehensible ways, exercises, through a secret ordering of things it has created subject to Itself, both severity in punishment, and mercy in forgiveness," ibid., chap. 7.

116 Ghazali, for instance, appears to be something of an occasionalist, denying any genuine causality to creatures of any kind. The statement that "God alone is efficient cause" is basic to his thinking. *See,* e.g., *Some Moral and Religious Teachings of Al-Ghazzali,* trans. S. N. Ali, 2d ed. rev. (Lahore, Pakistan: Sh. Muhammad Ashraf, 1960), chap. 2, pp. 48–51.

117 Philo *Moses* 2. 5.

118 *See* Ghazali, *Foundations,* sec. 1, pp. 6 and 7; see also *Teachings,* sec. 5, p. 111.

119 Augustine *The City of God* 5. 10; *GBWW,* Vol. 18, p. 216b–c.

120 Philo *On the Special Laws* 1. 65.

121 *See* Philo *Moses* 2. 188.

122 *See* Philo *On Creation* 2. 8, *Allegorical Interpretation* 3. 102, and *On Rewards and Punishments* 7. 44.

123 *See* in Augustine, e.g., *The Enchiridion* 4, "What we have neither had experience of through our own bodily senses, and have been unable to reach through the intellect, must undoubtedly be believed on the testimony of those witnesses by whom the Scriptures, justly called divine, were written; and who by divine assistance were enabled to see, or to foresee, the things in question."

In Ghazali, *see* e.g., *Foundations,* sec. 3, p. 89, "This is contrary to the Brahmans who say there is no use in sending prophets since reason renders it unnecessary. This is false because reason does not guide men to works which lead to salvation in the hereafter."

124 *See* in Augustine, e.g., *The Enchiridion* 118, "The history of God's people has been ordered according to His pleasure. . . . For the church existed at first before the Law, then under the Law, which was given by Moses, then under Grace, which was first made manifest in the coming of the Mediator [Jesus Christ]. Not indeed that this grace was absent previously, but in harmony with the arrangements of the time it was veiled and hidden. For none, even of the just men of old, could find salvation apart from the faith in Christ; nor unless He had been known to them, could their ministry have been used to convey prophecies concerning Him to us, some plain, others obscure."

125 *See* in Ghazali, e.g., *Foundations,* sec. 1, pp. 6 and 8, "We also attest that the Quran, the Bible, the Gospel, and Psalms are His [Allah's] books revealed to His apostles . . . God sent the unlettered Qurashite prophet Muhammed as an apostle to all . . . And by his law he abrogated the others' laws, except such of them as he confirmed. And he gave him precedence over all prophets . . . and declared incomplete any profession of faith which attests to unity, i.e., 'there is no God but Allah,' unless it is followed by the witness to the Apostle, namely, 'Muhammed is the Apostle of Allah'."

126 Philo *On the Virtues* 7. 35.

127 Philo *On Rewards and Punishments* 14. 84.

128 *See* Augustine, e.g., *The City of God* 17 and 18 [*GBWW,* Vol. 18, pp. 449–507], and *On True Religion* 5. 9–10; 25. 46–29. 52.

129 *See* Ghazali, e.g., *Foundations,* sec. 3, p. 55.

130 Such is opinion of H. A. Wolfson, *Philo,* 2: 215–16. This opinion seems to be verified by the texts: "Therefore, he [Abraham] is the first person spoken of as believing in God, since he first grasped a firm and unswerving conception of the truth that there is one Cause above all, and that it provides for the world, and all that there is therein. And having gained faith, the most sure and certain of the virtues, he gained with it all the other virtues." *On the Virtues* 39. 216; "Do not . . . claim that the unworthy possess the most perfect of virtues, faith. . . . to trust in God alone and join no other with Him is no easy matter. . . . nothing is so just and righteous as to put in God alone a trust which is pure and unalloyed." *Who Is the Heir of Divine Things* 18–19. 91–94. See also *On the Migration of Abraham* 46. 268–70.

[131] Philo *On the Migration of Abraham* 23. 130–32, and *On Abraham* 46. 268–70.

[132] *See* in Augustine, e.g., *The Enchiridion* 4–5, where Augustine's reply to the question "What holds the first place in religion?" is that "we begin in faith."

Ghazali, in *Foundations*, sec. 4, p. 102, while claiming that faith is perfected through good works, also asserts that "faith is in reality a work, in fact the best of works."

[133] *See* in Augustine, e.g., *The Enchiridion* 30, and in Ghazali, *Foundations*, sec. 4, p. 108.

[134] *See* in Augustine *The Enchiridion* 2 and 30, and in Ghazali, *Teachings*, chap. 6, p. 128, and chap. 7, pp. 142–44.

[135] Augustine *The City of God* 10. 5; *GBWW*, Vol. 18, pp. 301b–302a. "A sacrifice . . . is the visible sacrament or sacred sign of an invisible sacrifice . . . the sacrifice of a contrite heart."

Philo, in *Moses* 2. 107–108, writes, "If the worshipper is without kindly feeling or justice, the sacrifices are no sacrifices, the consecrated oblation is desecrated, the prayers are words of ill omen with utter destruction waiting upon them. . . . But, if he is pure of heart and just, the sacrifice stands firm, though the flesh is consumed, or rather, even if no victim at all is brought to the altar."

[136] Philo writes, in *On the Migration of Abraham* 16. 93, "We should look on all these outward observances as resembling the body, and their inner meanings as resembling the soul. It follows that, exactly as we have to take thought for the body, because it is the abode of the soul, so we must pay heed to the letter of the laws. If we keep and observe these, we shall gain a clearer conception of those things of which these are the symbols."

Something of the same analogy appears also in Ghazali, *Foundations*, sec. 4, pp. 116–19, and in Augustine *On Christian Doctrine* 3. 9; *GBWW*, Vol. 18, p. 661a–c.

[137] Philo *On the Virtues* 34. 181.

[138] Philo *On Abraham* 37. 208.

[139] *See* Philo *On the Virtues* 9. 51 and 17. 94.

[140] Philo *Every Good Man Is Free* 12. 75–83. He is referring to the Essenes.

[141] *See* Augustine *On the Christian Life* 6, 11, and 14.

[142] Augustine *The Enchiridion* 121.

[143] *See* Augustine *The Catholic and Manichean Ways of Life* 1. 28. 56 and 57.

[144] Ibid., 1. 15. 25 and 1. 25. 46.

[145] Ghazali, *Foundations*, sec. 4, p. 126.

[146] Ghazali, *Teachings*, pp. 112–13.

[147] *See* Ghazali, ibid., pp. 114–15.

[148] Ghazali, *Alchemy of Happiness*, chap. 8, p. 135.

[149] Philo *Allegorical Interpretation* 1. 15. 48–49; see also *The Confusion of Tongues* 25. 180.

[150] *See* Augustine, e.g., *On Christian Doctrine* 3. 33. 46 [*GBWW*, Vol. 18, p. 670b–c] and *The Enchiridion* 32.

[151] *See* note 116.

[152] The problem is especially acute for Ghazali, who speaks of "losing sight even of the duality of one's own self" in the highest stage of religious devotion, wherein one "gazes at the vision of the all-comprehensive, all-absorbing One." *Teachings*, pp. 125–26. However, *see* ibid., pp. 113–14, where he refers to "the airy nothings of pantheism" and calls them "vagaries of the imagination."

[153] *See* Philo *Who Is the Heir* 51–53. 249, 258, and 263–65; Augustine *Commentary on Psalm 41* 2–10, and the author's *The Image of God* (Dubuque: Priory Press, 1963), pp. 65–67; Ghazali, *Teachings*, pp. 34–35.

[154] *See*, e.g., Philo *On the Migration of Abraham* 31. 170–71, where he says, "The soul has reason to fear ascending in its own strength to the sight of Him that Is . . . lifted up as it is at once by ignorance and by daring . . . it is better to stay where we are, roaming, with the bulk of mankind, through this mortal life, rather than to lift ourselves heavenward, and incur shipwreck as imposters. This has been the fate of multitudes of sophists."

[155] *See*, e.g., *The Humanist Manifesto* (1933), where it is said that "Religion consists of those actions, purposes, and experiences which are humanly significant. Nothing human is alien to the religious. It includes labor, art, science, philosophy, love, friendship, recreation—all that is in its degree expressive of intelligently satisfying human living." In *The New Humanist*, vol. 6, no. 3.

[156] Auguste Comte, *The Catechism of Positive Religion*, trans. Richard Congreve (London, 1858), pp. 46–48. Comte's estimate of human history is based ultimately on his famous law of three stages of mankind's intellectual evolution in which the properly national element in man

gained steadily at the expense of his animality. According to this view of the evolution of humanity, theological fictions and metaphysical abstractions were being replaced by a positive science of facts and connecting laws governing the whole of phenomenal reality. *See* Harriet Martineau, *The Positive Philosophy of Auguste Comte* (London: John Chapman, 1853), pp. 1–2. A fuller development of Comte's philosophy of history can be found in the author's *Prophets of the West* (New York: Holt, Rinehart, and Winston, 1970), pp. 64–73.

[157] Comte, *The Catechism*, pp. 63 and 78. *See also* Comte's *A General View of Positivism*, chap. 6, p. 365.

[158] Feuerbach, *The Essence of Christianity*, chap. 27, pp. 270–71.

[159] Ibid., chap. 1, p. 25. "Religion itself, not indeed on the surface, but fundamentally, not in intention or according to its own supposition, but in its heart, in its essence, believes in nothing else than the truth and divinity of human nature." Ibid., Preface to second edition, p. xxxvi.

[160] Ibid., chap. 1, p. 32.

[161] Ibid., chap. 27, p. 271. *See also* chap. 18, p. 184. "My work ... the new philosophy ... being evolved from the nature of religion ... has in itself the true essence of religion—[it] is, in its very quality as a philosophy, a religion also." Ibid., Preface, pp. xlii–xliv.

[162] Comte, *A General View*, chap. 1, pp. 50–51 and 62–63.

[163] Ibid., chap. 6, pp. 368 and 371.

[164] *See*, e.g., Julian Huxley, *Religion without Revelation*, rev. ed. (New York: Harper & Brothers, 1957). For a brief exposition of Huxley's view, *see* the author's *Prophets of the West*, chap. 13, pp. 245–62.

[165] *See* Comte, *The Catechism*, pp. 8–11.

[166] Comte, *A General View*, chap. 6, p. 365.

[167] Feuerbach, *The Essence*, chap. 27, p. 271.

[168] Ibid., chap. 26, pp. 263–64.

[169] Ibid., pp. 268–69. In another work (*The Philosophy of the Future*), Feuerbach focuses on the I-Thou relationship as characteristic of ideal human relationships. He does not hesitate to say that "Man with man—the unity of I and thou—is God."

[170] *See* Karl Marx and Friedrich Engels, *On Religion* (New York: Schocken Books, 1964), esp. pp. 41–42, 89, and 94, and above all F. Engels, "Ludwig Feuerbach and the End of Classical German Philosophy," sec. 3 in ibid., p. 239.

[171] *See*, e.g., *The Enchiridion* 31 and *Arrian's Discourses of Epictetus* 2. 14 and 3. 21. Something of a quasi-mystical element is also present in Epictetus.

[172] References to the "mysteries" are frequent in Plotinus, for instance, and some consider it more nearly accurate to designate him as more of an "oriental mystic" than a Greek philosopher.

[173] *See*, e.g., *The Two Sources of Morality and Religion.*

[174] *See*, e.g., *Religion in the Making* and *Process and Reality.*

[175] *See*, e.g., *Luther on Galatians* 2:16 and 3:6.

[176] *See*, e.g., *The Reasonableness of Christianity*, pars. 21, 172, 185, 187, 212, 241.

[177] *See*, e.g., *On Religion: Speeches to Its Cultured Despisers*, which should be taken with his later *The Christian Faith.*

[178] *See*, e.g., Vlad Lossky, *The Mystical Theology of the Eastern Church.*

[179] *See*, e.g., R. M. Jones, *Studies in Mystical Religion* and *New Studies in Mystical Religion.*

[180] *See* Robert N. Bellah, "Civil Religion in America," *Daedelus*, Winter 1967, pp. 1–21, and R. E. Richey and D. G. Jones (eds.), *American Civil Religion* (New York: Harper & Row, 1974). Bellah's concept of "civil religion" must be carefully distinguished from that of Rousseau in *The Social Contract* (bk. 4, chap. 8). *See*, e.g., the text cited in footnote 75.

[181] Bertrand Russell, "My Mental Development," in *The Philosophy of Bertrand Russell*, ed. P. A. Schilpp, 4th ed. (LaSalle, Ill.: Open Court Publishing Co., 1971), p. 19.

[182] *Sermon 117* 3. 5; *see also* Augustine's *Commentary on Psalm 85* 12.

[183] *The Catechism of Positive Religion*, pp. 46–48.

[184] Definitions of religion abound, but most are definitions of this or that kind of religion. Some definitions do attempt to take in several of the kinds, but only a very few appear to cover the entire range of the five kinds. Hence, most definitions of religion are not relevant to the dialectical question of religion in general.

[185] Cf. J. S. Mill, "The Nature of Religion," in *Three Essays on Religion*, 2d. ed. (London: Longmans, Green, Reader and Dyer, 1874), pp. 38–41.

[186] Cf. Bosanquet, *The Value and Destiny of the Individual* (London: Macmillan and Co., 1913), p. 235, and *What Religion Is* (London: Macmillan and Co., 1920), p. 5. In this Bosanquet is following F. H. Bradley's position (*Appearance and Reality*).

[187] A worthwhile collection of contemporary essays on the concept of transcendence is to be found in H. W. Richardson and D. R. Cutler (eds.), *Transcendence* (Boston: Beacon Press, 1969).

[188] Marxists have developed a radically temporal concept of transcendence as *futurity; see* R. B. Norris, *God, Marx, and the Future: Dialogue with Roger Garaudy* (Philadelphia: Fortress Press, 1974).

[189] Augustine reserves completely the reverence of worship, or *latria*, for the one Creator-God of revelation alone. The reverence that is rightly given to creatures of God (including angels) is called *dulia*. Only *latria* is religious reverence strictly speaking. *See,* e.g., *The City of God* 10. 1–3 and 8. 27; *GBWW*, Vol. 18, pp. 298–301 and 284–85. However, since the good angels and the saints in eternity are united with God, a later Christian tradition speaks of a higher form of dulia, or *hyper-dulia*, in reference to the angels and saints. *See,* e.g., Thomas Aquinas, *Summa Theologica* 2. 2. 104. 3–4.

[190] *See,* e.g., G. M. A. Grube, *Plato's Thought* (Boston: Beacon Press, 1968), pp. 151–52.

[191] See *The Idea of the Holy*, especially chap. 4, "Mysterium Tremendum."

[192] Fear may be out of place in reverence for the One or *Brahman*, but wonder (awe) is not; *see* Otto, ibid., chap. 5, "The Analysis of 'Mysterium'."

[193] Comte, *A General View of Positivism*, chap. 6, p. 378.

[194] Though terms like *devotion* and *commitment* were considered, all in all *reverence* appears to be the most suitable term to designate the kind of relationship that religion is commonly conceived to be. *Reverence,* according to one authority, is deeper than *honor,* which is principally external, and *respect,* which is principally internal, while able to embrace both internal and external elements.

[195] Cf. C. J. Ducasse, *A Philosophical Scrutiny of Religion* (New York: Ronald Press Co., 1953), pp. 63–66; Bronislaw Malinowski, *Magic, Science, and Religion* (New York: Free Press, 1946), pp. 85–90; and J. G. Frazer, *Man, God, and Immortality* (New York: Macmillan, 1927), pp. 299–300.

[196] "Persons who spent whole days in prayer and sacrifice to ensure that their children should outlive them were termed 'superstitious' [from *superstes,* a survivor] and the word later acquired a wider application." Cicero *On the Nature of the Gods* 2. 28. 72.

NOTE TO THE READER

RELIGION is the subject of Chapter 79 of the *Syntopicon*, as GOD is the subject of Chapter 29. Most of the topics listed in these chapters contain references to matters discussed by Father Sullivan in his long essay. An overview of both subjects as treated in the Great Books will be found, of course, in the introductions to those chapters.

For related material in *GGB*, see T. S. Eliot's essay "Dante" in Vol. 5, pp. 371–403; Gustave Flaubert, "The Legend of St. Julian the Hospitaller," in Vol. 3, pp. 371–392; William James, "The Will to Believe," in Vol. 10, pp. 39–57; Abraham Lincoln, "Meditation on the Divine Will," in Vol. 6, p. 758; Isaac Singer, "The Spinoza of Market Street," in Vol. 3, pp. 466–80; and Leo Tolstoy, "The Death of Ivan Ilyitch," "The Three Hermits," and "What Men Live By," in Vol. 3, pp. 646–727.

PART FOUR

Reflections on a Great Books Author

The Philosophy of Kant

Anthony Quinton

Anthony Quinton was born in England in 1925. A student of history and, later, philosophy, he was educated at Stowe and at Christ Church College, Oxford. In 1949 he was named a fellow of All Souls College at the same university and, in 1955, of New College. His areas of interest are social and political philosophy, metaphysics and the theory of knowledge, and intellectual history.

Mr. Quinton, who at different times has been visiting professor at Swarthmore and Stanford, was this year a visiting professor with the graduate faculty of the New School for Social Research in New York. He has been Dawes Hicks lecturer to the British Academy, where he spoke on the British Hegelians, and has given the Gregynog lectures at the University of Wales, where his subject was the philosophy of the social sciences. He was also T. S. Eliot lecturer at the University of Kent, where he discussed conservative political thought in England from Richard Hooker to the present time, the subject of his forthcoming book, *The Politics of Imperfection*.

Mr. Quinton's books include *Utilitarian Ethics* (1973), a historical survey and critical discussion, mainly from Hume to the present, and *The Nature of Things* (1973), a general treatise on philosophical logic, the theory of knowledge, and metaphysics. His publications are in varying respects contributions also to intellectual history. He has contributed essays and reviews on philosophy, history, and literature to *The Times Literary Supplement, The New York Review of Books,* and other publications.

The place of Kant in the history of philosophy

I mmanuel Kant, who lived from 1724 to 1804, is the only philosopher of the modern age who is unquestionably of the same order of importance as Plato and Aristotle. To say this is not to endorse as correct all of his main doctrines, or even any of them. One reason for the judgment is simply the bulk and range of his original contributions to philosophy.* There is no significant, recognized part of the subject to which he did not have a distinctive contribution to make, with the marginal exception of formal logic. In the first great work of his philosophical maturity, the *Critique of Pure Reason*, he discusses all the leading issues of the theory of knowledge and metaphysics in a manner and with conclusions of revolutionary originality. In his *Critique of Practical Reason* and other ethical writings he covers the whole range of moral philosophy and the philosophy of action. In the *Critique of Judgement* he deals with aesthetics and with the kind of thinking that ascribes purposiveness to the contents of the natural world. In his *Anthropology* he advances a general theory of human nature (something most philosophers presuppose, rather than argue for explicitly); in his *Religion within the Limits of Reason Alone* he develops a philosophy of religion; in other writings of his mature (or "Critical" period) he considers politics and physical science.

There have been other philosophers in the modern age with as wide a range, and one at least of these, Hegel, is a philosopher of great importance and originality. What particularly singles Kant out from Hegel and other encyclopedically comprehensive philosophers is the fact that he was situated at a point of utmost strategic importance in the development of the subject. The two main and conflicting lines of philosophical thought that had been diverging ever farther apart from each other over the two preceding centuries were brought together by Kant in a heroic attempt at reconciliation, or synthesis. The unification that he hoped he had achieved proved unstable. Soon after his death his European, and in particular, German, successors returned to constructive metaphysical speculation of a kind which he

---

* See *GBWW*, Vol. 42.

had tried to show was invalid. At the same time British philosophers, after a brief dominance of the Scottish philosophy of common sense, a diluted and superficial version of Kant's philosophy, were preparing to return to the tradition of more or less skeptical empiricism whose initiators were Locke and Hume.

To make the questions Kant put to himself intelligible, the two opposed philosophical traditions that he tried to bring together, with a good deal of exclusion and adjustment, must be briefly described. The point of departure for both is the philosophy of Descartes, worked out in the first half of the seventeenth century (Descartes died in 1650). Descartes began and justified his thoroughgoing investigation into the whole range of our claims to knowledge by taking very seriously skeptical arguments against the most obvious source of that supposed knowledge: perception by the senses. The one belief which he found to resist all such skeptical undermining was the belief he had in his own existence and in the occurrence of the thoughts or mental states in which alone that existence is—according to him—essentially manifested. That I exist and think (whether or not there is anything apart from me and my thoughts) is an indubitable and indestructible certainty, Descartes held. From this first principle he derived a number of substantial and important conclusions. The first of these was that any belief which had the certifying characteristics of his first principle was as worthy of belief as it was. What he took to be comparably "clear and distinct" were, first, the propositions that report our immediate current experience, such as that I am in pain or that there is a red patch in the middle of my field of vision (whether any public, physical red thing exists independently of me or not), and, second, what he called truths evident to the natural light of reason, in other words, propositions which it would be an evident contradiction to suppose are false, such as that a triangle has three sides, or that if there is a thought there must be a thinker that thinks it.

A second conclusion was that the self of which he was indubitably certain is essentially a thinking thing, a mind, and only contingently or accidentally embodied, or a body. He asserted this on the ground that while he could consistently conceive that his body did not exist, he could not consistently suppose that his mind did not. A mind, as distinct from the body associated with it, does not have to die with that body, and Descartes clearly thought it did not.

Descartes went on to argue that God exists, first, because his existence is the only adequate explanation for the idea the mind has of him, and second, because, since existence is more perfect than nonexistence, the definition of God as the possessor of all perfections logically entails that he exists. Only when God's existence is assured in this way can we have good reason to trust any of the beliefs about the material world that our senses inspire us to accept. If our perceptions were not in fact caused by independently existing material things, more or less like the appearances present to our minds, God would, inconsistently with his perfection, be a deceiver.

This is so, Descartes maintains, because we have a strong inclination to suppose that the appearances present to our minds are caused by physical things in some respects like them.

The two traditions that stem from Descartes—the rationalism of continental Europe and British empiricism—move off in different directions from him. The rationalists, notably Spinoza and Leibniz, accentuate the contrast he discerned between the certainty with which pure reasoning establishes the truths of mathematics and such metaphysical propositions as that God exists, and the tenuous support the senses provide for our beliefs about the material world. The conclusion they draw is that sense experience is no more than confused thought, a weak substitute on which we rely because of the limitations of our finite intellects. True knowledge, they hold, can be achieved only by the kind of abstract demonstration that mathematics rests on. Thus, Spinoza's main work was called *Ethica: Ordine Geometrico Demonstrata*; that is: Ethics, proved in the geometrical manner. Even if the minute detail of the nature of the world cannot be demonstratively discovered by the finite human mind, this work argues, its main outlines, its principal types of constituent and the relations between them, can be discovered by abstract reasoning that is quite independent of the senses. It was this optimistic conception of the powers of pure reason that was the prime object of Kant's criticism in the *Critique of Pure Reason*.

The empiricists, on the other hand, combined Descartes's conviction that the senses tell us nothing directly or certainly about the external world with the view that anything we have reason to believe about what Hume called "matter of fact and existence" must depend for such justification as it has on experience—on the deliverances of the senses and of the introspective awareness we have of our own current mental states. Locke and Hume did not deny that certain knowledge can be obtained in mathematics by purely rational argument. But they took mathematical truth to be merely formal or conceptual in nature, to report only what Hume called the "relations of ideas," and to assert nothing about what actually exists. Descartes had already admitted this as far as mathematics was concerned, but he believed the style of demonstrative reasoning found in mathematics to be applicable also to factual questions about what exists.

The only factual truths we can know for certain, according to the empiricists, are the immediate deliverances of sensation and introspection. Everything else we can properly claim to believe about matters of fact must be inferred somehow from these fragmentary, subjective items of knowledge. The empiricists were especially preoccupied with three kinds of common knowledge we claim to possess: that of material objects, existing independently of our perception of them; that of general regularities or connections in nature; and that of the mind itself, considered as the continuing subject of the particular mental states of which we are aware in introspection. Locke tried to supply the needed justification for these common varieties of belief. He argued that we could infer from the impressions of our senses that there are material things which cause them and partly resemble them. But his arguments for this thesis were devastatingly criticized by Berkeley. Hume, with a mixture of despair and cheerful resignation, drew the skeptical conclusion that none of these kinds of common belief can be justified. All that can be done, he argued, is to explain the psychological machinery which leads us to *imagine* that there are material things with a continued existence distinct from us, that there are necessary causal connections between events, and that streams of consciousness are actually unitary and persisting minds. Each of these beliefs embodies some sort of imaginative fiction, Hume held. We are led to suppose that there are independent material objects by the measure of constancy and coherence that is to be found in our sense impressions, and we believe that there are necessary connections between events of different kinds because they have commonly occurred together in our previous experience.

Kant's philosophical education had been in a version of the philosophy of Leibniz presented in the rigidly organized textbooks of Wolff. The reading of Hume's *Enquiry concerning Human Understanding*, he said, awoke him from his "dogmatic slumber." What no doubt disposed Kant to be so affected by British empiricism was his admiration for Newton. Newton's *Principia* seemed to him, as it was, the greatest achievement of the human mind in its pursuit of the scientific knowledge of nature. But Newton's system of the world had a foundation in sense experience, the perceptually observed behavior of the constituents of the solar system and of the mechanical interactions of more accessible common objects. How could Newton's account of nature, depending as it did on experience and not just on pure reasoning, be vindicated against Hume's claim that the hidden inferences to material objects and causal relationships involved in Newton's fundamental factual evidence were not valid intellectual steps but only imaginative fictions?

Kant agreed with Hume that the immediate, fragmentary deliverances of sense impressions are essential ingredients in our knowledge of the world. Where he crucially differed from Hume was in holding that the passage of the mind from these impressions to its beliefs in objective things and causal connections is not an unjustifiable, if explainable, imaginative transition but is in accordance with principles for which proof of a new, "transcendental" kind is available. In simplest terms, Kant justifies the principles he affirms as necessary conditions of our having any orderly experience whatever. If we did not interpret our sensations as constituting a world of persisting objects, causally related to each other, they would be a shapeless, kaleidoscopic jumble. The human understanding is so constituted that it cannot but order the sensations given to it in that way.

What has just been sketched is the main positive doctrine of the *Critique of Pure Reason*. The doctrine seeks to prove that the presuppositions of the Newtonian conception of the physical world must be correct for any rational mind. In this first *Critique* it is preceded by a parallel account of mathematical knowledge, and it is followed by a lengthy critique of the pretensions of rationalistic metaphysics. Kant took it to be a consequence of his theory of knowledge that we could not prove any propositions about things in themselves, in particular that we could have no knowledge of the existence and nature of God or of the freedom and immortality of the soul. But he was far from indifferent to these topics. In the moral philosophy expounded in his *Groundwork of the Metaphysic of Morals* (1785) and, at greater length, in his *Critique of Practical Reason*, he argued that the existence of God and the freedom and immortality of the soul are indispensable presuppositions of genuine morality. If moral obligation is what the morally serious person takes it to be, an irresistible demand that action of certain kinds be performed for its own sake and not for any attractive or advantageous effects that action may produce, then God must exist and the soul be free and immortal. Everything turns here for Kant on the sense of obligation or duty. If duty is what it seems, the consequences about God and the soul follow, but Kant does not claim to prove that it is what it seems. In effect, he invites his readers to accept the description of duty he gives as a faithful account of their own moral experience. "I have limited knowledge," he says, "to make room for faith." But he insists that it is a *rational* faith which he invites us to share, and what he has to say about the nature of duty or obligation has a very coercive or demonstrative appearance.

Kant's German successors, while applauding the respects in which, as they saw it, he had corrected the skeptical excesses of empiricism, dissented from one disconcerting aspect of his philosophy. He maintained that the world of which we can have genuine mathematical and scientific knowledge is, as he put it, phenomenal. This is not to say that it is subjective, for it is the same order that is found in or imposed on their respective sensations by all rational minds. But it is still a world of appearance, behind which there is an unknowable order of things-in-themselves. Subsequent idealist philosophers, most notably Fichte, Schelling, and Hegel, rejected that idea. There were good grounds in Kant's own thinking for them to do so. They argued that true reality should not be conceived as something hidden behind the phenomenal world of science and common observation, that it is, rather, the infinite whole of which science and common observation give a limited, partial, and inadequate account. For these idealists, philosophy has such an infinite whole for its subject and should approach it by a method of reasoning superior to the abstractive procedure of natural science, which is foreshadowed in Kant's own "transcendental" method of philosophizing. At the time of his death, Kant was aware of this line of development and adopted an ambiguous attitude toward it: on the one hand hostile, on the other receptive to its influence.

Kant's importance was recognized in the German philosophical world from the moment in 1781 his *Critique of Pure Reason* was published, when he was fifty-seven years old. As has been said, his leading German successors, notably Fichte and Hegel, rejected one central element of his philosophy, the doctrine of the thing-in-itself. But materials for that rejection are to be found in the rest of Kant's thought and, in general, the post-Kantian idealism of nineteenth-century Germany presupposes the new mode of thinking that Kant had introduced and is unintelligible without it. By the mid-nineteenth century Hegel had fallen from favor. His most vehement and distinguished critic, Schopenhauer, saw himself as a direct continuator of Kant. Later still, in 1865, Otto Liebmann's appeal, "Back to Kant," initiated a period of something like half a century in which a modernized version of Kantianism occupied a dominating position in German academic philosophy, to be dislodged from that eminence at the end of the First World War by the growing phenomenological movement and, somewhat later, by the existentialism which came to be associated with phenomenology.

Kant's impact on the English-speaking philosophical world was much slower to develop and much more indirect. It was not simply the barrier of language that was responsible. Kant's German, in his main works at least, is of a particularly snarled, cumbrous, and technical character; the dialect of a professor writing for professors. In England, in the late eighteenth and early nineteenth centuries, philosophy was an avocation for independent men of letters rather than academics. Translations of Kant into English began to appear early in the nineteenth century. Coleridge took an interest in him, but even more in his idealist successors. De Quincey wrote an essay on, and indeed largely derived from, some rather trivial German biographies of Kant. Sir William Hamilton, the last and most learned of the Scottish philosophers of common sense, recognized Kant as some sort of ally but was content, like the rest of his school, to assert as self-evident what Kant had sought laboriously to prove. A more typical and Philistine response was that of James Mill, who, after a brief look at some book by Kant, observed, "I see well enough what poor Kant would be at."

The one part of the English-speaking world in which philosophy was practiced in the German professorial way in Kant's time was Scotland, and it was there that he was first to find informed recognition. The massive commentaries of Edward Caird interpreted Kant in a Hegelian manner, and the two German philosophers were inseparably bound together in the esteem of the British idealist movement that flourished from the 1870s until supplanted in the first two decades of the present century by the analytic and realistic philosophy of Bertrand Russell and G. E. Moore. T. H. Green, the chief originator of British idealism, called on his students to put aside their Mill and Spencer and to turn to Kant and Hegel.

Brought in with Hegel, Kant to some extent fell with him. Russell, the most influential figure of the first half of the century in Britain, regarded him as a disaster, judging him too much, perhaps, as the father of German idealism. In the years between the two wars there was scholarly commentary on Kant, particularly from Norman Kemp Smith, his ablest translator, but there was comparatively little interest in his doctrines on their own merits.

In the last twenty years, however, there has been a conspicuous revival of interest. P. F. Strawson compared the "descriptive metaphysics" of his own *Individuals*, published in 1959, in which he broke away from the piecemeal investigations of the hitherto dominant Wittgenstein and Austin to develop a general account of the "massive central core" of our thinking about the world, with the philosophical procedure of Aristotle and Kant. Consistent with this avowal of allegiance, Strawson went on in 1966, with *The Bounds of Sense*, to write the most penetrating and original of recent writings on Kant in the English language. Since then there has been a steady flow of informed and committed discussion of Kant's ideas.

Life and precritical writings

Kant was born in 1724 in Königsberg, in what was then East Prussia but is now absorbed into the Soviet Union, the city being renamed Kaliningrad. His father was a saddler of modest means. Kant was brought up, both at home and at school, in a somewhat oppressively severe religious atmosphere, that of the Pietist movement. This German analogue to English Methodism sought to enhance the devotional character of Protestantism, to make that faith more inward and practical, less a matter of formal, public subscription and of intellectual assent to theoretically formulated doctrine. It is often said that Kant rebelled against the religious system that was imposed on him early in life, and, no doubt, he was opposed to its depreciation of the intellect in favor of emotion and conduct. Nevertheless, his own mature views about the nature of religion, that it is a matter of faith resting on moral experience, and not susceptible of theoretical proof, is at any rate pietistic in its general form.

At the local university Kant studied under Martin Knutzen, who combined adherence to the philosophy of Leibniz's expositor Christian Wolff with a lively interest in natural science. Upon graduating, Kant worked for a number of years as a private tutor, but in 1755, at the age of thirty-one, he became a privatdocent (lecturer) at the University of Königsberg and was promoted to a professorship of logic and metaphysics in 1770. The year of his entry into a university career he completed his doctoral dissertation (*De Igne*—On Fire) and published his first book: *Universal Natural History and Theories of the Heavens*, in which the nebular hypothesis of Laplace's *Système du Monde* is anticipated.

The main stages of Kant's thought coincide neatly with the turning points of his career. His fifteen years as a privatdocent from 1755 to 1770 make up what is called his precritical period, as being that in which he is still working within the bounds of the official Leibniz-Wolff philosophy of his time and has not yet developed any of the characteristic doctrines of the mature philosophy of his three *Critiques*. His *Critique of Pure Reason* was not published until 1781, but in 1770, the year of his elevation to a chair, he published his *Inaugural Dissertation: On the Form and Principles of the Sensible and Intelligible World*. In that work the theory of space and time as "pure intuitions" of which we have necessary and nonempirical knowledge, the starting point of the first *Critique*, is developed, and the conclusion is drawn that the world accessible through our senses is "phenomenal" in nature, an appearance rather than reality proper. But at this stage Kant still believed that the reality lying behind it, the "intelligible world," could be known by the use of reason alone, conceived as operating independently of the senses and with the aid of concepts such as possibility and necessity, substance and cause, which are not derived from experience but are part of the mind's innate constitution, a view he was later to spend the second half of the *Critique of Pure Reason* in undermining.

Few of the works of Kant's precritical period are now much read. Their main interest lies in the occasional anticipations they offer of what is to be found in his mature work. Thus in the *Nova Dilucidato* of 1755 he criticizes the use made of the principle of sufficient reason by philosophers of the school of Leibniz. This foreshadows the important claim of the first *Critique* that the concept of cause can be properly applied only within the empirical world accessible to the senses, that it cannot be invoked to connect that world with the domain of the supersensible. In 1763, in an essay on proving the existence of God, Kant denies that God can be argued for as the first cause of the natural world. He goes on to reject two other proofs—the ontological proof of Saint Anselm and Descartes and the argument from design. These three proofs come up again for extended critical consideration in the first *Critique*. What does not reappear there is a fourth type of proof, which in 1763 Kant found acceptable, and which argues, rather ethereally, that thinking by its nature is an envisagement of possibility and that possibility must rest or be "grounded" on something that actually exists. This seems pretty questionable. It is generally agreed by philosophers, except for those who accept the ontological proof that Kant rejects, that it is possible that nothing might have existed at all. In that case it would still have been possible that something actually existed although nothing in fact did.

Two years later, in an essay on the distinctness of the principles of natural theology and morals, Kant raised for the first time in a fully general form the question that was continuously to preoccupy him: how is metaphysics —that is to say, knowledge of the world as it really is, or the world beyond the reach of the senses—possible? At this stage he is content to say that metaphysics is different from mathematics, although they are both purely rational, demonstrative sciences. Where mathematics starts from freely constructed notions, which then commonly turn out to have an application to objects, metaphysics must arrive at its concepts by reflection on the objects in which they are exemplified. By 1766, in *Dreams of a Spirit-Seer*, Kant's attitude to metaphysics is less favorable. He says of the visions of the mystic Swedenborg (his "spirit-seer") that they may derive from a spiritual world, but equally they may be just the fancies of a disordered brain. In either case they are held to be superior to metaphysics, as hitherto conceived, with its attempts to argue in a purely demonstrative way to large conclusions about the nature of the world in general.

In 1768, in an essay on space, the first sign is seen of the striking, original, and somewhat indigestible conception of space that is expounded in the first main section of the *Critique of Pure Reason*. Kant got from the mathematician Euler the idea that space is independent of and prior to matter, as Newton had maintained in his theory of the absolute nature of space. Kant's startling modification of this thesis was that space is not an ingredient of the objective, natural world but is something subjective, a universal propensity of the human mind which makes perception of an external world possible. In the *Inaugural Dissertation* of 1770, which is ordinarily taken to mark the end of Kant's precritical period, these ideas about space are developed further, a parallel position is taken about time, and the whole is combined with a new, and distinctly more optimistic, Leibnizian view about the possibility of metaphysics as a science of the intelligible or supersensible world. Space and time, Kant maintains here, as in the first *Critique*, are "pure intuitions," by which he means that they are unique individual objects or entities which are not met with in the world as we encounter it in sense perception but are rather forms that the mind imposes on the sensations it passively receives. They are, so to speak, the form of the window rather than the scene observed through it. Only if that is so, Kant holds, can the necessary truth of the propositions of geometry be accounted for.

It follows from this, Kant goes on, that the sensible world is only a phenomenon or appearance. Infected with subjectivity through the forms of spatiotemporal order the mind imposes on it, that world does not exist independent of the mind. Nevertheless, knowledge of things-in-themselves —of the real, intelligible world—is possible. (After 1768 Kant could read Leibniz's works in some fullness, instead of having to approach Leibniz's ideas largely through the desiccated intermediary of Wolff's textbooks. That may explain his endorsement of demonstrative reasoning as a way of acquiring knowledge of the real nature of the world only four years after his apparent dismissal of it in sardonic terms.)

But the positive metaphysical enthusiasm of the *Inaugural Dissertation* expressed a very short-lived mood. Within a year or two Kant was telling friends in letters that he was engaged in a major work in which the bounds of reason would be circumscribed. He had found a new role for the abstract concepts which he had just been saying were the vocabulary of a demonstrative science of the intelligible world. They, like the ideas of space and time, turned out, as he saw it, to be instruments by which the mind organizes its sensations, and not the means by which it can articulate for itself the character of a real world lying altogether beyond the reach of the senses.

Kant's promised book took eleven years to write. In fact, it was written in a few months, at a time when he came to feel he could delay no longer. The publication of the *Critique of Pure Reason* in 1781 was followed by a torrent of further works over the ensuing sixteen years. A simpler presentation of the *Critique*'s main ideas, the *Prolegomena to Any Future Metaphysic*, came out in 1783; the *Groundwork* appeared in 1785, and the *Critique of Practical Reason*, in which the ethical theory of the *Groundwork* was set out more fully, was published in 1788. A considerably revised second edition of the first *Critique* appeared in 1787. The system was completed in its broad outlines with the *Critique of Judgement* in 1790. In the midst of all this activity Kant also brought out his *Metaphysical Foundations of Natural Science* (1786).

In 1793 the publication of *Religion within the Limits of Reason Alone* soon brought unfavorable attention from the king of Prussia, Frederick the Great's nephew, Frederick William II. Kant had to promise to abstain from publishing anything on theological matters. In 1795 he brought out an essay on *Perpetual Peace*. His last major published work was his *Metaphysic of Morals* in 1797, but he continued writing up to his death in 1804, and in his final reflections, brought out eventually as the *Opus Postumum*, he seemed to be moving away from the position of his main works in the direction of the doctrines of his more idealistic juniors—for example Fichte—although he had officially rejected them.

Kant was a dry, methodical bachelor whose habits of life exhibited a legendary regularity. He never traveled outside his native province. Although his chief works are uglily written, he was capable of eloquence, and the wit that is recorded to have enlivened his lectures and the dinner tables of Königsberg is apparent here and there. He was a man of the utmost honor and integrity, with a large circle of friends and generally equable temperament that seems never to have interfered with the voluminous unrolling of his philosophical output. For all his influence as the initiator of what may be called the theoretical aspect of romanticism, which was as great in its way as that of Rousseau was on romanticism in practice—that is, as a mode of feeling, valuing, and acting—Kant was very much a man of the Enlightenment. In this respect the pictures that represent him in a neat white peruke with a long, formal coat and knee breeches give a correct impression. He sympathized with the revolutionaries of America and France and favored a republican form of government, in a cautiously theoretical way. He was by no means an orthodox Christian, for he set no great store by ritual, did not regard the Bible as the literally inspired word of God, and, in accordance with his emphasis on the autonomy of the true moral agent, took an implicitly unfavorable view of prayer. All in all, he is an unpromising subject for the psychobiographer. He is, nevertheless, the most important figure in postmedieval philosophy, approached but not equaled by Descartes and Hume. More than that, he came as near as anyone ever has to combining in himself the speculative originality of Plato with the encyclopedic thoroughness of Aristotle.

The Critique of Pure Reason

The introduction to Kant's first *Critique* presents its central problem in an uncompromisingly technical fashion. How, he asks, are synthetic a priori judgments possible? The answer he gives has a profound bearing on topics of the greatest and most direct human interest: the existence of God, the freedom of the will, and the immortality of the soul. The intellectual stimulus to Kant's reflections is the sorry figure that metaphysics cuts, in its attempt to prove these three things, beside the authoritatively certain and objective discoveries of pure mathematics, which has possessed this status since the time of Euclid, and natural science, which has finally acquired a solid title to intellectual respectability with the work of Newton. Mathematics and natural science give us knowledge of the sensible world: the first of its spatiotemporal form, the second of the laws of persistence and change in its content. But metaphysics presents a startlingly contrasted scene of unsettled and sterile disputation. Why, then, has transcendent metaphysics, the attempt to arrive by rational arguments at conclusions about what lies beyond the reach of the senses, failed? Has the whole project of traditional metaphysics from Parmenides to Leibniz been misconceived? Kant's eventual conclusion is that it has been.

At the same time there is another problem to be faced. The sensible world of persisting things in space and time, causally interacting with one another, is something we get to know about only through a flow of private sense impressions. The public world which we believe in is not directly given to us. Our conception of it is not a simple transcription of our sense experience but is, rather, some kind of constructive development of that experience. Kant distinguishes the primary data of our knowledge of matters of fact as *sensation* from the perceptual awareness we have of a public world of things in space and time, for which he reserves the term *experience*. That these are not only distinct but that the passage from one to the other is thoroughly problematic is, for Kant, the main upshot of the philosophy of Hume. The answer that he gives to Hume helps also to solve his first problem: how is transcendent metaphysics possible?

From the earliest times, philosophers have acknowledged a distinction between two kinds of proposition. On the one hand there are truths that are either self-evident or can be derived from self-evident truths by self-evidently valid steps of deductive inference. The most interesting propositions of this kind are the truths of mathematics. But there are others, such as "if his parents had no brothers his uncle must be an uncle by marriage." On the other hand there are propositions that are not about how things must be, but how they actually are—propositions that, even if true, could have been false. The central place among this group is held by singular propositions reporting the deliverances of the senses or of self-consciousness, such as "there is something red here" or "I am in pain." They are central since they supply whatever reasons we have for affirming general beliefs such as "all crows are black" or "water is composed of hydrogen and oxygen."

For all their differences, and on most points they were fundamentally opposed, Leibniz and Hume agreed about the nature of this basic distinction between the contents of our thought and the objects of our belief. Leibniz called them truths of reason and truths of fact; Hume called them propositions asserting relations between ideas and propositions about "matter of fact and existence." But they were at one in holding that propositions of the first kind were in two ways distinct from propositions of the second kind. In the first place, necessary truths could be discovered by thinking or reasoning alone, without reliance on the senses or introspection, which was not the case with contingent truths. Second, necessary truths were propositions whose denials are self-contradictory, whereas contingent truths could be conceived to be false without contradiction.

The fundamental technical idea of Kant's philosophy was that these two characteristics do not coincide. It is not true, he maintained, that every proposition that has one of the two properties has the other. In particular he maintained that there are propositions which are a priori, that is to say, do not depend on experience for their justification, and which at the same time are not *analytic*, that is to say, such that their denials are not self-contradictory. As nonanalytic, such propositions are synthetic. In other words, *synthetic* a priori propositions can and do exist. The importance of this claim is that, if it is correct, there are propositions that can be established a priori, without reliance on experience, which are nevertheless substantial and informative. They are thus distinct from analytic propositions, which are also a priori but which are true simply in virtue of the meanings of their constituent terms. Among such propositions are, for example, that "all bachelors are unmarried." Or, less obviously, there is the statement about the uncle by marriage, which is likewise analytic though at first glance it may not seem so. An analytic proposition is always verbal and without substantial content.

Kant contended that there are at least three important kinds of synthetic a priori propositions. First, there are the propositions of pure mathematics, which, he said, against Leibniz and Hume, are not analytic, although they are a priori. Second, there are what he called the "propositions of pure natural science," the presuppositions of the physicists' theory of the world, such as that, through all its changes, matter is indestructible or that every event has a cause. Third, there are the fundamental principles of morality. The contentions of traditional metaphysicians about the transcendent, supersensible world are not like any of these, Kant argues. If they were, they would have to be a priori, in view of their subject matter, and would have to be synthetic, as making substantial assertions about what actually exists. But, he goes on, the conditions that make synthetic a priori knowledge possible are not satisfied in this type of statement. In consequence, there are no valid propositions of transcendent metaphysics. The latter half of the first *Critique* is devoted to exposure of what Kant regards as the inevitable illusion that there are.

What are the conditions that make possible synthetic a priori propositions? Essentially they are that such propositions express the mode of operation of the human understanding in its work of organizing or "synthesizing" the data presented to it by sensation and introspection. These principles of intellectual organization and the concepts embodied in them, a priori concepts that Kant called *categories*, apply validly only to what is given to the outer and inner senses. They are forms which are empty without the matter supplied for them by the senses. It is failure to recognize this fact, Kant believes, that has led to the interminable sterility of metaphysical disputation.

In adopting this position, Kant believed he had navigated successfully between the contrary errors of Leibniz and Hume. Leibniz had wrongly supposed that pure reasoning could give us substantial information about the transcendent and supersensible world. He was right in thinking that reasoning alone could yield substantial knowledge, but wrong in thinking that such knowledge could be had of such subject matter. Hume, on the other hand, although correct in arguing that the principle of causality is not analytic, was wrong in failing to see that it is nevertheless a priori, capable of proof by reasoning alone, and not just an unjustifiable imaginative propensity of the human understanding.

It is time to consider Kant's arguments for this bold conclusion in more specific detail.

A. The aesthetic: space, time, and mathematics

Kant's account of mathematical knowledge, his first example of the synthetic a priori, is at the same time an account of our knowledge of space and time. The reason is that Kant takes the subject matter of the propositions of mathematics to be space and time. It is undoubtedly very plausible to regard the subject matter of geometry as space. Kant is somewhat furtive about the parallel connection between arithmetic and time. He arrives at his conclusions in this part of his philosophy from two different directions: on the one hand from reflections on the nature of mathematical propositions, on the other from reflections on the character of our ideas of space and time.

The main conclusion, in his own somewhat uninformative phrase, is that space and time are "pure intuitions." The idea involved can be expressed in a less mysterious way. What he means is that space and time are individual items or entities, indeed that they are unique individuals, and that they do not exist in independence of the human mind but instead are mental constructions. In other words, the human mind has an inbuilt propensity to arrange its sensations within a single space and a single time.

It may help to make this clearer if it is contrasted with other philosophical views about the nature of space and time. There are two principal issues that have to be decided with regard to space and time. First, are they self-subsistent things which would still exist without the objects and events that in fact occupy them, that is to say, *absolute*, or are they no more than the systems of relations in which objects and events stand to one another, that is to say, *relative*? Second, are they features or constituents of the world that exist in independence of the mind, that is to say, *objective*, or are they somehow imposed on the world as we experience it by the mind, that is to say, *subjective*? Newton had held that space and time are absolute and objective, Leibniz that they are relative and subjective; the usual opinion in recent times is that they are relative and objective. Kant adopts the remaining option, seeing them as independent of the objects and events in them but not as independent of the mind.

I said earlier that Kant reaches this conclusion from two different directions. The first and more straightforward is from an examination of space and time themselves. These are, he says, not concepts but individual entities; we can conceive them without the objects and events they in fact contain, but not vice versa; we cannot but conceive of them as unique; we inevitably conceive them as infinite in extent. The first two points are taken to show that they are absolute, the latter two that they are not empirical.

It can be reasonably argued that to the extent that these propositions are true they do not have the consequences that he draws from them. Space and time are conceived as individuals, as unique and as infinite. But it is not clear that they have to be conceived as unique. More important is the fact that they cannot be conceived as existing independently of the objects and events they contain. Space and time as individual entities are indeed constructions. What is empirically given to us is spatial relations between objects, such as *behind, beside*, and *above*, and temporal relations between events, *before* and *after*. In the light of these empirical facts of spatial and temporal relatedness we develop the notions of the totality of spatially related objects and of temporally related events. Although we do not experience space and time so conceived as wholes, they are still thought of as wholly composed of empirical ingredients.

Compare with space and time the notion of the human race. A family is a collection of human beings related by way of the relations of spouse and parent. It may be, if the story of Adam and Eve is true, or if there was at one time a single evolutionary leap from apehood to humanity, that the human race is a single family, that every human being is connected to every other by a chain of marital and parental relationships. The human family thus conceived is a unique individual and possibly, in one direction, an infinite one. It is not empirically given, but it is still an empirical object. What is more, it is inconceivable without the particular human beings who are its constituents. The parallel is not exact, but it points in the right direction. What it is designed to show is that the notion of a single, all-inclusive scheme of relations can still be empirically founded, despite having such large, speculative, abstract properties as uniqueness, all-inclusiveness, and infinity of extent.

The other angle from which Kant approaches his conclusion is his view about the nature of mathematical knowledge. He holds that the propositions of arithmetic and geometry are both synthetic and a priori. That they are a priori is shown by their imperviousness to empirical falsification: the propositions of mathematics are necessary truths; they can be arrived at by pure reasoning. On the other hand, Kant maintains, they are substantial and informative, for they tell us about the general nature of time, in the case of arithmetic, and of space, in the case of geometry.

As was said above, Kant's claim that arithmetic is the pure theory of time is hinted or insinuated, rather than properly argued for. The parallel claim about geometry and space seems self-justifying. But he does offer an additional argument for the synthetic a priori nature of arithmetic. The proposition that $7 + 5 = 12$ is not analytic, he says, because we do not "think" 12 when we "think" $7 + 5$. But this does not make his point. Someone could believe that they had 7 things and 5 other things without realizing that they had 12 things and even with the belief that they had some number of things other than 12. It would still be a contradiction to suppose that, having 7 + 5 things, they did not have 12, and that is the point at issue. Inconsistencies in belief do not always present themselves irresistibly to the minds of those who perpetrate them. A standard procedure in mathematical argument, after all, is reductio ad absurdum or indirect proof, in which a proposition is proved by showing that a contradiction logically follows from the supposition that it is false. That fact alone strongly suggests the analytical character of mathematical truth.

It is harder to show briefly what is wrong with Kant's assumption that geometry is the pure theory of space. But doubt is thrown on it by the fact that non-Euclidean geometrics have not only been formulated without inconsistency (that would show only that geometrical propositions, Euclidean or not, were not analytic) but have also been given a physical application. Einstein relied on experiment to show that physical space is not Euclidean but Riemannian. Light rays from remote celestial objects do not travel in Euclidean straight lines. We could say that they travel in Euclidean curves. It is simpler and more convenient to say that they travel in straight lines as defined in a non-Euclidean geometry. If we do that, we are treating a geometry as an empirical theory about the behavior of light rays, and in that case we interpret the sentence "light travels in straight lines" as analytic. But we could treat (Euclidean) geometry itself as analytic, and it would then be a synthetic and empirical falsehood to say that light travels in straight lines.

Kant's theory of space and time, and his connected account of the nature of mathematics, has been perhaps the least influential of the major parts of the *Critique of Pure Reason*. Leibniz, who for reasons of his own held space and time to be subjective, had prepared Kant's mind for that side of his doctrine, while Kant adhered to the view of Newton on the issue of whether space and time are absolute or relative. Curiously, this seems to have been the first part of the characteristic doctrines of the first *Critique* to occur to Kant, as is shown by its fairly thorough anticipation in the *Inaugural Dissertation*. In taking the spatial and temporal character of the world of experience to be imposed on it by the constitutional mode of working of the human mind, Kant arrived at a new view of the constructive role of the understanding in our thinking about the world that was subsequently developed in a much more plausible form with his theory of categories and a priori principles. To this we shall now turn.

B. The analytic of concepts: the categories

Kant begins his account of the role of the understanding in our experience from the argument of Locke and Hume that what we receive or is given to us in sensation is a series of ideas, as they called them, or representations, as he did. Yet the world we take ourselves to perceive, the world of experience proper and not just raw sensation, is not a kaleidoscopic flux (Kant calls that a mere "manifold"). The series of representations that we passively receive is, as he puts it, *synthesized*. This technical term appears to cover two distinguishable activities. The first is that of *organizing* our sensations into various kinds of systematically related patterns: some series of sensations we experience as stages in the history of persistent things, others as causal interactions. The second activity is that of *objectifying* what we perceive, of coming to think of it as making up an external world, independent of and distinguishable from ourselves and our own private, mental histories.

In the first edition of the *Critique of Pure Reason* Kant goes into a fair amount of narrative detail about the activity of synthesis. He notes three phrases or aspects of it: attention to our sensations, recollection of preceding sensations, and application of concepts to our sensations. In synthesis, that is to say, we attend to some series of sensations reaching back from the present some way into the past and recognize some pattern or order in the series thus attended to.

Hume had held that all our concepts must be derived from sensations and must rest on the directly perceived similarities between them. Where these similarities related single sensations, they supplied concepts of attributes or properties, such as redness and roundness. Where they related groups or series of sensations, they supplied concepts of serial relatedness, in particular those of constancy (or sameness of properties) and coherence (continuity of properties). What they could not supply were the concepts of continuity through gaps in perception and of existence distinct from perception, which are essential elements of our notion of a material thing. Sensation, again, could supply only the concept of regular succession; it could not supply the concept of necessary connection that Hume regarded as an essential part of our notion of cause.

Kant agreed that sensation could not supply us with concepts of objective things and causal connections. But instead of concluding, with Hume, that such concepts were no more than imaginative, and logically unjustifiable, extrapolations of the fragmentary suggestions of order in the flow of our sensations, he held that they are a priori *concepts* or *categories*, part of the constitutional apparatus which the mind produces from its own resources for the orderly interpretation of experience. The argument, in short, is this. What is given to us is a manifold of sensation. The world which we take ourselves to perceive is one of continuing, objective things, standing in causal relations to one another, and disposed in space and time. The passage from the one to the other is made possible by the fact that we arrange our sensations in a spatiotemporal order by applying the forms of intuition and conceive them as objective, persistent, causally related things by applying the categories. The common world of our experience proper, as contrasted with the mere flux of sensation, is thus a *phenomenal* world. It is the world as we represent it through our interpretation of it with the categories and forms of intuition, not the world as it is in itself. It is appearance, but it is organized, objectified appearance.

This is Kant's celebrated "transcendental deduction." If we are to have orderly experience of an objective world, as we do, and not a mere kaleidoscopic flux of sensations, we must apply organizing concepts to our sensations that are brought to them by the mind and are not derived from those sensations. Hume seemed to Kant to have shown that if we were confined to concepts derived directly from sensations, our conception of a world of objects and causal relationships could be no more than a kind of imaginative fiction, an unwarrantable leap beyond the evidence like that shown in the behavior of a primitive man who wonders how hard or how far off the sky is or what the things he sees in a mirror are like at the back.

A problem of justification nevertheless remains. Even if it is true that all human beings do confront experience with anticipatory inclinations to organize their sensations in certain ways, what makes this more than arbitrary cognitive prejudice? Kant's solution to that problem takes two forms. In the first place, he regards the human mind's order-imposing propensity as a universal feature of the human mind in general. The results of its exercise will thus be the same for everyone. Second, in what he calls his "metaphysical deduction of the categories," he connects the instruments of organization, the categories, with formal logic. Inasmuch as he takes the validity of formal logic to be absolute and unquestionable, he infers that the same kind of validity must extend to cover the categories that he sees as derivable from formal logic.

This alleged derivation is one of the less regarded parts of Kant's philosophy. Its unearthly formal symmetry inspires suspicions that the detail of the argument does little to assuage. According to Kant, formal logic authorizes a twelvefold classificatory scheme: four triads of logical forms. Under the aspect of quantity, judgments are either universal, particular, or singular;

under that of quality they are either affirmative, negative, or "infinite"; under that of relation they are either categorical, hypothetical, or disjunctive; under that of modality they are either problematic (possible), assertoric, or apodeictic (necessary). To each of these twelve logical forms, Kant maintains, a category corresponds.

The connecting link is the notion of judgment. The categories are what enable us to pass from raw sensation to objective judgments about the common world. Formal logic is the pure theory of the nature and relations of judgments in general. Formal logic is universally and absolutely valid. So, therefore, must be the corresponding "transcendental logic" which concerns the synthetic construction of judgments out of given sensations.

This reasoning, as is quite often the case with Kant, has a strikingly deductive appearance at first glance that does not survive closer inspection. In general, Kant's insights are more impressive than his power to supply them with rational justification. Formal logic concerns the relations of judgments to one another; "transcendental" logic, in the *Critique* at any rate, concerns the relations of judgments to sensation. (In the *Prolegomena*, however, "judgments of sensation" are allowed for as well as "judgments of experience.") The classification Kant assigns to formal logic is far from authoritative: to round it off symmetrically he has added some items (e.g., infinite quality) and substracted others (conjunctive relation). More important, perhaps, is that as far as formal logic is concerned the items within each triad are mutually exclusive. Every judgment must exemplify one, but only one, of the forms within each group of three. There is nothing corresponding to this in his account of the application of the categories.

So far, attention has been confined to Kant's view of the categories as the a priori concepts with which sensation is articulated and organized. There is also the matter of objectification to be considered. The manifold or flux of sensation contains in itself no distinction between subject and object. It is only as categorially articulated that experience embodies a distinction between the mind that is the subject of the experience and its independently existing objects. Kant's argument here is that in order to be assembled for categorization, sensations have to be thought of as the sensations of a single thinking subject, in other words, as "mine." They have to be brought under or included within what is mysteriously referred to as "the transcendental unity of apperception." But there can be no such conception of the unity of the self that is the subject of a series of sensations without a corresponding conception of an objective world, a not-self, existing independently of that subject.

There is obviously something in this. The conception of the self presupposes that of the not-self, and neither applies to the manifold of sensation. Insofar as, in articulating our sensations, we cancel out some sensations as not being constituents of the organized structure (i.e., as illusions) and imaginatively or conjecturally add other possible but unsensed sensations to fill out the pattern, we are committed to two receptacles that will serve to hold these differently wayward items: the self to contain the subtracted sensations, the not-self to contain the added ones. But that proves nothing about the source or validity of the organizing concepts employed in the business of patternmaking by subtraction and addition.

It is not necessary to go into the detail of Kant's systematic presentation of the categories, for most of it does not turn out to have much application. The first two triads, for example, yield, in the end, not six but only two principles of organization, which stand in a very remote relation indeed to the sixfold logical classification which Kant claims to underly them. It is not so much the categories themselves that are important for his general argument as the principles which declare their universal applicability, the topic of the Analytic of Principles, to which we turn now.

C. *The Analytic of Principles*

The categories are a priori concepts. They are brought to sensation by the human understanding and are not in any way derived from sensation. The result of this bringing together is experience proper, our consciousness of an objective world of persisting material objects, conceived as existing independently of that consciousness and as standing in causal relations to one another. Kant concludes that the categories are universally applicable to experience. The reasoning behind this claim is not altogether clear. He has, indeed, argued that there can be no experience of an ordered phenomenal world without synthesis. Second, he has argued that the indispensable instruments of synthesis are a priori concepts. But the metaphysical deduction must play a crucial part in his reasoning. For it claims to prove that a *particular set* of a priori concepts, those rather shakily derived from the "table of judgments" of formal logic, are the ones that have universal application.

Some philosophers of science have suggested that other categories fit the world better than Kant's. Instead of material things, the world should be seen as composed of processes or fields. These items are lawfully related, according to such philosophers, but not in a causal fashion. Kant does not consider this question of the possibility of alternative categorial schemes. His at any rate seems to be the one that is employed in common, everyday experience, and it is on evidence derived from such common experience that the theoretically speculative findings of physical theorists are founded.

More rebarbative terminology confronts the reader as he comes to study the Analytic of Principles. We hear first of Axioms of Intuition and Anticipations of Perception, which are described as the mathematical principles of the understanding. In each case what Kant gives is only a single principle; the suggested plurality of axioms and anticipations does not materialize.

Underneath this mystifying apparatus, something comparatively straightforward is to be found. The two principles affirmed are: (1) that all intuitions are extensive magnitudes, and (2) that all sensations have intensive magnitudes, or exhibit their properties to some degree. What the first amounts to is the assertion that the perceived world lends itself to mathematical representation or description. Its characteristics can be numerically measured, and the results of such measurement obey the laws of ordinary cardinal arithmetic. We can properly speak of one thing as being twice as large or heavy as another. This is, in fact, not true of all the characteristics we commonly ascribe to objects. One thing cannot be intelligibly described as being twice as red or warm or even colored as another. It is only what Locke called primary qualities, such as shape, size, position, and perhaps mass, the properties that are the subject matter of classical mechanics, which are cardinally or extensively measurable.

Kant derives this conclusion from his view that all objects are perceived or intuited by us in space and time, together with his principle that space and time are the true subject matter of mathematics. The connection of this with the logical notions falling within the triad of quantity (namely universality, particularity, singularity) is tenuous in the extreme, although there is a verbal connection with his actual topic here, the quantitative describability of the world. Nevertheless, a real and important question arises. Why is it that some properties of things are extensively measurable? Unless there were such properties, the great scientific revolution of the Renaissance would either never have occurred or would have been no different from cabbalism or thaumaturgy if it had.

The second principle, that all sensations have intensive magnitudes or possess their properties to some degree, so that we can say of similar sensations that one is more or less intensive than the other, is less significant. It may have some value in pointing out that some features of what there is may be quantitatively comparable even if they are not numerically measurable.

Most commentators on the Analytic of Principles largely confine themselves to the first and second of the Analogies of Experience. The general principle of the Analogies is that experience is possible only through the representation of a necessary connection of perceptions, which is a restatement of the doctrine of synthesis. The principle of the first analogy is that, in all changes, substance is permanent and the amount of it in nature is neither increased nor diminished. That of the second analogy is that all changes take place according to the law of the connection of cause and effect. Since the analogies of experience take up nearly twice as much space in Kant's exposition as the other three types of principle combined, the commentators' special attention to them is reasonable.

Kant argues for his principle of substance, which is simply the principle of the conservation of matter expressed in a philosophical idiom, from the premise that the world of our experience is a temporal sequence. Time itself cannot be perceived (a fact which counts against his earlier contention, in the Aesthetic, that it can be conceived apart from the events that occur in it), so our knowledge of temporal relations must be based on our perception of change in things. If there is to be change in things, the things themselves must persist through it. Therefore, the ultimate stuff of the world consists of things that persist eternally, all change being a matter of the rearrangement of this ultimate stuff.

As often in Kant, something important is going on here, even if it is not quite what Kant takes it to be. The principle that all change is rearrangement of something that in itself does not change is an assumption that guides our search for explanations in science and everyday life. To a very great extent it has been confirmed, but it does not seem to be a necessity of thought. Physicists have claimed, in fairly recent times, that in atomic transformations at very high temperatures a certain absolute loss of energy takes place, without leading to unintelligibility.

But that has very little to do with time. It does at any rate seem necessary to suppose that things endure through time to some extent if we are to be able to organize our perceptions as revealing a spatiotemporally unitary world. At any given moment we perceive an array of things spatially related to each other at that moment. If they are to be conceived as in the same space as the things perceived at another moment, there must be some things present in both momentary spaces (or overlapping the spaces of intermediate moments so as to establish a connection). There is a sense, then, in which there can be change only if there is persistence. But it need not be eternal persistence.

The second analogy of experience contains Kant's proof of the causal principle: every event has a cause. As far as the phenomenal world of our organized experience is concerned, Kant was a determinist. The crucial step in the proof is easy to state but puzzlingly elusive to interpret. There is, Kant rightly says, a distinction between the succession of our sensations (subjective succession) and the succession of actual events (objective succession). I may see the front of a house before I see its back, but that does not mean that its front actually precedes its back in the way that a boat's being upstream actually precedes its being downstream. What Kant concludes is that objective succession depends on there being a causal relationship between the temporally related items.

There is something in this. It is because we hold certain beliefs about the ways in which houses and boats on rivers behave that we conclude, in the two examples given, that while the boat has moved, the house has not changed. In general, the front of a house turns into the back of a house only in the most bizarre and unusual circumstances. Likewise, where there is a front there practically always is, outside film sets and recently bombed towns, a back at the same time. On the other hand, where there is a boat at one moment and a little later a boat that looks just like the first one a bit farther downstream, there is usually only one boat involved and not, for example, two similar, static boats at the two positions. Causal laws are, no doubt, among the general rules we rely on in deciding whether what is perceived successively exists successively, but there are rules of other kinds —for instance, rules about the normal persistence or normal accompaniments of things.

What is surely undeniable about Kant's view is that the organization of our sensations into a coherent world picture, by way of subtraction and addition, as was described earlier, requires the presence of regularities and the recognition by us of those regularities. Unless our sense impressions contained intimations of regularity, we could never sift and infer an orderly world from them. But to say that such regularities exist falls far short of determinism, the claim that there is a causal explanation for everything. Furthermore, the existence of tracts of regularity in our sense impressions is just a matter of contingent fact. It might not have been the case, and in that situation no distinction between the self and the not-self would have been drawn. Reality would then be just a kaleidoscopic flux of sensation, as it might be for a jellyfish in a turbulent sea. Also, the fact that there is some order-licensing regularity in our sensations is one thing; the fact that it underlies an order of substances, causally related to each other, is another. In other words, the discovery of an order in our sensations allowing for the distinction of the self from an objective world is not something that must have happened. Kant's account of the necessity of the a priori principles of the understanding seems to suggest that we could not fail to find an order in our sensations of the sort that we actually do find. Nevertheless, we do find such an order, and it is broadly of the kind that he says it is.

Kant concludes the analytic part of the *Critique of Pure Reason* with an account of the distinction between phenomena and noumena. The constructive role of the understanding in the building up of the world of our experience proper means that that world is not wholly independent of consciousness. It is, as Kant would say, independent of any particular consciousness but is not independent of consciousness in general. It is not subjective in the way that mere sensations are, they being peculiar to the minds to which they are present. But, although intersubjective, it is not fully objective. Although not mere appearance, it is still appearance, even if organized and present to all minds.

We must acknowledge, Kant infers, that there is something over and above the world of experience, the phenomenal world: namely, the world of things-in-themselves, or noumena. We can know, he says, that such a world of noumena exists, although we cannot say what it is like. To do that we should have to apply the categories to what is not given to us in sensation, and that is illegitimate.

Kant's explicit argument for noumena is of an unconvincingly verbal nature. The common world is a world of appearance, but there cannot be appearances unless there is something that appears. There is, in fact, a better reason for the conclusion he draws. Each mind's sensations are private to it. Even if each is disposed to apply the same constructive, world-articulating principles to the sensations it passively receives, it would not follow from that that the worlds they constructed would all turn out to be the same world. All that would follow is that each mind would construct a world of the same general form. To produce the desired coincidence of constructed worlds there must be some common pattern to the individual histories of sensation. It might be added that the passively received sensations require some explanation themselves. The mind does not make them. Who or what does?

If the various sets of sensations individual minds receive all have a common source, both their origin and their mutual correspondence are accounted for. But this solution is achieved at a heavy theoretical cost. In such a view, noumena are in effect taken to be the causes of sensations, and that involves what is for Kant the illegitimate application of the category of cause outside the realm of sensations. Moreover, for all Kant's reserve about the properties of noumena, in allowing that we can know that there are such things it allows that we can have some knowledge of what altogether transcends the given.

Kant's admission of the transcendent is minimal, but it is still substantial. It was this aspect of Kant's doctrine that proved most unacceptable to his leading German successors. They saw it, reasonably enough, as an unexpunged residue of the kind of metaphysics it was his main achievement to have undermined. What they did was to see mind in general or spirit (*Geist*), not only as the source of the constructive categories and principles of the intellect, but as the source, also, of the contents of the sensibility. Reality, they concluded, is an all-encompassing mind, an infinite or absolute mind of which finite, individual minds are fragmentary parts, limited regions in which the absolute mind attains *self*-consciousness.

D. The Dialectic: Kant's criticism of metaphysics

The upshot of the Aesthetic and Analytic of Kant's first *Critique* is that our substantial knowledge of the world, whether everyday or scientific, requires both passively received sensations and constructive contributions from the knowing mind. The first are provided by forms of pure intuition which endow sensations with a spatiotemporal arrangement, the second by categories whose application represents what is intuited as a system of enduring substances standing in causal relations to one another. Both elements are necessary for there to be knowledge. "Concepts without intuitions are empty," Kant says; "intuitions without concepts are blind." But there are also forms of knowledge in his scheme which are not instances of conceptualized intuition. There is the knowledge we have of analytic truths, which is of a purely formal nature, empty, but useful as allowing us to express our substantial knowledge in verbally different ways. It is what is involved in our recognition that "George is a bachelor" states the same fact as "George is an unmarried man." And then there is the philosophical knowledge which Kant claims to possess about the nature and workings of the human understanding. This is reflective, second-order knowledge about the conditions of ordinary, first-order knowledge.

Philosophical theories of knowledge must always find a place for themselves in the account they give of knowledge; they cannot afford to rule out the possibility of the kind of knowledge they themselves claim to be. Kant does not address himself to this issue very directly, and his position remains not wholly clear. Beyond ordinary empirical knowledge and knowledge of analytic truths, he seems to admit two kinds of knowledge that fall into neither of these classifications. One is synthetic a priori knowledge, expressed in the propositions of mathematics and in the presuppositions of science, such as the principles of conservation and causality; the other is his own special contribution, the knowledge he offers of the "transcendental" (but not "transcendent") explanation of these synthetic a priori truths. This explanation is a kind of cognitive metapsychology, a theory to the effect that the world inevitably appears to us as it does because of the intellectual machinery with which we construct it. It is certainly distinct from ordinary, empirical psychology which, it is suggested, applies the form of time and the categories to the deliverances of the inner sense or introspection. What it describes is not part of the world of appearance but a condition of there being any such world at all.

In the Dialectic—the long, concluding part of the *Critique of Pure Reason* —a general attack is mounted by Kant on the program of traditional metaphysics, which seeks to arrive at general truths about the world as it is in itself by means of purely rational argument. Yet in the positive part of the *Critique* he seems to be engaged in just such an activity himself, even if he is concerned with only one part of the world as it is, namely the human intellect.

Kant begins the Dialectic with a general diagnosis of what he regards as the illusion of transcendental metaphysics. The mind seeks explanations; it tries to discover the conditions that make it possible for what happens to happen. The activity of explanation comes to take on a serial form, and that inspires the inquiring mind to suppose that an ultimate explanation can be arrived at, something absolutely unconditioned that is the ultimate condition of everything else. As it turns out, this account of metaphysics applies moderately well to the second and third of the metaphysical disciplines Kant considers, but it does not discernibly do so to the first one, namely, "rational psychology," or the metaphysical theory of the soul.

The soul is the subject of the Paralogisms of Pure Reason, with which the main body of the Dialectic begins. What Kant has particularly in view here is the type of conclusion which Descartes draws from the infallible certitude of the proposition *cogito ergo sum*, "I think therefore I am." That proposition Descartes took as setting the limit of the possibilities of skeptical doubt— as a truth which even an all-powerful deceiver could not make him believe falsely, since it seemed a necessary condition of his believing anything. I know that I exist as a thinking being, Kant agrees. But, since I may be deceived in supposing that I have a body, I am in essence a thinking thing or substance, and only contingently, if at all, an embodied one.

This leads to an effective criticism of the detailed arguments of rational psychology. They conclude that the soul is a simple, unitary substance of a nonphysical nature. Kant objects that, although I have immediate and certain knowledge that I think whenever I am conscious at all, that does not mean there is a substantial entity called the self or soul with which in all consciousness I am directly acquainted. The "I" in "I think" is not like "the horse" in "the horse drinks." To be aware of the horse I have to apply the category of substance to a set of sensations, but there is no such awareness of the self involved in "I think," the accompaniment of all my acts of consciousness. The self, in Kant's view, is merely a formal unity, unlike the material unity which connects a set of sensations conceived as a horse. He admits, as he should, that one can conceive oneself as a material unity or empirical substance. The self so conceived is, however, the phenomenal self, the subject matter of empirical psychology. It is a kind of pattern which is found in, or imposed on, various collections of introspective experiences. It is, one might say, the self as object of consciousness. The self as subject of consciousness is something quite different. In that sense it is the mysteriously named "transcendental unity of apperception," or unity of consciousness, that was argued for in the Transcendental Deduction as the necessary correlate of our conception of "the unity of objects" or not-self.

As it turns out, there is yet a further self, the noumenal self, which is at once the reality behind the appearances present to inner sense and also the locus of our moral agency, the uncaused executor of free acts of will, which, unlike the phenomenal self, subject to time and the categories, does not fall within the deterministic realm of phenomenal nature. This third self, however, is not a possible object of knowledge; it is, rather, a presupposition of morality, as will be shown later.

Rational psychology concludes from the simplicity it ascribes to the soul that it is immortal. All coming into and going out of existence is rearrangement of that which is permanent. The soul is nonphysical and so not in space and so not divisible into parts. Therefore, it is impossible that the soul should come into or go out of existence. Against this Kant argues, in effect, that the phenomenal self is complex, since it is a categorized collection of the data of inner sense, and that the subject self, the "I" in the Cartesian "I think," is not a thing or substance at all.

The next section of the Dialectic, the Antinomies, is concerned with the alleged findings of rational cosmology or metaphysics of nature. In this field, exactly opposite conclusions are drawn about the infinite extent and divisibility of matter, the universal character of natural causation, and the existence of a first cause or absolutely necessary being. These conclusions are antinomies—inconsistent conclusions drawn, by valid argument, from seemingly irresistible premises.

One example from the first two, "mathematical," antinomies about the infinite extent and divisibility of the world will suffice to illustrate Kant's procedure here. Does the world have a beginning in time? It must have, because it is impossible to make sense of the idea that an infinite series of intervals of time has existed before now. It cannot have, since in that case there would have been empty time before it began with nothing in it to explain the fact of the world's beginning. It can reasonably be argued that neither of these arguments establishes its conclusion. To say the world had no beginning is not to say it began an infinitely long time ago (for that is to say it *did* have a beginning); it is to say that, however far back in time you go, something was actually happening then. On the other hand, although if it did have a beginning then certainly nothing existed before it did to explain why it came into existence when it did, it is not self-evident that there has to be an explanation for everything.

Similar arguments are used by Kant to show that the world has and has not a limit in space, and that what exists is and is not composed of absolutely simple parts. He arrives at two interesting conclusions. The first is that the only way to resolve the antinomies is by identifying some illegitimate conception in their premises. This, he believes, is the conception of the world as a whole. His general term for this conception, along with the conceptions of the substantial soul and of God, is "Idea of Reason." Ideas of Reason are categories employed, not in their legitimate manner to organize sensations, but in alleged application to what lies beyond the reach of the senses altogether. Ideas of Reason, Kant maintains, have no legitimate "constitutive" employment, cannot figure in significant, justifiable assertions, put forward as true. This is so because there can be no true statements, for which we can give justifying reasons, about things-in-themselves (apart, presumably from the contention that there *are* things-in-themselves).

Nevertheless, there is a point to the Ideas of Reason in connection with our pursuit of knowledge. Although they cannot be used to say that the world is of such-and-such a nature or contains such-and-such things, they still have what Kant calls a *regulative* employment. We cannot know whether the world is infinitely extended in space or time or not, but we should govern our investigations of it in accordance with the maxim: pursue your inquiries into the nature of the world without limit in space and time. This is to say that while the thesis that the world is limited spatiotemporally is no better and no worse than its antithesis that the world is unlimited, considered as a constitutive theory about the way the world is, the antithesis is the correct principle to adopt regulatively because it is of greater assistance to the scientific investigation of the world.

The third and final section of the Dialectic, the Ideal of Pure Reason, is concerned with rational theology, the metaphysical theory of God. Here Kant examines and rejects the three most notable of the traditional metaphysical proofs of God's existence. The first is the ontological argument, which is that, since God is defined as the possessor of all perfections, and existence is a perfection, it follows necessarily that God exists. In these terms, since existence is a defining or essential property, to assert that God does not exist is self-contradictory. Kant confronts Descartes's version of the ontological argument rather than the superior version in which it was advanced by Anselm, but his criticisms are at a sufficiently fundamental level to be fatal to Anselm, too. The second argument Kant rejects is the cosmological or causal proof. This he defines as the contention that it is impossible that everything that exists should do so contingently, dependent on the existence of something else, from which it would follow that at least something must exist necessarily, if anything exists at all. Finally, he examines the "physico-theological" proof, or argument from design, which is that the coherent and systematic character of the world implies that it is the purposive creation of a supremely intelligent and powerful being.

Here, as elsewhere in the Dialectic, Kant's criticisms of transcendent metaphysics, although interesting and powerful, do not stand in any discernible relation to the general account he gives of the erroneousness of traditional metaphysical reasoning. His general thesis is that transcendent metaphysics results from the illicit application of the categories beyond the range of possible experience. But his detailed objections to rational theology do not even try to show that its arguments commit this offense. Thus, against the ontological proof of God, he follows Hume in claiming that there is no difference between the idea of God and the idea of God as existing. He diagnoses what he, like Aquinas, regards as a sophistical verbal trick, as dependent on the mistaken notion that existence is a property. He argues that the cosmological proof is only a variant of the ontological proof and so collapses with it. Against the argument from design, for which he has a measure of sympathy ("this argument," he says, "always deserves to be mentioned with respect"), he shrewdly objects that at best it could prove that the natural world of our experience is the work of an *architect*, giving purposive form to already existing raw material, and not of a *creator* proper, bringing it into existence as a whole out of nothingness.

One kind of argument for God's existence, perhaps the most direct in its appeal to the theologically unsophisticated, does directly exemplify what he holds to be the general pattern of metaphysical error. This is the simple causal proof: there must be a cause for what there is; the world that we encounter, including ourselves, must have come from somewhere. A version of this, that there must be a limit to the series of causes stretching backward in time, is indeed rejected in the Antinomies, but only for being no more provable than, and thus as unprovable as, its opposite. But the hypothesis of an unexperienceable cause of everything that is experienced is an obvious application of the category of cause beyond the proper experiential limits of its employment.

In fact, just such an illicit application of the category of cause is rather firmly implied, although not explicitly affirmed, in Kant's distinction between phenomena and things-in-themselves. Unless the given sensations to which we apply the categories to construct the common phenomenal world are seen as somehow causally dependent on things-in-themselves, not only is their existence unexplained but the fact that distinct minds all synthesize their private sets of sensations in the same way, to produce a single phenomenal world, remains a mystery. It may have been some sense of this half-hidden deviation from his main antimetaphysical thesis that led Kant to be less than emphatic in relating the specific errors of transcendent metaphysicians to their offenses against the rules for the correct use of the categories.

Kant's ethics and moral theology

Kant's conclusion that demonstrative metaphysical reasoning cannot establish the existence of God, the freedom of the will, and the immortality of the soul is in no way an expression of lack of interest in these beliefs or, in the manner of later and more radical antimetaphysicians, an assertion of their meaninglessness. Not only did Kant regard these topics as those above all of concern to mankind, he also believed that they could be rationally defended. But their defense could not take the form of straightforward intellectual proof. They are, rather, presuppositions of morality, propositions that must be assumed to be true if we are to conceive our apparent experience of absolute and unconditional moral obligation as genuine.

The first step in this train of reasoning is to establish that moral experience does involve absolute obligation. This is the main task of Kant's brief but pregnant *Groundwork of the Metaphysic of Morals*, published in 1785, four years after the first *Critique*, and, carried out more systematically and at greater length, of the *Critique of Practical Reason* in 1788. In the *Groundwork*, the argument that freedom of the will is a precondition or, as Kant puts it, a postulate, of true morality which recognizes the absoluteness of obligation is added to the main development of his account of the nature of morality. In the *Critique of Practical Reason*, the postulates of God's existence and the soul's immortality are added to that of the freedom of the will. Finally, in 1793, in his *Religion within the Limits of Reason Alone*, Kant elaborates an interpretation of Christianity which endorses such of its doctrines as can be given a form in which they harmonize with his essentially moral conception of religion and rejects those aspects of Christian belief that strike him as irrational and anthropomorphic.

A. The nature of morality

Kant's *Groundwork* starts with the arresting sentence "Nothing can possibly be conceived in the world, or even out of it, which can be called good, without qualification, except a good will." To the extent that this remark is evidently true it means that the proper objects of primary moral evaluation are human motives, the characters they constitute, the virtues and vices they manifest—that actions enter the picture only insofar as they are conceived in the light of the motives that underlie them. To say that is to say, surely correctly, that actions in themselves, considered in a purely external way, as, for example, keepings of promises or tellings of the truth, are not, as such, morally good or bad, praiseworthy or blameworthy.

One can admit this while at the same time maintaining that actions in themselves can be characterized as right or wrong. In that case a wrong action, a comforting lie told to a dying man, for instance, could be morally good, and a right action, for instance an uncomfortable truth told in order to give pain, could be morally bad. Furthermore, the distinction could be admitted without the denial of any connection between rightness and moral goodness. An action, it might be held, is morally good if it is performed from a motive which usually leads to right action, and morally bad in the opposite circumstance. In that case the concept of the right is prior to that of the morally good.

Kant, however, apparently takes his initial proposition in a larger sense, seeming to mean that what is central or fundamental in morality is the will or motivation of moral agents. He rightly observes that virtuously motivated actions often have bad or unfortunate consequences and that this need not detract from their praiseworthiness. From this fact he derives the conclusion that the consequences of action have nothing whatever to do with its moral quality. But this is a rather wild inference. An activity can be dangerous even if, on a particular occasion, the agent comes to no harm from it. That does not in the least tend to show that the dangerousness of activities has nothing to do with their consequences. An activity is dangerous if it is likely to lead to harm to one who engages in it, even if, on a particular occasion, no harm comes to him.

Kant, at any rate, adopts what is called the deontological view that the moral value of actions is independent of their consequences. Other deontologists have been content at this point to maintain that the principles of right conduct are self-evident in the manner of logical or mathematical axioms and are not, as consequentialists suppose, rules justified by their tendency to maximize some kind of outcome such as the general happiness or welfare. Kant seeks to go further, to discover what he calls a supreme principle of morality, of which absolute principles of moral obligation are in some way exemplifications.

Inasmuch as the consequences of action are morally irrelevant, Kant holds, it cannot be the matter or content of a principle of conduct that makes it morally obligatory, but its form. This again is a questionable argumentative leap. Even if the consequences of truth telling—namely, the augmentation of true, and the diminution of false, beliefs—are irrelevant to the rightness of the practice, telling the truth is the material or content of the principle which serves to distinguish it from the inconsistent principle of telling lies or the independent principle of keeping promises.

The form of a principle of obligation is, Kant holds, the idea of lawfulness as such, an obscure contention which serves to introduce the notion of the categorical imperative. This is that one should always act in accordance with a principle that one could consistently recommend for universal adoption. Or, as Kant puts it, "I am never to act otherwise than so that I could also will that my maxim should become a universal law." His argument is that truth telling and promise keeping are validated by this categorical imperative because the opposite principles are, in his view, self-contradictory if proposed for universal adoption. If everyone always lied, the conditions of communication would break down, and no one would be able to tell lies or the truth. If everyone broke promises, the institution of promising would collapse.

These two examples are the most plausible applications of Kant's thesis, but neither of them works very well. Undoubtedly, universal lying or promise breaking would be likely in some way to undermine themselves. One possibility would be that each form of words would come to mean its contradictory in the lying case and that "I promise to" would come to mean "I promise not to." But to reject the absolute obligatoriness of truth telling is not to embrace its complete contrary: always tell lies. It might be to embrace, as most morally reasonable people do, the principle: always tell the truth unless substantial harm to others would follow from doing so. Or it might be to adopt the working rule of most of us in our morally feebler moments: always tell the truth unless it is clearly disadvantageous to one to do so. Neither of these watered-down principles of truth telling is in the least self-undermining, let alone self-contradictory. In the case of promise keeping, the point can be put more forcibly. If one has made a comparatively unimportant promise and, on the way to perform it, finds oneself able to avert a great evil only by breaking the promise, it is not merely not one's duty to keep the promise, it is one's duty to break it.

Kant goes on to argue that further kinds of morally approved conduct are covered by his supreme principle—for example, abstaining from suicide and cultivating one's talents. But universal suicide is, first, not the only alternative to the policy of universal abstention from it ("commit suicide only when life is unbearable" is a more reasonable one), and, second, there is nothing self-contradictory about it. If it is followed, there will be no more occasion for or possibility of affirming it. But if that is self-contradictory, so is the pursuit of virtue so complete that success would render moral injunctions otiose.

It should be noticed that Kant's applications of his supreme principle of morality to particular principles of conduct take no account of the will or motivation of agents on which such stress was laid at the outset of his argument. That aspect of his ethical doctrine is, however, reintroduced in the reasoning that leads up to the formulation of the categorical imperative. When he concludes that it is the form, not the matter or content, of principles of conduct that renders them obligatory, he expresses that conclusion in the words "duty is the necessity of acting out of reverence for the law."

He seems to interpret this dark saying in two distinct ways: first, as meaning that an action is a duty if it exemplifies a consistently universalizable principle; second, as meaning that to do one's duty is to do what one's sense of duty, one's desire to act in accordance with the moral law as such, impels one to do. The second interpretation really presupposes the first. One's desire to do one's duty cannot impel one to do anything in particular unless one has some antecedent notion of what one's duty is. Clearly it is one thing to act in a way that *is* consistently universalizable, another to act in a certain way *because* so to act is consistently universalizable. These are, in fact, Kant's answers to two distinct questions: What is a right action? What is a morally good and praiseworthy action?

If these questions are distinguished, as they must be for consistency, a rigid but intelligible theory of moral goodness follows. A right action is one that conforms to the categorical imperative; a morally good action is one performed because of that conformity. In practice, Kant admits the distinction, as when he writes of an innkeeper who gives the right change, either in order to secure a good reputation (a right act, nonmorally motivated) or because it is morally right to do so (a right action, morally motivated).

Kant adopts a starkly dualistic view of human nature in its active, practical aspect. Men are led to act either by inclination or by reason. The sole rational motive of action is the sense of duty, the desire to do what is right just because it is right. All other motives are inclinations, desires for ends which lie beyond the action itself. Some of these are attractive and even admirable, such as the desire for the happiness of others. Others are neutral (or discreditable where they conflict with the demands of the practical or moral reason), such as the desire for one's own personal advantage. The existence of such a thing as Kant's sole truly moral motive depends on Kant's view that the rightness of actions has nothing to do with the consequences of action, for if it were defined in terms of consequences of some kind, the desire to do right would be the desire for consequences of that kind.

There does seem to be, as a matter of psychological fact, such a thing as the desire to do what is right just because it is right, independent, or even in the teeth, of all other likes and dislikes. But this kind of desire does not seem to predominate in the most estimable moral personality. The Lord, it is said, loveth a cheerful giver. Kant's preference is for one whose altruistic acts are ground out by sheer effort of will.

Kant puts forward two other abstract moral propositions which he represents as expressions of the categorical imperative in different words. The first of these alternative formulations states that we should treat human beings as ends in themselves and never merely as means. The connection between this and the original version is tenuous but still marginally discernible. It lies in the fact that both mention the total community of all rational beings, the first saying we should act in accordance with rules that could be laws for such a community, the second that we should treat all human beings as members of such a community. Kant's equation seems to imply that we should recognize obligations only to other mature and rational moral agents. Duties to children and lunatics might be accommodated by stretching membership in the "kingdom of ends" so as to include in it potential or former rational beings. But there seems no way of providing for the duties most people recognize that they have toward animals.

In his final and allegedly most complete formulation of the categorical imperative, Kant asserts that we should act in accordance with laws we have legislated as sovereign members of a kingdom of ends. This introduces the notion of autonomy which plays a large part in his reasoning about the connection between morality and the freedom of the will. A moral system, according to Kant, is heteronomous if it founds morality on some desired consequence of action as happiness or perfection. In general, we act heteronomously whenever we act for the sake of some object of desire. Autonomous action is that which is motivated by the sense of duty alone and is therefore, in Kant's view, carried out in accordance with a law which we have legislated for ourselves. The connection between rationality and self-legislation is not at all obvious. We are, after all, constrained by the demands of rationality—although, to the extent that, as rational beings, we have internalized them, we impose them on ourselves. But are our desires not as much a constitutive part of ourselves as our reason? In complying with their demands, are we not self-determining beings? In the ordinary sense of the word we lack autonomy only to the extent that our actions are determined by the desires of *others*.

Kant seems to be guided by the belief that human beings are essentially rational but only contingently the possessors of desires. Thus, rational motivation is motivation by the real person, whereas allegedly heteronomous motivation by desire is, so to speak, only apparent or somehow accidental. Yet he also believes, inconsistently with this, that what distinguishes human beings from "holy wills" (angels?) who are purely rational, on one side, and animals, who are wholly driven by desire, on the other, is that they have both reason and desires. Indeed, for beings without both reason and desire there can be no moral problems. Angels are above morality, for there is nothing in them to lead them away from the action practical reason requires. Animals are below morality, for there is nothing in them to come into conflict with their inclinations.

The ethical theory of Kant reveals his strengths and weaknesses perhaps more forcefully than any other part of his works. On the credit side, he combines a determination to set out his ideas in a rationally systematic way with a clear sense of the concrete implications of his beliefs. On the debit side is the fact that much of his argument is exceedingly bad, proceeding more by a form of loose verbal association in spuriously argumentative disguise than by anything that deserves to be dignified with the name of deductive reasoning. There is a kind of corruption of thought here that is assisted by a professorial corruption of language. Behind it lies a tradition of oracular academicism and, more particularly, the fact that in his Prussian isolation Kant had no one from whose intelligent criticism he could benefit. In a more lively intellectual community he could never have got away with his polysyllabic sophisms. Socrates would have annihilated him.

Yet it may be just as well that Kant had no critical gadfly to interrupt his logically defective processes of reasoning. For, in spite of them, he was gifted with great imagination and insight. There are interesting connections between the doctrines he brings together, even if he fails to make clear what they are. A certain type of rigoristic dutifulness, a persisting strand of Western thinking about morality, is brought to its most articulate expression in Kant. His ideas, however muddled and inchoate, are always powerfully suggestive.

B. *The freedom of the will; the existence of God; the immortality of the soul*

A moral being, for Kant, is autonomous in that he acts in accordance with universal laws which he has legislated himself. Such a being cannot, therefore, be wholly motivated by desires or inclinations. Kant's position is that we cannot prove theoretically that there are such beings, that men are genuine moral agents. Nevertheless, reflection on the nature of moral obligation, he believes, makes clear that if there were any moral beings, this is what they would have to be like. Furthermore, there is an aspect of moral experience which at least strongly suggests to us that we are genuinely moral beings. This is the sense we feel, according to Kant, of the absolute and unconditional nature of our moral obligations. He cannot prove that this experience is veridical, although he plainly believes that it is. What he does claim to do is to show that it is possibly genuine and how it is so.

Kant's problem here arises fairly directly from the conclusions of the first *Critique*. There he asserts that the empirical self, which is the object of psychological investigation, and the human body, in association with which it acts on the world, are parts of the order of phenomenal nature and subject to causal law. Human action, in other words, to the extent that it can be scientifically observed and theoretically understood, is an element in a deterministic system. From this Kant concludes, without further ado, that in that aspect, at any rate, human action is not free. But freedom, he supposes, is a necessary precondition of moral obligation. Therefore, if the phenomenal account of man as a part of a deterministic natural order were the whole truth about him, he could not be a genuine moral being in the sense that Kant has expounded.

In his consideration of this subject, Kant is moving around in a philosophically well-trodden area. That fact may obscure the special peculiarities of his own position. It has been very widely supposed that if men's actions are causally determined, men cannot act freely and, therefore, are not true moral agents, subjects of binding moral obligation. Kant agrees with that thesis, but in his own way. A man, for him, is a moral agent and subject to obligation only if he is autonomous—in other words, capable of being moved to act by practical reason alone, not just by his conflicting inclinations. In the face of the supposed clash between determinism and moral agency, many have concluded that determinism cannot be wholly true, that it must be false at least as regards the voluntary actions of mature human beings. Kant does not quite take this step.

Instead he draws on his troublesomely metaphysical distinction between phenomena and noumena or things-in-themselves to argue that we can conceive ourselves in two distinct ways: as empirical selves, within the deterministic order of phenomenal nature, and as noumenal selves, outside it, in particular, outside the order of time. We can, he goes on, know ourselves only as empirical; but we can *think of* ourselves as noumenal, and must do so if we are to think of ourselves as genuine moral agents. Morality, as he puts it, is possible only "under the idea of freedom."

The very high level of abstraction at which Kant conducts his argument may tend to conceal its very surprising character. Can sense be made at all of the idea of an agent or will not operating in time? Is not action necessarily directed toward the future, conceived by the agent as open and so as offering him the possibility of choice? Surely the actions in whose moral evaluation we are interested are actions in the phenomenal, temporal world? Kant's account of the matter supplies no answer to these questions.

There is another problem. According to Kant we are free to the extent that we are autonomous. But we are autonomous just so far as we are motivated by practical reason, by the sense of duty. On this view, can there be such a thing as wrongdoing? For either actions are determined by desire alone and are thus morally indifferent since wholly causally determined, or they are determined by the sense of duty and in that case are worthy of praise. There appears no room for moral condemnation.

In his *Groundwork*, at any rate, Kant goes no further into the presuppositions of morality than this. There can be no moral obligation or agency unless there is autonomy, which he takes to imply freedom from causal determination. To think of ourselves as acting morally is to conceive ourselves as, in this sense, free. Since Kant believes he has shown that, as theoretically knowable, we are in all our actions causally determined, it follows that if we are to think of ourselves as free, we have to think of ourselves not as empirical beings but as noumena, and about ourselves in this aspect we can know nothing. Our freedom, then, remains ineliminably problematic, an assumption we have to make in taking ourselves to be moral agents, but not something we can know to be true. In his phrase, it is a "postulate of practical reason."

The other two great topics of transcendent metaphysics also turn out to be postulates of practical reason in Kant's second *Critique*: the existence of God and the immortality of the soul. Although virtue, the good will, is the only thing absolutely good in itself, it is not the complete or total good. That, Kant maintains, is a combination of virtue and happiness in which the two are proportionate. But empirically, in this world, the two do not coincide;

the wicked flourish, the virtuous suffer. There must, therefore, be a power that can bring about the complete good or *summum bonum*, and that is God. So the existence of God, Kant concludes, is a demand of practical reason. He recognizes that the existence of God is less intimately bound up with morality than freedom is. What Kant seems to be doing here is bringing in by the back door that identification of morality with enlightened self-interest which is a common feature of just the kind of heteronomous ethical theory from which he is most emphatically concerned to distinguish his own.

It might seem that if God is to proportion happiness to virtue in such a way as to correct the imbalance of reward evident in this world, the immortality of the soul must be taken to be also provided for. Unless the miswarded survive their deaths in this world, nothing can be done to rectify the account. But Kant approaches the problem from a different direction. Morality, he says, requires us to strive for complete virtue. But, because we are natural, desiring creatures, we can never do more than move toward that end, which is, indeed, an infinite process. Since we cannot be required to do what is impossible, it follows that we must have an infinite life. Of course, if we are right when we think of ourselves as noumenal beings, as we must if we are to be moral agents, we are in a way immortal, since the noumenal self is outside time.

The religious reassurance provided by Kant's elaboration of the presuppositions of genuine morality has a certain thinness. That is not a result of his insistence that God, freedom, and immortality are not matters of theoretical knowledge but only postulates of practical reason. Kant described himself as limiting knowledge to make room for faith, which suggests a kind of belief resting more on hope than on justifying grounds. His claim is that *if* our experience of absolute moral obligation is genuine, it must be the case that we are truly free agents and thus noumenal occupants of an intelligible world; and it seems, although less certainly, that there must be a God to proportion happiness to virtue and an unending afterlife in which the soul can achieve perfection. But Kant does not really entertain any doubt that our moral experience is what he takes it to be.

What makes Kant's theological conclusions insubstantial from the point of view of ordinary religious belief is that his reluctance to do more than state them baldly, to develop any general account of the supernatural order they intimate, suggests that he thinks of them less as statements of supernatural fact than as picturesque restatements of the general moral principles that underlie them: that we have absolute moral obligations, that virtue ought to be proportioned to happiness, that we ought to strive for perfect virtue.

The suggestion is confirmed by *Religion within the Limits of Reason Alone*, the late work which brought on Kant's head the disapproval of the Prussian king. This is an essentially modernistic treatment of religion in which the true content of assertions about God is held to be moral in character. To reverence God *is* to do one's duty; it is not something which supplies a particular kind of reason for dutiful action. Kant regards the liturgical and ritual aspects of religion as of negligible importance and adopts a somewhat disapproving attitude toward prayer. When Kant says that we are to look on duties as divine commands, what he means is simply that we must regard them as absolute and unconditional. Basic Christian dogmas are reinterpreted in the same spirit: the doctrine of the fall of man and original sin as a recognition of the innately self-interested aspect of human nature, the doctrine of the incarnation as an affirmation of the ideal of moral perfection. Kant's thoughts about religion plainly anticipate Hegel's notion that "religion imagines what philosophy thinks," but with an exclusively ethical emphasis that reappears in modern reinterpretations of religious theses in ultimately secular terms.

The Critique of Judgement: aesthetics and teleology

Kant begins the *Critique of Judgement* with an introduction which is designed to place its subject matter in a systematic relation to his other main works. As they stand, the two parts of the book—the first a study of aesthetics, the second a study of the attribution of purpose to nature and to the objects it contains—seem unconnected. It turns out, however, that a kind of purposiveness is, in Kant's view, a feature of the things we find beautiful.

There is no need to linger over the details of Kant's systematizing operations, which show great perseverance but provide little illumination. Briefly, he takes the first *Critique*, dealing with pure reason, to have considered understanding, or the faculty of knowledge, and the second to have considered practical reason, the faculty that orders desire. He then represents judgment, the faculty that gives order to feeling, as the connecting link between the other two. What he seems to have in mind is the solution to a problem left open by the findings of the two earlier *Critiques*.

The phenomenal world, of which alone we can have theoretical knowledge, is rigidly deterministic; yet, as moral agents, we have to conceive ourselves as free. If we can think of the world as purposive, we think of it as hospitable to the pursuit of ends, as a possible field of action. The apparent upshot of Kant's account of free moral agency is that we are free only as denizens of another, intelligible, but not sensible, world. However, there is a suggestion in his proposal for the reconciliation of freedom and causal necessity that it is the very same actions which can be conceived from two distinct points of view. In his account of action, Kant almost wholly concentrates on truly moral action, an essential feature of which, for him, is that it is *not* purposive. (If it were, it would be heteronomous.) But he allows that there is prudent or merely skillful action as well.

The main interest of the two parts of the third *Critique* is to be found within them, rather than in any alleged connection between them.

A. Aesthetic judgment

For Kant the central problem of aesthetics is not unlike the central problem of the first *Critique*. The earlier work can be seen as asking how it is that we can have knowledge of a common, objective world, when the given basis of our beliefs about matters of fact is private sensations. In the case of aesthetic judgments, the question is how they can claim universal validity when they rest on private experiences of satisfaction.

The somewhat obscure answer Kant returns to this question is of less interest than the analysis of aesthetic judgment that leads up to it. First, the judgment of beauty or taste reports a special, disinterested kind of satisfaction yielded by some contemplated object. This, broadly, is Shaftesbury's notion of what differentiates aesthetic from other kinds of pleasure. Second, such a judgment both claims to be valid for all and yet does not rest on reasons and cannot be argumentatively established. Third, the common feature of aesthetically satisfying things is that while they serve no actual purpose, they still have the form of a purposive thing—in Kant's phrase, they have "purposiveness without purpose."

Kant's fondness for abstraction serves him well in his aesthetic thinking, which is much more sophisticated than any aesthetic theorizing of comparable philosophic generality that had preceded it. He respects the integrity and autonomy of the domain of aesthetic interest and is wholly free from any tendency, of the sort which is to be found in its most extreme and childishly vulgar form in Tolstoy, to subordinate the aesthetic to the moral. On the other hand, Kant does not fall, in the opposite direction, into a Paterian aestheticism of exquisite pulses of feeling. (His temperament, one may well suppose, would more probably have led him to the previous, moralistic extreme.) Again, he strives admirably to navigate between over-generalizing properties peculiar only to one kind of aesthetic object (such as mimesis) and putting forward empty comprehensive formulae like "organic unity" and "significant form."

Part of the answer to Kant's central problem is supplied by the disinterestedness which he regards as a defining characteristic of aesthetic satisfaction. That at least detaches aesthetic judgment from the peculiarities of private concern. The idea that aesthetic judgment is somehow nonconceptual is a challenging and important one. It is, of course, possible to support aesthetic or critical evaluations with further consideration of the object evaluated, but that involves a fuller description of it to improve our awareness, not an identification of properties which bring it under a general canon of excellence.

Kant's answer to the question of how judgment based on feeling can still claim universal validity should be briefly sketched. It is that the formally purposive nature of aesthetic objects stimulates the imagination in a way that brings out the harmony between that faculty (which assembles our sensations for purposes of synthesis) and the understanding (which brings the assembled sensations under a concept). In effect, this is to say that an aesthetic object pleases because it somehow testifies to the intelligibility of the world, a rather strikingly intellectualistic account of the matter.

B. Teleological judgment

In the introduction to the third *Critique* Kant connects the urge of scientists to organize their findings into unitary and comprehensive systems with the idea of nature as a purposive whole. In pursuing their ideal of system, scientists are thinking of nature as adapted to the human mind, and to think that is to think of nature *as if* it were the product of a single intelligence, vastly greater than, but of the same general character as, our own intellects.

Purpose is discernible in nature both in the relations of things to one another (the purposiveness of nature as whole being simply the largest and most inclusive instance of this) and, as it were, within things, where the parts of the whole thing serve reciprocally as means to each other's ends. This kind of immanent, or, as Kant calls it, absolute, purposiveness is something we are inclined to ascribe to organisms for whose growth and activities no mechanical explanation is available.

In the first *Critique* Kant had argued that it is possible to experience only that which falls within a causal system, which seems to imply that everything we can think of as part of nature must be mechanically explainable. Kant does not very convincingly reconcile this fundamental conviction with his admission of teleological explanation in terms of purpose. At certain times he suggests that teleological explanation is a temporary makeshift, to be put up with until a proper mechanical explanation is available; at others, he indicates that it can coexist with a mechanical explanation, in something like the way in which, in his ethical theory, the freedom of human agents is held to coexist with causal determination. In the end he cannot bring himself to accord fully scientific status to teleology. It has to be understood in a more or less regulative way as a useful guide for the study of nature, but only as a preliminary to scientific knowledge proper.

Teleological explanation by "final causes" occupies a fundamental place in the thought of Aristotle. In proclaiming the barrenness of final causes, Bacon, to whom Kant dedicated his first *Critique*, was unequivocally asserting the principal assumption about method underlying the natural scientists of the seventeenth century. Reverent as he was toward the Newtonian system in which the scientific revolution culminated, Kant was characteristically open-minded enough to see that the final causality which was its chief bugbear still had a part to play in science.

The Critique of Judgement discusses interesting questions and contains, particularly in its aesthetic part, influential further developments of the main body of Kant's thought. But as a whole it has none of the systematic power of the theories of knowledge and ethics of the first two *Critiques*. It is really more a supplementary collection of additional reflections than the third part of a substantive grand design that Kant represents it as being.

Conclusion

The somewhat irregular course of Kant's influence was described earlier. It is present in the idealists who used him as a point of departure for a new kind of metaphysical thinking, in the vigorous revival of his thought in something much more like its original form by the neo-Kantian movement in Germany in the second half of the nineteenth century, and, finally, in the considerable growth of interest in his way of philosophizing that has taken place in the English-speaking philosophical world in recent years (inspired, probably, by the common interpretation of Wittgenstein's *Tractatus* as a work of transcendental philosophy in Kant's sense).

Considered as literature, his work is deplorable. No major philosopher since the close of the Middle Ages had written in such a crabbed and jargon-ridden manner. Indeed, most of the leading philosophers of the two centuries preceding him must be numbered among the greatest of prose writers: Bacon, Hobbes, Berkeley, and Hume in England, Descartes in France, Spinoza wherever Latin was read.

Kant is great enough to survive a comparison that is, in one dimension, so very unfavorable to him. He combined a marvelously sure sense of what was centrally at issue in the philosophy of his age with the creative power to produce an altogether new proposal for its resolution. That proposal is not easy to understand, particularly with regard to implications he does not pursue. For most people, it is even harder to believe. But for anyone who, like Bertrand Russell, takes one of the chief values of philosophy to be the enlargement of our conception of the possible, it must retain an inexhaustible fascination.

PART FIVE

Additions
to the
Great Books Library

The Comparison of Related Forms

D'Arcy Wentworth Thompson

Editor's Introduction

On Growth and Form in more than one respect is something of an exception in the literature of twentieth-century science. In an age when most scientific achievements are communicated in the form of papers or monographs, it is a book, large in size — 1,116 pages divided into seventeen chapters. Then, too, it is far-ranging in its scope and draws upon the writings of philosophers and poets as well as scientists from many ages, in many languages. Finally, not least in significance, it is clearly and beautifully written in a language not confined to the specialist alone but available to the general reader.

The book was written, the preface tells us, as "an easy introduction to the study of organic Form, by methods which are the common-places of physical science, which are by no means novel in their application to natural history, but which nevertheless naturalists are little accustomed to employ." At the time it was written, during the First World War, biologists tended to prefer historical or phylogenetic methods. Thompson's book marked a change toward the use of physical and mathematical methods — a path that is still being widened, as evident from the essay by Charles Oxnard on physical anthropology. His sole purpose, Thompson goes on to say, "is to correlate with mathematical statement and physical law certain of the simpler outward phenomena of organic growth and structure or form, while all the while regarding the fabric of the organism, *ex hypothesi* [hypothetically], as a material and mechanical configuration." But as a cautionary note, he further remarked that he "would not for the world be thought to believe that this is the only story which Life and her Children have to tell. One does not come by studying living things for a lifetime to suppose that physics and chemistry can account for them all."

The lifetime that he devoted to this study was a long one. D'Arcy Wentworth Thompson was born in Edinburgh, May 2, 1860, and died at his home in Scotland, June 21, 1948. His father, who gave the son all of his three names, was a professor of classics; his mother, Fanny Gamgee, the daughter of a veterinary surgeon. In 1863 the father went to Queen's College, Galway, as professor of Greek, and the child, motherless since birth, was left in the charge of his maternal grandfather. He claimed that he owed to this grandfather his interest in biology, just as he owed to his father his love of the classics. His early education was in Edinburgh, and after completing three years as a medical student there, he went in 1880 to Trinity College, Cambridge, where he studied with the group that was then laying the foundation of the Cambridge school of biology.

In 1884 he graduated and, although receiving high honors, he failed to win appointment as a fellow. He then took a position as professor of biology (later of natural history) at University College, Dundee, Scotland. Besides his regular teaching, he built up a museum of zoology, which became especially rich in specimens from the Arctic seas, brought back by the whalers who were still working out of that northeastern Scottish port. He wrote many papers on fish and oceanography and from 1898 to 1939 served as a scientific adviser to the Fishery Board of Scotland. In 1902 he was appointed the British representative on the International Council for the Exploration of the Sea. In 1917 he was called to fill the senior chair of natural history at St. Andrews University, where he remained for the rest of his life. Many honors were awarded him: fellowship in the Royal Society in 1916, a knighthood in 1937, and academic degrees from Boston to Delhi, from Aberdeen to Johannesburg. He loved teaching and continued to do so to the very end of his life.

Thompson was a classicist as well as a scientist. Apart from his many publications dealing directly with zoological subjects, he wrote extensively on the natural history of ancient writers. He produced *A Glossary of Greek Birds* in 1895, an annotated translation of Aristotle's *Historia Animalium* in 1910 (the translation of which is in *GBWW*, Vol. 9). In 1947 he published *A Glossary of Greek Fishes*. A selection of his articles and addresses was published under the title of *Science and the Classics* (1940).

In stature and appearance Thompson is described as huge and magnificent, a "kindly Jupiter," with a great spade beard and unshakable self-possession. An instance of this last was provided in a lecture given in India in 1946 on the skeletal structure of birds. To have at hand illustrative material of the points that he wished to make, "he held an angry hen tucked under one arm so that he could conveniently point out on a living specimen the salient features of his description. The remonstrances of his model disturbed not at all the easy flow of his speech." He married in 1901 and had three daughters. Ruth D'Arcy Thompson has written a biography under the title *D'Arcy Wentworth Thompson, The Scholar-Naturalist* (1958).

On Growth and Form was first published in 1917. The second edition appeared in 1942, prepared as was the first during yet another war, providing him with "solace and occupation, when service was debarred [him] by [his] years." The selection presented here is the seventeenth and concluding chapter of the work.

The Comparison of Related Forms

In the morphology of living things the use of mathematical methods and symbols has made slow progress; and there are various reasons for this failure to employ a method whose advantages are so obvious in the investigation of other physical forms. To begin with, there would seem to be a psychological reason, lying in the fact that the student of living things is by nature and training an observer of concrete objects and phenomena and the habit of mind which he possesses and cultivates is alien to that of the theoretical mathematician. But this is by no means the only reason; for in the kindred subject of mineralogy, for instance, crystals were still treated in the days of Linnaeus as wholly within the province of the naturalist, and were described by him after the simple methods in use for animals and plants: but as soon as Haüy shewed the application of mathematics to the description and classification of crystals, his methods were immediately adopted and a new science came into being.

A large part of the neglect and suspicion of mathematical methods in organic morphology is due to an ingrained and deep-seated belief that even when we seem to discern a regular mathematical figure in an organism, the sphere, the hexagon, or the spiral which we so recognise merely resembles, but is never entirely explained by, its mathematical analogue; in short, that the details in which the figure differs from its mathematical prototype are more important and more interesting than the features in which it agrees; and even that the peculiar aesthetic pleasure with which we regard a living thing is somehow bound up with the departure from mathematical regularity which it manifests as a peculiar attribute of life. This view

seems to me to involve a misapprehension. There is no such essential difference between these phenomena of organic form and those which are manifested in portions of inanimate matter.* The mathematician knows better than we do the value of an approximate result.† The child's skipping-rope is but an approximation to Huygens's catenary curve—but in the catenary curve lies the whole gist of the matter. We may be dismayed too easily by contingencies which are nothing short of irrelevant compared to the main issue; there is a *principle of negligibility*. Someone has said that if Tycho Brahé's instruments had been ten times as exact there would have been no Kepler, no Newton, and no astronomy.

---

* M. Bergson repudiates, with peculiar confidence, the application of mathematics to biology; cf. *Creative Evolution*, p. 21, "Calculation touches, at most, certain phenomena of organic destruction. Organic creation, on the contrary, the evolutionary phenomena which properly constitute life, we cannot in any way subject to a mathematical treatment." Bergson thus follows Bichat: "C'est peu connaître les fonctions animales que de vouloir les soumettre au moindre calcul, parceque leur instabilité est extrême. Les phénomènes restent toujours les mêmes, et c'est ce qui nous importe; mais leurs variations, en plus ou en moins, sont sans nombre" (*La Vie et la Mort*, p. 257).

† When we make a "first approximation" to the solution of a physical problem, we usually mean that we are solving one part while neglecting others. Geometry deals with *pure forms* (such as a straight line), defined by a single law; but these are few compared with the *mixed forms*, like the surface of a polyhedron, or a segment of a sphere, or any ordinary mechanical construction or any ordinary physical phenomenon. It is only in a purely mathematical treatment of physics that the "single law" can be dealt with alone, and the approximate solution dispensed with accordingly.

If no chain hangs in a perfect catenary and no raindrop is a perfect sphere, this is for the reason that forces and resistances other than the main one are inevitably at work. The same is true of organic form, but it is for the mathematician to unravel the conflicting forces which are at work together. And this process of investigation may lead us on step by step to new phenomena, as it has done in physics, where sometimes a knowledge of form leads us to the interpretation of forces, and at other times a knowledge of the forces at work guides us towards a better insight into form. After the fundamental advance had been made which taught us that the world was round, Newton shewed that the forces at work upon it must lead to its being imperfectly spherical, and in the course of time its oblate spheroidal shape was actually verified. But now, in turn, it has been shewn that its form is still more complicated, and the next step is to seek for the forces that have deformed the oblate spheroid. As Newton somewhere says, "Nature delights in transformations."

The organic forms which we can define more or less precisely in mathematical terms, and afterwards proceed to explain and to account for in terms of force, are of many kinds, as we have seen; but nevertheless they are few in number compared with Nature's all but infinite variety. The reason for this is not far to seek. The living organism represents, or occupies, a field of force which is never simple, and which as a rule is of immense complexity. And just as in the very simplest of actual cases we meet with a departure from such symmetry as could only exist under conditions of *ideal* simplicity, so do we pass quickly to cases where the interference of numerous, though still perhaps very simple, causes leads to a resultant complexity far beyond our powers of analysis. Nor must we forget that the biologist is much more exacting in his requirements, as regards form, than the physicist; for the latter is usually content with either an ideal or a general description of form, while the student of living things must needs be specific. Material things, be they living or dead, shew us but a shadow of mathematical perfection. The physicist or mathematician can give us perfectly satisfying expressions for the form of a wave, or even of a heap of sand; but we never ask him to define the form of any particular wave of the sea, nor the actual form of any mountain-peak or hill.

In this there lies a certain justification for a saying of Minot's, of the greater part of which, nevertheless, I am heartily inclined to disapprove. "We biologists," he says, "cannot deplore too frequently or too emphatically the great mathematical delusion by which men often of great if limited ability have been misled into becoming advocates of an erroneous conception of accuracy. The delusion is that no science is accurate until its results can be expressed mathematically. The error comes from the assumption that mathematics can express complex relations. Unfortunately mathematics have a very limited scope, and are based upon a few extremely rudimentary experiences, which we make as very little children and of which no adult has any recollection. The fact that from this basis men of genius have evolved wonderful methods of dealing with numerical relations should not blind us to another fact, namely, that the observational basis of mathematics is, psychologically speaking, very minute compared with the observational basis of even a single minor branch of biology. . . . While therefore here and there the mathematical methods may aid us, we need a kind and degree of accuracy of which mathematics is absolutely incapable. . . . *With human minds constituted as they actually are, we cannot anticipate that there will ever be a mathematical expression for any organ or even a single cell, although formulae will continue to be useful for dealing now and then with isolated details . . ." (op. cit. p. 19, 1911). It were easy to discuss and criticise these sweeping assertions, which perhaps had their origin and parentage in an* obiter dictum *of Huxley's, to the effect that "Mathematics is that study which knows nothing of observation, nothing of experiment, nothing of induction, nothing of causation" (cit. Cajori, Hist. of Elem. Mathematics, p. 283). But Gauss, "rex mathematicorum," called mathematics "a science of the eye"; and Sylvester assures us that "most, if not all, of the great ideas of modern mathematics have had their origin in observation"* (Brit. Ass. Address, *1869, and* Laws of Verse, *p. 120, 1870).*

For one reason or another there are very many organic forms which we cannot describe, still less define, in mathematical terms: just as there are problems even in physical science beyond the mathematics of our age. We never even seek for a formula to define this fish or that, or this or that vertebrate skull. But we may already use mathematical language to describe, even to define in general terms, the shape of a snail-shell, the twist of a horn, the outline of a leaf, the texture of a bone, the fabric of a skeleton, the stream-lines of fish or bird, the fairy lacework of an insect's wing. Even to do this we must learn from the mathematician to eliminate and to discard; to keep the type in mind and leave the single case, with all its accidents, alone; and to find in this sacrifice of what matters little and conservation of what matters much one of the peculiar excellences of the method of mathematics.*

In a very large part of morphology, our essential task lies in the comparison of related forms rather than in the precise definition of each; and the *deformation* of a complicated figure may be a phenomenon easy of comprehension, though the figure itself have to be left unanalysed and undefined. This process of comparison, of recognising in one form a definite permutation or *deformation* of another, apart altogether from a precise and adequate understanding of the original "type" or standard of comparison, lies within the immediate province of mathematics, and finds its solution in the elementary use of a certain method of the mathematician. This method is the Method of Coordinates, on which is based the Theory of Transformations.†

I imagine that when Descartes conceived the method of coordinates, as a generalisation from the proportional diagrams of the artist and the architect, and long before the immense possibilities of this analysis could be foreseen, he had in mind a very simple purpose; it was perhaps no more than to find a way of translating the *form* of a curve (as well as the position of a point) into *numbers* and into *words*. This is precisely what we do, by the method of coordinates, every time we study a statistical curve; and conversely, we translate numbers into form whenever we "plot a curve," to illustrate a table of mortality, a rate of growth, or the daily variation of temperature or barometric pressure. In precisely the same way it is possible to inscribe in a net of rectangular coordinates the outline, for instance, of a fish, and so to translate it into a table of numbers, from which again we may at pleasure reconstruct the curve.

But it is the next step in the employment of coordinates which is of special interest and use to the morphologist; and this step consists in the alteration, or deformation, of our system of coordinates, and in the study of the corresponding transformation of the curve or figure inscribed in the coordinate network.

Let us inscribe in a system of Cartesian coordinates the outline of an organism, however complicated, or a part thereof: such as a fish, a crab, or a mammalian skull. We may now treat this complicated figure, in general terms, as a function of x, y. If we submit our rectangular system to deformation on simple and recognised lines, altering, for instance, the direction of the axes, the ratio of x/y, or substituting for x and y some more com-

---

* Cf. W. H. Young, The mathematical method and its limitations, *Congresso dei Matematici*, Bologna, 1928.

† The mathematical Theory of Transformations is part of the Theory of Groups, of great importance in modern mathematics. A distinction is drawn between Substitution-groups and Transformation-groups, the former being discontinuous, the latter continuous—in such a way that within one and the same group each transformation is infinitely little different from another. The distinction among biologists between a mutation and a variation is curiously analogous.

plicated expressions, then we obtain a new system of coordinates, whose deformation from the original type the inscribed figure will precisely follow. In other words, we obtain a new figure which represents the old figure under a more or less homogeneous *strain,* and is a function of the new coordinates in precisely the same way as the old figure was of the original coordinates x and y.

The problem is closely akin to that of the cartographer who transfers identical data to one projection or another; and whose object is to secure (if it be possible) a complete correspondence, *in each small unit of area,* between the one representation and the other. The morphologist will not seek to draw his organic forms in a new and artificial projection; but, in the converse aspect of the problem, he will enquire whether two different but more or less obviously related forms can be so analysed and interpreted that each may be shewn to be a transformed representation of the other. This once demonstrated, it will be a comparatively easy task (in all probability) to postulate the direction and magnitude of the force capable of effecting the required transformation. Again, if such a simple alteration of the system of forces can be proved adequate to meet the case, we may find ourselves able to dispense with many widely current and more complicated hypotheses of biological causation. For it is a maxim in physics that an effect ought not to be ascribed to the joint operation of many causes if few are adequate to the production of it.

We might suppose that by the combined action of appropriate forces any material form could be transformed into any other: just as out of a "shapeless" mass of clay the potter or the sculptor models his artistic product; or just as we attribute to Nature herself the power to effect the gradual and successive transformation of the simple germ into the complex organism. But we need not let these considerations deter us from our method of comparison of *related* forms. We shall strictly

limit ourselves to cases where the transformation necessary to effect a comparison shall be of a simple kind, and where the transformed, as well as the original, coordinates shall constitute an harmonious and more or less symmetrical system. We should fall into deserved and inevitable confusion if, whether by the mathematical or any other method, we attempted to compare organisms separated far apart in Nature and in zoological classification. We are limited, both by our method and by the whole nature of the case, to the comparison of organisms such as are manifestly related to one another and belong to the same zoological class. For it is a grave sophism, in natural history as in logic, to make a transition into another kind.

Our enquiry lies, in short, just within the limits which Aristotle himself laid down when, in defining a "genus," he shewed that (apart from those superficial characters, such as colour, which he called "accidents") the essential differences between one "species" and another are merely differences of proportion, of relative magnitude, or (as he phrased it) of "excess and defect." "Save only for a difference in the way of excess or defect, the parts are identical in the case of such animals as are of one and the same genus; and by 'genus' I mean, for instance, Bird or Fish." And again: "Within the limits of the same genus, as a general rule, most of the parts exhibit differences . . . in the way of multitude or fewness, magnitude or parvitude, in short, in the way of excess or defect. For 'the more' and 'the less' may be represented as 'excess' and 'defect'."* It is precisely this difference of relative magnitudes, this Aristotelian "excess and defect" in the case of form, which our coordinate method is especially adapted to analyse, and to reveal and demonstrate as the main cause of what (again in the Aristotelian sense) we term "specific" differences.

The applicability of our method to particular cases will depend upon, or be further limited by, certain practical considerations or

---

* *Historia Animalium* 1. 1. [Cf. *GBWW,* Vol. 9, p. 7.]

qualifications. Of these the chief, and indeed the essential, condition is, that the form of the entire structure under investigation should be found to vary in a more or less uniform manner, after the fashion of an approximately homogeneous and isotropic body. But an imperfect isotropy, provided always that some "principle of continuity" run through its variations, will not seriously interfere with our method; it will only cause our transformed coordinates to be somewhat less regular and harmonious than are those, for instance, by which the physicist depicts the motions of a perfect fluid, or a theoretic field of force in a uniform medium.

Again, it is essential that our structure vary in its entirety, or at least that "independent variants" should be relatively few. That independent variations occur, that localised centres of diminished or exaggerated growth will now and then be found, is not only probable but manifest; and they may even be so pronounced as to appear to constitute new formations altogether. Such independent variants as these Aristotle himself clearly recognised: "It happens further that some have parts which others have not; for instance, some [birds] have spurs and others not, some have crests, or combs, and others not; but, as a general rule, most parts and those that go to make up the bulk of the body are either identical with one another, or differ from one another in the way of contrast and of excess and defect. For 'the more' and 'the less' may be represented as 'excess' or 'defect'."*

If, in the evolution of a fish, for instance, it be the case that its several and constituent parts—head, body and tail, or this fin and that fin—represent so many independent variants, then our coordinate system will at once become too complex to be intelligible; we shall be making not one comparison but several separate comparisons, and our general method will be found inapplicable. Now precisely this independent variability of parts and organs—here, there, and everywhere within the organism—would appear to be implicit in our ordinary accepted notions regarding variation; and, unless I am greatly mistaken, it is precisely on such a conception of the easy, frequent, and normally independent variability of parts that our conception of the process of natural selection is fundamentally based. For the morphologist, when comparing one organism with another, describes the differences between them point by point, and "character" by "character." If he is from time to time constrained to admit the existence of "correlation" between characters (as a hundred years ago Cuvier first shewed the way), yet all the while he recognises this fact of correlation somewhat vaguely, as a phenomenon due to causes which, except in rare instances, he can hardly hope to trace; and he falls readily into the habit of thinking and talking of evolution as though it had proceeded on the lines of his own descriptions, point by point, and character by character.[†]

With the "characters" of Mendelian genetics there is no fault to be found; tall and short, rough and smooth, plain or coloured are opposite tendencies or contrasting qualities, in plain logical contradistinction. But when the morphologist compares one animal with another, point by point or character by character, these are too often the mere

---

* Aristotle's argument is even more subtle and far-reaching; for the differences of which he speaks are not merely those between one bird and another, but between them all and the very type itself, or Platonic "idea" of a bird.

† Cf. H. F. Osborn, On the origin of single characters, as observed in fossil and living animals and plants, *Amer. Nat.* XLIX, pp. 193–239, 1915 (and other papers); *ibid.* p. 194, "Each individual is composed of a vast number of somewhat similar new or old characters, each character has its independent and separate history, each character is in a certain stage of evolution, each character is correlated with the other characters of the individual. ... The real problem has always been that of the origin and development of characters. Since the *Origin of Species* appeared, the terms variation and variability have always referred to single characters; if a species is said to be variable, we mean that a considerable number of the single characters or groups of characters of which it is composed are variable," etc.

outcome of artificial dissection and analysis. Rather is the living body one integral and indivisible whole, in which we cannot find, when we come to look for it, any strict dividing line even between the head and the body, the muscle and the tendon, the sinew and the bone. Characters which we have differentiated insist on integrating themselves again; and aspects of the organism are seen to be conjoined which only our mental analysis had put asunder. The coordinate diagram throws into relief the integral solidarity of the organism, and enables us to see how simple a certain kind of *correlation* is which had been apt to seem a subtle and a complex thing.

But if, on the other hand, diverse and dissimilar fishes can be referred as a whole to identical functions of very different coordinate systems, this fact will of itself constitute a proof that variation has proceeded on definite and orderly lines, that a comprehensive "law of growth" has pervaded the whole structure in its integrity, and that some more or less simple and recognisable system of forces has been in control. It will not only shew how real and deep-seated is the phenomenon of "correlation," in regard to form, but it will also demonstrate the fact that a correlation which had seemed too complex for analysis or comprehension is, in many cases, capable of very simple graphic expression. This, after many trials, I believe to be in general the case, bearing always in mind that the occurrence of independent or localised variations must sometimes be considered.

We are dealing in this chapter with the forms of related organisms, in order to shew that the differences between them are as a general rule simple and symmetrical, and just such as might have been brought about by a slight and simple change in the system of forces to which the living and growing organism was exposed. Mathematically speaking, the phenomenon is identical with one met with by the geologist, when he finds a bed of fossils squeezed flat or otherwise symmetrically deformed by the pressures to which they, and the strata which contain them, have been subjected. In the first step towards fossili-

sation, when the body of a fish or shellfish is silted over and buried, we may take it that the wet sand or mud exercises, approximately, a hydrostatic pressure —that is to say a pressure which is uniform in all directions, and by which the form of the buried object will not be appreciably changed. As the strata consolidate and accumulate, the fossil organisms which they contain will tend to be flattened by the vast superincumbent load, just as the stratum which contains them will also be compressed and will have its molecular arrangement more or less modified. But the deformation due to direct vertical pressure in a horizontal stratum is not nearly so striking as are the deformations produced by the oblique or shearing stresses to which inclined and folded strata have been exposed, and by which their various "dislocations"

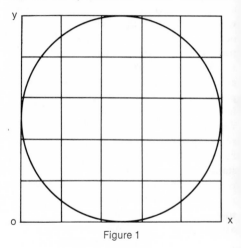

Figure 1

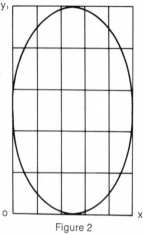

Figure 2

have been brought about. And especially in mountain regions, where these dislocations are especially numerous and complicated, the contained fossils are apt to be so curiously and yet so symmetrically deformed (usually by a simple shear) that they may easily be interpreted as so many distinct and separate "species." A great number of described species, and here and there a new genus (as the genus Ellipsolithes *for an obliquely deformed* Goniatite *or* Nautilus*), are said to rest on no other foundation.*

If we begin by drawing a net of rectangular equidistant coordinates (about the axes *x* and *y*), we may alter or *deform* this network in various ways, several of which are very simple indeed. Thus (1) we may alter the dimensions of our system, extending it along one or other axis, and so converting each little square into a corresponding and proportionate oblong (figs. 1, 2). It follows that any figure which we may have inscribed in the original net, and which we transfer to the new, will thereby be *deformed* in strict proportion to the deformation of the entire configuration, being still defined by corresponding points in the network and being throughout in conformity with the original figure. For instance, a circle inscribed in the original "Cartesian" net will now, after extension in the *y*-direction, be found elongated into an ellipse. In elementary mathematical language, for the original *x* and *y* we have substituted x_1 and cy_1, and the equation to our original circle, $x^2 + y^2 = a^2$, becomes that of the ellipse, $x_1^2 + c^2 y_1^2 = a^2$.

If I draw the cannon-bone of an ox (fig. 3, A), for instance, within a system of rectangular coordinates, and then transfer the same drawing, point for point, to a system in which for the *x* of the original diagram we substitute $x' = 2x/3$, we obtain a drawing (B) which is a very close approximation to the cannon-bone of the sheep. In other words, the main (and perhaps the only) difference between the two bones is simply that that of the sheep is elongated along the vertical axis as compared with that of the ox, in the proportion of 3/2. And similarly, the long slender cannon-bone of the giraffe (C) is referable to the

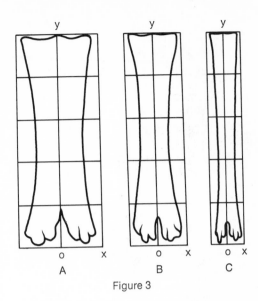

Figure 3

same identical type, subject to a reduction of breadth, or increase of length, corresponding to $x'' = x/3$.

(2) The second type is that where extension is not equal or uniform at all distances from the origin: but grows greater or less, as, for instance, when we stretch a *tapering* elastic band. In such cases, as I have represented it in fig. 4, the ordinate increases logarithmically, and for *y* we substitute ϵ^y. It is obvious that this logarithmic extension may involve both abscissae and ordinates, *x* becoming ϵ^x while *y* becomes ϵ^y. The circle in our original figure is now deformed into some such shape as that of fig. 5. This method of deformation is a common one, and will often be of

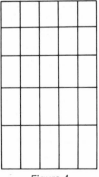

Figure 4

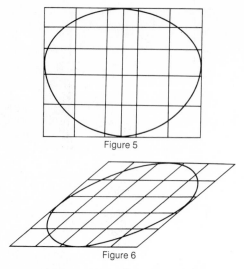

Figure 5

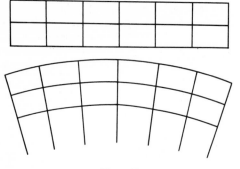

Figure 6

use to us in our comparison of organic forms.

(3) Our third type is the "simple shear," where the rectangular coordinates become "oblique," their axes being inclined to one another at a certain angle ω. Our original rectangle now becomes such a figure as that of fig. 6. The system may now be described in terms of the oblique axes X, Y; or may be directly referred to new rectangular coordinates ξ, η by the simple transposition $x = \xi - \eta \cot \omega$, $y = \eta \csc \omega$.

(4) Yet another important class of deformations may be represented by the use of radial coordinates, in which one set of lines are represented as radiating from a point or "focus," while the other set are transformed into circular arcs cutting the radii orthogonally. These radial coordinates are especially

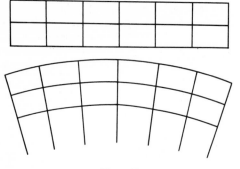

Figure 7

applicable to cases where there exists (either within or without the figure) some part which is supposed to suffer no deformation; a simple illustration is afforded by the diagrams which illustrate the flexure of a beam (fig. 7). In biology these coordinates will be especially applicable in cases where the growing structure includes a "node," or point where growth is absent or at a minimum; and about which node the rate of growth may be assumed to increase symmetrically. Precisely such a case is furnished us in a leaf of an ordinary dicotyledon. The leaf of a typical monocotyledon—such as a grass or a hyacinth, for instance—grows continuously from its base, and exhibits no node or "point of arrest." Its sides taper off gradually from its broad base to its slender tip, according to some law of decrement specific to the plant; and any alteration in the relative velocities of longitudinal and transverse growth will merely make the leaf a little broader or narrower, and will effect no other conspicuous alteration in its contour. But if there once come into existence a node, or "locus of no growth," about which we may assume growth —which in the hyacinth leaf was longitudinal and transverse—to take place radially and transversely to the radii, then we shall soon see the sloping sides of the hyacinth leaf give place to a more typical and "leaf-like" shape. If we alter the ratio between the radial and tangential velocities of growth—in other words, if we increase the angles between corresponding radii—we pass successively through the various configurations which the botanist describes as the lanceolate, the ovate, and the cordiform leaf. These successive changes may to some extent, and in appropriate cases, be traced as the individual leaf grows to maturity; but as a much more general rule, the balance of forces, the ratio between radial and tangential velocities of growth, remains so nicely and constantly balanced that the leaf increases in size without conspicuous modification of form. It is rather what we may call a long-period variation, a tendency for the relative velocities to alter from one generation to another, whose re-

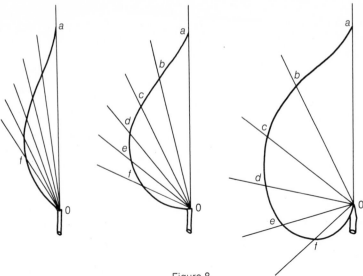

Figure 8

sult is brought into view by this method of illustration.

There are various corollaries to this method of describing the form of a leaf which may be here alluded to. For instance, the so-called unsymmetrical leaf* of a begonia, in which one side of the leaf may be merely ovate while the other has a cordate outline, is seen to be really a case of *unequal,* and not truly asymmetrical, growth on either side of the midrib. There is nothing more mysterious in its conformation than, for instance, in that of a forked twig in which one limb of the fork has grown longer than the other. The case of the begonia leaf is of sufficient interest to deserve illustration, and in fig. 9 I have outlined a leaf of the large *Begonia daedalea.* On the smaller left-hand side of the leaf I have taken at random three points *a*, *b*, *c*, and have measured the angles, *AOa,* etc., which the radii from the hilus of the leaf to these points make with the median axis. On the other side of the leaf I have marked the points *a'*, *b'*, *c'*, such that the radii drawn to this margin of the leaf are equal to the former, *Oa'* to *Oa,* etc. Now if the two sides of the leaf are mathematically similar to one another, it is obvious that the respective angles should be in continued proportion, i.e.,

as *AOa* is to *AOa',* so should *AOb* be to *AOb'.* This proves to be very nearly the case. For I have measured the three angles on one side, and one on the other, and have then compared, as follows, the calculated with the observed values of the other two:

	AOa	*AOb*	*AOc*
Observed values	12°	28.5°	88°
Calculated values	—	—	—
Observed values	—	—	—

	AOa'	*AOb'*	*AOc'*
Observed values	—	—	157°
Calculated values	21.5°	51.1°	—
Observed values	20	52	—

The agreement is very close, and what discrepancy there is may be amply accounted for, firstly, by the slight irregularity of the sinuous margin of the leaf; and secondly, by

---

* Cf. Sir Thomas Browne, in *The Garden of Cyrus:* "But why ofttimes one side of the leaf is unequall unto the other, as in Hazell and Oaks, why on either side the master vein the lesser and derivative channels stand not directly opposite, not at equall angles, respectively unto the adverse side, but those of one side do often exceed the other, as the Wallnut and many more, deserves another enquiry."

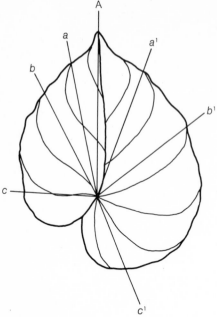

Figure 9. *Begonia daedalea.*

notice, lastly, that the shape of a solid fruit, such as an apple or a cherry, is a solid of revolution, developed from similar curves and to be explained on the same principle. In the cherry we have a "point of arrest" at the base of the berry, where it joins its peduncle, and about this point the fruit (in imaginary section) swells out into a cordate outline; while in the apple we have two such well-marked points of arrest, above and below, and about both of them the same conformation tends to arise. The bean and the human kidney owe their "reniform" shape to precisely the same phenomenon, namely, to the existence of a node or "hilus," about which the forces of growth are radially and symmetrically arranged. When the seed is small and the pod roomy, the seed may grow round, or nearly so, like a pea; but it is flattened and bean-shaped, or elliptical like a kidney-bean, when compressed within a narrow and elongated pod. If the original seed have any simple pattern, of the nature for instance of meridians or parallels of latitude, it is easy to see how these will suffer a conformal transformation, corresponding to the deformation of the sphere.

the fact that the true axis or midrib of the leaf is not straight but slightly curved, and therefore that it is curvilinear and not rectilinear triangles which we ought to have measured. When we understand these few points regarding the peripheral curvature of the leaf, it is easy to see that its principal veins approximate closely to a beautiful system of isogonal coordinates. It is also obvious that we can easily pass, by a process of shearing, from those cases where the principal veins start from the base of the leaf to those where they arise successively from the midrib, as they do in most dicotyledons.

It may sometimes happen that the node,* or "point of arrest," is at the upper instead of the lower end of the leaf-blade; and occasionally there is a node at both ends. In the former case, as we have it in the daisy, the form of the leaf will be, as it were, inverted, the broad, more or less heart-shaped, outline appearing at the upper end, while below the leaf tapers gradually downwards to an ill-defined base. In the latter case, as in *Dionaea,* we obtain a leaf equally expanded, and similarly ovate or cordate, at both ends. We may

We might go farther, and farther than we have room for here, to illustrate the shapes of leaves by means of radial coordinates, and even to attempt to define them by polar equations. In a former chapter we learned to look upon the curve of sines as an easy, gradual and natural transition—perhaps the simplest and most natural of all—from minimum to corresponding maximum, and so on alternately and continuously; and we found the same curve going round like the hands of a clock, when plotted on radial coordinates and (so to speak) prevented from leaving its place. Either way it represents a "simple harmonic motion." Now we have just seen an ordinary dicotyledonous leaf to have a "point

---

* "Node," in the botanical, not the mathematical, sense.

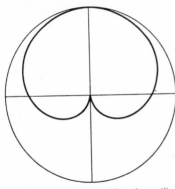

Figure 10. Curve resembling the outline of a reniform leaf: $r = \sin \theta/2$.

Figure 11. Violet leaf.

of arrest," or zero-growth in a certain direction, while in the opposite direction towards the tip it has grown with a maximum velocity. This progress from zero to maximum suggests one-half of the sine-curve; in other words, if we look on the outline of the leaf as a vector-diagram of its own growth, at rates varying from zero to zero in a complete circuit of 360°, this suggests, as a possible and very simple case, the plotting of $r = \sin \theta/2$. Doing so, we obtain a curve (fig. 10) closely resembling what the botanists call a *reniform* (or kidney-shaped) leaf, that is to say, with a cordate outline at the base formed of two "auricles," one on either side, and then rounded off with no projecting apex.* The ground-ivy and the dog-violet (fig. 11) illus-

trate such a leaf; and sometimes, as in the violet, the veins of the leaf show similar curves congruent with the outer edge. Moreover the violet is a good example of how the reniform leaf may be drawn out more and more into an acute and ovate form.

From $\sin \theta/2$ we may proceed to any other given fraction of θ, and plot, for instance, $r = \sin 5\theta/3$, as in fig. 12; which now no longer represents a single leaf but has become a diagram of the five petals of a pentamerous flower. Abbot Guido Grandi, a Pisan math-

---

* Fig. 10 illustrates the whole leaf, but only shows one-half of the sine-curve. The rest is got by reflecting the moiety already drawn in the horizontal axis ($\theta = \pi/2$).

Figure 12. Grandi's curves based on $r = \sin \frac{5}{3} \theta$, and illustrating the five petals of a simple flower.

Figure 13. Diagram illustrating a corolla of five petals, or of five lobes, are based on the equation $r = a + b \cos \theta$.

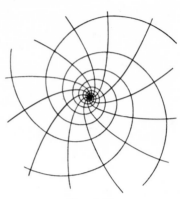

Figure 14. Outline of a compound leaf, like a horse-chestnut, based on a composite sine-curve, of the form $r = \sin \theta/2 . \sin n\theta$.

Figure 15

ematician of the early eighteenth century, drew such a curve and pointed out its botanical analogies; and we still call the curves of this family "Grandi's curves."

The gamopetalous corolla is easily transferred to polar coordinates, in which the radius vector now consists of two parts, the one a constant, the other expressing the amplitude (or half-amplitude) of the sine-curve; we may write the formula $r = a + b\cos n\theta$. In fig. 13 $n = 5$; in this figure, if the radius of the outermost circle be taken as unity, the outer of the two sinuous curves has $a : b$ as $9 : 1$, and the inner curve as $3 : 1$; while the five petals become separate when $a = b$, and the formula reduces to $r = \cos^2 5\theta/2$.

In fig. 14 we have what looks like a first approximation to a horse-chestnut leaf. It consists of so many separate leaflets, akin to the five petals in fig. 13; but these are now inscribed in (or have a *locus* in) the cordate or reniform outline of fig. 10. The new curve is, in short, a composite one; and its general formula is $r = \sin \theta/2 . \sin n\theta$. The small size of the two leaflets adjacent to the petiole is characteristic of the curve, and helps to explain the development of "stipules."

In this last case we have combined one curve with another, and the doing so opens out a new range of possibilities. On the outline of the simple leaf, whether ovate, lanceolate or cordate, we may superpose secondary sine-curves of lesser period and varying amplitude, after the fashion of a Fourier series; and the results will vary from a mere crenate outline to the digitate lobes of an ivy-leaf, or to separate leaflets such as we have just studied in the horse-chestnut. Or again, we may inscribe the separate petals of fig. 15 within a spiral curve, equable or equiangular as the case may be; and then, continuing the series on and on, we shall obtain a figure resembling the clustered leaves of a stonecrop, or the petals of a water-lily or other polypetalous flower.

Most of the transformations which we have hitherto considered (other than that of the simple shear) are particular cases of a general transformation, obtainable by the method of conjugate functions and equivalent to the projection of the original figure on a new plane. Appropriate transformations, on these general lines, provide for the cases of a coaxial system where the Cartesian coordinates are replaced by coaxial circles,

334

or a confocal system in which they are replaced by confocal ellipses and hyperbolas.

Yet another curious and important transformation, belonging to the same class, is that by which a system of straight lines becomes transformed into a conformal system of logarithmic spirals: the straight line $Y - AX = c$ corresponding to the logarithmic spiral $\theta - A \log r = c$ (fig. 15). This beautiful and simple transformation lets us at once convert, for instance, the straight conical shell of the Pteropod or the *Orthoceras* into the logarithmic spiral of the Nautiloid; it involves a mathematical symbolism which is but a slight extension of that which we have employed in our elementary treatment of the logarithmic spiral.

These various systems of coordinates, which we have now briefly considered, are sometimes called "isothermal coordinates," from the fact that, when employed in this particular branch of physics, they perfectly represent the phenomena of the conduction of heat, the contour lines of equal temperature appearing, under appropriate conditions, as the orthogonal lines of the coordinate system. And it follows that the "law of growth" which our biological analysis by means of orthogonal coordinate systems presupposes, or at least foreshadows, is one according to which the organism grows or develops along *stream-lines*, which may be defined by a suitable mathematical transformation.

When the system becomes no longer orthogonal, as in many of the following illustrations — for instance, that of *Orthagoriscus* (fig. 36) — then the transformation is no longer within the reach of comparatively simple mathematical analysis. Such departure from the typical symmetry of a "stream-line" system is, in the first instance, sufficiently accounted for by the simple fact that the developing organism is very far from being homogeneous and isotropic, or, in other words, does not behave like a perfect fluid. But though under such circumstances our coordinate systems may be no longer capable

of strict mathematical analysis, they will still indicate *graphically* the relation of the new coordinate system to the old, and conversely will furnish us with some guidance as to the "law of growth," or play of forces, by which the transformation has been effected.

Before we pass from this brief discussion of transformations in general, let us glance at one or two cases in which the forces applied are more or less intelligible, but the resulting transformations are, from the mathematical point of view, exceedingly complicated.

The "marbled papers" of the bookbinder are a beautiful illustration of visible "streamlines." On a dishful of a sort of semi-liquid gum the workman dusts a few simple lines or patches of colouring matter; and then, by passing a comb through the liquid, he draws the colour-bands into the streaks, waves, and spirals which constitute the marbled pattern, and which he then transfers to sheets of paper laid down upon the gum. By some such system of shears, by the effect of unequal traction or unequal growth in various directions and superposed on an originally simple pattern, we may account for the not dissimilar marbled patterns which we recognise, for instance, on a large serpent's skin. But it must be remarked, in the case of the marbled paper, that though the method of application of the forces is simple, yet in the aggregate the system of forces set up by the many teeth of the comb is exceedingly complex, and its complexity is revealed in the complicated "diagram of forces" which constitutes the pattern.

To take another and still more instructive illustration. To turn one circle (or sphere) into two circles (or spheres) would be, from the point of view of the mathematician, an extraordinarily difficult transformation; but, physically speaking, its achievement may be extremely simple. The little round gourd grows naturally, by its symmetrical forces of expansive growth, into a big, round, or somewhat oval pumpkin or melon.* But the Moorish husbandman ties a rag round its middle, and the same forces of growth, unaltered save for the presence of this trammel, now expand the globular structure into two superposed and connected globes. And again, by varying the position of the encircling band, or by applying several such ligatures instead of one, a great variety of artificial forms of "gourd" may be, and actually are, produced. It is clear, I think, that we may account for many ordinary biological processes of development or transformation of form by the existence of trammels or lines of constraint, which limit and determine the action of the expansive forces of growth that would otherwise be uniform and symmetrical. This case has a close parallel in the operations of the glass-blower, to which we have already, more than once, referred in passing.† The glass-blower starts his operations with a *tube,* which he first closes at one end so as to form a hollow vesicle, within which his blast of air exercises a uniform pressure on all sides; but the spherical conformation which this uniform expansive force would naturally tend to produce is modified into all kinds of forms by the trammels or resistances set up as the workman lets one part or another of his bubble be unequally heated or cooled. It was Oliver Wendell Holmes who first shewed this curious parallel between the operations of the glass-blower and those of Nature, when she starts, as she so often does, with a simple tube.‡ The alimentary canal, the arterial system including the heart, the central nervous system of the vertebrate, including the brain itself, all begin as simple tubular structures. And with them Nature does just what the glass-blower does, and, we might even say, no more than he. For she can expand the tube here and narrow it there; thicken its walls or thin them; blow off a lateral offshoot or caecal diverticulum; bend the tube, or twist and coil it; and infold or crimp its walls as, so to speak, she pleases. Such a form as that of the human stomach is easily explained when it is regarded from this point of view; it is simply an ill-blown

bubble, a bubble that has been rendered lopsided by a trammel or restraint along one side, such as to prevent its symmetrical expansion—such a trammel as is produced if the glass-blower lets one side of his bubble get cold, and such as is actually present in the stomach itself in the form of a muscular band.

The Florence flask, or any other handiwork of the glass-blower, is always beautiful, because its graded contours are, as in its living analogues, a picture of the graded forces by which it was conformed. It is an example of mathematical beauty, of which the machine-made, moulded bottle has no trace at all. An alabaster bottle is different again. It is no longer an unduloid figure of equilibrium. Turned on a lathe, it is a solid of revolution, and not without beauty; but it is not near so beautiful as the blown flask or bubble.

The gravitational field is part of the complex field of force by which the form of the organism is influenced and determined. Its share is seldom easy to define, but there is a resultant due to gravity in hanging breasts and tired eyelids and all the sagging wrinkles of the old. Now and then we see gravity at work in the normal construction of the body, and can describe its effect on form in a general, or qualitative, way. Each pair of ribs in man forms a hoop which droops of its own weight in front, so flattening the chest, and at the same time twisting the rib on either hand

---

* Analogous structural differences, especially in the fibrovascular bundles, help to explain the differences between (e.g.) a smooth melon and a cantelupe, or between various elongate, flattened and globular varieties. These breed true to type, and obey, when crossed, the laws of Mendelian inheritance. Cf. E. W. Sinnett, Inheritance of fruit-shape in Cucurbita, *Botan. Gazette,* LXXIV, pp. 95–103, 1922, and other papers.

† Where gourds are common, the glass-blower is still apt to take them for a prototype, as the prehistoric potter also did. For instance, a tall, annulated Florence oil-flask is an exact but no longer a conscious imitation of a gourd which has been converted into a bottle in the manner described.

‡ Cf. *Elsie Venner,* chap. II.

near its point of suspension.* But in the dog each costal hoop is dragged straight downwards, into a vertical instead of a transverse ellipse, and is even narrowed to a point at the sternal border.

We may now proceed to consider and illustrate a few permutations or transformations of organic form, out of the vast multitude which are equally open to this method of enquiry.

We have already compared in a preliminary fashion the metacarpal or cannon-bone of the ox, the sheep, and the giraffe (fig. 3); and we have seen that the essential difference in form between these three bones is a matter of relative length and breadth, such that, if we reduce the figures to an identical standard of length (or identical values of y), the breadth (or value of x) will be approximately two-thirds that of the ox in the case of the sheep and one-third that of the ox in the case of the giraffe. We may easily, for the sake of closer comparison, determine these ratios more accurately, for instance, if it be our purpose to compare the different racial varieties within the limits of a single species. And in such cases, by the way, as when we compare with one another various breeds or races of cattle or of horses, the ratios of

length and breadth in this particular bone are extremely significant.[†]

If, instead of limiting ourselves to the cannon-bone, we inscribe the entire foot of our several Ungulates in a coordinate system, the same ratios of x that served us for the cannon-bones still give us a first approximation to the required comparison; but even in the case of such closely allied forms as the ox and the sheep there is evidently something wanting in the comparison. The reason is that the relative elongation of the several parts, or individual bones, has not proceeded equally or proportionately in all cases; in other words, that the equations for x will not suffice without some simultaneous modification of the values of y (fig. 16). In such a case it may be found possible to satisfy the varying values of y by some logarithmic or other formula; but, even if that be possible, it will probably be somewhat difficult of discovery or verification in such a case as the present, owing to the fact that we have too few well-marked points of correspondence between the one object and the other, and that especially along the shaft of such long bones as the cannon-bone of the ox, the deer, the llama, or the giraffe there is a complete lack of easily recognisable corresponding points. In such a case a brief tabular statement of apparently corresponding values of y, or of those obviously corresponding values which coincide with the boundaries of the several bones of the foot, will, as in the following

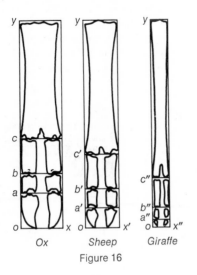

Ox   Sheep   Giraffe

Figure 16

---

* See T. P. Anderson Stuart, How the form of the thorax is partly determined by gravitation, *Proc. R.S.* XLIX, p. 143, 1891.

† This significance is particularly remarkable in connection with the development of speed, for the metacarpal region is the seat of very important leverage in the propulsion of the body. In a certain Scottish Museum there stand side by side the skeleton of an immense carthorse (celebrated for having drawn all the stones of the Bell Rock Lighthouse to the shore), and a beautiful skeleton of a racehorse, long supposed to be the actual skeleton of Eclipse. When I was a boy my grandfather used to point out to me that the cannon-bone of the little racer is not only relatively, but actually, longer than that of the great Clydesdale.

example, enable us to dispense with a fresh equation.

		a	b	c	d
y (Ox)	... 0	18	27	42	100
y' (Sheep)	... 0	10	19	36	100
y" (Giraffe)	... 0	5	10	24	100

This summary of values of y', coupled with the equations for the value of x, will enable us, from any drawing of the ox's foot, to construct a figure of that of the sheep or of the giraffe with remarkable accuracy.

That underlying the varying amounts of extension to which the parts or segments of the limb have been subject there is a law, or principle of continuity, may be discerned from such a diagram as fig. 17, where the values of y in the case of the ox are plotted as a straight line, and the corresponding values for the sheep (extracted from the table) are seen to form a more or less regular and even curve. This simple graphic result implies the existence of a comparatively simple equation between y and y'.

An elementary application of the principle of coordinates to the study of proportion, as we have here used it to illustrate the varying proportions of a bone, was in common use in the sixteenth and seventeenth centuries by artists in their study of the human form. The method is probably much more ancient, and may even be classical; it is fully described and put in practice by Albert Dürer in his *Geometry,* and especially in his *Treatise on Proportion.* In this latter work, the manner in which the human figure, features, and facial expres-

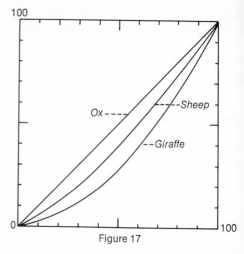

Figure 17

sion are all transformed and modified by slight variations in the relative magnitude of the parts is admirably and copiously illustrated (fig. 18).

In a tapir's foot there is a striking difference, and yet at the same time there is an obvious underlying resemblance, between the middle toe and either of its unsymmetrical lateral neighbours. Let us take the median terminal phalanx and inscribe its outline in a net of rectangular equidistant coordinates (fig. 19, *a*). Let us then make a similar network about axes which are no longer at right angles, but inclined to one another at an angle of about 50° (*b*). If into this new network we fill in, point for point, an outline precisely corresponding to our original drawing of the middle toe, we shall find that we have already represented the main

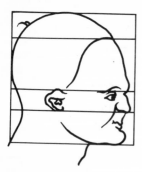 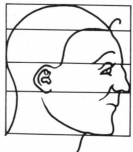 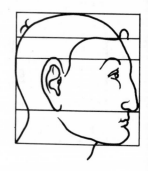

Figure 18. (After Albert Dürer.)

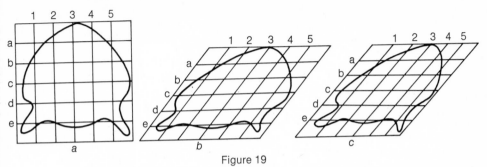

Figure 19

features of the adjacent lateral one. We shall, however, perceive that our new diagram looks a little too bulky on one side, the inner side, of the lateral toe. If now we substitute for our equidistant ordinates, ordinates which get gradually closer and closer together as we pass towards the median side of the toe, then we shall obtain a diagram which differs in no essential respect from an actual outline copy of the lateral toe (c). In short, the difference between the outline of the middle toe of the tapir and the next lateral toe may be almost completely expressed by saying that if the one be represented by rectangular equidistant coordinates, the other will be represented by oblique coordinates, whose axes make an angle of 50°, and in which the abscissal interspaces decrease in a certain logarithmic ratio. We treated our original complex curve or projection of the tapir's toe as a function of the form $F(x, y) = 0$. The figure of the tapir's lateral toe is a precisely identical function of the form $F(e^x, y_1) = 0$, where x_1, y_1 are oblique coordinate axes inclined to one another at an angle of 50°.

Dürer was acquainted with these oblique coordinates also, and I have copied two illustrative figures from his book.*

In fig. 21 I have sketched the common Copepod *Oithona nana*, and have inscribed it in a rectangular net, with abscissae three-fifths the length of the ordinates. Side by side (fig. 22) is drawn a very different Copepod,

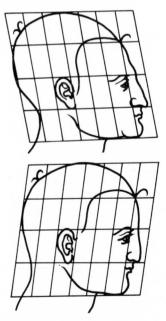

Figure 20. (After Albert Dürer.)

* It was these very drawings of Dürer's that gave to Peter Camper his notion of the "facial angle." Camper's method of comparison was the very same as ours, save that he only drew the axes, without filling in the network, of his coordinate system; he saw clearly the essential fact, that the skull *varies as a whole,* and that the "facial angle" is the index to a general deformation. "The great object was to shew that natural differences might be reduced to rules, of which the direction of the facial line forms the *norma* or canon; and that these directions and inclinations are always accompanied by correspondent form, size and position of the other parts of the cranium," etc.; from Dr T. Cogan's preface to Camper's work *On the Connexion between the Science of Anatomy and the Arts of Drawing, Painting and Sculpture* (1768?), quoted in Dr R. Hamilton's Memoir of Camper, in *Lives of Eminent Naturalists (Nat. Libr.),* Edinburgh, 1840.

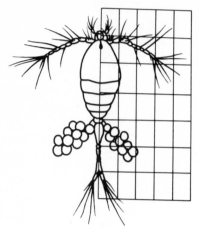

Figure 21. *Oithona nana.*

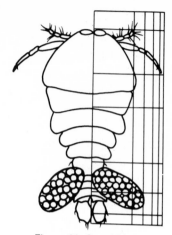

Figure 22. *Sapphirina.*

of the genus *Sapphirina*; and about it is drawn a network such that each coordinate passes (as nearly as possible) through points corresponding to those of the former figure. It will be seen that two differences are apparent. (1) The values of y in fig. 22 are large in the upper part of the figure, and diminish rapidly towards its base. (2) The values of x are very large in the neighbourhood of the origin, but diminish rapidly as we pass towards either side, away from the median vertical axis; and it is probable that they do so according to a definite, but somewhat complicated, ratio. If, instead of seeking for an actual equation, we simply tabulate our values of x and y in the second figure as compared with the first (just as we did in comparing the feet of the Ungulates), we get the dimensions of a net in which, by simply projecting the figure of *Oithona*, we obtain that of *Sapphirina* without further trouble, e.g.:

x (*Oithona*)	0	3	6	9	12	15	—
x' (*Sapphirina*)	0	8	10	12	13	14	—
y (*Oithona*)	0	5	10	15	20	25	30
y' (*Sapphirina*)	0	2	7	13	23	32	40

In this manner, with a single model or type to copy from, we may record in very brief space the data requisite for the production of approximate outlines of a great number of forms. For instance, the difference, at first sight immense, between the attenuated body of a *Caprella* and the thick-set body of a *Cyamus* is obviously little, and is probably nothing more than a difference of relative magnitudes, capable of tabulation by numbers and of complete expression by means of rectilinear coordinates.

The Crustacea afford innumerable instances of more complex deformations. Thus we may compare various higher Crustacea with one another, even in the case of such dissimilar forms as a lobster and a crab. It is obvious that the whole body of the former is elongated as compared with the latter, and that the crab is relatively broad in the region of the carapace, while it tapers off rapidly towards its attenuated and abbreviated tail. In a general way, the elongated rectangular system of coordinates in which we may inscribe the outline of the lobster becomes a shortened triangle in the case of the crab. In a little more detail we may compare the outline of the carapace in various crabs one with another: and the comparison will be found easy and significant, even, in many cases, down to minute details, such as the number and situation of the marginal spines, though these are in other cases subject to independent variability.

If we choose, to begin with, such a crab as *Geryon* (fig. 23, 1) and inscribe it in our equi-

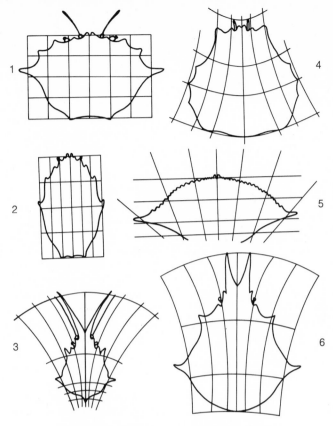

Figure 23. Carapaces of various crabs. 1, *Geryon;*
2, *Corystes;* 3, *Scyramathia;* 4, *Paralomis;* 5, *Lupa;*
6, *Chorinus.*

distant rectangular coordinates, we shall see that we pass easily to forms more elongated in a transverse direction, such as *Matuta* or *Lupa* (5), and conversely, by transverse compression, to such a form as *Corystes* (2). In certain other cases the carapace conforms to a triangular diagram, more or less curvilinear, as in fig. 23, 4, which represents the genus *Paralomis.* Here we can easily see that the posterior border is transversely elongated as compared with that of *Geryon,* while at the same time the anterior part is longitudinally extended as compared with the posterior. A system of slightly curved and converging ordinates, with orthogonal and logarithmically interspaced abscissal lines, as shewn in the figure, appears to satisfy the conditions.

In an interesting series of cases, such as the genus *Chorinus,* or *Scyramathia,* and in the spider-crabs generally, we appear to have just the converse of this. While the carapace of these crabs presents a somewhat triangular form, which seems at first sight more or less similar to those just described, we soon see that the actual posterior border is now narrow instead of broad, the broadest part of the carapace corresponding precisely, not to that which is broadest in *Paralomis,* but to that which was broadest in *Geryon;* while the most striking difference from the latter lies in an antero-posterior lengthening of the forepart of the carapace, culminating in a great elongation of the frontal region, with its two spines or "horns." The curved ordinates here converge posteriorly and diverge

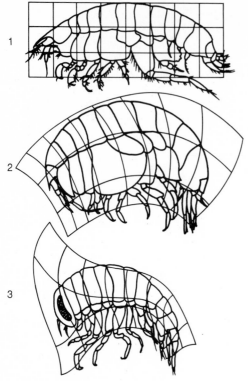

1

2

3

Figure 24. 1, *Harpinia plumosa* Kr.;
2, *Stegocephalus inflatus* Kr.; 3, *Hyperia galba.*

We put our method to a severer test when we attempt to sketch an entire and complicated animal than when we simply compare corresponding parts such as the carapaces of various Malacostraca, or related bones as in the case of the tapir's toes. Nevertheless, up to a certain point, the method stands the test very well. In other words, one particular mode and direction of variation is often (or even usually) so prominent and so paramount throughout the entire organism, that one comprehensive system of coordinates suffices to give a fair picture of the actual phenomenon. To take another illustration from the Crustacea, I have drawn roughly in fig. 24, 1 a little amphipod of the family Phoxocephalidae (*Harpinia* sp.). Deforming the coordinates of the figure into the curved orthogonal system in fig. 24, 2, we at once obtain a very fair representation of an allied genus, belonging to a different family of amphipods, namely *Stegocephalus*. As we proceed further from our type our coordinates will require greater deformation, and the resultant figure will usually be somewhat less accurate. In fig. 24, 3 I shew a network, to which, if we transfer our diagram of *Harpinia* or of *Stegocephalus*, we shall obtain a tolerable representation of the aberrant genus *Hyperia*, with its narrow abdomen, its reduced pleural lappets, its great eyes, and its inflated head.

widely in front (fig. 23, 3 and 6), while the decremental interspacing of the abscissae is very marked indeed.

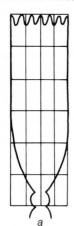
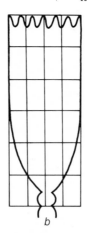
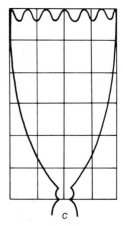

a
b
c

Figure 25. *a, Campanularia macroscyphus* Allm.; *b, Gonothyraea hyalina* Hincks; *c, Clytia Johnstoni* Alder.

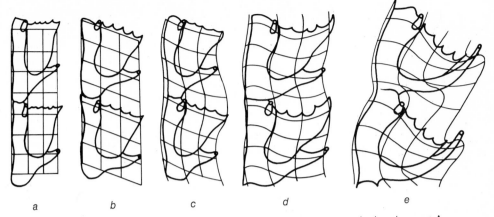

Figure 26. *a, Cladocarpus crenatus* F.; *b, Aglaophenia pluma* L.; *c, A. rhynchocarpa* A.; *d, A. cornuta* K.; *e, A. ramulosa* K.

The hydroid zoophytes constitute a "polymorphic" group, within which a vast number of species have already been distinguished; and the labours of the systematic naturalist are constantly adding to the number. The specific distinctions are for the most part based, not upon characters directly presented by the living animal, but upon the form, size and arrangement of the little cups, or "calycles," secreted and inhabited by the little individual polyps which compose the compound organism. The variations, which are apparently infinite, of these conformations are easily seen to be a question of relative magnitudes, and are capable of complete expression, sometimes by very simple, sometimes by somewhat more complex, coordinate networks.

For instance, the varying shapes of the simple wineglass-shaped cups of the Campanularidae are at once sufficiently represented and compared by means of simple Cartesian coordinates (fig. 25). In the two allied families of Plumulariidae and Aglaopheniidae the calycles are set unilaterally upon a jointed stem, and small cup-like structures (holding rudimentary polyps) are associated with the large calycles in definite number and position. These small calyculi are variable in number, but in the great majority of cases they accompany the large calycle in groups of three—two standing by

its upper border, and one, which is especially variable in form and magnitude, lying at its base. The stem is liable to flexure and, in a high degree, to extension or compression; and these variations extend, often on an exaggerated scale, to the related calycles. As a result we find that we can draw various systems of curved or sinuous coordinates, which express, all but completely, the configuration of the various hydroids which we inscribe therein (fig. 26). The comparative smoothness of denticulation of the margin of the calycle, and the number of its denticles, constitutes an independent variation, and requires separate description; we have already seen that this denticulation is in all probability due to a particular physical cause.

Among countless other invertebrate animals which we might illustrate, did space and time permit, we should find the bivalve molluscs shewing certain things extremely well. If we start with a more or less oblong shell, such as *Anodon* or *Mya* or *Psammobia*, we can see how easily it may be transformed into a more circular or orbicular, but still closely related form; while on the other hand a simple shear is well-nigh all that is needed to transform the oblong *Anodon* into the triangular, pointed *Mytilus, Avicula* or *Pinna*. Now suppose we draw the shell of *Anodon* in the usual rectangular coordinates, and deform this network into the corresponding oblique

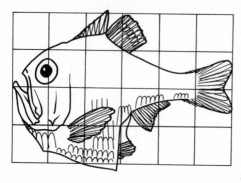

Figure 27. *Argyropelecus Olfersi.*

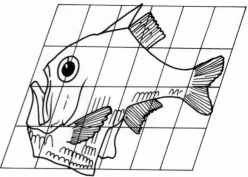

Figure 28. *Sternoptyx diaphana.*

coordinates of *Mytilus*, we may then proceed to draw within the same two nets the anatomy of the same two molluscs. Then of the two adductor muscles, coequal in *Anodon*, one becomes small, the other large, when transferred to the oblique network of *Mytilus*; at the same time the foot becomes stunted and the siphonal aperture enlarged. In short, having "transformed" one shell into the other we may perform an identical transformation on their contained anatomy: and so (provided the two are not too distantly related) deduce the bodily structure of the one from our knowledge of the other, to a first but by no means negligible approximation.

Among the fishes we discover a great variety of deformations, some of them of a very sim-

ple kind, while others are more striking and more unexpected. A comparatively simple case, involving a simple shear, is illustrated by figs. 27 and 28. The one represents, within Cartesian coordinates, a certain little oceanic fish known as *Argyropelecus Olfersi*. The other represents precisely the same outline, transferred to a system of oblique coordinates whose axes are inclined at an angle of 70°; but this is now (as far as can be seen on the scale of the drawing) a very good figure of an allied fish, assigned to a different genus, under the name of *Sternoptyx diaphana*. The deformation illustrated by this case of *Argyropelecus* is precisely analogous to the simplest and commonest kind of deformation to which fossils are subject as the result of shearing-stresses in the solid rock.

Fig. 29 is an outline diagram of a typical Scaroid fish. Let us deform its rectilinear

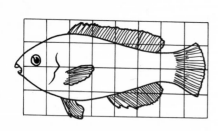

Figure 29. *Scarus* sp.

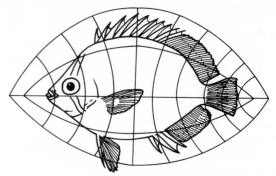

Figure 30. *Pomacanthus.*

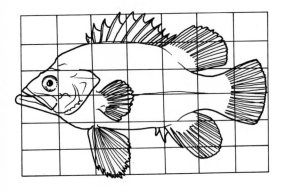

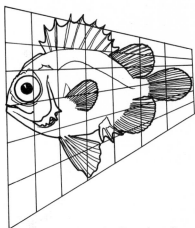

Figure 31. *Polyprion.*

Figure 32. *Pseudopriacanthus altus.*

coordinates into a system of (approximately) coaxial circles, as in fig. 30, and then filling into the new system, space by space and point by point, our former diagram of *Scarus*, we obtain a very good outline of an allied fish, belonging to a neighbouring family, of the genus *Pomacanthus.* This case is all the more interesting, because upon the body of our *Pomacanthus* there are striking colour bands, which correspond in direction very closely to the lines of our new curved ordinates. In like manner, the still more bizarre outlines of

other fishes of the same family of Chae-todonts will be found to correspond to very slight modifications of similar coordi-nates; in other words, to small variations in the values of the constants of the coaxial curves.

In figs. 31–34 I have represented another series of Acanthopterygian fishes, not very distantly related to the foregoing. If we start this series with the figure of *Polyprion*, in fig. 31, we see that the outlines of *Pseudopriacan-thus* (fig. 32) and of *Sebastes* or *Scorpaena* (fig.

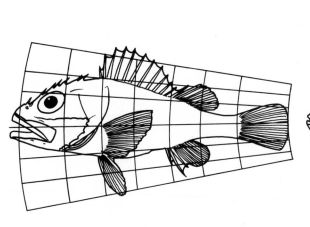

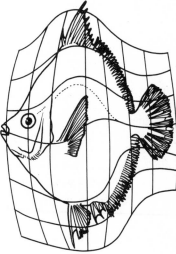

Figure 33. *Scorpaena* sp.

Figure 34. *Antigonia capros.*

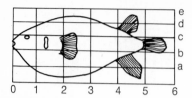

Figure 35. *Diodon.*

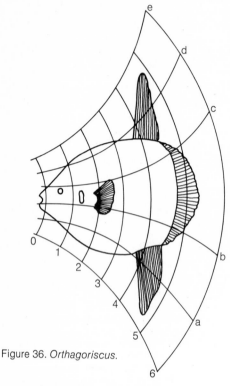

Figure 36. *Orthagoriscus.*

work, appears as a manifest representation of the closely allied, but very different looking, sunfish, *Orthagoriscus mola.* This is a particularly instructive case of deformation or transformation. It is true that, in a mathematical sense, it is not a perfectly satisfactory or perfectly regular deformation, for the system is no longer isogonal; but nevertheless, it is symmetrical to the eye, and obviously approaches to an isogonal system under certain conditions of friction or constraint. And as such it accounts, by one single integral transformation, for all the apparently separate and distinct external differences between the two fishes. It leaves the parts near to the origin of the system, the whole region of the head, the opercular orifice and the pectoral fin, practically unchanged in form, size and position; and it shews a greater and greater apparent modification of size and form as we pass from the origin towards the periphery of the system.

In a word, it is sufficient to account for the new and striking contour in all its essential details, of rounded body, exaggerated dorsal and ventral fins, and truncated tail. In like manner, and using precisely the same coordinate networks, it appears to me possible to shew the relations, almost bone for bone, of the skeletons of the two fishes; in other words, to reconstruct the skeleton of the one from our knowledge of the skeleton of the other, under the guidance of the same correspondence as is indicated in their external configuration.

33) are easily derived by substituting a system of triangular, or radial, coordinates for the rectangular ones in which we had inscribed *Polyprion.* The very curious fish *Antigonia capros,* an oceanic relative of our own boar-fish, conforms closely to the peculiar deformation represented in fig. 34.

Fig. 35 is a common, typical *Diodon* or porcupine-fish, and in fig. 36 I have deformed its vertical coordinates into a system of concentric circles, and its horizontal coordinates into a system of curves which, approximately and provisionally, are made to resemble a system of hyperbolas.* The old outline, transferred in its integrity to the new net-

The family of the crocodiles has had a special interest for the evolutionist ever since Huxley pointed out that, in a degree only second to the horse and its ancestors, it furnishes us with a close and almost unbroken series of transitional forms, running down in continu-

---

* The coordinate system of fig. 36 is somewhat different from that which I first drew and published. It is not unlikely that further investigation will further simplify the comparison, and shew it to involve a still more symmetrical system.

ous succession from one geological formation to another. I should be inclined to trans-
pose this general statement into other terms,
and to say that the Crocodilia constitute a
case in which, with unusually little complica-
tion from the presence of independent variants, the trend of one particular mode of
transformation is visibly manifested. If we exclude meanwhile from our comparison a few
of the oldest of the crocodiles, such as *Belo-
don*, which differ more fundamentally from
the rest, we shall find a long series of genera
in which we can refer not only the changing
contours of the skull, but even the shape and
size of the many constituent bones and their
intervening spaces or "vacuities," to one and
the same simple system of transformed coordinates. The manner in which the skulls of
various Crocodilians differ from one
another may be sufficiently illustrated by
three or four examples.

Let us take one of the typical modern
crocodiles as our standard of form, e.g. *C.
porosus*, and inscribe it, as in fig. 37, *a*, in the
usual Cartesian coordinates. By deforming
the rectangular network into a triangular
system, with the apex of the triangle a little
way in front of the snout, as in *b*, we pass to
such a form as *C. americanus*. By an exaggera-
tion of the same process we at once get an
approximation to the form of one of the
sharp-snouted, or longirostrine, crocodiles,
such as the genus *Tomistoma*; and, in the species figured, the oblique position of the orbits, the arched contour of the occipital border, and certain other characters suggest a
certain amount of curvature, such as I have
represented in the diagram (fig. 37, *b*), on the
part of the horizontal coordinates. In the still
more elongated skull of such a form as the
Indian Gavial, the whole skull has undergone a great longitudinal extension, or, in
other words, the ratio of x/y is greatly diminished; and this extension is not uniform, but
is at a maximum in the region of the nasal
and maxillary bones. This especially elongated region is at the same time narrowed in
an exceptional degree, and its excessive narrowing is represented by a curvature, convex
towards the median axis, on the part of the
vertical ordinates. Let us take as a last illustration one of the Mesozoic crocodiles, the
little *Notosuchus*, from the Cretaceous formation. This little crocodile is very different
from our type in the proportions of its skull.
The region of the snout, in front of and including the frontal bones, is greatly shortened; from constituting fully two-thirds of

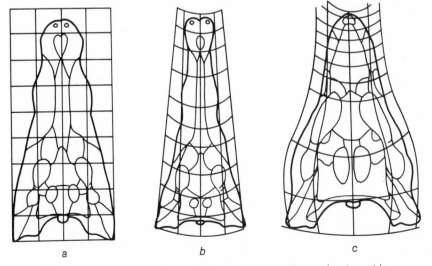

Figure 37. *a, Crocodilus porosus; b, C. americanus; c, Notosuchus terrestris.*

the whole length of the skull in *Crocodilus*, it now constitutes less than half, or, say, three-sevenths of the whole; and the whole skull, and especially its posterior part, is curiously compact, broad, and squat. The orbit is unusually large. If in the diagram of this skull we select a number of points obviously corresponding to points where our rectangular coordinates intersect particular bones or other recognisable features in our typical crocodile, we shall easily discover that the lines joining these points in *Notosuchus* fall into such a coordinate network as that which is represented in fig. 37, *c*. To all intents and purposes, then, this not very complex system, representing one harmonious "deformation," accounts for *all* the differences between the two figures, and is sufficient to enable one at any time to reconstruct a detailed drawing, bone for bone, of the skull of *Notosuchus* from the model furnished by the common crocodile.

The many diverse forms of Dinosaurian reptiles, all of which manifest a strong family likeness underlying much superficial diversity, furnish us with plentiful material for comparison by the method of transformations. As an instance, I have figured the pelvic bones of *Stegosaurus* and of *Camptosaurus* (fig. 38, *a*, *b*) to shew that, when the former is taken as our Cartesian type, a slight curva-

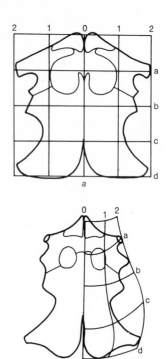

Figure 39. Shoulder-girdle of *Cryptocleidus*. *a*, young; *b*, adult.

ture and an approximately logarithmic extension of the *x*-axis brings us easily to the configuration of the other. In the original specimen of *Camptosaurus* described by Marsh,* the anterior portion of the iliac bone is missing; and in Marsh's restoration this part of the bone is drawn as though it came somewhat abruptly to a sharp point. In my figure I have completed this missing part of the bone in harmony with the general coordinate network which is suggested by our comparison of the two entire pelves; and I venture to think that the result is more natural in appearance, and more likely to be correct than was Marsh's conjectural restoration. It would seem, in fact, that there is an obvious field for the employment of the method of coordinates in this task of reproducing missing portions of a structure to the

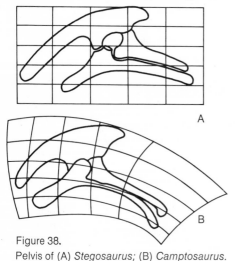

Figure 38.
Pelvis of (A) *Stegosaurus;* (B) *Camptosaurus.*

* *Dinosaurs of North America*, pl. LXXXI, etc., 1896.

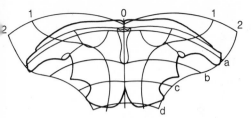

Figure 40. Shoulder-girdle of *Ichthyosaurus*.

proper scale and in harmony with related types. To this subject we shall presently return.

In fig. 39, *a, b*, I have drawn the shoulder-girdle of *Cryptocleidus*, a Plesiosaurian reptile, half-grown in the one case and full-grown in the other. The change of form during growth in this region of the body is very considerable, and its nature is well brought out by the two coordinate systems. In fig. 40 I have drawn the shoulder-girdle of an Ichthyosaur, referring it to *Cryptocleidus* as a standard of comparison. The interclavicle, which is present in *Ichthyosaurus*, is minute and hidden in *Cryptocleidus*; but the numerous other differences between the two forms, chief among which is the great elongation in *Ichthyosaurus* of the two clavicles, are all seen by our diagrams to be part and parcel of one general and systematic deformation.

Before we leave the group of reptiles we may glance at the very strangely modified skull of *Pteranodon*, one of the extinct flying reptiles, or Pterosauria. In this very curious

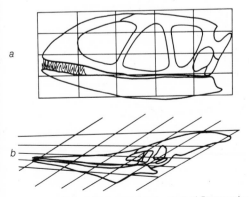

Figure 41. *a*, skull of *Dimorphodon*; *b*, skull of *Pteranodon*.

skull the region of the jaws, or beak, is greatly elongated and pointed; the occipital bone is drawn out into an enormous backwardly directed crest; the posterior part of the lower jaw is similarly produced backwards; the orbit is small; and the quadrate bone is strongly inclined downwards and forwards. The whole skull has a configuration which stands, apparently, in the strongest possible contrast to that of a more normal Ornithosaurian such as *Dimorphodon*. But if we inscribe the latter in Cartesian coordinates (fig. 41, *a*), and refer our *Pteranodon* to a system of oblique coordinates (*b*), in which the two coordinate systems of parallel lines become each a pencil of diverging rays, we make manifest a correspondence which extends uniformly throughout all parts of these very different-looking skulls.

We have dealt so far, and for the most part we shall continue to deal, with our coordinate method as a means of comparing one known structure with another. But it is obvious, as I have said, that it may also be employed for drawing hypothetical structures, on the assumption that they have varied from a known form in some definite way. And this process may be especially useful, and will be most obviously legitimate, when we apply it to the particular case of representing intermediate stages between two forms which are actually known to exist, in other words, of reconstructing the transitional stages through which the course of evolution must have successively travelled if it has brought about the change from some ancestral type to its presumed descendant. Some years ago I sent my friend, Mr Gerhard Heilmann of Copenhagen, a few of my own rough coordinate diagrams, including some in which the pelves of certain ancient and primitive birds were compared one with another. Mr Heilmann, who is both a skilled draughtsman and an able morphologist, returned me a set of diagrams which are a vast improvement on my own, and which are reproduced in figs. 42–47. Here we have, as ex-

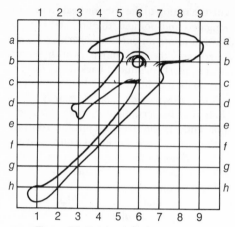

Figure 42. Pelvis of *Archaeopteryx*.

treme cases, the pelvis of *Archaeopteryx*, the most ancient of known birds, and that of *Apatornis*, one of the fossil "toothed" birds from the North American Cretaceous formations —a bird shewing some resemblance to the modern terns. The pelvis of *Archaeopteryx* is taken as our type, and referred accordingly to Cartesian coordinates (fig. 42); while the corresponding coordinates of the very different pelvis of *Apatornis* are represented in fig. 43. In fig. 44 the outlines of these two coordinate systems are superposed upon one another, and those of three intermediate and equidistant coordinate systems are interpolated between them. From each of these latter systems, so determined by direct interpolation, a complete coordinate diagram is drawn, and the corresponding outline of a pelvis is found from each of these systems of

coordinates, as in figs. 45, 46. Finally, in fig. 47 the complete series is represented, beginning with the known pelvis of *Archaeopteryx*, and leading up by our three intermediate hypothetical types to the known pelvis of *Apatornis*.

Among mammalian skulls I will take two illustrations only, one drawn from a comparison of the human skull with that of the higher apes, and another from the group of Perissodactyle Ungulates, the group which includes the rhinoceros, the tapir, and the horse.

Let us begin by choosing as our type the skull of *Hyrachyus agrarius* Cope, from the Middle Eocene of North America, as figured by Osborn in his Monograph of the Extinct Rhinoceroses* (fig. 48).

The many other forms of primitive rhinoceros described in the monograph differ from *Hyrachyus* in various details—in the characters of the teeth, sometimes in the number of the toes, and so forth; and they also differ very considerably in the general appearance of the skull. But these differences in the conformation of the skull, conspicuous as they are at first sight, will be found easy to bring under the conception of a simple and homogeneous transformation, such as would result from the application of some not very complicated stress. For instance, the corresponding coordinates of

* *Mem. Amer. Mus. of Nat. Hist.* I, III, 1898.

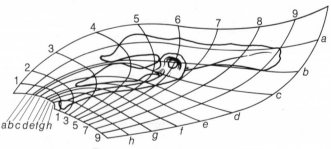

Figure 43. Pelvis of *Apatornis*.

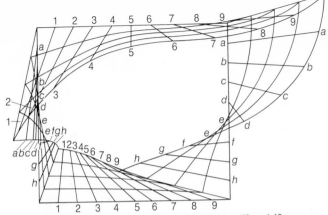

Figure 44. The coordinate systems of figures 42 and 43, with three intermediate systems interpolated.

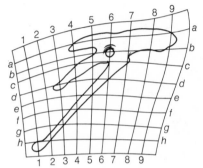

Figure 45. The first intermediate coordinate network, with its corresponding inscribed pelvis.

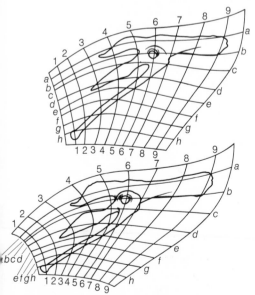

Figure 46. The second and third intermediate coordinate networks, with their corresponding inscribed pelves.

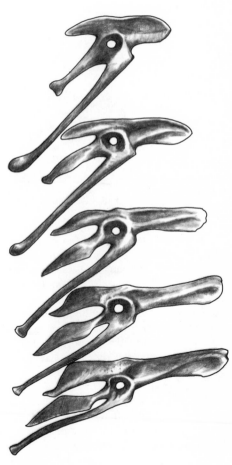

Figure 47. The pelvis of *Archaeopteryx* and of *Apatornis*, with three transitional types interpolated between them.

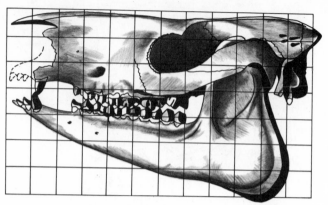

Figure 48. Skull of *Hyrachyus agrarius*. After Osborn.

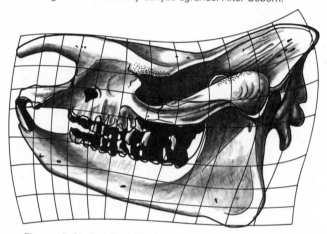

Figure 49. Skull of *Aceratherium tridactylum*. After Osborn.

Aceratherium tridactylum, as shewn in fig. 49, indicate that the essential difference between this skull and the former one may be summed up by saying that the long axis of the skull of *Aceratherium* has undergone a slight double curvature, while the upper parts of the skull have at the same time been subject to a vertical expansion, or to growth in somewhat greater proportion than the lower parts. Precisely the same changes, on a somewhat greater scale, give us the skull of an existing rhinoceros.

Among the species of *Aceratherium*, the posterior, or occipital, view of the skull presents specific differences which are perhaps more conspicuous than those furnished by the side view; and these differences are very strik-

ingly brought out by the series of conformal transformations which I have represented in fig. 50. In this case it will perhaps be noticed that the correspondence is not always quite accurate in small details. It could easily have been made much more accurate by giving a slightly sinuous curvature to certain of the coordinates. But as they stand, the correspondence indicated is very close, and the simplicity of the figures illustrates all the better the general character of the transformation.

By similar, and not more violent changes we pass easily to such allied forms as the Titanotheres (fig. 51); and the well-known series of species of *Titanotherium*, by which Professor Osborn has illustrated the evolu-

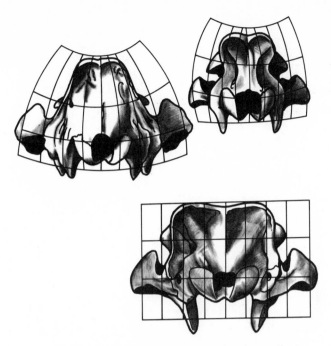

Figure 50. Occipital view of the skulls of various extinct rhinoceroses (*Aceratherium* spp.). After Osborn.

tion of this genus, constitutes a simple and suitable case for the application of our method.

But our method enables us to pass over greater gaps than these, and to discern the general, and to a very large extent even the detailed, resemblances between the skull of the rhinoceros and those of the tapir or the horse. From the Cartesian coordinates in which we have begun by inscribing the skull of a primitive rhinoceros, we pass to the tapir's skull (fig. 52), firstly, by converting the rectangular into a triangular network, by

which we represent the depression of the anterior and the progressively increasing elevation of the posterior part of the skull; and secondly, by giving to the vertical ordinates a curvature such as to bring about a certain longitudinal compression, or condensation, in the forepart of the skull, especially in the nasal and orbital regions.

The conformation of the horse's skull departs from that of our primitive Perissodactyle (that is to say our early type of rhinoceros, *Hyrachyus*) in a direction that is nearly the opposite of that taken by *Titanotherium*

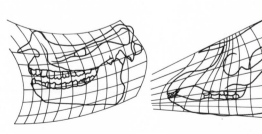

Figure 51. *Titanotherium robustum.*   Figure 52. Tapir's skull.

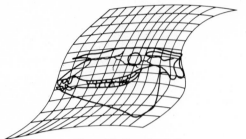

Figure 53. Horse's skull.

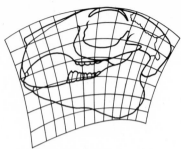

Figure 54. Rabbit's skull.

and by the recent species of rhinoceros. For we perceive, by fig. 53, that the horizontal coordinates, which in these latter cases become transformed into curves with the concavity upwards, are curved, in the case of the horse, in the opposite direction. And the vertical ordinates, which are also curved, somewhat in the same fashion as in the tapir, are very nearly equidistant, instead of being, as in that animal, crowded together anteriorly. Ordinates and abscissae form an oblique system, as is shewn in the figure. In this case I have attempted to produce the network beyond the region which is actually required to include the diagram of the

horse's skull, in order to shew better the form of the general transformation, with a part only of which we have actually to deal.

It is at first sight not a little surprising to find that we can pass, by a cognate and even simpler transformation, from our Perissodactyle skulls to that of the rabbit; but the fact that we can easily do so is a simple illustration of the undoubted affinity which exists between the Rodentia, especially the family of the Leporidae, and the more primitive Ungulates. For my part, I would go further; for I think there is strong reason to believe that the Perissodactyles are more closely

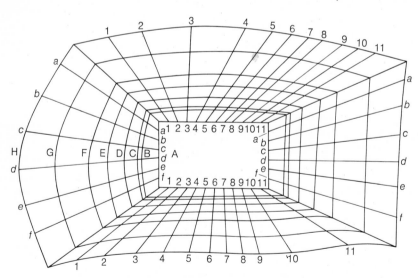

Figure 55. A, outline diagram of the Cartesian coordinates of the skull of *Hyracotherium* or *Eohippus*, as shewn in figure 56, A. H, outline of the corresponding projection of the horse's skull. B–G intermediate, or interpolated, outlines.

related to the Leporidae than the former are to the other Ungulates, or than the Leporidae are to the rest of the Rodentia. Be that as it may, it is obvious from fig. 54 that the rabbit's skull conforms to a system of coordinates corresponding to the Cartesian coordinates in which we have inscribed the skull of *Hyrachyus*, with the difference, firstly, that the horizontal ordinates of the latter are transformed into equidistant curved lines, approximately arcs of circles, with their concavity directed downwards; and secondly, that the vertical ordinates are transformed into a pencil of rays approximately orthogonal to the circular arcs. In short, the configuration of the rabbit's skull is derived from that of our primitive rhinoceros by the unexpectedly simple process of submitting the latter to a strong and uniform flexure in the downward direction (cf. fig. 48). In the case of the rabbit the configuration of the individual bones does not conform quite so well to the general transformation as it does when we are comparing the several Perissodactyles one with another; and the chief departures from conformity will be found in the size of the orbit and in the outline of the immediately surrounding bones. The simple fact is that the relatively enormous eye of the rabbit constitutes an independent variation, which cannot be brought into the general and fundamental transformation, but must be dealt with separately. The enlargement of the eye, like the modification in form and number of the teeth, is a separate phenomenon, which supplements but in no way contradicts our general comparison of the skulls taken in their entirety.

Before we leave the Perissodactyla and their allies, let us look a little more closely into the case of the horse and its immediate relations or ancestors, doing so with the help of a set of diagrams which I again owe to Mr Gerhard Heilmann.* Here we start afresh, with the skull (fig. 56, A) of *Hyracotherium* (or *Eohippus*), inscribed in a simple Cartesian network. At the other end of the series (H) is a skull

of *Equus*, in its own corresponding network; and the intermediate stages (B–G) are all drawn by direct and simple interpolation, as in Mr Heilmann's former series of drawings of *Archaeopteryx* and *Apatornis*. In this present case, the relative magnitudes are shewn, as well as the forms, of the several skulls. Alongside of these reconstructed diagrams are set figures of certain extinct "horses" (Equidae or Palaeotheriidae), and in two cases, viz. *Mesohippus* and *Protohippus* (M, P), it will be seen that the actual fossil skull coincides in the most perfect fashion with one of the hypothetical forms or stages which our method shews to be implicitly involved in the transition from *Hyracotherium* to *Equus*. In a third case, that of *Parahippus* (Pa), the correspondence (as Mr Heilmann points out) is by no means exact. The outline of this skull comes nearest to that of the hypothetical transition stage D, but the "fit" is now a bad one; for the skull of *Parahippus* is evidently a longer, straighter and narrower skull, and differs in other minor characters besides. In short, though some writers have placed *Parahippus* in the direct line of descent between *Equus* and *Eohippus*, we see at once that there is no place for it there, and that it must, accordingly, represent a somewhat divergent branch or offshoot of the Equidae.† It may be noticed, especially in the case of *Protohippus* (P), that the configuration of the angle of the jaw does not tally quite so accurately with that of our hypothetical diagrams as do

---

* These and also other coordinate diagrams will be found in Mr G. Heilmann's beautiful and original book *Fuglenes Afstamning*, 398 pp., Copenhagen, 1916; see especially pp. 368–380.

† Cf. W. B. Scott (*Amer. Journ. of Science*, XLVIII, pp. 335–374, 1894), "We find that any mammalian series at all complete, such as that of the horses, is remarkably continuous, and that the progress of discovery is steadily filling up what few gaps remain. So closely do successive stages follow upon one another that it is sometimes extremely difficult to arrange them all in order, and to distinguish clearly those members which belong in the main line of descent, and those which represent incipient branches. Some phylogenies actually suffer from an embarrassment of riches."

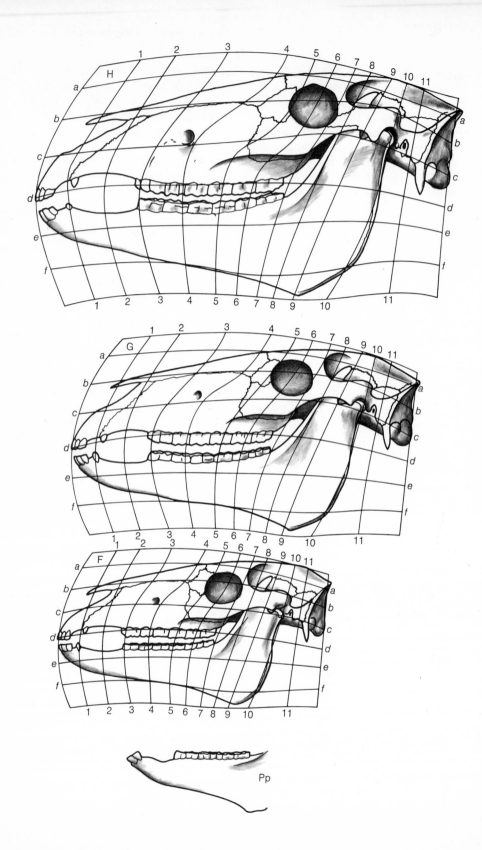

Pp

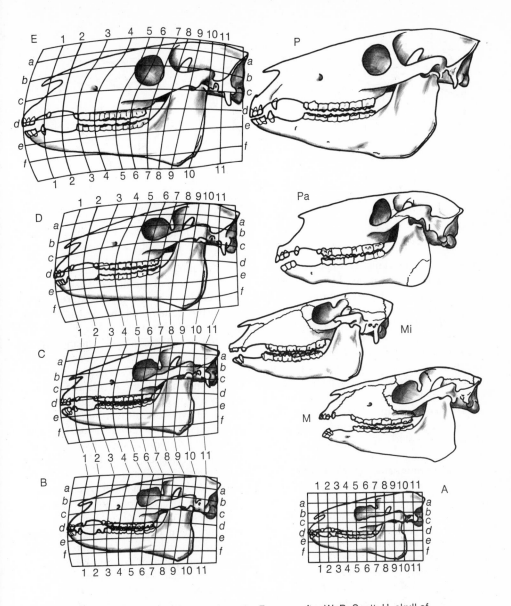

Figure 56. A, skull of *Hyracotherium,* from the Eocene, after W. B. Scott; H, skull of horse, represented as a coordinate transformation of that of *Hyracotherium,* and to the same scale of magnitude; B–G, various artificial or imaginary types, reconstructed as intermediate stages between A and H; M, skull of *Mesohippus,* from the Oligocene, after Scott, for comparison with C; P, skull of *Protohippus,* from the Miocene, after Cope, for comparison with E; Pp, lower jaw of *Protohippus placidus* (after Matthew and Gidley), for comparison with F; Mi, *Miohippus* (after Osborn), Pa, *Parahippus* (after Peterson), shewing resemblance, but less perfect agreement, with C and D.

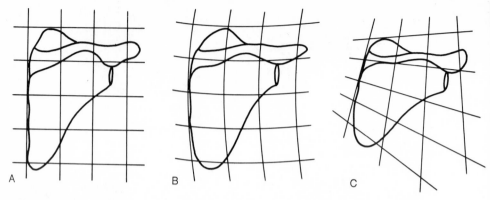

Figure 57. Human scapulae (after Dwight). A, Caucasian; B, Negro; C, North American Indian (from Kentucky Mountains).

other parts of the skull. As a matter of fact, this region is somewhat variable, in different species of a genus, and even in different individuals of the same species; in the small figure (Pp) of *Protohippus placidus* the correspondence is more exact.

In considering this series of figures we cannot but be struck, not only with the regularity of the succession of "transformations," but also with the slight and inconsiderable differences which separate each recorded stage from the next, and even the two extremes of the whole series from one another. These differences are no greater (save in regard to actual magnitude) than those between one human skull and another, at least if we take into account the older or remoter races; and they are again no greater, but if anything less, than the range of variation, racial and individual, in certain other human bones, for instance the scapula.*

The variability of this latter bone is great, but it is neither surprising nor peculiar; for it is linked with all the considerations of mechanical efficiency and functional modification which we dealt with in our last chapter. The scapula occupies, as it were, a focus in a very important field of force; and the lines of force converging on it will be very greatly modified by the varying development of the muscles over a large area of the body and of the uses to which they are habitually put.

Let us now inscribe in our Cartesian coordinates the outline of a human skull (fig. 58),

for the purpose of comparing it with the skulls of some of the higher apes. We know beforehand that the main differences between the human and the simian types depend upon the enlargement or expansion of the brain and brain-case in man, and the relative diminution or enfeeblement of his jaws. Together with these changes, the "facial angle" increases from an oblique angle to nearly a right angle in man, and the configuration of every constituent bone of the face and skull undergoes an alteration. We do not know to begin with, and we are not shewn by the ordinary methods of comparison, how far these various changes form part of one harmonious and congruent transformation, or whether we are to look, for instance, upon the changes undergone by the frontal, the occipital, the maxillary, and the mandibular regions as a congeries of separate modifications or independent variants. But as soon as we have marked out a number of points in the gorilla's or chimpanzee's skull, corresponding with those which our coordinate

* Cf. T. Dwight, The range of variation of the human scapula, *Amer. Nat.* XXI, pp. 627–638, 1887. Cf. also Turner, *Challenger Rep.* XLVII, on Human Skeletons, p. 86, 1886: "I gather both from my own measurements, and those of other observers, that the range of variation in the relative length and breadth of the scapula is very considerable in the same race, so that it needs a large number of bones to enable one to obtain an accurate idea of the mean of the race."

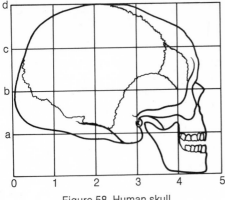

Figure 58. Human skull.

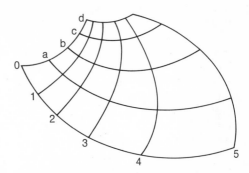

Figure 59. Coordinates of chimpanzee's skull, as a projection of the Cartesian coordinates of figure 58.

network intersected in the human skull, we find that these corresponding points may be at once linked up by smoothly curved lines of intersection, which form a new system of coordinates and constitute a simple "projection" of our human skull. The network represented in fig. 59 constitutes such a projection of the human skull on what we may call, figuratively speaking, the "plane" of the chimpanzee; and the full diagram in fig. 60 demonstrates the correspondence. In fig. 61 I have shewn the similar deformation in the case of a baboon, and it is obvious that the transformation is of precisely the same order, and differs only in an increased intensity or degree of deformation.* These anthropoid skulls, then, which we can transform one into another by a "continuous transformation," are admirable examples of what Listing called "topological similitude."

In both dimensions, as we pass from above downwards and from behind forwards, the corresponding areas of the network are seen to increase in a gradual and approximately logarithmic order in the lower as compared with the higher type of skull; and, in short, it becomes at once manifest that the modifications of jaws, brain-case, and the regions between are all portions of one continuous and integral process. It is of course easy to draw the inverse diagrams, by which the Cartesian

---

* The empirical coordinates which I have sketched in for the chimpanzee as a conformal transformation of the Cartesian coordinates of the human skull look as if they might find their place in an equipotential elliptic field. They are indeed closely analogous to some already figured by MM. Y. Ikada and M. Kuwaori, Some conformal representations by means of the elliptic integrals, *Sci. Papers Inst. Phys. Research, Tokyo*, XXVI, pp. 208–215, 1936: e.g. pl. XXXI*b*.

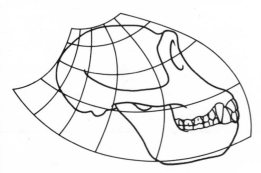

Figure 60. Skull of chimpanzee.

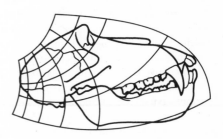

Figure 61. Skull of baboon.

coordinates of the ape are transformed into curvilinear and non-equidistant coordinates in man.*

From this comparison of the gorilla's or chimpanzee's with the human skull we realise that an inherent weakness underlies the anthropologist's method of comparing skulls by reference to a small number of axes. The most important of these are the "facial" and "basicranial" axes, which include between them the "facial angle." But it is, in the first place, evident that these axes are merely the principal axes of a system of coordinates, and that their restricted and isolated use neglects all that can be learned from the filling in of the rest of the coordinate network. And, in the second place, the "facial axis," for instance, as ordinarily used in the anthropological comparison of one human skull with another, or of the human skull with the gorilla's, is in all cases treated as a straight line; but our investigation has shewn that rectilinear axes only meet the case in the simplest and most closely related transformations; and that, for instance, in the anthropoid skull no rectilinear axis is homologous with a rectilinear axis in a man's skull, but what is a straight line in the one has become a certain definite curve in the other.

Mr Heilmann tells me that he has tried, but without success, to obtain a transitional series between the human skull and some prehuman, anthropoid type, which series (as in the case of the Equidae) should be found to contain other known types in direct linear sequence. It appears impossible, however, to obtain such a series, or to pass by successive and continuous gradations through such forms as Mesopithecus, Pithecanthropus, *Homo neanderthalensis*, and the lower or higher races of modern man. The failure is not the fault of our method. It merely indicates that no one straight line of descent, or of consecutive transformation, exists; but on the contrary, that among human and anthropoid types, recent and extinct, we have to do with a complex problem of divergent, rather than of continuous, variation. And in like manner, easy as it is to correlate the ba-

boon's and chimpanzee's skulls severally with that of man, and easy as it is to see that the chimpanzee's skull is much nearer to the human type than is the baboon's, it is also not difficult to perceive that the series is not, strictly speaking, continuous, and that neither of our two apes lies *precisely* on the same direct line or sequence of deformation by which we may hypothetically connect the other with man.

After easily transforming our coordinate diagram of the human skull into a corresponding diagram of ape or of baboon, we may effect a further transformation of man or monkey into dog no less easily; and we are thereby encouraged to believe that any two mammalian skulls may be compared with, or transformed into, one another by this method. There is something, an essential and indispensable something, which is common to them all, something which is the subject of all our transformations, and remains *invariant* (as the mathematicians say) under them all. In these transformations of ours every point may change its place, every line its curvature, every area its magnitude; but on the other hand every point and every line continues to exist, and keeps its relative order and position throughout all distortions and transformations. A series of points, a, b, c, along a certain line persist as corresponding points a', b', c', however the line connecting them may lengthen or bend; and as with points, so with lines, and so also with areas. Ear, eye and nostril, and all the other great landmarks of cranial anatomy, not only continue to exist but retain their relative order and position throughout all our transformations.

---

* Speaking of "diagrams in pairs," and doubtless thinking of his own "reciprocal diagrams," Clerk Maxwell says (in his article *Diagrams* in the *Encyclopaedia Britannica*): "The method in which we simultaneously contemplate two figures, and recognise a correspondence between certain points in the one figure and certain points in the other, is one of the most powerful and fertile methods hitherto known in science . . . It is sometimes spoken of as the method or principle of duality."

We can discover a certain *invariance*, somewhat more restricted than before, between the mammalian skull and that of fowl, frog or even herring. We have still something common to them all; and using another mathematical term (somewhat loosely perhaps) we may speak of the *discriminant characters* which persist unchanged, and continue to form the subject of our transformation. But the method, far as it goes, has its limitations. We cannot fit both beetle and cuttlefish into the same framework, however we distort it; nor by any coordinate transformation can we turn either of them into one another or into the vertebrate type. They are essentially different; there is nothing about them which can be legitimately compared. Eyes they all have, and mouth and jaws; but what we call by these names are no longer in the same order or relative position; they are no longer the same thing, there is no *invariant* basis for transformation. The cuttlefish eye seems as perfect, optically, as our own; but the lack of an invariant relation of position between them, or lack of true homology between them (as we naturalists say), is enough to shew that they are unrelated things, and have come into existence independently of one another.

As a final illustration I have drawn the outline of a dog's skull (fig. 62), and inscribed it in a network comparable with the Cartesian network of the human skull in fig. 58. Here we attempt to bridge over a wider gulf than we have crossed in any of our former comparisons. But, nevertheless, it is obvious that our method still holds good, in spite of the fact that there are various specific differences, such as the open or closed orbit, etc., which have to be separately described and accounted for. We see that the chief essential differences in plan between the dog's skull and the man's lie in the fact that, relatively speaking, the former tapers away in front, a triangular taking the place of a rectangular conformation; secondly, that, coincident with the tapering off, there is a progressive elongation, or pulling out, of the whole forepart of the skull; and lastly, as a minor difference, that the straight vertical ordinates of the human skull become curved, with their convexity directed forwards, in the dog. While the net result is that in the dog, just as in the chimpanzee, the brain-pan is smaller and the jaws are larger than in man, it is now conspicuously evident that the coordinate network of the ape is by no means intermediate between those which fit the other two. The mode of deformation is on different lines; and, while it may be correct to say that the chimpanzee and the baboon are more brute-like, it would be by no means accurate to assert that they are more dog-like, than man.

In this brief account of coordinate transformations and of their morphological utility I have dealt with plane coordinates only, and have made no mention of the less elementary subject of coordinates in three-dimensional space. In theory there is no difficulty whatso-

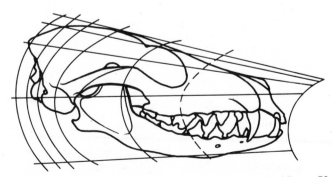

Figure 62. Skull of dog, compared with the human skull of figure 58.

ever in such an extension of our method; it is just as easy to refer the form of our fish or of our skull to the rectangular coordinates x, y, z, or to the polar coordinates ξ, η, ζ, as it is to refer their plane projections to the two axes to which our investigation has been confined. And that it would be advantageous to do so goes without saying, for it is the shape of the solid object, not that of the mere drawing of the object, that we want to understand; and already we have found some of our easy problems in solid geometry leading us (as in the case of the form of the bivalve and even of the univalve shell) quickly in the direction of coordinate analysis and the theory of conformal transformations. But this extended theme I have not attempted to pursue, and it must be left to other times, and to other hands. Nevertheless, let us glance for a moment at the sort of simple cases, the simplest possible cases, with which such an investigation might begin; and we have found our plane coordinate systems so easily and effectively applicable to certain fishes that we may seek among them for our first and tentative introduction to the three-dimensional field.

It is obvious enough that the same method of description and analysis which we have applied to one plane, we may apply to another: drawing by observation, and by a process of trial and error, our various cross-sections and the coordinate systems which seem best to correspond. But the new and important problem which now emerges is to *correlate* the deformation or transformation which we discover in one plane with that which we have observed in another: and at length, perhaps, after grasping the general principles of such correlation, to forecast approximately what is likely to take place in the third dimension when we are acquainted with two, that is to say, to determine the values along one axis in terms of the other two.

Let us imagine a common "round" fish, and a common "flat" fish, such as a haddock and a plaice. These two fishes are not as nicely adapted for comparison by means of plane coordinates as some which we have studied, owing to the presence of essentially

unimportant, but yet conspicuous differences in the position of the eyes, or in the number of the fins—that is to say in the manner in which the continuous dorsal fin of the plaice appears in the haddock to be cut or scolloped into a number of separate fins. But speaking broadly, and apart from such minor differences as these, it is manifest that the chief factor in the case (so far as we at present see) is simply the broadening out of the plaice's body, as compared with the haddock's, in the dorso-ventral direction, that is to say, along the y axis; in other words, the ratio x/y is much less (and indeed little more than half as great) in the haddock than in the plaice. But we also recognise at once that while the plaice (as compared with the haddock) is expanded in one direction, it is also flattened, or thinned out, in the other: y increases, but z diminishes, relatively to x. And furthermore, we soon see that this is a common or even a general phenomenon. The high, expanded body in our Antigonia or in our sun-fish or in a John Dory is at the same time flattened or *compressed* from side to side, in comparison with the related fishes which we have chosen as standards of reference or comparison; and conversely, such a fish as the skate, while it is expanded from side to side in comparison with a shark or dogfish, is at the same time flattened or *depressed* in its vertical section. We hasten to enquire whether there be any simple relation of *magnitude* discernible between these twin factors of expansion and compression; and the very fact that the two dimensions of breadth and depth tend to vary inversely assures us that, in the general process of deformation, the volume and the area of cross-section are less affected than are those two linear dimensions. Some years ago, when I was studying the weight-length coefficient in fishes, that is to say the coefficient k in the formula $W = kL^3$, I was not a little surprised to find that k (let us call it in this case k_1) was all but identical in two such different looking fishes as the haddock and the plaice: thus indicating that these two fishes have approximately the same *volume* when they are equal in *length*; or, in other words, that the extent to which the plaice has broadened is *just about compensated for* by the extent to which it has also got flattened or thinned. In short, if we might conceive of a haddock being transformed directly into a plaice, a very large part of the change would be accounted for by supposing the round fish to be "rolled out" into the flat one, as a baker rolls a piece of dough. This is, as it were, an extreme case of the *balancement des organes*, or "compensation of parts."

We must not forget, while we consider the "deformation" of a fish, that the fish, like the bird, is subject to certain strict limitations of form. What we happen to have found in a particular case was observed fifty years ago, and brought under a general rule, by a naval engineer studying fishes from the shipbuilder's point of view. Mr Parsons* compared the contours and the sectional areas of a number of fishes and of several whales; and he found the sectional areas to be always very much the same at the same proportional distances from the front end of the body.† Increase in depth was balanced (as we also have found) by diminution of breadth; and the magnitude of the "entering angle" presented to the water by the advancing fish was fairly constant. Moreover, according to Parsons, the position of the greatest cross-section is fixed for all species, being situated at 36 per cent. of the length behind the snout. We need not stop to consider such extreme cases as the eel or the globefish (*Diodon*), whose ways of propulsion and locomotion are materially modified. But it is certainly curious that no sooner do we try to correlate deformation in one direction with deformation in another, than we are led towards a broad generalisation, touching on hydrodynamical conditions and the limitations of form and structure which are imposed thereby.

Our simple, or simplified, illustrations carry us but a little way, and only half prepare us for much harder things. But interesting as the whole subject is we must meanwhile leave it alone; recognising, however, that if the difficulties of description and representation could be overcome, it is by means of such coordinates in space that we should at last obtain an adequate and satisfying picture of the processes of deformation and the directions of growth.

A note on pattern

We have had so much to do with the study of Form that *pattern* has been well-nigh left out of the account, although it is part of the same story. Like any other aspect of form, pattern is correlated with growth, and even determined by it. A feather, for example, which is equally and equidistantly striped to begin with, may have this simple striping transformed into a more complex pattern by the unequal but *graded* elongation of the feather. We need not go farther than the zebra for a characteristic pattern of stripes, nor need we seek a better illustration of how a common pattern may vary in related species.

A zebra's stripes may be broad or narrow, uniform or alternately dark and pale—these are minor or secondary diversities; but the pattern of the stripes shews more conspicuous differences than these, though the differences remain of a simple kind. A zebra's stripes fall into several series. One set covers the neck, including the mane, and extends backwards over the body and forwards on to the face; and these "body-stripes" are all that the extinct Quagga possessed. On the head they are interrupted by the ears and eyes, and end at a definite vertex on the forehead: from which, however, they run down the face in pairs, of which the first pair of all may or may not coalesce into a single median stripe

---

* H. de B. Parsons, Displacements and area-curves of fish, *Trans. Amer. Soc. of Mechan. Engineers*, IX, pp. 679–695, 1888.

† That is to say, if the areas of cross-section be plotted against their distances from the front end of the body, the results are very much alike for all the species examined. See also Selig Hecht, Form and growth in fishes, *Journ. Morph.* XXVII, pp. 379–400, 1916.

Figure 63. Zebra's head, to shew how the body-stripes extend to the face. From A. Rzasnicki.

(fig. 63). A second series runs up the foreleg, and where it meets the body we have the problem of how best to fit the horizontal leg-stripes and the vertical body-stripes together. There is only one way. A pair of body-stripes diverge apart and the upper leg-stripes fit in between, becoming at the same time chevron-shaped so as to adapt themselves to the space they have come to occupy. The stripes of the forelegs, and their manner of fitting on to the body-stripes, vary very little in the several species or varieties.

A third series of stripes ascends the hindlegs, in a fashion identical to begin with for all, but open to modification where these leg-stripes spread over the haunches; for here there may be great differences in the extent to which the leg-stripes compete with and interfere with, or (so to speak) encroach upon, the stripes of the body. The typical *Equus zebra* is easily recognised by the so-called "gridiron" on its rump; this is a dorsal continuation of the body-stripes, extending to the tail, but sharply cut off on either side by the stripes ascending from the leg (fig. 64, C). In Burchell's zebra the hindleg-stripes encroach still farther on the body, and even reach up to the rump, so that the gridiron is entirely cut away.* In the Abyssinian *Equus Grevyi*, all the stripes are very numerous, narrow and close-set. The body-stripes refuse, as

it were, to be encroached on or obliterated by those of the hindlegs; which latter are merely intercalated between them, chevron fashion, wedging in between the body-stripes as the foreleg-stripes are wont to do. It follows that in the middle of the haunch, over the region of the hip-joint, there is in this species a characteristic "focus," where the leg-stripes fit in between the lumbar and the caudal sections of the body-stripes. We may now add, as a fourth and last series, common to all kinds, the few stripes which surround the lips on either side, and wedge in between the stripes upon the face.

Conclusion

There is one last lesson which coordinate geometry helps us to learn; it is simple and easy, but very important indeed. In the study of evolution, and in all attempts to trace the descent of the animal kingdom, fourscore years' study of the *Origin of Species* has had an unlooked-for and disappointing result. It was hoped to begin with, and within my own recollection it was confidently believed, that the broad lines of descent, the relation of the main branches to one another and to the trunk of the tree, would soon be settled, and the lesser ramifications would be unravelled bit by bit and later on. But things have turned out otherwise. We have long known, in more or less satisfactory detail, the pedigree of horses, elephants, turtles, crocodiles and some few more; and our conclusions tally as to these, again more or less to our satisfaction, with the direct evidence of palaeonto-

---

* Ward's zebra and Grant's zebra are varieties of *Equus zebra*, the former with a very strong "gridiron," the latter with a mere vestige of the same: which is as much as to say that the leg-stripes encroach little in the one, and much in the other, on the hindmost body-stripes. Chapman's zebra is a form of *E. Burchelli*, with well-striped legs and faint intermediate striping. Cf. W. Ridgeway, on The differentiation of the three species of Zebra, *P.Z.S.* 1909, pp. 547–563; also (*int. al.*) Adolf Rzasnicki, *Zebry*, Warsaw, 1931.

logical succession. But the larger and at first sight simpler questions remain unanswered; for eighty years' study of Darwinian evolution has not taught us how birds descend from reptiles, mammals from earlier quadrupeds, quadrupeds from fishes, nor vertebrates from the invertebrate stock. The invertebrates themselves involve the selfsame difficulties, so that we do not know the origin of the echinoderms, of the molluscs, of the coelenterates, nor of one group of protozoa from another. The difficulty is not always quite the same. We may fail to find the actual links between the vertebrate groups, but yet their resemblance and their relationship, real though indefinable, are plain to see; there are gaps between the groups, but we can see, so to speak, across the gap. On the other hand, the breach between vertebrate and invertebrate, worm and coelenterate, coelenterate and protozoon, is in each case of another order, and is so wide that we cannot see across the intervening gap at all.

This failure to solve the cardinal problem of evolutionary biology is a very curious thing; and we may well wonder why the long pedigree is subject to such breaches of continuity. We used to be told, and were content to believe, that the old record was of necessity imperfect—we could not expect it to be otherwise; the story was hard to read because every here and there a page had been lost or torn away, like some *hiatus valde deflendus* in an ancient manuscript. But there is a deeper reason. When we begin to draw comparisons between our algebraic curves and attempt to

Figure 64. Zebra patterns. A, B, *Equus Burchelli;* C, *E. zebra;* D, *E. Grevyi.*

transform one into another, we find ourselves limited by the very nature of the case to curves having some tangible degree of relation to one another; and these "degrees of relationship" imply a *classification* of mathematical forms, analogous to the classification of plants or animals in another part of the *Systema Naturae*.

An algebraic curve has its fundamental formula, which defines the family to which it belongs; and its parameters, whose quantitative variation admits of infinite variety within the limits which the formula prescribes. With some extension of the meaning of parameters, we may say the same of the families, or genera, or other classificatory groups of plants and animals. We cross a boundary every time we pass from family to family, or group to group. The passage is easy at first, and we are led, *along definite lines*, to more and more subtle and elegant comparisons. But we come in time to forms which, though both may still be simple, yet stand so far apart that direct comparison is no longer legitimate. We never think of "transforming" a helicoid into an ellipsoid, or a circle into a frequency-curve. So it is with the forms of animals. We *cannot* transform an invertebrate into a vertebrate, nor a coelenterate into a worm, by any simple and legitimate deformation, nor by anything short of reduction to elementary principles.

A "principle of discontinuity," then, is inherent in all our classifications, whether mathematical, physical or biological; and the infinitude of possible forms, always limited, may be further reduced and discontinuity further revealed by imposing conditions — as, for example, that our parameters must be

whole numbers, or proceed by *quanta*, as the physicists say. The lines of the spectrum, the six families of crystals, Dalton's atomic law, the chemical elements themselves, all illustrate this principle of discontinuity. In short, nature proceeds *from one type to another* among organic as well as inorganic forms; and these types vary according to their own parameters, and are defined by physico-mathematical conditions of possibility. In natural history Cuvier's "types" may not be perfectly chosen nor numerous enough, but *types* they are; and to seek for stepping-stones across the gaps between is to seek in vain, for ever.

This is no argument against the theory of evolutionary descent. It merely states that formal resemblance, which we depend on as our trusty guide to the affinities of animals within certain bounds or grades of kinship and propinquity, ceases in certain other cases to serve us, because under certain circumstances it ceases to exist. Our geometrical analogies weigh heavily against Darwin's conception of endless small continuous variations; they help to show that discontinuous variations are a natural thing, that "mutations" — or sudden changes, greater or less — are bound to have taken place, and new "types" to have arisen, now and then. Our argument indicates, if it does not prove, that such mutations, occurring on a comparatively few definite lines, or plain alternatives, of physico-mathematical possibility, are likely to repeat themselves: that the "higher" protozoa, for instance, may have sprung not from or through one another, but severally from the simpler forms; or that the worm-type, to take another example, may have come into being again and again.

Religion within the Limits
of Reason Alone

Immanuel Kant

Editor's Introduction

Kant's concern for religion falls into two clearly marked periods: First, his early upbringing at home and preliminary schooling up until the time he entered the university at the age of sixteen; then, some fifty years later, an interval at the end of his life, after he had achieved great fame as the author of his three *Critiques*. During the long intervening period he showed little concern for religion and its problems, although the results of his work were indeed heavy for religious thought and practice.

Immanuel Kant was born on April 22, 1724, at Königsberg in East Prussia (since 1946 a part of the Soviet Union), and he remained in that remote province throughout his entire life. His parents were poor, but good simple people, adherents of the Pietist branch of the Lutheran church, which taught that religion belongs to the inner life, is expressed in devotion and the desire for spiritual and emotional rebirth, and demands steadfast observance of the moral law. The young Kant's intellectual abilities so impressed their pastor that he made it possible for the boy at the age of eight to enter the Pietist school. This was a Latin school that provided a good general education with heavy emphasis upon the study of the Bible. Its effect on Kant was antipathetic. By the time he was adolescent, he had come to find painful the devotional services that were required, especially the display of religious emotion, and after leaving the school he refused to have anything more to do with prayer and hymn singing for the rest of his life.

In 1740 Kant entered the University of Königsberg. Although nominally enrolled in the faculty of theology, he took few courses in that subject, turning his attention mainly to mathematics, physics, and the rationalist philosophy whose professors were actively arguing against their Pietist opponents. Amid such intellectual ferment, Kant decided to follow an academic career. The death of his father in 1746 compelled him to interrupt his studies and to support himself, which he did for some nine years as a private tutor. But in 1755 he was able to return to the university. He completed his degree, took up the position of privatdocent (lecturer), and began the career of teaching and writing that established him as Germany's leading philosopher and one of the most influential minds of all time.

Among his major writings, the *Critique of Pure Reason* appeared in 1781, the *Critique of Practical Reason* in 1788, and the *Critique of Judgement* in 1790.

Although not expressly concerned with religion, they were viewed by many as undermining its rational foundations. In the first, Kant claimed to have demolished the cogency and shown the impossibility of any rational proofs for the existence of God, the freedom of the will, and the immortality of the soul; in the third, he attacked the teleological argument from design. As a result, he came to be called the "Allzermalmende" (All-destroyer). Kant remained undisturbed, however, for he was confident that in the second *Critique* he had provided the only possible proofs for God, freedom, and immortality by showing that they are indispensable postulates for the moral life.

The religious repercussion of these works may well have contributed to his turning his attention to the idea of religion. He began to give lectures on the philosophy of religion and then in 1791 submitted for publication the first portion of *Religion within the Limits of Reason Alone*, which was his last major work. The considerable freedom of expression that Prussia had experienced under Frederick the Great had ended in 1786 with his death and the accession of Frederick William II. Censorship was established for all publications to ensure that they did not deviate from the teachings of the Bible. The first book of the *Religion* was granted the required permission as being mainly philosophical and directed only to scholars. But when Kant went on to submit the second book, he was met with a flat refusal on the ground that the work clearly contradicted the Bible. To evade the Berlin censors, Kant, on completing the next two books, presented the three books to the faculty at the University of Jena, which had the power to authorize for publication books on religion. With their imprimatur, he then published the entire work in four books at Königsberg in 1793. The king responded with a personal letter to Kant criticizing his "misuse of philosophy" and demanding that he give no further cause for such offense. Kant responded by promising to refrain henceforth from making any public statements about religion. He interpreted this as a personal promise to the king alone, however, and on the latter's death in 1797 he felt free to publish again on matters of religion. The next year he published the last major essay of his life, "The Conflict of the Faculties." This is a polemical work that criticizes the claim of the theological faculty in the universities to exercise a censoring authority over the teaching and researches of the other faculties. In effect, it was an application to the then current university situation of the teaching contained in the *Religion*.

Religion within the Limits of Reason Alone consists of four books. Kant's reputation as perhaps the most eminent representative of one of the most basic theories of religion rests mainly on Book Three. That book is reprinted here in the translation of Theodore M. Green and Hoyt H. Hudson, with the permission of the Open Court Publishing Company.

Religion within the Limits of Reason Alone

Book Three

The Victory of the Good over the Evil Principle, and the Founding of a Kingdom of God on Earth

The combat which every morally well-disposed man must sustain in this life, under the leadership of the good principle, against the attacks of the evil principle, can procure him, however much he exerts himself, no greater advantage than freedom from the *sovereignty* of evil. To become *free*, "to be freed from bondage under the law of sin, to live for righteousness"*—this is the highest prize he can win. He continues to be exposed, none the less, to the assaults of the evil principle; and in order to assert his freedom, which is perpetually being attacked, he must ever remain armed for the fray.

Now man is in this perilous state through his own fault; hence he is *bound* at the very least to strive with all his might to extricate himself from it. But how? That is the question. When he looks around for the causes and circumstances which expose him to this danger and keep him in it, he can easily convince himself that he is subject to these not because of his own gross nature, so far as he is here a separate individual, but because of mankind to whom he is related and bound. It is not at the instigation of the former that what should properly be called the *passions*, which cause such havoc in his original good predisposition, are aroused. His needs are but few and his frame of mind in providing for them is temperate and tranquil. He is poor (or considers himself so) only in his anxiety lest other men consider him poor and despise him on that account. Envy, the lust for power, greed, and the malignant inclinations bound up with these, be-

siege his nature, contented within itself, *directly he is among men*. And it is not even necessary to assume that these are men sunk in evil and examples to lead him astray; it suffices that they are at hand, that they surround him, and that they are men, for them mutually to corrupt each other's predispositions and make one another evil. If no means could be discovered for the forming of an alliance uniquely designed as a protection against this evil and for the furtherance of goodness in man—of a society, enduring, ever extending itself, aiming solely at the maintenance of morality, and counteracting evil with united forces—this association with others would keep man, however much, as a single individual, he may have done to throw off the sovereignty of evil, incessantly in danger of falling back under its dominion. As far as we can see, therefore, the sovereignty of the good principle is attainable, so far as men can work toward it, only through the establishment and spread of a society in accordance with, and for the sake of, the laws of virtue, a society whose task and duty it is rationally to impress these laws in all their scope upon the entire human race. For only thus can we hope for a victory of the good over the evil principle. In addition to prescribing laws to each individual, morally legislative reason also unfurls a banner of virtue as a rallying point for all who love the

---

* Cf. Romans 6 : 18: "Being then made free from sin, ye became the servants of righteousness."

good, that they may gather beneath it and thus at the very start gain the upper hand over the evil which is attacking them without rest.

A union of men under merely moral laws, patterned on the above idea, may be called an *ethical*, and so far as these laws are public, an *ethico-civil* (in contrast to a *juridico-civil*) society or an *ethical commonwealth*. It can exist in the midst of a political commonwealth and may even be made up of all its members (indeed, unless it is based upon such a commonwealth it can never be brought into existence by man). It has, however, a special and unique principle of union (virtue), and hence a form and constitution, which fundamentally distinguish it from the political commonwealth. At the same time there is a certain analogy between them, regarded as two commonwealths, in view of which the former may also be called an *ethical state, i.e.,* a *kingdom* of virtue (of the good principle). The idea of such a state possesses a thoroughly well-grounded objective reality in human reason (in man's duty to join such a state), even though, subjectively, we can never hope that man's good will will lead mankind to decide to work with unanimity towards this goal.

Division one: Philosophical account of the victory of the good principle in the founding of a kingdom of God on earth

I. Concerning the ethical state of nature

A *juridico-civil* (political) *state* is the relation of men to each other in which they all alike stand socially under *public juridical laws* (which are, as a class, laws of coercion). An *ethico-civil* state is that in which they are united under non-coercive laws, *i.e., laws of virtue* alone.

Now just as the rightful (but not therefore always righteous), *i.e., the juridical, state of* NATURE is opposed to the first, *the ethical state of* NATURE is distinguished from the second. In both, each individual prescribes the law for himself, and there is no external law to which he, along with all others, recognizes himself to be subject. In both, each individual is his own judge, and there exists no powerful *public* authority to determine with legal power, according to laws, what is each man's duty in every situation that arises, and to bring about the universal performance of duty.

In an already existing political commonwealth all the political citizens, as such, are in an *ethical state of nature* and are entitled to remain therein; for it would be a contradiction (*in adjecto*) for the political commonwealth to compel its citizens to enter into an ethical commonwealth, since the very concept of the latter involves freedom from coercion. Every political commonwealth may indeed wish to be possessed of a sovereignty, according to laws of virtue, over the spirits [of its citizens]; for then, when its methods of compulsion do not avail (for the human judge cannot penetrate into the depths of other men) their dispositions to virtue would bring about what was required. But woe to the legislator who wishes to establish through force a polity directed to ethical ends! For in so doing he would not merely achieve the very opposite of an ethical polity but also undermine his political state and make it insecure. The citizen of the political commonwealth remains therefore, so far as its legislative function is concerned, completely free to enter with his fellow-citizens into an ethical union in addition [to the political] or to remain in this kind of state of nature, as he may wish. Only so far as an ethical commonwealth must rest on *public* laws and possess a constitution based on these laws are those who freely pledge themselves to enter into this ethical state bound, not [indeed] to accept orders from the political power as to how they shall or shall not fashion this ethical constitution internally, but to agree to limitations, namely, to the condition that this constitution shall contain nothing which contradicts the duty of its members as *citizens of the state*—although when the ethical pledge is of the genuine sort the political limitation need cause no anxiety.

Further, because the duties of virtue apply to the entire human race, the concept of an ethical commonwealth is extended ideally to the whole of mankind, and thereby distinguishes itself from the concept of a political commonwealth. Hence even a large number of men united in that purpose can be called not the ethical commonwealth itself but only a particular society which strives towards harmony with all men (yes, finally with all rational beings) in order to form an absolute ethical whole of which every partial society is only a representation or schema; for each of these societies in turn, in its relation to others of the same kind, can be represented as in the ethical state of nature and subject to all the defects thereof. (This is precisely the situation with separate political states which are not united through a public international law.)

II. Man ought to leave his ethical state of nature in order to become a member of an ethical commonwealth

Just as the juridical state of nature is one of war of every man against every other, so too is the ethical state of nature one in which the good principle, which resides in each man, is continually attacked by the evil which is found in him and also in everyone else. Men (as was noted above) mutually corrupt one another's moral predispositions; despite the good will of each individual, yet, because they lack a principle which unites them, they recede, through their dissensions, from the common goal of goodness and, just as though they were *instruments of evil*, expose one another to the risk of falling once again under the sovereignty of the evil principle. Again, just as the state of a lawless external (brutish) freedom and independence from coercive laws is a state of injustice and of war, each against each, which a man ought to leave in order to enter into a politico-civil state[1]: so is the ethical state of nature one of *open* conflict between principles of virtue and a state of inner immorality which the natural

man ought to bestir himself to leave as soon as possible.

Now here we have a duty which is *sui generis*, not of men toward men, but of the human race toward itself. For the species of rational beings is objectively, in the idea of reason, destined for a social goal, namely, the promotion of the highest as a social good. But because the highest moral good cannot be achieved merely by the exertions of the single individual toward his own moral perfection, but requires rather a union of such individuals into a whole toward the same goal—into a system of well-disposed men, in which and through whose unity alone the highest moral good can come to pass—the idea of such a whole, as a universal republic based on laws of virtue, is an idea completely distinguished from all moral laws (which concern what we know to lie in our own power); since it involves working toward a whole regarding which we do not know whether, as such, it lies in our power or not. Hence this duty is distinguished from all others both in kind and in principle. We can already foresee that this duty will require the presupposition of another idea, namely, that of a higher moral Being through whose universal dispensation the forces of separate individuals,

---

[1] Hobbes' statement, *status hominum naturalis est* bellum *omnium in omnes*, is correct except that it should read, *est* status *belli*, etc. For even if one does not concede that actual *hostilities* are continually in progress between men who do not stand under external and public laws, yet the *state* (*status iuridicus*) is the same; *i.e.*, the relationship in and through which men are fitted for the acquisition and maintenance of rights—a state in which each wants to be the judge of what shall be his rights against others, but for which rights he has no security against others, and gives others no security: each has only his private strength. This is a state of war in which everyone must be perpetually armed against everyone else. Hobbes' second statement, *exeundum esse e statu naturali*, follows from the first; for this state is a continual infringement upon the rights of all others through man's arrogant insistence on being the judge in his own affairs and giving other men no security in their affairs save his own arbitrary will.

insufficient in themselves, are united for a common end. First of all, however, we must follow up the clue of that moral need [for social union] and see whither this will lead us.

III. The concept of an ethical commonwealth is the concept of a people of God under ethical laws

If an ethical commonwealth is to come into being, all single individuals must be subject to a public legislation, and all the laws which bind them must be capable of being regarded as commands of a common law-giver. Now if the commonwealth to be established is to be *juridical*, the mass of people uniting itself into a whole would itself have to be the law-giver (of constitutional laws), because legislation proceeds from the principle of *limiting the freedom of each to those conditions under which it can be consistent with the freedom of everyone else according to a common law*,[2] and because, as a result, the general will sets up an external legal control. But if the commonwealth is to be *ethical*, the people, as a people, cannot itself be regarded as the law-giver. For in such a commonwealth all the laws are expressly designed to promote the *morality* of actions (which is something *inner*, and hence cannot be subject to public human laws) whereas, in contrast, these public laws—and this would go to constitute a juridical commonwealth—are directed only toward the *legality* of actions, which meets the eye, and not toward (inner) morality, which alone is in question here. There must therefore be someone other than the populace capable of being specified as the public law-giver for an ethical commonwealth. And yet, ethical laws cannot be thought of as emanating *originally* merely from the will of this superior being (as statutes, which, had he not first commanded them, would perhaps not be binding), for then they would not be ethical laws and the duty proper to them would not be the free duty of virtue but the coercive duty of law. Hence only he can be thought of as highest law-giver of an ethical commonwealth with respect to whom all *true duties*,

hence also the ethical,[3] must be represented as *at the same time* his commands; he must therefore also be "one who knows the heart,"* in order to see into the innermost parts of the disposition of each individual and, as is necessary in every commonwealth, to bring it about that each receives whatever his actions are worth. But this is the concept of God as moral ruler of the world. Hence an ethical commonwealth can be thought of only as a people under divine commands, *i.e.*, as a *people of God*,† and indeed *under laws of virtue*.

We might indeed conceive of a people of God *under statutory laws*, under such laws that obedience to them would concern not the morality but merely the legality of acts. This would be a juridical commonwealth, of which, indeed, God would be the lawgiver (hence the *constitution* of this state would be theocratic); but men, as priests receiving His behests from Him directly, would build up an aristocratic *government*. Such a constitution, however, whose existence and form rest wholly on an historical basis, cannot settle the problem of the morally-legislative reason, the solution of which alone we are to effect; as an institution under politico-civil laws, whose lawgiver, though God, is yet external,

---

[2] This is the principle of all external rights.

[3] As soon as anything is recognized as a duty, even if it should be a duty imposed through the arbitrary will of a human law-giver, obedience to it is also a divine command. Of course one cannot call statutory civil laws divine commands; yet, when they are legitimate, *obedience* to them is still a divine command. The saying: "We ought to obey God rather than men" [cf. Acts 5 : 29], signifies merely that when men command anything which in itself is evil (directly opposed to the law of morality) we dare not, and ought not, obey them. But conversely, when a politico-civil law, itself not immoral, is opposed to what is held to be a divine statutory law, there are grounds for regarding the latter as spurious, since it contradicts a plain duty and since [the notion] that it is actually a divine command can never, by any empirical token, be accredited adequately enough to allow an otherwise established duty to be neglected on its account.

* Cf. Acts 1 : 24; 15 : 8; Luke 16 : 15.

† Cf. I Peter 2 : 10.

it will come under review in the historical section. Here we have to do only with an institution whose laws are purely inward—a republic under laws of virtue, *i.e.,* a people of God "zealous of good works."*

To such a *people* of God we can oppose the idea of a *rabble* of the evil principle, the union of those who side with it for the propagation of evil, and whose interest it is to prevent the realization of that other union—although here again the principle which combats virtuous dispositions lies in our very selves and is represented only figuratively as an external power.

IV. The idea of a people of God can be realized (through human organization) only in the form of a church

The sublime, yet never wholly attainable, idea of an ethical commonwealth dwindles markedly under men's hands. It becomes an institution which, at best capable of representing only the pure form of such a commonwealth, is, by the conditions of sensuous human nature, greatly circumscribed in its means for establishing such a whole. How indeed can one expect something perfectly straight to be framed out of such crooked wood?

To found a moral people of God is therefore a task whose consummation can be looked for not from men but only from God Himself. Yet man is not entitled on this account to be idle in this business and to let Providence rule, as though each could apply himself exclusively to his own private moral affairs and relinquish to a higher wisdom all the affairs of the human race (as regards its moral destiny). Rather must man proceed as though everything depended upon him; only on this condition dare he hope that higher wisdom will grant the completion of his well-intentioned endeavors.

The wish of all well-disposed people is, therefore, "that the kingdom of God come, that His will be done on earth."† But what preparations must they now make that it shall come to pass?

An ethical commonwealth under divine moral legislation is a *church* which, so far as it is not an object of possible experience, is called the *church invisible* (a mere idea of the union of all the righteous under direct and moral divine world-government, an idea serving all as the archetype of what is to be established by men). The *visible church* is the actual union of men into a whole which harmonizes with that ideal. So far as each separate society maintains, under public laws, an order among its members (in the relation of those who obey its laws to those who direct their obedience), the group, united into a whole (the church), is a *congregation* under authorities, who (called teachers or shepherds of souls) merely administer the affairs of the invisible supreme head thereof. In this function they are all called *servants* of the church, just as, in the political commonwealth, the visible overlord occasionally calls himself the highest servant of the state even though he recognizes no single individual over him (and ordinarily not even the people as a whole). The true (visible) church is that which exhibits the (moral) kingdom of God on earth so far as it can be brought to pass by men. The requirements upon, and hence the tokens of, the true church are the following:

1. *Universality,* and hence its numerical oneness; for which it must possess this characteristic, that, although divided and at variance in unessential opinions, it is none the less, with respect to its fundamental intention, founded upon such basic principles as must necessarily lead to a general unification in a single church (thus, no sectarian divisions).

2. Its *nature* (quality); *i.e., purity,* union under no motivating forces other than *moral* ones (purified of the stupidity of superstition and the madness of fanaticism).

3. Its *relation* under the principle of *freedom;* both the internal relation of its members to one another, and the external relation of the church to political power—both relations as

---

* Cf. Titus 2 : 14.
† Cf. Matthew 6 : 10; Luke 11 : 2.

in a *republic* (hence neither a *hierarchy*, nor an *illuminatism*, which is a kind of *democracy* through special inspiration, where the inspiration of one man can differ from that of another, according to the whim of each).

4. Its *modality*, the *unchangeableness* of its *constitution*, yet with the reservation that incidental regulations, concerning merely its *administration*, may be changed according to time and circumstance; to this end, however, it must already contain within itself *a priori* (in the idea of its purpose) settled principles. (Thus [it operates] under primordial laws, once [for all] laid down, as it were out of a book of laws, for guidance; not under arbitrary symbols which, since they lack authenticity, are fortuitous, exposed to contradiction, and changeable.)

An ethical commonwealth, then, in the form of a church, *i.e.*, as a mere *representative* of a city of God, really has, as regards its basic principles, nothing resembling a political constitution. For its constitution is neither *monarchical* (under a pope or patriarch), nor *aristocratic* (under bishops and prelates), nor *democratic* (as of sectarian *illuminati*). It could best of all be likened to that of a household (family) under a common, though invisible, moral Father, whose holy Son, knowing His will and yet standing in blood relation with all members of the household, takes His place in making His will better known to them; these accordingly honor the Father in him and so enter with one another into a voluntary, universal, and enduring union of hearts.

V. The constitution of every church originates always in some historical (revealed) faith which we can call ecclesiastical faith; and this is best founded on a holy scripture

Pure religious faith alone can found a universal church; for only [such] rational faith can be believed in and shared by everyone, whereas an historical faith, grounded solely on facts, can extend its influence no further than tidings of it can reach, subject to circumstances of time and place and dependent upon the capacity [of men] to judge the credibility of such tidings. Yet, by reason of a peculiar weakness of human nature, pure faith can never be relied on as much as it deserves, that is, a church cannot be established on it alone.

Men are conscious of their inability to know supersensible things; and although they allow all honor to be paid to faith in such things (as the faith which must be universally convincing to them), they are yet not easily convinced that steadfast diligence in morally good life-conduct is all that God requires of men, to be subjects in His kingdom and well-pleasing to Him. They cannot well think of their obligation except as an obligation to some *service* or other which they must offer to God—wherein what matters is not so much the inner moral worth of the actions as the fact that they are offered to God—to the end that, however morally indifferent men may be in themselves, they may at least please God through passive obedience. It does not enter their heads that when they fulfil their duties to men (themselves and others) they are, by these very acts, performing God's commands and are therefore in all their actions and abstentions, so far as these concern morality, *perpetually in the service of God,* and that it is absolutely impossible to serve God more directly in any other way (since they can affect and have an influence upon earthly beings alone, and not upon God). Because each great worldly lord stands in special need of being *honored* by his subjects and *glorified* through protestations of submissiveness, without which he cannot expect from them as much compliance with his behests as he requires to be able to rule them, and since, in addition, however gifted with reason a man may be, he always finds an immediate satisfaction in attestations of honor. we treat duty, so far as it is also a divine command, as the prosecution of a *transaction* with God, not with man. Thus arises the concept of a religion of *divine worship* as against the concept of a religion purely moral.

Since all religion consists in this, that in all our duties we look upon God as the lawgiver universally to be honored, the determining of religion, so far as the conformity of our attitude with it is concerned, hinges upon knowing *how God wishes* to be honored (and obeyed). Now a divine legislative will commands either through laws in themselves *merely statutory* or through *purely moral* laws. As to the latter, each individual can know of himself, through his own reason, the will of God which lies at the basis of his religion; for the concept of the Deity really arises solely from consciousness of His laws and from the need of reason to postulate a might which can procure for these laws, as their final end, all the results conformable to them and possible in a world. The concept of a divine will, determined according to pure moral laws alone, allows us to think of only *one* religion which is purely moral, as it did of only *one* God. But if we admit statutory laws of such a will and make religion consist of our obedience to them, knowledge of such laws is possible not through our own reason alone but only through revelation, which, be it given publicly or to each individual in secret, would have to be an *historical* and not a *pure rational* faith if it is to be propagated among men by tradition or writ. And even admitting divine statutory laws (laws which do not in themselves appear to us as obligatory but can be known as such only when taken as the revelation of God's will), pure *moral* legislation, through which the will of God is primordially engraved in our hearts, is not only the ineluctable condition of all true religion whatsoever but is also that which really constitutes such religion; statutory religion can merely comprise the means to its furtherance and spread.

If, then, the question: How does God wish to be honored? is to be answered in a way universally valid for each man, *regarded merely as man*, there can be no doubt that the legislation of His will ought to be solely *moral;* for statutory legislation (which presupposes a revelation) can be regarded merely as contingent and as something which never has applied or can apply to every man, hence as not binding upon all men universally. Thus, "not they who say Lord! Lord! but they who

do the will of God,"* they who seek to become well-pleasing to Him not by praising Him (or His envoy, as a being of divine origin) according to revealed concepts which not every man can have, but by a good course of life, regarding which everyone knows His will—these are they who offer Him the true veneration which He desires.

But when we regard ourselves as obliged to behave not merely as men but also as *citizens* in a divine state on earth, and to work for the existence of such a union, under the name of a church, then the question: How does God wish to be honored in *a church* (as a congregation of God)? appears to be unanswerable by reason alone and to require statutory legislation of which we become cognizant only through revelation, *i.e.,* an historical faith which, in contra-distinction to pure religious faith, we can call ecclesiastical faith.

For pure religious faith is concerned only with what constitutes the essence of reverence for God, namely, obedience, ensuing from the moral disposition, to all duties as His commands; a church, on the other hand, as the union of many men with such dispositions into a moral commonwealth, requires a *public* covenant, a certain ecclesiastical form dependent upon the conditions of experience. This form is in itself contingent and manifold, and therefore cannot be apprehended as duty without divine statutory laws. But the determination of this form must not be regarded forthwith as the concern of the divine Lawgiver; rather are we justified in assuming that it is the divine will that we should ourselves carry into effect the rational idea of such a commonwealth and that, although men may have tried many a type of church with unhappy result, yet on no account should they cease to strive after this goal, with new attempts if necessary, avoiding so far as possible the mistakes of the earlier

---

* Matthew 7 : 21: "Not every one that saith unto me, Lord, Lord, shall enter into the kingdom of heaven; but he that doeth the will of my Father which is in heaven."

ones—inasmuch as this task, which is for them a duty as well, is entirely committed to them alone. We therefore have no reason straightway to take the laws constituting the basis and form of any church as divine *statutory* laws; rather is it presumptuous to declare them to be such, in order to save ourselves the trouble of still further improving the church's form, and it is a usurpation of higher authority to seek, under pretense of a divine commission. to lay a yoke upon the multitude by means of ecclesiastical dogmas. Yet it would be as great self-conceit to deny peremptorily that the way in which a church is organized may perhaps be a special divine arrangement, if, so far as we can see, it is completely harmonious with the moral religion—and if, in addition, we cannot conceive how it could have appeared all at once without the requisite initiatory progress of the public in religious conceptions.

In the indecision over the problem of whether God or men themselves should found a church, there is evidenced man's propensity to *a religion of divine worship* (*cultus*) and—since such a religion rests upon arbitrary precepts—to belief in divine statutory laws, on the assumption that some divine legislation, not to be discovered through reason but calling for revelation, must supplement the best life-conduct (conduct which man is always free to adopt under the guidance of the pure moral religion). Herein consideration is given to the veneration of the Highest Being directly (and not by way of that obedience to His laws which is already prescribed to us by reason). Thus it happens that men will regard neither union into a church, nor agreement with respect to the form which it is to take, nor yet *public* institutions, as in themselves necessary for the promotion of the moral element in religion, but only, as they say, for the service of their God, through ceremonies, confessions of faith in revealed laws, and observance of the ordinances requisite to the form of the church (which is itself, after all, only a means). All these observances are at bottom morally indifferent actions; yet, just because they are to

be performed merely for His sake, they are held to be all the more pleasing to Him. In men's striving towards an ethical commonwealth, ecclesiastical faith thus naturally precedes[4] pure religious faith; *temples* (buildings consecrated to the public worship of God) were before *churches* (meeting-places for the instruction and quickening of moral dispositions), *priests* (consecrated stewards of pious rites) before *divines* (teachers of the purely moral religion); and for the most part they still are first in the rank and value ascribed to them by the great mass of people.

Since, then, it remains true once for all that a statutory *ecclesiastical faith* is associated with pure religious faith as its vehicle and as the means of public union of men for its promotion, one must grant that the preservation of pure religious faith unchanged, its propagation in the same form everywhere, and even a respect for the revelation assumed therein, can hardly be provided for adequately through *tradition,* but only through *scripture;* which, again, as a revelation to contemporaries and posterity, must itself be an object of esteem, for the necessities of men require this in order that they may be sure of their duty in divine service. A holy book arouses the greatest respect even among those (indeed, most of all among those) who do not read it, or at least those who can form no coherent religious concept therefrom; and the most sophistical reasoning avails nothing in the face of the decisive assertion, which beats down every objection: *Thus it is written.* It is for this reason that the passages in it which are to lay down an article of faith are called simply *texts.* The appointed expositors of such a scripture are themselves, by virtue of their occupation, like unto consecrated persons; and history proves that it has never been possible to destroy a faith grounded in scripture, even with the most devastating revolutions in the state, whereas the faith established upon tradition and ancient public observances has promptly met its downfall when the state was overthrown.

---

[4] Morally, this order ought to be reversed.

How fortunate,[5] when such a book, fallen into men's hands, contains, along with its statutes, or laws of faith, the purest moral doctrine of religion in its completeness—a doctrine which can be brought into perfect harmony with such statutes [which serve] as vehicles for its introduction). In this event, both because of the end thereby to be attained and because of the difficulty of rendering intelligible according to natural laws the origin of such enlightenment of the human race as proceeds from it, such a book can command an esteem like that accorded to revelation.

* * *

And now a few words touching this concept of a belief in revelation.

There is only *one* (true) *religion;* but there can be *faiths* of several kinds. We can say further that even in the various churches, severed from one another by reason of the diversity of their modes of belief, one and the same true religion can yet be found.

It is therefore more fitting (as it is more customary in actual practice) to say: This man is of this or that *faith* (Jewish, Mohammedan, Christian, Catholic, Lutheran), than: He is of this or that religion. The second expression ought in justice never to be used in addressing the general public (in catechisms and sermons), for it is too learned and unintelligible for them; indeed, the more modern languages possess no word of equivalent meaning. The common man always takes it to mean his ecclesiastical faith, which appeals to his senses, whereas religion is hidden within and has to do with moral dispositions.

One does too great honor to most people by saying of them: They profess this or that religion. For they know none and desire none—statutory ecclesiastical faith is all that they understand by the word. The so-called religious wars which have so often shaken the world and bespattered it with blood, have never been anything but wrangles over ecclesiastical faith; and the oppressed have complained not that they were hindered

from adhering to their religion (for no external power can do this) but that they were not permitted publicly to observe their ecclesiastical faith.

Now when, as usually happens, a church proclaims itself to be the one church universal (even though it is based upon faith in a special revelation, which, being historical, can never be required of everyone), he who refuses to acknowledge its (peculiar) ecclesiastical faith is called by it an *unbeliever* and is hated wholeheartedly; he who diverges therefrom only in part (in non-essentials) is called *heterodox* and is at least shunned as a source of infection. But he who avows [allegiance to] this church and yet diverges from it on essentials of its faith (namely, regarding the practices connected with it), is called, especially if he spreads abroad his false belief, a *heretic*,[6] and, as a rebel, such a man is held more culpable than a foreign foe, is expelled from the church with an anathema (like that which the Romans pronounced on him who crossed the Rubicon against the Senate's will) and is given over to all the gods of hell. The exclusive correctness of belief in

---

[5] An expression for everything wished for, or worthy of being wished for, which we can neither foresee nor bring about through our own endeavors according to the laws of experience; for which, therefore, if we wish to name its source, we can offer none other than a gracious Providence.

[6] According to the *Alphabetum Tibetanum* of Georgius, Mongols call Tibet "Tangut-Chazar," the land of the house-dwellers, to distinguish its inhabitants from themselves as nomads living in the desert under tents. From this has originated the name Chazars, and from this name that of a *Ketzer* [= heretic], since the Mongols adhered to the Tibetan faith (of the Lamas) which agrees with Manicheanism, perhaps even arose from it, and spread it in Europe during their invasions; whence, too, for a long time the names *Haeretici* and *Manichaei* were synonymous in usage. ["This etymological explanation is certainly incorrect. In all probability, *Ketzer* is related to *Gazzari,* the Lombardish word for *Kathari* = Καθαροι. The Kathari (the "pure ones") were the most important heretical sect with which the church in the Middle Ages (especially in the twelfth and thirteenth centuries) had to deal. The Manichaean element in the movement is unmistakable." (Note in Berlin Edition.)]

matters of ecclesiastical faith claimed by the church's teachers or heads is called *orthodoxy*. This could be sub-divided into *despotic (brutal)* or *liberal* orthodoxy.

If a church which claims that its ecclesiastical faith is universally binding is called a *catholic* church, and if that which protests against such claims on the part of others (even though oftentimes it would gladly advance similar claims itself, if it could) is called a *protestant* church, an alert observer will come upon many laudable examples of protestant Catholics and, on the other hand, still more examples, and offensive ones, of arch-catholic Protestants: the first, men of a cast of mind (even though it is not that of their church) *leading to self-expansion;* to which the second, with their *circumscribed* cast of mind, stand in sharp contrast—not at all to their own advantage.

VI. Ecclesiastical faith has pure religious faith as its highest interpreter

We have noted that a church lacks the most important mark of truth, namely, a rightful claim to universality, when it bases itself upon a revealed faith. For such a faith, being historical (even though it be far more widely disseminated and more completely secured for remotest posterity through the agency of scripture) can never be universally communicated so as to produce conviction. Yet, because of the natural need and desire of all men for something *sensibly tenable,* and for a confirmation of some sort from experience of the highest concepts and grounds of reason (a need which really must be taken into account when the universal *dissemination* of a faith is contemplated), some historical ecclesiastical faith or other, usually to be found at hand, must be utilized.

If such an empirical faith, which chance, it would seem, has tossed into our hands, is to be united with the basis of a moral faith (be the first an end or merely a means), an exposition of the revelation which has come into our possession is required, that is, a thorough-going interpretation of it in a sense

agreeing with the universal practical rules of a religion of pure reason. For the theoretical part of ecclesiastical faith cannot interest us morally if it does not conduce to the performance of all human duties as divine commands (that which constitutes the essence of all religion). Frequently this interpretation may, in the light of the text (of the revelation), appear forced—it may often really be forced; and yet if the text can possibly support it, it must be preferred to a literal interpretation which either contains nothing at all [helpful] to morality or else actually works counter to moral incentives.[7]

We shall find, too, that this has always been

_____

[7] As an illustration of this, take Psalm 59 : 11-16, where we find a *prayer* for *revenge* which goes to terrifying extremes. Michaelis (*Moral,* Part 2, p. 202) approves of this prayer, and adds: "The Psalms are *inspired;* if in them punishment is prayed for, it cannot be wrong, and *we must have no morality holier than the Bible.*" Restricting myself to this last expression, I raise the question as to whether morality should be expounded according to the Bible or whether the Bible should not rather be expounded according to morality. Without considering how the passage in the New Testament [cf. Matthew 5 : 21 ff., 44ff.], "It was said to them of old time, etc. . . . But I say unto you, Love your enemies, *bless them that curse you,* etc., . . ." which is also inspired, can agree with the other, I should try, as a first alternative, to bring the New Testament passage into conformity with my own self-subsistent moral principles (that perhaps the reference is here not to enemies in the flesh but rather to invisible enemies which are symbolized by them and are far more dangerous to us, namely, evil inclinations which we must desire to bring wholly under foot). Or, if this cannot be managed, I shall rather have it that this passage is not to be understood in a moral sense at all but only as applying to the relation in which the Jews conceived themselves to stand to God as their political regent. This latter interpretation applies to still another passage in the Bible, where it is written: "Vengeance is mine. I will repay, saith the Lord." [Cf. Romans 12 : 19; Deuteronomy 32 : 35]. This is commonly interpreted as a moral warning against private revenge, though probably it merely refers to the law, valid for every state, that satisfaction for injury shall be sought in the courts of justice of the overlord, where the judge's permission to the complainant to ask for a punishment as severe as he desires is not to be taken as approval of the complainant's craving for revenge.

done with all types of faith, old and new, some of them recorded in holy books, and that wise and thoughtful teachers of the people kept on interpreting them until, gradually, they brought them, as regards their essential content, into line with the universal moral dogmas. The moral philosophers among the Greeks, and later among the Romans, did exactly this with the fabulous accounts of the gods. They were able in the end to interpret the grossest polytheism as mere symbolic representation of the attributes of the single divine Being, and to supply the various wicked actions [of the gods] and the wild yet lovely fancies of the poets with a mystical meaning which made a popular faith (which it would have been very inadvisable to destroy, since atheism, still more dangerous to the state, might perhaps have resulted) approach a moral doctrine intelligible to all men and wholly salutary. The later Judaism, and even Christianity itself, consist of such interpretations, often very forced, but in both instances for ends unquestionably good and needful for all men. The Mohammedans (as Reland* shows) know very well how to ascribe a spiritual meaning to the description of their paradise, which is dedicated to sensuality of every kind; the Indians do exactly the same thing in the interpretation of their Vedas, at least for the enlightened portion of their people.

That this can be done without ever and again offending greatly against the literal meaning of the popular faith is due to the fact that, earlier by far than this faith, the predisposition to the moral religion lay hidden in human reason; and though its first rude manifestations took the form merely of practices of divine worship, and for this very purpose gave rise to those alleged revelations, yet these manifestations have infused even into the myths, though unintentionally, something from the nature of their supersensible origin. Nor can we charge such interpretations with dishonesty, provided we are not disposed to assert that the meaning which we ascribe to the symbols of the popular faith, even to the holy books, is exactly as

intended by them, but rather allow this question to be left undecided and merely admit the *possibility* that their authors may be so understood. For the final purpose even of reading these holy scriptures, or of investigating their content, is to make men better; the historical element, which contributes nothing to this end, is something which is in itself quite indifferent, and we can do with it what we like. (Historical faith "is dead, being alone";† that is, of itself, regarded as a creed, it contains nothing, and leads to nothing, which could have any moral value for us.)

Hence, even if a document is accepted as a divine revelation, the highest criterion of its being of divine origin will be: "All scripture given by inspiration of God is profitable for doctrine, for reproof, for correction, etc.";‡ and since this last, to wit, the moral improvement of men, constitutes the real end of all religion of reason, it will comprise the highest principle of all Scriptural exegesis. This religion is "the Spirit of God, who guides into all truth";§ and this it is which in *instructing* us also *animates* us with basic principles for action, and wholly subjects whatever Scripture may contain for historical faith to the rules and incentives of pure moral faith, which alone constitutes the element of genuine religion in each ecclesiastical faith. All investigation and interpretation of Scripture must from the start be based on a search for this Spirit in it, and "eternal life can be found therein only so far as it [Scripture] testifies of this principle."‖

Now placed beside this Scriptural interpreter, but subordinated to him, is another, namely, the *Scriptural scholar*. The authority of Scripture, as the most worthy instrument,

---

* Adrian Reland (1676–1718), a Dutch Orientalist, wrote *De religione mohammedica libri duo*, second edition, 1717; cf. 2. 17.

† Cf. James 2 : 17.

‡ Cf. II Timothy 3 : 16.

§ Cf. John 16 : 13: "Howbeit when he, the Spirit of truth, is come, he will guide you into all truth, etc."

‖ Cf. John 5 : 39: "Search the scriptures; for in them ye think ye have eternal life: and they are they which testify of me."

and at present the only instrument in the most enlightened portion of the world, for the union of all men into one church, constitutes the ecclesiastical faith, which, as the popular faith, cannot be neglected, because no doctrine based on reason alone seems to the people qualified to serve as an unchangeable norm. They demand divine revelation, and hence also an historical certification of its authority through the tracing back of its origin. Now human skill and wisdom cannot ascend so far as heaven in order itself to inspect the credentials validating the mission of the first Teacher. It must be content with evidence that can be elicited, apart from the content, as to the way in which such a faith has been introduced—that is, with human reports which must be searched out little by little from very ancient times, and from languages now dead, for evaluation as to their historical credibility. Hence *Scriptural scholarship* will [ever] be required to maintain in authority a church founded upon Holy Scripture, ([though] not a religion, which, to be universal, must always be founded upon reason alone), even though this scholarship settles no more than that there is nothing in the origin of Scripture to render impossible its acceptance as direct divine revelation; for this would suffice to provide security for those who fancy that they find in this idea [of a revealed Scripture] special fortification of their moral faith, and who therefore gladly accept it. Yet not only the *authentication* of Holy Scripture, but its *interpretation* as well, stands in need of scholarship, and for the same reason. For how are the unlearned, who can read it only in translation, to be certain of its meaning? Hence the expositor, in addition to being familiar with the original tongue, must also be a master of extended historical knowledge and criticism, in order that from the conditions, customs, and opinions (the popular faith) of the times in question he may be able to derive the means wherewith to enlighten the understanding of the ecclesiastical commonwealth.

Rational religion and Scriptural learning are thus the properly qualified interpreters

and trustees of a sacred document. It is obvious that they must on no account be hindered by the secular arm in the public use of their judgments and discoveries in this field, or bound to certain dogmas; for otherwise the *laity* would compel the *clergy* to concur in their opinion, which, after all, they have acquired only from the clergy's instruction. So long as the state takes care that there is no dearth of scholars and of men in morally good repute who have authority in the entire church body and to whose consciences the state entrusts this commission, it has done all that its duty and capacity require. But to insist that the legislator should carry this matter into the schools and concern himself with their quarrels (which, if they are not proclaimed from the pulpit, leave the church-public quite undisturbed)—such a burden the public cannot thrust upon him without arrogance, for it is beneath his dignity.

A third claimant contests the office of interpreter, the man who needs neither reason nor scholarship, but merely an inner *feeling*, to recognize the true meaning of Scripture as well as its divine origin. Now we certainly cannot deny that "he who follows its teachings and *does* what it commands will surely find that it is of God,"* and that the very impulse to good actions and to uprightness in the conduct of life, which the man who reads Scripture or hears it expounded must feel, cannot but convince him of its divine nature; for this impulse is but the operation of the moral law which fills man with fervent respect and hence deserves to be regarded as a divine command. A knowledge of laws, and of their morality, can scarcely be derived from any sort of feeling; still less can there be inferred or discovered from a feeling certain evidence of a direct divine influence; for the same effect can have more than one cause. In this case, however, the bare morality of the law (and the doctrine), known through reason, is the source [of the law's validity]; and

---

* Cf. John 7 : 17: "If any man will do his will, he shall know of the doctrine, whether it be of God, . . ."

even if this origin were no more than barely possible, duty demands that it be thus construed unless we wish to open wide the gates to every kind of fanaticism, and even cause the unequivocal moral feeling to lose its dignity through affiliation with fantasy of every sort. Feeling is private to every individual and cannot be demanded of others [even] when the law, from which and according to which this feeling arises, is known in advance; therefore one cannot urge it as a touchstone for the genuineness of a revelation, for it teaches absolutely nothing, but is merely the way in which the subject is affected as regards pleasure or displeasure—and on this basis can be established no knowledge whatever.

There is therefore no norm of ecclesiastical faith other than Scripture, and no expositor thereof other than pure *religion of reason* and *Scriptural scholarship* (which deals with the historical aspect of that religion). Of these, the first alone is *authentic* and valid for the whole world; the second is merely *doctrinal*, having as its end the transformation of ecclesiastical faith for a given people at a given time into a definite and enduring system. Under this system, historical faith must finally become mere faith in Scriptural scholars and their insight. This does not, indeed, particularly redound to the honor of human nature; yet it is a situation which can be corrected through public freedom of thought— and such freedom is the more justified since only if scholars submit their interpretations to public examination, while they themselves ever hope for and remain open and receptive to better insight, can they count on the community's confidence in their decisions.

VII. The gradual transition of ecclesiastical faith to the exclusive sovereignty of pure religious faith is the coming of the kingdom of God

The token of the true church is its *universality;* the sign of this, in turn, is its necessity and its determinability in only one possible way. Historical faith (which is based upon revelation, regarded as an experience) has only particular validity, to wit, for those who have

had access to the historical record upon which this faith rests; and like all empirical knowledge it carries with it the consciousness not that the object believed in *must* be so and not otherwise, but merely that it *is* so; hence it involves as well the consciousness of its contingency. Thus historical faith can become an ecclesiastical faith (of which there can be several), whereas only pure religious faith, which bases itself wholly upon reason, can be accepted as necessary and therefore as the only one which signalizes the *true* church.

When, therefore (in conformity with the unavoidable limitation of human reason) an historical faith attaches itself to pure religion, as its vehicle, but with the consciousness that it is only a vehicle, and when this faith, having become ecclesiastical, embraces the principle of a continual approach to pure religious faith, in order finally to be able to dispense with the historical vehicle, a church thus characterized can at any time be called the *true* church; but, since conflict over historical dogmas can never be avoided, it can be spoken of only as the church *militant*, though with the prospect of becoming finally the changeless and all-unifying church *triumphant!* We call the faith of every individual who possesses moral capacity (worthiness) for eternal happiness a *saving* faith. This also can be but a single faith; amid all diversity of ecclesiastical faiths [or creeds] it is discoverable in each of these in which, moving toward the goal of pure religious faith, it is practical. The faith of a religion of divine worship, in contrast, is a *drudging* and mercenary faith (*fides mercenaria, servilis*) and cannot be regarded as saving because it is not moral. For a moral faith must be free and based upon an ingenuous disposition of the heart (*fides ingenua*). Ecclesiastical faith fancies it possible to become well-pleasing to God through actions (of *worship*) which (though irksome) yet possess in themselves no moral worth and hence are merely acts induced by fear or hope—acts which an evil man also can perform. Moral faith, in contrast, presupposes that a morally good disposition is requisite.

Saving faith involves two elements, upon

which hope of salvation is conditioned, the one having reference to what man himself cannot accomplish, namely, undoing lawfully (before a divine judge) actions which he has performed, the other to what he himself can and ought to do, that is, leading a new life conformable to his duty. The first is the faith in an atonement (reparation for his debt, redemption, reconciliation with God); the second, the faith that we can become well-pleasing to God through a good course of life in the future. Both conditions constitute but one faith and necessarily belong together. Yet we can comprehend the necessity of their union only by assuming that one can be derived from the other, that is, either that the faith in the absolution from the debt resting upon us will bring forth good life-conduct, or else that the genuine and active disposition ever to pursue a good course of life will engender the faith in such absolution according to the law of morally operating causes.

Here now appears a remarkable antinomy of human reason with itself, whose solution, or, were this not possible, at least whose adjustment can alone determine whether an historical (ecclesiastical) faith must always be present as an essential element of saving faith, over and above pure religious faith, or whether it is only a vehicle which finally—however distant this future event may be—can pass over into pure religious faith.

1. If it is assumed that atonement has been made for the sins of mankind, it is indeed conceivable that every sinner would gladly have it applied to himself and that were it merely a matter of *belief* (which means no more than an avowal that he wishes the atonement to be rendered for him also), he would not for an instant suffer misgivings on this score. However, it is quite impossible to see how a reasonable man, who knows himself to merit punishment, can in all seriousness believe that he needs only to credit the news of an atonement rendered for him, and to accept this atonement *utiliter* (as the lawyers say), in order to regard his guilt as annihilated—indeed, so completely annihilated

(to the very root) that good life-conduct, for which he has hitherto not taken the least pains, will in the future be the inevitable consequence of this faith and this acceptance of the proffered favor. No thoughtful person can bring himself to believe this, even though self-love often does transform the bare wish for a good, for which man does nothing and can do nothing, into a hope, as though one's object were to come of itself, elicited by mere longing. Such a persuasion can be regarded as possible only if the individual regards this belief as itself instilled in him by heaven and hence as something concerning which he need render no further account to his reason. If he cannot think this, or if he is still too upright artificially to produce in himself such a confidence, as a mere means of ingratiation, he can only, with all respect for such a transcendent atonement, and with every wish that it be available for him also, regard it as conditioned. That is, he must believe that he must first improve his way of life, so far as improvement lies in his power, if he is to have even the slightest ground for hope of such a higher gain. Wherefore, since historical knowledge of the atonement belongs to ecclesiastical faith, while the improved way of life, as a condition, belongs to pure moral faith, *the latter must take precedence over the former.*

2. But if men are corrupt by nature, how can a man believe that by himself, try as hard as he will, he can make himself a new man well-pleasing to God, when—conscious of the transgressions of which up to the present he has been guilty—he still stands in the power of the evil principle and finds in himself no capacity adequate for future improvement? If he cannot regard justice, which he has provoked against himself, as satisfied through atonement by another, and cannot regard himself reborn, so to speak, through this faith and so for the first time able to enter upon a new course of life—and this would follow from his union with the good principle —upon what is he to base his hope of becoming a man pleasing to God? Thus faith in a merit not his own, whereby he is reconciled with God, must precede every effort to good

works. But this goes counter to the previous proposition [that good works must *precede* faith in divine atonement]. This contradiction cannot be resolved through insight into the causal determination of the freedom of a human being, *i.e.*, into the causes which bring it about that a man becomes good or bad; hence it cannot be resolved theoretically, for it is a question wholly transcending the speculative capacity of our reason. But practically, the question arises: What, in the use of our free will, comes first* (not physically but morally)? Where shall we start, *i.e.*, with a faith in what God has done on our behalf, or with what we are to do to become worthy of God's assistance (whatever this may be)? In answering this question we cannot hesitate in deciding for the second alternative.

The acceptance of the first requisite for salvation, namely, faith in a vicarious atonement, is in any case necessary only for the theoretical concept; in no other way can we *make comprehensible* to ourselves such absolution. In contrast, the necessity for the second principle is practical and, indeed, purely moral. We can certainly hope to partake in the appropriation of another's atoning merit, and so of salvation, only by qualifying for it through our own efforts to fulfil every human duty—and this obedience must be the effect of our own action and not, once again, of a foreign influence in the presence of which we are passive. For since the command to do our duty is unconditioned, it is also necessary that man shall make it, as maxim, the basis of his belief, that is to say that he shall begin with the improvement of his life as the supreme condition under which alone a saving faith can exist.

Ecclesiastical faith, being historical, rightly starts with the belief in atonement; but since it merely constitutes the vehicle for pure religious faith (in which lies the real end), the maxim of *action*, which in religious faith (being practical) is the condition, must take the lead, and the maxim of *knowledge*, or theoretical faith, must merely bring about the strengthening and consummation of the maxim of action.

In this connection it might also be remarked that, according to the ecclesiastical principle, the faith in a vicarious atonement would be imputed to man as a duty, whereas faith in good life-conduct, as being effected through a higher agency, would be reckoned to him as of grace. According to the other principle the order is reversed. For according to it the *good course of life*, as the highest condition of grace, is unconditioned *duty*, whereas atonement from on high is purely a *matter of grace*. Against the first faith is charged (often not unjustly) the *superstitious belief* of divine worship, which knows how to combine a blameworthy course of life with religion; against the second, *naturalistic unbelief*, which unites with a course of life, perhaps otherwise exemplary, indifference or even antagonism to all revelation. This [latter attitude] would constitute cutting the knot (by means of a practical maxim) instead of disentangling it (theoretically)—a procedure which is after all permitted in religious questions. However, the theoretical demand can be satisfied in the following manner.

The living faith in the archetype of humanity well-pleasing to God (in the Son of God) is bound up, *in itself*, with a moral idea of reason so far as this serves us not only as a guide-line but also as an incentive; hence it matters not whether I start with it as a *rational* faith, or with the principle of a good course of life. In contrast, the faith in the self-same archetype *in its* [*phenomenal*] *appearance* (faith in the God-Man), as an *empirical* (historical) faith, is not interchangeable with the principle of the good course of life (which must be wholly rational), and it would be quite a different matter to wish to start with such a faith[8] and to deduce the good course of life from it. To this extent, then, there would be a contradiction between the two propositions above. And yet, in the appearance of the God-Man [on earth], it is not that in him which strikes the senses and can be known

---

* *I.e.*, not in time.

[8] Which must base the existence of such a person on historical evidence.

through experience, but rather the archetype, lying in our reason, that we attribute to him (since, so far as his example can be known, he is found to conform thereto), which is really the object of saving faith, and such a faith does not differ from the principle of a course of life well-pleasing to God.

Here, then, are not two principles which in themselves so differ that to begin with the one, or the other, would be to enter upon opposing paths, but only one and the same practical idea from which we take our start, this idea representing the archetype now as found in God and proceeding from Him, and now, as found in us, but in both instances as the gauge for our course of life. The antinomy is therefore only apparent, since, through a misunderstanding, it regards the self-same practical idea, taken merely in different references, as two different principles. If one wished, however, to make the historical faith in the reality of such an appearance, taking place in the world on a single occasion, the condition of the only saving faith, there would, indeed, be two quite different principles (the one empirical, the other rational) regarding which a real conflict of maxims would arise—whether one should begin with and start out from the one or the other. This conflict no reason would ever be able to resolve.

The proposition: We must believe that there was once a man (of whom reason tells us nothing) who through his holiness and merit rendered satisfaction both for himself (with reference to his duty) and for all others (with their shortcomings, in the light of their duty), if we are to hope that we ourselves, though in a good course of life, will be saved by virtue of that faith alone—this proposition says something very different from the following: With all our strength we must strive after the holy disposition of a course of life well-pleasing to God, to be able to believe that the love (already assured us through reason) of God toward man, so far as man does endeavor with all his strength to do the

will of God, will make good, in consideration of an upright disposition, the deficiency of the deed, whatever this deficiency may be. The first belief is not in the power of everyone (even of the unlearned). History testifies that in all forms of religion this conflict between two principles of faith has existed; for all religions have involved expiation, on whatever basis they put it, and the moral predisposition in each individual has not failed, on its side, to let its claims be heard. Yet at all times the priests have complained more than the moralists: the former (with summons to the authorities to check the mischief) protesting loudly against the neglect of divine worship, which was instituted to reconcile the people with heaven and to ward off misfortune from the state; the latter complaining, on the other hand, about the decline of morals, a decline which they zealously set to the account of those means of absolution whereby the priests made it easy for anyone to make his peace with the Deity over the grossest vices. In point of fact, if an inexhaustible fund is already at hand for the payment of debts incurred or still to be incurred, so that man has merely to reach out (and at every claim which conscience makes one would be sure, first of all, to reach out) in order to free himself of sin, while he can postpone resolving upon a good course of life until he is first clear of those debts—if this were possible it is not easy to conceive any other consequences of such a faith. Yet were this faith to be portrayed as having so peculiar a power and so mystical (or magical) an influence, that although merely historical, so far as we can see, it is yet competent to better the whole man from the ground up (to make a new man of him) if he yields himself to it and to the feelings bound up with it, such a faith would have to be regarded as imparted and inspired directly by heaven (together with, and in, the historical faith), and everything connected even with the moral constitution of man would resolve itself into an unconditioned decree of God: "He hath mercy on whom he will, and whom he will he *hardeneth*,"[9]* which, taken according to the letter, is the *salto mortale* of human reason.

Hence a necessary consequence of the physical and, at the same time, the moral predisposition in us, the latter being the basis and the interpreter of all religion, is that in the end religion will gradually be freed from all empirical determining grounds and from all statutes which rest on history and which through the agency of ecclesiastical faith provisionally unite men for the requirements of the good; and thus at last the pure religion of reason will rule over all, "so that God may be all in all."† The integuments within which the embryo first developed into a human being must be laid aside when he is to come into the light of day. The leading-string of holy tradition with its appendages of statutes and observances, which in its time did good service, becomes bit by bit dispensable, yea, finally, when man enters upon his adolescence, it becomes a fetter. While he (the human race) "was a child he understood as a child" and managed to combine a certain amount of erudition, and even a philosophy ministering to the church, with the propositions which were bestowed on him without his cooperation: "but when he becomes a man he puts away childish things."‡ The humilating distinction between *laity* and *clergy* disappears, and equality arises from true freedom, yet without anarchy, because, though each obeys the (non-statutory) law which he prescribes to himself, he must at the same time regard this law as the will of a World-Ruler revealed to him through reason, a will which by invisible means unites all under one common government into one state—a state previously and inadequately represented and prepared for by the visible church. All this is not to be expected from an external revolution, because such an upheaval produces its effect tempestuously and violently, an effect, quite dependent on circumstances. Moreover whatever mistake has once been made in the establishment of a new constitution, is regretfully retained throughout hundreds of years, since it can

no longer be changed or at least only through a new (and at any time dangerous) revolution. The basis for the transition to that new order of affairs must lie in the principle that the pure religion of reason is a continually occurring divine (though not empirical) revelation for all men. Once this basis has been grasped with mature reflection, it is carried into effect, so far as this is destined to be a human task, through gradually advancing reform. As for revolutions which might hasten this progress, they rest in the hands of Providence and cannot be ushered in according to plan without damage to freedom.

We have good reason to say, however, that "the kingdom of God is come unto us"§ once the principle of the gradual transition of ecclesiastical faith to the universal religion of reason, and so to a (divine) ethical state on earth, has become general and has also gained somewhere a *public* foothold, even though the actual establishment of this state is still infinitely removed from us. For since this principle contains the basis for a continual approach towards such a consumma-

---

[9] This can, indeed, be interpreted as follows. No one can say with certainty why this man becomes good, that man evil (both comparatively), because the predisposition to one of these characters or the other often seems to be discoverable at birth, and because contingencies of life as well, which no one can foresee, seem to tip the scale. No more can one say what a man may develop into. In all this therefore we must entrust judgment to the All-Seeing; but this is expressed in the text as though His decree, pronounced upon men before they were born, had prescribed to each the role which he was some day to play. *Prevision* regarding the order of appearances is at the same time *predestination* for a World-Creator, when, in this connection, He is conceived of in terms of human senses. But in the supersensible order of things, according to the laws of freedom, where time drops out, it is only an *all-seeing knowledge*; and yet it is impossible to explain why one man conducts himself in one way, and another according to opposite principles and to harmonize [this knowledge of causes] with the freedom of the will.

* Cf. Romans 9 : 18.
† Cf. I Corinthians 15 : 28.
‡ Cf. I Corinthians 13 : 11.
§ Cf. Matthew 12 : 28.

tion, there lies in it (invisibly), as in a seed which is self-developing and in due time self-fertilizing, the whole, which one day is to illumine and to rule the world. But truth and goodness—and in the natural predisposition of every man there lies a basis of insight into these as well as a basis of heartfelt sympathy with them—do not fail to communicate themselves far and wide once they have become public, thanks to their natural affinity with the moral predisposition of rational beings generally. The obstacles, arising from political and civil causes, which may from time to time hinder their spread, serve rather to make all the closer the union of men's spirits with the good (which never leaves their thoughts after they have once cast their eyes upon it).[10]

Such, therefore, is the activity of the good principle, unnoted by human eyes but ever continuing—erecting for itself in the human race, regarded as a commonwealth under laws of virtue, a power and kingdom which sustains the victory over evil and, under its own dominion, assures the world of an eternal peace.

---

[10] Without either renouncing the service of ecclesiastical faith or attacking it, one can recognize its useful influence as a vehicle and at the same time deny to it, taken as the illusory duty of divine worship, all influence upon the concept of genuine (that is, moral) religion. Thus, amid the diversity of statutory forms of belief, a mutual compatibility of the adherents to these forms can be established through the basic principles of the one and only religion of reason, toward which the teachers of all such dogmas and observances should direct their interpretations; until, in time, by virtue of the true enlightenment (conformity to law, proceeding from moral freedom) which has now prevailed, the form of a debasing means of constraint can be exchanged, by unanimous consent, for an ecclesiastical form which squares with the dignity of a moral religion, to wit, the religion of a free faith. To combine a unity of ecclesiastical belief with freedom in matters of faith is a problem toward whose solution the idea of the objective unity of the religion of reason continually urges us, through the moral interest which we take in this religion; although, when we take human nature into account, there appears small hope of bringing this to pass in a visible church. It is an idea of reason

Division two: Historical account of the gradual establishment of the sovereignty of the good principle on earth

We can expect no *universal history* of religion (in the strictest meaning of the word) among men on earth; for, since it is based upon pure moral faith, it is not open to public view, and each man can become aware only in and for himself of the advances which he has made in it. Hence it is only of ecclesiastical faith that we can expect a universal historical account, in which its varied and changing form is compared with the single, unchanging, pure religious faith. At the point where the first of these publicly recognizes its dependence upon the qualifying conditions of the second and the necessity of conformity to them, the *church universal* commences to fashion itself into an ethical state of God and to march toward the consummation of this state under a steadfast principle which is one and the same for all men and for all times. We can see in advance that this history will be nothing but the narrative of the enduring conflict between the faith of divine worship and the

which we cannot represent through any [sensuous] intuition adequate to it, but which, as a practical regulative principle, does have objective reality, enabling it to work toward this end, *i.e.,* the unity of the pure religion of reason. In this it is like the political idea of the rights of a state so far as these are meant to relate to an international law which is universal and *possessed of power*. Here experience bids us give over all hope. A propensity seems to have been implanted (perhaps designedly) in the human race causing every single state to strive if possible to subjugate every other state and to erect a universal monarchy, but, when it has reached a certain size, to break up, of its own accord, into smaller states. In like manner every single church cherishes the proud pretension of becoming a church universal; yet as soon as it has extended itself and commenced to rule, a principle of *dis*solution and schism into different sects at once shows itself. [The premature and therefore (since it comes before men have become morally better) the harmful fusion of states into one is chiefly hindered—if we are permitted here to assume a design of Providence—through two mightily effective causes, namely, difference of tongues, and difference of religions.]

moral faith of religion, the first of which, as historical faith, man is continually inclined to put foremost, while, on the other hand, the second has never relinquished its claim to the priority to which it is entitled as the only faith bettering the soul—a claim which it will certainly, in the end, make good.

Now this historical account can have unity only if it is confined wholly to that portion of the human race in which the predisposition to the unity of the universal church is already approaching its [complete] development, that is, when the problem of the difference between the faiths of reason and of history has already been publicly propounded and its solution made a matter of the greatest moral importance; for an historical account merely of the dogmas of diverse peoples, whose faiths stand in no connection with one another, can reveal no [such example of] church unity. It cannot be taken as an instance of this unity that in one and the same people a certain new faith once arose and distinguished itself by name from the faith previously dominant, even though the latter afforded the *occasional* causes of the new product. For there must exist a unity of principle if we are to construe the succession of different types of belief following one another as modifications of one and the same church; and it is really with the history of this church that we are now concerned.

So we can deal, under this heading, only with the history of that church which contained within itself, from its first beginning, the seed and the principles of the objective unity of the true and *universal* religious faith, to which it is gradually brought nearer. And first of all it is evident that the Jewish faith stands in no essential connection whatever, *i.e.,* in no unity of concepts, with this ecclesiastical faith whose history we wish to consider, though the Jewish immediately preceded this (the Christian) church and provided the physical occasion for its establishment.

The *Jewish faith* was, in its original form, a collection of mere statutory laws upon which was established a political organization; for whatever moral additions were then or later

appended to it in no way whatever belong to Judaism as such. Judaism is really not a religion at all but merely a union of a number of people who, since they belonged to a particular stock, formed themselves into a commonwealth under purely political laws, and not into a church; nay, it was *intended* to be merely an earthly state so that, were it possibly to be dismembered through adverse circumstances, there would still remain to it (as part of its very essence) the political faith in its eventual reestablishment (with the advent of the Messiah). That this political organization has a theocracy as its basis (visibly, an aristocracy of priests or leaders, who boast of instructions imparted directly by God), and that therefore the name of God, who after all is here merely an earthly regent making absolutely no claims upon, and no appeals to, conscience, is respected—this does not make it a religious organization.

The proof that Judaism has not allowed its organization to become religious is clear. *First,* all its commands are of the kind which a political organization can insist upon and lay down as coercive laws, since they relate merely to external acts; and although the Ten Commandments are, to the eye of reason, valid as ethical commands even had they not been given publicly, yet in that legislation they are not so prescribed as to induce obedience by laying requirements upon the *moral disposition* (Christianity later placed its main emphasis here); they are directed to absolutely nothing but outer observance. From this it is also clear that, *second,* all the consequences of fulfilling or transgressing these laws, all rewards or punishments, are limited to those alone which can be allotted to all men in this world, and not even these [are distributed] according to ethical concepts, since both rewards and punishments were to reach a posterity which has taken no practical part in these deeds or misdeeds. In a political organization this may indeed be a prudent device for creating docility, but in an ethical organization it would be contrary to all right. Furthermore, since no religion can be conceived of which involves no belief in a future life, Judaism, which, when taken in its purity is seen to lack this belief, is not a religious faith at all. This can be further supported by the following remark. We can hardly question that the Jews, like other peoples, even the most savage, ought [normally] to have had a belief in a future life, and therefore in a heaven and a hell; for this belief automatically obtrudes itself upon everyone by virtue of the universal moral predisposition in human nature. Hence it certainly came about *intentionally* that the lawgiver of this people, even though he is represented as God Himself, *wished* to pay not the slightest regard to the future life. This shows that he must have wanted to found merely a political, not an ethical commonwealth; and to talk, in a political state, of rewards and punishments which cannot become apparent here in this life would have been, on that premise, a wholly inconsequential and unsuitable procedure. And though, indeed, it cannot be denied that the Jews may, subsequently, and each for himself, have framed some sort of religious faith which was mingled with the articles of their statutory belief, such religious faith has never been part and parcel of the legislation of Judaism. *Third,* Judaism fell so far short of constituting an era suited to the requirements of the *church universal,* or of setting up this universal church itself during its time, as actually to exclude from its communion the entire human race, on the ground that it was a special people chosen by God for Himself—[an exclusiveness] which showed enmity toward all other peoples and which, therefore, evoked the enmity of all. In this connection, we should not rate too highly the fact that this people set up, as universal Ruler of the world, a one and only God who could be represented through no visible image. For we find that the religious doctrines of most other peoples tended in the same direction and that these made themselves suspected of polytheism only by the *veneration* of certain mighty undergods subordinated to Him. For a God who desires merely obedience to commands for which absolutely no improved

moral disposition is requisite is, after all, not really the moral Being the concept of whom we need for a religion. Religion would be more likely to arise from a belief in many mighty invisible beings of this order, provided a people conceived of these as all agreeing, amid their "departmental" differences, to bestow their good pleasure only upon the man who cherishes virtue with all his heart—more likely, I say, than when faith is bestowed upon but one Being, who, however, attaches prime importance to mechanical worship.

We cannot, therefore, do otherwise than begin general church history, if it is to constitute a system, with the origin of Christianity, which, completely forsaking the Judaism from which it sprang, and grounded upon a wholly new principle, effected a thoroughgoing revolution in doctrines of faith. The pains which teachers of Christianity take now, and may have taken in the beginning, to join Judaism and Christianity with a connecting strand by trying to have men regard the new faith as a mere continuation of the old (which, they allege, contained in prefiguration all the events of the new)—these efforts reveal most clearly that their problem is and was merely the discovery of the most suitable means of *introducing* a purely moral religion in place of the old worship, to which the people were all too well habituated, without directly offending the people's prejudices. The subsequent dispensing with the corporal sign which served wholly to separate this people from others warrants the judgment that the new faith, not bound to the statutes of the old, nor, indeed, to any statutes whatever, was to comprise a religion valid for the world and not for one single people.

Thus Christianity arose suddenly, though not unprepared for, from Judaism. The latter, however, was no longer patriarchal and unmixed, standing solely upon its political constitution (for even this was by that time sorely unsettled), but was already interfused, by reason of moral doctrines gradually made public within it, with a religious faith—for this otherwise ignorant people had been able to receive much foreign (Greek) wisdom. This wisdom presumably had the further effect of enlightening Judaism with concepts of virtue and, despite the pressing weight of its dogmatic faith, of preparing it for revolution, the opportunity being afforded by the diminished power of the priests, who had been subjugated to the rule of a race* which regarded all foreign popular beliefs with indifference. The Teacher of the Gospel announced himself to be an ambassador from heaven. As one worthy of such a mission, he declared that servile belief (taking the form of confessions and practices on days of divine worship) is essentially vain and that moral faith, which alone renders men holy "as their Father in Heaven is holy"† and which proves its genuineness by a good courses of life, is the only saving faith. After he had given, in his own person, through precept and suffering even to unmerited yet meritorious death,[11] an example conforming to the archetype of a humanity alone pleasing to God, he is represented as returning to heaven, whence he came. He left behind him, by word of mouth, his last will (as in a testament); and, trusting in the power of the memory of his merit, teaching, and example, he was able to say that "he (the ideal of humanity well-pleasing to God) would still be with his disciples, even to the end of the world."‡ Were it a question of *historical belief* concerning the derivation and the rank, possibly supermundane, of his person, this doctrine would indeed stand in need of verification through miracles; although, as merely belonging to moral soul-improving faith, it can dispense with all such proofs of its truth. Hence, in a holy book miracles and mysteries find a place; the manner of making these known, in turn, is also miraculous, and demands a faith in history; which, finally, can be authenticated, and assured as to meaning and import, only by scholarship.

Every faith which, as an historical faith, bases itself upon books, needs for its security a *learned public* for whom it can be controlled, as it were, by writers who lived in those times

---

* *I.e.*, the Romans.

† Cf. Matthew 5 : 48; also I Peter 1 : 16.

[11]With which the public record of his life ends (a record which, as public, might serve universally as an example for imitation). The more secret records, added as a sequel, of his *resurrection* and *ascension*, which took place before the eyes only of his intimates, cannot be used in the interest of religion within the limits of reason alone without doing violence to their historical valuation. (If one takes these events merely as ideas of reason, they would signify the commencement of another life and entrance into the seat of salvation, *i.e.*, into the society of all the good.) This is so not merely because this added sequel is an historical narrative (for the story which precedes it is that also) but because, taken literally, it involves a concept, *i.e.*, of the materiality of all worldly beings, which is, indeed, very well suited to man's mode of sensuous representation but which is most burdensome to reason in its faith regarding the future. This concept involves both the *materialism of personality* in men (psychological materialism), which asserts that a personality can exist only as always conditioned by the same *body,* as well as the *materialism of necessary existence in a world,* a world which, according to this principle, must be *spatial* (cosmological materialism). In contrast, the hypothesis of the spirituality of rational world-beings asserts that the body can remain dead in the earth while the same person is still alive, and that man, as a spirit (in his non-sensuous quality), can reach the seat of the blessed without having to be transported to some portion or other of the endless space which surrounds the earth (and which is also called heaven). This hypothesis is more congenial to reason, not only because of the impossibility of making comprehensible a matter which thinks, but especially because of the contingency to which materialism exposes our existence after death by claiming that such existence depends solely upon the cohering of a certain lump of matter in a certain form, and denying the possibility of thinking that a simple substance can persist based upon its [own] nature. On the latter supposition (of spirituality) reason can neither take an interest in dragging along, through eternity, a body which, however purified, must yet (if the personality is to rest upon the body's identity) consist of the self-same stuff which constitutes the basis of its organization and for which, in life, it never achieved any great love; nor can it render conceivable that this calcareous earth, of which the body is composed, should be in heaven, *i.e.*, in another region of the universe, where presumably other materials might constitute the condition of the existence and maintenance of living beings.

‡ Cf. Matthew 28 : 20.

who are not suspected of a special agreement with the first disseminators of the faith, and with whom our present-day scholarship is connected by a continuous tradition. The pure faith of reason, in contrast, stands in need of no such documentary authentication, but proves itself. Now at the time of the revolution in question there was present among the people (the Romans), who ruled the Jews and who had spread into their very domain, a learned public from whom the history of the political events of that period has indeed been handed down to us through an unbroken series of writers. And although the Romans concerned themselves but little with the religious beliefs of their non-Roman subjects, they were by no means incredulous of the miracles alleged to have taken place publicly in their midst. Yet they made no mention, as contemporaries, either of these miracles or of the revolution which the miracles produced (in respect to religion) in the people under their dominion, though the revolution had taken place quite as publicly. Only later, after more than a generation, did they institute inquiries into the nature of this change of faith which had remained unknown to them hitherto (but which had occurred not without public commotion), but they did not inquire into the history of its first beginning, in order to learn this history from its own records. So from this period to the time when Christendom could furnish a learned public of its own, its history is obscure and we remain ignorant of what effect the teaching of Christianity had upon the morality of its adherents—whether the first Christians actually were morally improved men or just people of the common run. At any rate, the history of Christendom, from the time that it became a learned public itself, or at least part of the universal learned public, has served in no way to recommend it on the score of the beneficent effect which can justly be expected of a moral religion.

For history tells how the mystical fanaticism in the lives of hermits and monks, and the glorification of the holiness of celibacy, rendered great masses of people useless to the world; how alleged miracles accompanying all this weighed down the people with heavy chains under a blind superstition; how, with a hierarchy forcing itself upon free men, the dreadful voice of *orthodoxy* was raised, out of the mouths of presumptuous, exclusively "called," Scriptural expositors, and divided the Christian world into embittered parties over credal opinions on matters of faith (upon which absolutely no general agreement can be reached without appeal to pure reason as the expositor); how in the East, where the state meddled in an absurd manner with the religious statutes of the priests and with priestdom, instead of holding them within the narrow confines of a teacher's status (out of which they are at all times inclined to pass over into that of ruler)—how, I say, this state had finally to become, quite inescapably, the prey of foreign enemies, who at last put an end to its prevailing faith; how, in the West, where faith had erected its own throne, independent of worldly power, the civil order together with the sciences (which maintain this order) were thrown into confusion and rendered impotent by a self-styled viceroy of God; how both Christian portions of the world became overrun by barbarians, just as plants and animals, near death from some disease, attract destructive insects to complete their dissolution; how, in the West, the spiritual head ruled over and disciplined kings like children by means of the magic wand of his threatened excommunication, and incited them to depopulating foreign wars in another portion of the world (the Crusades), to the waging of war with one another, to the rebellion of subjects against those in authority over them, and to bloodthirsty hatred against their otherwise-minded colleagues in one and the same universal Christendom so-called; how the root of this discord, which even now is kept from violent outbreaks only through political interest, lies hidden in the basic principle of a despotically commanding ecclesiastical faith and still gives cause for dread of events like unto these—this history of Christendom (which indeed could not eventuate otherwise if erected upon an historical faith), when surveyed in a single glance, like a painting, might well justify the exclamation: *tantum religio potuit suadere malorum,** did not the fact still shine forth clearly from its founding that Christianity's first intention was really no other than to introduce a pure religious faith, over which no conflict of opinions can prevail; whereas that turmoil, through which the human race was disrupted and is still set at odds, arises solely from this, that what, by reason of an evil propensity of human nature, was in the beginning to serve merely for the introduction of pure religious faith, *i.e.*, to win over for the new faith the nation habituated to the old historical belief through its own prejudices, was in the sequel made the foundation of a universal world-religion.

If now one asks, What period in the entire known history of the church up to now is the best? I have no scruple in answering, *the present*. And this, because, if the seed of the true religious faith, as it is now being publicly sown in Christendom, though only by a few, is allowed more and more to grow unhindered, we may look for a continuous approximation to that church, eternally uniting all men, which constitutes the visible representation (the schema) of an invisible kingdom of God on earth. For reason has freed itself, in matters which by their nature ought to be moral and soul-improving, from the weight of a faith forever dependent upon the arbitrary will of the expositors, and has among true reverers of religion in all the lands of this portion of the world universally (though indeed not in all places publicly) laid down the following principles.

The *first* is the principle of reasonable *modesty* in pronouncements regarding all that goes by the name of revelation. For no one can deny the *possibility* that a scripture which, in practical content, contains much that is godly, may (with respect to what is historical in it) be regarded as a genuinely divine revelation. It is also possible that the union of men into one religion cannot feasibly be brought about or made abiding without a holy book and an ecclesiastical faith based

upon it. Moreover, the contemporary state of human insight being what it is, one can hardly expect a new revelation, ushered in with new miracles. Hence the most intelligent and most reasonable thing to do is from now on to use the book already at hand as the basis for ecclesiastical instruction and not to lessen its value through useless or mischievous attacks, yet meanwhile not forcing belief in it, as requisite to salvation, upon any man.

The *second* principle is this: that, since the sacred narrative, which is employed solely on behalf of ecclesiastical faith, can have and, taken by itself, ought to have absolutely no influence upon the adoption of moral maxims, and since it is given to ecclesiastical faith only for the vivid presentation of its true object (virtue striving toward holiness), it follows that this narrative must at all times be taught and expounded in the interest of morality; and yet (because the common man especially has an enduring propensity within him to sink into passive[12] belief) it must be inculcated painstakingly and repeatedly that true religion is to consist not in the knowing or considering of what God does or has done for our salvation but in what we must do to become worthy of it. This last can never be anything but what possesses in itself undoubted and *unconditional* worth, what therefore can alone make us well-pleasing to God,

* Lucretius *De rerum natura* 1. 101: "Such evil deeds could religion prompt!" (cf. *GBWW*, Vol. 12, p. 2.)
[12] One of the causes of this propensity lies in the principle of security; that the defects of a religion in which I am born and brought up, instruction therein not having been chosen by me nor in any way altered through my own ratiocination, are charged not to my account but to that of my instructors or teachers publicly appointed for the task. This is also a ground for our not easily giving our approval to a man's public change of religion: although here, no doubt, there is another (and deeper) ground, namely, that amid the uncertainty which every man feels within himself as to which among the historical faiths is the right one, while the moral faith is everywhere the same, it seems highly unnecessary to create a stir about the matter.

and of whose necessity every man can become wholly certain without any Scriptural learning whatever. Now it is the duty of rulers not to hinder these basic principles from becoming public. On the contrary, very much is risked and a great responsibility assumed by one who intrudes upon the process of divine Providence and, for the sake of certain historical ecclesiastical doctrines which at best have in their favor only a probability discoverable by scholars, exposes to temptation[13] the consciences of the subjects through the offer, or denial, of certain civil advantages otherwise open to all: all this, apart from the damage done thereby to a freedom which in this case is holy, can scarcely produce good citizens for the state. Who among those proffering themselves to hinder such a free development of godly predispositions to the world's highest good, or even proposing such a hindrance, would wish, after thinking it over in communion with his conscience, to answer for all the evil which might arise from such forcible encroachments, whereby the advance in goodness intended by the Governor of the world, though it can never be wholly destroyed through human might or human contrivance, may perhaps be checked for a long time, yea, even turned into a retrogression!

---

[13] When a government wishes to be regarded as not coercing man's conscience because it merely prohibits the *public utterance* of his religious opinions and hinders no one from *thinking* to himself in secrecy whatever he sees fit, we usually jest about it and say that in this the government grants no freedom at all, for it cannot in any case hinder thinking. Yet what the greatest secular power cannot do, spiritual power can—that is, forbid thought itself and really hinder it; it can even lay such a compulsion—the prohibition even to think other than it prescribes—upon those in temporal authority over it. For because of men's propensity to the servile faith of divine worship, which they are automatically inclined not only to endow with an importance greater than that of moral faith (wherein man serves God truly through the performance of his duties) but also to regard as unique and compensating for every other deficiency, it is always easy for the custodians of orthodoxy, the shepherds of souls, to instil into their

As regards its guidance by Providence, the kingdom of heaven is represented in this historical account not only as being brought ever nearer, in an approach delayed at certain times yet never wholly interrupted, but also as arriving. When to this narrative is added (in the Apocalypse) a prophecy (like those in the Sibylline books) of the consummation of this great world-change, in the image of a visible kingdom of God on earth (under the government of His representative and viceroy, again descended to earth), and of the happiness which is to be enjoyed under him in this world after the separation and expulsion of the rebels who once again seek to withstand him, and also of the complete extirpation of these rebels and their leader, and when, thus, the account closes with *the end of the world,* all this may be interpreted as a symbolical representation intended merely to enliven hope and courage and to increase our endeavors to that end.

The Teacher of the Gospel revealed to his disciples the kingdom of God on earth only in its glorious, soul-elevating moral aspect, namely, in terms of the value of citizenship in a divine state, and to this end he informed them of what they had to do, not only to achieve it themselves but to unite with all others of the same mind and, so far as possi-

flock a pious terror of the slightest swerving from certain dogmas resting on history, and even of all investigation—a terror so great that they do not trust themselves to allow a doubt concerning the doctrines forced upon them to arise, even in their thoughts, for this would be tantamount to lending an ear to the evil spirit. True, to become free from this compulsion one needs but *to will* (which is not the case when the sovereign compels public confessions); but it is precisely this willing against which a rule has been interposed internally. Such forcing of conscience is indeed bad enough (for it leads to inner hypocrisy); yet it is not as bad as the restriction of external freedom of belief. For the inner compulsion must of itself gradually disappear through the progress of moral insight and the consciousness of one's own freedom, from which alone true respect for duty can arise, whereas this external pressure hinders all spontaneous advances in the ethical community of believers—which constitutes the being of the true church—and subjects its form to purely political ordinances.

ble, with the entire human race. Concerning happiness, however, which constitutes the other part of what man inevitably wishes, he told them in advance not to count on it in their life on earth. Instead he bade them be prepared for the greatest tribulations and sacrifices; yet he added (since man cannot be expected, while he is alive, wholly to renounce what is physical in happiness): "Rejoice and be exceeding glad: for great is your reward in heaven."* The supplement, added to the history of the church, dealing with man's future and final destiny, pictures men as ultimately *triumphant, i.e.,* as crowned with happiness while still here on earth, after all obstacles have been overcome. The separation of the good from the evil, which, during the progress of the church toward its consummation, would not have conduced to this end (since their mixture with one another was needed, partly to spur the good on to virtue, partly to withdraw the bad from evil through the others' example), is represented as following upon the completed establishment of the divine state and as its last consequence; whereto is added, as the final proof of the state's stability and might, its victory over all external foes who are also regarded as forming a state (the state of hell). With this all earthly life comes to an end, in that "the last enemy (of good men), death, is destroyed";† and immortality commences for both parties, to the salvation of one, the dam-

nation of the other. The very form of a church is dissolved, the viceroy becomes at one with man who is raised up to his level as a citizen of heaven, and so God is all in all.[14]

This sketch of a history of after-ages, which themselves are not yet history, presents a beautiful ideal of the moral world-epoch, brought about by the introduction of true universal religion and in faith *foreseen* even to its culmination—which we cannot *conceive* as a culmination in experience, but can merely *anticipate, i.e.,* prepare for, in continual progress and approximation toward the highest good possible on earth (and in all of this there is nothing mystical, but everything moves quite naturally in a moral fashion). The appearance of the Antichrist, the milennium, and the news of the proximity of the end of the world—all these can take on, before reason, their right symbolic meaning; and to represent the last of these as an event not to be seen in advance (like the end of life, be it far or near) admirably expresses the necessity of standing ready at all times for the end and indeed (if one attaches the intellectual meaning to this symbol) really to consider ourselves always as chosen citizens of a divine (ethical) state. "When, therefore, cometh the kingdom of God?"‡ "The kingdom of God cometh not in visible form. Neither shall they say, Lo here; or lo there! *For, behold, the kingdom of God is within you,*" (Luke 17 : 21–22).[15]

---

* Cf. Matthew 5 : 12. Luther's translation reads *belohnet* instead of Kant's *vergolten.*

† Cf. I Corinthians 15 : 26.

[14] This expression (if one sets aside what is mysterious, what reaches out beyond the limits of all possible experience, and what belongs to sacred *history* and so in no way applies to us practically) can be taken to mean that historical faith, which, as ecclesiastical, stands in need of a sacred book as a leading-string for men, but, for that very reason, hinders the unity and universality of the church, will itself cease and pass over into a pure religious faith equally obvious to the whole world. To this end we ought even now to labor industriously, by way of continuously setting free the pure religion from its present shell, which as yet cannot be spared.

Not that it is to cease (for as a vehicle it may

perhaps always be useful and necessary) but that it be able to cease; whereby is indicated merely the inner stability of the pure moral faith.

‡ Cf. Luke 17 : 20-21: "And when he was demanded of the Pharisees when the kingdom of God should come, he answered them and said, the kingdom of God cometh not with observation. Neither shall, etc."

[15] Here a kingdom of God is represented not according to a particular covenant (*i.e.,* not Messianic) but *moral* (knowable through unassisted reason). The former (*regnum divinum pactitium*) had to draw its proofs from history; and there it is divided into the *Messianic* kingdom according to the *old* and according to the *new* covenant. Now it is worthy of notice that the followers of the former (the Jews) have continued to maintain themselves as such, though scattered throughout the world;

395

General observation

Investigation into the inner nature of all kinds of faith which concern religion invariably encounters a *mystery, i.e.,* something *holy* which may indeed be *known* by each single individual but cannot be *made known* publicly, that is, shared universally. Being something *holy,* it must be moral, and so an object of reason, and it must be capable of being known from within adequately for practical use, and yet, as something *mysterious,* not for theoretical use, since in this case it would have to be capable of being shared with everyone and made known publicly.

Belief in what we are yet to regard as a holy mystery can be looked upon as *divinely prompted* or as *a pure rational faith.* Unless we are impelled by the greatest need to adopt the first of these views, we shall make it our maxim to abide by the second. Feelings are not knowledge and so do not indicate [the presence of] a mystery; and since the latter is related to reason, yet cannot be shared universally, each individual will have to search for it (if ever there is such a thing) solely in his own reason.

It is impossible to settle, *a priori* and objectively, whether there are such mysteries or not. We must therefore search directly in the inner, the subjective, part of our moral predisposition to see whether any such thing is to be found in us. Yet we shall not be entitled to number among the holy mysteries the *grounds* of morality, which are inscrutable to

---

whereas the faith of other religious fellowships has usually been fused with the faith of the people among whom they have been scattered. This phenomenon strikes many as so remarkable that they judge it to be impossible according to the nature of things, but to be an extraordinary dispensation for a special divine purpose. Yet a people which has a written religion (sacred books) never fuses together in one faith with a people (like the Roman Empire, then the entire civilized world) possessing no such books but only rites; instead, sooner or later it makes proselytes. This is the reason why, after the Babylonian captivity (following which, it seems, their sacred books were for the first time read publicly), the Jews were no longer chargeable with their propensity to run after strange gods; though the Alexandrian culture, which must also have had an influence upon them, could have been favorable to their giving this propensity a systematic form. Thus also the Parsees, followers of the religion of Zoroaster, have kept their faith up to the present despite their dispersion; for their *dustoors* [high priests] possessed the Zendavesta. These Hindus, on the other hand, who under the name of gipsies are scattered far and wide, have not escaped a mixture with foreign faiths, for they came from the dregs of the people (the Pariahs) who are forbidden even to read in the sacred books of the Hindus. What the Jews would not have achieved of themselves, the Christian and later the Mohammedan religions brought about— especially the former; for these religions presupposed the Jewish faith and the sacred books belonging to it (even though Mohammedanism declares that these books have been falsified). For the Jews could ever and again seek out their old docu-

ments among the Christians (who had issued forth from them) whenever, in their wanderings, the skill in reading these books, and so the desire to possess them, was lost, as may often have happened, and when they merely retained the memory of having formerly possessed them. Hence we find no Jews outside the countries referred to, if we except the few on the coast of Malabar and possibly a community in China (and of these the first could have been in continual commercial relation with their co-religionists in Arabia). Although it cannot be doubted that they spread throughout those rich lands [*i.e.,* lands not Christian or Mohammedan], yet, because of the lack of all kinship between their faith and the types of belief found there, they came wholly to forget their own. To base edifying remarks upon this preservation of the Jewish people, together with their religion, under circumstances so disadvantageous to them, is very hazardous, for both sides believe that they find in it [confirmation of] their own opinions. One man sees in the continuation of the people to which he belongs, and in his ancient faith which remained unmixed despite the dispersion among such diverse nations, the proof of a special beneficent Providence saving this people for a future kingdom on earth; the other sees nothing but the warning ruins of a disrupted state which set itself against the coming of the kingdom of heaven— ruins, however, which a special Providence still sustains, partly to preserve in memory the ancient prophecy of a Messiah arising from this people, partly to offer, in this people, an example of punitive justice [visited upon it] because it stiff-neckedly sought to create a political and not a moral concept of the Messiah.

us; for we can thus classify only that which we can know but which is incapable of being communicated publicly, whereas, though morality can indeed be communicated publicly, its cause remains unknown to us. Thus freedom, an attribute of which man becomes aware through the determinability of his will by the unconditioned moral law, is no mystery, because the knowledge of it can be *shared* with everyone; but the ground, inscrutable to us, of this attribute is a mystery because this ground is *not given* us as an object of knowledge. Yet it is this very freedom which, when applied to the final object of practical reason (the realization of the idea of the moral end), alone leads us inevitably to holy mysteries.[16]

The idea of the highest good, inseparably bound up with the purely moral disposition, cannot be realized by man himself (not only in the matter of the happiness pertaining thereto, but also in the matter of the union of men necessary for the end in its entirety); yet he discovers within himself the duty to work for this end. Hence he finds himself impelled to believe in the cooperation or management of a moral Ruler of the world, by means of which alone this goal can be reached. And now there opens up before him the abyss of a mystery regarding what God may do [toward the realization of this end], whether indeed *anything* in general,

and if so, *what* in particular should be ascribed to God. Meanwhile man knows concerning each duty nothing but what he must himself do in order to be worthy of that supplement, unknown, or at least incomprehensible, to him.

This idea of a moral Governor of the world is a task presented to our practical reason. It concerns us not so much to know what God is in Himself (His nature) as what He is for us as moral beings; although in order to know the latter we must conceive and comprehend all the attributes of the divine nature (for instance, the unchangeableness, omniscience, omnipotence, etc. of such a Being) which, in their totality, are requisite to the carrying out of the divine will in this regard. Apart from this context we can know nothing about Him.

Now the universal true religious belief conformable to this requirement of practical reason is belief in God (1) as the omnipotent Creator of heaven and earth, *i.e.*, morally as *holy* Legislator, (2) as Preserver of the human race, its *benevolent* Ruler and moral Guardian, (3) as Administrator of His own holy laws, *i.e.*, as *righteous* Judge.

This belief really contains no mystery, because it merely expresses the moral relation of God to the human race; it also presents itself spontaneously to human reason everywhere and is therefore to be met with in the

---

[16] Similarly, the *cause* of the universal gravity of all matter in the world is unknown to us, so much so, indeed, that we can even see that we shall never know it: for the very concept of gravity presupposes a primary motive force unconditionally inhering in it. Yet gravity is no mystery but can be made public to all, for its *law* is adequately known. When Newton represents it as similar to divine omnipresence in the [world of] appearance (*omnipraesentia phaenomenon*), this is not an attempt to explain it (for the existence of God in space involves a contradiction), but a sublime analogy which has regard solely to the union of corporeal beings with a world-whole, an incorporeal cause being here attributed to this union. The same result would follow upon an attempt to comprehend the self-sufficing principle of the union of rational beings in the world into an ethical state, and to explain

this in terms of that principle. All we know is the duty which draws us toward such a union; the possibility of the achievement held in view when we obey that duty lies wholly beyond the limits of our insight.

There are mysteries which are hidden things in nature (*arcana*), and there can be mysteries (secrecies, *secreta*) in politics which *ought* not to be known publicly; but both *can*, after all, become known to us, inasmuch as they rest on empirical causes. There can be no mystery with respect to what all men are in duty bound to know (*i.e.*, what is moral); only with respect to that which God alone can do and the performance of which exceeds our capacity, and therefore our duty, can there be a genuine, that is, a holy mystery (*mysterium*) of religion; and it may well be expedient for us merely to know and understand that there is such a mystery, not to comprehend it.

religion of most civilized peoples.[17] It is present likewise in the concept of a people regarded as a commonwealth, in which such a threefold higher power (*pouvoir*) will always be descried, except that this commonwealth is here represented as ethical: hence this threefold quality of the moral Governor of the human race, which in a juridico-civil state must of necessity be divided among three different departments [legislative, executive, and judicial], can be thought of as combined in one and the same Being.[18]

And since this faith which, on behalf of religion in general, has cleansed the moral relation of men to the Supreme Being from harmful anthropomorphism, and has harmonized it with the genuine morality of a people of God, was first set forth in a particular (the Christian) body of doctrine and only therein made public to the world, we can call the promulgation of these doctrines a revelation of the faith which had hitherto remained hidden from men through their own fault.

These doctrines assert, *first,* that we are to look upon the Supreme Lawgiver as one who

commands not *mercifully* or with *forbearance* (indulgently) for men's weakness, or *despotically* and merely according to His unlimited right; and we are to look upon His laws not as arbitrary and as wholly unrelated to our concepts of morality, but as laws addressed to man's holiness. *Second,* we must place His beneficence not in an unconditioned *good-will* toward His creatures but in this, that He first looks upon their moral character, through which they can be *well-pleasing* to Him, and only then makes good their inability to fulfil this requirement of themselves. *Third,* His justice cannot be represented as *beneficent* and *exorable* (for this involves a contradiction); even less can it be represented as dispensed by Him in his character of *holy* Lawgiver (before Whom no man is righteous); rather, it must be thought of as beneficence which is limited by being conditioned upon men's agreement with the holy law so far as they, as *sons of men,* may be able to measure up to its requirement. In a word, God wills to be served under three specifically different moral aspects. The naming of the different (not physically, but morally different) per-

---

[17] In the sacred prophetic story of "the last things," the *judge of the world* (really he who will separate out and take under his dominion, as his own, those who belong to the kingdom of the good principle) is not represented and spoken of as God but as the Son of Man. This seems to indicate that *humanity itself,* knowing its limitation and its frailty, will pronounce the sentence in this selection [of the good from the bad]—a benevolence which yet does not offend against justice. In contrast, the Judge of men, represented in His divinity (the Holy Ghost), *i.e.,* as He speaks to our conscience according to the holy law which we know, and in terms of our own reckoning, can be thought of only as passing judgment according to the rigor of the law. For we ourselves are wholly ignorant of how much can be credited, in our behalf, to the account of our frailty, and have moreover before our eyes nothing but our transgression, together with the consciousness of our freedom, and the violation of duty for which we are wholly to blame; hence we have no ground for assuming benevolence in the judgment passed upon us.

[18] We cannot discover the cause for the agreement of so many ancient peoples in this idea, unless it is that the idea is present universally in hu-

man reason whenever man wants to conceive of civil government or (by analogy therewith) of world government. The religion of Zoroaster had these three divine persons, Ormazd, Mithra, and Ahriman; that of the Hindus had Brahma, Vishnu, and Siva—but with this difference, that Zoroastrians represent the third person as creator, not only of *evil* so far as it is punishment, but even of *moral evil* for which man is punished, whereas the Hindus represent him as merely judging and punishing. The religion of Egypt had its Ptah, Kneph, and Neith, of whom, so far as the obscurity of the earliest records of this people allows of conjecture, the first was intended to represent spirit, distinguished from matter, as *World-Creator,* the second, a principle of sustaining and *ruling* benevolence, the third, wisdom setting limits to this benevolence, *i.e., justice.* The Goths honored their Odin (father of all), their Freya (also Freyer, beneficence), and Thor, the judging (punishing) god. Even the Jews seem to have followed these ideas during the last period of their hierarchical constitution. For in the complaint of the Pharisees that Christ had called himself a *Son of God,* they seem to have attached no special weight of blame to the doctrine that God had a son, but merely to Christ's having wished to be this son of God.

sons of one and the same Being expresses this not ineptly. This symbol of faith gives expression also to the whole of pure moral religion which, without this differentiation, runs the risk of degenerating into an anthropomorphic servile faith, by reason of men's propensity to think of the Godhead as a human overlord (because in man's government rulers usually do not separate these three qualities from one another but often mix and interchange them).

But if this very faith (in a divine tri-unity) were to be regarded not merely as a representation of a practical idea but as a faith which is to describe what God is in Himself, it would be a mystery transcending all human concepts, and hence a mystery of revelation, unsuited to man's powers of comprehension; in this account, therefore, we can declare it to be such. Faith in it, regarded as an extension of the theoretical knowledge of the divine nature, would be merely the acknowledgment of a symbol of ecclesiastical faith which is quite incomprehensible to men or which, if they think they can understand it, would be anthropomorphic, and therefore nothing whatever would be accomplished for moral betterment. Only that which, in a practical context, can be thoroughly understood and comprehended, but which, taken theologically (for the determining of the nature of the object in itself), transcends all our concepts, is a mystery (in one respect) and can yet (in another) be revealed. To this type belongs what has just been mentioned; and this can be divided into three mysteries revealed to us through our reason.

1. The mystery of the divine *call* (of men, as citizens, to an ethical state). We can conceive of the universal *unconditioned* subjection of men to the divine legislation only so far as we likewise regard ourselves as God's *creatures;* just as God can be regarded as the ultimate source of all natural laws only because He is the creator of natural objects. But it is absolutely incomprehensible to our reason how beings can be *created* to a free use of their powers; for according to the principle of causality we can assign to a being, regarded as having been brought forth, no inner ground for his actions other than that which the producing cause has placed there, by which, then, (and so by an external cause) his every act would be determined, and such a being would therefore not be free. So the legislation which is divine and holy, and therefore concerns free beings only, cannot through the insight of our reason be reconciled with the concept of the creation of such beings; rather must one regard them even now as existing free beings who are determined not through their dependence upon nature by virtue of their creation but through a purely moral necessitation possible according to laws of freedom, *i.e.*, a call to citizenship in a divine state. Thus the call to this end is morally quite clear, while for speculation the possibility of such a calling is an impenetrable mystery.

2. The mystery of *atonement*. Man, as we know him, is corrupt and of himself not in the least suited to that holy law. And yet, if the goodness of God has called him, as it were, into being, *i.e.*, to exist in a particular manner (as a member of the kingdom of Heaven), He must also have a means of supplementing, out of the fullness of His own holiness, man's lack of requisite qualifications therefor. But this contradicts spontaneity (which is assumed in all the moral good or evil which a man can have within himself), according to which such a good cannot come from another but must arise from man himself, if it is to be imputable to him. Therefore, so far as reason can see, no one can, by virtue of the superabundance of his own good conduct and through his own merit, take another's place; or, if such vicarious atonement is accepted, we would have *to assume it* only from the moral point of view, since for ratiocination it is an unfathomable mystery.

3. The mystery of *election*. Even if that vicarious atonement be admitted as possible, still a morally-believing acceptance of it is a determination of the will toward good that already presupposes in man a disposition which is pleasing to God; yet man, by reason

399

of his natural depravity, cannot produce this within himself through his own efforts. But that a heavenly *grace* should work in man and should accord this assistance to one and not to another, and this not according to the merit of works but by an unconditioned *decree;* and that one portion of our race should be destined for salvation, the other for eternal reprobation—this again yields no concept of a divine justice but must be referred to a wisdom whose rule is for us an absolute mystery.

As to these mysteries, so far as they touch the moral life-history of every man—how it happens that there is a moral good or evil at all in the world, and (if the evil is present in all men and at all times) how out of evil good could spring up and be established in any man whatever, or why, when *this* occurs in some, others remain deprived thereof—of this God has revealed to us nothing and can reveal nothing since we would not *understand* it.[19] It is as though we wished to *explain* and to *render comprehensible* to ourselves in terms of a man's freedom what happens to him; on this question God has indeed revealed His will through the moral law in us, but the *causes* due to which a free action on earth occurs or does not occur He has left in that obscurity in which human investigation must leave whatever (as an historical occurrence, though yet springing from freedom) ought to be conceived of according to the laws of cause and effect.[20] But all that we need concerning the objective rule of our behavior is adequately revealed to us (through reason and Scripture), and this revelation is at the same time comprehensible to every man.

That, through the moral law, man is called to a good course of life; that, through unquenchable respect for this law lying in him, he finds in himself justification for confidence in this good spirit and for hope that, however it may come about, he will be able to satisfy this spirit; finally, that, comparing the last-named expectation with the stern command of the law, he must continually test himself as though summoned to account before a judge—reason, heart, and con-

science all teach this and urge its fulfilment. To demand that more than this be revealed to us is presumptuous, and were such a revelation to occur, it could not rightly be reckoned among man's universal needs.

Although that great mystery, comprising in one formula all that we have mentioned, can be made comprehensible to each man through his reason as a practical and necessary religious idea, we can say that, in order to become the moral basis of religion, and particularly of a public religion, it was, at that time, first revealed when it was *publicly* taught and made the symbol of a wholly new religious epoch. *Ceremonial formulas* are usually couched in a language of their own, intended only for those who belong to a particular union (a guild or society), a language at times mystical and not understood by everyone, which properly (out of respect) ought to be made use of only for a

---

[19] We commonly have no misgivings in requiring of novices in religion a belief in mysteries; for the fact that we do not *comprehend* them, *i.e.,* that we cannot see into the possibility of their objective existence, could no more justify our refusal to accept them than it could justify our not accepting, say, the procreative capacity of organisms, which likewise no man comprehends yet which we cannot on that account refuse to admit, even though it is and will remain a mystery to us. But we *understand* very well what this expression means to convey and we have an empirical concept of this capacity, together with the consciousness that it harbors no contradiction. Now we can with justice require of every mystery offered for belief that we *understand* what it is supposed to mean; and this does not happen when we merely understand the words by which it is designated *one by one, i.e.,* attaching a meaning to each word—rather, these words, taken together in one concept, must admit of another meaning and not, thus taken in conjunction, frustrate all thought. It is unthinkable that God could allow this knowledge to come to us through *inspiration* whenever we on our part wish earnestly for it; for such knowledge cannot inhere in us at all because our understanding is by nature unsuited to it.

[20] Hence we understand perfectly well what freedom is, practically (when it is a question of duty), whereas we cannot without contradiction even think of wishing to understand theoretically the causality of freedom (or its nature).

ceremonial act (as, for instance, when some one is to be initiated as a member of a society which is exclusive). But the highest goal of moral perfection of finite creatures—a goal to which man can never completely attain —is love of the law.

The equivalent in religion of this idea would be an article of faith, "God is love": in Him we can *revere* the loving One (whose love is that of moral *approbation* of men so far as they measure up to His holy law)—the *Father;* in Him also, so far as He reveals Himself in His all-inclusive idea, the archetype of humanity reared and beloved by Him, we can revere His *Son;* and finally, so far as He makes this approbation dependent upon men's agreement with the condition of that approving love, and so reveals love as based upon wisdom, we can revere the *Holy Ghost.*[21] Not that we should actually *invoke* Him in terms of this multiform personality (for to do so would suggest a diversity of entities, whereas He is ever but single); but we can call

upon him in the name of that object loved of Him, which He Himself esteems above all else, with which to enter into moral union is [our] desire and also [our] duty. Over and above this, the theoretical avowal of faith in the divine nature under this threefold character is part of what is merely the classic formula of an ecclesiastical faith, to be used for the distinguishing of this faith from other modes of belief deriving from historical sources. Few men are in the position of being able to combine with this faith a concept [of the Trinity] which is clear and definite (open to no misinterpretation); and its exposition concerns, rather, teachers in their relation to one another (as philosophical and scholarly expositors of a Holy Book), that they may agree as to its interpretation, since not everything in it is suited to the common capacity of comprehension, nor to the needs of the present, and since a bare literal faith in it hurts rather than improves the truly religious disposition.

---

[21] This Spirit, in and through which the love of God, as the Author of salvation (really our own responding love proportioned to His), is combined with the fear of God as Lawgiver, *i.e.,* the conditioned with the condition, and which can therefore be represented as "issuing forth from both," ["As it is expressed in the Western (Augustinian) form of the doctrine of the Trinity; whereas the Eastern form asserts the emanance of the Holy Ghost from the Father alone. Cf. John 15 : 26." (Note in the Berlin Edition.)], not only "leads to all truth" [cf. John 16 : 13] (obedience to duty), but is also the real Judge of men (at the bar of conscience). For judgment can be interpreted in two ways, as concerning either merit and lack of merit, or guilt and absence of guilt. God, regarded as *love* (in His Son), judges men so far as merit is attributable to them over and above their indebtedness, and here the verdict is: *worthy,* or *unworthy.* He separates out as His own those to whom such merit can still be accredited. Those who are left depart emptyhanded. On the other hand the sentence of the Judge in terms of *justice* (of the Judge properly so called, under the name of the Holy Ghost) upon those for whom no merit is forthcoming, is *guilty* or *not guilty, i.e.,* condemnation or acquittal. This *judging* signifies first of all the *separation* of the deserving from the undeserving, both parties competing for a prize (salvation). By *desert* is here meant moral excellence, not in relation to the law

(for in the eyes of the law no balance of obedience to duty over and above our indebtedness can accrue to us), but only in comparison with other men on the score of their moral disposition. And *worthiness* always has a merely negative meaning (not unworthiness), that is, the moral receptivity for such goodness.

Hence he who judges in the first capacity (as *brabeuta* [one who presided at public games and assigned the prizes]) pronounces a judgment of choice between *two* persons (or parties) striving for the prize (of salvation); while he who judges in the second capacity (the real judge) passes sentence upon *one and the same* person before a court (conscience) which declares the final verdict between the prosecution and the defense. If now it is admitted that, though indeed all men are guilty of sin, some among them may be able to achieve merit, then the verdict of *Him who judges from love* becomes effective. In the absence of this judgment, only a *verdict of rejection* could follow, whose inescapable consequence would be the *judgment of condemnation* (since the man now falls into the hands of Him who judges in righteousness). It is thus, in my opinion, that the apparently contradictory passages, "The Son will come again to judge the quick and the dead" [cf. II Timothy 4 : 1], and, "God sent not his Son into the world to condemn the world; but that the world through him might be saved" (John 3 : 17), can be reconciled, and they can agree with the other passage which reads, "He that believeth not in him is condemned *already*" (John 3 : 18), namely, by the Spirit, of whom it is said: "He will judge the world because of sin and righteousness." [Cf. John 16 : 8: ". . . he will reprove the world of sin and of righteousness and of judgment."] Anxious solicitude over such distinctions in the domain of bare reason, for whose sake they have really been instituted here, might well be regarded as a useless and burdensome subtlety; and it would indeed be such if it were directed to an inquiry into the divine nature. But since men are ever prone, in matters of religion, to appeal, respecting their transgressions, to divine benignity, though they cannot circumvent His righteousness, and since a *benign judge,* as one and the same person, is a contradiction in terms, it is very evident that, even from a practical point of view, men's concepts on this subject must be very wavering and lacking in internal coherence, and that the correction and precise determination of these concepts is of great practical importance.

The Utility of Religion

John Stuart Mill

Editor's Introduction

While Mill's name stands high—stands first, perhaps—on any list of the great Victorian minds, his eminence derives more from his writings on politics and philosophy, on social questions and even literature, than from anything he had to say about religion. In fact, he published nothing on this subject during his lifetime, or at any rate nothing specific; it was treated incidentally in certain of his other works. Only after his death did a volume appear entitled *Three Essays on Religion*, of which the second essay appears here (the first, "Nature," may be found in *GGB*, Vol. 10), and which revealed that he had turned his attention to religious topics on more than one occasion. Even then, the attention was indirect, a function of his concern with other matters. Mill was not a believer, at least with respect to anything supernatural. The only religion he professed was what he called (after Comte) the Religion of Humanity, to which he came as a moral philosopher and student of society. Yet it was to such a religion, for him, that those preoccupations ultimately led, and his reflections on it, brief as they are, and minor by comparison with those he brought to bear on other subjects, constitute an interesting and by no means unimportant extension of his thought.

"The Utility of Religion" was written in the 1850s, during the period of Mill's life when he was married to Harriet Taylor, whose influence on his ideals of life and happiness he regarded as profound, and who served to some extent as his collaborator in his writings of this time. From the same period came the essay subsequently published as *Utilitarianism* (1863; *GBWW*, Vol. 43, pp. 443–76). This was a defense of the moral aspects of philosophic radicalism, the system of thought Mill had inherited from his father, James Mill (1773–1836), and from his father's mentor, the philosopher and social theorist Jeremy Bentham (1748–1831). In the course of it, Mill argues that all persons should be instilled with a regard for their fellows strong enough to create in them "a feeling of unity" with mankind which could be "taught as a religion." Such an assertion brought him necessarily into conflict with orthodox religious conceptions, to which he addresses himself here.

No question was of greater moment to the Victorians than the one he raises, which is whether, supposing religion in any particular form to be untrue, it may nevertheless be a socially necessary belief, indispensable to the morals and the mental stability of mankind. This is as much as to ask whether religion is not, after all, a vital lie. Many of Mill's contemporaries thought of it in such terms, and no one's views on the subject could have been more seriously considered than his, had he chosen—that may have been why, not wishing to be diverted from other concerns, he did not choose—to offer them while he lived.

Because Mill in his other writings rejected the idea that the moral code by which men live must have a supernatural basis—because he argued, on the contrary, that this code is, or ought to be, a work of education and convention—it was thought by some that he had contradicted himself and betrayed his rationalist principles in the third of the essays in *Three Essays on Religion,* called "Theism." In this work, written near the end of his life, Mill allowed the possibility of an intelligent creator of the world, conceded that hope, if not belief, as to the immortality of the soul might be rationally sustained, and accepted, as consistent with purely human ends, the habit of seeking approval from such a figure as Christ for the conduct of life. Whether these admissions are inconsistent with the position taken in "The Utility of Religion" is for the present reader to decide. It should be pointed out, however, that Mill was ever sensitive to the demands of feeling, that he did not think a morally good life could be led in defiance of them, and that if he found men better disposed to one another from religious sentiments he was not likely to object. The point for him was that the striving for moral excellence and the work of making the world a better place in which to live should go on. Indeed, he regarded the possibility of this as the chief reason men might have to feel gratitude toward God. For it seemed to Mill, as he rather wryly said, that "if man had not the power, by the exercise of his own energies, for the improvement both of himself and his outward circumstances, to do for himself and other creatures vastly more than God had in the first instance done, the Being who called him into existence would deserve something very different from thanks at his hands."

The Utility of Religion

It has sometimes been remarked how much has been written, both by friends and enemies, concerning the truth of religion, and how little, at least in the way of discussion or controversy, concerning its usefulness. This, however, might have been expected; for the truth, in matters which so deeply affect us, is our first concernment. If religion, or any particular form of it, is true, its usefulness follows without other proof. If to know authentically in what order of things, under what government of the universe it is our destiny to live, were not useful, it is difficult to imagine what could be considered so. Whether a person is in a pleasant or in an unpleasant place, a palace or a prison, it cannot be otherwise than useful to him to know where he is. So long, therefore, as men accepted the teachings of their religion as positive facts, no more a matter of doubt than their own existence or the existence of the objects around them, to ask the use of believing it could not possibly occur to them. The utility of religion did not need to be asserted until the arguments for its truth had in a great measure ceased to convince. People must either have ceased to believe, or have ceased to rely on the belief of others, before they could take that inferior ground of defence without a consciousness of lowering what they were endeavouring to raise. An argument for the utility of religion is an appeal to unbelievers, to induce them to practise a well meant hypocrisy, or to semi-believers to make them avert their eyes from what might possibly shake their unstable belief, or finally to persons in general to abstain from expressing any doubts they may feel, since a fabric of immense importance to mankind is so insecure at its foundations, that men must hold their breath in its neighbourhood for fear of blowing it down.

In the present period of history, however, we seem to have arrived at a time when, among the arguments for and against religion, those which relate to its usefulness assume an important place. We are in an age of weak beliefs, and in which such belief as men have is much more determined by their wish to believe than by any mental appreciation of evidence. The wish to believe does not arise only from selfish but often from the most disinterested feelings; and though it cannot produce the unwavering and perfect reliance which once existed, it fences round all that remains of the impressions of early education; it often causes direct misgivings to fade away by disuse; and above all, it induces people to continue laying out their lives according to doctrines which have lost part of their hold on the mind, and to maintain towards the world the same, or a rather more demonstrative attitude of belief, than they thought it necessary to exhibit when their personal conviction was more complete.

If religious belief be indeed so necessary to mankind, as we are continually assured that it is, there is great reason to lament, that the intellectual grounds of it should require to be backed by moral bribery or subornation of the understanding. Such a state of things is most uncomfortable even for those who may, without actual insincerity, describe themselves as believers; and still worse as regards those who, having consciously ceased to find the evidences of religion convincing, are withheld from saying so lest they should aid in doing an irreparable injury to mankind. It is a most painful position to a conscientious and cultivated mind, to be drawn in contrary directions by the two noblest of all objects of pursuit, truth, and the general good. Such a conflict must inevitably produce a growing indifference to one or other of these objects, most probably to both. Many who could render giant's service both to truth and to mankind if they believed that they could serve the one without loss to the other, are either totally paralysed, or led to confine their exertions to matters of minor detail, by the apprehension that any real freedom of speculation, or any considerable strengthening or enlargement of the thinking faculties of mankind at large, might, by making them unbelievers, be the surest way to render them vicious and miserable. Many, again, having observed in others or experienced in themselves elevated feelings which they imagine incapable of emanating from any other source than religion, have an honest aversion to anything tending, as they think, to dry up the fountain of such feelings. They, therefore, either dislike and disparage all philosophy, or addict themselves with intolerant zeal to those forms of it in which intuition usurps the place of evidence, and internal feeling is made the test of objective truth. The whole of the prevalent metaphysics of the present century is one tissue of suborned evidence in favour of religion; often of Deism only, but in any case involving a misapplication of noble impulses and speculative capacities, among the most deplorable of those wretched wastes of human faculties which make us wonder that enough is left to keep mankind progressive, at however slow a pace. It is time to consider, more impartially and therefore more deliberately than is usually done, whether all this straining to prop up beliefs which require so great an expense of intellectual toil and ingenuity to keep them standing, yields any sufficient return in human well being; and whether that end would not be better served by a frank recognition that certain subjects are inaccessible to our faculties, and by the application of the same mental powers to the strengthening and enlargement of those other sources of virtue and happiness which

stand in no need of the support or sanction of supernatural beliefs and inducements.

Neither, on the other hand, can the difficulties of the question be so promptly disposed of, as sceptical philosophers are sometimes inclined to believe. It is not enough to aver, in general terms, that there never can be any conflict between truth and utility; that if religion be false, nothing but good can be the consequence of rejecting it. For, though the knowledge of every positive truth is an useful acquisition, this doctrine cannot without reservation be applied to negative truth. When the only truth ascertainable is that nothing can be known, we do not, by this knowledge, gain any new fact by which to guide ourselves; we are, at best, only disabused of our trust in some former guidemark, which, though itself fallacious, may have pointed in the same direction with the best indications we have, and if it happens to be more conspicuous and legible, may have kept us right when they might have been overlooked. It is, in short, perfectly conceivable that religion may be morally useful without being intellectually sustainable: and it would be a proof of great prejudice in any unbeliever to deny, that there have been ages, and that there are still both nations and individuals, with regard to whom this is actually the case. Whether it is the case generally, and with reference to the future, it is the object of this paper to examine. We propose to inquire whether the belief in religion, considered as a mere persuasion, apart from the question of its truth, is really indispensable to the temporal welfare of mankind; whether the usefulness of the belief is intrinsic and universal, or local, temporary, and, in some sense, accidental; and whether the benefits which it yields might not be obtained otherwise, without the very large alloy of evil, by which, even in the best form of the belief, those benefits are qualified.

With the arguments on one side of the question we all are familiar: religious writers have not neglected to celebrate to the utmost the advantages both of religion in general and of their own religious faith in particular.

But those who have held the contrary opinion have generally contented themselves with insisting on the more obvious and flagrant of the positive evils which have been engendered by past and present forms of religious belief. And, in truth, mankind have been so unremittingly occupied in doing evil to one another in the name of religion, from the sacrifice of Iphigenia to the Dragonnades of Louis XIV (not to descend lower), that for any immediate purpose there was little need to seek arguments further off. These odious consequences, however, do not belong to religion in itself, but to particular forms of it, and afford no argument against the usefulness of any religions except those by which such enormities are encouraged. Moreover, the worst of these evils are already in a great measure extirpated from the more improved forms of religion; and as mankind advance in ideas and in feelings, this process of extirpation continually goes on: the immoral, or otherwise mischievous consequences which have been drawn from religion, are, one by one, abandoned, and, after having been long fought for as of its very essence, are discovered to be easily separable from it. These mischiefs, indeed, after they are past, though no longer arguments against religion, remain valid as large abatements from its beneficial influence, by showing that some of the greatest improvements ever made in the moral sentiments of mankind have taken place without it and in spite of it, and that what we are taught to regard as the chief of all improving influences, has in practice fallen so far short of such a character, that one of the hardest burdens laid upon the other good influences of human nature has been that of improving religion itself. The improvement, however, has taken place; it is still proceeding, and for the sake of fairness it should be assumed to be complete. We ought to suppose religion to have accepted the best human morality which reason and goodness can work out, from philosophical, christian, or any other elements. When it has thus freed itself from the pernicious consequences which result from its

identification with any bad moral doctrine, the ground is clear for considering whether its useful properties are exclusively inherent in it, or their benefits can be obtained without it.

This essential portion of the inquiry into the temporal usefulness of religion, is the subject of the present Essay. It is a part which has been little treated of by sceptical writers. The only direct discussion of it with which I am acquainted, is in a short treatise, understood to have been partly compiled from manuscripts of Mr. Bentham,* and abounding in just and profound views; but which, as it appears to me, presses many parts of the argument too hard. This treatise, and the incidental remarks scattered through the writings of M. Comte, are the only sources known to me from which anything very pertinent to the subject can be made available for the sceptical side of the argument. I shall use both of them freely in the sequel of the present discourse.

The inquiry divides itself into two parts, corresponding to the double aspect of the subject; its social, and its individual aspect. What does religion do for society, and what for the individual? What amount of benefit to social interests, in the ordinary sense of the phrase, arises from religious belief? And what influence has it in improving and ennobling individual human nature?

The first question is interesting to everybody; the latter only to the best; but to them it is, if there be any difference, the more important of the two. We shall begin with the former, as being that which best admits of being easily brought to a precise issue.

To speak first, then, of religious belief as an instrument of social good. We must commence by drawing a distinction most commonly overlooked. It is usual to credit religion *as such* with the whole of the power inherent in *any* system of moral duties inculcated by education and enforced by opinion.

---

* "Analysis of the Influence of Natural Religion on the Temporal Happiness of Mankind." By Philip Beauchamp.

Undoubtedly mankind would be in a deplorable state if no principles or precepts of justice, veracity, beneficence, were taught publicly or privately, and if these virtues were not encouraged, and the opposite vices repressed, by the praise and blame, the favourable and unfavourable sentiments, of mankind. And since nearly everything of this sort which does take place, takes place in the name of religion; since almost all who are taught any morality whatever, have it taught to them *as* religion, and inculcated on them through life principally in that character; the effect which the teaching produces as teaching, it is supposed to produce as religious teaching, and religion receives the credit of all the influence in human affairs which belongs to any generally accepted system of rules for the guidance and government of human life.

Few persons have sufficiently considered how great an influence this is; what vast efficacy belongs naturally to any doctrine received with tolerable unanimity as true, and impressed on the mind from the earliest childhood as duty. A little reflection will, I think, lead us to the conclusion that it is this which is the great moral power in human affairs, and that religion only seems so powerful because this mighty power has been under its command.

Consider first, the enormous influence of authority on the human mind. I am now speaking of involuntary influence; effect on men's conviction, on their persuasion, on their involuntary sentiments. Authority is the evidence on which the mass of mankind believe everything which they are said to know, except facts of which their own senses have taken cognizance. It is the evidence on which even the wisest receive all those truths of science, or facts in history or in life, of which they have not personally examined the proofs. Over the immense majority of human beings, the general concurrence of mankind, in any matter of opinion, is all powerful. Whatever is thus certified to them, they believe with a fulness of assurance which they do not accord even to the evidence of their senses when the general opinion of mankind stands in opposition to it. When, therefore, any rule of life and duty, whether grounded or not on religion, has conspicuously received the general assent, it obtains a hold on the belief of every individual, stronger than it would have even if he had arrived at it by the inherent force of his own understanding. If Novalis could say, not without a real meaning, "My belief has gained infinitely to me from the moment when one other human being has begun to believe the same," how much more when it is not one other person, but all the human beings whom one knows of. Some may urge it as an objection, that no scheme of morality has this universal assent, and that none, therefore, can be indebted to this source for whatever power it possesses over the mind. So far as relates to the present age, the assertion is true, and strengthens the argument which it might at first seem to controvert; for exactly in proportion as the received systems of belief have been contested, and it has become known that they have many dissentients, their hold on the general belief has been loosened, and their practical influence on conduct has declined: and since this has happened to them notwithstanding the religious sanction which attached to them, there can be no stronger evidence that they were powerful not as religion, but as beliefs generally accepted by mankind. To find people who believe their religion as a person believes that fire will burn his hand when thrust into it, we must seek them in those Oriental countries where Europeans do not yet predominate, or in the European world when it was still universally Catholic. Men often disobeyed their religion in those times, because their human passions and appetites were too strong for it, or because the religion itself afforded means of indulgence to breaches of its obligations; but though they disobeyed, they, for the most part, did not doubt. There was in those days an absolute and unquestioning completeness of belief, never since general in Europe.

Such being the empire exercised over mankind by simple authority, the mere belief and testimony of their fellow creatures; consider next how tremendous is the power of education; how unspeakable is the effect of bringing people up from infancy in a belief, and in habits founded on it. Consider also that in all countries, and from the earliest ages down to the present, not merely those who are called, in a restricted sense of the term, the educated, but all or nearly all who have been brought up by parents, or by any one interested in them, have been taught from their earliest years some kind of religious belief, and some precepts as the commands of the heavenly powers to them and to mankind. And as it cannot be imagined that the commands of God are to young children anything more than the commands of their parents, it is reasonable to think that any system of social duty which mankind might adopt, even though divorced from religion, would have the same advantage of being inculcated from childhood, and would have it hereafter much more perfectly than any doctrine has it at present, society being far more disposed than formerly to take pains for the moral tuition of those numerous classes whose education it has hitherto left very much to chance. Now it is especially characteristic of the impressions of early education, that they possess what it is so much more difficult for later convictions to obtain—command over the feelings. We see daily how powerful a hold these first impressions retain over the feelings even of those, who have given up the opinions which they were early taught. While on the other hand, it is only persons of a much higher degree of natural sensibility and intellect combined than it is at all common to meet with, whose feelings entwine themselves with anything like the same force round opinions which they have adopted from their own investigations later in life; and even when they do, we may say with truth that it is because the strong sense of moral duty, the sincerity, courage and self-devotion which enabled them to do so, were themselves the fruits of early impressions.

The power of education is almost boundless: there is not one natural inclination which it is not strong enough to coerce, and, if needful, to destroy by disuse. In the greatest recorded victory which education has ever achieved over a whole host of natural inclinations in an entire people—the maintenance through centuries of the institutions of Lycurgus—it was very little, if even at all, indebted to religion: for the Gods of the Spartans were the same as those of other Greek states; and though, no doubt, every state of Greece believed that its particular polity had at its first establishment, some sort of divine sanction (mostly that of the Delphian oracle), there was seldom any difficulty in obtaining the same or an equally powerful sanction for a change. It was not religion which formed the strength of the Spartan institutions: the root of the system was devotion to Sparta, to the ideal of the country or State: which transformed into ideal devotion to a greater country, the world, would be equal to that and far nobler achievements. Among the Greeks generally, social morality was extremely independent of religion. The inverse relation was rather that which existed between them; the worship of the Gods was inculcated chiefly as a social duty, inasmuch as if they were neglected or insulted, it was believed that their displeasure would fall not more upon the offending individual than upon the state or community which bred and tolerated him. Such moral teaching as existed in Greece had very little to do with religion. The Gods were not supposed to concern themselves much with men's conduct to one another, except when men had contrived to make the Gods themselves an interested party, by placing an assertion or an engagement under the sanction of a solemn appeal to them, by oath or vow. I grant that the sophists and philosophers, and even popular orators, did their best to press religion into the service of their special objects, and to make it be thought that the sentiments of whatever kind, which they were engaged in inculcating, were particularly acceptable to the Gods, but this never seems the primary consideration in any case save

411

those of direct offence to the dignity of the Gods themselves. For the enforcement of human moralities secular inducements were almost exclusively relied on. The case of Greece is, I believe, the only one in which any teaching, other than religious, has had the unspeakable advantage of forming the basis of education: and though much may be said against the quality of some part of the teaching, very little can be said against its effectiveness. The most memorable example of the power of education over conduct, is afforded (as I have just remarked) by this exceptional case; constituting a strong presumption that in other cases, early religious teaching has owed its power over mankind rather to its being early than to its being religious.

We have now considered two powers, that of authority, and that of early education, which operate through men's involuntary beliefs, feelings and desires, and which religion has hitherto held as its almost exclusive appanage. Let us now consider a third power which operates directly on their actions, whether their involuntary sentiments are carried with it or not. This is the power of public opinion; of the praise and blame, the favour and disfavour, of their fellow creatures; and is a source of strength inherent in any system of moral belief which is generally adopted, whether connected with religion or not.

Men are so much accustomed to give to the motives that decide their actions, more flattering names than justly belong to them, that they are generally quite unconscious how much those parts of their conduct which they most pride themselves on (as well as some which they are ashamed of), are determined by the motive of public opinion. Of course public opinion for the most part enjoins the same things which are enjoined by the received social morality; that morality being, in truth, the summary of the conduct which each one of the multitude, whether he himself observes it with any strictness or not, desires that others should observe towards him. People are therefore easily able to flatter themselves that they are acting from the motive of conscience when they are doing in obedience to the inferior motive, things which their conscience approves. We continually see how great is the power of opinion in opposition to conscience; how men "follow a multitude to do evil;" how often opinion induces them to do what their conscience disapproves, and still oftener prevents them from doing what it commands. But when the motive of public opinion acts in the same direction with conscience, which, since it has usually itself made the conscience in the first instance, it for the most part naturally does; it is then, of all motives which operate on the bulk of mankind, the most overpowering.

The names of all the strongest passions (except the merely animal ones) manifested by human nature, are each of them a name for some one part only of the motive derived from what I here call public opinion. The love of glory; the love of praise; the love of admiration; the love of respect and deference; even the love of sympathy, are portions of its attractive power. Vanity is a vituperative name for its attractive influence generally, when considered excessive in degree. The fear of shame, the dread of ill repute or of being disliked or hated, are the direct and simple forms of its deterring power. But the deterring force of the unfavourable sentiments of mankind does not consist solely in the painfulness of knowing oneself to be the object of those sentiments; it includes all the penalties which they can inflict: exclusion from social intercourse and from the innumerable good offices which human beings require from one another; the forfeiture of all that is called success in life; often the great diminution or total loss of means of subsistence; positive ill offices of various kinds, sufficient to render life miserable, and reaching in some states of society as far as actual persecution to death. And again the attractive, or impelling influence of public opinion, includes the whole range of what is commonly meant by ambition: for, except in times of lawless military violence, the objects of social ambition can only be attained by means of the good opinion and favourable disposition of our fellow-creatures; nor, in nine cases out of ten, would those objects be even desired, were it not for the power they confer over the sentiments of mankind. Even the pleasure of self-approbation, in the great majority, is mainly dependent on the opinion of others. Such is the involuntary influence of authority on ordinary minds, that persons must be of a better than ordinary mould to be capable of a full assurance that they are in the right, when the world, that is, when *their* world, thinks them wrong: nor is there, to most men, any proof so demonstrative of their own virtue or talent as that people in general seem to believe in it. Through all departments of human affairs, regard for the sentiments of our fellow-creatures is in one shape or other, in nearly all characters, the pervading motive. And we ought to note that this motive is naturally strongest in the most sensitive natures, which are the most promising material for the formation of great virtues. How far its power reaches is known by too familiar experience to require either proof or illustration here. When once the means of living have been obtained, the far greater part of the remaining labour and effort which takes place on the earth, has for its object to acquire the respect or the favourable regard of mankind; to be looked up to, or at all events, not to be looked down upon by them. The industrial and commercial activity which advance civilization, the frivolity, prodigality, and selfish thirst of aggrandizement which retard it, flow equally from that source. While as an instance of the power exercised by the terrors derived from public opinion, we know how many murders have been committed merely to remove a witness who knew and was likely to disclose some secret that would bring disgrace upon his murderer.

Any one who fairly and impartially considers the subject, will see reason to believe that those great effects on human conduct, which are commonly ascribed to motives derived directly from religion, have mostly for their proximate cause the influence of human opinion. Religion has been powerful not by its intrinsic force, but because it has wielded that additional and more mighty power. The effect of religion has been immense in giving a direction to public opinion: which has, in many most important respects, been wholly determined by it. But without the sanctions superadded by public opinion, its own proper sanctions have never, save in exceptional characters, or in peculiar moods of mind, exercised a very potent influence, after the times had gone by, in which divine agency was supposed habitually to employ temporal rewards and punishments. When a man firmly believed that if he violated the sacredness of a particular sanctuary he would be struck dead on the spot, or smitten suddenly with a mortal disease, he doubtless took care not to incur the penalty: but when any one had had the courage to defy the danger, and escaped with impunity, the spell was broken. If ever any people were taught that they were under a divine government, and that unfaithfulness to their religion and law would be visited from above with temporal chastisements, the Jews were so. Yet their history was a mere succession of lapses into Paganism. Their prophets and historians, who held fast to the ancient beliefs (though they gave them so liberal an interpretation as to think it a sufficient manifestation of God's displeasure towards a king if any evil happened to his great grandson), never ceased to complain that their countrymen turned a deaf ear to their vaticinations; and hence, with the faith they held in a divine government operating by temporal penalties, they could not fail to anticipate (as Mirabeau's father without such prompting, was able to do on the eve of the French Revolution) *la culbute générale;* an expectation which, luckily for the credit of their prophetic powers, was fulfilled; unlike that of the Apostle John, who in the only intelligible prophecy in the Revelations, foretold to the city of the seven hills a fate like that of Nineveh and Babylon; which prediction remains to this hour unaccomplished. Unquestionably the conviction which experience in time forced on all but the very ignorant, that divine punishments

413

were not to be confidently expected in a temporal form, contributed much to the downfall of the old religions, and the general adoption of one which without absolutely excluding providential interferences in this life for the punishment of guilt or the reward of merit, removed the principal scene of divine retribution to a world after death. But rewards and punishments postponed to that distance of time, and never seen by the eye, are not calculated, even when infinite and eternal, to have, on ordinary minds, a very powerful effect in opposition to strong temptation. Their remoteness alone is a prodigious deduction from their efficacy, on such minds as those which most require the restraint of punishment. A still greater abatement is their uncertainty, which belongs to them from the very nature of the case: for rewards and punishments administered after death, must be awarded not definitely to particular actions, but on a general survey of the person's whole life, and he easily persuades himself that whatever may have been his peccadilloes, there will be a balance in his favour at the last. All positive religions aid this self-delusion. Bad religions teach that divine vengeance may be bought off, by offerings, or personal abasement; the better religions, not to drive sinners to despair, dwell so much on the divine mercy, that hardly any one is compelled to think himself irrevocably condemned. The sole quality in these punishments which might seem calculated to make them efficacious, their overpowering magnitude, is itself a reason why nobody (except a hypochondriac here and there) ever really believes that he is in any very serious danger of incurring them. Even the worst malefactor is hardly able to think that any crime he has had it in his power to commit, any evil he can have inflicted in this short space of existence, can have deserved torture extending through an eternity. Accordingly religious writers and preachers are never tired of complaining how little effect religious motives have on men's lives and conduct, notwithstanding the tremendous penalties denounced.

Mr. Bentham, whom I have already mentioned as one of the few authors who have written anything to the purpose on the efficacy of the religious sanction, adduces several cases to prove that religious obligation, when not enforced by public opinion, produces scarcely any effect on conduct. His first example is that of oaths. The oaths taken in courts of justice, and any others which from the manifest importance to society of their being kept, public opinion rigidly enforces, are felt as real and binding obligations. But university oaths and custom-house oaths, though in a religious point of view equally obligatory, are in practice utterly disregarded even by men in other respects honourable. The university oath to obey the statutes has been for centuries, with universal acquiescence, set at nought: and utterly false statements are (or used to be) daily and unblushingly sworn to at the Custom-house, by persons as attentive as other people to all the ordinary obligations of life. The explanation being, that veracity in these cases was not enforced by public opinion. The second case which Bentham cites is duelling; a practice now, in this country, obsolete, but in full vigour in several other christian countries; deemed and admitted to be a sin by almost all who, nevertheless, in obedience to opinion, and to escape from personal humiliation, are guilty of it. The third case is that of illicit sexual intercourse; which in both sexes, stands in the very highest rank of religious sins, yet not being severely censured by opinion in the male sex, they have in general very little scruple in committing it; while in the case of women, though the religious obligation is not stronger, yet being backed in real earnest by public opinion, it is commonly effectual.

Some objection may doubtless be taken to Bentham's instances, considered as crucial experiments on the power of the religious sanction; for (it may be said) people do not really believe that in these cases they shall be punished by God, any more than by man. And this is certainly true in the case of those university and other oaths, which are habitually taken without any intention of keeping them. The oath, in these cases, is regarded as a mere formality, destitute of any serious meaning in the sight of the Deity; and the most scrupulous person, even if he does reproach himself for having taken an oath which nobody deems fit to be kept, does not in his conscience tax himself with the guilt of perjury, but only with the profanation of a ceremony. This, therefore, is not a good example of the weakness of the religious motive when divorced from that of human opinion. The point which it illustrates is rather the tendency of the one motive to come and go with the other, so that where the penalties of public opinion cease, the religious motive ceases also. The same criticism, however, is not equally applicable to Bentham's other examples, duelling, and sexual irregularities. Those who do these acts, the first by the command of public opinion, the latter with its indulgence, really do, in most cases, believe that they are offending God. Doubtless, they do not think that they are offending him in such a degree as very seriously to endanger their salvation. Their reliance on his mercy prevails over their dread of his resentment; affording an exemplification of the remark already made, that the unavoidable uncertainty of religious penalties makes them feeble as a deterring motive. They are so, even in the case of acts which human opinion condemns: much more, with those to which it is indulgent. What mankind think venial, it is hardly ever supposed that God looks upon in a serious light: at least by those who feel in themselves any inclination to practise it.

I do not for a moment think of denying that there are states of mind in which the idea of religious punishment acts with the most overwhelming force. In hypochondriacal disease, and in those with whom, from great disappointments or other moral causes, the thoughts and imagination have assumed an habitually melancholy complexion, that topic, falling in with the pre-existing tendency of the mind, supplies images well fitted to drive the unfortunate sufferer even to madness. Often, during a temporary state

of depression, these ideas take such a hold of the mind as to give a permanent turn to the character; being the most common case of what, in sectarian phraseology, is called conversion. But if the depressed state ceases after the conversion, as it commonly does, and the convert does not relapse, but perseveres in his new course of life, the principal difference between it and the old is usually found to be, that the man now guides his life by the public opinion of his religious associates, as he before guided it by that of the profane world. At all events, there is one clear proof how little the generality of mankind, either religious or worldly, really dread eternal punishments, when we see how, even at the approach of death, when the remoteness which took so much from their effect has been exchanged for the closest proximity, almost all persons who have not been guilty of some enormous crime (and many who have) are quite free from uneasiness as to their prospects in another world, and never for a moment seem to think themselves in any real danger of eternal punishment.

With regard to the cruel deaths and bodily tortures, which confessors and martyrs have so often undergone for the sake of religion, I would not depreciate them by attributing any part of this admirable courage and constancy to the influence of human opinion. Human opinion indeed has shown itself quite equal to the production of similar firmness in persons not otherwise distinguished by moral excellence; such as the North American Indian at the stake. But if it was not the thought of glory in the eyes of their fellow-religionists, which upheld these heroic sufferers in their agony, as little do I believe that it was, generally speaking, that of the pleasures of heaven or the pains of hell. Their impulse was a divine enthusiasm—a self-forgetting devotion to an idea: a state of exalted feeling, by no means peculiar to religion, but which it is the privilege of every great cause to inspire; a phenomenon belonging to the critical moments of existence, not to the ordinary play of human motives, and from which nothing can be inferred as to the efficacy of the ideas which it sprung from, whether religious or any other, in overcoming ordinary temptations, and regulating the course of daily life.

We may now have done with this branch of the subject, which is, after all, the vulgarest part of it. The value of religion as a supplement to human laws, a more cunning sort of police, an auxiliary to the thief-catcher and the hangman, is not that part of its claims which the more highminded of its votaries are fondest of insisting on: and they would probably be as ready as any one to admit, that if the nobler offices of religion in the soul could be dispensed with, a substitute might be found for so coarse and selfish a social instrument as the fear of hell. In their view of the matter, the best of mankind absolutely require religion for the perfection of their own character, even though the coercion of the worst might possibly be accomplished without its aid.

Even in the social point of view, however, under its most elevated aspect, these nobler spirits generally assert the necessity of religion, as a teacher, if not as an enforcer, of social morality. They say, that religion alone can teach us what morality is; that all the high morality ever recognized by mankind, was learnt from religion; that the greatest uninspired philosophers in their sublimest flights, stopt far short of the christian morality, and whatever inferior morality they may have attained to (by the assistance, as many think, of dim traditions derived from the Hebrew books, or from a primaeval revelation) they never could induce the common mass of their fellow citizens to accept it from them. That, only when a morality is understood to come from the Gods, do men in general adopt it, rally round it, and lend their human sanctions for its enforcement. That granting the sufficiency of human motives to make the rule obeyed, were it not for the religious idea we should not have had the rule itself.

There is truth in much of this, considered as matter of history. Ancient peoples have generally, if not always, received their morals, their laws, their intellectual beliefs, and even their practical arts of life, all in short which tended either to guide or to discipline them, as revelations from the superior powers, and in any other way could not easily have been induced to accept them. This was partly the effect of their hopes and fears from those powers, which were of much greater and more universal potency in early times, when the agency of the Gods was seen in the daily events of life, experience not having yet disclosed the fixed laws according to which physical phenomena succeed one another. Independently, too, of personal hopes and fears, the involuntary deference felt by these rude minds for power superior to their own, and the tendency to suppose that beings of superhuman power must also be of superhuman knowledge and wisdom, made them disinterestedly desire to conform their conduct to the presumed preferences of these powerful beings, and to adopt no new practice without their authorization either spontaneously given, or solicited and obtained.

But because, when men were still savages, they would not have received either moral or scientific truths unless they had supposed them to be supernaturally imparted, does it follow that they would now give up moral truths any more than scientific, because they believed them to have no higher origin than wise and noble human hearts? Are not moral truths strong enough in their own evidence, at all events to retain the belief of mankind when once they have acquired it? I grant that some of the precepts of Christ as exhibited in the Gospels—rising far above the Paulism which is the foundation of ordinary Christianity—carry some kinds of moral goodness to a greater height than had ever been attained before, though much even of what is supposed to be peculiar to them is equalled in the Meditations of Marcus Antoninus, which we have no ground for believing to have been in any way indebted to Christianity. But this benefit, whatever it amounts to, has been gained. Mankind have entered into the possession of it. It has become the property of humanity, and cannot now be lost by anything short of a return to primae-val barbarism. The "new commandment to love one another";* the recognition that the greatest are those who serve, not who are served by, others; the reverence for the weak and humble, which is the foundation of chivalry, they and not the strong being pointed out as having the first place in God's regard, and the first claim on their fellow men; the lesson of the parable of the Good Samaritan; that of "he that is without sin let him throw the first stone"; the precept of doing as we would be done by; and such other noble moralities as are to be found, mixed with some poetical exaggerations, and some maxims of which it is difficult to ascertain the precise object; in the authentic sayings of Jesus of Nazareth; these are surely in sufficient harmony with the intellect and feelings of every good man or woman, to be in no danger of being let go, after having been once acknowledged as the creed of the best and foremost portion of our species. There will be, as there have been, shortcomings enough for a long time to come in acting on them; but that they should be forgotten, or cease to be operative on the human conscience, while human beings remain cultivated or civilized, may be pronounced, once for all, impossible.

On the other hand, there is a very real evil consequent on ascribing a supernatural origin to the received maxims of morality. That origin consecrates the whole of them, and protects them from being discussed or criticized. So that if among the moral doctrines received as a part of religion, there be any which are imperfect—which were either erroneous from the first, or not properly limited and guarded in the expression, or which, unexceptionable once, are no longer suited to the changes that have taken place in human relations (and it is my firm belief that in so-called christian morality, instances of all these kinds are to be found) these doctrines are considered equally binding on the conscience with the noblest, most permanent and most universal precepts of Christ. Wherever morality is supposed to be of supernatu-

ral origin, morality is stereotyped; as law is, for the same reason, among believers in the Koran.

Belief, then, in the supernatural, great as are the services which it rendered in the early stages of human development, cannot be considered to be any longer required, either for enabling us to know what is right and wrong in social morality, or for supplying us with motives to do right and to abstain from wrong. Such belief, therefore, is not necessary for social purposes, at least in the coarse way in which these can be considered apart from the character of the individual human being. That more elevated branch of the subject now remains to be considered. If supernatural beliefs are indeed necessary to the perfection of the individual character, they are necessary also to the highest excellence in social conduct: necessary in a far higher sense than that vulgar one, which constitutes it the great support of morality in common eyes.

Let us then consider, what it is in human nature which causes it to require a religion; what wants of the human mind religion supplies, and what qualities it developes. When we have understood this, we shall be better able to judge, how far these wants can be otherwise supplied and those qualities, or qualities equivalent to them, unfolded and brought to perfection by other means.

The old saying, *Primus in orbe Deos fecit timor*, I hold to be untrue, or to contain, at most, only a small amount of truth. Belief in Gods had, I conceive, even in the rudest minds, a more honourable origin. Its universality has been very rationally explained from the spontaneous tendency of the mind to attribute life and volition, similar to what it feels in itself, to all natural objects and phenomena which appear to be self-moving. This was a plausible fancy, and no better theory could be formed at first. It was naturally

* Not, however, a new commandment. In justice to the great Hebrew lawgiver, it should always be remembered that the precept, to love thy neighbour as thyself, already existed in the Pentateuch; and very surprising it is to find it there.

persisted in so long as the motions and operations of these objects seemed to be arbitrary, and incapable of being accounted for but by the free choice of the Power itself. At first, no doubt, the objects themselves were supposed to be alive; and this belief still subsists among African fetish-worshippers. But as it must soon have appeared absurd that things which could do so much more than man, could not or would not do what man does, as for example to speak, the transition was made to supposing that the object present to the senses was inanimate, but was the creature and instrument of an invisible being with a form and organs similar to the human.

These beings having first been believed in, fear of them necessarily followed; since they were thought able to inflict at pleasure on human beings great evils, which the sufferers neither knew how to avert nor to foresee, but were left dependent, for their chances of doing either, upon solicitations addressed to the deities themselves. It is true, therefore, that fear had much to do with religion: but belief in the Gods evidently preceded, and did not arise from, fear: though the fear, when established, was a strong support to the belief, nothing being conceived to be so great an offence to the divinities as any doubt of their existence.

It is unnecessary to prosecute further the natural history of religion, as we have not here to account for its origin in rude minds, but for its persistency in the cultivated. A sufficient explanation of this will, I conceive, be found in the small limits of man's certain knowledge, and the boundlessness of his desire to know. Human existence is girt round with mystery: the narrow region of our experience is a small island in the midst of a boundless sea, which at once awes our feelings and stimulates our imagination by its vastness and its obscurity. To add to the mystery, the domain of our earthly existence is not only an island in infinite space, but also in infinite time. The past and the future are alike shrouded from us: we neither know the origin of anything which is, nor its final destination. If we feel deeply interested in knowing that there are myriads of worlds at an immeasurable, and to our faculties inconceivable, distance from us in space; if we are eager to discover what little we can about these worlds, and when we cannot know what they are, can never satiate ourselves with speculating on what they may be; is it not a matter of far deeper interest to us to learn, or even to conjecture, from whence came this nearer world which we inhabit; what cause or agency made it what it is, and on what powers depend its future fate? Who would not desire this more ardently than any other conceivable knowledge, so long as there appeared the slightest hope of attaining it? What would not one give for any credible tidings from that mysterious region, any glimpse into it which might enable us to see the smallest light through its darkness, especially any theory of it which we could believe, and which represented it as tenanted by a benignant and not a hostile influence? But since we are able to penetrate into that region with the imagination only, assisted by specious but inconclusive analogies derived from human agency and design, imagination is free to fill up the vacancy with the imagery most congenial to itself; sublime and elevating if it be a lofty imagination, low and mean if it be a grovelling one.

Religion and poetry address themselves, at least in one of their aspects, to the same part of the human constitution: they both supply the same want, that of ideal conceptions grander and more beautiful than we see realized in the prose of human life. Religion, as distinguished from poetry, is the product of the craving to know whether these imaginative conceptions have realities answering to them in some other world than ours. The mind, in this state, eagerly catches at any rumours respecting other worlds, especially when delivered by persons whom it deems wiser than itself. To the poetry of the supernatural, comes to be thus added a positive belief and expectation, which unpoetical minds can share with the poetical. Belief in a God or Gods, and in a life after death, becomes the canvas which every mind, according to its capacity, covers with such ideal pictures as it can either invent or copy. In that other life each hopes to find the good which he has failed to find on earth, or the better which is suggested to him by the good which on earth he has partially seen and known. More especially, this belief supplies the finer minds with material for conceptions of beings more awful than they *can* have known on earth, and more excellent than they probably *have* known. So long as human life is insufficient to satisfy human aspirations, so long there will be a craving for higher things, which finds its most obvious satisfaction in religion. So long as earthly life is full of sufferings, so long there will be need of consolations, which the hope of heaven affords to the selfish, the love of God to the tender and grateful.

The value, therefore, of religion to the individual, both in the past and present, as a source of personal satisfaction and of elevated feelings, is not to be disputed. But it has still to be considered, whether in order to obtain this good, it is necessary to travel beyond the boundaries of the world which we inhabit; or whether the idealization of our earthly life, the cultivation of a high conception of what *it* may be made, is not capable of supplying a poetry, and, in the best sense of the word, a religion, equally fitted to exalt the feelings, and (with the same aid from education) still better calculated to ennoble the conduct, than any belief respecting the unseen powers.

At the bare suggestion of such a possibility, many will exclaim, that the short duration, the smallness and insignificance of life, if there is no prolongation of it beyond what we see, makes it impossible that great and elevated feelings can connect themselves with anything laid out on so small a scale: that such a conception of life can match with nothing higher than Epicurean feelings, and the Epicurean doctrine "Let us eat and drink, for to-morrow we die."

Unquestionably, within certain limits, the maxim of the Epicureans is sound, and applicable to much higher things than eating and drinking. To make the most of the present for all good purposes, those of enjoyment among the rest; to keep under control those mental dispositions which lead to undue sacrifice of present good for a future which may never arrive; to cultivate the habit of deriving pleasure from things within our reach, rather than from the too eager pursuit of objects at a distance; to think all time wasted which is not spent either in personal pleasure or in doing things useful to oneself or others; these are wise maxims, and the "carpe diem" doctrine, carried thus far, is a rational and legitimate corollary from the shortness of life. But that because life is short we should care for nothing beyond it, is not a legitimate conclusion; and the supposition, that human beings in general are not capable of feeling deep and even the deepest interest in things which they will never live to see, is a view of human nature as false as it is abject. Let it be remembered that if individual life is short, the life of the human species is not short; its indefinite duration is practically equivalent to endlessness; and being combined with indefinite capability of improvement, it offers to the imagination and sympathies a large enough object to satisfy any reasonable demand for grandeur of aspiration. If such an object appears small to a mind accustomed to dream of infinite and eternal beatitudes, it will expand into far other dimensions when those baseless fancies shall have receded into the past.

Nor let it be thought that only the more eminent of our species, in mind and heart, are capable of identifying their feelings with the entire life of the human race. This noble capability implies indeed a certain cultivation, but not superior to that which might be, and certainly will be if human improvement continues, the lot of all. Objects far smaller than this, and equally confined within the limits of the earth (though not within those of a single human life), have been found sufficient to inspire large masses and long successions of mankind with an enthusiasm capable of ruling the conduct, and colouring the whole life. Rome was to the entire Roman people, for many generations as much a religion as Jehovah was to the Jews; nay, much more, for they never fell off from their worship as the Jews did from theirs. And the Romans, otherwise a selfish people, with no very remarkable faculties of any kind except the purely practical, derived nevertheless from this one idea a certain greatness of soul, which manifests itself in all their history where that idea is concerned and nowhere else, and has earned for them the large share of admiration, in other respects not at all deserved, which has been felt for them by most noble-minded persons from that time to this.

When we consider how ardent a sentiment, in favourable circumstances of education, the love of country has become, we cannot judge it impossible that the love of that larger country, the world, may be nursed into similar strength, both as a source of elevated emotion and as a principle of duty. He who needs any other lesson on this subject than the whole course of ancient history affords, let him read Cicero *de Officiis*. It cannot be said that the standard of morals laid down in that celebrated treatise is a high standard. To our notions it is on many points unduly lax, and admits capitulations of conscience. But on the subject of duty to our country there is no compromise. That any man, with the smallest pretensions to virtue, could hesitate to sacrifice life, reputation, family, everything valuable to him, to the love of country is a supposition which this eminent interpreter of Greek and Roman morality cannot entertain for a moment. If, then, persons could be trained, as we see they were, not only to believe in theory that the good of their country was an object to which all others ought to yield, but to feel this practically as the grand duty of life, so also may they be made to feel the same absolute obligation towards the universal good. A morality grounded on large and wise views of the good of the whole, neither sacrificing the individual to the aggregate nor the aggregate to the individual, but giving to duty on the one hand and to freedom and spontaneity on

the other their proper province, would derive its power in the superior natures from sympathy and benevolence and the passion for ideal excellence: in the inferior, from the same feelings cultivated up to the measure of their capacity, with the superadded force of shame. This exalted morality would not depend for its ascendancy on any hope of reward; but the reward which might be looked for, and the thought of which would be a consolation in suffering, and a support in moments of weakness, would not be a problematical future existence, but the approbation, in this, of those whom we respect, and ideally of all those, dead or living, whom we admire or venerate. For, the thought that our dead parents or friends would have approved our conduct is a scarcely less powerful motive than the knowledge that our living ones do approve it: and the idea that Socrates, or Howard or Washington, or Antoninus, or Christ, would have sympathized with us, or that we are attempting to do our part in the spirit in which they did theirs, has operated on the very best minds, as a strong incentive to act up to their highest feelings and convictions.

To call these sentiments by the name morality, exclusively of any other title, is claiming too little for them. They are a real religion; of which, as of other religions, outward good works (the utmost meaning usually suggested by the word morality) are only a part, and are indeed rather the fruits of the religion than the religion itself. The essence of religion is the strong and earnest direction of the emotions and desires towards an ideal object, recognized as of the highest excellence, and as rightfully paramount over all selfish objects of desire. This condition is fulfilled by the Religion of Humanity in as eminent a degree, and in as high a sense, as by the supernatural religions even in their best manifestations, and far more so than in any of their others.

Much more might be added on this topic; but enough has been said to convince any one, who can distinguish between the intrinsic capacities of human nature and the forms in which those capacities happen to have been historically developed, that the sense of unity with mankind, and a deep feeling for the general good, may be cultivated into a sentiment and a principle capable of fulfilling every important function of religion and itself justly entitled to the name. I will now further maintain, that it is not only capable of fulfilling these functions, but would fulfil them better than any form whatever of supernaturalism. It is not only entitled to be called a religion: it is a better religion than any of those which are ordinarily called by that title.

For, in the first place, it is disinterested. It carries the thoughts and feelings out of self, and fixes them on an unselfish object, loved and pursued as an end for its own sake. The religions which deal in promises and threats regarding a future life, do exactly the contrary: they fasten down the thoughts to the person's own posthumous interests; they tempt him to regard the performance of his duties to others mainly as a means to his own personal salvation; and are one of the most serious obstacles to the great purpose of moral culture, the strengthening of the unselfish and weakening of the selfish element in our nature; since they hold out to the imagination selfish good and evil of such tremendous magnitude, that it is difficult for any one who fully believes in their reality, to have feeling or interest to spare for any other distant and ideal object. It is true, many of the most unselfish of mankind have been believers in supernaturalism, because their minds have not dwelt on the threats and promises of their religion, but chiefly on the idea of a Being to whom they looked up with a confiding love, and in whose hands they willingly left all that related especially to themselves. But in its effect on common minds, what now goes by the name of religion operates mainly through the feelings of self-interest. Even the Christ of the Gospels holds out the direct promise of reward from heaven as a primary inducement to the noble and beautiful beneficence towards our fellow-creatures which he so impressively incul-

cates. This is a radical inferiority of the best supernatural religions, compared with the Religion of Humanity; since the greatest thing which moral influences can do for the amelioration of human nature, is to cultivate the unselfish feelings in the only mode in which any active principle in human nature can be effectually cultivated, namely by habitual exercise: but the habit of expecting to be rewarded in another life for our conduct in this, makes even virtue itself no longer an exercise of the unselfish feelings.

Secondly, it is an immense abatement from the worth of the old religions as means of elevating and improving human character, that it is nearly, if not quite impossible for them to produce their best moral effects, unless we suppose a certain torpidity, if not positive twist in the intellectual faculties. For it is impossible that any one who habitually thinks, and who is unable to blunt his inquiring intellect by sophistry, should be able without misgiving to go on ascribing absolute perfection to the author and ruler of so clumsily made and capriciously governed a creation as this planet and the life of its inhabitants. The adoration of such a being cannot be with the whole heart, unless the heart is first considerably sophisticated. The worship must either be greatly overclouded by doubt, and occasionally quite darkened by it, or the moral sentiments must sink to the low level of the ordinances of Nature: the worshipper must learn to think blind partiality, atrocious cruelty, and reckless injustice, not blemishes in an object of worship, since all these abound to excess in the commonest phenomena of Nature. It is true, the God who is worshipped is not, generally speaking, the God of Nature only, but also the God of some revelation; and the character of the revelation will greatly modify and, it may be, improve the moral influences of the religion. This is emphatically true of Christianity; since the Author of the Sermon on the Mount is assuredly a far more benignant Being than the Author of Nature. But unfortunately, the believer in the christian revelation is obliged to believe that the same being is the author of both. This, unless he resolutely averts his mind from the subject, or practises the act of quieting his conscience by sophistry, involves him in moral perplexities without end; since the ways of his Deity in Nature are on many occasions totally at variance with the precepts, as he believes, of the same Deity in the Gospel. He who comes out with least moral damage from this embarrassment, is probably the one who never attempts to reconcile the two standards with one another, but confesses to himself that the purposes of Providence are mysterious, that its ways are not our ways, that its justice and goodness are not the justice and goodness which we can conceive and which it befits us to practise. When, however, this is the feeling of the believer, the worship of the Deity ceases to be the adoration of abstract moral perfection. It becomes the bowing down to a gigantic image of something not fit for us to imitate. It is the worship of power only.

I say nothing of the moral difficulties and perversions involved in revelation itself; though even in the Christianity of the Gospels, at least in its ordinary interpretation, there are some of so flagrant a character as almost to outweigh all the beauty and benignity and moral greatness which so eminently distinguish the sayings and character of Christ. The recognition, for example, of the object of highest worship, in a being who could make a Hell; and who could create countless generations of human beings with the certain foreknowledge that he was creating them for this fate. Is there any moral enormity which might not be justified by imitation of such a Deity? And is it possible to adore such a one without a frightful distortion of the standard of right and wrong? Any other of the outrages to the most ordinary justice and humanity involved in the common christian conception of the moral character of God, sinks into insignificance beside this dreadful idealization of wickedness. Most of them too, are happily not so unequivocally deducible from the very words of Christ as to be indisputably a part of christian doctrine. It may be doubted, for instance, whether

Christianity is really responsible for atonement and redemption, original sin and vicarious punishment: and the same may be said respecting the doctrine which makes belief in the divine mission of Christ a necessary condition of salvation. It is nowhere represented that Christ himself made this statement, except in the huddled-up account of the Resurrection contained in the concluding verses of St. Mark, which some critics (I believe the best), consider to be an interpolation. Again, the proposition that "the powers that be are ordained of God" and the whole series of corollaries deduced from it in the Epistles, belong to St. Paul, and must stand or fall with Paulism, not with Christianity. But there is one moral contradiction inseparable from every form of Christianity, which no ingenuity can resolve, and no sophistry explain away. It is, that so precious a gift, bestowed on a few, should have been withheld from the many: that countless millions of human beings should have been allowed to live and die, to sin and suffer, without the one thing needful, the divine remedy for sin and suffering, which it would have cost the Divine Giver as little to have vouchsafed to all, as to have bestowed by special grace upon a favoured minority. Add to this, that the divine message, assuming it to be such, has been authenticated by credentials so insufficient, that they fail to convince a large proportion of the strongest and most cultivated minds, and the tendency to disbelieve them appears to grow with the growth of scientific knowledge and critical discrimination. He who can believe these to be the intentional shortcomings of a perfectly good Being, must impose silence on every prompting of the sense of goodness and justice as received among men.

It is, no doubt, possible (and there are many instances of it) to worship with the intensest devotion either Deity, that of Nature or of the Gospel, without any perversion of the moral sentiments: but this must be by fixing the attention exclusively on what is beautiful and beneficent in the precepts and spirit of the Gospel and in the dispensations of Nature, and putting all that is the reverse as entirely aside as if it did not exist. Accordingly, this simple and innocent faith can only, as I have said, co-exist with a torpid and inactive state of the speculative faculties. For a person of exercised intellect, there is no way of attaining anything equivalent to it, save by sophistication and perversion, either of the understanding or of the conscience. It may almost always be said both of sects and of individuals, who derive their morality from religion, that the better logicians they are, the worse moralists.

One only form of belief in the supernatural—one only theory respecting the origin and government of the universe—stands wholly clear both of intellectual contradiction and of moral obliquity. It is that which, resigning irrevocably the idea of an omnipotent creator, regards Nature and Life not as the expression throughout of the moral character and purpose of the Deity, but as the product of a struggle between contriving goodness and an intractable material, as was believed by Plato, or a Principle of Evil, as was the doctrine of the Manicheans. A creed like this, which I have known to be devoutly held by at least one cultivated and conscientious person of our own day, allows it to be believed that all the mass of evil which exists was undesigned by, and exists not by the appointment of, but in spite of the Being whom we are called upon to worship. A virtuous human being assumes in this theory the exalted character of a fellow-labourer with the Highest, a fellow-combatant in the great strife; contributing his little, which by the aggregation of many like himself becomes much, towards that progressive ascendancy, and ultimately complete triumph of good over evil, which history points to, and which this doctrine teaches us to regard as planned by the Being to whom we owe all the benevolent contrivance we behold in Nature. Against the moral tendency of this creed no possible objection can lie: it can produce on whoever can succeed in believing it, no other than an ennobling effect. The evidence for it, indeed, if evidence it can be called, is too shadowy and unsubstantial, and the prom-

ises it holds out too distant and uncertain, to admit of its being a permanent substitute for the religion of humanity; but the two may be held in conjunction: and he to whom ideal good, and the progress of the world towards it, are already a religion, even though that other creed may seem to him a belief not grounded on evidence, is at liberty to indulge the pleasing and encouraging thought, that its truth is possible. Apart from all dogmatic belief, there is for those who need it, an ample domain in the region of the imagination which may be planted with possibilities, with hypotheses which cannot be known to be false; and when there is anything in the appearances of nature to favour them, as in this case there is (for whatever force we attach to the analogies of Nature with the effects of human contrivance, there is no disputing the remark of Paley, that what is good in nature exhibits those analogies much oftener than what is evil), the contemplation of these possibilities is a legitimate indulgence, capable of bearing its part, with other influences, in feeding and animating the tendency of the feelings and impulses towards good.

One advantage, such as it is, the supernatural religions must always possess over the Religion of Humanity; the prospect they hold out to the individual of a life after death. For, though the scepticism of the understanding does not necessarily exclude the Theism of the imagination and feelings, and this, again, gives opportunity for a hope that the power which has done so much for us may be able and willing to do this also, such vague possibility must ever stop far short of a conviction. It remains then to estimate the value of this element—the prospect of a world to come—as a constituent of earthly happiness. I cannot but think that as the condition of mankind becomes improved, as they grow happier in their lives, and more capable of deriving happiness from unselfish sources, they will care less and less for this flattering expectation. It is not, naturally or generally, the happy who are the most anxious either for a prolongation of the present life, or for a life hereafter: it is those who never have been happy. They who have had their happiness can bear to part with existence: but it is hard to die without ever having lived. When mankind cease to need a future existence as a consolation for the sufferings of the present, it will have lost its chief value to them, for themselves. I am now speaking of the unselfish. Those who are so wrapped up in self that they are unable to identify their feelings with anything which will survive them, or to feel their life prolonged in their younger cotemporaries and in all who help to carry on the progressive movement of human affairs, require the notion of another selfish life beyond the grave, to enable them to keep up any interest in existence, since the present life, as its termination approaches, dwindles into something too insignificant to be worth caring about. But if the Religion of Humanity were as sedulously cultivated as the supernatural religions are (and there is no difficulty in conceiving that it might be much more so), all who had received the customary amount of moral cultivation would up to the hour of death live ideally in the life of those who are to follow them: and though doubtless they would often willingly survive as individuals for a much longer period than the present duration of life, it appears to me probable that after a length of time different in different persons, they would have had enough of existence, and would gladly lie down and take their eternal rest. Meanwhile and without looking so far forward, we may remark, that those who believe the immortality of the soul, generally quit life with fully as much, if not more, reluctance, as those who have no such expectation. The mere cessation of existence is no evil to any one: the idea is only formidable through the illusion of imagination which makes one conceive oneself as if one were alive and feeling oneself dead. What is odious in death is not death itself, but the act of dying, and its lugubrious accompaniments: all of which must be equally undergone by the believer in immortality. Nor can I perceive that the sceptic loses by his scepticism any real and valuable consolation

except one; the hope of reunion with those dear to him who have ended their earthly life before him. That loss, indeed, is neither to be denied nor extenuated. In many cases it is beyond the reach of comparison or estimate; and will always suffice to keep alive, in the more sensitive natures, the imaginative hope of a futurity which, if there is nothing to prove, there is as little in our knowledge and experience to contradict.

History, so far as we know it, bears out the opinion, that mankind can perfectly well do without the belief in a heaven. The Greeks had anything but a tempting idea of a future state. Their Elysian fields held out very little attraction to their feelings and imagination. Achilles in the Odyssey expressed a very natural, and no doubt a very common sentiment, when he said that he would rather be on earth the serf of a needy master, than reign over the whole kingdom of the dead. And the pensive character so striking in the address of the dying emperor Hadrian to his soul, gives evidence that the popular conception had not undergone much variation during that long interval. Yet we neither find that the Greeks enjoyed life less, nor feared death more, than other people. The Buddhist religion counts probably at this day a greater number of votaries than either the Christian or the Mahomedan. The Buddhist creed recognises many modes of punishment in a future life, or rather lives, by the transmigration of the soul into new bodies of men or animals. But the blessing from Heaven which it proposes as a reward, to be earned by perseverance in the highest order of virtuous life, is annihilation; the cessation, at least, of all conscious or separate existence. It is impossible to mistake in this religion, the work of legislators and moralists endeavouring to supply supernatural motives for the conduct which they were anxious to encourage; and they could find nothing more transcendant to hold out as the capital prize to be won by the mightiest efforts of labour and self-denial, than what we are so often told is the terrible idea of annihilation. Surely this is a proof that the idea is not really or naturally terrible; that not philosophers only, but the common order of mankind, can easily reconcile themselves to it, and even consider it as a good; and that it is no unnatural part of the idea of a happy life, that life itself be laid down, after the best that it can give has been fully enjoyed through a long lapse of time; when all its pleasures, even those of benevolence, are familiar, and nothing untasted and unknown is left to stimulate curiosity and keep up the desire of prolonged existence. It seems to me not only possible but probable, that in a higher, and, above all, a happier condition of human life, not annihilation but immortality may be the burdensome idea; and that human nature, though pleased with the present, and by no means impatient to quit it, would find comfort and not sadness in the thought that it is not chained through eternity to a conscious existence which it cannot be assured that it will always wish to preserve.

The Golden Flower Pot

E. T. A. Hoffmann

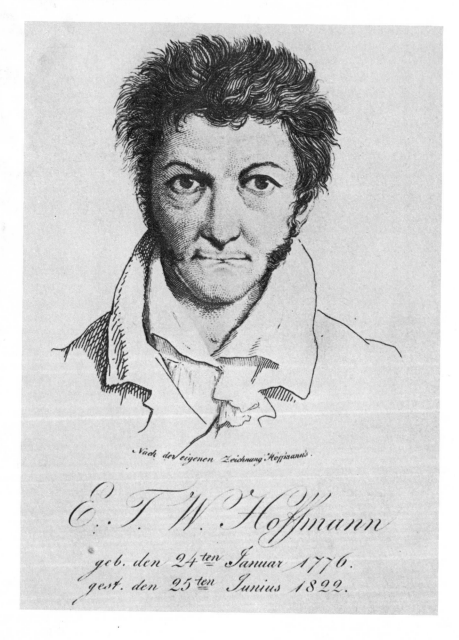

Nach der eigenen Zeichnung Hoffmanns.

E. T. W. Hoffmann
geb. den 24ten Januar 1776.
gest. den 25ten Junius 1822.

Editor's Introduction

"The Golden Flower Pot" is one ("The Nutcracker" is another) of what are known as the Tales of Hoffmann, a collection of stories by Ernst Theodor Amadeus Hoffmann (1776–1822) that date from the second decade or so of the nineteenth century and have as their subject the supernatural and fantastic. The stories treat these old and enduring human concerns with a confidence and power peculiar to their time. At an earlier period of history the adventures they describe would have been regarded as errant ravings if not diabolical apparitions. Later, they would seem to be the stuff of abnormal psychology. Only during the age we have come to call Romantic, of which Hoffmann saw the beginning if not the end, were they likely to have inspired the combination of enthusiasm and intensity he devoted to them. They are, as stories, often strange and even mystifying. Yet they work in the way Hoffmann intended that they should, and no one who has ever read them comes away without a sense that he has looked at marvelous if sometimes rather terrifying things.

Hoffmann, like Kant, was born in Königsberg, East Prussia, and attended the university there while Kant was still its dominant intellectual figure. It was not philosophy that Hoffmann studied, however, but law, with much time given to music, painting, and literature, all of which he seems to have pursued with equal diligence. In 1795, when he had completed his studies, he took examinations for the Prussian civil service, which he entered the following year, and in which he seemed likely to have a promising career. But shortly afterward his involvement in a scandalous love affair, the first of a series of personal difficulties in which he became entangled, made it necessary for him to leave town, and while he subsequently held minor official positions in a number of different places during his relatively short life, he never settled in any one spot, nor did he become the comfortable, respected public functionary he might have been. Instead he endeavored to develop first one and then another of his many talents, and at various times gained reputation as a composer and critic of music, as a caricaturist, and as a writer of novels and plays, in each of which occupations he had as much success as adverse circumstances, an excitable temper, spendthrift ways, and an excessive fondness for drink would allow.

Music was Hoffmann's first love. At Warsaw, in 1804, he founded an orchestra and conducted works of Mozart, whom he liked so much that he changed his middle name from Wilhelm to Amadeus, and Beethoven, of whom he was an early and perceptive admirer. He also composed works of his own, among them an opera and several symphonies. Later, at Bamberg in southern Germany, where he lived from 1808 to 1813, he created musical settings for the plays of Shakespeare, Calderón, and others, which he presented at a theater of which he was the director.

The Tales by which he is best known were written from 1813 on, after he had moved to Berlin, where for a time he had an appointment as an administrator and judge. After they had appeared first in various periodicals, the stories, or at least the best of them, were brought out in four volumes as *Die Serapions-brüder* (The Serapion Brethren) between 1819 and 1821. "The Golden Flower Pot," which is generally regarded as the finest of them, and is certainly the longest, was also one of the earliest. Its meaning, assuming it is some kind of allegory, has been much debated. In the tradition of a *märchen*, or German literary myth, it may be supposed to have something to do with the awakening of the imagination, or the birth of poetry, and at any rate certain Romantic ideas, such as that the loss of faith can be destructive, that there is a connection between madness and human misery, and that art and life are incompatible, are evident in it. What is most remarkable about the story, however, is the way the real world in which it begins turns gradually into a fantastic vision, without its being clear just how or where the shift is accomplished. Hoffmann was justly proud of his ability to turn this trick.

The translation of the story that appears here is by Thomas Carlyle, who thought highly of Hoffmann's work. Poe and Hawthorne admired him also and seem to have taken something from him, as did Dostoevsky, who said that Hoffmann had taught him much about psychology. But it is in the musical settings that his writings chiefly survive. Besides Tchaikovsky's ballet, there is Offenbach's opera (1881), based on an adaptation of certain of the tales by Alexandre Dumas, with its well-known "Barcarolle." There are also a ballet by Delibes and an opera in the present century by Hindemith which are based on the tales. There is even a piano work by Schumann called "Kreisleriana" that pays homage to the pseudonym of Johannes Kreisler, under which Hoffmann published some of the best musical criticism of his time. These several borrowings and acknowledgments are the more touching in that, while Hoffmann's tales are nowadays sometimes read, and at least one of them is almost universally known, none of his own musical compositions is any longer played, nor is either of the two operas he composed ever performed.

The Golden Flower Pot

First Vigil

The Mishaps of the Student Anselmus. Conrector Paulmann's Tobacco-box, and the Gold-green Snakes

On Ascension-day, about three o'clock in the afternoon, there came a young man running through the Schwarzthor, or Black Gate, out of Dresden, and right into a basket of apples and cakes, which an old and very ugly woman was there exposing to sale. The crash was prodigious; all that escaped being squelched to pieces was scattered away, and the street-urchins joyfully divided the booty which this quick gentleman had thrown them. At the murder-shriek which the crone set up, her gossips, leaving their cake and brandy tables, encircled the young man, and with plebeian violence stormfully scolded him: so that, for shame and vexation, he uttered no word, but merely held out his small, and by no means particularly well-filled purse, which the crone eagerly clutched, and stuck into her pocket. The firm ring now opened; but as the young man started off, the crone called after him: "Ay, run, run thy ways, thou Devil's bird! To the Crystal run! to the Crystal!" The squealing, creaking voice of the woman had something unearthly in it: so that the promenaders paused in amazement, and the laugh, which at first had been universal, instantly died away. The Student Anselmus, for the young man was no other, felt himself, though he did not in the least understand these singular phrases, nevertheless seized with a certain involuntary horror; and he quickened his steps still more, to escape the curious looks of the multitude, which were all turned towards him. As he worked his way through the crowd of well-dressed people, he heard them murmuring on all sides: "Poor young fellow! Ha! what a cursed beldam it is!" The mysterious words of the crone had oddly enough given this ludicrous adventure a sort of tragic turn; and the youth, before unobserved, was now looked after with a certain sympathy. The ladies, for his fine shape and handsome face, which the glow of inward anger was rendering still more expressive, forgave him this awkward step, as well as the dress he wore, though it was utterly at variance with all mode. His pike-grey frock was shaped as if the tailor had known the modern form only by hearsay; and his well-kept black satin lower habiliments gave the whole a certain pedagogic air, to which the gait and gesture of the wearer did not at all correspond.

The Student had almost reached the end of the alley which leads out to the Linke Bath; but his breath could stand such a rate no longer. From running, he took to walking; but scarcely did he yet dare to lift an eye from the ground; for he still saw apples and cakes dancing round him; and every kind look from this or that fair damsel was to him but the reflex of the mocking laughter at the Schwarzthor. In this mood, he had got to the entrance of the Bath: one group of holiday people after the other were moving in. Music of wind-instruments resounded from the place, and the din of merry guests was growing louder and louder. The poor Student Anselmus was almost on the point of weeping; for he too had expected, Ascension-day having always been a family-festival with him, to participate in the felicities of the Linkean paradise; nay, he had purposed even to go the length of a half *portion* of coffee with rum, and a whole bottle of double beer; and that he might carouse at his ease, had put more money in his purse than was entirely convenient or advisable. And now, by this fatal step into the apple-basket, all that he had about him had been swept away. Of coffee, of double or single beer, of music, of looking at the bright damsels; in a word, of all his fancied enjoyments, there was now nothing more to be said. He glided slowly past; and at last turned down the Elbe road, which at that time happened to be quite solitary.

Beneath an elder-tree, which had grown out through the wall, he found a kind green resting-place: here he sat down, and filled a pipe from the Sanitätsknaster, or Health-tobacco-box, of which his friend the Conrector Paulmann had lately made him a present. Close before him, rolled and chafed the gold-dyed waves of the fair Elbe-stream: behind this rose lordly Dresden, stretching, bold and proud, its light towers into the airy sky; which again, farther off, bent itself down towards flowery meads and fresh springing woods; and in the dim distance, a range of azure peaks gave notice of remote Bohemia. But, heedless of this, the Student Anselmus, looking gloomily before him, blew forth his smoky clouds into the air. His chagrin at length became audible, and he said: "Of a truth, I am born to losses and crosses for my life long! That in boyhood, at Odds or Evens, I could never once guess the right way; that my bread and butter always fell on the buttered side; of all these sorrows I will not speak: but is it not a frightful destiny, that now, when, in spite of Satan, I have become a student, I must still be a jolthead as before? Do I ever put a new coat on, without the first day smearing it with tallow, or on some ill-fastened nail or other, tearing a cursed hole in it? Do I ever bow to any Councillor or any lady, without pitching the hat out of my hands, or even sliding away on the smooth pavement, and shamefully oversetting? Had I not, every market-day, while in Halle, a regular sum of from three to four groschen to pay for broken pottery, the Devil putting it into my head to walk straight forward, like a leming-rat? Have I ever once got to my college, or any place I was appointed to, at the right time? What availed it that I set out half an hour before, and planted myself at the door, with the knocker in my hand? Just as the clock is going to strike, souse! some Devil pours a wash-basin down on me, or I bolt against some fellow coming out, and get myself engaged in endless quarrels till the time is clean gone.

"Ah! well-a-day! whither are ye fled, ye blissful dreams of coming fortune, when I proudly thought that here I might even reach the height of Privy Secretary? And has not my evil star estranged from me my best patrons? I learn, for instance, that the Councillor, to whom I have a letter, cannot suffer cropt hair; with immensity of trouble, the barber fastens me a little cue to my hindhead; but at the first bow, his unblessed knot gives way, and a little shock, running snuffing about me, frisks off to the Privy Councillor with the cue in its mouth. I spring after it in terror; and stumble against the table, where he has been working while at breakfast; and cups, plates, ink-glass, sand-box, rush jingling to the floor, and a flood of chocolate and ink overflows the Relation he has just been writing. 'Is the Devil in the man?' bellows the furious Privy Councillor, and shoves me out of the room.

"What avails it that Conrector Paulmann gave me hopes of a writership: will my malignant fate allow it, which everywhere pursues me? Today even! Do but think of it! I was purposing to hold my good old Ascension-day with right cheerfulness of soul: I would stretch a point for once; I might have gone, as well as any other guest, into Linke's Bath, and called out proudly: 'Marqueur! a bottle of double-beer; best sort, if you please!' I might have sat till far in the evening; and, moreover, close by this or that fine party of well-dressed ladies. I know it, I feel it! heart would have come into me, I should have been quite another man; nay, I might have carried it so far, that when one or other of them asked: 'What o'clock may it be?' or 'What is it they are playing?' I should have started up with light grace, and without overturning my glass, or stumbling over the bench, but in a curved posture, moving one step and a half forward, I should have answered: 'Give me leave, mademoiselle! it is the overture of the *Donanweibchen*'; or, 'It is just going to strike six.' Could any mortal in the world have taken it ill of me? No! I say; the girls would have looked over, smiling so roguishly; as they always do when I pluck up heart to show them that I too understand the light tone of society, and know how ladies should be spoken to. And now the Devil himself leads me into that cursed apple-basket, and now must I sit moping in solitude, with nothing but a poor pipe of——" Here the Student Anselmus was interrupted in his soliloquy by a strange rustling and whisking, which rose close by him in the grass, but soon glided up into the twigs and leaves of the elder-tree that stretched out over his head. It was as if the evening wind were shaking the leaves; as if little birds were twittering among the branches, moving their little wings in capricious flutter to and fro. Then he heard a whispering and lisping; and it seemed as if the blossoms were sounding like little crystal bells. Anselmus listened and listened. Ere long, the whispering, and lisping, and tinkling, he himself knew not how, grew to faint and half-scattered words:

"'Twixt this way, 'twixt that; 'twixt branches, 'twixt blossoms, come shoot, come twist and twirl we! Sisterkin, sisterkin! up to the shine; up, down, through and through, quick! Sun-rays yellow; evening-wind whispering; dew-drops pattering; blossoms all singing: sing we with branches and blossoms! Stars soon glitter; must down: 'twixt this way, 'twixt that, come shoot, come twist, come twirl we, sisterkin!"

And so it went along, in confused and confusing speech. The Student Anselmus thought: "Well, it is but the evening-wind, which to-night truly is whispering distinctly enough." But at that moment there sounded over his head, as it were, a triple harmony of clear crystal bells: he looked up, and perceived three little Snakes, glittering with green and gold, twisted round the branches, and stretching out their heads to the evening

sun. Then, again, began a whispering and twittering in the same words as before, and the little Snakes went gliding and caressing up and down through the twigs; and while they moved so rapidly, it was as if the elder-bush were scattering a thousand glittering emeralds through the dark leaves.

"It is the evening sun which sports so in the elder-bush," thought the Student Anselmus; but the bells sounded again; and Anselmus observed that one Snake held out its little head to him. Through all his limbs there went a shock like electricity; he quivered in his inmost heart: he kept gazing up, and a pair of glorious dark-blue eyes were looking at him with unspeakable longing; and an unknown feeling of highest blessedness and deepest sorrow was like to rend his heart asunder. And as he looked, and still looked, full of warm desire, into these kind eyes, the crystal bells sounded louder in harmonious accord, and the glittering emeralds fell down and encircled him, flickering round him in thousand sparkles, and sporting in resplendent threads of gold. The Elder-bush moved and spoke: "Thou layest in my shadow; my perfume flowed round thee, but thou understood'st it not. The perfume is my speech, when Love kindles it." The Evening Wind came gliding past, and said: "I played round thy temples, but thou understood'st me not. That breath is my speech, when Love kindles it." The Sun-beam broke through the clouds, and the sheen of it burnt, as in words: "I overflowed thee with glowing gold, but thou understood'st me not: That glow is my speech, when Love kindles it."

And, still deeper and deeper sunk in the view of these glorious eyes, his longing grew keener, his desire more warm. And all rose and moved around him, as if awakening to glad life. Flowers and blossoms shed their odours round him; and their odour was like the lordly singing of a thousand softest voices; and what they sung was borne, like an echo, on the golden evening clouds, as they flitted away, into far-off lands. But as the last sun-beam abruptly sank behind the hills, and the twilight threw its veil over the scene, there came a hoarse deep voice, as from a great distance:

"Hey! hey! what chattering and jingling is that up there? Hey! hey! who catches me the ray behind the hills? Sunned enough, sung enough. Hey! hey! through bush and grass, through grass and stream. Hey! hey! Come dow-w-n, dow-w-w-n!"

So faded the voice away, as in murmurs of a distant thunder; but the crystal bells broke off in sharp discords. All became mute; and the Student Anselmus observed how the three Snakes, glittering and sparkling, glided through the grass towards the river; rustling and hustling, they rushed into the Elbe; and over the waves where they vanished, there crackled up a green flame, which, gleaming forward obliquely, vanished in the direction of the city.

Second Vigil

How the Student Anselmus was looked upon as drunk and mad. The crossing of the Elbe. Bandmaster Graun's Bravura. Conradi's Stomachic Liqueur, and the bronzed Apple-woman

"The gentleman is ailing some way!" said a decent burgher's wife, who, returning from a walk with her family, had paused here, and, with crossed arms, was looking at the mad pranks of the Student Anselmus. Anselmus had clasped the trunk of the elder-tree, and was calling incessantly up to the branches and leaves: "O glitter and shine once more, ye dear gold Snakes: let me hear your little bell-voices once more! Look on me once more, ye kind eyes; O once, or I must die in pain and warm longing!" And with this, he was sighing and sobbing from the bottom of his heart most pitifully; and in his eagerness and impatience, shaking the elder-tree to and fro; which, however, instead of any reply, rustled quite stupidly and unintelligibly with its leaves; and so rather seemed, as it were, to make sport of the Student Anselmus and his sorrows.

"The gentleman is ailing some way!" said

the burgher's wife; and Anselmus felt as if you had shaken him out of a deep dream, or poured ice-cold water on him, that he might awaken without loss of time. He now first saw clearly where he was; and recollected what a strange apparition had assaulted him, nay, so beguiled his senses, as to make him break forth into loud talk with himself. In astonishment, he gazed at the woman; and at last snatching up his hat, which had fallen to the ground in his transport, was for making off in all speed. The burgher himself had come forward in the meanwhile; and, setting down the child from his arm on the grass, had been leaning on his staff, and with amazement listening and looking at the Student. He now picked up the pipe and tobacco-box which the Student had let fall, and, holding them out to him, said: "Don't take on so dreadfully, my worthy sir, or alarm people in the dark, when nothing is the matter, after all, but a drop or two of christian liquor: go home, like a pretty man, and take a nap of sleep on it."

The Student Anselmus felt exceedingly ashamed; he uttered nothing but a most lamentable Ah!

"Pooh! Pooh!" said the burgher, "never mind it a jot; such a thing will happen to the best; on good old Ascension-day a man may readily enough forget himself in his joy, and gulp down a thought too much. A clergyman himself is no worse for it: I presume, my worthy sir, you are a *Candidatus.*—But, with your leave, sir, I shall fill my pipe with your tobacco; mine went done a little while ago."

This last sentence the burgher uttered while the Student Anselmus was about putting up his pipe and box; and now the burgher slowly and deliberately cleaned his pipe, and began as slowly to fill it. Several burgher girls had come up: these were speaking secretly with the woman and each other, and tittering as they looked at Anselmus. The Student felt as if he were standing on prickly thorns, and burning needles. No sooner had he got back his pipe and tobacco-box, than he darted off at the height of his speed.

All the strange things he had seen were

clean gone from his memory; he simply recollected having babbled all manner of foolish stuff beneath the elder-tree. This was the more frightful to him, as he entertained from of old an inward horror against all soliloquists. It is Satan that chatters out of them, said his Rector; and Anselmus had honestly believed him. But to be regarded as a *Candidatus Theologiae*, overtaken with drink on Ascension-day! The thought was intolerable.

Running on with these mad vexations, he was just about turning up the Poplar Alley, by the Kosel garden, when a voice behind him called out: "Herr Anselmus! Herr Anselmus! for the love of Heaven, whither are you running in such haste?" The Student paused, as if rooted to the ground; for he was convinced that now some new mischance would befall him. The voice rose again: "Herr Anselmus, come back, then: we are waiting for you here at the water!" And now the Student perceived that it was his friend Conrector Paulmann's voice: he went back to the Elbe; and found the Conrector, with his two daughters, as well as Registrator Heerbrand, all on the point of stepping into their gondola. Conrector Paulmann invited the Student to go with them across the Elbe, and then to pass the evening at his house in the Pirna suburb. The Student Anselmus very gladly accepted this proposal; thinking thereby to escape the malignant destiny which had ruled over him all day.

Now, as they were crossing the river, it chanced that, on the farther bank, in the Anton garden, a fire-work was just going off. Sputtering and hissing, the rockets went aloft, and their blazing stars flew to pieces in the air, scattering a thousand vague shoots and flashes round them. The Student Anselmus was sitting by the steersman, sunk in deep thought; but when he noticed in the water the reflection of these darting and wavering sparks and flames, he felt as if it was the little golden Snakes that were sporting in the flood. All the wonders that he had seen at the elder-tree again started forth into his heart and thoughts; and again that unspeak-able longing, that glowing desire, laid hold of him here, which had before agitated his bosom in painful spasms of rapture.

"Ah! is it you again, my little golden Snakes? Sing now, O sing! In your song let the kind, dear, dark-blue eyes, again appear to me—Ah! are ye under the waves, then?"

So cried the Student Anselmus, and at the same time made a violent movement, as if he were for plunging from the gondola into the river.

"Is the Devil in you, sir?" exclaimed the steersman, and clutched him by the coat-breast. The girls, who were sitting by him, shrieked in terror, and fled to the other side of the gondola. Registrator Heerbrand whispered something in Conrector Paulmann's ear, to which the latter answered at considerable length, but in so low a tone, that Anselmus could distinguish nothing but the words: "Such attacks more than once?—Never heard of it." Directly after this, Conrector Paulmann also rose; and then sat down, with a certain earnest, grave, official mien, beside the Student Anselmus, taking his hand, and saying: "How are you, Herr Anselmus?" The Student Anselmus was like to lose his wits, for in his mind there was a mad contradiction, which he strove in vain to reconcile. He now saw plainly that what he had taken for the gleaming of the golden Snakes was nothing but the image of the fireworks in Anton's garden: but a feeling unexperienced till now, he himself knew not whether it was rapture or pain, cramped his breast together; and when the steersman struck through the water with his helm, so that the waves, curling as in anger, gurgled and chafed, he heard in their din a soft whispering: "Anselmus! Anselmus! seest thou not how we still skim along before thee? Sisterkin looks at thee again: believe, believe, believe in us!" And he thought he saw in the reflected light three green-glowing streaks; but then, when he gazed, full of fond sadness, into the water, to see whether these gentle eyes would not again look up to him, he perceived too well that the shine proceeded only from the windows in the neighbouring houses. He was sitting mute in his place, and inwardly battling with himself, when Conrector Paulmann repeated, with still greater emphasis: "How are you, Herr Anselmus?"

With the most rueful tone, Anselmus replied: "Ah! Herr Conrector, if you knew what strange things I have been dreaming, quite awake, with open eyes, just now, under an elder-tree at the wall of Linke's garden, you would not take it amiss of me that I am a little absent, or so."

"Ey, ey, Herr Anselmus!" interrupted Conrector Paulmann, "I have always taken you for a solid young man: but to dream, to dream with your eyes wide open, and then, all at once, to start up for leaping into the water! This, begging your pardon, is what only fools or madmen could do."

The Student Anselmus was deeply affected at his friend's hard saying; then Veronica, Paulmann's eldest daughter, a most pretty blooming girl of sixteen, addressed her father: "But, dear father, something singular must have befallen Herr Anselmus; and perhaps he only thinks he was awake, while he may have really been asleep, and so all manner of wild stuff has come into his head, and is still lying in his thoughts."

"And, dearest Mademoiselle! Worthy Conrector!" cried Registrator Heerbrand, "may one not, even when awake, sometimes sink into a sort of dreaming state? I myself have had such fits. One afternoon, for instance, during coffee, in a sort of brown study like this, in the special season of corporeal and spiritual digestion, the place where a lost *Act* was lying occurred to me, as if by inspiration; and last night, no farther gone, there came a glorious large Latin paper tripping out before my open eyes, in the very same way."

"Ah! most honoured Registrator," answered Conrector Paulmann; "you have always had a tendency to the *Poetica*; and thus one falls into fantasies and romantic humours."

The Student Anselmus, however, was particularly gratified that in this most troublous situation, while in danger of being considered drunk or crazy, any one should take his part; and though it was already pretty dark, he thought he noticed, for the first time, that Veronica had really very fine dark-blue eyes, and this too without remembering the strange pair which he had looked at in the elder-bush. On the whole, the adventure under the elder-bush had once more entirely vanished from the thoughts of the Student Anselmus; he felt himself at ease and light of heart; nay, in the capriciousness of joy, he carried it so far, that he offered a helping hand to his fair advocate, Veronica, as she was stepping from the gondola; and without more ado, as she put her arm in his, escorted her home with so much dexterity and good luck, that he only missed his footing once, and this being the only wet spot in the whole road, only spattered Veronica's white gown a very little by the incident.

Conrector Paulmann failed not to observe this happy change in the Student Anselmus; he resumed his liking for him, and begged forgiveness for the hard words which he had let fall before. "Yes," added he, "we have many examples to show that certain fantasms may rise before a man, and pester and plague him not a little; but this is bodily disease, and leeches are good for it, if applied to the right part, as a certain learned physician, now deceased, has directed." The Student Anselmus knew not whether he had been drunk, crazy, or sick; but at all events the leeches seemed entirely superfluous, as these supposed fantasms had utterly vanished, and the Student himself was growing happier and happier, the more he prospered in serving the pretty Veronica with all sorts of dainty attentions.

As usual, after the frugal meal, came music; the Student Anselmus had to take his seat before the harpsichord, and Veronica accompanied his playing with her pure clear voice: "Dear Mademoiselle," said Registrator Heerbrand, "you have a voice like a crystal bell!"

"That she has not!" ejaculated the Student Anselmus, he scarcely knew how. "Crystal bells in elder-trees sound strangely!

strangely!" continued the Student Anselmus, murmuring half aloud.

Veronica laid her hand on his shoulder, and asked: "What are you saying now, Herr Anselmus?"

Instantly Anselmus recovered his cheerfulness, and began playing. Conrector Paulmann gave a grim look at him; but Registrator Heerbrand laid a music-leaf on the frame, and sang with ravishing grace one of Bandmaster Graun's bravura airs. The Student Anselmus accompanied this, and much more; and a fantasy duet, which Veronica and he now fingered, and Conrector Paulmann had himself composed, again brought all into the gayest humour.

It was now pretty late, and Registrator Heerbrand was taking up his hat and stick, when Conrector Paulmann went up to him with a mysterious air, and said: "Hem!— Would not you, honoured Registrator, mention to the good Herr Anselmus himself— Hem! what we were speaking of before?"

"With all the pleasure in nature," said Registrator Heerbrand, and having placed himself in the circle, began, without farther preamble, as follows:

"In this city is a strange remarkable man, people say he follows all manner of secret sciences; but as there are no such sciences, I rather take him for an antiquary, and along with this, for an experimental chemist. I mean no other than our Privy Archivarius Lindhorst. He lives, as you know, by himself, in his old sequestered house; and when disengaged from his office, he is to be found in his library, or in his chemical laboratory, to which, however, he admits no stranger. Besides many curious books, he possesses a number of manuscripts, partly Arabic, Coptic, and some of them in strange characters, which belong not to any known tongue. These he wishes to have copied properly; and for this purpose he requires a man who can draw with the pen, and so transfer these marks to parchment, in Indian ink, with the highest strictness and fidelity. The work is carried on in a separate chamber of his house, under his own oversight; and besides free board during the time of business, he pays his man a speziesthaler, or specie-dollar, daily, and promises a handsome present when the copying is rightly finished. The hours of work are from twelve to six. From three to four, you take rest and dinner.

"Herr Archivarius Lindhorst having in vain tried one or two young people for copying these manuscripts, has at last applied to me to find him an expert drawer; and so I have been thinking of you, dear Herr Anselmus, for I know that you both write very neatly, and likewise draw with the pen to great perfection. Now, if in these bad times, and till your future establishment, you could like to earn a speziesthaler in the day, and this present over and above, you can go tomorrow precisely at noon, and call upon the Archivarius, whose house no doubt you know. But be on your guard against any blot! If such a thing falls on your copy, you must begin it again; if it falls on the original, the Archivarius will think nothing to throw you over the window, for he is a hot-tempered gentleman."

The Student Anselmus was filled with joy at Registrator Heerbrand's proposal; for not only could the Student write well and draw well with the pen, but this copying with laborious caligraphic pains, was a thing he delighted in beyond aught else. So he thanked his patron in the most grateful terms, and promised not to fail at noon tomorrow.

All night the Student Anselmus saw nothing but clear speziesthalers, and heard nothing but their lovely clink. Who could blame the poor youth, cheated of so many hopes by capricious destiny, obliged to take counsel about every farthing, and to forego so many joys which a young heart requires! Early in the morning he brought out his black-lead pencils, his crow-quills, his Indian ink; for better materials, thought he, the Archivarius can find nowhere. Above all, he mustered and arranged his caligraphic masterpieces and his drawings, to show them to the Archivarius, in proof of his ability to do what he wished. All prospered with the Student; a peculiar happy star seemed to be presiding over him; his neckcloth sat right at the very first trial; no tack burst; no loop gave way in his black silk stockings; his hat did not once fall to the dust after he had trimmed it. In a word, precisely at half-past eleven, the Student Anselmus, in his pike-grey frock, and black satin lower habiliments, with a roll of caligraphies and pen-drawings in his pocket, was standing in the Schlossgasse, or Castlegate, in Conradi's shop, and drinking one— two glasses of the best stomachic liqueur; for here, thought he, slapping on the still empty pocket, for here speziesthalers will be chinking soon.

Notwithstanding the distance of the solitary street where the Archivarius Lindhorst's antique residence lay, the Student Anselmus was at the front-door before the stroke of twelve. He stood here, and was looking at the large fine bronze knocker; but now when, as the last stroke tingled through the air with loud clang from the steeple-clock of the Kreuzkirche, or Cross-church, he lifted his hand to grasp this same knocker, the metal visage twisted itself, with horrid rolling of its blue-gleaming eyes, into a grinning smile. Alas, it was the Applewoman of the Schwarzthor! The pointed teeth gnashed together in the loose jaws, and in their chattering through the skinny lips, there was a growl as of: "Thou fool, fool, fool!—Wait, wait!—Why did'st run!—Fool!" Horror-struck, the Student Anselmus flew back; he clutched at the door-post, but his hand caught the bell-rope, and pulled it, and in piercing discords it rung stronger and stronger, and through the whole empty house the echo repeated, as in mockery: "To the crystal, fall!" An unearthly terror seized the Student Anselmus, and quivered through all his limbs. The bell-rope lengthened downwards, and became a white transparent gigantic serpent, which encircled and crushed him, and girded him straiter and straiter in its coils, till his brittle paralysed limbs went crashing in pieces, and the blood spouted from his veins, penetrating into the transparent body of the serpent, and dyeing it red. "Kill me! Kill me!" he would have cried, in his horrible agony; but the cry was only a stifled gurgle in his throat. The serpent lifted its head, and laid its long peaked tongue of glowing brass on the breast of Anselmus; then a fierce pang suddenly cut asunder the artery of life, and thought fled away from him. On returning to his senses, he was lying on his own poor truckle-bed; Conrector Paulmann was standing before him, and saying: "For Heaven's sake, what mad stuff is this, dear Herr Anselmus?"

Third Vigil

Notices of Archivarius Lindhorst's Family. Veronica's blue Eyes. Registrator Heerbrand

"The Spirit looked upon the water, and the water moved itself, and chafed in foaming billows, and plunged thundering down into the Abysses, which opened their black throats, and greedily swallowed it. Like triumphant conquerors, the granite Rocks lifted their cleft peaky crowns, protecting the Valley, till the Sun took it into his paternal bosom, and clasping it with his beams as with glowing arms, cherished it and warmed it. Then a thousand germs, which had been sleeping under the desert sand, awoke from their deep slumber, and stretched out their little leaves and stalks towards the Sun their father's face; and like smiling infants in green cradles, the flowrets rested in their buds and blossoms, till they too, awakened by their father, decked themselves in lights, which their father, to please them, tinted in a thousand varied hues.

"But in the midst of the Valley was a black Hill, which heaved up and down like the breast of man when warm longing swells it. From the Abysses mounted steaming vapours, and rolled themselves together into huge masses, striving malignantly to hide the father's face: but he called the Storm to him, which rushed thither, and scattered them away; and when the pure sunbeam rested again on the bleak Hill, there started from it, in the excess of its rapture, a glorious Fire-lily, opening its fair leaves like gentle lips to receive the kiss of its father.

"And now came a gleaming Splendour into the Valley; it was the youth Phosphorus; the Lily saw him, and begged, being seized with warm longing love: 'Be mine for ever, thou fair youth! For I love thee, and must die if thou forsake me!' Then spake the youth Phosphorus: 'I will be thine, thou fair flower; but then wilt thou, like a naughty child, leave father and mother; thou wilt know thy play-mates no longer, wilt strive to be greater and stronger than all that now rejoices with thee as thy equal. The longing which now be-neficently warms thy whole being, will be scattered into a thousand rays, and torture and vex thee; for sense will bring forth senses; and the highest rapture, which the Spark I cast into thee kindles, will be the hopeless pain wherein thou shalt perish, to spring up anew in foreign shape. This spark is Thought!'

" 'Ah!' mourned the Lily, 'can I not be thine in this glow, as it now burns in me; not still be thine? Can I love thee more than now; could I look on thee as now, if thou wert to annihilate me?' Then the youth Phosphorus kissed the Lily; and as if penetrated with light, it mounted up in flame, out of which issued a foreign Being, that hastily flying from the Valley, roved forth into endless Space, no longer heeding its old playmates, or the youth it had loved. This youth mourned for his lost beloved; for he too loved her, it was love to the fair Lily that had brought him to the lone Valley; and the gran-ite Rocks bent down their heads in participa-tion of his grief.

"But one of these opened its bosom, and there came a black-winged Dragon flying out of it, and said: 'My brethren, the Metals are sleeping in there; but I am always brisk and waking, and will help thee.' Dashing up and down on its black pinions, the Dragon at last caught the Being which had sprung from the Lily; bore it to the Hill, and encircled it with his wing; then was it the Lily again; but Thought, which continued with it, tore asunder its heart; and its love for the youth

Phosphorus was a cutting pain, before which, as if breathed on by poisonous vapours, the flowrets which had once rejoiced in the fair Lily's presence, faded and died.

"The youth Phosphorus put on a glittering coat of mail, sporting with the light in a thou-sand hues, and did battle with the Dragon, who struck the cuirass with his black wing, till it rung and sounded; and at this loud clang the flowrets again came to life, and like varie-gated birds fluttered round the Dragon, whose force departed; and who, thus being vanquished, hid himself in the depths of the Earth. The Lily was freed; the youth Phos-phorus clasped her, full of warm longing, of heavenly love; and in triumphant chorus, the flowers, the birds, nay, even the high granite Rocks, did reverence to her as the Queen of the Valley."

"By your leave, worthy Herr Archivarius, this is Oriental bombast," said Registrator Heerbrand: "and we beg very much you would rather, as you often do, give us some-thing of your own most remarkable life, of your travelling adventures, for instance; above all, something true."

"What the deuce, then?" answered Ar-chivarius Lindhorst: "True? This very thing I have been telling, is the truest I could dish out for you, good people, and belongs to my life too, in a certain sense. For I come from that very Valley; and the Fire-Lily, which at last ruled as queen there, was my great-great-great-great-grandmother; and so, properly speaking, I am a prince myself." All burst into a peal of laughter. "Ay, laugh your fill," continued Archivarius Lindhorst: "To you this matter, which I have related, cer-tainly in the most brief and meagre way, may seem senseless and mad; yet, notwithstanding this, it is meant for anything but incoherent, or even allegorical, and it is, in one word, literally true. Had I known, however, that the glorious love-story, to which I owe my exis-tence, would have pleased you so ill, I might have given you a little of the news my brother brought me on his visit yesterday."

"How, how is this? Have you a brother, then, Herr Archivarius? Where is he? Where lives he? In his Majesty's service too? Or perhaps a private scholar?" cried the company from all quarters.

"No!" replied the Archivarius, quite cool, and composedly taking a pinch of snuff, "he has joined the bad side; he has gone over to the Dragons."

"What do you please to mean, dear Herr Archivarius?" cried Registrator Heerbrand: "Over to the Dragons?"—"Over to the Dragons?" resounded like an echo from all hands.

"Yes, over to the Dragons," continued Archivarius Lindhorst: "it was sheer desperation, I believe. You know, gentlemen, my father died a short while ago; it is but three hundred and eighty-five years since at most, and I am still in mournings for it. He had left me, his favourite son, a fine onyx; this onyx, right or wrong, my brother would have: we quarrelled about it, over my father's corpse; in such unseemly wise that the good man started up, out of all patience, and threw my wicked brother down stairs. This stuck in our brother's stomach, and so without loss of time he went over to the Dragons. At present, he keeps in a cypress wood, not far from Tunis: he has got a famous mystic carbuncle to watch there, which a dog of a necromancer, who has set up a summer-house in Lapland, has an eye to; so my poor brother only gets away for a quarter of an hour or so, when the necromancer happens to be out looking after the salamander-bed in his garden, and then he tells me in all haste what good news there are about the Springs of the Nile."

For the second time, the company burst out into a peal of laughter: but the Student Anselmus began to feel quite dreary in heart; and he could scarcely look in Archivarius Lindhorst's parched countenance, and fixed earnest eyes, without shuddering internally in a way which he could not himself understand. Moreover, in the rude and strangely metallic sound of Archivarius Lindhorst's voice there was something mysteriously piercing for the Student Anselmus, and he felt his very bones and marrow tingling as the Archivarius spoke.

The special object, for which Registrator Heerbrand had taken him into the coffee-house, seemed at present not to be attainable. After that accident at Archivarius Lindhorst's door, the Student Anselmus had withstood all inducements to risk a second visit: for, according to his own heart-felt conviction, it was only chance that had saved him, if not from death, at least from the danger of insanity. Conrector Paulmann had happened to be passing through the street at the time when Anselmus was lying quite senseless at the door, and an old woman, who had laid her cake and apple-basket to a side, was busied about him. Conrector Paulmann had forthwith called a chair, and so got him carried home. "Think of me what you will," said the Student Anselmus, "consider me a fool or not: I say, the cursed visage of that witch at the Schwarzthor grinned on me from the door-knocker. What happened after I would rather not speak of: but had I recovered from my swoon and seen that infernal Apple-wife beside me (for the old woman whom you talk of was no other), I should that instant have been struck by apoplexy, or have run stark mad." All persuasions, all sensible arguments on the part of Conrector Paulmann and Registrator Heerbrand, profited nothing; and even the blue-eyed Veronica herself could not raise him from a certain moody humour, in which he had ever since been sunk. In fact, these friends regarded him as troubled in mind, and meditated expedients for diverting his thoughts; to which end, Registrator Heerbrand thought, there could nothing be so serviceable as this employment of copying Archivarius Lindhorst's manuscripts. The business, therefore, was to introduce the Student in some proper way to Archivarius Lindhorst; and so Registrator Heerbrand, knowing that the Archivarius used to visit a certain coffee-house almost nightly, had invited the Student Anselmus to come every evening to that same coffee-house, and drink a glass of beer and smoke a pipe, at his the Registrator's charges, till such time as Archivarius Lindhorst should in one way or another see him, and the bargain for this copying work be settled; which offer the Student Anselmus had most gratefully accepted. "God will reward you, worthy Registrator, if you bring the young man to reason!" said Conrector Paulmann. "God will reward you!" repeated Veronica, piously raising her eyes to heaven, and vividly thinking that the Student Anselmus was already a most pretty young man, even without any reason.

Now accordingly, as Archivarius Lindhorst, with hat and staff, was making for the door, Registrator Heerbrand seized the Student Anselmus briskly by the hand, and with him stepping in the way, he said: "Most esteemed Herr Archivarius, here is the Student Anselmus, who has an uncommon talent in calligraphy and drawing, and will undertake the copying of your rare manuscripts."

"I am most particularly glad to hear it," answered Archivarius Lindhorst sharply; then threw his three-cocked military hat on his head; and shoving Registrator Heerbrand and the Student Anselmus to a side, rushed down stairs with great tumult, so that both of them were left standing much bamboozled, gaping at the room-door, which he had slammed in their faces, till the bolts and hinges of it rung again.

"It is a very strange old gentleman," said Registrator Heerbrand. "Strange old gentleman," stammered the Student Anselmus, with a feeling as if an ice-stream were creeping over all his veins, and he were stiffening into a statue. All the guests, however, laughed, and said: "Our Archivarius has got into his high key today: tomorrow, you shall see, he is mild as a lamb again, and speaks not a word, but looks into the smoke-vortexes of his pipe, or reads the newspapers: you must not mind these freaks."

"That is true too," thought the Student Anselmus: "who would mind such a thing, after all? Did not the Archivarius tell me he was most particularly glad to hear that I would undertake the copying of his manuscripts; and why did Registrator Heerbrand step directly in his way, when he was going

home? No, no, he is a good man at bottom this Privy Archivarius Lindhorst, and surprisingly liberal. A little curious or so in his figures of speech; but what is that to me? Tomorrow by the stroke of twelve I go to him, though fifty bronzed Apple-wives should try to hinder me!"

Fourth Vigil

Melancholy of the Student Anselmus. The Emerald Mirror. How Archivarius Lindhorst flew off in the shape of a Kite, and the Student Anselmus met nobody

To thee thyself, favourable reader, I may well venture the question, Whether thou in thy time hast not had hours, nay, days and weeks, in which all thy customary trading and transacting raised a most vexing dissatisfaction in thy soul; and all that thou wert wont to look upon as worthy and important, now seemed paltry and unprofitable? Thou knewest not, at this season, what to do, or whither to turn; a dim feeling that somewhere, and some time or other, there must be a higher wish fulfilled, a wish overstepping the circle of all earthly joys, and which the spirit, like a strictly-nurtured and timid child, durst not even utter, still swelled thy breast; and in this longing for the unknown Somewhat, which, wherever thou wentest or stoodest, hovered round thee like an airy dream with thin translucent forms melting away in thy sharper glance, thou wert mute for all that environed thee here below. Thou glidest to and fro with troubled look, like a hopeless lover; and all that thou sawest men attempting or attaining, in the noisy vortex of their many-coloured existence, awakened in thee no sorrow and no joy, as if thou hadst neither part nor lot in this sublunary world.

If such, favourable reader, has at any time been thy humour, then from thy own experience thou knowest the state into which the Student Anselmus had now fallen. On the whole, I could wish much, courteous reader, that it were in my power to bring the Student

Anselmus with proper vividness before thy eyes. For in the Night-watches, which I spend in recording his highly singular history, I have still so much of the marvellous, which like a spectral vision may remove into faint remoteness the week-day life of common mortals, to lay before thee, that I fear thou wilt come, in the end, to believe neither in the Student Anselmus, nor in Archivarius Lindhorst; nay, wilt even entertain some unfounded doubts as to Registrator Heerbrand and Conrector Paulmann, though the last two estimable persons, at least, are yet walking the pavement of Dresden. Make an effort, favourable reader—while in the Fairy region full of glorious Wonders, which with subduing thrills calls forth the highest rapture and the deepest horror; nay, where the Earnest Goddess herself will waft aside her veil, so that we seem to look upon her countenance (but a smile often glimmers through her earnest glance; and this is that jestful teasing, which sports with us in all manner of perplexing enchantments, as mothers in nursing and dandling their dearest children)—in this region, which the spirit so often, at least in dreams, lays open to us, do thou make an effort, favourable reader, again to recognise the well-known shapes which, even in common life, are daily, in fitful brightness, hovering round thee. Thou wilt then find that this glorious kingdom lies much closer at hand, than thou wert wont to suppose; which I now very heartily desire, and am striving to show thee in the singular story of the Student Anselmus.

So, as was hinted, the Student Anselmus, ever since that evening when he met with Archivarius Lindhorst, had been sunk in a dreamy musing, which rendered him insensible to every outward touch from common life. He felt how an unknown Something was awakening his inmost soul, and calling forth that rapturous pain, which is even the mood of Longing that announces a loftier existence to man. He delighted most when he could rove alone through meads and woods; and as if loosened from all that fettered him to his necessitous life, could, so to speak, again find

himself in the manifold images which mounted from his soul.

It happened once, that in returning from a long ramble, he passed by that notable elder-tree; under which, as if taken with faery, he had formerly beheld so many marvels. He felt himself strangely attracted by the green kindly sward; but no sooner had he seated himself on it, than the whole vision which he had then seen as in a heavenly trance, and which had since as if by foreign influence been driven from his mind, again came floating before him in the liveliest colours, as if he had a second time been looking on it. Nay, it was clearer to him now than ever, that the gentle blue eyes belonged to the gold-green Snake, which had wound itself through the middle of the elder-tree; and that from the turnings of its taper body all those glorious crystal tones, which had filled him with rapture, must needs have broken forth. As on Ascension-day, he now again clasped the elder-tree to his bosom, and cried into the twigs and leaves: "Ah, once more shoot forth, and turn and wind thyself among the twigs, thou little fair green Snake, that I may see thee! Once more look at me with thy gentle eyes! Ah, I love thee, and must die in pain and grief, if thou return not!" All, however, remained quite dumb and still; and as before, the elder-tree rustled quite unintelligibly with its twigs and leaves. But the Student Anselmus now felt as if he knew what it was that so moved and worked within him, nay, that so tore his bosom in the pain of an infinite longing. "What else is it," said he, "but that I love thee with my whole heart and soul, and even to the death, thou glorious golden little Snake; nay, that without thee I cannot live, and must perish in hopeless woe, unless I find thee again, unless I have thee as the beloved of my heart. But I know it, thou shalt be mine; and then all that glorious dreams have promised me of another higher world shall be fulfilled."

Henceforth the Student Anselmus, every evening, when the sun was scattering its bright gold over the peaks of the trees, was to be seen under the elder-bush, calling from the depths of his heart in most lamentable tones into the branches and leaves, for a sight of his beloved, of his little gold-green Snake. Once as, according to custom, he was going on with this, there stood before him suddenly a tall lean man, wrapped up in a wide light-grey surtout, who, looking at him with his large fiery eyes, exclaimed: "Hey, hey, what whining and whimpering is this? Hey, hey, this is Herr Anselmus that was to copy my manuscripts." The Student Anselmus felt not a little terrified at this strong voice, for it was the very same which on Ascension-day had called: "Hey, hey, what chattering and jingling is this," and so forth. For fright and astonishment, he could not utter a word. "What ails you then, Herr Anselmus," continued Archivarius Lindhorst, for the stranger was no other; "what do you want with the elder-tree, and why did you not come to me, and set about your work?"

In fact, the Student Anselmus had never yet prevailed upon himself to visit Archivarius Lindhorst's house a second time, though, that evening, he had firmly resolved on doing it. But now at this moment, when he saw his fair dreams torn asunder, and that too by the same hostile voice which had once before snatched away his beloved, a sort of desperation came over him, and he broke out fiercely into these words: "You may think me mad or not, Herr Archivarius; it is all one to me: but here in this bush, on Ascension-day, I saw the gold-green Snake—ah! the for ever beloved of my soul; and she spoke to me in glorious crystal tones; and you, you, Herr Archivarius, cried and shouted so horribly over the water."

"How is this, sweet sir?" interrupted Archivarius Lindhorst, smiling quite inexpressibly, and taking snuff.

The Student Anselmus felt his breast getting great ease, now that he had succeeded in beginning this strange story; and it seemed to him as if he were quite right in laying the whole blame upon the Archivarius, and that it was he, and no other, who had so thundered from the distance. He courageously proceeded: "Well, then, I will tell you the whole mystery that happened to me on Ascension-evening; and then you may say and do, and withal think of me whatever you please." He accordingly disclosed the whole miraculous adventure, from his luckless oversetting of the apple-basket, till the departure of the three gold-green Snakes over the river; and how the people after that had thought him drunk or crazy. "All this," so ended the Student Anselmus, "I actually saw with my eyes; and deep in my bosom are those dear voices, which spoke to me, still sounding in clear echo: it was nowise a dream; and if I am not to die of longing and desire, I must believe in these gold-green Snakes; though I see by your smile, Herr Archivarius, that you hold these same Snakes as nothing more than creatures of my heated and overstrained imagination."

"Not at all," replied the Archivarius, in the greatest peace and composure; "the gold-green Snakes, which you saw in the elder-bush, Herr Anselmus, were simply my three daughters; and that you have fallen over head and ears in love with the blue eyes of Serpentina the youngest, is now clear enough. Indeed, I knew it on Ascension-day myself: and as I on that occasion, sitting busied with my writing at home, began to get annoyed with so much chattering and jingling, I called to the idle minxes that it was time to get home, for the sun was setting, and they had sung and basked enough."

The Student Anselmus felt as if he now merely heard in plain words something he had long dreamed of; and though he fancied he observed that elder-bush, wall and sward, and all objects about him were beginning slowly to whirl round, he took heart, and was ready to speak; but the Archivarius prevented him; for sharply pulling the glove from his left hand, and holding the stone of a ring, glittering in strange sparkles and flames before the Student's eyes, he said: "Look here, Herr Anselmus; what you see may do you good."

The Student Anselmus looked in, and O wonder! the stone threw a beam of rays round it, as from a burning focus; and the rays wove themselves together into a clear gleaming crystal mirror; in which, with many windings, now flying asunder, now twisted together, the three gold-green Snakes, were dancing and bounding. And when their taper forms, glittering with a thousand sparkles, touched each other, there issued from them glorious tones, as of crystal bells; and the mid-most of the three stretched forth her little head from the mirror, as if full of longing and desire, and her dark-blue eyes said: "Knowest thou me then; believest thou in me, Anselmus? In Belief alone is Love: canst thou love?"

"O Serpentina! Serpentina!" cried the Student Anselmus in mad rapture; but Archivarius Lindhorst suddenly breathed on the mirror, and with an electric sputter the rays sank back into their focus; and on his hand there was now nothing but a little emerald, over which the Archivarius drew his glove.

"Did you see the golden Snakes, Herr Anselmus?" said the Archivarius.

"Ah, good Heaven, yes!" replied the Student, "and the fair dear Serpentina."

"Hush!" continued Archivarius Lindhorst, "enough at one time: for the rest, if you resolve on working with me, you may see my daughter often enough; or rather I will grant you this real satisfaction, if you stick tightly and truly to your task, that is to say, copy every mark with the greatest clearness and correctness. But you do not come to me at all, Herr Anselmus, though Registrator Heerbrand promised I should see you forthwith, and I have waited several days in vain."

Not till the mention of Registrator Heerbrand's name did the Student Anselmus again feel as if he were really standing with his two legs on the ground, and he were really the Student Anselmus, and the man talking to him really Archivarius Lindhorst. The tone of indifference, with which the latter spoke, in such rude contrast with the strange sights which, like a genuine necromancer, he had called forth, awakened a certain horror in the Student, which the piercing look of these fiery eyes, beaming

from their bony sockets in the lean puckered visage, as from a leathern case, still farther aggravated; and the Student was again forcibly seized with the same unearthly feeling, which had before gained possession of him in the coffee-house, when Archivarius Lindhorst had talked so wildly. With a great effort he retained his self-command, and as Archivarius again asked: "Well, why have you not come to me?" the Student exerted his whole energies, and related to him all that had happened at the street-door.

"Dear Herr Anselmus," said the Archivarius, when the narrative was finished; "dear Herr Anselmus, I know this Applewife of whom you speak: she is a fatal slut of a creature that plays all manner of freaks on me; but that she should have bronzed herself, and taken the shape of a door-knocker, to deter pleasant visitors from calling, is indeed very bad, and truly not to be endured. Would you please, however, worthy Herr Anselmus, if you come tomorrow at noon, and notice aught more of this grinning and growling, just to be so good as drop me a driblet or two of this liquor on her nose; it will put all to rights immediately. And now, adieu, dear Herr Anselmus! I go somewhat fast, therefore I would not advise you to think of returning with me. Adieu, till we meet!—Tomorrow at noon!"

The Archivarius had given the Student Anselmus a little vial, with a gold-coloured fluid in it; and he walked rapidly off; so rapidly, that in the dusk, which had now come on, he seemed rather to be floating down to the valley than stepping down to it. Already he was near the Kosel garden; the wind got within his wide greatcoat, and drove the breasts of it asunder; so that they fluttered in the air like a pair of large wings; and to the Student Anselmus, who was looking full of amazement at the course of the Archivarius, it seemed as if a large bird were spreading out its pinions for rapid flight. And now, while the Student kept gazing into the dusk, a white-grey kite with creaking cry soared up into the air; and he now saw clearly that the white flutter which he had looked upon, as the retiring Archivarius must have been this very kite, though he still could not understand where the Archivarius had vanished so abruptly.

"Perhaps he may have flown away in person, this Herr Archivarius Lindhorst," said the Student Anselmus to himself; "for I now see and feel clearly, that all these foreign shapes of a distant wondrous world, which formerly I never saw except in quite peculiarly remarkable dreams, have now come forth into my waking life, and are making their sport of me. But be this as it will! Thou livest and glowest in my breast, thou lovely, gentle Serpentina; thou alone canst still the infinite longing which now rends my soul in pieces. Ah, when shall I see thy kind eyes, dear, dear Serpentina!" So cried the Student Anselmus quite aloud.—"That is a vile unchristian name!" murmured a bass voice beside him, which belonged to some home-going promenader. The Student Anselmus, reminded in right season where he was, hastened off at a quick pace; thinking to himself: "Were it not a proper misfortune now if Conrector Paulmann or Registrator Heerbrand were to meet me?"—But neither of these gentlemen met him.

Fifth Vigil

Die Frau Hofräthinn Anselmus. Cicero de Officiis. *Meer-cats, and other vermin. The Equinox*

"There is nothing in the world to be made of this Anselmus," said Conrector Paulmann; "all my good advices, all my admonitions, are fruitless; he will apply himself to nothing; though he is a fine classical scholar too, and that is the foundation of all."

But Registrator Heerbrand, with a sly, mysterious smile, replied: "Let Anselmus have his time, dear Conrector! he is a strange subject this Anselmus, but there is much in him; and when I say much, I mean a Privy Secretary, or even a Court-councillor, a Hofrath."

"Hof—" began Conrector Paulmann, in the deepest amazement; the word stuck in his throat.

"Hush! hush!" continued Registrator Heerbrand, "I know what I know. These two days he has been with Archivarius Lindhorst, copying manuscripts; and last night the Archivarius meets me at the coffee-house, and says: 'You have sent me a proper man, good neighbour! There is stuff in him!' And now think of Archivarius Lindhorst's influence— Hush! hush! we will talk of it this time twelve-month." And with these words the Registrator, his face still wrinkled into the same sly smile, went out of the room; leaving the Conrector speechless from astonishment and curiosity, and fixed, as if by enchantment, in his chair.

But on Veronica this dialogue had made a still deeper impression. "Did I not know all along," thought she, "that Herr Anselmus was a most clever and pretty young man, out of whom something great was to come? Were I but certain that he really liked me! But that night when we crossed the Elbe, did he not twice press my hand? Did he not look at me, in our duet, with such particular glances, that pierced into my very heart? Yes, yes! he really likes me; and I——" Veronica gave herself up, as young maidens are wont, to sweet dreams of a gay future. She was Mrs. Hofrath, Frau Hofräthinn; she occupied a fine house in the Schlossgasse, or in the Neumarkt, or in the Moritzstrasse; the fashionable hat, the new Turkish shawl, became her admirably; she was breakfasting in the balcony in an elegant negligée, giving orders to her cook for the day: "And see, if you please, not to spoil that dish; it is the Hofrath's favourite." Then passing beaux glanced up, and she heard distinctly: "Well, it is a heavenly woman, that Hofräthinn; how prettily the lace cap sets her!" Mrs. Privy Councillor Ypsilon sends her servant to ask if it would please the Frau Hofräthinn to drive as far as the Linke Bath to-day? "Many compliments; extremely sorry I am engaged to tea already with the Presidentinn Tz." Then comes the Hofrath Anselmus back from his office; he is dressed in the top of the mode: "Ten, I declare," cries he, making his gold watch repeat, and giving his young lady a kiss. "How goes it, little wife? Guess what I have here for thee?" continues he, roguishly toying; and draws from his waistcoat-pocket a pair of beautiful earrings, fashioned in the newest style, and puts them on in place of the old ones. "Ah! the pretty, dainty earrings!" cried Veronica aloud; and started up from her chair, throwing aside her work, to see these fair earrings with her own eyes in the glass.

"What is this, then?" said Conrector Paulmann, roused by the noise from his deep study of *Cicero de Officiis*, and almost dropping the book from his hand; "are we taking fits, like Anselmus?" But at this moment, the Student Anselmus, who, contrary to his custom, had not been seen for several days, entered the room, to Veronica's astonishment and terror; for, in truth, he seemed altered in his whole bearing. With a certain precision, which was far from usual in him, he spoke of new tendencies of life which had become clear to his mind, of glorious prospects which were opening for him, but which many a one had not the skill to discern. Conrector Paulmann, remembering Registrator Heerbrand's mysterious speech, was still more struck, and could scarcely utter a syllable, till the Student Anselmus, after letting fall some hints of urgent business at Archivarius Lindhorst's, and with elegant adroitness kissing Veronica's hand, was already down stairs, off and away.

"This was the Hofrath already," murmured Veronica to herself: "and he kissed my hand, without sliding on the floor, or treading on my foot, as he used! He threw me the softest look too; yes, he really likes me!"

Veronica again gave way to her dreaming; yet now, it was as if a hostile shape were still coming forward among these lovely visions of her future household life as Frau Hofräthinn, and the shape were laughing in spiteful mockery, and saying: "This is all very stupid and trashy stuff, and lies to boot; for Anselmus will never, never, be Hofrath, and thy husband; he does not love thee in the least, though thou hast blue eyes, and a fine figure, and a pretty hand." Then an ice-stream poured over Veronica's soul; and a deep sorrow swept away the delight with which, a little while ago, she had seen herself in the lace cap and fashionable earrings. Tears almost rushed into her eyes, and she said aloud: "Ah! it is too true; he does not love me in the least; and I shall never, never, be Frau Hofräthinn!"

"Romance crotchets! Romance crotchets!" cried Conrector Paulmann; then snatched his hat and stick, and hastened indignantly from the house. "This was still wanting," sighed Veronica; and felt vexed at her little sister, a girl of twelve years, because she sat so unconcerned, and kept sewing at her frame, as if nothing had happened.

Meanwhile it was almost three o'clock; and now time to trim the apartment, and arrange the coffee-table: for the Mademoiselles Oster had announced that they were coming. But from behind every work-box which Veronica lifted aside, behind the note-books which she laid away from the harpsichord, behind every cup, behind the coffee-pot which she took from the cupboard, that shape peeped forth, like a little mandrake, and laughed in spiteful mockery, and snapped its little spider fingers, and cried: "He will not be thy husband! he will not be thy husband!" And then, when she threw all away, and fled to the middle of the room, it peered out again, with long nose, in gigantic bulk, from behind the stove, and snarled and growled: "He will not be thy husband!"

"Dost thou hear nothing, sister? dost thou see nothing?" cried Veronica, shivering with affright, and not daring to touch aught in the room. Fränzchen rose, quite grave and quiet, from her broidering-frame, and said: "What ails thee today, sister? Thou art throwing all topsyturvy, and jingling and tingling. I must help thee, I see."

But here the lively visitors came tripping in with brisk laughter; and the same moment, Veronica perceived that it was the stove-handle which she had taken for a shape; and the creaking of the ill-shut stove-door for those spiteful words. Yet, thus violently seized with an inward horror, she could not so directly recover her composure, that the strange excitement, which even her paleness and agitated looks betrayed, was not noticed by the Mademoiselles Oster. As they at once cut short their merry narratives, and pressed her to tell them what, in Heaven's name, had happened, Veronica was obliged to admit that certain strange thoughts had come into her mind; and suddenly, in open day, a dread of spectres, which she did not use to feel, had got the better of her. She described in such lively colours how a little grey mannikin, peeping out of all the corners of the room, had mocked and plagued her, that the Mademoiselles Oster began to look round with timid glances, and start all manner of unearthly notions. But Fränzchen entered at this moment with the steaming coffee-pot; and the whole three, taking thought again, laughed outright at their folly.

Angelica, the elder of the Osters, was engaged to an officer: the young man had joined the army; but his friends had been so long without news of him, that there was too little doubt of his being dead, or at least grievously wounded. This had plunged Angelica into the deepest sorrow; but today she was merry, even to extravagance; a state of things which so much surprised Veronica, that she could not but speak of it, and inquire the reason. "Dear girl," said Angelica, "dost thou fancy that my Victor is not still in my heart and my thoughts? It is for him I am so gay—O Heaven! so happy, so blessed in my whole soul! For my Victor is well: in a little while he comes, advanced to be Rittmeister, and adorned with the honours which his boundless courage has won him. A deep, but by no means dangerous wound, in the right arm, which he got too by a sword-cut from a French hussar, prevents him from writing; and the rapid change of quarters, for he will not consent to leave his regiment, still makes it impossible for him to send me tidings. But tonight he receives a fixed order to withdraw, till his wound be cured. Tomorrow he sets out for home; and just as he is stepping into the coach, he learns his promotion to be Rittmeister."

"But, dear Angelica," interrupted the other, "how knowest thou all this already?"

"Do not laugh at me, my friend," continued Angelica; "and surely thou wilt not laugh; for might not the little grey mannikin, to punish thee, peep forth from behind the mirror there? In a word, I cannot lay aside my belief in certain mysterious things, since often enough in life they have come before my eyes, I might say, into my very hands. For example, I cannot reckon it so strange and incredible as many others do, that there should be people gifted with a certain faculty of prophecy, which, by sure means known to themselves, they may put in action. In the city, here, is an old woman, who possesses this gift to a high degree. It is not, as with others of her tribe, by cards, or melted lead, or grounds of coffee, that she divines to you; but after certain preparations, in which you yourself bear a part, she takes a polished metallic mirror, and there rises in it the strangest mixture of figures and forms, all intermingled; these she interprets, and so answers your question. I was with her last night, and got those tidings of my Victor, in which I have not doubted for a moment."

Angelica's narrative threw a spark into Veronica's soul, which instantly kindled with the thought of consulting this same old prophetess about Anselmus and her hopes. She learned that the crone was called Frau Rauerin, and lived in a remote street near the Seethor; that she was not to be seen except on Tuesdays, Thursdays, and Fridays, from seven o'clock in the evening, but then, indeed, through the whole night till sunrise; and that she liked best if her customers came alone. It was Thursday even now, and Veronica determined, under pretext of accompanying the Osters home, to visit this old woman, and lay the case before her.

Accordingly, no sooner had her friends, who lived in the Neustadt, parted from her at the Elbe-bridge, than she hastened with winged steps towards the Seethor; and, ere long, she had reached the remote narrow street described to her, and at the end of it perceived the little red house in which Frau Rauerin was said to live. She could not rid herself of a certain dread, nay, of a certain horror, as she approached the door. At last she summoned resolution, in spite of inward terror, and made bold to pull the bell: the door opened, and she groped through the dark passage for the stair which led to the upper story, as Angelica had directed. "Does Frau Rauerin live here?" cried she, into the empty lobby, as no one appeared; and instead of answer, there rose a long clear "Mew!" and a large black Cat, with its back curved up, and whisking its tail to and fro in wavy coils, stept on before her, with much gravity, to the door of the apartment, which, on a second mew, was opened.

"Ah, see! Art thou here already, daughter? Come in, love; come in!" exclaimed the advancing figure, the aspect of which was rooting Veronica to the floor. A long lean woman, wrapped in black rags!—while she spoke, her peaked projecting chin wagged this way and that; her toothless mouth, overshadowed by the bony hawk-nose, twisted itself into a ghastly smile, and gleaming cat's-eyes flickered in sparkles through the large spectacles. From a party-coloured clout wrapped round her head, black wiry hair was sticking out; but what deformed her haggard visage to absolute horror, was two large burnmarks which ran from the left cheek, over the nose. Veronica's breathing stopped; and the scream, which was about to lighten her choked breast, became a deep sigh, as the witch's skeleton hand took hold of her, and led her into the chamber. Here all was awake and astir; nothing but din and tumult, and squeaking, and mewing, and croaking, and piping all at once, on every hand. The crone struck the table with her fist, and screamed: "Peace, ye vermin!" And the meer-cats, whimpering, clambered to the top of the high bed; and the little meer-swine all ran beneath the stove, and the raven fluttered up to the round mirror; and the black Cat, as if the rebuke did not apply to him, kept sitting at his ease on the

cushion-chair, to which he had leapt directly after entering.

So soon as quiet was obtained, Veronica took heart; she felt less dreary and frighted than without in the lobby; nay, the crone herself seemed not so hideous. For the first time, she now looked round the room. All manner of odious stuffed beasts hung down from the ceiling: strange unknown household implements were lying in confusion on the floor; and in the grate was a blue scanty fire, which only now and then sputtered up in yellow sparkles; and at every sputter, there came a rustling from above, and monstrous bats, as if with human countenances, in distorted laughter, went flitting to and fro; at times, too, the flame shot up, licking the sooty wall, and then there sounded cutting howling tones of woe, which shook Veronica with fear and horror. "With your leave, Mamsell!" said the crone, knitting her brows, and seizing a brush; with which, having dipt it in a copper skillet, she then besprinkled the grate. The fire went out; and as if filled with thick smoke, the room grew pitch-dark: but the crone, who had gone aside into a closet, soon returned with a lighted lamp; and now Veronica could see no beasts or implements in the apartment; it was a common meanly furnished room. The crone came up to her, and said with a creaking voice: "I know what thou wantest here, little daughter: tush, thou wouldst have me tell thee whether thou shalt wed Anselmus, when he is Hofrath."

Veronica stiffened with amazement and terror; but the crone continued: "Thou hast told me the whole of it at home, at thy papa's, when the coffee-pot was standing before thee: I was the coffee-pot; didst thou not know me? Daughterkin, hear me! Give up, give up this Anselmus: 'tis a nasty creature; he trod my little sons to pieces, my dear little sons, the Apples with the red cheeks, that glide away, when people have bought them, whisk! out of their pockets again, and roll back into my basket. He trades with the Old One: 'twas but the day before yesterday, he poured that cursed Auripigment on my face, and I had nigh gone blind with it. Thou may'st see the burnmarks yet. Daughterkin, give him up, give him up! He loves thee not, for he loves the gold-green Snake; he will never be Hofrath, for he has joined the Salamanders, and he means to wed the green Snake: give him up, give him up!"

Veronica, who had a firm, steadfast spirit of her own, and could soon conquer girlish terror, now drew back a step, and said, with a serious resolute tone: "Old dame! I heard of your gift of looking into futurity; and wished, perhaps too curiously and thoughtlessly, to learn from you whether Anselmus, whom I love and value, could ever be mine. But if, instead of fulfilling my desire, you keep vexing me with your foolish unreasonable babble, you are doing wrong; for I have asked of you nothing but what, as I well know, you grant to others. Since, as it would seem, you are acquainted with my inmost thoughts, it might perhaps have been an easy matter for you to unfold to me much that now pains and grieves my mind; but after your silly slander of the good Anselmus, I care not for talking farther with you. Goodnight!"

Veronica was hastening away; but the crone, with tears and lamentation, fell upon her knees; and, holding the young lady by the gown, exclaimed: "Veronica! Veronica! hast thou forgot old Liese, then? Her who has so often carried thee in her arms, and nursed and dandled thee?"

Veronica could scarcely believe her eyes; for here, in truth, was her old nurse, defaced only by greater age, and chiefly by the two burns; old Liese in person, who had vanished from Conrector Paulmann's house, some years ago, no one knew whither. The crone, too, had quite another look now: instead of the ugly many-pieced clout, she had on a decent cap; instead of the black rags, a gay printed bedgown; she was neatly dressed, as of old. She rose from the floor; and, taking Veronica in her arms, proceeded: "What I have just told thee may seem very mad; but, unluckily, it is too true. Anselmus has done me much mischief, though against his will: he has fallen into Archivarius Lindhorst's

hands, and the Old One means to marry him with his daughter. Archivarius Lindhorst is my deadliest enemy: I could tell thee thousands of things about him; which, however, thou wouldst not understand, or, at best, be too much frightened at. He is the Wise Man, it seems; but I am the Wise Woman: let this stand for that! I see now, thou lovest this Anselmus heartily; and I will help thee with all my strength, that so thou mayest be happy, and wed him like a pretty bride, as thou wishest."

"But tell me, for Heaven's sake, Liese ———" interrupted Veronica.

"Hush! child, hush!" cried the old woman, interrupting in her turn: "I know what thou wouldst say; I have become what I am, because it was to be so; I could do no other. Well, then! I know the means which will cure Anselmus of his frantic love for the green Snake, and lead him, the prettiest Hofrath, into thy arms; but thou thyself must help."

"Speak it out, Liese; I will do aught and all, for I love Anselmus much!" whispered Veronica, scarce audibly.

"I know thee," continued the crone, "for a courageous child: I could never frighten thee to sleep with the *Wauwau*; for that instant, thy eyes were open to what the *Wauwau* was like. Thou wouldst go without a light into the darkest room; and many a time, with papa's powder-mantle, hast thou terrified the neighbours' children. Well, then, if thou art in earnest about conquering Archivarius Lindhorst and the green Snake by my art; if thou art in earnest about calling Anselmus by the name of Hofrath and thy husband; then, at the next Equinox, about eleven at night, glide from thy father's house, and come hither: I will go with thee to the crossing of the roads, which cut the fields hard by here: we shall provide the needful; and whatever wonders thou mayest see, shall do thee no whit of harm. And now, love, good-night: Papa is waiting for thee to supper."

Veronica hastened away: she had the firmest purpose not to neglect the night of the Equinox; "for," thought she, "old Liese is right; Anselmus has got entangled in strange fetters; but I will free him from them, and call him mine for ever and aye; mine he is, and shall be, the Hofrath Anselmus."

Sixth Vigil

Archivarius Lindhorst's Garden, with some Mockbirds. The Golden Pot. English current-hand. Pothooks. The Prince of the Spirits

"It may be, after all," said the Student Anselmus to himself, "that the superfine strong stomachic liqueur, which I took somewhat freely in Monsieur Conradi's, might really be the cause of all these shocking fantasms, which so tortured me at Archivarius Lindhorst's door. Therefore, I will go quite sober today; and so bid defiance to whatever farther mischief may assail me." On this occasion, as before when equipping himself for his first call on Archivarius Lindhorst, the Student Anselmus put his pen-drawings, and caligraphic masterpieces, his bars of Indian ink, and his well-pointed crow-pens, into his pockets; and was just turning to go out, when his eye lighted on the vial with the yellow liquor, which he had received from Archivarius Lindhorst. All the strange adventures he had met with again rose on his mind in glowing colours; and a nameless emotion of rapture and pain thrilled through his breast. Involuntarily he exclaimed, with a most piteous voice: "Ah, am not I going to the Archivarius solely for a sight of thee, thou gentle lovely Serpentina!" At that moment, he felt as if Serpentina's love might be the prize of some laborious perilous task which he had to undertake; and as if this task were no other than the copying of the Lindhorst manuscripts. That at his very entrance into the house, or more properly, before his entrance, all manner of mysterious things might happen, as of late, was no more than he anticipated. He thought no more of Conradi's strong water; but hastily put the vial of liquor in his waist-coat-pocket, that he might act strictly by the Archivarius' directions, should the bronzed Apple-woman again take it upon her to make faces at him.

And did not the hawk-nose actually peak itself, did not the cat-eyes actually glare from the knocker, as he raised his hand to it, at the stroke of twelve? But now, without farther ceremony, he dribbled his liquor into the pestilent visage; and it folded and moulded itself, that instant, down to a glittering bowl-round knocker. The door went up: the bells sounded beautifully over all the house: "Klingling, youngling, in, in, spring, spring, klingling." In good heart he mounted the fine broad stair; and feasted on the odours of some strange perfumery, that was floating through the house. In doubt, he paused on the lobby; for he knew not at which of these many fine doors he was to knock. But Archivarius Lindhorst, in a white damask night-gown, stept forth to him, and said: "Well, it is a real pleasure to me, Herr Anselmus, that you have kept your word at last. Come this way, if you please; I must take you straight into the Laboratory." And with this he stept rapidly through the lobby, and opened a little side-door, which led into a long passage. Anselmus walked on in high spirits, behind the Archivarius; they passed from this corridor into a hall, or rather into a lordly greenhouse: for on both sides, up to the ceiling, stood all manner of rare wondrous flowers, nay, great trees with strangely formed leaves and blossoms. A magic dazzling light shone over the whole, though you could not discover whence it came, for no window whatever was to be seen. As the Student Anselmus looked in through the bushes and trees, long avenues appeared to open in remote distance. In the deep shade of thick cypress groves, lay glittering marble fountains, out of which rose wondrous figures, spouting crystal jets that fell with pattering spray into the gleaming lily-cups; strange voices cooed and rustled through the wood of curious trees; and sweetest perfumes streamed up and down.

The Archivarius had vanished: and Anselmus saw nothing but a huge bush of glowing fire-lilies before him. Intoxicated with the sight and the fine odours of this fairy-garden, Anselmus stood fixed to the spot. Then began on all sides of him a giggling and laughing; and light little voices railed and mocked him: "Herr Studiosus! Herr Studiosus! how came you hither? Why have you dressed so bravely, Herr Anselmus? Will you chat with us for a minute, how grandmammy sat squelching down upon the egg, and young master got a stain on his Sunday waistcoat?—Can you play the new tune, now, which you learned from Daddy Cockadoodle, Herr Anselmus?—You look very fine in your glass perriwig, and post-paper boots." So cried and chattered and sniggered the little voices, out of every corner, nay, close by the Student himself, who now observed that all sorts of party-coloured birds were fluttering above him, and jeering him in hearty laughter. At that moment, the bush of fire-lilies advanced towards him; and he perceived that it was Archivarius Lindhorst, whose flowered night-gown, glittering in red and yellow, had so far deceived his eyes.

"I beg your pardon, worthy Herr Anselmus," said the Archivarius, "for leaving you alone: I wished, in passing, to take a peep at my fine cactus, which is to blossom tonight. But how like you my little house-garden?"

"Ah, Heaven! Immeasurably pretty it is, most valued Herr Archivarius," replied the Student; "but these party-coloured birds have been bantering me a little."

"What chattering is this?" cried the Archivarius angrily into the bushes. Then a huge grey Parrot came fluttering out, and perched itself beside the Archivarius on a myrtle-bough; and looking at him with an uncommon earnestness and gravity through a pair of spectacles that stuck on its hooked bill, it creaked out: "Don't take it amiss, Herr Archivarius; my wild boys have been a little free or so; but the Herr Studiosus has himself to blame in the matter, for ———"

"Hush! hush!" interrupted Archivarius Lindhorst; "I know the varlets; but thou must keep them in better discipline, my friend!—Now, come along, Herr Anselmus."

And the Archivarius again stept forth, through many a strangely decorated chamber; so that the Student Anselmus, in following him, could scarcely give a glance at all the glittering wondrous furniture, and other unknown things, with which the whole of them were filled. At last they entered a large apartment; where the Archivarius, casting his eyes aloft, stood still; and Anselmus got time to feast himself on the glorious sight, which the simple decoration of this hall afforded. Jutting from the azure-coloured walls rose gold-bronze trunks of high palm-trees, which wove their colossal leaves, glittering like bright emeralds, into a ceiling far up: in the middle of the chamber, and resting on three Egyptian lions, cast out of dark bronze, lay a porphyry plate; and on this stood a simple Golden Pot, from which, so soon as he beheld it, Anselmus could not turn away an eye. It was as if, in a thousand gleaming reflexes, all sorts of shapes were sporting on the bright polished gold: often he perceived his own form, with arms stretched out in longing—ah! beneath the elder-bush—and Serpentina was winding and shooting up and down, and again looking at him with her kind eyes. Anselmus was beside himself with frantic rapture.

"Serpentina! Serpentina!" cried he aloud; and Archivarius Lindhorst whirled round abruptly, and said: "How now, worthy Herr Anselmus? If I mistake not, you were pleased to call for my daughter; she is quite in the other side of the house at present, and indeed just taking her lesson on the harpsichord. Let us go along."

Anselmus, scarcely knowing what he did, followed his conductor; he saw or heard nothing more, till Archivarius Lindhorst suddenly grasped his hand, and said: "Here is the place!" Anselmus awoke as from a dream, and now perceived that he was in a high room, all lined on every side with bookshelves, and nowise differing from a common library and study. In the middle stood a large writing-table, with a stuffed arm-chair before it. "This," said Archivarius Lindhorst, "is your work-room for the present: whether you may work, some other time, in the blue library, where you so suddenly called out my daughter's name, I yet know not. But now I could wish to convince myself of your ability to execute this task appointed you, in the way I wish it and need it." The Student here gathered full courage; and not without internal self-complacence in the certainty of highly gratifying Archivarius Lindhorst, pulled out his drawings and specimens of penmanship from his pocket. But no sooner had the Archivarius cast his eye on the first leaf, a piece of writing in the finest English style, than he smiled very oddly, and shook his head. These motions he repeated at every following leaf, so that the Student Anselmus felt the blood mounting to his face; and at last, when the smile became quite sarcastic and contemptuous, he broke out in downright vexation: "The Herr Archivarius does not seem contented with my poor talents."

"Dear Herr Anselmus," said Archivarius Lindhorst, "you have indeed fine capacities for the art of caligraphy; but, in the meanwhile, it is clear enough, I must reckon more on your diligence and good-will, than on your attainments in the business."

The Student Anselmus spoke largely of his often-acknowledged perfection in this art, of his fine Chinese ink, and most select crow-quills. But Archivarius Lindhorst handed him the English sheet, and said: "Be judge yourself!" Anselmus felt as if struck by a thunderbolt, to see his hand-writing look so: it was miserable, beyond measure. There was no rounding in the turns, no hair-stroke where it should be; no proportion between the capital and single letters; nay, villainous school-boy pot-hooks often spoiled the best lines. "And then," continued Archivarius Lindhorst, "your ink will not stand." He dipt his finger in a glass of water, and as he just skimmed it over the lines, they vanished without vestige. The Student Anselmus felt as if some monster were throttling him: he could not utter a word. There stood he, with the unlucky sheet in his hand; but Archivarius Lindhorst laughed aloud, and said:

"Never mind it, dearest Herr Anselmus; what you could not perfect before, will perhaps do better here. At any rate, you shall have better materials than you have been accustomed to. Begin, in Heaven's name!"

From a locked press, Archivarius Lindhorst now brought out a black fluid substance, which diffused a most peculiar odour; also pens, sharply pointed and of strange colour, together with a sheet of especial whiteness and smoothness; then at last an Arabic manuscript: and as Anselmus sat down to work, the Archivarius left the room. The Student Anselmus had often copied Arabic manuscripts already; the first problem, therefore, seemed to him not so very difficult to solve. "How these pot-hooks came into my fine English current-hand, Heaven, and Archivarius Lindhorst, know best," said he; "but that they are not from *my* hand, I will testify to the death!" At every new word that stood fair and perfect on the parchment, his courage increased, and with it his adroitness. In truth, these pens wrote exquisitely well; and the mysterious ink flowed pliantly, and black as jet, on the bright white parchment. And as he worked along so diligently, and with such strained attention, he began to feel more and more at home in the solitary room; and already he had quite fitted himself into his task, which he now hoped to finish well, when at the stroke of three the Archivarius called him into the side-room to a savoury dinner. At table, Archivarius Lindhorst was in special gaiety of heart: he inquired about the Student Anselmus' friends, Conrector Paulmann, and Registrator Heerbrand, and of the latter especially he had store of merry anecdotes to tell. The good old Rhenish was particularly grateful to the Student Anselmus, and made him more talkative than he was wont to be. At the stroke of four, he rose to resume his labour; and this punctuality appeared to please the Archivarius.

If the copying of these Arabic manuscripts had prospered in his hands, before dinner, the task now went forward much better; nay, he could not himself comprehend the rapidity and ease, with which he succeeded in transcribing the twisted strokes of this foreign character. But it was as if, in his inmost soul, a voice were whispering in audible words: "Ah! couldst thou accomplish it, wert thou not thinking of *her*, didst thou not believe in *her* and in her love?" Then there floated whispers, as in low, low, waving crystal tones, through the room: "I am near, near, near! I help thee: be bold, be steadfast, dear Anselmus! I toil with thee, that thou mayest be mine." And as, in the fulness of secret rapture, he caught these sounds, the unknown characters grew clearer and clearer to him; he scarcely required to look on the original at all; nay, it was as if the letters were already standing in pale ink on the parchment, and he had nothing more to do but mark them black. So did he labour on, encompassed with dear inspiring tones as with soft sweet breath, till the clock struck six, and Archivarius Lindhorst entered the apartment. He came forward to the table, with a singular smile; Anselmus rose in silence: the Archivarius still looked at him, with that mocking smile: but no sooner had he glanced over the copy, than the smile passed into deep solemn earnestness, which every feature of his face adapted itself to express. He seemed no longer the same. His eyes, which usually gleamed with sparkling fire, now looked with unutterable mildness at Anselmus; a soft red tinted the pale cheeks; and instead of the irony which at other times compressed the mouth, the softly-curved graceful lips now seemed to be opening for wise and soul-persuading speech. The whole form was higher, statelier; the wide nightgown spread itself like a royal mantle in broad folds over his breast and shoulders; and through the white locks, which lay on his high open brow, there winded a thin band of gold.

"Young man," began the Archivarius in solemn tone, "before thou thoughtest of it, I knew thee, and all the secret relations which bind thee to the dearest and holiest of my interests! Serpentina loves thee; a singular destiny, whose fateful threads were spun by enemies, is fulfilled, should she be thine, and thou obtain, as an essential dowry, the Golden Pot, which of right belongs to her. But only from effort and contest can thy happiness in the higher life arise; hostile Principles assail thee; and only the interior force with which thou shalt withstand these contradictions can save thee from disgrace and ruin. Whilst labouring here, thou art passing the season of instruction: Belief and full knowledge will lead thee to the near goal, if thou but hold fast, what thou hast well begun. Bear *her* always and truly in thy thoughts, her who loves thee; then shalt thou see the marvels of the Golden Pot, and be happy for ever more. Fare thee well! Archivarius Lindhorst expects thee tomorrow at noon in thy cabinet. Fare thee well!" With these words Archivarius Lindhorst softly pushed the Student Anselmus out of the door, which he then locked; and Anselmus found himself in the chamber where he had dined, the single door of which led out to the lobby.

Altogether stupefied with these strange phenomena, the Student Anselmus stood lingering at the street-door; he heard a window open above him, and looked up: it was Archivarius Lindhorst, quite the old man again, in his light-grey gown, as he usually appeared. The Archivarius called to him: "Hey, worthy Herr Anselmus, what are you studying over there? Tush, the Arabic is still in your head. My compliments to Herr Conrector Paulmann, if you see him; and come tomorrow precisely at noon. The fee for this day is lying in your right waistcoat-pocket." The Student Anselmus actually found the clear speziesthaler in the pocket indicated; but he took no joy in it. "What is to come of all this," said he to himself, "I know not: but if it be some mad delusion and conjuring work that has laid hold of me, the dear Serpentina still lives and moves in my inward heart; and before I leave her, I will die altogether; for I know that the thought in me is eternal, and no hostile Principle can take it from me: and what else is this thought but Serpentina's love?"

Seventh Vigil

How Conrector Paulmann knocked the Ashes out of his Pipe, and went to Bed. Rembrandt and Höllenbreughel. The Magic Mirror; and Dr. Eckstein's Prescription for an unknown Disease

At last Conrector Paulmann knocked the ashes out of his pipe, and said: "Now, then, it is time to go to bed."—"Yes, indeed," replied Veronica, frightened at her father's sitting so late; for ten had struck long ago. No sooner, accordingly, had the Conrector withdrawn to his study and bed-room, and Fränzchen's heavy breathing signified that she was asleep, than Veronica, who, to save appearances, had also gone to bed, rose softly, softly, out of it again; put on her clothes, threw her mantle round her, and glided out of doors.

Ever since the moment when Veronica had left old Liese, Anselmus had continually stood before her eyes; and it seemed as if a foreign voice, unknown to herself, were ever and anon repeating in her soul that his reluctance sprang from a hostile person holding him in bonds, which, by secret means of magical art, Veronica might break. Her confidence in old Liese grew stronger every day; and even the impression of unearthliness and horror by degrees softened down, so that all the mystery and strangeness of her relation to the crone appeared before her only in the colour of something singular, romantic, and so not a little attractive. Accordingly, she had a firm purpose, even at the risk of being missed from home, and encountering a thousand inconveniences, to front the adventure of the Equinox. And now, at last, the fateful night, in which old Liese had promised to afford comfort and help, was come; and Veronica, long used to thoughts of nightly wandering, was full of heart and hope. With winged speed, she flew through the solitary streets; heedless of the storm which was howling in the air, and dashing thick rain-drops in her face.

With stifled droning clang, the Kreuzthurm clock struck eleven, as Veronica, quite wetted, reached old Liese's house. "Art come, dear! wait, love; wait, love—" cried a voice from above; and instantly the crone, laden with a basket, and attended by her Cat, was also standing at the door. "We will go, then, and do what is proper, and can prosper in the night, which favours the work." So speaking, the crone with her cold hand seized the shivering Veronica, to whom she gave the heavy basket to carry, while she herself produced a little cauldron, a trevet, and a spade. On their reaching the open fields, the rain had ceased, but the storm had become louder; howlings in a thousand tones were flitting through the air. A horrible heart-piercing lamentation sounded down from the black clouds, which rolled themselves together, in rapid flight, and veiled all things in thickest darkness. But the crone stept briskly forward, crying in a shrill harsh voice: "Light, light, my lad!" Then blue forky gleams went quivering and sputtering before them; and Veronica perceived that it was the Cat emitting sparks, and bounding forward to light the way; while his doleful ghastly screams were heard in the momentary pauses of the storm. Her heart was like to fail; it was as if ice-cold talons were clutching into her soul: but, with a strong effort, she collected herself; pressed closer to the crone, and said: "It must all be accomplished now, come of it what may!"

"Right, right, little daughter!" replied the crone; "be steady, like a good girl; thou shalt have something pretty, and Anselmus to boot."

At last the crone paused, and said: "Here is the place!" She dug a hole in the ground, then shook coals into it, put the trevet over them, and placed the cauldron on the top of it. All this she accomplished with strange gestures, while the Cat kept circling round her. From his tail there sputtered sparkles, which united into a ring of fire. The coals began to burn; and at last blue flames rose up round the cauldron. Veronica was ordered to lay off her mantle and veil, and to cower down beside the crone, who seized her hands, and pressed them hard, glaring with her fiery eyes, at the maiden. Ere long the strange materials (whether flowers, metals, herbs, or beasts, you could not determine), which the crone had taken from her basket, and thrown into the cauldron, began to seeth and foam. The crone quitted Veronica; then clutched an iron ladle, and plunged it into the glowing mass, which she began to stir; while Veronica, as she directed, was to look steadfastly into the cauldron, and fix her thoughts on Anselmus. But now the crone threw fresh ingredients, glittering pieces of metal, a lock of hair which Veronica had cut from her head, and a little ring which she had long worn, into the pot; while she howled in dread yelling tones through the gloom, and the Cat in quick incessant motion, whimpered and whined.——————

I could wish much that thou, favourable reader, hadst on this twenty-third of September been thyself travelling towards Dresden. In vain, when late night sank down, did the people try to retain thee at the last stage: the friendly host represented to thee that the storm and the rain were too bitter, and moreover, that it was not safe for unearthly reasons to rush away in the dark, in the night of the Equinox; but thou regardedst him not, thinking within thyself: "I will give the postillion a whole thaler of drink-money, and so, at latest, by one o'clock reach Dresden; where, in the *Golden Angel*, or in the *Helmet*, or in the *City of Naumburg*, a well-readied supper and a soft bed await me." And now, as thou art driving hither through the dark, thou suddenly observest in the distance a most strange flickering light. Coming nearer, thou perceivest a ring of fire; and in the midst of it, beside a pot, out of which thick vapour is mounting with quivering red flashes and sparkles, sit two most diverse forms. Right through the fire goes thy road: but the horses snort, and stamp, and rear; the postillion curses and prays, and scourges his cattle withal; they stir not from the spot. Involuntarily thou leapest out of thy carriage, and hurriest a few steps forward. And now thou clearly beholdest the dainty gentle maiden, who, in her white thin night-dress, is kneeling by the cauldron. The storm has loosened her braids, and the long chestnut-brown hair is floating free in the wind. Full in the dazzling fire of the flame flickering up under the trevet, stands the angelic face; but in the horror which has overflowed it with an ice-stream, it is stiffened to the paleness of death; and by the updrawn eyebrows, by the mouth in vain opened for the shriek of anguish, which cannot find its way from the bosom compressed with nameless torture, thou perceivest her affright, her horror: her soft small hands she holds aloft spasmodically pressed together, as if she were calling with prayers her guardian angel, to deliver her from the monsters of the Pit, which in obedience to this potent spell are forthwith to appear! There kneels she, motionless as a figure of marble. Over against her sits cowering on the ground, a long, shrivelled, copper-yellow crone, with peaked hawk-nose, and glistering cat-eyes; from the black cloak, which is huddled round her, stick forth her naked skinny arms; stirring the Hell-broth, she laughs and cries with creaking voice, through the raging bellowing storm. I can well believe that in thee too, favourable reader, though otherwise unacquainted with fear and dread, there might have arisen at the aspect of this Rembrandt or Höllenbreughel picture, here standing forth alive, some unearthly feelings; nay, that for very horror the hairs of thy head might have risen on end. But thy eye could not turn away from the gentle maiden, entangled in these infernal doings; and the electric stroke, that quivered through all thy nerves and fibres, kindled in thee with the speed of lightning the courageous thought of defying the mysterious powers of the fire-circle; and in this thought, thy horror disappeared; nay, the thought itself sprang up from that very horror as its product. Thy heart felt as if thou thyself wert one of those guardian angels, to whom the maiden, terrified to death, was praying; nay, as if thou must instantly lug forth thy pocket-pistol, and without more ceremony blow the hag's brains out. But while thou wert thinking of all this most vividly, thou criedst aloud "Holla!" or "What's the matter here?" or "What's adoing there?" The postillion blew a clanging blast on his horn; the witch ladled about in her brewage, and in a trice the whole had vanished in thick smoke. Whether thou wouldst then have found the maiden, whom with most heart-felt longing thou wert groping for in the darkness, I cannot say: but the spell of the witch thou hadst of a surety destroyed, and undone the magic circle into which Veronica had thoughtlessly entered.

Alas! Neither thou, favourable reader, nor any other man either drove or walked this way, on the twenty-third of September, in the tempestuous witch-favouring night; and Veronica must abide by the cauldron, in deadly terror, till the work was near its close. She heard, indeed, what howling and raging there was around her; how all sorts of hateful voices bellowed and bleated, and yelled and hummed; but she opened not her eyes, for she felt that the sight of the abominations and the horrors with which she was encircled might drive her into incurable destroying madness. The hag had ceased to stir the pot: its smoke grew fainter and fainter; and at last, nothing but a light spirit-flame was burning in the bottom. Then the beldam cried: "Veronica, my child! my darling! look into the grounds there! What seest thou? What seest thou?"

Veronica could not answer, yet it seemed as if all manner of perplexed shapes were dancing and whirling in the cauldron; and on a sudden, with friendly looks and reaching her his hand, rose the Student Anselmus from the cavity of the vessel. She cried aloud: "It is Anselmus! It is Anselmus!"

Instantly the crone turned the cock fixed at the bottom of the cauldron, and glowing metal rushed forth, hissing and bubbling, into a little mould which she had placed beside it. The hag now sprang aloft; and shrieked, capering about with wild horrific gestures: "It is done! It is done! Thanks, my pretty lad; hast watched?—Pooh, pooh, he is coming! Bite him to death! Bite him to

death!" But there sounded a strong rushing through the air: it was as if a huge eagle were pouncing down, striking round him with his pinions; and there shouted a tremendous voice: "Hey, hey, vermin!—It is over! It is over!—Home with ye!" The crone sank down with bitter howling; but Veronica's sense and recollection forsook her.

On her returning to herself, it was broad day, she was lying in her bed, and Fränzchen was standing before her with a cup of steaming tea, and saying to her: "But tell me then, sister, what in all the world ails thee? Here have I been standing this hour, and thou lying senseless, as if in the heat of a fever, and moaning and whimpering till we are frightened to death. Father has not gone to his class, this morning, because of thee; he will be here directly with the Doctor."

Veronica took the tea in silence: and while drinking it, the horrid images of the night rose vividly before her eyes. "So it was all nothing but a wild dream that tortured me? Yet last night, I surely went to that old woman; it was the twenty-third of September too? Well, I must have been very sick last night, and so fancied all this; and nothing has sickened me but my perpetual thinking of Anselmus and the strange old wife who gave herself out for Liese, but was no such thing, and only made a fool of me with that story."

Fränzchen, who had left the room, again came in with Veronica's mantle, all wet, in her hand. "Do but look, sister," said she, "what a sight thy mantle is! There has the storm overnight blown up the window, and overset the chair where thy mantle was hanging; and so the rain has come in, and wetted it all for thee."

This speech sank heavy on Veronica's heart; for she now saw that it was no dream which had tormented her; but that she had really been with the witch. Anguish and horror took hold of her at the thought; and a fever-frost quivered through all her frame. In spasmodic shuddering, she drew the bed-clothes close over her; but with this, she felt something hard pressing on her breast, and on grasping it with her hand, it seemed like a medallion: she drew it out, so soon as Fränzchen went away with the mantle; it was a little, round, bright-polished metallic mirror. "This is a present from the woman," cried she eagerly; and it was as if fiery beams were shooting from the mirror, and penetrating into her inmost soul with benignant warmth. The fever-frost was gone; and there streamed through her whole being an unutterable feeling of contentment and cheerful delight. She could not but remember Anselmus; and as she turned her thoughts more and more intensely on him, behold he smiled on her with friendly looks out of the mirror, like a living miniature portrait. But ere long she felt as if it were no longer the image which she saw; no! but the Student Anselmus himself alive and in person. He was sitting in a stately chamber, with the strangest furniture, and diligently writing. Veronica was about to step forward, to pat his shoulder, and say to him: "Herr Anselmus, look round; it is I!" But she could not; for it was as if a fire-stream encircled him; and yet when she looked more narrowly, this fire-stream was nothing but large books with gilt leaves. At last Veronica so far succeeded that she caught Anselmus' eye: it seemed as if he needed, in gazing at her, to bethink himself who she was; but at last he smiled and said: "Ah! Is it you, dear Mademoiselle Paulmann! But why do you please now and then to take the form of a little Snake?" At these strange words, Veronica could not help laughing aloud; and with this she awoke as from a deep dream; and hastily concealed the little mirror, for the door opened, and Conrector Paulmann with Doctor Eckstein entered the room. Doctor Eckstein stept forward to the bedside; felt Veronica's pulse with long profound study, and then said: "Ey! Ey!" Thereupon he wrote out a prescription; again felt the pulse; a second time said: "Ey! Ey!" and then left his patient. But from these disclosures of Doctor Eckstein's, Conrector Paulmann could not clearly make out what it was that particularly ailed Veronica.

Eighth Vigil

The Library of the Palm-trees. Fortunes of an unhappy Salamander. How the Black Quill caressed a Parsnip, and Registrator Heerbrand was much overtaken with Liquor

The Student Anselmus had now worked several days with Archivarius Lindhorst; these working hours were for him the happiest of his life; still encircled with lovely tones, with Serpentina's encouraging voice, he was filled and overflowed with a pure delight, which often rose to highest rapture. Every strait, every little care of his needy existence, had vanished from his thoughts; and in the new life, which had risen on him as in serene sunny splendour, he comprehended all the wonders of a higher world, which before had filled him with astonishment, nay, with dread. His copying proceeded rapidly and lightly; for he felt more and more as if he were writing characters long known to him; and he scarcely needed to cast his eye upon the manuscript, while copying it all with the greatest exactness.

Except at the hour of dinner, Archivarius Lindhorst seldom made his appearance; and this always precisely at the moment when Anselmus had finished the last letter of some manuscript: then the Archivarius would hand him another, and directly after, leave him, without uttering a word; having first stirred the ink with a little black rod, and changed the old pens with new sharp-pointed ones. One day, when Anselmus, at the stroke of twelve, had as usual mounted the stair, he found the door through which he commonly entered, standing locked; and Archivarius Lindhorst came forward from the other side, dressed in his strange flower-figured night-gown. He called aloud: "Today come this way, good Herr Anselmus; for we must to the chamber where Bhogovotgita's masters are waiting for us."

He stept along the corridor, and led Anselmus through the same chambers and halls as at the first visit. The Student Anselmus again felt astonished at the marvellous beauty of the garden: but he now perceived that many of the strange flowers, hanging on the dark bushes, were in truth insects glancing with lordly colours, hovering up and down with their little wings, as they danced and whirled in clusters, caressing one another with their antennae. On the other hand again, the rose and azure-coloured birds were odoriferous flowers; and the perfume which they scattered, mounted from their cups in low lovely tones, which, with the gurgling of distant fountains, and the sighing of the high groves and trees, mingled themselves into mysterious accords of a deep unutterable longing. The mock-birds, which had so jeered and flouted him before, were again fluttering to and fro over his head, and crying incessantly with their sharp small voices: "Herr Studiosus, Herr Studiosus, don't be in such a hurry! Don't peep into the clouds so! They may fall about your ears—He! He! Herr Studiosus, put your powder-mantle on; cousin Screech-Owl will frizzle your toupee!" And so it went along, in all manner of stupid chatter, till Anselmus left the garden.

Archivarius Lindhorst at last stept into the azure chamber: the porphyry, with the Golden Pot, was gone; instead of it, in the middle of the room, stood a table overhung with violet-coloured satin, upon which lay the writing-ware already known to Anselmus; and a stuffed arm-chair, covered with the same sort of cloth, was placed beside it.

"Dear Herr Anselmus," said Archivarius Lindhorst, "you have now copied me a number of manuscripts, rapidly and correctly, to my no small contentment: you have gained my confidence; but the hardest is yet behind; and that is the transcribing or rather painting of certain works, written in a peculiar character; I keep them in this room, and they can only be copied on the spot. You will, therefore, in future, work here; but I must recommend to you the greatest foresight and attention; a false stroke, or, which may Heaven forfend, a blot let fall on the original, will plunge you into misfortune."

Anselmus observed that from the golden trunks of the palm-trees, little emerald leaves projected: one of these leaves the Archivarius took hold of; and Anselmus could not but perceive that the leaf was in truth a roll of parchment, which the Archivarius unfolded, and spread out before the Student on the table. Anselmus wondered not a little at these strangely intertwisted characters; and as he looked over the many points, strokes, dashes, and twirls in the manuscript, he almost lost hope of ever copying it. He fell into deep thoughts on the subject.

"Be of courage, young man!" cried the Archivarius; "if thou hast continuing Belief and true Love, Serpentina will help thee."

His voice sounded like ringing metal; and as Anselmus looked up in utter terror, Archivarius Lindhorst was standing before him in the kingly form, which, during the first visit, he had assumed in the library. Anselmus felt as if in his deep reverence he could not but sink on his knee; but the Archivarius stept up the trunk of a palm-tree, and vanished aloft among the emerald leaves. The Student Anselmus perceived that the Prince of the Spirits had been speaking with him, and was now gone up to his study; perhaps intending, by the beams which some of the Planets had despatched to him as envoys, to send back word what was to become of Anselmus and Serpentina.

"It may be too," thought he farther, "that he is expecting news from the Springs of the Nile; or that some magician from Lapland is paying him a visit: me it behoves to set diligently about my task." And with this, he began studying the foreign characters on the roll of parchment.

The strange music of the garden sounded over to him, and encircled him with sweet lovely odours; the mock-birds too he still heard giggling and twittering, but could not distinguish their words, a thing which greatly pleased him. At times also it was as if the leaves of the palm-trees were rustling, and as if the clear crystal tones, which Anselmus on that fateful Ascension-day had heard under the elder-bush, were beaming and flitting through the room. Wonderfully strengthened by this shining and tinkling, the Student Anselmus directed his eyes and thoughts more and more intensely on the superscription of the parchment roll; and ere long he felt, as it were from his inmost soul, that the characters could denote nothing else than these words: *Of the marriage of the Salamander with the green Snake.* Then resounded a louder triphony of clear crystal bells: "Anselmus! dear Anselmus!" floated to him from the leaves; and, O wonder! on the trunk of the palm-tree the green Snake came winding down.

"Serpentina! Serpentina!" cried Anselmus, in the madness of highest rapture; for as he gazed more earnestly, it was in truth a lovely glorious maiden that, looking at him with those dark-blue eyes, full of inexpressible longing, as they lived in his heart, was hovering down to meet him. The leaves seemed to jut out and expand; on every hand were prickles sprouting from the trunk; but Serpentina twisted and winded herself deftly through them; and so drew her fluttering robe, glancing as if in changeful colours, along with her, that, plying round the dainty form, it nowhere caught on the projecting points and prickles of the palm-tree. She sat down by Anselmus on the same chair, clasping him with her arm, and pressing him towards her, so that he felt the breath which came from her lips, and the electric warmth of her frame.

"Dear Anselmus!" began Serpentina, "thou shalt now soon be wholly mine; by thy Belief, by thy Love, thou shalt obtain me, and I will bring thee the Golden Pot, which shall make us both happy for evermore."

"O thou kind lovely Serpentina!" said Anselmus, "If I have but thee, what care I for all else! if thou art but mine, I will joyfully give in to all the wondrous mysteries that have beset me ever since the moment when I first saw thee."

"I know," continued Serpentina, "that the strange and mysterious things, with which my father, often merely in the sport of his humour, has surrounded thee, have raised distrust and dread in thy mind; but now, I

hope, it shall be so no more; for I come at this moment to tell thee, dear Anselmus, from the bottom of my heart and soul, all and sundry to a tittle that thou needest to know for understanding my father, and so for seeing clearly what thy relation to him and to me really is."

Anselmus felt as if he were so wholly clasped and encircled by the gentle lovely form, that only with her could he move and live, and as if it were but the beating of her pulse that throbbed through his nerves and fibres; he listened to each one of her words till it sounded in his inmost heart, and, like a burning ray, kindled in him the rapture of Heaven. He had put his arm round that daintier than dainty waist; but the changeful glistering cloth of her robe was so smooth and slippery, that it seemed to him as if she could at any moment wind herself from his arms, and glide away. He trembled at the thought.

"Ah, do not leave me, gentlest Serpentina!" cried he; "thou art my life."

"Not now," said Serpentina, "till I have told thee all that in thy love of me thou canst comprehend:

"Know then, dearest, that my father is sprung from the wondrous race of the Salamanders; and that I owe my existence to his love for the green Snake. In primeval times, in the Fairyland Atlantis, the potent Spirit-prince Phosphorus bore rule; and to him the Salamanders, and other Spirits of the Elements, were plighted. Once on a time, the Salamander, whom he loved before all others (it was my father), chanced to be walking in the stately garden, which Phosphorus' mother had decked in the lordliest fashion with her best gifts; and the Salamander heard a tall Lily singing in low tones: 'Press down thy little eyelids, till my Lover, the Morning-wind, awake thee.' He stept towards it: touched by his glowing breath, the Lily opened her leaves; and he saw the Lily's daughter, the green Snake, lying asleep in the hollow of the flower. Then was the Salamander inflamed with warm love for the fair Snake; and he carried her away from the

Lily, whose perfumes in nameless lamentation vainly called for her beloved daughter throughout all the garden. For the Salamander had borne her into the palace of Phosphorus, and was there beseeching him: 'Wed me with my beloved, and she shall be mine for evermore.' — 'Madman, what askest thou!' said the Prince of the Spirits; 'Know that once the Lily was my mistress, and bore rule with me; but the Spark, which I cast into her, threatened to annihilate the fair Lily; and only my victory over the black Dragon, whom now the Spirits of the Earth hold in fetters, maintains her, that her leaves continue strong enough to enclose this Spark, and preserve it within them. But when thou claspest the green Snake, thy fire will consume her frame; and a new Being rapidly arising from her dust, will soar away and leave thee.'

"The Salamander heeded not the warning of the Spirit-prince: full of longing ardour he folded the green Snake in his arms; she crumbled into ashes; a winged Being, born from her dust, soared away through the sky. Then the madness of desperation caught the Salamander; and he ran through the garden, dashing forth fire and flames; and wasted it in his wild fury, till its fairest flowers and blossoms hung down, blackened and scathed; and their lamentation filled the air. The indignant Prince of the Spirits, in his wrath, laid hold of the Salamander, and said: 'Thy fire has burnt out, thy flames are extinguished, thy rays darkened: sink down to the Spirits of the Earth; let these mock and jeer thee, and keep thee captive, till the Fire-element shall again kindle, and beam up with thee as with a new being from the Earth.' The poor Salamander sank down extinguished: but now the testy old Earth-spirit, who was Phosphorus' gardener, came forth and said: 'Master! who has greater cause to complain of the Salamander than I? Had not all the fair flowers, which he has burnt, been decorated with my gayest metals; had I not stoutly nursed and tended them, and spent many a fair hue on their leaves? And yet I must pity the poor Salamander; for it was but love, in which thou, O Master, hast full often been entangled, that drove him to despair, and made him desolate the garden. Remit him the too harsh punishment!' — 'His fire is for the present extinguished,' said the Prince of the Spirits; 'but in the hapless time, when the Speech of Nature shall no longer be intelligible to degenerate man; when the Spirits of the Elements, banished into their own regions, shall speak to him only from afar, in faint, spent echoes; when, displaced from the harmonious circle, an infinite longing alone shall give him tidings of the Land of Marvels, which he once might inhabit while Belief and Love still dwelt in his soul: in this hapless time, the fire of the Salamander shall again kindle; but only to manhood shall he be permitted to rise, and entering wholly into man's necessitous existence, he shall learn to endure its wants and oppressions. Yet not only shall the remembrance of his first state continue with him, but he shall again rise into the sacred harmony of all Nature; he shall understand its wonders, and the power of his fellow-spirits shall stand at his behest. Then, too, in a Lily-bush, shall he find the green Snake again: and the fruit of his marriage with her shall be three daughters, which, to men, shall appear in the form of their mother. In the spring season these shall disport themselves in the dark Elder-bush, and sound with their lovely crystal voices. And then if, in that needy and mean age of inward stuntedness, there shall be found a youth who understands their song; nay, if one of the little Snakes look at him with her kind eyes; if the look awaken in him forecastings of the distant wondrous Land, to which, having cast away the burden of the Common, he can courageously soar; if, with love to the Snake, there rise in him belief in the Wonders of Nature, nay, in his own existence amid these Wonders, then the Snake shall be his. But not till three youths of this sort have been found and wedded to the three daughters, may the Salamander cast away his heavy burden, and return to his brothers.' — 'Permit me, Master,' said the Earth-spirit, 'to make these three daughters a present, which may glorify their life with the husbands they shall find. Let each of them receive from me a Pot, of the fairest metal which I have; I will polish it with beams borrowed from the diamond; in its glitter shall our Kingdom of Wonders, as it now exists in the Harmony of universal Nature be imaged back in glorious dazzling reflection; and from its interior, on the day of marriage, shall spring forth a Fire-lily, whose eternal blossoms shall encircle the youth that is found worthy, with sweet wafting odours. Soon too shall he learn its speech, and understand the wonders of our kingdom, and dwell with his beloved in Atlantis itself.'

"Thou perceivest well, dear Anselmus, that the Salamander of whom I speak is no other than my father. Spite of his higher nature, he was forced to subject himself to the paltriest contradictions of common life; and hence, indeed, often comes the wayward humour with which he vexes many. He has told me now and then, that, for the inward make of mind, which the Spirit-prince Phosphorus required as a condition of marriage with me and my sisters, men have a name at present, which, in truth, they frequently enough misapply: they call it a childlike poetic character. This character, he says, is often found in youths, who, by reason of their high simplicity of manners, and their total want of what is called knowledge of the world, are mocked by the populace. Ah, dear Anselmus! beneath the Elder-bush, thou understoodest my song, my look: thou lovest the green Snake, thou believest in me, and wilt be mine for evermore! The fair Lily will bloom forth from the Golden Pot; and we shall dwell, happy, and united, and blessed, in Atlantis together!

"Yet I must not hide from thee that in its deadly battle with the Salamanders and Spirits of the Earth, the black Dragon burst from their grasp, and hurried off through the air. Phosphorus, indeed, again holds him in fetters; but from the black Quills, which, in the struggle, rained down on the ground, there sprung up hostile Spirits, which on all hands set themselves against the Salamanders and

Spirits of the Earth. That woman who so hates thee, dear Anselmus, and who, as my father knows full well, is striving for possession of the Golden Pot; that woman owes her existence to the love of such a Quill (plucked in battle from the Dragon's wing) for a certain Parsnip beside which it dropped. She knows her origin and her power; for, in the moans and convulsions of the captive Dragon, the secrets of many a mysterious constellation are revealed to her; and she uses every means and effort to work from the Outward into the Inward and unseen; while my father, with the beams which shoot forth from the spirit of the Salamander, withstands and subdues her. All the baneful principles which lurk in deadly herbs and poisonous beasts, she collects; and, mixing them under favourable constellations, raises therewith many a wicked spell, which overwhelms the soul of man with fear and trembling, and subjects him to the power of those Demons, produced from the Dragon when it yielded in battle. Beware of that old woman, dear Anselmus! She hates thee; because thy childlike pious character has annihilated many of her wicked charms. Keep true, true to me; soon art thou at the goal!"

"O my Serpentina! my own Serpentina!" cried the Student Anselmus, "how could I leave thee, how should I not love thee for ever!" A kiss was burning on his lips; he awoke as from a deep dream: Serpentina had vanished; six o'clock was striking, and it fell heavy on his heart that today he had not copied a single stroke. Full of anxiety, and dreading reproaches from the Archivarius, he looked into the sheet; and, O wonder! the copy of the mysterious manuscript was fairly concluded; and he thought, on viewing the characters more narrowly, that the writing was nothing else but Serpentina's story of her father, the favourite of the Spirit-prince Phosphorus, in Atlantis, the Land of Marvels. And now entered Archivarius Lindhorst, in his light-grey surtout, with hat and staff: he looked into the parchment on which Anselmus had been writing; took a large pinch of snuff, and said with a smile: "Just as I

459

thought!—Well, Herr Anselmus, here is your speziesthaler; we will now to the Linke Bath: do but follow me!" The Archivarius stept rapidly through the garden, in which there was such a din of singing, whistling, talking, that the Student Anselmus was quite deafened with it, and thanked Heaven when he found himself on the street.

Scarcely had they walked twenty paces, when they met Registrator Heerbrand, who companionably joined them. At the Gate, they filled their pipes, which they had about them: Registrator Heerbrand complained that he had left his tinder-box behind, and could not strike fire. "Fire!" cried Archivarius Lindhorst, scornfully; "here is fire enough, and to spare!" And with this he snapped his fingers, out of which came streams of sparks, and directly kindled the pipes.—"Do but observe the chemical knack of some men!" said Registrator Heerbrand; but the Student Anselmus thought, not without internal awe, of the Salamander and his history.

In the Linke Bath, Registrator Heerbrand drank so much strong double beer, that at last, though usually a good-natured quiet man, he began singing student songs in squeaking tenor; he asked every one sharply, Whether he was his friend or not? and at last had to be taken home by the Student Anselmus, long after the Archivarius Lindhorst had gone his ways.

Ninth Vigil

How the Student Anselmus attained to some Sense. The Punch Party. How the Student Anselmus took Conrector Paulmann for a Screech-Owl, and the latter felt much hurt at it. The Ink-blot, and its Consequences

The strange and mysterious things which day by day befell the Student Anselmus, had entirely withdrawn him from his customary life. He no longer visited any of his friends, and waited every morning with impatience, for the hour of noon, which was to unlock his

paradise. And yet while his whole soul was turned to the gentle Serpentina, and the wonders of Archivarius Lindhorst's fairy kingdom, he could not help now and then thinking of Veronica; nay, often it seemed as if she came before him and confessed with blushes how heartily she loved him; how much she longed to rescue him from the phantoms, which were mocking and befooling him. At times he felt as if a foreign power, suddenly breaking in on his mind, were drawing him with resistless force to the forgotten Veronica; as if he must needs follow her whither she pleased to lead him, nay, as if he were bound to her by ties that would not break. That very night after Serpentina had first appeared to him in the form of a lovely maiden; after the wondrous secret of the Salamander's nuptials with the green Snake had been disclosed, Veronica came before him more vividly than ever. Nay, not till he awoke, was he clearly aware that he had but been dreaming; for he had felt persuaded that Veronica was actually beside him, complaining with an expression of keen sorrow, which pierced through his inmost soul, that he should sacrifice her deep true love to fantastic visions, which only the distemper of his mind called into being, and which, moreover, would at last prove his ruin. Veronica was lovelier than he had ever seen her; he could not drive her from his thoughts: and in this perplexed and contradictory mood he hastened out, hoping to get rid of it by a morning walk.

A secret magic influence led him on the Pirna gate: he was just turning into a cross street, when Conrector Paulmann, coming after him, cried out: "Ey! Ey!—Dear Herr Anselmus!—*Amice! Amice!* Where, in Heaven's-name, have you been buried so long? We never see you at all. Do you know, Veronica is longing very much to have another song with you. So come along; you were just on the road to me, at any rate."

The Student Anselmus, constrained by this friendly violence, went along with the Conrector. On entering the house, they were met by Veronica, attired with such neatness and attention, that Conrector Paulmann, full of amazement, asked her: "Why so decked, Mamsell? Were you expecting visitors? Well, here I bring you Herr Anselmus."

The Student Anselmus, in daintily and elegantly kissing Veronica's hand, felt a small soft pressure from it, which shot like a stream of fire over all his frame. Veronica was cheerfulness, was grace itself; and when Paulmann left them for his study, she contrived, by all manner of rogueries and waggeries, so to uplift the Student Anselmus, that he at last quite forgot his bashfulness, and jigged round the room with the light-headed maiden. But here again the Demon of Awkwardness got hold of him: he jolted on a table, and Veronica's pretty little work-box fell to the floor. Anselmus lifted it; the lid had started up; and a little round metallic mirror was glittering on him, into which he looked with peculiar delight. Veronica glided softly up to him; laid her hand on his arm, and pressing close to him, looked over his shoulder into the mirror also. And now Anselmus felt as if a battle were beginning in his soul: thoughts, images flashed out—Archivarius Lindhorst—Serpentina—the green Snake—at last the tumult abated, and all this chaos arranged and shaped itself into distinct consciousness. It was now clear to him that he had always thought of Veronica alone; nay, that the form which had yesterday appeared to him in the blue chamber, had been no other than Veronica; and that the wild legend of the Salamander's marriage with the green Snake had merely been written down by him from the manuscript, but nowise related in his hearing. He wondered not a little at all these dreams; and ascribed them solely to the heated state of mind into which Veronica's love had brought him, as well as to his working with Archivarius Lindhorst, in whose rooms there were, besides, so many strangely intoxicating odours. He could not but laugh heartily at the mad whim of falling in love with a little green Snake; and taking a well-fed Privy Archivarius for a Salamander: "Yes, yes! It is Veronica!" cried he aloud; but on turning round his head, he looked right into Veronica's blue eyes, from which warmest love was beaming. A faint soft Ah! escaped her lips, which at that moment were burning on his.

"O happy I!" sighed the enraptured Student: "What I yesternight but dreamed, is in very deed mine today."

"But wilt thou really wed me, then, when thou art Hofrath?" said Veronica.

"That I will," replied the Student Anselmus; and just then the door creaked, and Conrector Paulmann entered with the words:

"Now, dear Herr Anselmus, I will not let you go today. You will put up with a bad dinner; then Veronica will make us delightful coffee, which we shall drink with Registrator Heerbrand, for he promised to come hither."

"Ah, best Herr Conrector!" answered the Student Anselmus, "are you not aware that I must go to Archivarius Lindhorst's and copy?"

"Look you, *Amice*!" said Conrector Paulmann, holding up his watch, which pointed to half-past twelve.

The Student Anselmus saw clearly that he was much too late for Archivarius Lindhorst; and he complied with the Conrector's wishes the more readily, as he might now hope to look at Veronica the whole day long, to obtain many a stolen glance, and little squeeze of the hand, nay, even to succeed in conquering a kiss. So high had the Student Anselmus' desires now mounted; he felt more and more contented in soul, the more fully he convinced himself that he should soon be delivered from all the fantastic imaginations, which really might have made a sheer idiot of him.

Registrator Heerbrand came, as he had promised, after dinner; and coffee being over, and the dusk come on, the Registrator, puckering his face together, and gaily rubbing his hands, signified that he had something about him, which, if mingled and reduced to form, as it were, paged and titled, by Veronica's fair hands, might be pleasant to them all, on this October evening.

"Come out, then, with this mysterious substance which you carry with you, most valued Registrator," cried Conrector Paulmann. Then Registrator Heerbrand shoved his hand into his deep pocket, and at three journeys, brought out a bottle of arrack, two citrons, and a quantity of sugar. Before half an hour had passed, a savoury bowl of punch was smoking on Paulmann's table. Veronica drank their health in a sip of the liquor; and ere long there was plenty of gay, good-natured chat among the friends. But the Student Anselmus, as the spirit of the drink mounted into his head, felt all the images of those wondrous things, which for some time he had experienced, again coming through his mind. He saw the Archivarius in his damask night-gown, which glittered like phosphorus; he saw the azure room, the golden palm-trees; nay, it now seemed to him as if he must still believe in Serpentina: there was a fermentation, a conflicting tumult in his soul. Veronica handed him a glass of punch; and in taking it, he gently touched her hand. "Serpentina! Veronica!" sighed he to himself. He sank into deep dreams; but Registrator Heerbrand cried quite aloud: "A strange old gentleman, whom nobody can fathom, he is and will be, this Archivarius Lindhorst. Well, long life to him! Your glass, Herr Anselmus!"

Then the Student Anselmus awoke from his dreams, and said, as he touched glasses with Registrator Heerbrand: "That proceeds, respected Herr Registrator, from the circumstance, that Archivarius Lindhorst is in reality a Salamander, who wasted in his fury the Spirit-prince Phosphorus' garden, because the green Snake had flown away from him."

"How? what?" inquired Conrector Paulmann.

"Yes," continued the Student Anselmus; "and for this reason he is now forced to be a Royal Archivarius; and to keep house here in Dresden with his three daughters, who, after all, are nothing more than little gold-green Snakes, that bask in elder-bushes, and traitorously sing, and seduce away young people, like as many syrens."

"Herr Anselmus! Herr Anselmus!" cried Conrector Paulmann, "is there a crack in your brain? In Heaven's name, what monstrous stuff is this you are babbling?"

"He is right," interrupted Registrator Heerbrand: "that fellow, that Archivarius, is a cursed Salamander, and strikes you fiery snips from his fingers, which burn holes in your surtout like red-hot tinder. Ay, ay, thou art in the right, brotherkin Anselmus; and whoever says No, is saying No to me!" And at these words Registrator Heerbrand struck the table with his fist, till the glasses rung again.

"Registrator! Are you frantic?" cried the wroth Conrector. "Herr Studiosus, Herr Studiosus! what is this you are about again?"

"Ah!" said the Student, "you too are nothing but a bird, a screech-owl, that frizzles toupees, Herr Conrector!"

"What?—I a bird?—A screech-owl, a frizzler?" cried the Conrector, full of indignation: "Sir, you are mad, born mad!"

"But the crone will get a clutch of him," cried Registrator Heerbrand.

"Yes, the crone is potent," interrupted the Student Anselmus, "though she is but of mean descent; for her father was nothing but a ragged wing-feather, and her mother a dirty parsnip: but the most of her power she owes to all sorts of baneful creatures, poisonous vermin which she keeps about her."

"That is a horrid calumny," cried Veronica, with eyes all glowing in anger: "old Liese is a wise woman; and the black Cat is no baneful creature, but a polished young gentleman of elegant manners, and her cousin-german."

"Can *he* eat Salamanders without singeing his whiskers, and dying like a candle-snuff?" cried Registrator Heerbrand.

"No! no!" shouted the Student Anselmus, "that he never can in this world; and the green Snake loves me, and I have looked into Serpentina's eyes."

"The Cat will scratch them out," cried Veronica.

"Salamander, Salamander beats them all,

all," hollowed Conrector Paulmann, in the highest fury: "But am I in a madhouse? Am I mad myself? What unwise stuff am I chattering? Yes, I am mad too! mad too!" And with this, Conrector Paulmann started up; tore the peruke from his head, and dashed it against the ceiling of the room; till the battered locks whizzed, and, tangled into utter disorder, rained down the powder far and wide. Then the Student Anselmus and Registrator Heerbrand seized the punch-bowl and the glasses; and, hallooing and huzzaing, pitched them against the ceiling also, and the sherds fell jingling and tingling about their ears.

"*Vivat* the Salamander!—*Pereat, pereat* the crone!—Break the metal mirror!—Dig the cat's eyes out!—Bird, little Bird, from the air —*Eheu—Eheu—Evoe—Evoe*, Salamander!" So shrieked, and shouted, and bellowed the three, like utter maniacs. With loud weeping, Fränzchen ran out; but Veronica lay whimpering for pain and sorrow on the sofa.

At this moment the door opened: all was instantly still; and a little man, in a small grey cloak, came stepping in. His countenance had a singular air of gravity; and especially the round hooked nose, on which was a huge pair of spectacles, distinguished itself from all the noses ever seen. He wore a strange peruke too; more like a feather-cap than a wig.

"Ey, many good-evenings!" grated and cackled the little comical mannikin. "Is the Student Herr Anselmus among you, gentlemen?—Best compliments from Archivarius Lindhorst; he has waited today in vain for Herr Anselmus; but tomorrow he begs most respectfully to request that Herr Anselmus would not miss the hour."

And with this, he went out again; and all of them now saw clearly that the grave little mannikin was in fact a grey Parrot. Conrector Paulmann and Registrator Heerbrand raised a horse-laugh, which reverberated through the room; and in the intervals, Veronica was moaning and whimpering, as if torn by nameless sorrow; but, as to the Student Anselmus, the madness of inward horror was darting through him; and unconsciously he ran through the door, along the streets. Instinctively he reached his house, his garret. Ere long Veronica came in to him, with a peaceful and friendly look, and asked him why, in the festivity, he had so vexed her; and desired him to be upon his guard against imaginations, while working at Archivarius Lindhorst's. "Good-night, good-night, my beloved friend!" whispered Veronica, scarce audibly, and breathed a kiss on his lips. He stretched out his arms to clasp her, but the dreamy shape had vanished, and he awoke cheerful and refreshed. He could not but laugh heartily at the effects of the punch; but in thinking of Veronica, he felt pervaded by a most peaceful feeling. "To her alone," said he within himself, "do I owe this return from my insane whims. In good sooth, I was little better than the man who believed himself to be of glass; or he who durst not leave his room for fear the hens should eat him, as he was a barleycorn. But so soon as I am Hofrath, I marry Mademoiselle Paulmann, and be happy, and there's an end of it."

At noon, as he walked through Archivarius Lindhorst's garden, he could not help wondering how all this had once appeared so strange and marvellous. He now saw nothing past common; earthen flowerpots, quantities of geraniums, myrtles, and the like. Instead of the glittering partycoloured birds which used to flout him, there were nothing but a few sparrows, fluttering hither and thither, which raised an unpleasant unintelligible cry at sight of Anselmus. The azure room also had quite a different look; and he could not understand how that glaring blue, and those unnatural golden trunks of palm-trees, with their shapeless glistening leaves, should ever have pleased him for a moment. The Archivarius looked at him with a most peculiar ironical smile, and asked: "Well, how did you like the punch last night, good Anselmus?"

"Ah, doubtless you have heard from the grey Parrot how——" answered the Student Anselmus, quite ashamed; but he stopt short, bethinking him that this appearance of the Parrot was all a piece of jugglery.

"I was there myself," said Archivarius Lindhorst; "did you not see me? But, among the mad pranks you were playing, I had nigh got lamed: for I was sitting in the punch-bowl, at the very moment when Registrator Heerbrand laid hands on it, to dash it against the ceiling; and I had to make a quick retreat into the Conrector's pipe-head. Now, adieu, Herr Anselmus! Be diligent at your task; for the lost day also you shall have a spezies-thaler, because you worked so well before."

"How can the Archivarius babble such mad stuff?" thought the Student Anselmus, sitting down at the table to begin the copying of the manuscript, which Archivarius Lindhorst had as usual spread out before him. But on the parchment roll, he perceived so many strange crabbed strokes and twirls all twisted together in inexplicable confusion, offering no resting-point for the eye, that it seemed to him well nigh impossible to copy all this exactly. Nay, in glancing over the whole, you might have thought the parchment was nothing but a piece of thickly veined marble, or a stone sprinkled over with lichens. Nevertheless he determined to do his utmost; and boldly dipt in his pen: but the ink would not run, do what he liked; impatiently he spirted the point of his pen against his nail, and—Heaven and Earth!—a huge blot fell on the outspread original! Hissing and foaming, rose a blue flash from the blot; and crackling and wavering, shot through the room to the ceiling. Then a thick vapour rolled from the walls; the leaves began to rustle, as if shaken by a tempest; and down out of them darted glaring basilisks in sparkling fire; these kindled the vapour, and the bickering masses of flame rolled round Anselmus. The golden trunks of the palm-trees became gigantic snakes, which knocked their frightful heads together with piercing metallic clang; and wound their scaly bodies round Anselmus.

"Madman! suffer now the punishment of what, in capricious irreverence, thou hast done!" So cried the frightful voice of the crowned Salamander, who appeared above the snakes like a glittering beam in the midst of the flame: and now the yawning jaws of the snakes poured forth cataracts of fire on Anselmus; and it was as if the fire-streams were congealing about his body, and changing into a firm ice-cold mass. But while Anselmus' limbs, more and more pressed together, and contracted, stiffened into powerlessness, his sense passed away. On returning to himself, he could not stir a joint: he was as if surrounded with a glistening brightness, on which he struck if he but tried to lift his hand—Alas! He was sitting in a well-corked crystal bottle, on a shelf, in the library of Archivarius Lindhorst.

Tenth Vigil

Sorrows of the Student Anselmus in the Glass Bottle. Happy Life of the Cross Church Scholars and Law Clerks. The Battle in the Library of Archivarius Lindhorst. Victory of the Salamander, and Deliverance of the Student Anselmus

Justly may I doubt whether thou, favourable reader, wert ever sealed up in a glass bottle; or even that any vivid tormenting dream ever oppressed thee with such necromantic trouble. If so were the case, thou wilt keenly enough figure out the poor Student Anselmus' woe: but shouldst thou never have even dreamed such things, then will thy quick fancy, for Anselmus' sake and mine, be obliging enough still to enclose itself for a few moments in the crystal. Thou art drowned in dazzling splendour; all objects about thee appear illuminated and begirt with beaming rainbow hues: all quivers and wavers, and clangs and drones, in the sheen; thou art swimming, motionless and powerless as in a firmly congealed ether, which so presses thee together that the spirit in vain gives orders to the dead and stiffened body. Weightier and weightier the mountain burden lies on thee; more and more does every breath exhaust the little handful of air, that still played up and down in the narrow space; thy pulse throbs madly; and cut through with horrid anguish, every nerve is quivering and bleeding in this deadly agony. Have pity, favourable reader, on the Student Anselmus! Him this inexpressible torture laid hold of in his glass prison: but he felt too well that death could not relieve him; for did he not awake from the deep swoon into which the excess of pain had cast him, and open his eyes to new wretchedness, when the morning sun shone clear into the room? He could move no limb; but his thoughts struck against the glass, stupifying him with discordant clang; and instead of the words, which the spirit used to speak from within him, he now heard only the stifled din of madness. Then he exclaimed in his despair: "O Serpentina! Serpentina! save me from this agony of Hell!" And it was as if faint sighs breathed around him, which spread like green transparent elder-leaves over the glass; the clanging ceased; the dazzling perplexing glitter was gone, and he breathed more freely.

"Have not I myself solely to blame for my misery? Ah! Have not I sinned against thee, thou kind, beloved Serpentina? Have not I raised vile doubts of thee? Have not I lost my Belief; and with it, all, all that was to make me so blessed? Ah! Thou wilt now never, never be mine; for me the Golden Pot is lost, and I shall not behold its wonders any more. Ah! But once could I see thee; but once hear thy kind sweet voice, thou lovely Serpentina!"

So wailed the Student Anselmus, caught with deep piercing sorrow: then spoke a voice close by him: "What the devil ails you, Herr Studiosus? What makes you lament so, out of all compass and measure?"

The Student Anselmus now perceived that on the same shelf with him were five other bottles, in which he perceived three Cross Church Scholars, and two Law Clerks.

"Ah, gentlemen, my fellows in misery," cried he, "how is it possible for you to be so calm, nay, so happy, as I read in your cheerful looks? You are sitting here corked up in glass bottles, as well as I, and cannot move a finger; nay, not think a reasonable thought, but there rises such a murder-tumult of clanging and droning, and in your head itself a tumbling and rumbling enough to drive one mad. But doubtless you do not believe in the Salamander, or the green Snake."

"You are pleased to jest, Mein Herr Studiosus," replied a Cross Church Scholar; "we have never been better off than at present: for the speziesthalers which the mad Archivarius gave us for all manner of pot-hook copies, are chinking in our pockets; we have now no Italian choruses to learn by heart; we go every day to Joseph's or other houses of call, where the double-beer is sufficient, and we can look a pretty girl in the face; so we sing like real Students, *Gaudeamus igitur*, and are contented in spirit!"

"They of the Cross are quite right," added a Law Clerk; "I too am well furnished with speziesthalers, like my dearest colleague beside me here; and we now diligently walk about on the Weinberg, instead of scurvy Act-writing within four walls."

"But, my best, worthiest masters!" said the Student Anselmus, "do you not observe, then, that you are all and sundry corked up in glass bottles, and cannot for your hearts walk a hairsbreadth?"

Here the Cross Church Scholars and the Law Clerks set up a loud laugh, and cried: "The Student is mad; he fancies himself to be sitting in a glass bottle, and is standing on the Elbe-bridge and looking right down into the water. Let us go along!"

"Ah!" sighed the Student, "they have never seen the kind Serpentina; they know not what Freedom, and life in Love, and Belief, signifies; and so by reason of their folly and low-mindedness, they feel not the oppression of the imprisonment into which the Salamander has cast them. But I, unhappy I, must perish in want and woe, if she, whom I so inexpressibly love, do not deliver me!"

Then waving in faint tinkles, Serpentina's voice flitted through the room: "Anselmus! believe, love, hope!" And every tone beamed into Anselmus' prison; and the crystal yielded to his pressure, and expanded, till the breast of the captive could move and heave.

The torment of his situation became less and less, and he saw clearly that Serpentina still loved him; and that it was she alone, who had rendered his confinement tolerable. He disturbed himself no more about his inane companions in misfortune; but directed all his thoughts and meditations on the gentle Serpentina. Suddenly, however, there arose on the other side a dull croaking repulsive murmur. Ere long he could observe that it proceeded from an old coffee-pot, with half-broken lid, standing over against him on a little shelf. As he looked at it more narrowly, the ugly features of a wrinkled old woman by degrees unfolded themselves; and in a few moments, the Apple-wife of the Schwarzthor stood before him. She grinned and laughed at him, and cried with screeching voice: "Ey, Ey, my pretty boy, must thou lie in limbo now? To the crystal thou hast run: did not I tell thee long ago?"

"Mock and jeer me; do, thou cursed witch!" said the Student Anselmus, "thou art to blame for it all; but the Salamander will catch thee, thou vile Parsnip!"

"Ho, ho!" replied the crone, "not so proud, good readywriter! Thou hast squelched my little sons to pieces, thou hast burnt my nose; but I must still like thee, thou knave, for once thou wert a pretty fellow; and my little daughter likes thee too. Out of the crystal thou wilt never come unless I help thee: up thither I cannot clamber; but my cousin gossip the Rat, that lives close behind thee, will eat the shelf in two; thou shalt jingle down, and I catch thee in my apron, that thy nose be not broken, or thy fine sleek face at all injured: then I carry thee to Mamsell Veronica; and thou shalt marry her, when thou art Hofrath."

"Avaunt, thou devil's brood!" cried the Student Anselmus full of fury; "it was thou alone and thy hellish arts that brought me to the sin which I must now expiate. But I bear it all patiently: for only here can I be, where the kind Serpentina encircles me with love and consolation. Hear it, thou beldam, and despair! I bid defiance to thy power: I love Serpentina, and none but her for ever; I will not be Hofrath, will not look at Veronica, who by thy means entices me to evil. Can the green Snake not be mine, I will die in sorrow and longing. Take thyself away, thou filthy rook! Take thyself away!"

The crone laughed, till the chamber rung: "Sit and die then," cried she: "but now it is time to set to work; for I have other trade to follow here." She threw off her black cloak, and so stood in hideous nakedness; then she ran round in circles, and large folios came tumbling down to her; out of these she tore parchment leaves, and rapidly patching them together in artful combination, and fixing them on her body, in a few instants she was dressed as if in strange party-coloured harness. Spitting fire, the black Cat darted out of the ink-glass, which was standing on the table, and ran mewing towards the crone, who shrieked in loud triumph, and along with him vanished through the door.

Anselmus observed that she went towards the azure chamber; and directly he heard a hissing and storming in the distance; the birds in the garden were crying; the Parrot creaked out: "Help! help! Thieves! thieves!" That moment the crone returned with a bound into the room, carrying the Golden Pot on her arm, and with hideous gestures, shrieking wildly through the air; "Joy! joy, little son!—Kill the green Snake! To her, son! To her!"

Anselmus thought he heard a deep moaning, heard Serpentina's voice. Then horror and despair took hold of him: he gathered all his force, he dashed violently, as if nerve and artery were bursting, against the crystal; a piercing clang went through the room, and the Archivarius in his bright damask night-gown was standing in the door.

"Hey, hey! vermin!—Mad spell!—Witchwork!—Hither, holla!" So shouted he: then the black hair of the crone started up in tufts; her red eyes glanced with infernal fire, and clenching together the peaked fangs of her abominable jaws, she hissed: "Hiss, at him! Hiss, at him! Hiss!" and laughed and neighed in scorn and mockery, and pressed the Golden Pot firmly towards her, and threw out of it handfuls of glittering earth on the Archivarius; but as it touched the nightgown, the earth changed into flowers, which rained down on the ground. Then the lilies of the nightgown flickered and flamed up; and the Archivarius caught these lilies blazing in sparky fire and dashed them on the witch; she howled for agony, but still as she leapt aloft and shook her harness of parchment the lilies went out, and fell away into ashes.

"To her, my lad!" creaked the crone: then the black Cat darted through the air, and soused over the Archivarius' head towards the door; but the grey Parrot fluttered out against him; caught him with his crooked bill by the nape, till red fiery blood burst down over his neck; and Serpentina's voice cried: "Saved! Saved!" Then the crone, foaming with rage and desperation, darted out upon the Archivarius: she threw the Golden Pot behind her, and holding up the long talons of her skinny fists, was for clutching the Archivarius by the throat: but he instantly doffed his nightgown, and hurled it against her. Then, hissing, and sputtering, and bursting, shot blue flames from the parchment leaves, and the crone rolled round in howling agony, and strove to get fresh earth from the Pot, fresh parchment leaves from the books, that she might stifle the blazing flames; and whenever any earth or leaves came down on her, the flames went out. But now, from the interior of the Archivarius issued fiery crackling beams, and darted on the crone.

"Hey, hey! To it again! Salamander! Victory!" clanged the Archivarius' voice through the chamber; and a hundred bolts whirled forth in fiery circles round the shrieking crone. Whizzing and buzzing flew Cat and Parrot in their furious battle; but at last the Parrot, with his strong wing, dashed the Cat to the ground; and with his talons transfixing and holding fast his adversary, which, in deadly agony, uttered horrid mews and howls, he, with his sharp bill, picked out his glowing eyes, and the burning froth spouted from them. Then thick vapour streamed up from the spot where the crone, hurled to the ground, was lying under the nightgown: her howling, her terrific, piercing cry of lamentation, died away in the remote distance. The smoke, which had spread abroad with irresistible smell, cleared off; the Archivarius picked up his nightgown; and under it lay an ugly Parsnip.

"Honoured Herr Archivarius, here let me offer you the vanquished foe," said the Parrot, holding out a black hair in his beak to Archivarius Lindhorst.

"Very right, my worthy friend," replied the Archivarius: "here lies my vanquished foe too: be so good now as manage what remains. This very day, as a small douceur, you shall have six cocoa-nuts, and a new pair of spectacles also, for I see the Cat has villainously broken the glasses of these old ones."

"Yours for ever, most honoured friend and patron!" answered the Parrot, much delighted; then took the Parsnip in his bill, and fluttered out with it by the window, which Archivarius Lindhorst had opened for him.

The Archivarius now lifted the Golden Pot, and cried, with a strong voice, "Serpentina! Serpentina!" But as the Student Anselmus, joying in the destruction of the vile beldam who had hurried him into misfortune, cast his eyes on the Archivarius, behold, here stood once more the high majestic form of the Spirit-prince, looking up to him with indescribable dignity and grace. "Anselmus," said the Spirit-prince, "not thou, but a hostile Principle, which strove destructively to penetrate into thy nature, and divide thee against thyself, was to blame for thy unbelief. Thou hast kept thy faithfulness: be free and happy." A bright flash quivered through the spirit of Anselmus: the royal triphony of the crystal bells sounded stronger and louder than he had ever heard it: his nerves and fibres thrilled; but, swelling higher and higher, the melodious tones rang through the room; the glass which enclosed Anselmus broke; and he rushed into the arms of his dear and gentle Serpentina.

Eleventh Vigil

Conrector Paulmann's anger at the Madness which had broken out in his Family. How Registrator Heerbrand became Hofrath; and, in the keenest Frost, walked about in Shoes and silk Stockings. Veronica's Confessions. Betrothment over the steaming Soup-plate

"But tell me, best Registrator! how the cursed punch last night could so mount into our heads, and drive us to all manner of *allotria?*" So said Conrector Paulmann, as he next morning entered his room, which still lay full of broken sherds; with his hapless peruke, dissolved into its original elements, floating in punch among the ruin. For after the Student Anselmus ran out of doors, Conrector Paulmann and Registrator Heerbrand had still kept trotting and hobbling up and down the room, shouting like maniacs, and butting their heads together; till Fränzchen, with much labour, carried her vertiginous papa to bed; and Registrator Heerbrand, in the deepest exhaustion, sunk on the sofa, which Veronica had left, taking refuge in her bedroom. Registrator Heerbrand had his blue handkerchief tied about his head; he looked quite pale and melancholic, and moaned out: "Ah, worthy Conrector, not the punch which Mamsell Veronica most admirably brewed, no! but simply that cursed Student is to blame for all the mischief. Do you not observe that he has long been *mente captus?* And are you not aware that madness is infectious? One fool makes twenty; pardon me, it is an old proverb: especially when you have drunk a glass or two, you fall into madness quite readily, and then involuntarily you manoeuvre, and go through your exercise, just as the crack-brained fugleman makes the motion. Would you believe it, Conrector? I am still giddy when I think of that grey Parrot!"

"Grey fiddlestick!" interrupted the Conrector: "it was nothing but Archivarius Lindhorst's little old Famulus, who had thrown a grey cloak over him, and was seeking the Student Anselmus."

"It may be," answered Registrator Heerbrand; "but, I must confess, I am quite downcast in spirit; the whole night through there was such a piping and organing."

"That was I," said the Conrector, "for I snore loud."

"Well, may be," answered the Registrator: "but, Conrector, Conrector! Ah, not without cause did I wish to raise some cheerfulness among us last night—And that Anselmus has spoiled all! You know not—O Conrector, Conrector!" And with this, Registrator Heerbrand started up; plucked the cloth from his head, embraced the Conrector, warmly pressed his hand, and again cried, in quite heart-breaking tone: "O Conrector, Conrector!" and snatching his hat and staff, rushed out of doors.

"This Anselmus comes not over my threshold again," said Conrector Paulmann; "for I see very well, that, with this moping madness of his, he robs the best gentlemen of their senses. The Registrator is now over with it too: I have hitherto kept safe; but the Devil, who knocked hard last night in our carousal, may get in at last, and play his tricks with me. So *Apage, Satanas!* Off with thee, Anselmus!" Veronica had grown quite pensive; she spoke no word; only smiled now and then very oddly, and liked best to be alone. "She too has Anselmus in her head," said the Conrector, full of spleen: "but it is well that he does not show himself here; I know he fears me, this Anselmus, and so he never comes."

These concluding words Conrector Paulmann spoke aloud; then the tears rushed into Veronica's eyes, and she said, sobbing: "Ah! how can Anselmus come? He has long been corked up in the glass bottle."

"How? What?" cried Conrector Paulmann. "Ah Heaven! Ah Heaven! she is doting too, like the Registrator: the loud fit will soon come! Ah, thou cursed, abominable, thrice-cursed Anselmus!" He ran forth directly to Doctor Eckstein; who smiled, and again said: "Ey! Ey!" This time, however, he prescribed nothing; but added, to the little he had uttered, the following words, as he walked away: "Nerves! Come round of itself. Take the air; walks; amusements; theatre; playing *Sonntagskind, Schwestern von Prag*. Come round of itself."

"So eloquent I have seldom seen the Doctor," thought Conrector Paulmann; "really talkative, I declare!"

Several days and weeks and months were gone; Anselmus had vanished; but Registrator Heerbrand also did not make his appearance: not till the fourth of February, when the Registrator, in a new fashionable coat of the finest cloth, in shoes and silk stockings, notwithstanding the keen frost, and with a large nosegay of fresh flowers in his hand, did enter precisely at noon into the parlour of Conrector Paulmann, who wondered not a little to see his friend so dizened. With a solemn air, Registrator Heerbrand stept forward to Conrector Paulmann; embraced him with the finest elegance, and then said: "Now at last, on the Saint's-day of your beloved and most honoured Mamsell Veronica, I will tell you out, straight forward, what I have long had lying at my heart. That evening, that unfortunate evening, when I put the ingredients of our noxious punch in my pocket, I purposed imparting to you a piece of good news, and celebrating the happy day in convivial joys. Already I had learned that I was to be made Hofrath; for which promotion I have now the patent, *cum nomine et sigillo Principis*, in my pocket."

"Ah! Herr Registr — Herr Hofrath Heerbrand I meant to say," stammered the Conrector.

"But it is you, most honoured Conrector," continued the new Hofrath; "it is you alone that can complete my happiness. For a long time, I have in secret loved your daughter, Mamsell Veronica; and I can boast of many a kind look which she has given me, evidently showing that she would not cast me away. In one word, honoured Conrector! I, Hofrath Heerbrand, do now entreat of you the hand of your most amiable Mamsell Veronica, whom I, if you have nothing against it, purpose shortly to take home as my wife."

Conrector Paulmann, full of astonishment, clapped his hands repeatedly, and cried: "Ey, Ey, Ey! Herr Registr — Herr Hofrath, I meant to say — who would have thought it? Well, if Veronica does really love you, I for my share cannot object: nay, perhaps, her present melancholy is nothing but concealed love for you, most honoured Hofrath! You know what freaks they have!"

At this moment Veronica entered, pale and agitated, as she now commonly was. Then Hofrath Heerbrand stept towards her; mentioned in a neat speech her Saint's-day, and handed her the odorous nosegay, along with a little packet; out of which, when she opened it, a pair of glittering earrings beamed up to her. A rapid flying blush tinted her cheeks; her eyes sparkled in joy, and she cried: "O Heaven! These are the very earrings which I wore some weeks ago, and thought so much of."

"How can this be, dearest Mamsell," interrupted Hofrath Heerbrand, somewhat alarmed and hurt, "when I bought these jewels not an hour ago, in the Schlossgasse, for current money?"

But Veronica heeded him not; she was standing before the mirror to witness the effect of the trinkets, which she had already suspended in her pretty little ears. Conrector Paulmann disclosed to her, with grave countenance and solemn tone, his friend Heerbrand's preferment and present proposal. Veronica looked at the Hofrath with a searching look, and said: "I have long known that you wished to marry me. Well, be it so! I promise you my heart and hand; but I must now unfold to you, to both of you, I mean, my father and my bridegroom, much that is lying heavy on my heart; yes, even now, though the soup should get cold, which I see Fränzchen is just putting on the table."

Without waiting for the Conrector's or the Hofrath's reply, though the words were visibly hovering on the lips of both, Veronica continued: "You may believe me, best father, I loved Anselmus from my heart, and when

Registrator Heerbrand, who is now become Hofrath himself, assured us that Anselmus might probably enough get some such length, I resolved that he and no other should be my husband. But then it seemed as if alien hostile beings were for snatching him away from me: I had recourse to old Liese, who was once my nurse, but is now a wise woman, and a great enchantress. She promised to help me, and give Anselmus wholly into my hands. We went at midnight on the Equinox to the crossing of the roads: she conjured certain hellish spirits, and by aid of the black Cat, we manufactured a little metallic mirror, in which I, directing my thoughts on Anselmus, had but to look, in order to rule him wholly in heart and mind. But now I heartily repent having done all this; and here abjure all Satanic arts. The Salamander has conquered old Liese; I heard her shrieks; but there was no help to be given: so soon as the Parrot had eaten the Parsnip, my metallic mirror broke in two with a piercing clang." Veronica took out both the pieces of the mirror, and a lock of hair from her work-box, and handing them to Hofrath Heerbrand, she proceeded: "Here, take the fragments of the mirror, dear Hofrath; throw them down, tonight, at twelve o'clock, over the Elbe-bridge, from the place where the Cross stands; the stream is not frozen there: the lock, however, do you wear on your faithful breast. I here abjure all magic: and heartily wish Anselmus joy of his good fortune, seeing he is wedded with the green Snake, who is much prettier and richer than I. You, dear Hofrath, I will love and reverence as becomes a true honest wife."

"Alack! Alack!" cried Conrector Paulmann, full of sorrow; "she is cracked, she is cracked; she can never be Frau Hofräthinn; she is cracked!"

"Not in the smallest," interrupted Hofrath Heerbrand; "I know well that Mamsell Veronica has had some kindness for the loutish Anselmus; and it may be that in some fit of passion, she has had recourse to the wise

woman, who, as I perceive, can be no other than the card-caster and coffee-pourer of the Seethor; in a word, old Rauerin. Nor can it be denied that there are secret arts, which exert their influence on men but too balefully; we read of such in the Ancients, and doubtless there are still such; but as to what Mamsell Veronica is pleased to say about the victory of the Salamander, and the marriage of Anselmus with the green Snake, this, in reality, I take for nothing but a poetic allegory; a sort of song, wherein she sings her entire farewell to the Student."

"Take it for what you will, best Hofrath!" cried Veronica; "perhaps for a very stupid dream."

"That I nowise do," replied Hofrath Heerbrand; "for I know well that Anselmus himself is possessed by secret powers, which vex him and drive him on to all imaginable mad freaks."

Conrector Paulmann could stand it no longer; he broke loose: "Hold! For the love of Heaven, hold! Are we again overtaken with the cursed punch, or has Anselmus' madness come over us too? Herr Hofrath, what stuff is this you are talking? I will suppose, however, that it is love which haunts your brain: this soon comes to rights in marriage; otherwise, I should be apprehensive that you too had fallen into some shade of madness, most honoured Herr Hofrath; then what would become of the future branches of the family, inheriting the *malum* of their parents? But now I give my paternal blessing to this happy union; and permit you as bride and bridegroom to take a kiss."

This happened forthwith; and thus before the presented soup had grown cold, was a formal betrothment concluded. In a few weeks, Frau Hofräthinn Heerbrand was actually, as she had been in vision, sitting in the balcony of a fine house in the Neumarkt, and looking down with a smile on the beaux, who passing by turned their glasses up to her, and said: "She is a heavenly woman, the Hofräthinn Heerbrand."

Twelfth Vigil

Account of the Freehold Property to which Anselmus removed, as Son-in-law of Archivarius Lindhorst; and how he lives there with Serpentina. Conclusion.

How deeply did I feel, in the centre of my spirit, the blessedness of the Student Anselmus, who now, indissolubly united with his gentle Serpentina, has withdrawn to the mysterious Land of Wonders, recognised by him as the home towards which his bosom, filled with strange forecastings, had always longed. But in vain was all my striving to set before thee, favourable reader, those glories with which Anselmus is encompassed, or even in the faintest degree to shadow them forth to thee in words. Reluctantly I could not but acknowledge the feebleness of my every expression. I felt myself enthralled amid the paltrinesses of everyday life; I sickened in tormenting dissatisfaction; I glided about like a dreamer; in brief, I fell into that condition of the Student Anselmus, which, in the Fourth Vigil, I have endeavoured to set before thee. It grieved me to the heart, when I glanced over the Eleven Vigils, now happily accomplished, and thought that to insert the Twelfth, the keystone of the whole, would never be vouchsafed me. For whensoever, in the night season, I set myself to complete the work, it was as if mischievous Spirits (they might be relations, perhaps cousins-german, of the slain witch) held a polished glittering piece of metal before me, in which I beheld my own mean Self, pale, over-watched, and melancholic, like Registrator Heerbrand after his bout of punch. Then I threw down my pen, and hastened to bed, that I might behold the happy Anselmus and the fair Serpentina at least in my dreams. This had lasted for several days and nights, when at length quite unexpectedly I received a note from Archivarius Lindhorst, in which he addressed me as follows:

"Respected Sir—It is well known to me that you have written down, in Eleven Vigils, the singular fortunes of my good son-in-law Anselmus, whilom Student, now Poet; and are at present cudgelling your brains very sore, that in the Twelfth and Last Vigil you may tell somewhat of his happy life in Atlantis, where he now lives with my daughter, on the pleasant Freehold, which I possess in that country. Now, notwithstanding I much regret that hereby my own peculiar nature is unfolded to the reading world; seeing it may, in my office as Privy Archivarius, expose me to a thousand inconveniences; nay, in the Collegium even give rise to the question: How far a Salamander can justly, and with binding consequences, plight himself by oath, as a Servant of the State? and how far, on the whole, important affairs may be intrusted to him, since, according to Gabalis and Swedenborg, the Spirits of the Elements are not to be trusted at all?—notwithstanding, my best friends must now avoid my embrace; fearing lest, in some sudden anger, I dart out a flash or two, and singe their hair-curls, and Sunday frocks; notwithstanding all this, I say, it is still my purpose to assist you in the completion of the Work, since much good of me and of my dear married daughter (would the other two were off my hands also!) has therein been said. Would you write your Twelfth Vigil, therefore, then descend your cursed five pair of stairs, leave your garret, and come over to me. In the blue palmtree-room, which you already know, you will find fit writing materials; and you can then, in few words, specify to your readers, what you have seen; a better plan for you than any long-winded description of a life, which you know only by hearsay. With esteem,

"Your obedient servant,
"The Salamander Lindhorst,
"P. T. Royal Archivarius."

This truly somewhat rough, yet on the whole friendly note from Archivarius Lindhorst, gave me high pleasure. Clear enough it seemed, indeed, that the singular manner in which the fortunes of his son-in-law had been revealed to me, and which I, bound to silence, must conceal even from thee, favourable reader, was well known to this peculiar old gentleman; yet he had not taken it so ill as I might readily have apprehended. Nay, here was he offering me his helpful hand in the completion of my work; and from this I might justly conclude, that at bottom he was not averse to have his marvellous existence in the world of spirits thus divulged through the press.

"It may be," thought I, "that he himself expects from this measure, perhaps, to get his two other daughters the sooner married: for who knows but a spark may fall in this or that young man's breast, and kindle a longing for the green Snake; whom, on Ascension-day, under the elder-bush, he will forthwith seek and find? From the woe which befell Anselmus, when inclosed in the glass bottle, he will take warning to be doubly and trebly on his guard against all Doubt and Unbelief."

Precisely at eleven o'clock, I extinguished my study-lamp; and glided forth to Archivarius Lindhorst, who was already waiting for me in the lobby.

"Are you there, my worthy friend? Well, this is what I like, that you have not mistaken my good intentions: do but follow me!"

And with this he led the way through the garden, now filled with dazzling brightness, into the azure chamber, where I observed the same violet table, at which Anselmus had been writing.

Archivarius Lindhorst disappeared: but soon came back, carrying in his hand a fair golden goblet, out of which a high blue flame was sparkling up. "Here," said he, "I bring you the favourite drink of your friend the Bandmaster, Johannes Kreisler.[1] It is burning arrack, into which I have thrown a little sugar. Sip a touch or two of it: I will doff my night-gown, and to amuse myself and enjoy your worthy company while you sit looking and writing, I shall just bob up and down a little in the goblet."

"As you please, honoured Herr Archivarius," answered I: "but if I am to ply the liquor, you will get none."

"Don't fear that, my good fellow," cried the Archivarius; then hastily threw off his night-gown, mounted, to my no small amazement, into the goblet, and vanished in the blaze. Without fear, softly blowing back the flame, I partook of the drink: it was truly precious!

———

Stir not the emerald leaves of the palm-trees in soft sighing and rustling, as if kissed by the breath of the morning wind. Awakened from their sleep, they move, and mysteriously whisper of the wonders, which from the far distance approach like tones of melodious harps! The azure rolls from the walls, and floats like airy vapour to and fro; but dazzling beams shoot through it; and whirling and dancing, as in jubilee of childlike sport, it mounts and mounts to immeasurable height, and vaults itself over the palm-trees. But brighter and brighter shoots beam on beam, till in boundless expanse opens the grove where I behold Anselmus. Here glowing hyacinths, and tulips, and roses, lift their fair heads; and their perfumes, in loveliest sound, call to the happy youth: "Wander, wander among us, our beloved; for thou understandest us! Our perfume is the Longing of Love: we love thee, and are thine for ever-more!" The golden rays burn in glowing tones: "We are Fire, kindled by Love. Perfume is Longing; but Fire is Desire: and dwell we not in thy bosom? We are thy own!" The dark bushes,

———

[1] An imaginary musical enthusiast of whom Hoffmann has written much; under the fiery sensitive wayward character of this crazy Bandmaster, presenting, it would seem, a shadowy likeness of himself. The *Kreisleriana* occupy a large space among these *Fantasy-pieces*; and Johannes Kreisler is the main figure in *Kater Murr*, Hoffmann's favourite but unfinished work. In the third and last volume, Kreisler was to end, not in composure and illumination, as the critics would have required, but in utter madness; a sketch of a wild, flail-like scarecrow, dancing vehemently and blowing soap-bubbles, and which had been intended to front the last title-page, was found among Hoffmann's papers, and engraved and published in his *Life and Remains.*—Ed.

he high trees rustle and sound: "Come to us, thou loved, thou happy one! Fire is Desire; but Hope is our cool Shadow. Lovingly we rustle round thy head: for thou understandest us, because Love dwells in thy breast!" The brooks and fountains murmur and patter: "Loved one, walk not so quickly by: look into our crystal! Thy image dwells in us, which we preserve with Love, for thou hast understood us." In the triumphal choir, bright birds are singing: "Hear us! Hear us! We are Joy, we are Delight, the rapture of Love!" But anxiously Anselmus turns his eyes to the glorious Temple, which rises behind him in the distance. The fair pillars seem trees; and the capitals and friezes acanthus leaves, which in wondrous wreaths and figures form splendid decorations. Anselmus walks to the Temple: he views with inward delight the variegated marble, the steps with their strange veins of moss. "Ah, no!" cries he, as if in the excess of rapture, "she is not far from me now; she is near!" Then advances Serpentina, in the fulness of beauty and grace, from the Temple; she bears the Golden Pot, from which a bright Lily has sprung. The nameless rapture of infinite longing glows in her meek eyes; she looks at Anselmus, and says: "Ah! Dearest, the Lily has sent forth her bowl: what we longed for is fulfilled; is there a happiness to equal ours?" Anselmus clasps her with the tenderness of warmest ardour: the Lily burns in flaming beams over his head. And louder move the trees and bushes; clearer and gladder play the brooks; the birds, the shining insects dance in the waves of perfume: a gay, bright rejoicing tumult, in the air, in the water, in the earth, is holding the festival of Love! Now rush sparkling streaks, gleaming over all the bushes; diamonds look from the ground like shining eyes: strange vapours are wafted hither on sounding wings: they are the Spirits of the Elements, who do homage to the Lily, and proclaim the happiness of Anselmus. Then Anselmus raises his head, as if encircled with a beamy glory. Is it looks? Is it words? Is it song? You hear the sound: "Serpentina! Belief in thee, Love of thee has

unfolded to my soul the inmost spirit of Nature! Thou hast brought me the Lily, which sprung from Gold, from the primeval Force of the world, before Phosphorus had kindled the spark of Thought; this Lily is Knowledge of the sacred Harmony of all Beings; and in this do I live in highest blessedness for evermore. Yes, I, thrice happy, have perceived what was highest: I must indeed love thee for ever, O Serpentina! Never shall the golden blossoms of the Lily grow pale; for, like Belief and Love, this Knowledge is eternal."

———

For the vision, in which I had now beheld Anselmus bodily, in his Freehold of Atlantis, I stand indebted to the arts of the Salamander; and most fortunate was it that, when all had melted into air, I found a paper lying on the violet table, with the foregoing statement of the matter, written fairly and distinctly by my own hand. But now I felt myself as if transpierced and torn in pieces by sharp sorrow. "Ah, happy Anselmus, who has cast away the burden of week-day life, who in the love of thy kind Serpentina fliest with bold pinion, and now livest in rapture and joy on thy Freehold in Atlantis! while I—poor I!—must soon, nay, in few moments, leave even this fair hall, which itself is far from a Freehold in Atlantis; and again be transplanted to my garret, where, enthralled among the pettinesses of necessitous existence, my heart and my sight are so bedimmed with thousand mischiefs, as with thick fog, that the fair Lily will never, never be beheld by me."

Then Archivarius Lindhorst patted me gently on the shoulder, and said: "Soft, soft, my honoured friend! Lament not so! Were you not even now in Atlantis; and have you not at least a pretty little copyhold Farm there, as the poetical possession of your inward sense? And is the blessedness of Anselmus aught else but a Living in Poesy? Can aught else but Poesy reveal itself as the sacred Harmony of all Beings, as the deepest secret of Nature?"

PICTURE CREDITS

*Key to abbreviations used to indicate location of pictures on page: r.—right; l.—left; t.—top; b.—bottom; c.—center; *—courtesy. Abbreviations are combined to indicate unusual placement.*

—**FRONTISPIECE** Jean-Claude Lejeune —**7** Roy Stevens —**17** Jack Novak—Photri —**19** (l.) * Chicago Symphony Orchestra (r.) * Metropolitan Opera Association (b.) * The Guthrie Theater —**35, 39** Jean-Claude Lejeune —**41** (c) Bern Schwartz —**53** * British Tourist Authority —**60** Martha Swope —**61** (t.) * The Joffrey Ballet (b.) Martha Swope —**77** Alinari —**111** From *Optical Transformations* by H. Lipson, Academic Press, London, New York, San Francisco (1972) —**113** From Article 1 by H. C. Becker et. al., *Annals of the New York Academy of Sciences*, vol. 157 (1969) —**114** * From "Image Transmission and Image Processing in Radiol-ogy" by Manfred Pfeiler in *Automatic Interpretation and Classification of Images*, edited by A. Grasseli, Academic Press (1969) —**115** (t.) * Karl J. Scheibengraber, University of Wisconsin—Milwaukee (b.) * From *Optical Data Processing* by A. R. Shulman, John Wiley & Sons (1970) —**154** Gene Fenn —**170** (t., b.l.) Christian Vioujard/Gamma—Liaison (b.c., b.r.) Jean-Philippe Reverdot —**204** Raymond Cox —**278** Janet Stone —**320** * From the portrait in the collection of the Royal Society of Edinburgh —**368, 404, 426** Radio Times Hulton Picture Library